THE
PLATONISM
OF
SHELLEY

A STUDY OF PLATONISM
AND THE POETIC MIND

JAMES A. NOTOPOULOS

1969
OCTAGON BOOKS
New York

For

My Mother and Father

ΦΙΛΟΤΕΚΝΟΙΣ

And to
the Memory of

Harry de Forest Smith

Preface

THIS STUDY of Shelley's Platonism is the result of a desire to see how Platonism, the most poetical of all philosophies, gives what Horace has called *rem,* substance, to the poet's imagination, thought, and emotion. Although there have been many studies of the Platonism of English poets, the writer has felt that the problem of Platonism in poetry goes deeper than a routine tracing of sources of influence. This important literary criticism must be rooted in an understanding of the complex nature and meaning of Platonism, how it works, shapes thought, and is transmuted into poetry in the alchemy of the creative mind. Once the critic realizes that Platonism is not a static standard of reference to which one may mechanically refer a passage, much of the confusion and polemic as to whether Shelley is a Platonist or a pseudo Platonist will cease. The writer has avoided taking part in the literary quarrels between classicism and romanticism, humanism and naturalism, in which Shelley's Platonism unfortunately is entangled. Platonism should be studied in the context of the creative process. Criticism should understand Plato's ideas not only as they are found in Plato but also as they are creatively assimilated by the poetic mind.

The writer has tried to probe into the Platonic mind and depict the complex processes that are at work there. The results are far from satisfactory, and in trying to understand the complexity of Shelley's Platonism the writer has from time to time found the partial truth in Burke's dictum that "a clear idea is therefore another name for a little idea." The realm of Shelley's Platonism is too often the "cavern of man's tractless spirit," the "dim cave of human thought." Sometimes it is impossible to decide whether a passage is Platonic and, if so, to unravel the twist which Shelley's symbolic mind has given to it, or to decide whether the Platonism of a passage is the independent creation of Shelley's own mind or derived directly or indirectly from Plato. If the success in understanding the complexity of Shelley's Platonism is limited, the writer will be satisfied with partial success provided he has asked the right questions, has explored Shelley's Platonism in the way all study of the Platonic tradition should be approached.

This study is a development of the writer's interest in the philosophic problem of the relation of Platonism and the "poetic" mind in philosophy, poetry, or religion. The writer stated his conclusions in a paper which appeared in the *Journal of Philosophy;* this paper appears now with some changes as the first chapter and main thesis of the book. The book itself is the result of the writer's desire not to remain content with an abstract evaluation of the problem, but to study the problem and apply his principles and conclusions in the laboratory of the concrete and dynamic richness of a creative mind. Though not professionally trained in the field of English poetry, he chose Shelley, since in the study of that poet the writer's own training in and love for Plato and the classics would be of distinct advantage, for a full understanding of Shelley, above all poets in the realm of English literature, requires a knowledge of Plato and the classics which the poet read in the original with delight and creative profit.

The thesis which is explicit and implicit in this book is that Plato, a philosopher-poet, helped Shelley, a poet-philosopher, give birth to the natural Platonism in his own soul. Shelley was one who had to have a philosophy to express in his poetry. When this philosophy was the radical revolutionary thought of the eighteenth century, his poetry reads like poetic pamphlets; when Shelley's own ideal philosophy was awakened, shaped by, and derived from Plato and the Platonic tradition, then he wrote some of the best Platonic poetry in English literature, such as *Prometheus Unbound, Adonais, Epipsychidion,* not to speak of the *Hymn to Intellectual Beauty* and *Mont Blanc.* Shelley's debt to Plato is like that aptly expressed by Bernard of Chartres: "We are like dwarfs, sitting on the shoulders of giants, in order that we may see things more numerous and more distant than they could see, not, certainly, by reason of the sharpness of our own vision or the tallness of our bodies, but because we are lifted and raised on high by the greatness of giants." Shelley was lifted and raised on high by the greatness of Plato, and because of this Shelley's greatness deserves a detailed study of his Platonism.

The above quotation can also be applied, *mutatis mutandis,* to the writer and the aid he has received in the pursuit of this study. In his undergraduate days he was lifted and raised on high by the greatness of Professor Harry de Forest Smith, an inspiring professor of Greek at Amherst, who initiated him into Plato and the Platonic tradition even to the extent of first suggesting to him a study of Shelley's Platonism as the best laboratory for a study of the Platonic tradition. In the pursuit of this work the writer saw things more numerous and distant than he alone could see because of the long list of Shelley scholars and editors who shaped the historical perspective of this study. In particular he is indebted to the late Professor N. I. White for his unfailing assistance and advice, and his generous offer of a typescript of the Journal of Shelley and Mary and the Diary of Jane Claire Clairmont which enabled him to penetrate deeper into the history of the contact of Shelley's mind with Plato and the Platonic tradition. Furthermore, he is greatly indebted to Professor White's masterful biography of Shelley for information and interpretation of Shelley's life and poetry. Scholars, no less than Shelley's poets, "are a very cameleonic race; they take the colour not only of what they feed on, but of the very leaves under which they pass." To list individually the writer's indebtedness to other sources would be to enumerate most of the bibliography of Shelley; like Shelley's chameleonic poet, the writer has profited even from their very notes.

He is also indebted to the editors of the Julian edition of Shelley's *Works* and Charles Scribner's Sons for permission to quote and use Shelley's translations from Plato as given in that edition; this text forms, when Shelley's own manuscripts or Mary's transcriptions of them are not available, the basis for the critical edition of Shelley's translations from Plato given herein. The need for such an edition is stated in the introduction to the third part of this volume.

The writer is grateful in particular to Sir John C. E. Shelley-Rolls for permission to make use of new material for Shelley's Platonism which first appeared in the limited privately printed editions of Shelley's translation of the *Banquet* and Shelley's *Verse and Prose*. The Bodleian Library has kindly given permission to use and has furnished photographic reproductions of Mary's transcript of Shelley's translation of the *Symposium* and other hitherto unpublished Platonic material in Shelley's notebooks recently given to the Bodleian by Sir John C. E. Shelley-Rolls. Furthermore, the writer is indebted to the editors of the *Journal of Philosophy, MLN, MLR, PMLA,* and *CW* for permission to fit into the organic whole of this study some Plato-Shelley articles and notes by the writer which first appeared in these periodicals. The passages quoted from the Loeb Classical Library translation of Plato are reprinted by permission of the President and Fellows of Harvard College, whose courtesy is appreciated. The writer acknowledges gratefully permission from the following publishers to quote from books in their lists: Alfred A. Knopf: N. I. White's *Shelley;* John Murray: R. Glynn Grylls's *Claire Clairmont;* Houghton Mifflin Co.: W. E. Peck's *Shelley, His Life and*

Work and J. L. Lowes's *The Road to Xanadu;* Princeton University Press: Herbert Agar's *Milton and Plato;* University of California Press: Paul Shorey's *Platonism, Ancient and Modern;* Oxford University Press: R. Glynn Grylls's *Mary Shelley,* A. H. Koszul's *Shelley's Prose in the Bodleian Manuscript,* Robert Bridges's *The Testament of Beauty,* F. H. Bradley's *Principles of Logic* and *English Literature and the Classics;* Constable and Co. Ltd.: *The Halliford Edition of the Works of Thomas Love Peacock;* The University of Oklahoma Press: *The Letters of Mary W. Shelley,* collected and edited by F. L. Jones; The Warburg Institute: Raymond Klibansky's *The Continuity of the Platonic Tradition during the Middle Ages.* The Greek in some of the quotations is printed without accents in strict conformity with the practice of Thomas Taylor, Peacock, Hogg, and Shelley.

Finally it is a duty and a pleasure to acknowledge the aid received from Dr. Remsen B. Ogilby, late president of Trinity College; Mrs. Harold Schatz and Miss Mary Moore Beale, of the staff of the Trinity College Library; Miss Evelyn Andersen, who prepared the manuscript; and Professor John C. E. Taylor. The careful patience and skill of the staff of the Duke University Press deserve the greatest gratitude.

Conscious that *nescit vox missa reverti,* the writer in no way imputes any of the errors in this book to Professors N. I. White and Morse S. Allen, who have read and improved the manuscript. He is indebted to his wife for sound judgment and encouragement, and finally to Shelley's own *Hellas,* that "tempestuous herald of victory," ἐν τούτῳ νίκα for the courage to dare let his mind deal with things eternal while the "Anarchs of the world of darkness" rage about us.

James Anastasios Notopoulos

Hartford, Conn.
March 25, 1949.

Contents

[xi]

CONTENTS

Part I

SHELLEY AND THE THREE STRANDS OF PLATONISM

Chapter I

Platonism and the Poetic Mind

"Represent them then, as it were, by a line divided."—*Republic,* 509d

OUR INTEREST in Platonism weaves itself into the eternal and temporal of its texture; the Platonic Eros of our minds leads some to adventure in the realm of Truth and Being, and others to follow the adventure of the Platonic tradition in the progress of civilization. Failure, however, to base any discussion of Platonism on clarity of distinction results either in confusion or at best in only partial illumination.

The history of Platonism is written with vagueness as to degree and kind. The natural Platonism in human nature, i.e., the common awareness of certain fundamental problems which agitate the human mind, is overlooked as the source of Plato's Platonism. A person who has never read Plato is called a Platonist, whereas one who has read him but differs from him runs the risk of being a pseudo-Platonist. The part is often mistaken for the whole. Hybrids are found in Platonism and called weeds. The judges of Platonism range all the way from specialists who demand a shibboleth to the synoptic-minded who lose the part in the whole, and sweep away any distinction between the natural universal Platonism, its "literal" expression by Plato, and its influence in the form of a tradition. He who is to be the historian of Platonism must fully understand these distinctions, for they serve as a measure for the evaluation of degree and kind of Platonism.

When one looks at the fountain of light, he is dazzled. Hence the apprehension of Platonism must be through degrees or levels. There are three levels in the realm of Platonism or in the Platonic tradition:[1] (a) indirect Platonism, or the adventure of Plato's thought as a tradition in the mind and history of Europe; (b) direct or "literal" Platonism, the philosophy of Plato as expressed in the Dialogues; and (c) Platonism as philosophy itself, the source of Plato's thought in the very nature of things. Though these levels are divided for purposes of evaluation, they

[1] Though Platonism and the Platonic tradition are not the same thing specifically, in the generic sense they are synonymous and are used interchangeably by many writers to mean both the philosophy of Plato and its influence as a tradition.

are continuous in the life of Platonism. The relation of the first to the second level and of the second to the third is, as it were, the relation of an image to the original. The student of Platonism must go through an experience of ἀναγνώρισις, or recognition, and realize that the image cannot be understood without reference to the direct Platonism of the Dialogues. In turn, the Platonism of the Dialogues cannot be understood without the venture into philosophy.

Without an insight into this final supreme level, our knowledge of the other two levels is confused and limited. To understand Platonism as an activity of certain fundamental ideas in the mind and history of Europe, we must try to understand the nature of its eternal element, and vice versa; the historian of Platonism must understand that the history of the ideas depends on the nature of the ideas, that history needs philosophy as philosophy needs history. Furthermore, though few are the individuals who have a clear insight into the third level of Platonism, every thinking person has a dim apprehension of it, so that it is possible for the student of Plato to distinguish between (1) the Platonist who is influenced by Plato indirectly, through Plato's plastic interpenetration in the thought and history of civilization; (2) the Platonist who studies, accepts, and is directly influenced by Plato's thought as contained in the Dialogues; and (3) the Platonist who has Plato's wonder, inspiration, and insight into the same realm of speculation. Similarly it is possible for the historian of Platonism to recognize those who combine natural with direct Platonism, or direct with indirect, or those who combine all three. Without this ability to distinguish levels or to perceive levels in combination, the historian of Platonism may be compared to a mariner without a compass.

The charting of the three levels of Platonism will be illustrated in the case of Shelley. The validity of their distinction, however, and the nature of each level require illumination. The levels can best be understood through the symbolism of image and original. That indirect Platonism is an image of the direct Platonism of the Dialogues is obvious; that the Platonism of the Dialogues is itself an image and was regarded as such by Plato himself has not been clear. In a significant passage in the seventh Epistle, Plato says that the object of writing philosophy is to discover and reveal nature rather than create it: "καὶ τὴν φύσιν εἰς φῶς πᾶσιν προαγαγεῖν" (341d). Though no student of Plato accepts his philosophy as a passive image, it is well to consider this remark in its proper Platonic context.

It is evident that Plato hints in this passage the truth that the creator is first a discoverer, that philosophy is a medium of approach or communication, a midwifery, ἡ μαιευτικὴ τέχνη, as he calls it. Like the poet in the *Ion,* the philosopher is a medium of communication from one realm to another, a note in the scale of τὰ μεταξύ. The Greek usually does not suffer from deterministic egoism; it is the Gods, the Muses, who speak; he is simply the medium. The poet, the artist, is the means to an end, the expression of Being. If "the Lord is my Light" is the conviction of religious experience, if the Muses are the source of the poet, reality, τὸ ὄν, is the Lord and Muse of the philosopher. Thus the above remark of Plato is consonant with the belief of the Greek that, though art and philosophy are creations in so far as they express in form what was nonbeing or latent in consciousness, they really *image* imperfectly something that is in them, yet beyond them. The importance and significance of this lies in looking upon Plato as a discoverer, and his thought as an image, nearer to the sun of Being, but still an image. His thought takes the form of hypotheses, images reflecting his insights into Being. He realized that one cannot write the truth, hence the image, the likeness, the "suggestion respecting the nature of essence."[2] Plato's image of truth is magical, full of artistic brilliance. Through this magic many historians of Platonism become like the prisoners in the Cave of the *Republic* and mistake the image for the original. Because of its merit, excellence, and art, they conceive of Platonism as a standard rather than as a notebook of discovery, an experimental adventure of Eros, a movement of thought to apprehend truth. For us Plato is a flower and we the bees, but for Plato himself his thought is an image of Being, ever seeking it as the bee does the flower. It is important for the understanding of the Platonic tradition to recognize this fact.

We must transcend the partial stage of εἰκασία, which confuses an image with the original and views Platonism as an absolutism in thought. As Professor Demos points out, ". . . thought is a telic phenomenon; it is movement with a direction."[3] This is the state of mind appropriate to the third level of Platonism and is characteristic of Plato's thought. Plato is a creative force within a creative realm. His concepts are not final. They are partial images bright with insight into the realm of Being. As art, the Dialogues of Plato are finalities; but as philosophy they are thought in process, images of an adventure into philosophy. The image of Platonism as expressed in the Dialogues is only one of

[2] *Phaedrus,* 276.
[3] Raphael Demos, "The Rhythm of Thought," *Philosophical Review,* XLII (1933), 274.

many possible images. It is a sample. But it is so appealing that it leads to synecdoche, a study of philosophy from a part of it. But we must realize that it is not the whole. The image of philosophy in the Dialogues is partial. In the felicitous words of Whitehead, it "exemplifies the grandeur of the wider truth arising from the very nature of the order of things"; it is an instance of the "general form of the forms of thought, and, like the air we breathe, such a form is so translucent, and so pervading, and so seemingly necessary, that only by extreme effort can we become aware of it."[4]

The difficulty, however, of grasping "the wider truth" and the "general form of the forms of thought" is greater than that of the awareness or consciousness of the existence of the realm of which the Platonism of the Dialogues is the image. The original of this image is reality; the general form in which it presents itself to the philosopher is the nature of the world of Being and Becoming, and the relation or medium connecting the eternality of Being with the fluency of Becoming. This is the third level of Platonism. Anyone who tries to apprehend it is a Platonist by virtue of his sharing with Plato the same movement, direction of thought, the general form of it which Plato first formulated. In the *Sophist* Plato defines Being as a power or force (247e).[5] It is very suggestive to think of the third level of Platonism as endowed with a power of magnetism and influence which persuades minds to wonder and speculate about the nature of this realm. Anyone who reads Plato is impressed with the immovable persuasive movement of Being. He has the feeling that the thoughts of the man are an effluence of the creativity of Being; that the philosopher is the "receptacle" of these thoughts. Eros is the vitalizing rhythm of communication between the philosopher and Being. The apprehension or realization of this is not the solitary privilege of one mind, not, as it were, Adam enjoying exclusive rights to Paradise. Rather it is the common privilege of any mind capable of entering the realm. Hence many are the minds which are conscious of the third level of Platonism, and many were the Platonists before Plato. It is not *identity* of their philosophies with that of Plato which determines whether they are Platonists, but rather *similar* awareness, doubt, question, and intuition into the same problems that Plato first fully discovered.

It is in this light that we must understand Whitehead's remark that "the safest general characterization of the European philosophical tradition is that it consists of a series of footnotes to Plato."[6] He does not

[4] A. N. Whitehead, *Adventures of Ideas* (New York, 1933), pp. 14, 19.
[5] Cf. Joseph Souilhé, *Étude sur le terme Δύναμις dans les Dialogues de Platon* (Paris, 1919).
[6] A. N. Whitehead, *Process and Reality* (New York, 1930), p. 63.

mean that the European philosophical tradition is one of imitation, but rather one of participation in the problems that Plato became aware of and pondered, in the living thought prior to his magical verbalization of it. Of further significance in this connection is Whitehead's remark:

Centuries ago Plato divined the seven main factors interwoven in fact: The Ideas, The Physical Elements, The Psyche, The Eros, The Harmony, The Mathematical Relations, The Receptacle. All philosophical systems are endeavours to express the interweaving of these components. Of course, it is most unscholarly to identify our modern notions with these archaic thoughts of Plato. For us everything has a subtle difference. But for all these differences, human thought is now endeavouring to express *analogous elements* in the composition of nature. It only dimly discerns, it misdescribes, and it wrongly associates. But always there remain the *same beacons* that lure.[7]

This statement of the most Platonic of modern philosophers is illuminating. It is not imitation of Plato, but the lure of the same beacons that determines the real Platonist.[8]

The reason for calling the third level Platonism rather than philosophy, or, to be exact, a certain kind of philosophy, is the genius, the persuasive and enshadowing vitality, of Plato's thought. In the same way that Christ, a living image of God but not the Father himself, so taught and lived as to color and give the religion of the Western World his name,[9] so Plato, whose philosophy is a living image of Being, became identified with the European philosophical tradition to the extent that it "consists of a series of footnotes to Plato."

To understand the difference between the second and third levels of Platonism, one must be aware of the theory of symbolism implicit in Plato's philosophy. Truth is not grasped immediately, but through stages. Truth is glimpsed through insight, thought; in turn, the insight or the thought is expressed through λόγος either as the spoken word or as the written word. The written word or the book is thus an image of an image. This explains Socrates's position on the superiority of the living word over the written word. The dualism of the living word

---

[7] Whitehead, *Adventures of Ideas*, p. 203. Italics inserted.

[8] It is the story of the lure of the third level rather than the Platonic tradition of the first level that explains the title of J. H. Muirhead's book, *The Platonic Tradition in Anglo-Saxon Philosophy* (New York, 1931). If one is not aware of the various levels of Platonism, the book is confusing, for there is little of the Platonism of the first or second level in it. In vain does the reader await the appearance of Plato in the story of idealism. It is the concern of the idealists with the problem of appearance and reality that accounts for the title.

[9] The analogy gains when it is realized that the sects of this religion are as diverse as the systems of philosophy.

and the written word is exemplified in the third and second levels of Platonism. The difference is one of thought as thought, and thought as formulated and expressed in the written word. The Platonism of the Dialogues is the formulation, in a fixed form, of the third level, thought as living process. This second level is thought become immanent, thought as a thing. The beauty of written Platonism lies in the fact that the expression is both universal and particular. It grasps the abstract aspect of thought with ordinary language, and the concrete side of it with art. It contains the "here and now" and the "beyond" as well. The Platonism of the Dialogues is a fusion of thought as process and thought as a thing. The movement of mind and emotion to grasp Being is caught and "prehended" in language, concept, myth. But thought, though fixed and caught so that it can be studied by all minds in common, is still vital, for Plato endows it with a variety of concepts and myths. It is due to this variety of expression for each intuition that the living word is not lost completely in the written word and that Plato has been able to influence thought in general.

The Platonism of the Dialogues is the fixation in art of insights into truth. The form of the dialogue is appropriate for the reflection of thought as movement. It, too, is thought in movement. The Dialogues are, as it were, the "receptacle" of Plato's insights; they are dramatizations of thought through which Being finds expression. The notions of the Ideas, the Physical Elements, the Psyche, the Eros, the Harmony, the Mathematical Relations, the Receptacle—all *image* Being, the general form of thought. But the Dialogues are more than a passive receptacle mirroring the order of things. Plato is creative and adds a quickening and harmonizing spirit. To say that the Platonism of the Dialogues is merely an image is to use too limited a word. *Image* is passive, but Plato is a creative force. To the reflection of the eternal he adds the temporal, which is most vividly presented in the form of the personal Plato: the Plato who tells us of his master, his friends, his reaction to the politics and art of the day, his taste, his personal experience. The important point is to know which is the personal Plato and which is the Plato imaging reality, to distinguish the movement and direction of his thought from the conceptual expression of it in the form of notions and suggestions concerning the nature of essence. We must not mistake the image for the original, Plato's formulation of thought with thought itself. Likewise we must not confuse the second level of Platonism with the third, in the same way that we must be careful not to confuse the Plato of tradition with the Plato of the Dialogues. The importance of charting the three levels of Platonism is the necessity of having a criterion of judgment whereby we realize that there are natural Platonists in philosophy or literature who belong to the creative and dynamic or literary tradition which Plato exemplifies, as well as Platonists of the imitative tradition. If the former are called Platonists, the reason is that Plato was genius enough to enshadow pervasively the realm with his name, because he was the efficient cause of its expression.

The story of the influence of Platonism on the thought and history of civilization constitutes the first level of Platonism. It is specifically known as the Platonic tradition. It starts with Aristotle, who began the "canalization" of it into specific grooves; it is transferred to Alexandria, where Platonic scholarship begins; then it joins the stream of Christianity and forms and permeates its theology. In the medieval period it feeds the imagination; in the Renaissance it gives form or substance or inspiration to movements, creeds, literature, and thought. This deterministic influence of Platonism owes its vitality to the creative persuasion of Plato's thought. It is a δύναμις, an impregnating force. The ideas of Plato are not, as it were, mental furniture, but ideas as causes, activities, molding the ideas with which they come in contact. Sometimes they constitute the very character and mentality of a plastic tradition. It is a changing tradition, entering into this or that mentality of an epoch and forming either its mystical, its religious, its artistic, or its metaphysical character. It has a rhythm of appearance and disappearance, as Whitehead points out. It is tradition in process, molding the formulation of other traditions.

The difference between the first and second levels of Platonism is again that of image and original. The Platonic tradition is the imitation, adaptation, conscious or unconscious, of the Platonism of Plato. It is the adventure of his ideas in thought and history. It is utilitarian in character, for it is used in the purposes of men, in their beliefs, formulation of creeds, and pleasures. It is, furthermore, a selective tradition to suit an immediate purpose or interest. Sometimes it is Plato the religious, the mystic; sometimes it is Plato the cosmologist, the poet, the logician. It is invariably a fusion, a coalescence, a Platonism arising from a union of its elements with the nature and temperament of the user, as well as with his environment or age.

The seed of Platonism in the Platonic tradition sometimes falls on fertile soil and sometimes on rock. Sometimes it is an inert, servile imitation without the warmth and creative vitality of the original, and sometimes it is an incarnate renascent spirit beating on the shores of human life in successive waves of specialization. In the medieval ages it is scholastic; in the Renaissance it is an outburst of fresh thought and activity. Sometimes the Platonic tradition takes the form of the working out of suggestions and hints found in Plato. For example, the relation of God to the world in Christian theology is formulated in part on Plato's suggestions of the possible relations of the eternal world with the temporal world. Sometimes it is the formation of patterns or systems based on Plato for purposes of teaching, civilizing, enlightening, or improving. The authority of Plato is often dragged in to sanction doctrines plucked from his philosophy and formalized into a creed.

Careful scrutiny is required to recognize the affinity of the Platonic tradition to Plato. In contrast to the second and third levels of Platonism, where philosophic speculation is the state of mind appropriate for the apprehension of their objects, the first level requires a historical state of mind endowed with the tools of scholarship to discern the ideas of Plato in the thought and actions of men. It must be able to untangle motivating ideas from events, examine them, write the story of their transmission, their coloration, their fertilization, and their nexus with events as they happen. Furthermore, the student of the Platonic tradition must be possessed of a sense of distinction, of an insight into genus and species. But just as in the Divided Line of the *Republic* we cannot understand the image without reference to the original, so the Platonic tradition cannot be understood without reference to the Platonism of the Dialogues, nor, ultimately, without reference to philosophy, the sun of its Being. The states of mind appropriate to each level are integrally related, as in their object.

The three levels are a necessary context for the understanding of Platonism, if not of Plato. They are essential to its history and its activity as a force in the world of thought and action. Their distinction prevents confusion in the use of the word *Platonism,* and the clarity that results increases our understanding of a vital force in our lives. Examples, taken from English poetry, illustrate simply the levels of Platonism. The first, illustrating the third level of Platonism, is taken from Wordsworth:

> And I have felt
> A presence that disturbs me with the joy
> Of elevated thoughts; a sense sublime
> Of something far more deeply interfused,
> Whose dwelling is the light of setting suns,
> And the round ocean and the living air,

And the blue sky, and the mind of man:
A motion and a spirit, that impels
All thinking things, all objects of all thought,
And rolls through all things. Therefore am I still
A lover of meadows and the woods,
And mountains; and of all that we behold
From this green earth.[10]

It is evident that the source of this poetry is not an inspiration from the Dialogues, nor from the influence of the Platonic tradition. It owes its source to a natural poetic insight in the realm of "Being." It is a spontaneous mood similar to Plato's, an awareness of the real presence of the eternal in the temporal. Though similar, it is an impassionate, direct flight to Beauty on the wings of its own being and not those of Plato or the Platonic tradition. That the experience is personal and not derivative is obvious. It seeks of its own nature the third and ultimate level of Platonism.

The example illustrating the second level of Platonism is taken from Bridges's *The Testament of Beauty:*

As some perfected flower, Iris or Lily, is born
patterning heav'nly beauty, a pictur'd idea
that hath no other expression for us, nor coud hav:
for thatt which Lily or Iris tell cannot be told
by poetry or by music in their secret tongues,
nor is discerptible in logic, but is itself
an absolute piece of Being, and we know not,
nay, nor search not by what creativ miracle
the soul's language is writ in perishable forms—
yet are we aware of such existences crowding,
mysterious beauties unexpanded, unreveal'd
phantasies intangible investing us closely,
hid only from our eyes by skies that will not clear;
activ presences, striving to force an entrance,
like bodiless exiled souls in dumb urgence pleading
to be brought to birth in our conscient existence,
as if our troubled lot wer the life they long'd for;
even as poor mortals thirst for immortality:—
And every divination of Natur or reach of Art
is nearer attainment to the divine plenitude
of understanding, and in moments of Vision
their unseen company is the breath of Life:—[11]

[10] *Lines, Composed a Few Miles Above Tintern Abbey,* ll. 93-105.
[11] *The Testament of Beauty,* I, 670-691.

We see the affinity of this poetry to the Platonism of the Platonic Dialogues, to the theory of ideas, to Eros. It is a graceful poetic transcription of Plato's thought, not servile in imitation nor yet possessing the spontaneity of Wordsworth's moods. It is the poetry of a man who has lived long with Plato, read him, thought about him until he is inspired to express in poetry the Eros of such a union. It is a poetry inspired by Plato himself, and this is the main characteristic of the second level of Platonism.

The poetry illustrating the first level, the Platonic tradition, is reflected in the following lines of Shakespeare:

> How sweet the moonlight sleeps upon this bank!
> Here will we sit, and let the sounds of music
> Creep in our ears: soft stillness and the night
> Become the touches of sweet harmony.
> Sit, Jessica: look, how the floor of heaven
> Is thick inlaid with patines of bright gold:
> There's not the smallest orb which thou behold'st
> But in his motion like an angel sings,
> Still quiring to the young eyed cherubins;
> Such harmony is in the immortal souls;
> But, whilst this muddy vesture of decay
> Doth grossly close it in, we can not hear it.[12]

The ultimate source of Lorenzo's discourse on music is to be found in Plato's *Timaeus,* a dialogue that had much influence on English literature. The adventure of the Pythagorean doctrine of harmony as the purgation of the soul, as an intermediary between the Soul of Man and the Soul of the World, the substitution of angels and cherubim for the Siren on each of the planetary rings who sings in monotone her proper note of the octave is an example of Platonism floating as a vast mass of traditional lore in the England of Shakespeare's youth. Though there is no evidence that Shakespeare read the *Timaeus,* he was just the man to be influenced by it.

Philosophers and poets, however, cannot be entirely pigeon-holed into this or that level of Platonism. There are degrees of Platonism as of any other standard of value. It is the realization of the degree, of what an outburst of the spirit itself is, as distinguished from an imitation of it, that determines the value. Thus while some Platonists fall into one

[12] *The Merchant of Venice,* V, i, 54-65; for this example, see John Burnet, *Essays and Addresses* (New York, 1930), pp. 163-168; E. M. W. Tillyard, *The Elizabethan World Picture* (London, 1943), pp. 38-47, 94-99.

definite level of Platonism, there are a very few who ascend and descend the Divided Line of Platonism like arpeggios. Shelley is the outstanding Platonist in English literature. He reveals a natural and authentic adventure into the realm of Being, both a direct knowledge of Plato and the interpenetration of the Platonic tradition in the inherited pattern of our thought. His Platonism is the attainment of the three levels.[13] In his work we will find the state of mind and object of each kind of Platonism. From the contemplation of Shelley's Platonism we will best understand how Plato is forever living because he is forever inspiriting his insights and inspiration into kindred spirits of all time. And from the contemplation of Platonism in Shelley we will best understand how Plato is not a static god but a dynamic creator.

[13] For a detailed listing and discussion of the three levels of Platonism in Shelley, *vide infra*, pp. 171-371.

Chapter II

Shelley's Natural Platonism

"Testimonia animae naturaliter Platonicae."

"A POET," says Shelley, "is the combined product of such internal powers as modify the nature of others; and of such external influences as excite and sustain these powers; he is not one, but both."[1] No better explanation is needed for the relation of Shelley's natural Platonism to direct and indirect Platonism. Shelley is the product of both; and, though for purposes of analysis we separate the various kinds of Platonism, the living soul of Shelley's Platonism is a unity of all three. Sometimes natural Platonism is revealed as an operation of his own mind, untouched by the external influence of Plato or the Platonic tradition. In one of the earliest of Shelley's poems we have an example of natural Platonism:

> Congenial minds will seek their kindred soul,
> E'en though the tide of time has roll'd between;
> They mock weak matter's impotent control,
> And seek of endless life the eternal scene.[2]

Quite often Shelley's natural Platonism is excited and sustained by the poet's constant contact with Plato and the Platonic tradition. The relation of Shelley's natural Platonism to the direct and indirect Platonism can most significantly be illustrated by the application, *mutatis mutandis,* of the Cave myth in the *Republic* to Shelley. Though natural Platonism is one of the essential characteristics of Shelley's poetic nature, we find it, in his early life, a chained prisoner in the cave of Radicalism, the French Revolution, and Godwinism. In the contemplation of these doctrines, under the conditions described in the *Republic,*[3] Shelley's

[1] *The Complete Works of Percy Bysshe Shelley,* Newly edited by Roger Ingpen and Walter E. Peck in Ten Volumes, Published for The Julian Editions (London and New York, 1926-1929), II, 174 (hereinafter referred to as Julian *Works*).

[2] *Fragment, Supposed to be an Epithalamium of Francis Ravaillac and Charlotte Cordé,* ll. 42-45.

[3] *Republic,* 514 ff.; for Shelley and the French Revolution, see Amiyakumar Sen, *Studies in Shelley* (Calcutta, 1936), pp. 271-335.

natural Platonism remains a latent force; like Plato's prisoner, it was eventually freed and then emerged into the sunlight of its true nature. The loosening of the bonds was brought about by Shelley's own maturing experience, the influence of Plato-loving friends, and his contact with direct and indirect Platonism.[4] All these contributed to the turning around of the eye of the mind, as Plato puts it, towards the light and sun of Platonism. It is important to point out, as Plato does in the case of the released prisoner, that the turning around of Shelley's soul by the forces mentioned is not a way of putting Platonism into a soul empty of Platonism. It is rather, as Plato says, "an art of . . . effective shifting or conversion of the soul, not an art of producing vision in it, but on the assumption that it possesses vision but does not rightly direct it and does not look where it should, an art of bringing this about."[5] Shelley's Platonism is not adventitious, but an indwelling power in his soul.

This is clearly seen in the case of the *Hymn to Intellectual Beauty* and other poems. Though the title of the *Hymn to Intellectual Beauty* is derived from the Platonic tradition, the source of the poem lies in the natural Platonism of Shelley's nature.[6] The poem records an experience of conversion[7] which occurred six years before, during Shelley's stay at Syon House Academy. The "unseen Power," whose shadow he saw in the world about him, remained quiescent until the beauty of Switzerland stirred him into expression. But, like Goethe, Shelley was possessed of two souls: natural Platonism and the soul of rebellion nurtured on eighteenth-century materialism. The materialistic doctrine of Necessity,[8] influenced by circumstances in Shelley's life favorable to its growth, found early and predominant expression. But soon the poet's heart triumphed over his head. Shelley's conflict between natural Platonism and materialism finds matchless analogy in a passage from Bradley:

That the glory of this world in the end is appearance leaves the world more glorious, if we feel it is a show of some fuller splendour; but the sensuous curtain is a deception and a cheat, if it hides some colourless movement of atoms, some spectral woof of impalpable abstractions, or unearthly ballet of bloodless categories. Though dragged to such conclusions, we can not embrace them. Our principles may be true, but they are not reality. They no more *make* that Whole which commands our devotion, than some shredded

[4] *Vide supra,* p. 46.

[5] *Republic,* 518d (Shorey's translation in Loeb Classical Library).

[6] *Vide infra,* pp. 18-19, 196; cf. William Temple, "Plato's Vision of the Ideas," *Mind,* XVII (1908), 505, where he views this poem as the record of an analogous experience.

[7] See N. I. White, *The Best of Shelley* (New York, 1932), pp. 473-474.

[8] See N. I. White, *Shelley* (New York, 1940), 2 vols., II, index, *s. v.* Necessity.

dissection of human tatters *is* that warm and breathing beauty of flesh which our hearts found delightful.[9]

Shelley found the breathing beauty of natural Platonism more delightful than materialism, and we soon find him "gifting," as Mary says, "the material universe with a soul and a voice." With *Alastor,* written in 1815, we find the quest of Ideal Beauty emerging with clearer manifestations and formulation. In the *Hymn to Intellectual Beauty* we find a conjunction of Shelley's natural Platonism with the Platonic tradition which aided in evoking the latent mood, giving syllables to its yearning, shaping its expression of natural Platonic intuitions and insights through the traditional concepts and symbols of Platonism. The poem is a magical fusion of a natural Platonic experience with a Platonic concept. The shadow of Intellectual Beauty which

> Gives grace and truth to life's unquiet dream[10]

began to haunt Shelley's soul more frequently. The reading and translation of the *Symposium* stimulated Shelley to express his quest for the ideal in the more precise concepts and formulas of direct Platonism. The *Prometheus Unbound, The Witch of Atlas, Epipsychidion,* and *The Sensitive Plant* are infused with conceptions, symbols, and language of direct and indirect Platonism which express Shelley's search for Ideal Beauty in a beautiful woman.[11] Finally in the *Adonais* we have the perfect fusion of natural, direct, and indirect Platonism. No poet who did not have natural Platonism in his soul could have given such perfect expression to the quintessence of Platonism, nor could any poet with natural Platonism in his soul give such perfect expression to it without the aid of Platonic concept, language, and feeling. A comparison with other Platonic poetry in English literature shows how sterile the Platonic tradition can be if, as Shelley says, poets possess "the form, whilst they want the spirit of those whom, it is alleged, they imitate."[12] The *Adonais,* like the *Hymn to Intellectual Beauty,* is a nondramatic testament of Shelley's natural Platonism felicitously wedded to the beauty of direct and indirect Platonism. Thus Shelley's contact with Plato and the Platonic tradition not only turned his soul around from the contemplation of the shadows of materialism to "the contemplation of essence and the brightest region of being,"[13] but also, like the Socratic midwife,

---

[9] F. H. Bradley, *Principles of Logic* (London, 1922), II, 591; cf. "the sensuous curtain is a deception and a cheat" with Shelley's *Sonnet,* 1818.

[10] *Hymn to Intellectual Beauty,* l. 36.   [11] Cf. White, *Shelley,* II, 439-444.

[12] Julian *Works,* II, 173.

[13] *Republic,* 518c.

helped Shelley give birth and expression to the Platonic ideas in his own soul.

In the creative process of Shelley's natural, direct, and indirect Platonism a new amalgam of Platonism is formed which is *sui generis*. Sometimes it can be measured by the yardstick of the Platonic tradition; sometimes it is intangible in the form of atmosphere, mood, *arrière pensée*. It is often combined with many non-Platonic qualities. Shelley's Platonism, therefore, is not and cannot be Plato's Platonism. The truly creative process is not strictly imitative; it involves assimilation, change, coloration.[14] Shelley himself is conscious of this and states it as a credo in the Preface to the *Prometheus Unbound*. In Shelley natural Platonism is sometimes similar to Plato's and sometimes different; it is protean in character, even as was Shelley himself.

Shelley's Platonism demands a new study of its Platonic and non-Platonic qualities. It demands a new understanding which does away with the Procrustean criticism to which it has often been subjected. "Procrustean" is the word because those critics who see Shelley as a Platonist cut off the protruding and embarrassing differences from Plato, while those who do not see him as a Platonist cut off the qualities similar to Plato. Our aim in this survey of Shelley's Platonism is to understand it as it is, with its similarities and differences from Plato; not abstracted but studied in the context of Shelley's life and character.

Natural Platonism in Shelley consists of what Coleridge calls "modes of inmost being,"[15] which are not derivative from Plato. Their cognate nature can be illustrated by the Yankee farmer who upon returning a volume of Plato borrowed from Emerson said, "That man has a good many of my idees."[16] The natural Platonism in Shelley concerns itself with a mode of inmost being common to poetry and philosophy. The poet and the philosopher have certain cognate insights. The poet's mind is naturally Platonic when it tries to find something eternal amid the temporal and passing phenomena of the world of time and space. Shelley's early sentiment:

> They mock weak matter's impotent control,
> And seek of endless life the eternal scene,

which is later to blossom into

> Heaven's light forever shines, Earth's shadows fly,[17]

[14] Cf. Epictetus, *Encheiridion*, 46, 2: "Sheep eat grass, but they do grow not grass but wool on their backs."

[15] *Coleridge's Works*, ed. W. G. Shedd (New York, 1853), III, 490.

[16] Paul Shorey, *Platonism, Ancient and Modern* (Berkeley, Calif., 1938), p. 155. (All subsequent references to Shorey, unless otherwise specified, are to this work.)

[17] *Fragment, Supposed to Be an Epithalamium of Francis Ravaillac and Charlotte Cordé*, ll. 44-45; *Adonais*, l. 461.

is at the very heart of his natural Platonism. It is an inmost mode of being which finds countless echoes in other poets, such as:

> Authentic tidings of invisible things;
> Of ebb and flow, and ever-during power;
> And central peace, subsisting at the heart
> Of endless agitation.[18]

The basic element, therefore, in Shelley's natural Platonism which he shares with Plato and other poets is the intuition, which developed with experience and study into a concept and belief, that the life of man in the world of time and space is an unsubstantial shadow, a "painted veil" as Shelley calls it, of an ideal world. Life, as man knows it, is all change; we come into being and perish; the processes of nature reveal the same experience: the seasons come and go, and though they bring similar experiences they are not the same; what once was joy has turned into sorrow, hope into disappointment. Thus change characterizes not only nature but all human experiences.[19] Man shifts and flounders in this unsteady, contradictory world of illusions. In contrast to this world there is a permanent reality, eternal, unchanged through every change. This eternal reality is beyond time and space; it transcends generation and decay. All the eternal values of life, truth, beauty, goodness, perfection, are essences of the Ideal world. Beautiful objects in the world of time and space pass and fade, but Ideal Beauty knows naught of the seasons.

The natural Platonism of the poet seeks and yearns for this permanent reality. In its quest he finds an immanent-transcendent relationship existing between the two worlds. The Ideal world is transcendent, above and beyond the relative world. If this Ideal world is to be partially realized or attained by man, it has somehow to be in the relative world and yet beyond it at the same time. Beauty must be in the beautiful flower in order that the flower might be beautiful, yet Ideal Beauty must be beyond it lest Beauty perish and decay with the flower. So, too, God must be within the world in order that His qualities may grace this world, yet He must also be above and beyond it lest He partake of the evanescent qualities of this world. The immanent and transcendent relation between these two worlds of natural Platonism[20] can be brought about only by the soul of man, which is a portion the divine and

---

[18] Wordsworth, *The Excursion*, IV, 1144-1147.

[19] Cf. Shelley's *Mutability* and White, *The Best of Shelley*, p. 471.

[20] Cf. A. M. D. Hughes, "The Theology of Shelley," *Proceedings of the British Academy*, XXIV (1938), 195 ff.

eternal in us. Therefore the poet's soul both feels the sorrows and pains of the relative world and, because of its divine nature, also has insight and apprehension of the Ideal world. Thus the poet's soul is, like Plato's Eros, the connecting link between the two worlds of natural Platonism.

The poet, the philosopher, the theologian—all have an intuitive grasp of this natural Platonism; all are aware of these two realms and their interrelation through the soul. Yet their common awareness finds different expression; each expresses the same intuition through the faculty that is characteristic of him: the poet through emotion, sense-laden thought and imagination; the philosopher through reason; the theologian through faith. The character of the apprehending soul also affects the object. The poet will dramatize Platonic values through the symbolism of flesh and blood; Emilia Viviani, for example, is the incarnation of Platonic Beauty and Love. The philosopher will find Intellectual Beauty in a logical and ontological essence, whereas the theologian will find it in the love of God. Thus the absolute world of natural Platonism is colored by the quality of the seeker's soul. Natural Platonism is not a static code of thought or intuition. The common awareness of an immaterial reality behind this world is given different expression by the diverse poetic, philosophic, and religious approaches to the common goal.

The pursuit of Ideal Beauty constitutes the essential character of Shelley's natural Platonism. "I always seek," he says, "in what I see the manifestation of something beyond the present and tangible object."[21] At the sight of it his soul sprouted wings, as Plato would say, and was possessed of an ever-present desire to fly to the Absolute. Bagehot calls him the poet of "peculiar removed essences." Shelley's yearning and pursuit of an unattainable ideal became the driving passion of his poetry. Feeling that life is a "painted veil," an unreal pageant, he passionately sought for the Ideal Beauty whose shadows he saw pervading the universe. The pursuit of the Ideal takes on a complex form. Any attempt to find logical consistency in the many and varied expressions of natural Platonism in Shelley will end in failure. Shelley for the most part pursues the Ideal on two planes: in the concrete and in the abstract. In some poems the beauty of the particular absorbs him; he could contemplate the Ideal only through its earthly image. In his own life he pursued Ideal Beauty through what he thought was its embodiment in various women. The story of his loves—Harriet Grove, Harriet Westbrook, Elizabeth Hitchener, Mary Godwin, Claire Clairmont, Emilia

[21] Julian *Works*, IX, 340.

Viviani, Jane Williams—is the story of his attempts to find the Ideal in the concrete. His failure to ascend to the empyrean heights of Platonism lies in the fact that the symbolism of the earthly is the unruly horse which prevents the chariot of his soul from ascending to the heaven of true Platonism. Shelley became aware of his failure and confessed in his later life, "I think one is always in love with something or other; the error, and I confess it is not easy for spirits cased in flesh and blood to avoid it, consists in seeking in a mortal image the likeness of what is perhaps eternal."[22] Yet it is the pursuit of the Ideal through earthly imagery that constitutes one of the charms of the natural Platonism of his poetry. The particular, the here and now, the image form the natural approach to the Ideal for most human beings, and Shelley's natural Platonism is attractive because, as De Sanctis says of the miracle of Greek art, "the concept is buried and entirely forgotten in the image."[23] But Shelley's mind sought the Ideal in the abstract as well as in concrete symbols. Mary Shelley in her note to the 1839 edition of Shelley's poems strikes one of the keynotes of Shelley's natural Platonism when she says:

He loved to idealize reality; . . . few of us understand or sympathize with the endeavour to ally the love of abstract beauty, and adoration of abstract good, the τὸ ἀγαθὸν καὶ τὸ καλόν of the Socratic philosophers, with our sympathies with our kind. In this Shelley resembled Plato; both taking more delight in the abstract and the ideal, than in the special and tangible. This did not result from imitation: for it was not till Shelley resided in Italy that he made Plato his study.[24]

Shelley himself attests to his use of abstract symbolism. In the Preface to *Prometheus Unbound* he says:

The imagery which I have employed will be found, in many instances, to have been drawn from the operations of the human mind, or from those external actions by which they are expressed. . . . Poetical abstractions are beautiful and new, not because the portions of which they are composed had no previous existence in the mind of man or in nature, but because the whole produced by their combination has some intelligible and beautiful analogy with those sources of emotion and thought.[25]

[22] *Ibid.*, X, 401; for Shelley's disappointment with Emilia Viviani, see R. M. Smith, *The Shelley Legend* (New York, 1945), p. 306; for a study of Shelley's transcendentalism, see H. N. Fairchild, *The Romantic Quest* (New York, 1931), pp. 373-401.

[23] Francesco De Sanctis, *History of Italian Literature* (New York, 1931), I, 72.

[24] Julian *Works*, I, xiii; for a study of this tendency in Shelley, see O. W. Firkins, *Power and Elusiveness in Shelley* (Minneapolis, Minn., 1937).

[25] Julian *Works*, II, 172-173; cf. *ibid.*, X, 69: "Strong passion expresses itself in metaphor borrowed from objects alike remote or near. . . ."

These poetical abstractions which are the product of "internal powers" constitute a large body of abstract symbols which Shelley used in his search for Ideal Beauty. Thus the natural Platonism of his most Platonic poems like *Alastor, Laon and Cythna, Prince Athanase, Prometheus Unbound* consists of a search for Ideal Beauty in Platonic abstractions like the "One," Cythna, and

> Asia, thou light of life,
> Shadow of beauty unbeheld.[26]

These women are the abstract symbols of Platonic Love even as the women in his life were the concrete symbols of it. But the repertoire of abstract symbols is not confined to these abstractions. It includes such words as Form, Soul, Adoration, Winged Persuasions, Veiled Destinies, and many others.[27] When a critic like Shorey says of Shelley, "There is an order of minds in which imagination and feeling are more stimulated by the abstract and the vague than by the concrete and particular,"[28] he is pointing out a characteristic of Shelley which arises more from his natural Platonism than from his understanding or use of Plato. This search for the Ideal through two sets of symbols, the concrete and the abstract, is characteristic of Shelley's natural Platonism.

It has never been clearly recognized that Shelley's conceptions of the immortality of the soul, of Platonic Love, of the Absolute are all natural consequences and protean aspects of his natural Platonism. Most of Shelleyan criticism has pointed out the affinities between Shelley's and Plato's belief in the immortality of the soul. Shelley's belief in the immortality of the soul is inconstant; it swings from the pole of affirmation to that of denial. The influence of materialistic thought and Shelley's own philosophical analysis of life and death combined with hatred of Christianity as an institution led him to deny the immortality of the soul. The imperious necessity, however, of being a poet quite often led Shelley into an affirmation of the immortality of the soul. This affinity, though influenced by the *Phaedo,* is a natural one. The poet cannot be possessed of an innate quest of the eternal without in time realizing that materialism is alien to this mood and that the concept of the immortality of the soul is intrinsically derived from and even dictated by the mood of natural Platonism. Even though historically Shelley's belief in the immortality of the soul shows the marked influence of Plato and others, the realization of the latent mood should not be mistaken for a derivative idea. We should keep in mind that Shelley's natural Platonism

[26] *Prometheus Unbound,* III, iii, 6-7.
[27] Cf. White, *Shelley,* II, 437.   [28] Shorey, *op. cit.,* p. 41.

could not find true or satisfying expression if he did not believe that
Being was characterized by eternal life not only with respect to its own
essence but also with respect to the soul which sought it.

What is true of the immortality of the soul is also true of Shelley's
Platonic Love. When Shelley defines love as "the universal thirst for a
communion not merely of the senses, but of our whole nature, intellectual,
imaginative and sensitive,"[29] and as "a going out of our own nature,
and an identification of ourselves with the beautiful which exists in
thought, action, or person, not our own,"[30] we see direct Platonic influence. But when we see how largely autobiographical is his poetry, how
many of his loves in poetry are a projection into the abstract of the concrete loves of his own life, we realize how we are led to Shelley's own
heart as the source of this thirst for a communion with the beautiful and
intellectual. Shelley's expression of the soul's communion and identification with Intellectual Beauty was influenced by Plato and the Platonic
tradition, which gave to his work inspiration, subject matter, theme,
and symbol. But the fact that he never imitated Plato's conception of
Love accounts in the main for the independent character of Shelley's
Platonism.

Clutton-Brock, who calls Shelley "the poet of Platonism, the one
writer, besides Plato, who can make it beautiful," says of him: "He is
in love, not with a theory, but with a vision. The absolute becomes the
Life of Life, the child of light whose limbs are burning through the
vest that seems to hide them. . . . For him the Absolute was not a word
but a world and a wind blew from it laden with its scent. The wind
that we hear and breathe in his poetry."[31] This passion for the Absolute is likewise an aspect of natural Platonism. The Absolute is created
in Shelley's own image; it is now a spirit, now a woman, now an abstract
unity of Platonic dialectic; sometimes it is emotional, sometimes mystical
or intellectual. Shelley's imagination sees it through change:

> I change, but I cannot die. . . .[32]

He feels it rather than knows it:

> And all feel, yet see thee never.[33]

The Absolute in Shelley would never have Plato's sanction even if

---

[29] Julian *Works,* VII, 228.

[30] *Ibid.,* VII, 118; cf. Floyd Stovall, "Shelley's Doctrine of Love," *PMLA,* XLV (1930),
283-303; White, *Shelley,* II, 441-444.

[31] Arthur Clutton-Brock, "Percy Bysshe Shelley," *Times Literary Supplement* (London),
July 6, 1922, pp. 433-434.

[32] *The Cloud,* l. 76.   [33] *Prometheus Unbound,* II, v, 64.

The One remains, the many change and pass[34]

is a good Platonic doctrine. Shelley's Absolute is not objective but subjective; its philosophical mélange is filled with the poet's desires, moods, visions of escape, and longings. Yet this passionate pursuit of the Absolute in Shelley springs from the same ground as Plato's. In the *Theaetetus* Plato says: "Evils can never pass away; for there must always remain something which is antagonistic to good. Having no place among the gods in heaven, of necessity they hover around the mortal nature, and this earthly sphere. Wherefore we ought to fly away from earth to heaven as quickly as we can; and to fly away is to become like God, as far as this is possible: and to become like him is to become holy, just, and wise."[35] Shelley, too, seeks to escape the evils of this earth and fly to his absolute heavens, which are all that this earth is not. Shelley's Absolute, despite many similarities,[36] is not the same as Plato's, but what is the same is the deep-rooted dissatisfaction with the earthly and the desire to flee to the heavenly.

Besides these major modes of inmost being which Shelley shares with Plato, there are certain others more or less connected and forming part of natural Platonism. Plato and Shelley exhibit some remarkable similarities in the symbolic communication of their similar insights. Plato used certain symbols like light and darkness, shadow and substance, the cavern, the sun, the moon for a more vivid and picturesque presentation of his thought. These symbols passed into the stream of the Platonic tradition, whence many of them find their way into Shelley's expression. But not all of them are derivative, for Shelley had a natural gift for creating images, similes, and metaphors.[37] Some of this imagery, ranging all the way from sensuous to abstract imagery, is cognate to Platonic imagery and is born in the imagination of natural Platonism. For example, the image of the cloud in Shelley's poem of the same name is a natural symbol for flux and permanence. It is used by Shelley to express a Platonic insight:

I change, but I cannot die.

Similarly, we find much of Shelley's imagery like the stream, cave, and veil used in expressing Platonic insights. The obscurity which often arises from Shelley's imagery is partly due to the vigorous imagination

[34] *Adonais*, l. 460.   [35] *Theaetetus,* 176a-b.
[36] Hughes, *op. cit.*, pp. 196-203.
[37] Cf. Julian *Works*, II, 172; for a study of Shelley's symbolism, see W. B. Yeats, *Ideas of Good and Evil*[2] (London, 1903), pp. 111-141; A. T. Strong, *Three Studies in Shelley* (Oxford, 1921), pp. 67-106.

of his natural Platonism, which, like Plato's god who is "forever geome-
trizing,"[38] is forever forcing the symbolism of mind and nature to yield
fresh, unconventional, and satisfying expression to natural Platonism.
When one examines the symbolism of *Mont Blanc, The Cloud, The
Sensitive Plant,* and others, he will discover Shelley's capacity for creating
natural Platonic symbols. Thus besides using the traditional images of
Platonism, Shelley created new symbols to express the same insights.

What is true of symbols is also true of their expansion into myths or
poetic dramas. Both Plato and Shelley have a genius for myth-making.
The communication of insights through dramatic narrative form, like
the myth of the Cave, of the Charioteer, of Er, constitutes one of the
striking characteristics of Plato's expression. Similarly, Shelley relies on
dramatic tales, allegory, and myths to express insights which he shares
in common with Plato. Thus similarity of insight results quite often
in similarity of expression.

Another manifestation of natural Platonism is the passion for reform
which characterizes both Plato and Shelley. Their dissatisfaction with
this world is connected with the natural Platonist's inability to accept the
world of relativity and its evils without trying to recreate it after his
ideal vision of perfection. Any analysis of Shelley's passion for reform
which is not related to the natural Platonism of his mind results in a
misunderstanding of its true source. Shelley's reform differs widely from
Plato's in its form and application; but this difference must not blind us
to the similarity of their source in the Platonist's dissatisfaction and impatience with the relative world. This dissatisfaction does not lead to
futility but rather to a re-creation of the future. In discussing Shelley's
Platonic Love, Professor White has pointed out the dependence of Shelley's reform on Platonism. "The thirst for Intellectual Beauty," he says,
"and the desire to free oneself, and the world, from evil and ignorance
were really one and the same thing. That is why, in the *Hymn to Intellectual Beauty,* Shelley describes his youthful awakening to a sense
of mission as a devotion to Intellectual Beauty, and in the prefatory poem
to *The Revolt of Islam* describes it as the beginning of a crusade against
tyranny."[39] The interdependence of reform and natural Platonism thus
forms another link in the chain of Shelleyan characteristics emanating
from this pervasive mood of natural Platonism. Shelley's similarities
to Plato with respect to the immortality of the soul, love, God, the Absolute, symbolism, and reform are due to the presence in both men of an
inward living mood of natural Platonism which dictated Shelley's funda-

[38] Plutarch, *Quaes. Conv.,* VIII, 2, 1.   [39] White, *Shelley,* II, 444.

mental similarity to Plato. Once it is realized that this similarity is not derivative in its nature, we make great strides in understanding, not only the similarities, but also the differences between Shelley and Plato.

The differences between Plato and Shelley have led many critics to call Shelley a pseudo-Platonist. Such critics do not understand the source of these differences in natural Platonism.[40] Now it is possible to point out all of Shelley's differences from Plato and still interpret them as objectively as we do in noting different species of the same genus. As was pointed out in the discussion of natural Platonism, the poet, the philosopher, and the theologian pursue the ideal and eternal, but they differ in the element of the soul used in apprehending it. It is apparent, as Plato points out in the *Republic,* that one element predominates in one man's soul and another in another's. The logical element predominates over emotion in the philosopher's soul, whereas emotion and imagination predominate in the poet's soul. This explains Shelley's difference from Plato. In the pursuit of the Ideal Plato uses the rational faculty, whereas Shelley subordinates it to emotion and imagination; the self-control of reason and logic gives way to unrestrained fantasy.

Moreover, much has been made of Shelley's Neoplatonism. Some critics[41] see in Shelley the great shadow of Neoplatonism. They attribute this to his reading of the Neoplatonists, or the influence of the Neo-platonic tradition upon Shelley. Though there is considerable evidence that Shelley was in contact with the Neoplatonic tradition, there is no evidence that he read any of the Neoplatonists. Notwithstanding all this it has not been sufficiently or clearly realized that Romanticism has closer affinities to Neoplatonism than to Platonism, that Shelley's soul is also naturally Neoplatonic. The natural affinities between Shelley and the Neoplatonic soul are great. Both make use of the rational faculty, but they mingle with it emotion, fancy, imagination, and mysticism in greater proportion than is found in Plato. The presence of these elements in the soul results in a different expression of Platonism. In Shorey's description of the Neoplatonic mind we find many counterparts to Shelley:

The Neo-Platonic mind combines with its dialectical impulse certain needs and aptitudes vaguely designated by such words as scholasticism, mysticism, enthusiasm, asceticism, pantheism, symbolism, and the imaginative personification of abstractions. . . . Abstraction is strangely akin to the poetic imagination, metaphor, symbolism, and the mythopoeic faculty. . . . There is an order

[40] For an ancient illustration of such a misunderstanding, see Shorey, *op. cit.,* p. 73.

[41] E.g., Carl Grabo, *The Magic Plant* (Chapel Hill, 1936); see references in index under Neoplatonism; cf. pp. 240-241, *infra.*

of minds in which imagination and feeling are more stimulated by the abstract and the vague than by the concrete and particular. . . . The order of intelligible and intelligent gods, intra- and extracosmic divinities of Iamblichus and Julian, the "thrones, dominations, princedoms, virtues, powers" of Dionysius the Areopagite, are of the same family as Shelley's Desires and Adorations, Winged Persuasions, and Veiled Destinies (*Adonais,* XIII, 1-2). . . . And the play of abstractions not only gives pleasurable exercise to the logical instinct, and stimulates the personifying imagination in poetry, but the abstractions become to the Neo-Platonic mind symbols of otherwise ineffable and inexpressible meanings. The Neo-Platonist is, like Dante, Milton, Swedenborg, Blake, Shelley, and Plato himself in some moods, a symbolist.[42]

Thus though Plato, Plotinus, and Shelley are all possessed of natural Platonism, Shelley and Neoplatonism belong to one species and Plato to another species of the same genus of natural Platonism. The differentiating factor is the compounding of reason with more nonrational faculties in Neoplatonism and Shelley than in Plato.

As a result there follow inevitably certain differences in the expression of Plato's and Shelley's natural Platonism. Foremost is the substitution of emotion, ecstasy, dreams, and fantasy for the intellectual and moral discipline of Plato. In *Jude the Obscure* Thomas Hardy has stated with neatness one of the essential differences between Plato and Shelley:

". . . Their supreme desire is to be together—to share each other's emotions, and fancies, and dreams."
"Platonic!" [replies Gillingham]
"Well, no. Shelleyan would be nearer to it. They remind me of Laon and Cythna."[43]

Thus even though Shelley was for the most part intellectual and pursued Intellectual Beauty, he sometimes went about it in a most unPlatonic and most unintellectual way. Soul-dissolving ecstasies are a far cry from "that which the reason itself lays hold of by the power of dialectics . . . making no use whatever of any object of sense but only of pure ideas moving on through ideas to ideas and ending with ideas."[44] Shelley, as an *amator furiosus,* is far removed from Plato's conception of Platonic Love.

Shelley furthermore "has the romantic wish to be infinite."[45] This again is to be explained by the predominance of the emotional over the logical and dialectical, which proceeds with definition no matter how

[42] Shorey, *op. cit.,* pp. 40-41.
[43] Thomas Hardy, *Jude the Obscure* (New York and London, 1923), pp. 274-275.
[44] *Republic,* 511b-c.
[45] Harry Levin, *The Broken Column* (Cambridge, Mass., 1931), p. 54.

far it advances into the infinite. This wish to be infinite is characteristic of the soul impatient with the slow progress of reason and eager to pursue its ends immediately rather than mediately. It is the same cause which underlies Plato's and Shelley's difference with respect to reform. Plato would reform society through the slow progress of reason, whereas Shelley's emotional impatience would uproot institutions and tyrants by the fiat of revolution.

Irving Babbitt, one of the most trenchant critics of Romanticism, has undertaken to show the fundamental differences between Plato and Rousseau, the representative figure of European Romanticism.[46] These differences would also apply to Shelley, who shares, according to Babbitt, the essential characteristics of Rousseau's Romanticism.

Platonic characteristics:	Rousseauistic or Romantic characteristics:
Unity of insight	Unity of instinct
Discipline of intellectual faculties	View of life as above all emotional
Concentration of the will	Expansion of feelings; mood of melting into nature
Intellect	Revery, the spontaneous, the instinctive
Impossibility of friendship between man and nature	Return to nature
Firm distinctions established by the intellect and enforced by the will between the planes of being	Confusion of the planes of flesh and spirit
Distinction between an earthly and an Uranian Aphrodite	Confusion of the two
Powers of illusion in the service of the reason	Powers of illusion in the service of the senses

These differences, being a part of the quarrel between Humanism and Romanticism, are subject to dispute. But even if we grant their validity, it is necessary to have a clearer understanding of their effect on the nature of Shelley's Platonism. If these characteristics are not abstracted from the nature of Plato and Shelley, it will be seen that those listed as Platonic are characteristics of one type of Platonism and those listed as Romantic are characteristics of another. Plato is characterized by an integrating intellect which subordinates all of the soul to the absolute

[46] Irving Babbitt, *The New Laokoön* (Boston and New York, 1910). The differences cited in the parallel columns are excerpted and summarized from the fifth chapter of this work, "Platonists and Pseudo-Platonists," pp. 87-114.

rule of the intellect. It makes a hierarchical empire of values which are apprehended by the rational faculty of the soul. On the other hand Shelley is characterized by a mind wherein emotion and feeling are dominant over intellect. One way of apprehending the Ideal is more natural to one mind and another to another. It is not a question of what one would, but rather what one can apprehend with the kind of soul he has. Both, through the kind of soul each has, obey the imperious necessity, imposed by natural Platonism, of pursuing the Ideal.

The judges of Platonism who are unaware of natural Platonism and its various modes of apprehension will use Plato's philosophical expression as the standard of reference, and every Platonism that deviates from it will be called spurious. Hence the judgments of those who condemn Shelley as a pseudo-Platonist[47] confuse natural Platonism with Plato's expression of it. They take Plato's direct Platonism as a fixed dogma, an absolute standard, little realizing that it is only the earliest and most perfect expression of the natural Platonism of humanity and that Shelley's Platonism is a cognate expression of it. An understanding of this truth will result in the recognition of Plato's and Shelley's Platonism as two species of the same genus. The wise critic, with no a priori predispositions, who understands the nature of Platonism will abstain from calling Shelley a pseudo-Platonist. He will enjoy the "pure emergence into visibility of the invisible soul"[48] of both Plato's and Shelley's natural Platonism. He will enjoy the identity in difference, the varied expressions of natural Platonism to which man's heart is intuitively attuned; he will rejoice in the perfect and luminous expressions which a philosopher-poet and a poet-philosopher have given to it. In their Platonism he will "behold now the height and amplitude of the Eternal Worth, seeing it hath made itself so many mirrors in which it breaks, while remaining one in itself as before."[49]

[47] Shorey, op. cit., p. 227; P. E. More, Platonism[2] (Princeton, 1926), pp. 294-296; Douglas Bush, Mythology and the Romantic Tradition in English Poetry (Cambridge, Mass., 1937), p. 156; Walter Bagehot, Works (Hartford, 1889), I, 106; J. R. Ullman, Mad Shelley (Princeton, 1933), pp. 103-105; J. A. Symonds, Shelley (London, 1878), p. 142.

[48] Franz Werfel, Embezzled Heaven (New York, 1940), p. 6.

[49] Dante, Paradiso, xxix, 142-145.

Chapter III

The Direct Platonism of Shelley

"The mind becomes that which it contemplates."
Prince Athanase, Frag. 2, l. 15

A SURVEY OF Shelley's reading, translation of, and observations on Plato is essential in determining the character of his direct Platonism. As in the case of Shelley's natural Platonism, we must study his direct Platonism in the context of his life and temperament. Shelley's study of Plato varies in its frequency, intensity, and re-creative assimilation. A study of Shelley's direct Platonism in the various years of his life will enable us to see approximately when and where he is in or out of Platonic focus, when Plato's influence is likely to be strong or weak, and what compositions are likely to reflect the influence of the particular dialogue of Plato Shelley had just read or was reading at the time of the composition.

Shelley's study of Plato is divided into two periods: the first, from his school days at Eton to the renascence of Platonic study at Marlow in 1817; the second, from 1817 until the time of his death in 1822, during which interval Plato in the original becomes Shelley's constant companion. During the first period Shelley knew Plato, mostly at Oxford, through poor translations which included that of Thomas Taylor, the self-tutored evangelist of Neoplatonism who plays an important part in Shelley's Platonism.[1] The second period is characterized by more direct, enthusiastic reading and translation from Plato. The two periods of his Platonism can thus be contrasted in depth of understanding as well as extent of reading. Each period, in turn, is made up of a series of years in Shelley's life which reveal similarity in the nature of their Platonic study. Each year, however, is not a complete index of Shelley's intellectual affinities with Plato, for the movement of his thought in the Platonic realm is not always recorded. By using the references to Plato in his own and his friends' writings we can determine the specific trend and rhythm of Shelley's Platonism in each period.

[1] J. A. Notopoulos, "Shelley and Thomas Taylor," *PMLA,* LI (1936), 502-517.

Shelley's first introduction to Plato was through James Lind, physician to the royal household at Windsor, who befriended Shelley at Eton.[2] Thomas Medwin, who took an interest in Shelley's Platonism,[3] mentions Shelley's statement that he read the *Symposium* with Dr. Lind.[4] It is of interest to note that this reading of Plato was not part of his academic work, for in that day the classical curriculum of Eton consisted mainly of "Homer, Vergil, Horace, and Ovid and the Greek Testament."[5] Shelley's introduction to Plato was through the friendship of an old man, "Free, calm-spirited, full of benevolence, and even of youthful ardour."[6] Dr. Lind must have instilled in Shelley more of an enthusiasm for Plato than an illuminating understanding of the text. Medwin said that Shelley's knowledge of Greek was superficial at this time,[7] and in view of his later request for Plato with a translation,[8] it is doubtful whether the initiation into the *Symposium* was in the original. The reading of the dialogue with Dr. Lind became a memorable event, for Shelley refers to the occasion in *Prince Athanase:*

> Then Plato's words of light in thee and me
> Lingered like moonlight in the moonless east,
> For we had just read—thy memory
>
> Is faithful now—the Story of the Feast;
> And Agathon and Diotima seemed
> From death and [dark] released. . . .[9]

After Eton Shelley entered Oxford in the fall of 1810 as Leicester Scholar of University College. There he met Thomas Jefferson Hogg, who became a Plato-loving and Plato-sharing friend of his. Although

[2] Thomas Medwin, *Revised Life of Shelley*, ed. H. B. Forman (London, 1913), p. 33; it is doubtful whether Dr. Lind was part of the faculty at Eton, as Medwin states. See White, *Shelley*, I, 47-48.

[3] *Vide infra*, pp. 385, 508.

[4] For a discussion of this problem, *vide infra*, p. 381.

[5] White, *Shelley*, I, 36.

[6] Thomas Jefferson Hogg, *The Life of Shelley*, ed. Humbert Wolfe (London, 1933), I, 35. (All references to Thomas Jefferson Hogg, *The Life of Shelley*; Edward John Trelawny, *The Recollections of Shelley and Byron*; and Thomas Love Peacock, *Memoirs of Shelley* are to Humbert Wolfe's combined edition, *The Life of Percy Bysshe Shelley* [London, 1933], 2 vols.)

[7] See Medwin, *op. cit.*, pp. 20-22, 34-38, for an account of Shelley's classical education at this time. A rough calculation by Professor White of Shelley's classical reading at Eton shows that he got through 75,000 lines of Greek and Latin prose and poetry (*Shelley*, I, 36).

[8] Julian *Works*, IX, 35.

[9] *Prince Athanase*, Frag. 3, ll. 61-66. For the identification of Zonoras with Dr. Lind, see White, *Shelley*, I, 573 n. 60.

classical reading was the foundation of education at Oxford, Shelley did not distinguish himself in classical studies.[10] His knowledge of Greek was inferior to his knowledge of Latin, and it was not until later years that he became proficient in the language of Plato. This limitation in the knowledge of Greek accounts for his use of translation in reading Plato at Oxford.

Shelley's study of Plato at Oxford was also self-chosen, for Plato was not part of the curriculum. It was not until 1847 that Plato begins to appear in the set papers of the *Literae Humaniores* of the Oxford Honours Schools.[11] The neglect of Plato in England during the seventeenth, eighteenth, and the early part of the nineteenth centuries is striking.[12] Thomas Gray deplored this neglect at Cambridge.[13] The only good thing which the *Edinburgh Review* had to say of Thomas Taylor's translation of Plato was that he undertook "to elucidate for his countrymen the Grecian philosophers," who were badly neglected.[14] Hogg, writing to Shelley in Italy, remarks, "Plato is unfortunately little read, even by scholars, which is much to be regretted, as he is, perhaps, the most edifying of the Greeks, and his style is so easy and simple."[15] Peacock and J. S. Mill give cumulative evidence of the neglect of Plato in England.[16] When seen in this context, Shelley's study of Plato is extraordinary for an undergraduate who asked his tutor, "Must I care about Aristotle? what if I do not mind Aristotle?"[17]

[10] Shelley's classical scholarship at Oxford was by no means trifling. Hogg informs us that Shelley read the Attic tragedians, particularly Euripides, and that he amused himself by turning the prose of Livy and Sallust into Latin heroic or elegiac verse. Shelley also competed for the Prize Poem, the subject being the Parthenon (Julian *Works*, VIII, 55, 135 n. 3; Hogg, *op. cit.*, I, 86, 134).

[11] Geoffrey Mure, "Oxford and Philosophy," *Philosophy*, XII (1938), 296-297; it must be noted, however, that *Platonis Dialogi V* (Oxford, 1745), edited by N. Forster, appears as part of the term reading for students at Magdalen College at the end of the eighteenth century (*Reminiscences of Oxford Men*, ed. A. T. Quiller-Couch [Oxford, 1892], p. 137).

[12] See F. B. Evans III, "Platonic Scholarship in Eighteenth-Century England," *MP*, XLI (1943), 103: "Some indication of how greatly his fame had diminished may be seen in the fact that, although the Renaissance had produced about thirty editions and translations of his *opera omnia*, only one version of the whole works, an Italian translation, appeared between 1602 and the last years of the eighteenth century."

[13] See *Correspondence of Thomas Gray*, ed. Paget Toynbee and Leonard Whibley (Oxford, 1935), III, 1295.

[14] *Edinburgh Review*, XIV (1809), 189-190.

[15] Letter to Shelley, dated June 15, 1821, in *Shelley and Mary*, p. 642.

[16] The Halliford Edition of the *Works of Thomas Love Peacock*, ed. H. F. B. Brett-Smith and C. E. Jones (London, 1924-1934), VIII, 202-203; see Vol. IV, *Crotchet Castle*, p. 95 (this edition will be referred to in the following notes as Halliford *Works*); J. S. Mill, *Monthly Repository*, n.s. VIII (1834), 89.

[17] Hogg, *op. cit.*, I, 70.

The story of Shelley's study of Plato at Oxford is told by Hogg, whose biography of Shelley forms an important source of our knowledge of Shelley's Platonism.

It is hazardous to speak of his earliest efforts as a Platonist, lest they should be confounded with his subsequent advancement; it is not easy to describe his first introduction to the exalted wisdom of antiquity without borrowing inadvertently from the knowledge which he afterwards acquired. . . . It seems laughable, but it is true, that our knowledge of Plato was derived solely from Dacier's translation of a few of the dialogues, and from an English version of that French translation; we had never attempted a single sentence in the Greek. Since that time, however, I believe few of our countrymen have read the golden works of that majestic philosopher in the original language more frequently and more carefully than ourselves; and few, if any, with more profit than Shelley. Although the source, whence flowed our earliest taste of the divine philosophy, was scanty and turbid, the draught was not the less grateful to our lips: our zeal in some measure atoned for our poverty. . . . It has been affirmed that "it was not until Shelley resided in Italy that he made Plato his study." It is quite true that he had not read much of the dialogues in the original Greek before; but he had long been familiar with his philosophy by means of translations; and he had imbibed, at a very early age, his doctrines and theories at second hand.[18]

The specific translations of Plato used by Shelley at Oxford were, according to Hogg, the English version of the French translation by Dacier of the *Phaedo* and several other dialogues of Plato; a French translation of the *Republic;* the translations of Floyer Sydenham and "several of the publications of the learned and eccentric Platonist, Thomas Taylor."[19] It is very probable that Shelley's copy of Thomas Taylor's translation of *Cratylus, Phaedo, Parmenides,* and *Timaeus* (London, 1793), found among his books,[20] was one of these several publications of Taylor.

In order to understand the fundamental weakness of the first period of Shelley's Platonism the nature of translation must be briefly examined. Thought is a process involving many stages in the process of communication. In the case of Platonic translation there is a series of stages between Plato's own insight and its reception by Shelley. We have first Plato's own insight into the realm of truth; then Plato's own verbal expression of this insight; then we have a translation of Plato's thought,

---

[18] *Ibid.,* I, 73, 121; II, 44-45; for other references to Shelley's Platonism, see I, 72-74, 86, 121-122, 129, 133, 144-145, 147-148, 166; II, 76, 145.

[19] *Ibid.,* I, 121.

[20] *The Shelley Correspondence in the Bodleian Library,* ed. R. H. Hill (Oxford, 1926), p. 47.

as expressed in the Dialogues, into another language; this stage involves, in turn, the degree of insight that the translator has into Plato's thought, then the re-expression of this insight into another language; and finally we have Shelley's own insight into the translator's own insight into Plato. Between the first and final stage we have Plato's thought refracted through individually colored stages, until it becomes four and, in the case of the English versions of the French translation, even five degrees removed from the original insight. The quality of the translator in the third stage in the process of translation is shown in Thomas Taylor, whose translation Coleridge described as "incomprehensible English" and which, besides being inaccurate in translation, interpreted Plato through obscure Neoplatonism, and prevented Shelley from ever seeing anything but a dim, distorted, and tradition-crusted Plato.[21] Shelley's knowledge of Plato through such translations accounts in part for the corresponding qualities of Shelley's Platonism of the first period.

The specific dialogues read in these translations are considerable in number. According to Hogg, "The English version of the French translation by Dacier of the *Phaedo,* and several other dialogues of Plato, was the first book we had, and this we read together several times very attentively at Oxford."[22] This work, which formed the main source of Shelley's knowledge of Plato at Oxford, is worthy of examination for an appraisal of the quantity and quality of Platonism which Shelley studied attentively. The title-page of this work reads: *"The Works of Plato Abridg'd: With an Account of His Life, Philosophy, Morals, and Politicks. Together with a Translation of his Choicest Dialogues, Viz. Of Human Nature, Prayer, Wisdom, Holiness, What one ought to do, Immortality of the Soul, Valour, Philosophy.* In Two Volumes. Illustrated with Notes. By M. Dacier. Translated from the French by several Hands. The Third Edition, Corrected. London, 1772."[23] It contains a translation of *"The first Alcibiades, Of the Nature of Man; The second Alcibiades, Of Prayer;* Theages, *Of Wisdom;* Eutyphron, *Of Holiness; An Abridgment of the first Alcibiades; An Abridgment of the second Alcibiades; An Abridgment of Eutyphron; The Apology* of Socrates; Crito, *Of what we ought to do;* Phedon, *Of the Immortality of the Soul;* Laches, *Of Valour;* Protagoras, *Against the Sophists;* The Rivals, *Of Philosophy."*

[21] Cf. Notopoulos, "Shelley and Thomas Taylor," *PMLA,* LI (1936), 505-508.

[22] Hogg, *op. cit.,* I, 121; for the popularity of the *Phaedo* in the eighteenth century, see Evans, "Platonic Scholarship in Eighteenth-Century England," *MP,* XLI (1943), 104.

[23] For other editions, see J. W. Moss, *A Manual of Classical Bibliography*[2] (London, 1837), II, 448.

It also contains what Hogg called "secondhand abstracts." These consist in this work of "A Discourse concerning Plato" and "The Life of Plato, with An Account of the Principal of his Opinions in Philosophy." A reading of these introductions corroborates what Hogg says of them: "It would be absurd to affirm that a profound, accurate, critical knowledge of the author may be acquired through the medium of translations, and at second hand by abstracts and abridgments."[24] A comparison of these translations with those of Shelley shows the difference between the Plato Shelley read at Oxford and the Plato he found by reading the original. One is reminded of the sea-god Glaucus in Plato's *Republic* (611d), "whose first nature can hardly be made out by those who catch glimpses of him, because the original members of his body are broken off and mutilated and crushed and in every way marred by the waves, and other parts have attached themselves to him, accretions of shells and sea-weed and rocks, so that he is more like any wild creature than what he was by nature." The "accretions of shells and sea-weed" in these introductions consist of statements that Moses is "the Model on which Plato forms his wise man," a doctrine which stems from the Neopythagorean Noumenios who asks, "What is Plato but Moses speaking Attic?" (frag. 13); of judgments that Plato "has corrupted the Truths with which he was illuminated by God"; of Neoplatonic and Christian interpolations and interpretations of Plato; of a conflation of Platonism with Egyptian philosophy and Jewish religion, which goes back to the time when Egyptian priests and Alexandrian Jews sought the sources of Platonism in their own past. If one wants to see how Shelley's Platonism of this period resembles Plato's Cave wherein Shelley's mind was seeing the unreal shadows of Plato rather than Plato himself, he has but to read the long "Account of Plato's Life and Philosophy" which is given in the introduction. There he will meet with a Plato whose substance is turned to shadow and whose shadow is deepened to substance. In this account Shelley found summaries of Plato's main doctrines and quotations from many dialogues. In particular it contains a summary of the *Timaeus,* which is refracted through the prisms of Neoplatonism, Christianity, and Cabalism; many informative statements from the *Laws,* the *Republic,* the *Symposium;* a discussion of the immortality of the soul with its associative doctrines of reminiscence, metempsychosis, its tripartite division, and the doctrine of Daemon or Genius; and finally a short account of the various Neoplatonists with a brief statement of

[24] Hogg, *op. cit.,* I, 121. The secondhand abstracts and abridgments were those contained in Dacier's edition (*vide supra*, p. 33, n. 23) and probably *A Synopsis; or, General View of the Works of Plato* (London, 1759), by Floyer Sydenham.

their philosophy. "Turbid" indeed was this draught of Platonism which Shelley drank.

This compendium of Plato's life and thought together with a translation of ten dialogues, which Hogg says were read "several times," shows that Shelley's acquaintance with Plato was considerable. Of the dialogues in this collection the *Phaedo* made the most impression. In a variant corroboration of the previous statement Hogg states, "Shelley was never weary of reading, or of listening to me whilst I read, passages from the dialogues contained in this collection [Dacier's], and especially from the *Phaedo,* and he was vehemently excited by the striking doctrines which Socrates unfolds, especially by that which teaches that all our knowledge consists of reminiscences of what we had learned in a former existence."[25] Of this vehement excitement Hogg gives ample testimony.[26] In addition to these dialogues, Shelley read the *Republic* in the French translation of Pillonnière or Grou.[27] "We perused," continues Hogg, "with infinite pleasure the elegant translation of Floyer Sydenham."[28] Sydenham had translated the *Ion* (1759), *The Greater Hippias* (1759), *The Lesser Hippias* (1761), *The Banquet* (Part I, 1761; Part II, 1767), *The Rivals* (1769), *Meno* (1769), *The First Alcibiades* (1773), *Second Alcibiades* (1776), and *Philebus* (Part I, 1779; Part II, 1780).[29] Some of these dialogues were contained in Dacier's translation and consequently can be eliminated. The word "elegant" in Hogg's description of the translation may possibly refer to dialogues which made use of this style. If this is the case, then Shelley very likely "perused" the *Banquet* and the *Ion.* The influence of the *Banquet* on Shelley's subsequent compositions makes it likely that the *Banquet* was reread at Oxford in Sydenham's translation. In addition to these translations Hogg records that they had "several of the publications of the learned and eccentric Platonist, Thomas Taylor." One of these must have been *The Cratylus, Phaedo, Parmenides, and Timaeus of Plato,* tr. from the Greek by T. Taylor, with notes on the *Cratylus,* and an explanatory introduction to each dialogue (London, 1793), which is now in the Bodleian Library. What the other publications were we do not know; they may have been Neoplatonic translations or translations of some of Plato's dialogues like the *Phaedrus*

---

[25] Hogg, *op. cit.,* I, 73.

[26] *Ibid.,* I, 73, 144-145, 147-148.

[27] *La République,* traduite par De la Pillonnière (London, 1726); *La République,* traduite du Grec, par J. Grou, 2 vols. (Amsterdam, 1763).

[28] Hogg, *op. cit.,* I, 121; for an account of Floyer Sydenham, see Evans, "Platonic Scholarship in Eighteenth-Century England," *MP,* XLI (1943), 106-107.

[29] See Moss, *op. cit.,* II, 449-450; for the intense reading activity of Shelley at Oxford, see Hogg, *op. cit.,* I, 84-85.

(1792).[30] We have some evidence that Shelley was acquainted at Oxford with Taylor's volume containing the *Timaeus*. Hogg, in chiding the poet for his never-ending creation of a paper navy, said, "Shelley, there is no use in talking to you; you are the Demiurgus of Plato!"[31] The allusion would not have been understood by Shelley had he not been acquainted with this dialogue, either through Taylor's translation or through the summary of the *Timaeus* in Dacier's introduction. The letter to Lord Ellenborough (1812) is evidence of the influence of the *Apology*. "Socrates," says Hogg, "as he is delineated by Plato, and whose boast it was that he knew nothing, was his prototype."[32] The specific reading, then, of *Alcibiades I* and *II*, *Theages*, *Euthyphro*, *Apology*, *Phaedo*, *Crito*, *Laches*, *Protagoras*, *Rivals*, *Republic* and probable reading of the *Banquet*, *Ion*, *Parmenides*, *Cratylus*, and *Timaeus* constitute one of the high-water marks of Shelley's study of Plato at Oxford.

This reading, moreover, was accompanied by enthusiastic discussion and passionate belief. In our picture of Shelley's Platonism we must not forget the extent to which oral Platonism is a part of the direct Platonism. His discussion of Plato and Platonic themes left a marked impression on his friends. "There were times," says Hogg, "when a visitor, who had listened to the glowing discourses delivered with a more intense ardour, would have hailed a young Platonist, breathing forth the ideal philosophy, and in his pursuit of the intellectual world entirely overlooking the material, or noticing it only to contemn it."[33] Shelley in particular was obsessed with the doctrine of reminiscence in the *Phaedo*.

He often rose [says Hogg], paced slowly about the room, shook his long wild locks, and discoursed in a solemn tone and with a mysterious air, speculating concerning our previous condition. . . . Every true Platonist, he used to say, must be a lover of children, for they are our masters and instructors in philosophy: the mind of a new-born infant, so far from being, as Locke affirms, a sheet of blank paper, is a pocket edition, containing every dialogue, a complete Elzevir Plato, if we can fancy such a pleasant volume.[34]

[30] For a bibliography of Taylor's writings, see Ruth Balch, *Thomas Taylor the Platonist 1758-1835, List of Original Works and Translations compiled for use in the Newberry Library* (Chicago, 1917). The writer is informed by Dr. W. E. Peck that he once had in his possession Hogg's copy of Thomas Taylor's Neoplatonic translations.

[31] Hogg, *op. cit.*, I, 63.

[32] *Ibid.*, II, 76; cf. Julian *Works*, V, 284 ff., where the *Apology* figures in Shelley's letter to Lord Ellenborough.

[33] Hogg, *op. cit.*, I, 72-73.

[34] *Ibid.*, I, 73, 147; cf. 144-145; the "complete Elzevir Plato" refers to the classical texts issued by the house of Elzevir. See Alphonse Willems, *Les Elzevirs, histoire et annales typographiques* (Brussels, 1880). The Elzevirs issued no edition of Plato.

The extent to which Shelley carried this doctrine forms the choicest illustration of Platonic faith in the entire Platonic tradition. Again it is Hogg who relates the incident:

One Sunday we had been reading Plato together so diligently, that the usual hour of exercise passed away unperceived: we sallied forth hastily to take the air for half an hour before dinner. In the middle of Magdalen Bridge we met a woman with a child in her arms. Shelley was more attentive at that instant to our conduct in a life that was past, or to come, than to a decorous regulation of the present, according to the established usages of society, in that fleeting moment of eternal duration, styled the nineteenth century. With abrupt dexterity he caught hold of the child. The mother, who might well fear that it was about to be thrown over the parapet of the bridge into the sedgy waters below, held it fast by its long train.

"Will your baby tell us anything about pre-existence, madam?" he asked, in a piercing voice, and with a wistful look.

The mother made no answer, but, perceiving that Shelley's object was not murderous, but altogether harmless, she dismissed her apprehension, and relaxed her hold.

"Will your baby tell us anything about pre-existence, madam?" he repeated with unabated earnestness.

"He cannot speak, sir," said the mother seriously.

"Worse and worse," cried Shelley, with an air of deep disappointment, shaking his long hair most pathetically about his young face; "but surely the babe can speak if he will, for he is only a few weeks old. He may fancy perhaps that he cannot, but it is only a silly whim; he cannot have forgotten entirely the use of speech in so short a time; the thing is absolutely impossible."

"It is not for me to dispute with you, gentlemen," the woman meekly replied, her eye glancing at our academical garb; "but I can safely declare that I never heard him speak, nor any child, indeed, of his age."

It was a fine placid boy; so far from being disturbed by the interruption, he looked up and smiled. Shelley pressed his fat cheeks with his fingers, we commended his healthy appearance and his equanimity, and the mother was permitted to proceed, probably to her satisfaction, for she would doubtless prefer a less speculative nurse. Shelley sighed as we walked on.

"How provokingly close are those new-born babes!" he ejaculated; "but it is not the less certain, notwithstanding the cunning attempts to conceal the truth, that all knowledge is reminiscence: the doctrine is far more ancient than the times of Plato, and as old as the venerable allegory that the Muses are the daughters of Memory; not one of the nine was ever said to be the child of Invention!"[35]

[35] Hogg, op. cit., I, 147-148.

Shelley's enthusiasm for Plato at this time is also revealed in the translation of an epigram of Plato which Shelley published in the *Oxford University and City Herald* on March 9, 1811.[36] The translation marks the first appearance of Shelley as a translator of Plato.

Shelley's academic career at Oxford ended when he was dismissed for his pamphlet on atheism. In his brief stay there he read Plato enthusiastically in poor translations and became acquainted with many dialogues and their doctrines. In particular he was impressed with the *Phaedo*, the *Republic*, and the *Symposium*, and a survey of his Platonism shows that these dialogues exercised the greatest influence on his work.[37] Shelley read them in translation at Oxford, and then reread them in the original in the interval of 1817-20. The knowledge and influence of these dialogues on Shelley's compositions from 1810 to 1817, a period in which there is no definite reading of Plato, shows the truth of Medwin's observation that "his memory was prodigious."[38]

After Shelley's expulsion from Oxford, Godwinism became ascendant. The perfectibility of human nature and the ascription of evil to the desolating power of positive institutions replaced the philosophy of Plato. While in this mood Shelley's rebellion against tradition extended even to the value of classical learning. He wrote to Godwin, who himself was fond of the classics,[39] "I am not sufficiently vain and dogmatical to say *now* I have *no* doubts on the deleteriousness of classical education; but it certainly is my opinion—nor has your last letter sufficed to refute it, that the evils of acquiring Greek and Latin considerably overbalance the benefits."[40] But this mood, like many others, was not to last long. The change was one of emphasis rather than love for the classics. Shelley, like Hogg, continued after Oxford "his humanizing studies . . . which had been so rudely, illegally, and insolently interrupted by the petty despots of my university."[41] The classics still continued to furnish themes and allusions in Shelley's work.[42]

In November of 1812, while in London,[43] Shelley made the acquaintance of Thomas Love Peacock, a poet, novelist, and a colossus of classical learning.[44] Peacock stimulated and guided Shelley's classical reading

[36] D. F. MacCarthy, *Shelley's Early Life: From Original Sources* (London, 1872), p. 62. See also pp. 566-567, *infra*, and White, *Shelley*, I, 110.

[37] *Vide infra*, pp. 171-371, *passim*.   [38] Medwin, *op. cit.*, 75.

[39] See H. N. Brailsford, *Shelley, Godwin, and Their Circle* (London, 1913), p. 81.

[40] Julian *Works*, IX, 12.   [41] Hogg, *op. cit.*, I, 361.

[42] Julian *Works*, VIII, 83-84, 128.

[43] See Halliford *Works*, I, l-li; White, *Shelley*, I, 242, and II, 637-638 n. 47.

[44] A glance at Peacock's classicism reveals the nature of the influence which he was to exercise on Shelley. Classical reading was a lifelong passion with Peacock. It

and was responsible for Shelley's Platonic renascence in 1817. He formed an antidote to that Godwinism which could not satisfy the innate idealism of Shelley's poetic nature even though it might have satisfied Shelley

---

started in Chertsey and was continued at the British Museum, where, like Housman, he spent many hours of his leisure in reading Greek and Latin authors. In Wales we find him reading a Greek dramatist and exciting "the wonder of the farmers . . . by reading two books at once" (Halliford *Works*, I, liv). In 1812 he devoted himself to the translation of a number of choruses from the Greek tragedians (Halliford *Works*, VII, Appendix I). We have an example of their influence on Shelley. In his confusion and suffering between his old feeling for Harriet and his new passion for Mary Godwin, he wrote Peacock, "I am always repeating to myself your lines from Sophocles:

> 'Man's happiest lot is not to be:
> And when we tread life's thorny steep
> Most blest are they, who earliest free
> Descend to death's eternal sleep' "

(Peacock, *Memoirs of Percy Bysshe Shelley*, II, 336). "Your lines" here means Peacock's translation of the *Choral Ode on the Evils of Life*, which Shelley memorized after his reading of Peacock's translation. These verse translations may have influenced Shelley's habit of translating from the Greek. During the interval that Peacock was associated with Shelley many of the classical authors on Shelley's reading list, such as Nonnus, Pausanias, Apuleius, and others, were Peacock's favorite authors (*vide infra*, pp. 49 n. 85-50 n. 89). In *Melincourt*, written by Peacock in 1816, Mr. Forester (Shelley) advises, "Read ancient books, the only source of permanent happiness left in this degenerate world" (Halliford *Works*, II, 272; cf. *ibid.*, II, 384). Shelley later echoes this in a letter to Hogg: "I have employed Greek in large doses, and I consider it the only sure remedy for diseases of the mind" (Julian *Works*, VII, 311). We can see the depth and intensity of the classical influence with which Shelley came in contact in Peacock's prospectus on classical education (Halliford *Works*, VIII, Appendix II), which expresses his revolt against the grammarian's approach to the classics, a point of view equally shared by Shelley (see Hogg, *op. cit.*, I, 86, II, 61-62), and in the diary which Peacock kept from July 7 to August 26, 1818 (Halliford *Works*, VIII, Appendix III). He continued this ardor till his death. Macaulay, who met him many years afterward, said, "I met Peacock; a clever fellow, and a good scholar. . . . We had out Aristophanes, Aeschylus, Sophocles, and several other old fellows, and tried each other's quality pretty well. We are both strong enough in these matters for gentlemen. But he is editing the *Supplices*. Aeschylus is not to be edited by a man whose Greek is only a secondary pursuit" (Halliford *Works*, I, clxxiv). Peacock's friendship with Thomas Taylor, his classical aloofness from such works as Godwin's *Mandeville*, which Shelley describes as "shaking the deepest soul," his hours of reading Greek with Shelley are indicative of his classical influence upon Shelley, which was all the more effective because it was integrally bound up with friendship. Peacock is largely responsible for Shelley's taking up Greek again, which "did more than anything else to turn a mixture of magnanimous crusader and eccentric crank into a poet" (Bush, *Mythology and the Romantic Tradition in English Poetry*, p. 131).

The friendship of Shelley and Peacock requires a few words of explanation, if we are to understand how Peacock influenced Shelley. Though Peacock had the capacity to understand Shelley's idealism, he could not approve of his treatment of Harriet. He accepted the elopement of Shelley and Mary as a *fait accompli* and tried not to let his personal views on the matter interfere with his relations with Shelley. Mary, however, was sensitive to his preference for Harriet and in her Journal expresses her reaction by omitting all reference to him for a considerable period of time (cf. Halliford *Works*, I, lxii; *The Letters of Mary W. Shelley*, ed. F. L. Jones, I, 7 n. 2, 21, 30). This prejudice and omission prevents us not only from getting a complete picture of the friendship of Peacock and Shelley, but also deprives us of much information about their classical reading.

the reformer.[45]   He helped to guide Shelley out of the confusion of revolutionary thought into the field of classical beauty.

The immediate influence of this friendship is seen in Shelley's book orders. On July 29, 1812, still smarting from his expulsion at Oxford, he wrote a letter to Godwin on the evils of classical learning. But on December 17, 1812, after he had made the acquaintance of Peacock,[46] he wrote two letters to Thomas Hookham, Jr., Peacock's friend and publisher, asking in the first letter for Herodotus, Thucidydes, Zenophon [sic], Plutarch, with Latin or English translations subjoined;[47] and in

---

Their friendship is characterized by constancy on the part of Peacock but by a variable attitude on the part of Shelley, who at times was angry with Peacock and saw him according to his own moods (see Halliford Works, I, lxiii-lxiv). There were certain temperamental differences and similarities between Peacock and Shelley which must be mentioned for a fuller understanding of Shelley's classicism. When Shelley introduced Peacock to the Boinville circle, Mrs. Newton found him "a cold scholar, who . . . has neither taste nor feeling. This Shelley will perceive sooner or later, for his warm nature craves sympathy" (Halliford Works, I, lv). Shortly after, Shelley wrote to Hogg that "his enthusiasm is not very ardent" (Julian Works, IX, 81). Peacock was the only one of Shelley's many friends who appreciated and understood Shelley's enthusiasm without being carried away. He possessed a common-sense stability which often angered Shelley but never alienated him. Shelley appreciated this difference of temperament, for Peacock tells how, in pointing to a similarity of their friendship to the fifth stanza of Wordsworth's "Stanzas Written in a Pocket Copy of Thomson's Castle of Indolence," Shelley said, "It was a remarkable instance of Wordsworth's insight into nature, that he should have made intimate friends of two imaginary characters so essentially dissimilar" (Halliford Works, VIII, 79). Their friendship developed on the basis of certain similarities and differences. Idealistic and romantic, they shared a realm of similar ideas. Peacock's common sense saw the futility of the realization of these ideas in the world about him, yet he never ceased yearning for them as a romantic satirist, as his novels and poems show; Shelley, on the other hand, was impatient and impetuous in his attempts to realize them. This difference made Peacock able to serve Shelley in practical matters, as their lives illustrate. The similarities of their temperaments made them see eye to eye on many matters: both despised formal education, the grammarian's approach to the classics; both were freethinkers in religion and loved freedom; Shelley found in Peacock "an amiable man of great learning, considerable taste, an enemy to every shape of tyranny and superstitious imposture" (Julian Works, IX, 209), qualities which formed the basis of their friendship. His admiration for Peacock's classical learning was the gate through which Hellenism and Platonism entered to stimulate and stir to creation similar tendencies latent in his soul. (For a detailed account of their friendship, see J. J. Mayoux, Un Epicurien anglais: Thomas Love Peacock [Paris, 1933], pp. 85 ff.; J. G. Merriam, "Shelley and Thomas Love Peacock," an unpublished M.A. thesis in the Trinity College Library.)

[45] This view of the relation of Shelley to Godwin is based on Amiyakumar Sen's Godwin and Shelley; for a brief summary of it, see The Year's Work in English Studies, XI (1930), 314-315.

[46] Shelley first met Peacock in London early in November, 1812. Although at the time Shelley ordered these books he had seen Peacock not more than three or four times (see White, Shelley, I, 242), the book list shows that these meetings were devoted in part to classical discussions and suggestions for reading.

[47] Julian Works, IX, 34; for Shelley's passion for buying books, see Hogg, op. cit., I, 358-359.

the second letter, written the same day, he asks for "Marcus Antoninus [Marcus Aurelius], Seneca's Works, Plato (with a translation)."[48] Again on December 24 he wrote to Clio Rickman asking, among other books, for seventeen classical authors ranging from Aeschylus to little-known authors like Lucius Florus, "original and translation, if possible, united."[49] Of the nearly seventy different works ordered from these booksellers, most of the nonclassical books and the classical authors in the first letter to Hookham are suggestions of Godwin in a letter, dated December 10, to Shelley, who had asked him to recommend a plan of reading and study.[50] But the inclusion of works by Monboddo, Sir William Drummond, and Horne Tooke, three favorite authors of Peacock,[51] shows that some of the books requested were at the suggestion of Peacock. Only Peacock among Shelley's friends at this time knew the byways of the classics shown in such authors as Procopius, Celsus, Ptolemaeus, Diodorus Siculus, Lucius Florus, Justin of Samaria. Whether the order for Plato was due to Shelley's own desire to read Plato again, or to Godwin's or Peacock's suggestion, cannot be known. Shelley's weakness in Greek at this period is evident in his request for a translation to accompany the original. The Plato translation that he received from Hookham was probably the Bipont text with Ficino's Latin translation.[52] Even if

---

[48] Julian Works, IX, 35.   [49] Ibid., IX, 36.

[50] White, Shelley, I, 276, 648 n. 69; cf. Edward Dowden, The Life of Percy Bysshe Shelley (London, 1886), I, 336.

[51] Carl Van Doren, Life of Thomas Love Peacock (London, 1911), p. 56; for Drummond, Horne Tooke, and Lord Monboddo, see Mayoux, op. cit., pp. 53-67, 80.

[52] The request for "Plato (with a translation)" would exclude Thomas Taylor's translation, which was simply an English translation without the Greek text (The Works of Plato, viz. His Fifty-Five Dialogues, and Twelve Epistles, Translated from the Greek; Nine of the Dialogues by the Late Floyer Sydenham, and the Remainder, by Thomas Taylor, with occasional Annotations on the Nine Dialogues Translated by Sydenham, and Copious Notes by the Latter Translator; in which is given the Substance of Nearly All the Existing Greek MS. Commentaries on the Philosophy of Plato, and a considerable portion of such as are already published, In Five Volumes, London: Printed for Thomas Taylor, By R. Wilks, Chancery-Lane; and sold by E. Jeffery, and R. H. Evans, Pall-Mall, 1804). Even though this edition had a limited sale (see F. B. Evans III, "Thomas Taylor, Platonist of the Romantic Period," PMLA, LV [1940], 1070), it is probable that Shelley, who was acquainted with Taylor, had a copy of it or had seen it among the books of Peacock, who was a friend of Taylor. It is most likely that the edition he received from his bookseller was Πλάτων /Platonis Philosophi/Quae Exstant/Graece Ad Editionem Henrici Stephani/Accurate Expressa/Cum Marsilii Ficini Interpretatione/Accedit Varietas Lectionis/Stüdiis Societatis Bipontinae/Biponti/Ex Typographia Societatis/12 vols./1781-1787. The Latin translation would have been satisfactory to Shelley, who was very proficient in Latin, as may be seen in his Journal entry for one day in February, 1815: "In the evening read Livy, p. 385, 2nd vol., half; 1,200 pages in seventeen days. . . . At night read Livy, pp. 385-450. 'Seneca.'" Shelley used this text of Plato at Marlow, Bagni di Lucca, and during the rest of his stay in Italy (vide infra, pp. 382, 555). It is not known whether he carried this copy of Plato from place to place or purchased a new copy. "When

Shelley did not receive his copy of Plato in time for it to affect the composition of *Queen Mab,* the influence of his reading of Plato at Oxford lingered. The theme of the poem is anti-Platonic, but, at least in the eyes of Hogg, "*Queen Mab* is the production of a Platonist incontestably; and if the great master of the Academy were to read it, he would once more acknowledge the author for a disciple—for a favoured and a favourite one."[53] Even in the most un-Platonic of Shelley's poems he is still a Platonist to his Plato-loving and Plato-sharing friend. The presence of Platonism in *Queen Mab,* side by side with materialism, shows that this judgment of Hogg, though hyperbolic, is not entirely wrong. A significant aspect of Shelley's Platonism is seen in the fact that all his friends were impressed with it and left many testaments of it in their memoirs, letters, and biographies.

---

he changed his residence," says Hogg, "and he often changed it . . . he hastily chose some new domicile, where he resolved to remain 'for ever'; thither his books were at once dispatched, but with so wild a precipitance, and such headlong hurry, that ancients and moderns alike missed their way. And when he, on the spur of the moment, quitted his eternal abode, as he was wont, the books were left behind to follow him to his lately elected and perpetual home: but they sometimes remained unheeded" (Hogg, *op. cit.,* I, 358-359; cf. II, 26). But even if his Plato was left behind, as was the case at Tanyrallt, he bought new copies. "No matter," says Professor White, "how many books he may have left behind at various lodgings, Shelley never required more than a few days to assemble a respectable library at his next stop. In the little sitting-room on Half-Moon Street books were arranged in rows on the floor, they occupied the recesses on either side of the fireplace, were piled in disorder on tables and chairs, and were heaped up under the tables" (*Shelley,* I, 309). Whether or not Shelley took the copy he received at Tanyrallt with him to London in April, 1813, is not known. The Bipont edition which he used at Marlow (*vide infra,* p. 47) may have been carried along from place to place after Shelley ordered and presumably received it at Tanyrallt in 1813. On the other hand he may have forgotten it when he moved to London and failed to buy another copy until 1817, a fact which may account for his not reading Plato from 1812 to 1817. The first and tenth volume of his Bipont edition were packed at Marlow on February 6, 1818, and were used at Bagni di Lucca for his reading and translation of Plato. He loaned his Plato (probably the tenth volume of his Bipont edition) to Byron in Venice in the fall of 1818 and at his departure wrote him a note asking for its return. Upon receiving it he started reading the *Republic* at Venice. The edition from which he made his translations of the *Republic* in Florence in 1819 was Massey's edition of the *Republic.* The reason for this is now apparent. Shelley had left with Peacock all except the first and tenth volumes of his Bipont edition of Plato (the *Republic* is in the sixth and seventh volumes of this edition). It is apparent that Shelley's appetite for Plato had increased, and he now bought Massey's edition of the *Republic* and later a folio edition of Plato's works, which we find him using at Pisa (*vide infra,* n. 175). Of all his copies of Plato, only his copy of Taylor's translation of *The Cratylus, Phaedo, Parmenides and Timaeus of Plato* (London, 1793) has survived and is now in the Bodleian Library (see *The Shelley Correspondence in the Bodleian Library,* p. 47). Leigh Hunt received his copy of the *Republic* (*vide infra,* p. 564). If his Bipont edition of Plato could be found, perhaps it might contain marginalia such as his copies of Herodotus and Xenophon show (see W. E. Peck, *Shelley, His Life and Work* [Boston and New York, 1927], II, 348-355); such marginalia would enrich considerably our knowledge of Shelley's direct Platonism.

[53] Hogg, *op. cit.,* II, 45.

After Shelley's departure from Wales on February 26, 1813, the study of Plato wanes as far as our sources show. There is no mention of his reading of Plato in 1813 or 1814. It is very probable, as Professor White points out, that Shelley received and read most of the books at Tanyrallt. His assumption is based "upon Shelley's obviously serious and thorough reading habits and upon acquaintance with many of them which he demonstrated later."[54] If a statement of Mrs. Godwin, contained in a letter to Mrs. Mason, is applicable to Shelley's relations with Godwin at this time, we have evidence of some reading of the Plato translation that Shelley received from Hookham. Mrs. Godwin writes:

I remember Mr. Godwin telling him once that he was too young to be so certain he was in the right—that he ought to have more experience before being so dogmatic and then he said some Saint, St. Cyril I think, but I know the name began with C., had spoken most wisely that Humility was Truth. Mr. Shelley laughed and said he would listen to Socrates or Plato but not to a Saint as he could not see any merit in Past Ages except in the Pagan republic of Athens.[55]

This enthusiasm for Plato may well be a reflection of his reading of Plato in London in 1813 or 1814.[56]

But even though there is no definite evidence for direct Platonism, the indirect Platonic tradition is marked in Shelley's reading of this period.[57] Shelley read Diogenes Laertius's *Lives of the Philosophers,* which contains, besides the life of Plato, a comprehensive summary of Plato's thought. His reading of Petrarch, Tasso, and Ariosto in Italian, which he began at this time, exposed him to an attractive presentation of Platonic Love. The reading of many of Cicero's philosophical works, Drummond's *Academical Questions,* Berkeley's works, Wordsworth's *The Excursion,* and Wieland's *Agathon* and *Peregrine Proteus* put Shelley in contact with a considerable amount of poetically attractive indirect Platonism. In particular the reading of Wieland's *Agathon* in

[54] White, *Shelley,* I, 276, 648 n. 69; Dowden is also of the opinion that Shelley read this translation: "While Harriet . . . was thus falling away from her interest in things of the mind, Shelley . . . studied in a translation the dialogues of Plato" (*op. cit.,* I, 405).

[55] R. Glynn Grylls, *Claire Clairmont* (London, 1939), pp. 279-280.

[56] Though Shelley visited London from Bishopsgate (1815 to 1816) and Marlow (1817), the attitude toward Christianity in this letter belongs to the earlier days of his friendship with Godwin in London in 1813 and 1814. For Shelley's later view on Christianity, see the *Essay on Christianity.*

[57] For the indirect Platonism in the writings which Shelley read, *vide infra,* pp. 83-86, 88, 97-98, 121-126, 139-144, 162-167. For Shelley's reading of the authors listed in this paragraph, see White, *Shelley,* II, 539-540, and index, pp. cviii-cxii; and entries in the Journal of Shelley and Mary.

the Boinville circle had a profound effect, as we shall see, on the nature and expression of Shelley's Platonism in poems like *Alastor, Laon and Cythna,* and *Hymn to Intellectual Beauty.* Hogg's account of how "the glowing young Platonic poet" embraced this work as "the testament of Platonism"[58] is valuable evidence as to the continuation of Platonism even when Shelley was not reading Plato directly.

In the summer of 1815 Shelley moved from the troubled atmosphere of London to Bishopsgate, where he resided until his departure for the Continent in May, 1816. This period, which was one of the most peaceful in Shelley's life, was devoted to study and writing. An examination of the list of books read by Shelley in 1815[59] shows that of the fifty-three works read that year, eleven were by classical authors, the rest mostly English literature and history, and Italian poetry. If compared with his earlier list of books ordered in 1812, the reading shows a considerable decline in Godwinian literature and the rise of poetry and literature. This was in great part due to the constant association with literary and scholarly friends like Peacock and Hunt, who were frequent visitors at Bishopsgate. Peacock says of this period, "The whole of the winter 1815-16 was passed quietly at Bishopsgate. Mr. Hogg often walked down from London; and I, as before, walked over from Marlow. This winter was, as Mr. Hogg expressed it, a mere Atticism. Our studies were exclusively Greek."[60] This finds corroboration not only in Peacock's novels, where we get a graphic reflection of Shelley's enthusiasm for Greek,[61]

[58] Hogg, *op. cit.,* II, 144-145.   [59] White, *Shelley,* II, 540-541.

[60] Peacock, *Memoirs,* II, 341; cf. Mayoux, *op. cit.,* pp. 122-126; *The Athenians,* ed. W. S. Scott (London, 1943), p. 55 *et passim.*

[61] We may see a picture of these three friends in the three philosophers of *Headlong Hall,* walking in the woods. Mr. Foster (Shelley) of *Headlong Hall,* written in 1815, and Mr. Scythrop Glover (Shelley) of *Nightmare Abbey* speak frequently of their interest in and love for Greek. Mr. Forester (Shelley) in *Melincourt,* written in 1816, reflects Shelley's new interest in Greek:

SIR TELEGRAPH PAXARETT.
'. . . What shall I do to kill time?'
MR. FORESTER.
'Read ancient books, the only source of permanent
happiness left in this degenerate world.' "

(Halliford *Works,* II, 272; cf. "I have employed Greek in large doses, and I consider it the only sure remedy for diseases of the mind," Julian *Works,* VII, 311.) This is echoed again when he tells Mr. Fax (Peacock): "In a state of society so corrupted as that in which we live, the best instructors and companions are ancient books; and these are best studied in . . . congenial solitudes" (Halliford *Works,* II, 384-385). Furthermore, when introduced to Anthelia in her extensive classical library, Mr. Fax apologizes for his friend's very evident excitement by assuring his bewildered hostess, "My friend's enthusiasm, Miss Melincourt, usually runs away with him when any allusion is made to ancient Greece" (*ibid.,* II, 169). Discounting dramatic invention, these pictures of Shelley which Peacock gives us show the depth and intensity of Shelley's renascent Hellenism; cf. Shelley's letters, Mary's Journal, and reading lists for 1815 to 1817.

but also in Mary's Journal, where the entry for March 1 reads: "In the evening Peacock comes. Talk about types, editions, and Greek letters all the evening." There is no evidence that Shelley read Plato during this "Attic winter of study," but it served to bring Shelley closer to Plato. The growth of Shelley's interest in Greek was shortly to include the reading of Plato in the original.

Though direct Platonism is absent for this period, an exceptionally large portion of Shelley's reading for 1815 is permeated and influenced by Plato and the Platonic tradition.[62]   His reading included Seneca's *Works,* two volumes of Plutarch (in Italian), Ariosto's *Orlando Furioso,* Tasso's *Gerusalemme Liberata,* Bacon's *Novum Organum,* Sir Thomas Browne's *Religio Medici,* Spenser's *Faerie Queene,* Milton's *Paradise Lost* and *Paradise Regained,* Gibbon's *Decline and Fall of the Roman Empire,* Wordsworth's *Poems,* Southey's *Curse of Kehama,* Coleridge's *Poems,* and Rousseau's *Reveries.* The delineation of the Platonism of these works, as shown in the next chapter, shows that Shelley found in them the essence of Platonism. The presence of Platonism in Shelley's works written at this period shows that even if he had not read Plato in the original, Platonism affected him indirectly through its influence on the works he read.[63]

Shelley's life of peace and study, however, was punctuated with debts and troubles in financing Godwin. He found relief in Switzerland, where he continued his classical reading. Mary's Journal and reading list for 1816 show that Shelley kept contact with the Platonic tradition through his reading of Apuleius's *Apologia,* containing an epigram of Plato which Shelley translated, Lucian's *Works,* Montaigne's *Essays,* and Rousseau's *Émile,* which, as the next chapter will show,[64] are important sources of indirect Platonism, and, in the case of Montaigne's *Essays,* of direct Platonism in the form of significant quotations from Plato. But again there is no mention of any reading of Plato in this year, and this at a time when he wrote the *Hymn to Intellectual Beauty.* This corroborates the natural Platonic character of the poem in seeing through the image of nature the manifestation of unearthly Beauty. Its expression was influenced by the language, concept, and imagery of the Platonic tradition, with which Shelley had been in contact to a considerable extent in 1815. The experience described in the poem prepared Shelley for his passionate reception of a cognate expression in the *Symposium*

[62] For Shelley's reading of these authors, see White, *Shelley,* II, 540-541, and index, pp. cviii-cxii; Adolph Droop, *Die Belesenheit Percy Bysshe Shelleys* (Weimar, 1906).

[63] For the indirect Platonism in these, *vide infra,* pp. 83, 103-105, 108-111, 114-119, 131, 134-136, 152-167.

[64] *Vide infra,* pp. 85, 86 n. 30, 112-114, 135.

and *Phaedrus*. It was like finding the other half of his soul as described in the *Symposium*.[65]

The year 1817 marks the beginning of the renascence of direct Platonism in Shelley. Up to this time Platonism was but the strong overtone of his reading at Oxford. Even the intellectual activities with Peacock include no mention of Plato. But with 1817 both friends ventured forth upon Platonic reading and used Platonic themes in their compositions. When Shelley took a house at Marlow, only a few minutes' walk from Peacock, they became constant companions in rowing, sailing, walking, and reading. A contemporary witness writes, "He ... kept no company but Mr. Peacock's and that of his boat, and was never seen in the house but he had a book in his hand, and was reading as he went along."[66] Mary, who, as an expression of her dislike for Peacock, omits references to him in her Journal from 1815 through the greater part of 1817, writes, "Peacock drinks tea here . . . . Peacock spends the evening here."[67] Peacock's influence is seen in the reading of Plato and the increase in Shelley's classical reading. The reading list for 1817 in Mary's Journal shows that Shelley read the "Symposium of Plato (Greek)."[68] Individual entries in the Journal show that Mary should have included several more works of Plato, for in her entry for February 23 she writes ". . . Shelley reads 'Waverly,' 'Tales of my Landlord,' and several of the works of Plato." What these several works of Plato were is not definitely known. It is unlikely that this entry includes the *Symposium*, for Mary's entry for Wednesday, August 13—"Shelley writes; reads Plato's 'Convivium' "—shows that this dialogue was read at the suggestion of Peacock, who was reading the *Symposium* in July. The influence of Plato on compositions written in 1817 and 1818 shows that the several works may have been the *Menexenus* (a dialogue popular in the eighteenth century), a portion of which Shelley translated in 1817,[69] possibly the *Apology,* or portions of the *Republic* and *Phaedo*.[70] Included in Shelley's reading for this year, though not specified by Mary, is the reading of a considerable portion of the *Phaedrus*. Hogg says, " I remember going up to London with him from Marlow one morning; he took a volume of Plato with him, and we read a good deal of it together, sitting side by side on the top of the coach. Phaedrus, I am pretty sure, was the dia-

---

[65] *Symposium*, 191d.   [66] Quoted in Peck, *op. cit.*, I, 527.

[67] Cf. Journal entries for November 3, 30, 1817; Mayoux, *op. cit.*, p. 129; Smith, *The Shelley Legend*, p. 4.

[68] White, *Shelley*, II, 544.   [69] *Vide infra*, pp. 487-489.

[70] See Shelley's preface to his translation of the *Symposium*, where he refers to the *Phaedo* (Julian *Works*, VII, 161-162; for the reference to the *Republic*, see *Note on the Republic*, p. 501, *infra*).

logue on beauty."[71] This considerable reading of Plato in 1817 marks the opening of the second period of Shelley's Platonism, which shows a consistent and enthusiastic study of Plato in each of the succeeding years until his death.

It is a question whether Shelley read all these works in the original or in translation. There is evidence that most of Shelley's readings in Plato this year were in the Greek. In Hogg's statement concerning the reading of the *Phaedrus*[72] we have information that Shelley read the *Phaedrus* in the original in the Bipont edition aided by the Latin translation of Ficino, which is found below the Greek text. That he also read the *Symposium* in this edition is evident from the page references in Shelley's "Note on the *Banquet* of Plato," dated 1817, which refer definitely to the speech of Agathon.[73] The page reference in this note to the Greek rather than Ficino's Latin translation shows that Shelley read the dialogue in Greek, resorting, as his later translation shows, to Ficino's Latin for help in passages he found difficult or could not understand. The amount of reading listed for February 23 in Mary's entry shows that the reading of the "several works of Plato" was probably in Ficino's Latin translation. The speed with which he read books and his facility in Latin[74] make it likely that he could finish several dialogues of Plato in addition to his other reading listed for that day.

All this extensive reading of Plato, both in the original and translation, marks the beginning of a renascence in his Platonic study. We find a reflection of this interest in Plato in the statements of various friends who associated with Shelley at Marlow. Hogg reports, "A pocket edition of Plato, of Plutarch, of Euripides . . . was his ordinary companion; and he read the text straightforward for hours."[75] Leigh Hunt, referring to the days at Marlow, where Shelley's study was adorned with a cast, as large as life, of Aphrodite Urania, says that he lived "as much like Plato himself as any of his theories resemble Plato. . . . His book was generally Plato."[76] Horace Smith gives a similar picture:

[71] Hogg, *op. cit.*, I, 121-122.   [72] *Ibid.*

[73] *Vide infra*, p. 555.

[74] Note amount of Livy read in seventeen days, p. 41 n. 52, *supra*.

[75] Hogg, *op. cit.*, I, 86; the authors cited show that this observation applies to Shelley at Marlow in 1817; cf. Mary's entries for reading of Euripides and Plutarch, April 10, July 9, 1817; and *The Athenians*, p. 41.

[76] *The Autobiography of Leigh Hunt* (Oxford, 1928), pp. 320, 322; R. Brimley Johnson, *Shelley—Leigh Hunt* (London, 1928), p. 38; see also *Correspondence of Leigh Hunt*, I, 122, Leigh Hunt to Shelley, August 4, 1818: "Pray tell me, in special, of Raphael's pictures; . . . of the School of Athens, with all the philosophers and Shelleyites of old in it"; cf. Raymond Klibansky, *The Continuity of the Platonic Tradition during the Middle Ages* (London, 1939), Plate 5.

"The weather being fine, the whole party sallied forth to stroll upon the Heath, where I attached myself to Shelley, and gradually drawing him apart, enjoyed with him a long and uninterrupted conversation. His principal discourse . . . was Plato, for whose character, writings, and philosophy he expressed an unbounded admiration."[77]

Shelley himself was very expressive of his enthusiasm for Plato. *Prince Athanase* was directly inspired by the reading of the *Symposium*, as the plot and the lines on Agathon and Diotima show.[78] In a letter to Godwin on December 7 praising his *Mandeville*, Shelley compares it to "the speech of Agathon in the Symposium of Plato."[79] Agathon's speech left such an impression upon him that he refers to it in his "Note on the *Banquet* of Plato" as "the wonderful description of Love in Plato" and makes a memorandum to compose a poem entitled *Agathon*.[80] Agathon's speech haunted Shelley until it found direct paraphrase in

> Ah, sister! Desolation is a delicate thing:
> It walks not on the earth, it floats not on the air,
> But treads with lulling footstep, and fans with silent wing
> The tender hopes which in their hearts the best and gentlest bear.[81]

Yet with all this reading and enthusiasm very little direct Platonism reaches Shelley's work with the directness and purity of these lines. The cause and effect of literary influence is not so simple or direct. Even if it is possible by textual reference to isolate the direct influence of Plato in Shelley's work, as the above lines show, yet in the creative process it will be found fused with natural and indirect Platonism. In 1817 Shelley read, side by side with Plato, a number of works like Berkeley, Coleridge's *Biographia Literaria*, the "Story of Psyche in Apuleius," Spenser's *Faerie*

---

[77] A. H. Beavan, *James and Horace Smith* (London, 1899), p. 138. Horace Smith, a broker on the Stock Exchange, was interested in literature and visited Shelley at Marlow in 1817; see also the remarks of Mr. Madocks of Marlow (C. S. Middleton, *Shelley and His Writings* [London, 1858], II, 98-99) that Shelley had been wont to "stay with him by the hour, talking, in his wild, earnest way, on all kinds of topics . . . on politics, on poetry, on the sublimities of the inspired writings, on the divinity of love. . . ." The latter two topics are probably reflections of the *Phaedrus* and *Symposium*. Cf. "Note on the Poems of 1817," by Mrs. Shelley: "He was eloquent when philosophy or politics, or taste were the subjects of conversation" (Julian *Works*, III, 171).

[78] *Vide infra*, pp. 51, 228.

[79] Julian *Works*, IX, 260. Cf. Shelley's review *On Godwin's "Mandeville"*: "It is . . . clothed in such enchanting melody of language, as seems, scarcely less than the writings of Plato, to realize those lines of Milton:—
　　　　　　　How charming is divine Philosophy!"
(*ibid.*, VI, 221).

[80] *Ibid.*, VII, 160; cf. p. 555, *infra*.

[81] *Prometheus Unbound*, I, 772-775; cf. *Adonais*, ll. 208-216.

Queene, Godwin's *Mandeville,* and Peacock's *Rhododaphne.*[82] With the exception of the first two works, the rest, as will be shown,[83] contain a poetic and romantic transmutation of Platonic Love in a form which was highly attractive to Shelley. The presence of the Platonic tradition in these works tended to dilute, infuse, and romantically interpret through the symbolism of woman the direct Platonism of the dialogues which Shelley read. Thus even though Shelley was reading Plato he was seeing him through the eyes of the poetically attractive Platonic tradition; even though he read of incorporeal, intellectual Love in the *Symposium,* its incarnation and dramatization through Henrietta in Godwin's *Mandeville* gave him more exciting inspiration. This refraction of direct Platonism through the medium of romantic literature can most clearly be illustrated by the influence of Peacock's Platonism on Shelley.

There can be no doubt that the reading of the *Symposium* by Shelley in 1817 was due to Peacock. In an undated letter postmarked "16 Jy 1817, Marlow," Peacock writes to Hogg, "I am reading the Συμποσιον of Plato, in which I have found one passage perfectly wonderful. I did not think there was such a combination of επεα πτεροεντα in the world, not even in Greek."[84] This dialogue figures prominently in Peacock's works: in *Headlong Hall,* written during the "Attic" year, we have a direct reference to Plato and the theory of Love;[85] in *Melincourt,* written during 1816, a few months before the composition of *Rhododaphne,* the *Symposium* figures prominently as the title of a chapter. In the works of Peacock written after *Melincourt* the references to the *Symposium* and its theory of Heavenly and Earthly Love are many and

[82] See White, *Shelley,* II, index, pp. cviii-cxii; entries in the Journal of *Shelley and Mary.*

[83] *Vide infra,* pp. 51-54, 86 n. 30, 105, 147.

[84] *The Athenians,* p. 36. On the reverse of the flap there is a pen-and-ink sketch of Plato by Peacock (cf. *Shelley at Oxford,* p. 57).

[85] Mr. Escot (Peacock), the deteriorationist, entered into a profound soliloquy, in which he examined "whether a philosopher ought to be in love?" and decided this point "affirmatively against Plato and Lucretius" (Halliford *Works,* I, 91). The reference to the theory of Love and the mention of Plato and Lucretius in connection with it are indicative that Peacock as early as 1816 was interested in the Platonic theory of Love. This doctrine was already familiar in English literature, but the association of it with Plato and Lucretius shows that these authors were the immediate source during the time that *Headlong Hall* was being composed. Shelley, who had finished Lucretius on July 29, 1816 (see entry in Journal of *Shelley and Mary,* p. 102), wrote to Hogg on July 6, 1817, "I am well acquainted with Lucretius. . . . The 4th book is perhaps the finest. The whole of that passage about love is full of irresistible energy of language as well as the profoundest truth" (Julian *Works,* IX, 231). This interest in Lucretius and Plato's conception of Love is also reflected in the opening of Canto VII of *Rhododaphne,* showing that the germ of the idea was already in Peacock's mind as early as 1816.

varied.[86] As the epitaph to his erring daughter Mary Meredith shows:

Χθόνιος μὲν Ἔρως ταχέως λήσμων·
μνήμων ὁ δ' ἀπ' οὐρανοῦ αἰεί.

Aphrodite Urania and Pandemos even became a part of his own life.[87] The influence of this doctrine of the *Symposium* on *Rhododaphne*, which was finished before November 28,[88] marks a definite point of contact where a romantic interpretation of the doctrine of the *Symposium* affects Shelley's creation. Shelley, who had read the *Symposium* a few months earlier, saw how beautifully its doctrines could be transmuted into poetry by a poet-scholar like Peacock, with whom Shelley had been reading the same authors who furnished the sources and inspiration for *Rhododaphne*.[89] Shelley was enchanted by the poem; he read it aloud, he

[86] In *Crotchet Castle* (1831), one of the most delightful episodes is that concerning the *Symposium* and its Pandemian and Uranian Venus in which Mr. Crotchet satirizes English cant by filling his house with the Greek Venus in all her forms. Mr. Crotchet, pointing to the half-draped figure of Uranian Venus, says, ". . . that figure realises the finest imaginings of Plato, and is the personification of the most refined and exalted feeling of which the human mind is susceptible; the love of pure, ideal, intellectual beauty" (Halliford *Works,* IV, 95). It is interesting to note in this connection that at Marlow Shelley "used to sit in a study adorned with casts, as large as life, of the Vatican Apollo, and the celestial Venus" (Leigh Hunt, *Autobiography,* p. 320; it is probable that it is to these statues that Mary has reference in her letters of 1817; see *The Letters of Mary W. Shelley,* collected and edited by F. L. Jones [Norman, Okla., 1944]; I, 24, 27). *Gryll Grange* (1861) carries on the theme of Ideal Beauty and alludes to various doctrines of the *Symposium* (Halliford *Works,* V, 94, 96, 150, 217-218).

[87] Halliford *Works,* I, cxci. I suspect that Peacock, an enemy of Greek accents, did not use them in his writing.

[88] Julian *Works,* IX, 254.

[89] On November 28 Shelley wrote to Hogg, "Peacock has finished his poem, which is a story of classical mystery and magic—the transfused essence of Lucian, Petronius, and Apuleius" (Julian *Works,* IX, 254). These authors, who form the sources of the poem (cf. Mayoux, *op. cit.,* pp. 134-135, 247), are part of both friends' reading. On Monday, May 8, 1817, Shelley wrote to Hogg, "I send you Plutarch. Peacock is reading Lucian. I am in the midst of Apuleius. . . . Peacock is equally enchanted with it" (R. Glynn Grylls, *Mary Shelley* [London, 1938], pp. 278-279; Shelley read Lucian September 29, October 21-22, November 10-14, and December 5, 1816; he read Plutarch August 18-20, November 17-19, 25-28, 1816). Furthermore, we find Shelley also sending an order on August 3, 1817, for Taylor's translation of Pausanias (Julian *Works,* IX, 235; White, *Shelley,* II, 462), who is one of the sources of *Rhododaphne* (Peacock was reading Pausanias in July, 1817; see *The Athenians,* p. 36; see also Halliford *Works,* VII, 5-6, 92-93: "That Love was the principal deity of Thespia we learn from Pausanias. . . . Both these festivals [Thespiae, Helicon] are noticed by Pausanias, who mentions likewise the three statues of Love . . . and those of Venus and Phryne by Praxiteles"). This reading of Shelley and Peacock furnishes evidence of the parallel classical interests of these two friends at this time. Another example of the close and intimate intellectual friendship between these two is in Shelley's ordering of Nonnus's *Dionysiaca* in two letters dated December 7 and 23, 1817 (Julian *Works,* IX, 257, 273). This work was a favorite of Peacock (see Halliford *Works,* I, lxxix-lxxx, and index under Nonnus, *Dionysiaca; Shelley at Oxford,* p. 60).

asked Mary to make a transcription of it[90] for him, and finally, just before he left London for Italy, he wrote a review of the poem which reflects his admiration for Peacock's scholarship and Platonism. "We sit," he writes, "with Plato by old Ilissus under the sacred Plane tree among the sweet scent of flowering sallows. . . . This it is to be a scholar; this it is to have read Homer and Sophocles and Plato. . . . Plato says, with profound allegory, that Love is not itself beautiful, but seeks the possession of beauty; this idea seems embodied in the deformed dwarf who bids, with a voice as from a trumpet, Anthemion enter."[91]

It is evident that *Prince Athanase,* written after December 5, immediately after the reading of *Rhododaphne,*[92] reflects not only the *Symposium* but also Peacock's poem with its themes of "intellectual soul," sensuous and intellectual beauty, and the incarnation of Platonic abstractions in the form of woman. The similarity of the plot of *Prince Athanase* to *Rhododaphne* makes it obvious that Shelley composed this poem after an enthusiastic reading of *Rhododaphne*. *Prince Athanase* had as its original title *Pandemos and Urania,* and the first sketch of its plot, according to Mary, was as follows:

Athanase seeks through the world the One whom he may love. He meets, in the ship in which he is embarked, a lady who appears to him to embody his ideal of love and beauty. But she proves to be Pandemos, or the earthly and unworthy Venus; who, after disappointing his cherished dreams and hopes, deserts him. Athanase, crushed by sorrow, pines and dies. "On his deathbed, the lady who can really reply to his soul comes and kisses his lips" *(The Deathbed of Athanase)*. . . . This slender note is all we have to aid our imagination in shaping out the form of the poem, such as its author imagined.[93]

[90] Entries for December 4-10, 1817, in the Journal show that Mary is copying *Rhododaphne*.

[91] Julian *Works*, VI, 273-275; Mary finished Shelley's review of *Rhododaphne* on February 23, 1818; Peacock refers to *Phaedrus* in *Rhododaphne* (Halliford *Works*, VII, 93).

[92] Shelley had finished reading *Rhododaphne* by November 28, when he wrote about it to Hogg, for he had Mary transcribing the poem on December 4, and he himself was reading Godwin's *Mandeville* on December 2. *Prince Athanase* was "written at Marlow in 1817, towards the close of the year. . . . Part I is dated by Mrs. Shelley, 'December, 1817,' the remainder, 'Marlow, 1817.' The verses were probably rehandled in Italy during the following year" (*The Complete Poetical Works of Percy Bysshe Shelley,* ed. Thomas Hutchinson [London, 1927], p. 156). It now appears that *Prince Athanase* was not started until after December 5; *vide infra,* pp. 224-225.

[93] Julian *Works*, III, 146. For the influence of *Ahrimanes* on *Laon and Cythna* (composed between April and September, 1817, at Marlow), see Halliford *Works*, I, lxxvii; cf. K. N. Cameron, "Shelley and Ahrimanes," *MLQ*, III (1942), 287-295. For the influence of *Rhododaphne* on Shelley's *Fiordispina* (1820), see Mayoux, *op. cit.,* p. 135. For the influence of even the phraseology on Shelley, see *Rhododaphne,* I, 2: "Round Thespian Love's hypaethral fane," and Shelley's "Their temples were mostly upaethric" (Julian *Works*, X, 26).

The poem, Mary claims, "was a good deal modelled on *Alastor,*" but a comparison of the sketch of its plot shows so close a similarity to Peacock's *Rhododaphne* that its derivative inspiration and dependence on it can hardly be doubted. Thus we see here an example of how Shelley, even when he was reading Plato, was influenced by the poetically attractive Platonism of Peacock's poem.

Because Peacock was a good classical scholar it need not be assumed that his Platonism was pure and direct. The Plato to whom Shelley was introduced by Peacock's poem was the Neoplatonically interpreted Plato of Thomas Taylor, who was a close friend of Peacock and affectionately called him "Greeky-Peaky."[94] His appearance in *Melincourt* as the learned mythologist who quotes Orphic Hymns, his advocacy of a return to classical polytheism, of which *Rhododaphne* is an example, his dislike of formal education, Greek accents, and other opinions which Peacock shared, are all an index of Thomas Taylor's influence on Peacock.[95] *Rhododaphne,* whose theme is the struggle of Anthemion between Uranian Love, represented by Calliröe, and Pandemian Love, represented by Rhododaphne, is not simply a poetic transcription of Plato's Intellectual Love and Beauty but is rather a magical potpourri of Neoplatonic Orphism, "the transfused essence of Lucian, Petronius, and Apuleius,"[96] as Shelley called it. The contamination of the stream of Heavenly and Earthly Beauty by the "mystery and magic" of these authors, who appear in both Shelley's and Peacock's reading, reveals the kind of Platonism to which Shelley was introduced. To understand how much of this mixture is the Orphic Neoplatonism of Taylor and how it reached Shelley, one may compare Peacock's note to page 9, line 14, of the poem (in the Halliford edition) with Thomas Taylor's preface to his translation of Pausanias, to which Peacock refers in the preface to *Rhododaphne,* and Shelley in a letter to his bookseller dated August 3, 1817.[97] The sources of *Rhododaphne* cannot be understood

[94] Halliford *Works,* I, xciv-xcviii; Mayoux, *op. cit.,* pp. 214-215; cf. "How is 'Peaky with his Greeky'?," *The Athenians,* pp. 71-72.

[95] Notopoulos, "Shelley and Thomas Taylor," *PMLA,* LI (1936), 510. Porphyry also appears in Peacock's reading at this time; see *The Athenians,* p. 36.

[96] *Vide supra,* p. 50 n. 89, *infra,* p. 86 n. 30; Halliford *Works,* VII, Preface to *Rhododaphne,* pp. 3, 92-93, where Peacock quotes Apuleius.

[97] Peacock's note is full of learned Neoplatonic information and interpretation: "Primogenial, or Creative Love, in the Orphic mythology, is the first born of Night and Chaos, the most ancient of the gods, and the parent of all things. According to Aristophanes, Night produced an egg in the bosom of Erebus, and golden-winged Love burst in due season from the shell. The Egyptians, as Plutarch informs us in his Erotic dialogue [*Amatorius,* 764b], recognised three distinct powers of Love: the Uranian, or Heavenly; the Pandemian, Vulgar or Earthly; and the Sun. That the identity of the Sun and Primogenial Love

without it. Its theological and mythological information and atmosphere emanate from the Neoplatonists whom Taylor considers the true inter-preters of Plato. Taylor, who is classed by Coleridge among "dream-ers,"[98] is the glass through which both Peacock and Shelley saw Plato

---

was recognised by the Greeks, appears from the community of their epithets in mythological poetry, as in this Orphic line: Πρωτογονος Φαεθων περιμηκεος ηερος υιος. Lactantius observes that Love was called Πρωτογονος, which signifies both first-produced and first-producing, because nothing was born before him, but all things have proceeded from him. Primogenial Love is represented in antiques mounted on the back of a lion, and, being of Egyptian origin, is traced by the modern astronomical interpreters of mythology to the Leo of the Zodiac; Uranian Love, in the mythological philosophy of Plato, is the deity or genius of pure mental passion for the good and the beautiful; and Pandemian Love, of ordinary sexual attachment" (Halliford *Works*, VII, 91).

In the notes of Thomas Taylor's translation of Pausanias (*Description of Greece*, 1794, 3 vols.), to whom Peacock refers in his preface to *Rhododaphne* (Halliford *Works*, VII, 5, 6, 92, 93), we see the affinities of Peacock's note with the potpourri of Greek religion, mythology, and the Neoplatonists whom Taylor considers the true interpreters of Plato. A glance at Taylor's notes on Celestial Venus, e.g., Pausanias III, 200-201, 206, and his notes on the *Symposium* and *Cratylus* (*Works of Plato*, III, 460, V, 641 ff.) reveal the extent to which Taylor permeates the background of the poem. In particular we may note one passage. Taylor, in speaking of the order of divinities, says, ". . . each of which series comprehends in itself many essences differing from each other; such as the angelical, daemoniacal, heroical, nymphical, and the like. The lowest powers therefore of these orders, have communion with the human race: for the extremities of first, are connascent with the summits of secondary natures. And they contribute to our other natural operations, and to the production of our species. On this account, it frequently is seen that from the mixture of these powers with men heroes are generated, who appear to possess a certain prerogative above human nature. But not only a daemoniacal genus of this kind, physically sympathizes with men, but a different genus sympathizes with other animals, as Nymphs with trees, others with fountains, and others with stags, or serpents" (*Works of Plato*, V, 685-686). Peacock was deeply influenced by such mytho-logical doctrines, which play a large part in the learned mythology of Taylor. Hunt, writing to Mary (Julian *Works*, X, 65 n. 2), says, "Hogg and Peacock generally live here every Sunday . . . we pass very pleasant afternoons talking of mythology and the Greeks." Peacock's poetry is to a degree poetic improvisations on Greek mythology. *Rhododaphne* is permeated with it; Peacock's affinity with "a daemoniacal genus . . . which sympathizes with other animals, as Nymphs with trees," finds expression in a projected Nympholeptic tale which he abandoned on seeing the announcement of Horace Smith's "Amarynthus the Nympholept" (see Halliford *Works*, VIII, 462-463, for a prose abstract of the plan of the poem). Shelley wrote to him on August 16, 1818: "Pray, are you yet cured of your Nympholepsy? 'Tis a sweet disease: but one as obstinate and dangerous as any—even when the Nymph is a Poliad. Whether such be the case or not, I hope your nym-pholeptic tale is not abandoned" (Julian *Works*, IX, 320). Thus it is seen that Peacock's poetry is the flowering of Taylor's polytheism and Neoplatonic mythology, of which *Rhododaphne* is an excellent example. The influence of Taylor on Peacock is further seen in the note on δαίμονες in the *Genius of Thames* (1812), which Shelley read (Julian *Works*, IX, 19 n. 5). A comparision of this note with Taylor's note on the *Symposium* shows similarity of conception (cf. Halliford *Works*, VI, 371-372, and *Works of Plato*, III, 685-686). These strands of romantic Neoplatonism in Peacock emanate mostly from Taylor, and they are important as a source which also affected Shelley through his friend-ship with Peacock and admiration of his poetry.

[98] *Letters of Samuel Taylor Coleridge*, ed. E. H. Coleridge (London, 1895), I, 181.

darkly. When it is realized how the natural Romantic temperament of both poets felt at home in the suggestive shadows of Taylor's pagan phantasms, it is understandable why so much of their Platonism is really Neoplatonic. "Among true and real friends all is common," says Shelley,[99] paraphrasing Plato's dictum κοινὰ γὰρ τὰ τῶν φίλων (*Phaedrus*, 279c); and Peacock's friendship with Taylor, and in turn Shelley's friendship with Peacock, inevitably resulted in Shelley's absorption of considerable Neoplatonism. Thus Peacock was not only instrumental in Shelley's reading of Plato at this period but also in transfusing to Shelley the Neoplatonic setting of the doctrine of Heavenly and Earthly Love. If this atmosphere of Neoplatonism is thickened not only by the large amount of Neoplatonism in Coleridge's *Biographia Literaria*, which Shelley read in 1817, but also by the similar conceptions of Platonic Love in Godwin's *Mandeville*, which Shelley rhapsodically admired, we can see how Shelley saw "Plato's words of light," not in the sunlight of their true being, but as Neoplatonic "moonlight in the moonless east."[100]

Yet the reading of Plato and other authors in Greek under Peacock's guidance resulted in a new attitude of mind in Shelley:

> This hour will in thy memory
> Be a dream of days forgotten long,
> We soon shall dwell by the azure sea
> Of serene and golden Italy,
> Or Greece, the Mother of the free;
> And I will teach thine infant tongue
> To call upon those heroes old
> In their own language, and will mould
> Thy growing spirit in the flame
> Of Grecian lore.[101]

These lines, addressed to his young son in 1817, show, in Shelley's own words, the conscious realization of the influence of Peacock, who guided Shelley's classical reading and effected the transition from reading Greek authors in translation to reading them in the original. The poem is an unconscious tribute to Peacock for opening new vistas of poetry to Shelley. He showed Shelley how to call on Plato in his "own language," a service which was to have profound implications on Shelley's future poetry.

Shelley's departure for Italy on March 11, 1818, marks only the transference to Italy of his enthusiastic study of Plato at Marlow. Shelley's

[99] Julian *Works*, VI, 245.   [100] *Prince Athanase*, Frag. 3 l. 62.
[101] *To William Shelley*, ll. 42-50.

extensive readings in Plato at Marlow, as shown by Mary's Journal and the testimony of his friends, proves that we must take with reservation Mrs. Shelley's statement that "it was not till Shelley resided in Italy that he made Plato his study."[102] We must therefore date the beginning of the second period of Shelley's Platonism from 1817 at Marlow and consider the study and translation of Plato in Italy as merely the continuation of an intellectual love begun at Marlow.

We have detailed evidence as to Shelley's continuation of his study of Plato and the specific content of his readings in Plato in a letter of Peacock to Hogg, postmarked 28 April, 1818, after Shelley's departure for the Continent. Peacock writes: "Shelley has left behind him some volumes of Plato, but he has taken with him the 1st. and 10th. and the Symposium is in the latter. I have not heard a word of Shelley since his departure."[103] This information enables us to identify the dialogues contained in these two volumes which formed the substance of Shelley's reading of Plato in Italy. The first volume of the Bipont edition of Plato contains the *Euthyphro, Apology, Crito, Phaedo,* and Diogenes Laertius's *Life of Plato,* along with Fabricius's notes on Plato. The tenth volume contains the *De anima mundi* of Timaeus of Locri, the *Critias, Parmenides, Symposium,* and *Phaedrus.* In view of Shelley's intense reading of Plato in Italy we can be sure that he read all these dialogues and more, for he supplemented these two volumes with an edition of the *Republic* and a folio edition of all of Plato's works. At any rate we can look upon these two volumes of the Bipont edition as potential sources of Platonic influence on Shelley's writings in Italy.

From the time the Shelleys packed their books on February 6 until they arrived at Bagni di Lucca on June 11 there is no mention of any reading of Plato. In his wanderings during this interval, however, Shelley read Dante, Wieland's *Aristippus,* Ariosto, Euripides's *Hippolytus,* Sophocles's *Ajax* and *Electra,* and thus showed that he not only continued his study of Greek but also came in contact with the Platonic tradition, particularly in the case of Wieland's *Aristippus.* But it was not until Shelley settled at Bagni di Lucca, and the trunkful of books, containing his Plato, arrived, that he began his intensive study of the classics. "We read a good deal here," he writes. . . . "I have been reading scarcely anything but Greek."[104] The entries in Mary's Journal corroborate this. Entries for June 13 to 17 record the reading of Xenophon's *Memorabilia,* which later led to the composition of the fragment *On*

---

[102] Julian *Works,* I, xiii.
[103] W. S. Scott, *Shelley at Oxford* (London, 1944), pp. 58-59.
[104] Julian *Works,* IX, 312, 315.

the Daemon of Socrates;[105] entries for June 17 to July 6 record the reading of Aristophanes and Abbé Barthélemy's *The Travels of Anacharsis the Younger in Greece,* a compendium of Greek civilization which contained excellent summary chapters on Socrates, the *Republic,* and *Timaeus.*[106] The reading of Xenophon's *Memorabilia* and Barthélemy's *Anacharsis,* both rich in their Socratic and Platonic content, may have stimulated Shelley's decision to translate the *Symposium.*

Shelley's life at Bagni di Lucca was spent in delightful solitude; he found delight in bathing in a mountain pool, riding through magnificent scenery, and reading, but with all this he was not creative.[107] He chose as a stepping stone to poetic creation the translation of Plato's *Symposium.* "I am employed just now," he says, "having little better to do, in translating into my fainting and inefficient periods the divine eloquence of Plato's *Symposium.*"[108] Like a fountain his heart pours forth enthusiasm for Plato. "Plato," he writes, "exhibits the rare union of close and subtle logic, with the Pythian enthusiasm of poetry, melted by the splendour and harmony of his periods into one irresistible stream of musical impressions which hurry the persuasions onward, as in a breathless career. His language is that of an immortal spirit, rather than a man."[109] This and other similar statements of praise in his letters[110] show that Plato had now become a god for him, and that translation was a form of worship, a Platonic daemon,[111] as it were, who would bring Shelley close to his god and his god close to Shelley.

Using the Bipont edition as his text,[112] Shelley began the translation of the *Symposium* on July 9, devoting the mornings to the task. Mary's Journal entries from July 9 on[113] are a succession of "Shelley translates the *Symposium*" with several additions of "he reads a part of it to me." On July 17 she enters: "Shelley finishes the translation of the 'Symposium'"; on July 20 she notes that Shelley has finished correcting the *Symposium* and she has begun transcribing it, a task which was not completed until August 6. The completion of the translation in eight days shows that Shelley was already familiar with the text in Marlow, and that the translation, which was aided by recourse to Ficino's Latin translation, was not a laborious, meticulous, plodding, and painstaking task, but a rapid, spirited, and vivid version.[114] The translation of the

[105] See marginalia in Shelley's copy of *Memorabilia* (Peck, *op. cit.,* II, 350) and p. 506, *infra;* for interest in Socrates's Daemon, see M. L. Clarke, *Greek Studies in England, 1700-1830* (Cambridge, 1945), p. 114.

[106] *Vide infra,* pp. 132-133.   [107] Julian *Works,* IX, 314.

[108] *Ibid.,* IX, 312.   [109] *Ibid.,* VII, 161.

[110] Cf. *ibid.,* IX, 317, 320; X, 130; VII, 311.

[111] Cf. *Symposium,* 202d-203a.   [112] *Vide infra,* p. 398.

[113] *Vide infra,* p. 382.   [114] *Vide infra,* pp. 395-398.

Symposium was one of the most important things in Shelley's poetic life.[115] It is valuable not only in itself but also for its influence on Shelley's subsequent poetry. The dialogue permeated Shelley's mind with its poetic and philosophic content, the allusions to it in his poetry and prose are unparalleled in number and importance,[116] and most of Shelley's direct Platonism can be traced to it.

Shelley's enthusiasm for this dialogue is shown not only in his reading and translation of it and its influence on his work, but also in his effort to interpret a phase of it which was not tolerated and therefore, in the eyes of Shelley, not understood by modern society. Though Shelley translated the entire of the *Symposium,* delicate caution had to be exercised in the matter of publication. The scene of the homosexual attempt of Alcibiades on Socrates, which was omitted by Mary in the publication of the translation, was an obstacle to a better appreciation of the masterpiece of Plato. We get an insight into the reaction of the British to the subject in several statements of Shelley's friends. In Peacock's *Crotchet Castle* the Reverend Dr. Folliott expresses the British reaction to offensive elements in the *Symposium:* "I am aware, sir, that Plato, in his Symposium discourseth very eloquently touching the Uranian and Pandemian Venus: but you must remember that, in our Universities, Plato is held to be little better than a misleader of youth; and they have shown their contempt for him, not only by never reading him . . . but even by never printing a complete edition of him."[117] Hogg, in a letter to Shelley recommending him to read the *Gorgias,* gives a variant expression of the same reaction.[118] Keenly aware of this prejudice, Shelley took it as his duty to explain to Mary and all society the practice among the Greeks illustrated by this episode in the *Symposium.* At first he thought that the translation in itself would be self-explanatory. In a letter to the Gisbornes on July 16 he speaks of his translation of the *Symposium* undertaken "only as an exercise or perhaps to give Mary some idea of the manners and feelings of the Athenians—so different on many subjects from that of any other community that ever existed."[119] But he soon realized that the translation in itself was insufficient to achieve this purpose and therefore decided to write an introductory essay to his translation. In a letter to Peacock on July 25 he speaks of his translation and says, "I am writing a prefatory essay."[120] In another letter to Peacock on August 16 he amplifies this statement:

I am proceeding to employ myself on a discourse, upon the subject of which the "Symposium" treats, considering the subject with reference to the dif-

---

[115] *Vide infra,* p. 392.
[117] Halliford *Works,* IV, 95.
[119] Julian *Works,* IX, 312.

[116] *Vide infra,* pp. 171-371, *passim.*
[118] *Vide infra,* pp. 68-69.
[120] *Ibid.,* IX, 315; *vide infra,* p. 383.

ference of sentiments respecting it, existing between the Greeks and modern nations: a subject to be handled with that delicate caution which either I cannot or I will not practice in other matters, but which here I acknowledge to be necessary. Not that I have any serious thought of publishing either this discourse or the "Symposium," at least till I return to England, when we may discuss the propriety of it.[121]

Shelley succeeded admirably in explaining to Mary this episode of the *Symposium*. On August 17, 1818, she wrote to Maria Gisborne, to whom she later read Shelley's translation,[122] "Shelley translated the Symposium in ten days (an anecdote for Mr. Beilby). It is a most beautiful piece of writing,—I think you will be delighted with it.—It is true that in many particulars it shocks our present manners, but no one can be a reader of the works of antiquity unless they can transport themselves from these to other times and judge not by our but by their morality."[123] But in 1840 when Mary came to publish the translation and the introductory essay, she deleted the episode from the translation; and, although the essay was completed by Shelley, she published it as a fragment which consists merely of the introduction to the subject.[124] With the publication now of both pieces in their entirety[125] we can appreciate Shelley both as a translator and as an interpreter of Plato to modern society. With his characteristic intellectual courage Shelley attempts in the essay to have Plato understood, not in abstraction, but in the context of his time and society. After an introduction which is remarkable for the comprehensive statement of the legacy of Greece to civilization he proceeds to give to modern society an interesting explanation of ancient pederasty. Recognizing the differences between the ancients and modern society on the subject, Shelley aimed at breaking down the barriers of misunderstanding. This is a prerequisite for any understanding of the *Symposium;* in the concluding paragraph Shelley writes, "This slight sketch was undertaken to induce the reader to cast off the cloak of his self-flattering prejudices and forbid the distinction of manners, which he has endeavoured to preserve in the translation of the ensuing piece, interfere with his delight or his instruction."[126] The essay forms a good introduction to the subject and deserves recognition in Platonic scholarship. For his

[121] *Ibid.*, IX, 320; cf. IX, 317.

[122] Mary records in her Journal for August 27, 1818: "Read the 'Symposium' to Mrs. Gisborne"; on August 28 she enters, "Finish reading the 'Symposium' to Mrs. Gisborne."

[123] *The Letters of Mary W. Shelley*, ed. F. L. Jones, I, 56. The reference to Mr. Beilby is to an Englishman whom the Shelleys met at Leghorn and of whom there is mention in the Journal entries for May 17 and June 5, 1818.

[124] *Vide infra*, pp. 388-390.   [125] *Vide infra*, p. 390.

[126] *Vide infra*, p. 413

translation of the dialogue, which has been described as "the poetry of a philosopher rendered by the prose of a poet,"[127] and for his effort to have this masterpiece of Plato understood by modern society Shelley deserves great praise.

The *Symposium,* however, is not the sole expression of his interest in Plato at Bagni di Lucca. Writing to William Godwin from Bagni di Lucca on July 25, 1818, Shelley says, "I have been constantly occupied in literature but have written little—except for some translations from Plato."[128] The use of the plural indicates that he began some other dialogue contained in the two volumes of the Bipont Plato. Shelley was probably tired of translation at this point and gave it up for the reading of Herodotus, which occupied him from July 20 to August 2. But the attraction for Plato was still strong. On August 4 Mary records her own and Shelley's reading of the *Phaedrus:* "Read . . . Plato, 'Phaedrus,' p. 380; Horace. Shelley reads 'Phaedrus' of Plato." The reading of the *Phaedrus,* which, as the Journal shows, was continued the following day, left its impress on Shelley. On August 16 he writes to Peacock: "What a wonderful passage there is in 'Phaedrus'—the beginning, I think, of one of the speeches of Socrates in praise of poetic madness, and in definition of what poetry is, and how a man becomes a poet."[129] These passages were to find re-expression in *A Defence of Poetry,* a work greatly influenced by the *Phaedrus.* In view of Mary's listing of this dialogue as read in 1820, this and the previous reading of the dialogue at Marlow must have consisted of selections rather than the whole of the dialogue.[130]

Shelley's enthusiasm for Plato turned into a missionary zeal, and we find him trying to have his household and friends share the delight he found in Plato. As her entry for August 4 shows, Mary, who had begun her study of Greek at his instigation,[131] was led to read the *Phaedrus.* In her preface to the *Collected Poems,* 1839, her comments on Shelley's Platonism reveal the extent of her introduction to Plato by Shelley.[132] Her pride in Shelley's translation of the *Symposium,* which

[127] *Vide infra,* p. 397.

[128] Julian *Works,* IX, 317.

[129] *Ibid.,* IX, 320-321; cf. Peacock's note, *Memoirs,* II, 398, which gives a translation of *Phaedrus,* 245a (p. 317 in Bipont text), the passage alluded to by Shelley in this letter. It is obvious that page 380 in Mary's Journal marks her own reading of the *Phaedrus* and not Shelley's (p. 380 in the Bipont edition, Volume X = Stephanus pagination 274d-275a). Shelley refers twice to the *Phaedrus* in the manuscript of the *Discourse on the Manners of the Antient Greeks Relative to the Subject of Love.*

[130] This is corroborated by the fact that Shelley read Theocritus from August 7 to 13, as the Journal shows.

[131] See Journal entries for September 18 to 25, 1814, for Mary's and Claire's detailed account of their Greek studies; also White, *Shelley,* I, 366-367.

[132] *Vide infra,* pp. 378-380.

she transcribed, is shown in her reading of it to Mrs. Gisborne; and her cryptic entry of ψηττα λιψαι[133] in her Journal for April 28, 1819, shows that she also read the dialogue in the original. Shelley also tried to have Byron share his love for Plato. Sometime during his reunion with Byron in Venice in August, 1818, when the two friends spent many pleasant hours in the Lido in conversation and discussion of their writings and literature in general, Shelley loaned his copy of Plato to Byron, no doubt with the recommendation that he read the *Symposium* and *Phaedrus,* which are found in the tenth volume of the Bipont edition. Elizabeth Atkins's study of Byron's Platonism[134] has shown that Byron was "indebted to Shelley for arousing his interest and so introducing him to the dialogues." Byron's poetry and conversations reflect considerable Platonism which he absorbed from Shelley's own writings, night-long discussions of philosophy with Shelley, and the reading of Plato's dialogues prompted, as we now see, by Shelley's loan of his own copy of Plato. Byron read the *Symposium* and the *Laches,* and his writings show the influence of the *Phaedo,* the *Phaedrus,* the *Republic,* and the *Timaeus.* Though by temperament Byron was antipathetic to Plato's doctrine of Love (cf. *Don Juan,* Canto I, cxvi), he found much to admire in the personality and thought of Socrates. Thus Shelley's Ficino-like enthusiasm for Plato had a very real influence upon Byron.

Shelley, however, missed his Plato, and on October 17, while at Venice on a last visit with the Hoppners and Byron, he wrote a note to Byron: "I am so dreadfully sleepy that I cannot come to-night. Will you have the goodness to send us 'The Fudge Family,' the 'Quarterly' and my Plato. . . ."[135] Byron returned his Plato at once, for Shelley later read the *Phaedrus* in this volume. On October 20 Mary records: "Shelley begins the 'Republic of Plato,'" which he read in Massey's edition of the *Republic.* This reading was not completed until 1820, as Mary's reading list shows.[136] Shelley continued the reading of the *Republic* during his journey to Ferrara and Rome, as Mary's entries for November 7 and 9 show.[137] The reading was discontinued at Rome in favor of writing

---

[133] *Vide infra,* p. 547.

[134] "Points of Contact between Byron and Socrates," *PMLA,* XLI (1926), 402-423.

[135] White, *Shelley,* II, 460.

[136] We have evidence of Shelley's renewed interest in the *Republic* in the *Essay on Christianity* (*vide infra,* pp. 329-330) and in notes (*vide infra,* p. 501).

[137] The effect of this reading of the *Republic* is seen in a letter to Peacock from Naples, January 26, 1819: "I consider Poetry very subordinate to moral and political science, and if I were well, certainly I should aspire to the latter" (Julian *Works,* X, 21; cf. *Symposium,* 209a), and in Preface to *Prometheus Unbound:* "Should I live to accomplish what I purpose, that is, produce a systematical history . . . of the genuine elements of human society, let not the advocates of injustice and superstition flatter themselves that I should take Aeschylus rather than Plato as my model" (Julian *Works,* II, 175).

the Platonic tale *The Coliseum,* which he started on November 25. No other readings of Plato appear in Mary's Journal for the rest of the year, which was spent in considerable sightseeing around Naples.

The translations and readings from Plato left Shelley, despite his poor health at the time, in a mood of Platonic exaltation. "You know," he writes Peacock from Ferrara on November 7, "I always seek in what I see the manifestation of something beyond the present and tangible object."[138] This basic note of natural Platonism was evoked both by the beautiful scenery,[139] which finds sublime expression in his letters, and the direct Platonism which influenced its expression. The inspired and inspiriting Platonism of the *Symposium,* quickened by Ideal Beauty, haunting him through its images in the lovely Italian scenery, left its deep impress on Shelley's compositions. The first act of *Prometheus Unbound,* composed in September and October, 1818, shortly after the translation of the *Symposium,* shows one of the loveliest expressions of the essence of that dialogue. From the earthly shadows of Ideal Beauty,

> . . . . create he can
> Forms more real than living man,
> Nurslings of immortality![140]

The influence of the *Symposium* is also shown in the plan for *The Coliseum,* which Shelley started at Rome on November 25. It was to be a tale of Platonic love modeled after Diotima.[141] The pervasive influence of the *Symposium,*[142] which Shelley used as a stimulating exercise for future creation, shows what Plato can do in giving substance to a poet who is by nature receptive to Platonism. The rise to a peak of Shelley's direct Platonism in 1818 is reflected in a proportional rise in the influence of Platonism in Shelley's compositions of 1818.[143]

Shelley's study of Plato is continued in 1819, though it is not so diversified or intense as the previous year. Mary's Journal shows no reading of Plato until Shelley's arrival in Florence. The interval between his departure from Naples on November 27, 1818, until his arrival at Florence on October 2, 1819, is spent in a sequence of travel with stopovers at Rome, Leghorn, and Villa Valsovano. During this interval his reading in the classics is less extensive. The dejection at Naples,[144] sightseeing,

[138] Julian *Works,* IX, 340.

[139] Cf. commentary on Julian *Works,* X, 26, given on pp. 363-364, *infra.*

[140] *Prometheus Unbound,* I, 747-749; cf. *ibid.,* III, iii, 50-56.

[141] Julian *Works,* V, viii-ix.

[142] For the influence of Plato on Shelley's change of philosophy, see White, *Shelley,* II, 135-137.

[143] *Vide infra,* pp. 76, 228, 230-245, 334-339.   [144] See White, *Shelley,* II, 68-82.

the death of William, and his new passion for Spanish and Calderón account for the decrease in classical reading. Yet the decrease was slight, as his readings in Livy, Plutarch's *Lives,* Lucretius, and the Greek tragedians show. There may have been some reading of Plato during this interval, for Mary discontinued the Journal after June 4, when William became very ill, and renewed it on August 4, Shelley's birthday.[145] The entries in the Journal for Shelley's readings at Florence are confined mostly to two works, the Earl of Clarendon's history and Plato's *Republic.* Entries for the reading of Plato's *Republic* occur on October 9, 10, 24, 28, November 2, and November 6 through 9. The reading of the *Republic* may have continued later in the year, for Mary enters for December 31: "I have not kept my Journal all this time; but I have little to say, except that on the morning of Friday, November 12, little Percy Florence was born." The entries for Shelley's readings up to their departure for Pisa on January 26, 1820, show that Shelley had stopped his reading of the *Republic* before the beginning of the year, and turned to the reading of the Bible and Sophocles. It is evident that Shelley's reading of the *Republic* was merely a continuation of his reading in Venice (October 20), in Ferrara (November 7), and Rome (November 9). This serial reading continued through 1820, when it was finally completed and so noted by Mary in her list of books read by Shelley in 1820. The text which Shelley used in translating the fragments of the *Republic* was Massey's.[146] Shelley had left with Peacock the sixth and seventh volumes of the Bipont edition, which contained the *Republic.* As the fragments of the translation and his references to the *Republic* in the letter concerning Carlile and in *The Moral Teachings of Jesus Christ* show,[147] the second and third books of the *Republic* left a deep impression on Shelley. The fragments from the *Republic* which Shelley translated consist of twenty passages, "the opinions and views of Plato," says Mrs. Shelley, "enounced in the *Republic* which appeared remarkable to Shelley . . . with the addition in some instances of his own observation on them."[148] The choice of the passages reveals examples of important truths, which he translated not for publication but as statements of truths or ideas to be used later in his own works.[149]

---

[145] Note Shelley's search for Platonic beauty in the galleries at Florence; his aim is to observe in statuary and painting "the degree in which . . . that ideal beauty of which we have so intense yet so obscure an apprehension, is realised in external forms" (Julian *Works,* X, 94).

[146] *Vide infra,* p. 564.

[147] *Vide infra,* p. 493.   [148] Julian *Works,* V, xii-xiii.

[149] *Vide infra,* pp. 341, 354, 493. For a similar example of Shelley's use of such passages, see his translation of two passages from the *Ion* in the MS of a *Defence of Poetry* (A. H. Koszul, *Shelley's Prose in the Bodleian Manuscripts* [London, 1910], pp. 121-122).

The year 1820 is the *annus mirabilis* of Shelley's direct Platonism. When Shelley moved to Pisa on January 26, 1820, he fitted up a study which included Plato, as Medwin shows:

Shelley's library was a very limited one. He used to say that a good library consisted not of many books, but a few chosen ones; and asking him what he considered such, he said, "I will give you my list . . . : The Greek Plays, Plato, Lord Bacon's Works, Shakspeare, The Old Dramatists, Milton, Göthe and Schiller, Dante, Petrarch and Boccaccio, and Machiavelli and Guicciardini,—not forgetting Calderon; and last, yet first, the Bible."[150]

Sensitive to the lack of appreciation of his poetry, Shelley turned to these "few select spirits" while reading was, as he described it to Mrs. Gisborne, as "quenching a thirst ever to be renewed."[151] We have an independent corroboration of this in Medwin's description of Shelley at Pisa:

He was indeed ever engaged in composition or reading, scarcely allowing himself time for exercise or air; a book was his companion the first thing in the morning, the last thing at night. He told me he always read himself to sleep. Even when he walked on the *Argine,* his favourite winter walk, he read—sometimes through the streets, and generally had a book on the table by his side at dinner, if his temperate meal could be called one. . . . he arose fresh in the morning to his task; the silence of the night invited him to pursue it, and he could truly say that food and rest were not preferred to it. No part gave him uneasiness but the last, for then he grieved that the work was done. He was indeed an indefatigable Student. So little impression did that which contributes one of the main delights of ordinary mortals, make on him, that he sometimes asked, "Mary, have I dined?"[152]

As Mary's Journal and reading list for 1820 show, Shelley's reading was mostly in the literature of Greece, with Plato predominant. She lists the *Republic,* the *Phaedo,* and the *Phaedrus* among Shelley's reading for 1820.[153] The individual entries in the Journal give us the approximate time for the reading of each of these dialogues. Shortly after Shelley's arrival at Pisa Mary's entries for February 14, 16, 17, 19 run: "Shelley reads Plato." The Plato covered by these entries must be the *Phaedrus,* for her entry for May 2 is: "Shelley finishes Phaedrus." Shelley read this dialogue in sections. He began it with Hogg at Marlow, where he read considerably in it; in this reading he evidently had not reached section 245, for his letter to Peacock on August 16, 1818, which reflects his reading of the dialogue on August 4 and 5, refers to this passage. On

[150] Medwin, *op. cit.,* p. 255.   [151] Julian *Works,* X, 164; IV, 8, l. 174.
[152] Medwin, *op. cit.,* pp. 268-269; cf. *ibid.,* p. 75.
[153] White, *Shelley,* II, 545.

August 5 he evidently laid aside the *Phaedrus* and turned to other readings. On his arrival in Pisa on January 26, 1820, he reread the entire dialogue or started somewhere after section 245 and in the four readings listed by Mary finished the remainder of the dialogue. Shelley's list of readings in the entries from February 9 to May 2 shows that the latter must be the case, for during this interval he was reading the *Aeneid* slowly and was also reading Godwin's *Political Justice;* at the same time he and Mary were translating Spinoza together.

A week after he finished the *Phaedrus* Mary enters for May 9: "Shelley reads 'Phaedon,' having read 'Phaedrus.' " No other entries appear for the *Phaedo,* but it must have been finished by September 4, when Mary enters: "Shelley . . . reads the 'Republic' of Plato." This is further corroborated by the fact that Shelley, who was praising and guiding Gisborne's classical reading, writes to him in November, 1820: "I send you the Phaedon and Tacitus."[154] Concurrent with his reading, or after the completion of the *Phaedo,* Shelley translated a portion of it. In a letter to Hogg from Bagni di Pisa on October 20, 1821, he writes: "I read . . . Plato perpetually: and have translated the *Symposium,* the *Ion,* and part of the *Phaedon.*"[155] On the surface, the listing of the translations might indicate a chronological order, in which case the translation of the *Phaedo* did not take place until some time in 1821 after the translation of the *Ion.* But Shelley's sending of his copy of the *Phaedo* to Gisborne in November, 1820, shows that he made the translation before sending the book away. The prior listing of the translation of the *Symposium* and *Ion* is then accounted for by the fact that they were completed translations in contrast to the *Phaedo,* which was incomplete. The manuscript of the *Phaedo* translation has not survived. It may have been loaned to Medwin, who took considerable interest in Shelley's writings. The possibility of this loan is seen in Shelley's later letter to Medwin asking him if he has his translation of the *Symposium.*[156] Shelley's interest in the *Phaedo* dates back to his Oxford days when its doctrines found favor with him. He shows evidence of having read part of it in 1817 or 1818, for in his preface to his translation of the *Symposium* he says, "This Apollodorus appears, both from the style in which he is represented in this piece, as well as from a passage in the *Phaedon,* to have been a person of an impassioned and enthusiastic disposition."[157]

---

[154] Julian *Works,* X, 220; Shelley no doubt sent to Gisborne the first volume of the Bipont edition containing, besides the *Phaedo,* the *Euthyphro, Apology,* and *Crito.* When he read the *Crito* later, he probably used the folio edition of Plato; *vide infra,* p. 68 n. 175.

[155] Scott, *Shelley at Oxford,* p. 64.   [156] Julian *Works,* X, 317.

[157] Julian *Works,* VII, 162.

The passage referred to is *Phaedo,* 59a, where Apollodorus is shown as giving way to tears on the last day of Socrates on this earth. Though Shelley had read the *Phaedo* earlier in translation and knew its essential doctrines through the Platonic tradition, the reading of it in the original and the translation of a portion, which helped to impress its content deeper on his mind, had a marked influence upon his compositions of 1820 to 1822. The reflection of its reading in the fragment *On a Passage in Crito,* written between October 22, 1820, and March 15, 1821, and the influence of its theme of immortality on *Adonais* and *Hellas* show the importance of the reading of this dialogue in the original.[158]

Shelley's continued and sustained interest in Plato is also shown in his completion of the *Republic.* That his reading in the *Republic* may have started earlier than September 4, the first entry of its reading in the Journal, seems probable because, after another entry of its reading on September 9, Mary begins the *Georgics* with Shelley on September 16, and Shelley's readings for September 21 to 23 and for October 1 consist largely of Lord Monboddo's *Antient Metaphysics* and Gillies's *History of Greece.* At any rate the *Republic* was the last of the three works of Plato read during the year. The impression which the *Republic* left on Shelley is seen in his letter to Hogg dated October 20, 1821: "Do you know the πολιτεια, & especially the sixth book of it? His speculations on civil society are surely the foundations of the politics, & if ever the world is to be arranged on another System than that of the several members of it destroying & tormenting one another for sake of the pleasures of sense, or from the force of habit & imitation; it must start from some such principles."[159] The completion of the reading of this dialogue marked a lifelong interest in it starting from his Oxford days. Though he found it "replete with considerable errors of speculation," some of which he pointed out in his writings, yet he called it "the greatest repository of important truths of all the works of Plato."[160] From it he drew many ideas in his writings, particularly those written after his various readings of it in the original in 1818 to 1820. As the *Symposium* and *Phaedrus* were the favorites of Shelley the poet and artist, so the *Republic* was the favorite dialogue of Shelley the reformer. His "passion for reforming the world"[161] and his passion for seeking in what he saw "the manifestations of something beyond the present tangible," both found vital sustenance in the *Republic.* Thus Shelley found in

---

[158] *Vide infra,* pp. 291, 304, 502.
[160] *Vide infra,* p. 501.
[159] Scott, *Shelley at Oxford,* p. 64.
[161] Julian *Works,* II, 174.

Plato nourishment for both the artist and the reformer in his nature. This Platonism, which was considerably increased by the reading of Lord Monboddo's *Antient Metaphysics* and Gillies's *History of Greece*, two important sources of indirect Platonism,[162] constitutes the high-water mark of Platonism in Shelley's life. It is reflected as intense enthusiasm in Shelley's letters of the time: "I read Plato forever," he writes Gisborne;[163] to Peacock he writes: "I have been reading nothing but Greek and Spanish. Plato and Calderón have been my gods."[164] He was so delighted with Plato and Calderón that in wishing to be the physician of Keats's body and soul he wanted to keep the one warm, and to teach the other Greek and Spanish so that Plato and Calderón could be Keats's gods as well.[165] Such an enthusiasm for Plato was more than mere words, as is shown in the reading and translation of these dialogues and their influence on Shelley's compositions.

The year 1821 is noteworthy in Shelley's Platonism, not only for a great many Platonically influenced works like *A Defence of Poetry*, *Epipsychidion*, and *Adonais*, but also for the considerable reading and translation from Plato.[166] No sooner had Shelley finished with the *Republic* than he started on the *Ion*. The Journal for 1821 contains no entries for its reading, but we know of it from a letter to Peacock dated February 15, 1821, where Shelley tells him that he delayed answering his essay on the *Four Ages of Poetry* because he was at the moment of its arrival reading Plato's *Ion*.[167] Shelley's enthusiasm for it is reflected in his recommendation of it to Peacock. Shelley evidently read the *Ion* in January, 1821, between the composition of the *Epipsychidion*, sometime in January, 1821, and that of *A Defence of Poetry*, in March, 1821, which shows direct allusions to the dialogue.[168] We have considerable evidence of the influence of this dialogue on Shelley in Medwin as well as in *A Defence of Poetry*, the manuscript of which contains two fragments which are now shown to be the translation of two passages from the *Ion*, made while Shelley was reading the dialogue or soon after his reading of it.[169]

Shelley thought so much of this dialogue that he made a complete translation of it.[170] Mary, who first published the translation in 1840, said, "Shelley left the *Ion* imperfect," and she completed the translation,

---

[162] *Vide infra*, pp. 130-131.
[163] Julian *Works*, X, 334.
[164] *Ibid.*, X, 223.
[165] *Ibid.*, X, 212.
[166] With one exception the Journal has no entries in 1821 for any of Shelley's reading of or translation from Plato.
[167] Julian *Works*, X, 234.
[168] *Vide infra*, p. 462.
[169] *Vide infra*, p. 482.
[170] *Vide infra*, p. 467.

marking with brackets, some of which the printer unfortunately omitted, the passages which she translated. The later discovery of Claire Clairmont's transcription of Shelley's translation of the dialogue shows that Shelley made, with the exception of the quotations from Homer, a complete translation.

We also have evidence that Shelley read a portion of Plato's *Laws* in the interval between the reading of the *Ion* and the commencement of the composition of *A Defence of Poetry*. Koszul states that "On ff. 88 v rev. and 87 rev. Shelley transcribed the delightful passage in Plato's *Leges* (ii. 653-654) which contrasts the disordinate cries and motions of children and animals with the human aspirations after rhythm and harmony, and attributes the latter to the teaching of the Muses, Apollo and Dionysos."[171] The position of the passage in the earliest draft of *A Defence of Poetry (MS Shelley, d. 1)* gives us a clue to the date of the reading. It is found immediately after Fragments I and II, which have been shown to be translations from the *Ion*. These passages are found on f. 91 v rev., f. 91 rev., f. 89 v rev.; the transcription from the *Laws* is found on ff. 88 v rev. and 87 rev., whereas the first draft of the essay begins on f. 86 v rev. The position of the transcription shows that Shelley had started the *Laws* sometime after the reading of the *Ion*. Like the two passages from the *Ion,* this transcription from the *Laws* left its influence on the introductory sections of the essay. The transcription shows that Shelley read as far as the second book of Plato's *Laws;* whether he continued it afterwards is not known. We have evidence in Mary's Journal of Shelley's enthusiastic study of Plato after he finished the essay. On April 19, 1821, Mary writes: "Shelley goes to the Baths. Reads Plato." The omission of specific reference leaves us in the dark as to the dialogue he was reading. It may refer to a continuation of the *Laws,* whose political nature and reform legislation must have appealed to Shelley.

The wide range of Shelley's reading in Plato is also shown in his reading or rereading of the *Crito* which resulted in a note *On a Passage in Crito.* This note can be dated sometime in the interval between Medwin's first stay with Shelley at Pisa, October 22, 1820, and March 15, 1821, or his second stay, November 15, 1821, and after.[172] The variant repetition of a phrase in this note in a canceled paragraph of a section of *Fragments on Metaphysics and Morals,* dated 1821,[173] and the direct

---

[171] Koszul, *op. cit.,* p. 122.

[172] *Vide infra,* p. 502.

[173] Koszul, *op. cit.,* p. 145 n. 2; Notopoulos, "The Dating of Shelley's Prose," *PMLA,* LVIII (1943), 488.

reference to Socrates's death in the *Phaedo,* which Shelley read in 1820, make it likely that Shelley read the *Crito* and wrote the note in the 1821 portion of Medwin's first stay.[174]   The reference in the note to *Apology* 36d7 shows that Shelley was intimately acquainted with or had just been rereading the *Apology* in 1821.[175]

Even though Hogg was far away in England, we find him still guiding Shelley's reading of Plato in 1821 through enthusiastic recommendations.   In a letter from London, dated June 15, 1821, Hogg wrote:

> I am going on in my usual routine of terms, circuits, sessions, and vacations, as much addicted as ever to the use of strong walks, and more prone than ever to Greek. . . . On Saturday last Peacock called upon me at eleven, to take a little stroll; . . . we soon forgot our toils in some supper, and complimented our legs on having carried us over 80 miles in three days. I need hardly add that we propitiated the far-darting King by a garland and an inscription, in Bisham Wood, which we hope to show you some day: ΣΜΙΝΘΕΕΙ. As touching Greek, I took upon me to read Demosthenes through; a great undertaking, but which I have nearly completed, for of the 1492 closely printed pages, in which the orator's δεινοτης is condensed, I have read 1344. Amongst other things, I have lately read the Αλκιβιαδης α and β of Plato, and his Γοργιας; if you do not know these dialogues, I recommend you to read them, especially Γοργιας, which, in my opinion, is the best of all his wonderful works. It ought to be translated and published with notes; it could not but succeed, as it is as interesting as a novel, and applicable to many things now passing in the world.   Plato is unfortunately little read, even by scholars, which is much to be regretted, as he is, perhaps, the most edifying of the Greeks and his style is so easy and simple.   That he should be shunned at Universities is natural enough, for reasons which he himself gives in the dialogue in question. I know no book more adapted to kindle a light in the minds of young persons incompatible with the darkness that now overshadows the earth, but, as a most ungrammatical and illogical writer says, "και το φως εν τη σκοτια

---

[174] If Shelley read the *Crito* in the folio edition of Plato (see Julian *Works,* VII, 312), then he may have written the fragment sometime between May 8 and November 1, 1821, when he was at Bagni di Pisa (see White, *Shelley,* II, 289-290, 611 n. 2).

[175] An apparent difficulty arises as to Shelley's reading of the *Crito* and *Apology* at this time.   The first volume of the Bipont edition, which was sent to Gisborne sometime in November, 1820, contained, besides the *Phaedo,* the *Euthyphro, Apology,* and *Crito.* But we have evidence that Shelley had already missed the volume he sent to Gisborne and substituted for it a poorer edition containing the same dialogues. In a letter to Hogg, dated October 20, 1821, Shelley speaks of having to put up with "a folio of *Plato* whose incredible contractions & abominable inaccuracy torment me to death." An examination of the text of Plato to which this description might apply points either to the folio edition of Stephanus (Paris, 1578), or more likely to Lugd. folio 1590 and Francof. 1602, which were popular though inaccurate reprints of Stephanus's edition (for a list of the folio editions of Plato, see Moss, *A Manual of Classical Bibliography,*[2] II, 423-427. It is likely therefore that Shelley read the *Crito* and *Apology* in this text.

φαινει, και ἡ σκοτια αυτο ου κατελαβεν. Ἐν τῷ κοσμῳ ην, και ο κοσμος αυτον ουκ εγνω." I suppose there is a public library at Pisa, where you can procure, or at least go and read, books, for even a confined shoe is less piteous than a confined library, and all private libraries must be too tight, unless the possessor be as rich as Gibbon. I supply my poverty by the library of the British Museum, where I find everything that man ever wrote or devil printed; when you return you may augment your wealth from the same treasury. . . . Remember me kindly to Mary, who deserves much praise for her industry in learning Greek, and believe me, my dear friend

Yours ever faithfully,
J. J. Hogg

I have become a great botanist, or rather lover of botany, and I herborize and collect dried specimens at a great rate, and find it a great amusement. If you meet with any curious plants, either wild or cultivated, save some seed, or dry a little bit; some day or other you will be able to send, or bring them to me. I inclose a little flower from Marlow.[176]

This letter deserves quotation, for Shelley's letter in reply summarizing his study of Plato can best be understood in the context of Hogg's letter. On October 20, 1821, Shelley wrote from Bagni di Pisa:

MY DEAR FRIEND,

. . . . I addict myself but little to walks of any length,—but wander about the edges of the hills some times with my book, and live in a total intellectual solitude. . . . I have employed Greek in large doses, & I consider it the only sure remedy for diseases of the mind. I read the tragedians, *Homer* & *Plato* perpetually, & have translated the *Symposium,* the *Ion,* & part of the *Phaedon.* I selected the first piece on account of the surpassing graces of the composition, but I have no intention of publishing it. The *Gorgias* is now open before me, and I shall read it with double interest from the views which you suggest about it. Do you know the πολιτεια & especially the sixth book of it? His speculations on civil society are surely the foundations of the politics, & if ever the world is to be arranged upon another System than that of the several members of it destroying & tormenting one another for the sake of the pleasures of sense, or from the force of habit & imitation; it must start from some such principles.

I congratulate you on your demosthenic energy—to me the feat appears to require the σθενος of an entire δημος —I have tried a philippic; I find it horribly difficult,—but I shall gather up my courage & assail him again.

I receive with delight your Milkwort—It reposes between the leaves of

---

[176] *Shelley and Mary* (London, 1882), pp. 640-643; the Greek is a quotation from the Gospel According to St. John, 1: 5, 10-11. Hogg, like Shelley and Peacock, did not use Greek accents. Cf. *The Athenians,* pp. 58-59, for Hogg's reading of the *Republic* and a reflection of similar sentiments.

a folio *Plato,* whose incredible contractions & abominable inaccuracy torment me to death, as I have only 3 vols. of my own edition as yet here. I send you a flower which grows on the mountain. . . . How much I envy your walks—though I fear my health would hardly allow me to share in them. I am glad to hear that you do not neglect the rites of the true religion. Your letter awakened my sleeping devotion, & the same evening I ascended alone the high mountain behind my house & suspended a garland, & raised a small turf altar to the mountain-walking Pan (παν ὀρειβάτεις) . . . .

Ever most sincerely yours,
P. B. SHELLEY[177]

This exchange of correspondence between these classical friends not only breathes of the aroma of their Marlow atmosphere but is also a note-worthy index of Shelley's Platonic activities and the degree in which Hogg influenced Shelley, not only in the immediate reading of the *Gorgias* and Demosthenes, but also in Shelley's mountain ritual to Pan.

In his statement of Platonic activities, Shelley merely mentions the most important of his Platonic readings, for the *Phaedrus* and other lesser readings in Plato are omitted. His appraisal of the *Republic* is a reply to Hogg's statement of Plato's value to modern society, a senti-ment which he also expressed in a note on the *Republic.* Shelley also affirms Hogg's statement about the beauty of Plato's style by praising the artistry of the *Symposium,* which led him to translate it. As to the folio of Plato, in which Hogg's milkwort "reposed,"[178] the description of its contractions fits, as we have seen, one of the cheaper but inaccurate re-prints of Stephanus's edition. The text of the *Gorgias* which Shelley had before him as he wrote is one of the three volumes[179] which he had brought with him to Bagni di Pisa, where he stayed from May 8, 1821, until November 1.[180] The remaining volumes, excluding the copy of *Phaedo* which he sent to Gisborne, were left in his library at Pisa, four miles away. That Shelley read the *Gorgias* is evident not only from this letter but from *Charles the First,* which he began towards the close of 1819, resumed in January, 1822, and finally laid aside by June of the same year. Lines 384-386 are a direct allusion to *Gorgias,* 464d-3 and 521e,[181]

---

[177] *Shelley at Oxford,* pp. 63-65. ὀρειβάτεις is either Shelley's error or an error in transcription for ὀρειβάτης (mountain-walking). For the fondness of Peacock, Hogg, and Leigh Hunt for Pan, see *Shelley at Oxford,* p. 61; *The Athenians,* p. 44.

[178] The past tense of this verb shows that the *Gorgias* before him was not part of the folio.

[179] The *Gorgias* is found in the fourth volume of the Bipont edition. This volume also includes the *Ion,* the *Philebus,* and the *Meno.* It is possible that Shelley may have asked Peacock to send the missing volumes of the Bipont edition, for he speaks of three volumes now. *Vide supra,* p. 70.

[180] White, *Shelley,* II, 289-290, 611 n. 2.   [181] *Vide infra,* p. 311.

and show Shelley's thoughtful reading of the dialogue. Thus to his Platonic readings of 1821 we may add the *Gorgias,* which does not appear in Mary's Journal, and Shelley's translations of Plato's epigrams, most of which can be dated in 1820-1821.[182] Shelley, who took Plato to be a poet, did not fail to give beautiful renditions of Plato's poetry.

A survey of Shelley's readings of Plato and translations shows that 1821 continues the *annus mirabilis* of 1820. The evidence indicates that his statement to Hogg: "I read . . . Plato perpetually," is, like his similar statement to Gisborne in 1820, no idle boast. In depth and range his study of Plato becomes one of the most important factors in understanding the sources of the great works of poetry and prose which he wrote during 1821 and 1822. The direct and vivid interrelation of his reading of Plato with the re-creation of its thought in his work[183] makes it imperative that we go to Plato for a deeper understanding of it. The *Epipsychidion* shows clearly the influence of the *Symposium* and the *Phaedrus; A Defence of Poetry* shows the influence of the *Symposium,* the *Ion,* the *Phaedrus,* the *Republic,* the *Timaeus,* the *Philebus; Adonais* shows the influence of the *Symposium,* the *Gorgias,* the *Republic,* the *Phaedo,* the *Timaeus; Hellas* shows the influence of the *Republic,* the *Symposium,* the *Phaedo,* the *Statesman; Charles the First* shows the influence of the *Phaedrus,* the *Republic,* and the *Gorgias.* These compositions cannot be understood without the *Symposium,* the *Phaedrus,* the *Phaedo,* the *Republic,* the *Ion,* and the *Gorgias,* which Shelley read in the original from 1818 to 1821. His debt to Plato in these works is consciously proclaimed in *Hellas,* when he refers to Jesus's relation to

> . . . Plato's sacred light,
> Of which my spirit was a burning morrow.[184]

His study of Plato continues with the same intensity in 1822, although the Journal and our other sources of evidence give no specific readings in Plato except the *Gorgias,* the reading of which probably extended into 1822. On January 14, 1822, Trelawny joined the Shelley circle, and though essentially a man of action, he gives us an interesting picture of the depth and extent of Shelley's study of Plato: "Shelley's thirst for knowledge was unquenchable. He set to work on a book, or pyramid of books, his eyes glistening with an energy as fierce as that of the most sordid gold-digger who works at a rock of quartz, crushing his way through all

---

[182] *Vide infra,* pp. 508-509.
[183] *Vide infra,* pp. 275-310.
[184] Prologue to *Hellas,* ll. 94-95.

impediments, no grain of the pure ore escaping his eager scrutiny."[185]
Of these books Plato was a favorite author, as Trelawny's picture of
Byron and Shelley at Pisa shows. "On returning to Pisa," he says, "I
found the two poets going through the same routine of habits they had
adopted before my departure; the one getting out of bed after noon. . . .
The other was up at six or seven, reading Plato, Sophocles, or Spinoza."[186]
Medwin, who again joined the Shelley group on November 15, 1821,
corroborates Shelley's enthusiastic study of Plato at this period.[187]

Plato's doctrines "through a thousand channels of manifest or im-
perceptible operation"[188] were by now victorious over Shelley's materialism. He agrees with Moore "that the doctrines of the French, and
Material Philosophy, are as false as they are pernicious."[189] He supplants this philosophy with that of Plato and Bacon. On a trip to Leghorn with Trelawny he said, "With regard to the great question, the
System of the Universe, I have no curiosity on the subject. I am content
to see no farther into futurity than Plato and Bacon. My mind is tranquil; I have no fears and some hopes. In our present gross material state
our faculties are clouded—when Death removes our clay coverings the
mystery will be solved."[190] This statement with its definite allusion to
Phaedo (63e-69e) reveals the extent to which Shelley absorbed Plato's
philosophy.

When the Shelleys moved to Lerici on the Gulf of Spezzia on April 26,
they took a house close to the sea; Shelley's fondness for boating led him
to buy a boat, which arrived on May 12. Shelley carried his study of
Plato with him on board the boat. Trelawny gives a picture of the struggle between Plato and seamanship aboard this boat. "I went out for a
sail in Shelley's boat to see how they would manage her. It was great
fun to witness Williams teaching the poet how to steer, and other points
of seamanship. As usual, Shelley had a book in hand, saying he could
read and steer at the same time, as one was mental, the other mechanical."

---

[185] Trelawny, *op. cit.*, II, 190; cf. *ibid.*, II, 195, 203, and Dowden, *op. cit.*, II, 502 n.
[186] Trelawny, *op. cit.*, II, 206. For a similar picture, see Medwin, *op. cit.*, p. 436: "Byron
was so sensible of his inability to cope with him, that he always avoided coming to a trial
of their strength in controversy . . . for Shelley was what Byron could not be, a close,
logical, and subtle reasoner, much of which he owed . . . to his constant study of Plato,
whose system of getting his adversary into admissions, and thus entangling him in his
own web, he followed."
[187] Medwin, *op. cit.*, pp. 349-350, 435.   [188] Julian *Works*, III, 8.
[189] *Ibid.*, X, 378.
[190] Trelawny, *op. cit.*, II, 199; cf. Mary's poem "The Choice" for the same phrase:
                    "while thy earthly dress
            Encompassed still thy soul's rare loveliness."
                                        (Grylls, *op. cit.*, p. 298)

The book was Plato. On this occasion the mainsheet was jammed and the boat became unmanageable because of Shelley's bad seamanship and preoccupation with Plato. "Williams," continues Trelawny, "blew up the poet for his neglect and inattention to orders, and the nautical terms so tickled his fancy that he even put his beloved Plato in his pocket, and gave up his mind to fun and frolic."[191]

The Triumph of Life, written for the most part on board the boat, foreshadows a deeper understanding of Plato, had Shelley lived. He realized an un-Platonic error in his life, which he expresses in a letter to Gisborne, June 18, 1822.[192] On the threshold of his death he realized that "all discontent with the *less* (to use a Platonic sophism) supposes the sense of a just claim to the *greater*."[193] He realized that the *less* meant the world in all its fragmentary glimpses of the ideal and that the *greater* meant the world of Being. It meant that he finally understood that

> The One remains, the many change and pass;
> Heaven's light forever shines, Earth's shadows fly;
> Life, like a dome of many-coloured glass,
> Stains the white radiance of Eternity.[194]

But it was fated that he should die young. On July 6 Jane Williams wrote a letter to him which ended with these words: "Why do you talk of never enjoying moments like the past? Are you going to join your friend Plato . . . ? *Buona notte.*"[195] Two days later he went to join him. In *The Triumph of Life* Shelley's triumphal car of Platonic vision mounted the ultimate level that he had been permitted to know, for he was shortly drowned in the boat in which he had spent many pleasant hours reading; copies of Sophocles and Keats were found in his pockets, but Plato was in his heart.

This is the story of Shelley's direct Platonism woven from the strands

---

[191] Trelawny, *op. cit.,* II, 209-210; Disraeli made use of this passage in his description of the death of Marmion Herbert (Shelley) in *Venetia.* Disraeli writes: "The sea had washed on the beach another corpse, the form of Marmion Herbert. It would appear that he had made no struggle to save himself, for his hand was locked in his waistcoat, where, at the moment, he had thrust the *Phaedo,* showing that he had been reading to the last, and was meditating on immortality when he died" (Benjamin Disraeli, *Venetia* [London, 1858], p. 323; quoted in *The Shelley Society's Papers,* First Series, No. 1 [London, 1888], p. 131).

[192] Julian *Works,* X, 401.

[193] *Ibid.,* X, 371.   [194] *Adonais,* ll. 460-463.

[195] Marshall, *op. cit.,* I, 367. Jane Williams is another among Shelley's many friends who were impressed by Shelley's Platonism. The letter probably alludes to Shelley's contemplation of death, his meeting it with the attitude of the philosopher, which he had evidently discussed with Jane.

of information left by the poet himself, Mary's Journal, and the testament of his friends. The story, however, is incomplete. Shelley never left a complete record of what he read. Even Mary's Journal, from which we get our most complete evidence, is very deficient in its account of Shelley's direct Platonism. It has no entries, for example, of Shelley's reading of the *Ion* or its translation, of his reading of the *Menexenus, Crito, Laws,* or *Gorgias.* If we compare its Plato entries in 1818–1822 with Shelley's statement, "I read Plato forever," we realize how fragmentary the Journal is in its listings. We must supply the gaps, vouched for by Shelley's "Plato forever" statement, by glancing at the influence of dialogues, other than those listed in our sources, on Shelley's compositions. By examining his work we may, like archaeologists examining stones, reconstruct additional columns in the Parthenon of Shelley's direct Platonism. For example, we have no record in our sources of Shelley's reading of Plato's *Statesman;* yet as Tillyard has shown,[196] the mystic retrograde return from age to infancy and then to death in *Prometheus Unbound,* Act II, scene v, lines 98-102, is a reflection of *Statesman,* 270d, e. Thus, if we grant the similarity and acknowledge its source in Plato, we are forced to list the *Statesman* in whole or part as one of Shelley's readings for 1817 to 1819. A survey of the influence of Platonism on Shelley's compositions shows that in addition to the dialogues definitely read by Shelley we must include some other dialogues. The works of Shelley composed in the following years show the influence of these additional dialogues:

Statesman	in *Prometheus Unbound* (1819)?
Apology	in *On a Passage in Crito* (1821)
Timaeus	in *Adonais* (1821), *On Devil and Devils* (1821),
	A Defence of Poetry (1821), *Hellas* (1821)

But even if we include these dialogues in Shelley's readings from Plato, the list may not be complete. All of Shelley's readings in Plato may not be transmuted into poetic influence, for the poetic process does not utilize everything that the poet reads; it is eclectic, using only those dialogues which contain material suitable for poetry. Thus though Shelley may have read nearly all of Plato, his work shows mainly the influence of the *Symposium, Phaedrus, Phaedo, Ion,* and *Republic,* dialogues rich in poetical thought and reform.

Integrating our evidence into a composite picture, we may show Shelley's direct Platonism in the following table:

[196] *Times Literary Supplement,* Sept. 29, 1932, p. 691.

Year	Place	Definite Reading (*Translation)	Probable Reading	Inference from Influence on Shelley's Works	Notes and Translations
1808?-10	Eton	*Symposium*			Plato Epigram
1810-11	Oxford	*Alcibiades I**	*Parmenides*?*		
		*Alcibiades II**	*Cratylus*?*		
		*Theages**	*Timaeus*?*		
		*Euthyphro**	*Banquet*?*		
		*Apology**	*Ion*?*		
		*Crito**			
		*Phaedo**			
		*Laches**			
		*Protagoras**			
		*The Rivals**			
		*Republic**			
		Abridgement of Plato's Philosophy, Morals, and Politics* (Summaries and quotations mostly from *Timaeus, Laws, Republic, Epistles, Symposium*)			
1812-16					Translation of an epigram of Plato, cited in the *Apologia* of Apuleius (1816)
1817	Marlow	*Symposium*			*Note on Banquet of Plato*
		Phaedrus (part)			
		"Several of the works of Plato"*			*Menexenus* (part)
		*Menexenus**	*Apology*?*		
			Republic?* (part)		
			Phaedo?* (part)		
1818	Bagni di Lucca	*Symposium*			*Symposium* *Note on Republic*
	Venice	*Republic* (part)			
	Ferrara	*Republic* (part)			
	Rome	*Republic* (part)			
1819	Florence	*Republic* (part)		Statesman?	*Republic* (part) *On the Daemon of Socrates* (Xenophon's *Memorabilia*)
1820	Pisa	*Phaedrus* (complete)			*Phaedo* (part)
		Phaedo (complete)			Epigrams of Plato
		Republic (completed)			
1821	Pisa	*Ion*		Apology?	*Ion* and notes
		Crito		Timaeus or	*On a Passage*
		Laws		Timaei Locri, De	*in Crito*
		Gorgias		Anima Mundi	
1822		*Gorgias* (continued)		Parmenides	

If we now translate this table into a graph showing the rise and fall in the rhythm of Platonic study in the various years of the poet's life, we have Shelley's direct Platonism represented by the solid line.

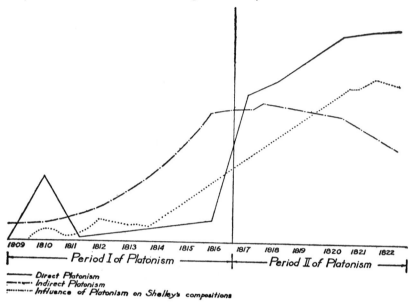

— Direct Platonism
—·—·— Indirect Platonism
·········· Influence of Platonism on Shelley's compositions

The graph of the solid line enables us to see approximately when and where in his life Shelley is in or out of Platonic focus, when Plato's influence is likely to be weak or strong, and finally to determine in what compositions the reflection of direct Platonism is likely to be found. The dotted line in the chart represents graphically the amount and intensity of Plato's influence on Shelley, as revealed in the survey of Platonism found in the compositions of the various years of his life. The amount of Platonism that Shelley re-created in his own work is small in comparison with what he read, but a comparison of the solid and dotted lines in the chart shows, with the exception of the years 1812 to 1817, a cause-and-effect relationship which is remarkably similar in the rhythm of reading and influence. This similarity reveals the integral relation of influence with the reading of an author; it shows once more that "poet is heir to poet now as of yore."[197] Being by nature studious, sensitive to poetic philosophy, equipped by temperament to understand a philosopher who was also a poet, Shelley found in Plato a sure guide to the attainment of his ideals and the expression of his own natural Platonism.

[197] *Bacchylides,* Frag. 5 (Snell).

His study of Plato may be looked upon as a force which developed his mind and poetry, as a haven of realization for a restless spirit that wandered through the literature of all ages seeking "for a communion . . . of our whole nature, intellectual, imaginative and sensitive"[198] His intense longing for sympathy found in Plato an understanding spirit. His perception in Plato "of the shadow of Intellectual Beauty and their common aspiration toward a more complete unity with Intellectual Beauty"[199] forms the heart of Shelley's direct and natural Platonism.

The broken line in the chart represents the indirect Platonic tradition in Shelley. Its sources are Shelley's reading of books strongly influenced by Plato and the Platonic tradition. Shelley was constantly in contact with the Platonic tradition both when he was not reading and when he was reading Plato in translation and in the original. The rise in Platonic influence on Shelley's works in 1812-1817, when Shelley was not reading Plato directly, is to be explained by Shelley's reading of books deeply impregnated by the Platonic tradition. In the next chapter will be shown the nature, content, and importance for Shelley of this Platonic tradition.

[198] Julian *Works*, VII, 228.
[199] White, *Shelley*, II, 444.

Chapter IV

The Indirect Platonism of Shelley

"Substances were thinned away into shadows, while everywhere shadows were deepened into substances."—COLERIDGE

A STUDY OF the sources of Shelley's indirect Platonism involves an almost synoptic survey of the Platonic tradition. This is imposed by the nature of Shelley's encyclopedic reading, which extends to almost every period, nation, and author influenced by the Platonic tradition. As the list of Shelley's recorded reading shows, he was a great reader. Hogg gives us a picture of Shelley's reading habits. "He was to be found," he says, "book in hand, at all hours; reading in season and out of season; at table, in bed, and especially during a walk; not only in the quiet country, and in retired paths, not only at Oxford, in the public walks, and High Street, but in the most crowded thoroughfares of London. It is no exaggeration to affirm, that out of the twenty-four hours, he frequently read sixteen."[1] It is obvious, as Professor Lane Cooper once remarked, that one "cannot be a reader of books without reading some one who has read Plato, or at second hand or third remove has received the Platonic stimulation." The authors Shelley read reflect the various phases of the Platonic tradition—aesthetic, religious, cosmological, and metaphysical. A brief account of the Platonic tradition in periods and authors not directly connected with Shelley's reading is necessary by virtue of the fact that authors like Boethius, whom Shelley did not read, influenced the Platonism of authors like Dante and Spenser, whom he did read. Thus we are confronted with a tradition which resembles the chain of magnetized rings in Plato's *Ion*.

The Platonic tradition in Shelley is very complex and may be likened once more to a number of streams pouring into rivers which ultimately reach the sea. The many become one, and the Platonic tradition in Shelley can be traced with respect to contributory streams; but once they

[1] Hogg, *op. cit.,* I, 84-85; for another picture of Shelley in London in 1813, cf.: "There was a little projecting window in Half-Moon Street, in which Shelley might be seen from the street all day long, book in hand, with lively gestures and bright eyes" (Hogg to Mrs. Shelley, May 29, 1841, *Shelley and Mary,* p. 1228).

enter Shelley's mind, it is almost impossible to trace from what particular stream the waters came.   The best clue to the source and origin of indirect Platonism in Shelley is to be found by examining Shelley's compositions written concurrently with or after the reading of an author deeply imbued with Platonism.   If Shelley is enthusiastic about an author who attractively presents the Platonic tradition, we have a possible direct source of Platonic influence, for Shelley creatively assimilates the object of his enthusiasm.   This is the closest approximation to specific sources for the elements in Shelley's indirect Platonism.   But at its best our source remains a guess; the operation of the poetic mind with respect to its source does not admit of scientific precision or classification.   The poetic mind can retain ideas in suspension and evoke them into being in the very process of creation long after the reading of an author.   Moreover, certain doctrines of Platonism, like the world soul, Platonic Love, the music of the spheres, the immortality of the soul, became common property and part of the intellectual atmosphere into which every cultured mind is born.   Shelley could have garnered these ideas from any number of authors, as is true even of such phrases as "plastic stress" and "Intellectual Beauty," which can be narrowed down to a limited number of authors in Shelley's reading list.

The indirect tradition of Platonism is paradoxically filled with direct Platonism; thus our troubles in tracing precisely the sources of Platonism in Shelley are increased.   The authors whom Shelley read contain many direct doctrines of Plato, sometimes in the form of direct quotation, paraphrase, or reference to specific dialogues.   These *disiecta membra* of our philosopher reach Shelley in such abundance that we can truthfully say that Shelley could have knowledge through this medium of most of the important thoughts of Plato.   The reading of authors embodying this Platonic information shows that Shelley's direct Platonism was constantly enriched even in periods when he was not reading Plato himself. Therefore it can with difficulty be maintained that a certain passage in Shelley does not show the influence of a particular dialogue because Shelley had not read this dialogue at the time.   From his early years Shelley was acquainted with all the leading doctrines of Plato through the presence of these doctrines in authors whom he read.   But it is to be noted that this informational Platonism, when abstracted from the artistic context of Plato's Dialogues, had on the whole little influence on Shelley unless it received an artistic and intellectually stimulating presentation in the author he was reading.   Therefore the influence of the direct Platonism found in authors he read depended on Shelley's enthusiastic assimilation of these authors.

The complex relations of indirect Platonism to direct Platonism are again shown in the fact that indirect Platonism colors Shelley's mind even when he is reading Plato directly. An example of this was shown in the influence of Peacock's Platonism at a time when Shelley had just read the *Symposium* in the original Greek. A comparison of direct and indirect Platonic reading in the composite chart shows that Shelley is influenced by both at the same time. Even when he is reading the *Symposium,* his own poetry may be influenced, not by Plato's conception of Platonic Love, but by the Platonic Love of the European tradition which extracted the concept from the *Symposium* and *Phaedrus* and made something altogether new out of it which Shelley found more to his own taste and liking. Thus the Platonic tradition may be derivative, but it is also plastic and re-creative. Plato is like the wine that the priestess gives in Rabelais's Temple of Bacbuc: though it comes from the same fountain, it tastes according to the imagination of those who drink it. Shelley was as much influenced by indirect as by direct Platonism, for temperamentally he had many qualities in common with the Platonic tradition, particularly with respect to the doctrine of love.

But regardless of the complex nature of the Platonic tradition and the difficulty of tracing Shelley's Platonism to a specific source in the Platonic tradition, it is obvious that Shelley's mind is as derivative and dependent upon the Platonic tradition as it is original. Shelley's poetry is not simply an unpremeditated art. The best appraisal of the significance of the Platonic tradition for Shelley is his own testament in the Preface of *Prometheus Unbound:*

The cloud of mind is discharging its collected lightning. . . . As to imitation, poetry is a mimetic art. It creates, but it creates by combination and representation . . . . one great poet is a masterpiece of nature which another not only ought to study but must study. He might as wisely and as easily determine that his mind should no longer be the mirror of all that is lovely in the visible universe, as exclude from his contemplation the beautiful which exists in the writings of a great contemporary. . . . A poet is the combined product of such internal powers as modify the nature of others; and of such external influences as excite and sustain these powers; he is not one, but both. Every man's mind is, in this respect, modified by all the objects of nature and art; by every word and every suggestion which he ever admitted to act upon his consciousness; it is the mirror upon which all forms are reflected, and in which they compose one form. Poets, not otherwise than philosophers, painters, sculptors, and musicians, are, in one sense, the creators, and, in another, the creations, of their age. From this subjection the loftiest do not escape.[2]

Though Shelley is primarily referring to contemporaries, his words apply equally to Plato, who because of his genius is the contemporary of every great thinker and poet. Shelley was attracted equally by Plato and by his image in the Platonic tradition; sometimes he was influenced by Plato directly and sometimes by the Platonic tradition; sometimes the influence is perceived in crystal clearness, but at other times Plato and the Platonic tradition are lost as distinct elements in the alembic of Shelley's mind. They appear indistinguishable from Shelley's own natural Platonism, which they often awakened into expression by their stimulating influence. Like scientists, we may study the component facts that go into the making of a mind, but it is the magic artistry of beauty to fuse the constituent elements, derived and original, into an indistinguishable unity of loveliness. Such is the case with Shelley's poetry. Analysis of the elements of Platonism in Shelley's poetry merely increases our knowledge of the creative process and enriches our knowledge of the whole through a study of its parts. Therefore an analysis and appraisal of the Platonic tradition in Shelley is essential for a comprehensive study of his Platonism.

ANCIENT PLATONISM

Shelley's contact with the Platonic tradition really begins with writers prior to Plato, for many elements in Plato are found in earlier writers with whose thought or writings Shelley was acquainted. Through his reading of Hesiod's *Works and Days* Shelley became acquainted with the Prometheus myth and the cycles of degeneration from the Golden Age, which also appear in Plato and later in Virgil's *Fourth Eclogue*.[3] Shelley's contact with the pre-Socratics who affected Plato is worthy of note. Shelley's interest in Pythagoras, probably the result of his interest in vegetarianism, is reflected in his order of Pythagoras from his bookseller on December 24, 1812.[4] If he received and read a traditionally interpreted Pythagoras, he would absorb information about catharsis, immortality of the soul, mystical doctrines, and notions like the music of the spheres. Shelley's knowledge of other pre-Socratic philosophers, as shown in his prose, is derived from his reading of Diogenes Laertius's *Lives of the Philosophers,* the account of the pre-Socratics in Cicero's

[2] Julian *Works,* II, 173-174.
[3] Hesiod, *Works and Days,* ll. 48-58, 109-201; Virgil, *Eclogue IV.*
[4] Julian *Works,* IX, 36.

treatises like the *Tusculan Disputations* and *De natura deorum,* treatises like Lord Monboddo's *Antient Metaphysics,* and Abbé Barthélemy's *Travels of Anacharsis,* all of which are found in Shelley's reading.[5]

XENOPHON, ARISTOTLE

The Platonic tradition actually begins with Xenophon, who probably made use of Plato's minor dialogues as source material for his *Memorabilia.*[6] Shelley's fragment *On the Daemon of Socrates* is a direct reflection of his reading of the *Memorabilia,* from which he supplemented his knowledge of Socrates.[7] Though Aristotle is opposed to Plato in many ways, he shares many of his thoughts, conveying even in his opposition information about Plato.[8] Shelley translated a section of the *Ethics* and read some other treatises of Aristotle at Oxford.[9]

ANCIENT SCHOOLS OF PHILOSOPHY

The Platonic tradition in the New Academy, Stoicism, Epicureanism, and Skepticism marks the beginning of significant changes in the doctrines of Plato.[10] Plato's thought undergoes the eclectic and adaptive changes which characterize the vital philosophy of a suggestive thinker who asks many fundamental questions and gives answers capable of further development. The names of various members of these schools are found in Shelley's philosophical essays. The sources of Shelley's knowledge of them are partly primary and partly secondary. He sent for Epicurus from his bookseller in 1812;[11] he read Lucretius, who despite a different outlook has many contacts with Plato;[12] he absorbed

[5] For Shelley's reading of these authors, see White, *Shelley,* II, Appendix VI, and index, pp. cviii-cxii.

[6] See *Plato's Phaedo,* ed. John Burnet (Oxford, 1911), Introduction, pp. xx-xxii.

[7] Cf. J. A. Notopoulos, "The Dating of Shelley's Notes and Translations from Plato," *MLR,* XXXIV (1939), 247-248. Entries in the Journal for the reading of the *Memorabilia* occur on June 13-17, 1818.

[8] See Charles Werner, *Aristote et l'idealisme platonicien* (Paris, 1910); Werner Jaeger, *Aristotle, Fundamentals of the History of His Development* (Oxford, 1934); Paul Shorey, *Platonism, Ancient and Modern* (Berkeley, Calif., 1938), p. 6; Raymond Klibansky, *The Continuity of the Platonic Tradition during the Middle Ages* (London, 1939), pp. 22, 40, Plates 3-5; C. H. Haskins, *The Renaissance of the Twelfth Century* (Cambridge, Mass., 1927), chap. xi.

[9] Carlos Baker, "Shelley's Translation from Aristotle," *MLN,* LXI (1946), 405-406; Kenneth N. Cameron, "Shelley and Aristotle," *Notes and Queries,* CXC (1946), 80; Hogg, *op. cit.,* I, 163; cf. *ibid.,* I, 70. Shelley also came in contact with Aristotle's philosophy in the extensive account of it in Albertus Magnus, in Dante, and in Lord Monboddo's *Antient Metaphysics.*

[10] Cf. F. W. Bussell, *The School of Plato* (London, 1896); Shorey, *op. cit.,* pp. 8-35; Henri Auguste Alline, *Histoire du texte de Platon* (Paris, 1915), pp. 134-173; Friedrich Solmsen, *Plato's Theology* (Ithaca, 1942), pp. 183-188.

[11] Julian *Works,* IX, 36.

[12] For Shelley's reading of Lucretius, see White, *Shelley,* II, index, p. lvi.

Platonic Stoicism from his reading of Cicero, Virgil, Seneca, and Plutarch;[13] he read accounts of these philosophic systems in Monboddo's *Antient Metaphysics,* in Bacon, and in various other writers who refer to them directly.

CICERO

In his role of a transmitter of Plato's thought to the Romans, Cicero served as one of the few vital contacts between Plato and European thought in ages when knowledge of Plato was limited.[14]   His influence upon Shelley may be traced not only in Shelley's reading of the essays, but also in the reading of many writers who derived their Platonism from Cicero.   Shelley read Cicero[15] at a time when he was not reading Plato, and some of the Platonism in Shelley's compositions written in 1814 and 1815 may emanate from Cicero.   In his reading list for 1814 appear Cicero's *Collectanea,* which must have included some of Cicero's philosophical works, for in a letter dated August 15, 1815, Shelley writes, "I have read some of the Orations of Cicero. . . . on the whole I consider them inferior in the interest they produced to those of his metaphysical essays which I have read."[16]   He continued his study of these essays in 1815, for he mentions in a letter dated September, 1815, that he proceeds slowly with Cicero's philosophic dialogues.[17]   We have evidence that he read the *De natura deorum,* the *Tusculan Disputations,* and *Somnium Scipionis.*[18]   His serious study of Cicero is reflected in his reference to and Latin quotations from the *De natura deorum* in *A Refutation of Deism,* and in the manuscript of *Fragment on God.*[19] This direct knowledge of Cicero forms an important source of Shelley's indirect Platonism.[20]

---

[13] Shorey, *op. cit.,* pp. 20-21; R. M. Jones, *The Platonism of Plutarch* (Menasha, Wis., 1916); *Virgil Aeneid VI,* ed. Sir Frank Fletcher (Oxford, 1941), pp. xxiv, 83-84.

[14] For Cicero and Plato, see references cited by Shorey, *op. cit.,* chap. i n. 49; Klibansky, *op. cit.,* pp. 22, 28, 32, 40; Alline, *op. cit.,* p. 135 n. 1; J. E. Sandys, *A History of Classical Scholarship* (Cambridge, 1903), I, 265-267; Thelma B. DeGraff, "Plato in Cicero," *Classical Philology,* XXXV (1940), 143-153 (this article contains all direct references in Cicero to Plato); Shorey, *op. cit.,* pp. 33-35; cf. Paul Friedlander, "Socrates Enters Rome," *American Journal of Philology,* LXVI (1945), 337-351.

[15] For Shelley's reading of Cicero, see White, *Shelley,* II, index, p. xv; Julian *Works,* X, 445.

[16] Julian *Works,* IX, 115-116; cf. *ibid.,* IX, 81.   [17] *Ibid.,* IX, 119.

[18] White, *Shelley,* I, 407, II, 540; the presence in the MS of *Fragment on God* of quotations from Cicero's *De natura deorum* (cf. *PMLA,* LVIII [1943], 484) and references to this dialogue in *A Refutation of Deism* show that this was one of the "many of Cicero's philosophical works" which Shelley read.   The reference to *mavis errare cum Platone* (Julian *Works,* X, 234) shows that *Tusculan Disputations* may have been included in Shelley's reading.

[19] Julian *Works,* VI, 30; A. Koszul, *Shelley's Prose in the Bodleian Manuscripts,* p. 124.

[20] Cf. Thaddaeus Zielinski, *Cicero im Wandel der Jahrhunderte²* (Leipzig and Berlin, 1908); E. K. Rand, *Founders of the Middle Ages* (Cambridge, Mass., 1928), *passim* (index,

Because Cicero, like Plato, was "readable and therefore read," he forms a magnetic chain of Platonic influence; and his importance in the Platonic tradition in Shelley deserves more than mere mention.

Always a student of philosophy, Cicero undertook to make available to the Roman people the rich treasure of Greek philosophy. In this mission Plato, whom he calls the "deus philosophorum," plays an important role. Cicero, like Shelley, rendered service to the Platonic tradition through his translation of the *Protagoras* and *Timaeus*. Shaping Latin into a philosophical medium, Cicero succeeded in transmuting through his essays the leading doctrines of Platonism, some of them in the form of factual information and others blended in with the philosophy of the various post-Platonic schools. A survey of Cicero's essays shows that Shelley in his reading of them came in contact with the leading features of Platonism. Plato's cosmology as developed in the *Timaeus* is briefly summarized in the *De natura deorum;* Cicero's *De republica* and *De legibus* include more Platonism than the mere Platonic titles; the *Somnium Scipionis* is an inspired counterpart of the vision of Er in the *Republic;* the immortality of the soul, the dualism of body and soul, and the respective worth of each in the Platonic scale of values, the astronomy and theology of the *Timaeus,* its doctrine of a sentient universe, the doctrine of the self-motion of the soul, and the doctrine of ideas and of reminiscence are interspersed throughout Cicero's work. Some of Cicero's Platonism is a direct, brief, and summary statement of Plato's views on various subjects; some of it is in the form of direct quotation from Plato's Dialogues; some of it is paraphrase; and some is Platonized Stoicism, with the view of which school Cicero is often sympathetic. In general, Cicero's Platonism is not only wide and extensive, covering almost a complete outline of Plato's thought, but is also a highly accurate transmission. As a result much of the Platonism which Shelley absorbed from Cicero is clear and direct, lacking of course the rich and poetic artistry of Plato. Its importance for Shelley lies in the fact that, absorbed as information, it forms an important source of Platonism for those works composed before 1817, when Shelley began to read Plato again.

Cicero is also important as the transmitter of Platonism fused with other systems of philosophy. Of these the most important is Stoicism,

pp. 356-357); Karl Mras, *Macrobius' Kommentar zu Ciceros Somnium* (Berlin, 1933); A. B. Modersohn, "Cicero im englischen Geistleben des 16 Jahrhunderts," *Herrig's Archiv für das Studium der Neueren Sprachen und Literaturen,* CXLIX (N.S. XLIX) (1925-1926), 33-51, 219-245; N. E. Nelson, "Cicero's *De Officiis* in Christian Thought: 300-1300," *University of Michigan Publications, Language and Literature,* X (1933), 59-160; J. C. Rolfe, *Cicero and His Influence* (Boston, 1923).

which adapted much of Platonism in the development of its own philosophy. The changes that Platonism underwent in Stoicism, the New
Academy, and Roman eclecticism mark the beginning of indirect Platonism which is complex and mixed with influences and contributions
of different minds and ages. Cicero is the medium through which this
type of Platonism reached Shelley.

Shelley's knowledge of the Platonic tradition in its early development
is also enriched by many other ancient writers influenced by Plato. A
poetically attractive presentation of the Platonic doctrine of the World
Soul, Plato's doctrine of the immortality of the soul, its relation to the
body, its purification, and an account of its transmigration are to be found
in the sixth book of the *Aeneid*, which Shelley read on January 6 and 24,
1818; similarly the Golden Age in the *Fourth Eclogue*, to which Shelley
refers directly in note 7 to *Hellas*, was suggested directly or indirectly
by Plato's *Statesman*, 268d ff.[21] His reading of Lucretius brought him
in contact with some aspects of Platonism.[22] Shelley also read Seneca's
works, and in his essays and in particular in letters 58 and 65 he found
much Platonism.[23] He sent for and probably read Polybius, whose
philosophy of politics, in particular the cycles of the form of government,
is derived from Plato.[24] Shelley's possible reading of Longinus would
introduce him to an analysis of Plato's sublimity, which is a favorite
topic in Shelley's writings.[25] From Lucian, who is not a Platonist,
Shelley absorbed the refracted Platonism contained in the references and
satiric caricature of its thought.[26] He also read Diogenes Laertius's *Lives
of the Philosophers*, which contains a compendium of Plato's life and
thought.[27] Though this is a factual account of Plato, it forms an im-

[21] For the Platonism in the sixth book of the *Aeneid* (ll. 784-751), see *P. Vergilius
Maro Aeneis Buch VI*[3], ed. Eduard Norden (Leipzig and Berlin, 1934), pp. 17-48, *passim;*
H. E. Butler, *The Sixth Book of the Aeneid* (Oxford, 1920), pp. 25-32, 228-231, 233;
Virgil Aeneid VI, ed. Sir Frank Fletcher (Oxford, 1941), pp. xii-xxiv, 83-87. For the
Platonic source of the Golden Age in the *Fourth Eclogue*, see H. J. Rose, *The Eclogues of
Vergil* (Berkeley and Los Angeles, 1942), pp. 183-186, 258 n. 61; *vide infra*, p. 253.
[22] Cf. Paul Shorey, "Plato, Lucretius, and Epicurus," *Harvard Studies in Classical
Philology*, XII (1901), 201-210.
[23] Cf. White, *Shelley*, II, 541.
[24] Julian *Works*, IX, 36; cf. Shorey, *Platonism, Ancient and Modern*, p. 33; E. K. Rand,
The Building of Eternal Rome (Cambridge, Mass., 1933), pp. 10-12.
[25] A reference to Longinus in Claire Clairmont's Diary (entry for April 14, 1818),
may indicate Shelley's guiding hand in her choice of reading; see Preface to *Laon and
Cythna* for reference to Longinus (Julian *Works*, I, 245).
[26] W. H. Tackaberry, "Lucian's Relation to Plato and the Post-Aristotelian Philosophers,"
The University of Toronto Studies, Philology and Literature Series, No. 9 (1930). For
a list of quotations and allusions to Plato in Lucian, see F. W. Householder, Jr., *Literary
Quotation and Allusion in Lucian* (New York, 1941), pp. 34-36.
[27] See White, *Shelley*, II, 540; the Bipont edition of Plato, which Shelley owned, also
contained Diogenes Laertius's *Life of Plato* (I, iii-lx).

portant source of informational Platonism for Shelley in the period before he read Plato enthusiastically. Plutarch is also a channel through which the Platonic tradition flowed into Shelley.[28] The two essays περὶ σαρκοφαγίας, which Shelley translated, contain several Platonic references among their Orphic and Pythagorean conceptions.[29] They constitute along with Apuleius[30] a transition to Neoplatonism.

NEOPLATONISM

The indirect tradition of Platonism in Shelley is as much Neoplatonic in character as Platonic. Neoplatonism, as the shadow of Platonism, is often mistaken for Platonism itself.[31] Its central thought is admirably summarized in Paul Shorey's *Platonism, Ancient and Modern:*

Everything exists by virtue of the inherent tendency of the plenitude of ungrudging Being in the higher to radiate, illuminate, emanate, overflow, and impart itself to the lower. In this process or procession the higher remains unchanged while the lower turns back towards and reflects that which brings it forth, somewhat as, psychologically speaking, the mind turns back to and reflects upon itself. The highest is the ineffable One (of Plato's *Parmenides*) identical with the Idea of the Good in the *Republic,* though in its unknowable unity it cannot properly be said to be either good or intelligent. The second principle, emanating from this, is the Nous, or intellect, answering to the Demiourgos, or creator, in Plato's *Timaeus*. The ideas that are the prototypes of all created things and constitute the intelligible world are in this Nous. They are the thoughts of God, or, to put it in Aristotelian terminology, the intellect is identical with its ideas, and God is self-thinking thought. In the poetical, cosmogonical myth of Plato's *Timaeus,* the Demiourgos creates the soul of the world; that is, in Plotinus' translation, soul is the emanation of intellect and the third and last member of the triad or trinity. Human souls, though endowed with freedom, are parts or detach-

---

[28] See Julian *Works*, IX, 81-82; for Plutarch's Platonism, *vide supra*, note 13.

[29] See *Moralia*, 996b, 998a.

[30] For Shelley's reading of Apuleius (the story of Psyche in the *Golden Ass*, IV, 28—VI, 24), see White, *Shelley*, II, 543, and R. Glynn Grylls, *Mary Shelley*, p. 279; for the Platonism in this story, see Richard Foerster, "Platons Phaedros und Apuleius," *Philologus*, LXXV (1918), 134-155. A recently discovered translation of an epigram of Plato which Shelley says he found in Apuleius's *Apologia* (*vide infra*, pp. 568-569) shows that we must include Apuleius's *Apologia* among the books read by Shelley in 1816. For the important statement of the Platonic Heavenly vs. Earthly Love in this work, see *Apologia*, 12.

[31] For Neoplatonism and the Neoplatonic tradition, see Shorey, *Platonism, Ancient and Modern*, pp. 36-61 and nn. (all subsequent references to Shorey, unless otherwise specified, are to this work); Charles Bigg, *Neoplatonism* (London, 1895); Thomas Whittaker, *The Neo-Platonists*[2] (Cambridge, 1928); W. R. Inge, *The Philosophy of Plotinus*[2] (London, 1923), 2 vols.; Solmsen, *op. cit.*, pp. 187-189; A. H. Armstrong, *The Architecture of the Intelligible Universe in the Philosophy of Plotinus* (Cambridge, 1940); *The Essence of Plotinus*, based on the translation of Stephen Mackenna, compiled by Grace H. Turnbull (New York, 1934), pp. 249-271.

ments of the soul. Extended first matter is the final and faintest irradiation of Being, and as such, through its weakness, the ultimate principle of evil, which is merely negation, and nothing positive. All good, true, and beautiful things are explicable as the restoration of the soul to its native purity, or the dominance and irradiation of the material by the ideal. All evil and unbeautiful things are the clogging and imbruting of the soul, or the obscuration of the idea, by matter. The order here set forth as in time really belongs to timeless eternity, and expresses the true nature and abiding relations of existence.[32]

In the expression of this philosophy Neoplatonism makes considerable use of symbolism, abstraction, mysticism, and dialectic, which ever refine its content by an abstruse hierarchical ascent. It possesses the quality of increasing in emotion as it decreases in sense and meaning. Platonism is a dialectical advance from sensation to a comprehensive knowledge, never forsaking logical development until it reaches its highest flight; it subordinates emotion, mysticism, symbolism to reason. In Neoplatonism we have the development of certain nuclei in Plato's thought, like the problem of the One and the Many in the *Parmenides,* the cosmology of the *Timaeus,* and the psychology of the *Phaedo* and *Phaedrus;* Neoplatonism starts from these basic notions, expands them, interpolates Gnostic, Hermetic, and Cabalistic ideas, symbols, and emotions alien to its pristine character, and is so intertwined with Platonism that it is difficult for the historian of Platonism to distinguish the two. Its central doctrine of emanation—the relation of the One and the Many through mystical integrations, daemons, spirits—and its development of Intellectual Beauty tend to make it appealing to philosophical poetry, the cosmic imagination, and pantheistic emotions, which love the twilight of mysticism, symbolism, and allegory. Though Neoplatonism may use Plato's basic concepts, yet by setting them in a different context of emotion and metaphysical imagination, it changes Platonism into a system of thought which appeals more to the poetical mind than strict Platonism itself. As a historian of Greek philosophy has said:

Nothing can be imagined more imposing than this wondrous procession of forms defiling from the Absolute One whither thought cannot soar to the abysmal infinitudes of possibility which thought cannot sound—from the self-developing consciousness of Reason as it breaks and flames and multiplies into a whole universe of being and life and thought, ever returning, by the very law of their production, to the source whence they have sprung—onward and outward on the wings of the cosmic Soul, through this visible world,

[32] Shorey, *op. cit.,* pp. 48-49; for the relations of the Neoplatonic One to Plato, see E. R. Dodds, "The *Parmenides* of Plato and the Origin of the Neo-Platonic One," *Classical Quarterly,* XXII (1928), 129-142; for the doctrine of emanation, see Dodds's edition of *Proclus, The Elements of Theology* (Oxford, 1933), pp. 212-214.

where they reappear as images of intellectual beauty in the eternal revolution of the starry spheres above, in the everlasting reproduction of organic species below, in the loveliest thoughts and actions of the loveliest human souls— till the utmost limits of their propagation and dispersion have been reached, till the last faint rays of existence die out in the dark and void region that extends to infinity beyond.[33]

As a philosophy Neoplatonism had qualities which fused easily with the various phases of Christianity, with the mentality of the Middle Ages, with the pagan, poetic, and philosophic outburst of the Renaissance, and finally with Romanticism. The channels through which Neoplatonism influenced Shelley are many and difficult to trace. Shelley was acquainted to a certain extent with the origin and development of Neoplatonism up to the Renaissance through the account of it in Gibbon's *Decline and Fall of the Roman Empire* and in Lord Monboddo's *Antient Metaphysics*. Neoplatonism reached him indirectly through its influence on almost every writer who is included in the history of the Platonic tradition. Among them are Augustine, Dante, Petrarch, Albertus Magnus, Chaucer, Spenser, Milton, Wieland, Coleridge, and many others whom Shelley read. An account of the Neoplatonism in these writers will be given in connection with the Platonic tradition, for the two traditions are so fused that even if these authors knew Plato they often interpreted him in the light of Neoplatonism.

The Neoplatonic tradition influenced Shelley most directly through Thomas Taylor,[34] the English Ficino, who uncritically but ardently devoted himself to the elucidation of Plato through the Neoplatonists. Shelley not only used Taylor's translation, but even made the acquaintance of this pagan Neoplatonist who influenced his vegetarianism and polytheism. If Shelley did not read any translations of Plotinus, or the commentaries of Proclus, he could absorb the essence of their Neoplatonism from Taylor's notes and introductions to his translation of Plato. Shelley's knowledge of Plato through these translations forms one of the important sources of his Neoplatonism.

Even when Shelley read Plato directly in the Greek, the association with Neoplatonism lingered. In Neoplatonism Shelley found an atmosphere more congenial to his own nature. To what extent he was natu-

---

[33] Alfred William Benn, *The Greek Philosophers*[2] (London, 1914), pp. 575-576.

[34] See J. A. Notopoulos, "Shelley and Thomas Taylor," *PMLA*, LI (1936), 502-517; another factor in bringing Shelley and Thomas Taylor together may be seen in the fact that Mary's mother, Mary Wollstonecraft, and a friend resided with Thomas Taylor for three months, and often heard him explain the doctrines of Plato (F. B. Evans III, "Thomas Taylor, Platonist of the Romantic Period," *PMLA*, LV [1940], 1064-1065).

rally predisposed to Neoplatonism has been considered in the study of his
natural Platonism, but here it need only be pointed out that in his cosmic
emotions, pantheism, daemons, spirits, love for abstract symbolism, and
allegory, Shelley leans more toward Neoplatonism than Platonism. The
Neoplatonic influences which reached Shelley through Thomas Taylor
and other authors affected by Neoplatonism were more sympathetic to
Shelley's temperament than was logical Platonism.

AUGUSTINE

Intermediate between the Platonism of the ancient world and the
Middle Ages are two important figures, Augustine and Boethius. Shelley
probably read some of Augustine[35] and felt the influence of Boethius
through Dante,[36] Petrarch, and Chaucer. These two transitional figures
are of some importance in the account of the Platonic tradition in Shelley.
Christianity and Platonism were fused into a powerful tradition which
influenced Christian and secular thought.[37] The Christian Apologists
and Fathers like Jerome, Justin the Martyr, Ambrose, and Augustine
were attracted to Platonism on account of many cognate doctrines.
Augustine, "the Christian Plato,"[38] was converted from Manichaeism
by his reading of the *libri Platonici* (Plotinus's *Enneads* and Porphyry),
which he could read in Marius Victorinus's translation;[39] he also ab-

[35] Shelley prefixed to *Alastor* a line from St. Augustine (*Confessions*, III, chap. i), which
also appears on page 196 in his notes at the end of Claire Clairmont's Diary for August-
November, 1814.

[36] For Augustine and Dante, see Rand, *op. cit.*, pp. 251-284.

[37] For Platonism and Christianity, see Caesar Morgan, *An Investigation of the Trinity
of Plato and of Philo Judaeus, and of the effects which an attachment to their writings
had upon . . . the Fathers of the Christian Church* (London, 1853); [Georg] C[hristian
Benedict] Ackermann, *The Christian Element in Plato and the Platonic Philosophy*, trans.
by S. R. Asbury (Edinburgh, 1861); Ernest Havet, *Le Christianisme et ses origines* (Paris,
1878-1884), Vols. I-II: *L'Hellénisme;* Charles Bigg, *The Christian Platonists of Alexandria*
(Oxford, 1886) and *Neoplatonism*, chap. xxv; Edwin Hatch, *The Influence of Greek Ideas
and Usages upon the Christian Church*[3] (London, 1891), pp. 129, 239, 240-243, 246-247;
K. K. Krogh-Tonning, *Essays I: Plato als Vorläufer des Christentums* (Kempten, 1906);
William Temple, *Plato and Christianity* (London, 1916), pp. 75-102; T. H. Billings, *The
Platonism of Philo Judaeus* (Chicago, 1919); G. P. Adams, *Idealism and the Modern Ages*
(New Haven, 1919), pp. 65-87; A. Kurfess, "Lactantius und Plato," *Philologus*, LXXVIII
(1923), 381-392; W. R. Inge, *The Platonic Tradition in English Religious Thought* (New
York, 1926); Joachim Meifort, *Der Platonismus bei Clemens Alexandrinus* (Tübingen,
1928); J. S. Hoyland, *The Great Forerunner, Studies in the Interrelation of Platonism and
Christianity* (London, 1928); Constantin Ritter, *Platonismus und Christentum* (Tübingen,
1934); Hans Willms, Εἰκών; *eine begriffsgeschichtliche Untersuchung zum Platonismus*
(Münster, 1935), 1. *Philon von Alexandreia; mit einer Einleitung über Platon und die
Zwischenzeit;* Shorey, *op. cit.*, pp. 62-87; Klibansky, *op. cit.*, Plates 2-4; Solmsen, *op. cit.*,
pp. 189-193.

[38] Rand, *op. cit.*, p. 256.

[39] Klibansky, *op. cit.*, p. 23; *Confessions*, VIII, 2; cf. VII, 9. For Augustine and the Pla-

sorbed some Platonism from such Latin authors as Cicero, Seneca, Apuleius, and Macrobius, and from Chalcidius's translation of the first part of the *Timaeus*. After his conversion Augustine saw many parallels between Plato and Christianity, such as the compatibility of Plato's cosmology with the Christian account; only the mystery of the Incarnation stood in the way of a complete harmony between Christianity and Platonism. Many of the rungs of the ladder by which Augustine ascended toward God were Platonic. The structure of his theology, the relation of God to the world, is essentially based on the cognate foundation of both Platonism and Christianity, appearance and reality. Augustine's estimate of Plato is seen in his statement: "Hunc Platonem . . . non heroibus tantum, sed etiam diis ipsis praeferendum esse non dubito."[40] Through Augustine Christianity was largely Platonized; the importance of this for Shelley is seen in his *Essay on Christianity*, which dwells on the close relationship of Christ and Plato.[41] Though at certain periods of his life an enemy of Christianity, Shelley absorbed considerable indirect Platonism through its presence in the Christian tradition.

BOETHIUS

After Augustine the most important channel through which the Platonic tradition passed to the Middle Ages is Boethius.[42] There is no evidence that Shelley read him directly, though he read an account of his life and a summary of the *Consolation* in Gibbon's *Decline and Fall of the Roman Empire*.[43] Boethius, however, is important for the Platonic tradition in Shelley. Many of the sources of Shelley's Platonism, like Dante, Chaucer, and Spenser, are themselves dependent on Boe-

---

tonic tradition, see L. Grandgeorge, *Saint Augustin et le Néo-Platonisme* (Paris, 1896); Prosper Alfaric, *L'Évolution intellectuelle de Saint Augustin*, I: *Du manichéisme au néoplatonisme* (Paris, 1918); Charles Boyer, *Christianisme et Néoplatonisme dans la formation de Saint Augustin* (Paris, 1920): Abbé Régis Jolivet, *Saint Augustin et le Néo-Platonisme chrétien* (Paris, 1932); Jakob Barion, *Plotin und Augustinus* (Berlin, 1935); Paul Henry, "Augustine and Plotinus," *Journal of Theological Studies*, XXXVIII (1937), 1-23, and *Plotin et l'Occident, Firmicus Maternus, Marius Victorinus, Saint Augustin et Macrobe* (Louvain, 1934); *Bibliographie zum Nachleben der Antike*, Bibliothek Warburg (London, 1934), Nos. 579-581, 583, 595, 598, 602; *ibid.*, II (London, 1938), Nos. 636-638; Sister Mary Patricia Garvey, *Saint Augustine: Christian or Neo-Platonist?* (Milwaukee, 1939); P. O. Kristeller, "Augustine and the Early Renaissance," *Review of Religion*, VIII (1944), 339-358.

[40] *De civitate Dei*, II, 14.

[41] Cf. Julian *Works*, VII, 127.

[42] For Boethius and the Platonic tradition, see H. R. Patch, *The Tradition of Boethius* (New York, 1935), pp. 32, 117-120, 141; Rand, *op. cit.*, pp. 142 ff., 314 n. 20; Klibansky, *op. cit.*, pp. 23-24; *Boethius*, ed. and trans. H. F. Stewart and E. K. Rand (Loeb Classical Library), index, *s.v.* Plato.

[43] Edward Gibbon, *The History of the Decline and Fall of the Roman Empire*, ed. J. B. Bury (London, 1898), IV, 201-202.

thius,[44] whose importance for the Middle Ages is seen in the existence of close to four hundred manuscripts in the libraries of mediaeval Europe. Boethius's intention to translate the whole of Plato into Latin was cut short when he was condemned to death by the Emperor Theodoric. While waiting for death in prison he transmuted many of Plato's thoughts into the noble prose and poetry of the *Consolatio*. Because of its poetic and philosophic appeal the *Consolatio* became one of the main sources of the Platonic tradition in the Middle Ages. "No part of the Consolatio," says Klibansky, "was more frequently quoted and discussed and commented on by Latin writers than the Platonic metrum, *O qui perpetua mundum ratione gubernas*,"[45] which is a poetic summary of the *Timaeus*. The diffusion of this and other Platonic doctrines through the *Consolatio* forms an important chapter in the Platonic tradition.

PLATONISM IN THE MIDDLE AGES

Shelley had very little sympathy or admiration for the Middle Ages. His only direct contact with the Platonism of the Middle Ages is Albertus Magnus, of whom Shelley says in a letter dated June 3, 1812, "I . . . pored over the reveries of Albertus Magnus and Paracelsus, the former of which I read in Latin, and probably gained more knowledge of that language from that source than from all the discipline of Eton." Though Albertus Magnus is a rich source of Platonism in the Middle Ages,[46]

[44] For Boethius and Dante, see Rocco Murari, *Dante e Boezio: contributo allo studio delle fonti dantesche* (Bologna, 1905); G. A. L. Baur, *Boetius und Dante* (Leipzig, 1874); Patch, *op. cit.*, pp. 43-44, 92. For Boethius and Chaucer, see Patch, *op. cit.*, pp. 66-73; B. L. Jefferson, *Chaucer and the Consolation of Philosophy of Boethius* (Princeton, 1917); for Boethius and Spenser, see B. E. C. Davis, *Edmund Spenser* (Cambridge, 1933), pp. 226, 234, 241.

[45] Klibansky, *op. cit.*, p. 33.

[46] For the Platonism of Albertus Magnus, see Leopold Gaul, *Alberts des Grossen Verhältnis zu Plato, Beiträge zur Geschichte der Philosophie des Mittelalters*, XII, No. 1 (Münster, 1913); *Bibliographie zum Nachleben der Antike*, Bibliothek Warburg (London, 1934), Band I, No. 750. For the Platonism of the Middle Ages in general, see Pierre Rousselot, *Pour l'histoire du problème de l'amour au moyen âge* (Münster, 1908); Clemens Baeumker, *Der Platonismus im Mittelalter* (Munich, 1916) and "Mittelalterlicher und Renaissance-Platonismus," *Joseph Schlecht . . . Festgabe* (Munich and Freising, 1917), pp. 1-13; Ernst Hoffmann, "Platonismus und Mittelalter," *Vorträge der Bibliothek Warburg*, III (1923-1924) (Leipzig and Berlin, 1926), 17-82; Hugo Koch, *Pseudo-Dionysius Areopagita in seinen Beziehungen zum Neuplatonismus und Mysterienwesen* (Mainz, 1900); H. O. Taylor, *The Mediaeval Mind*⁴ (London, 1927), 2 vols.; C. H. Haskins, *Studies in the History of Mediaeval Science*² (Cambridge, Mass., 1927); Etienne Gilson, *La Philosophie au Moyen-Âge* (Paris, 1930); Walther Aschenbach, *Die platonische Geschichts Philosophie als Fundament der Mittelalterlichen* (Quakenbrück, 1932); Dodds's edition of *Proclus, The Elements of Theology* (Oxford, 1933), Introduction, pp. xxvi-xxxiii; J. M. Parent, *La Doctrine de la Creation dans l'École de Chartres* (Paris, 1938); Alline, *op. cit.*, pp. 174-280; Klibansky, *op. cit.*, and "Plato's *Parmenides* in the Middle Ages and the Renaissance," *Mediaeval and Renaissance Studies*, I, 2 (1943), 281-330; Shorey, *op. cit.*, pp. 88-117, nn. on pp. 244-245.

we must look more to its reflection in the poetry of Dante and Petrarch, who in general helped to form the character of much of European literature and thought which Shelley absorbed in his reading. An example of this may be cited. The *Liber de Pomo,* largely Platonic in character, was not only an official textbook in Paris in 1225 but was also admired by Dante, who was a favorite poet of Shelley.[47] Hence a brief account of the Platonism of the Middle Ages is essential for a complete understanding of the indirect Platonic tradition in Shelley.

The Middle Ages are characterized by an almost Greekless knowledge of Plato and by a continuous tradition of Platonism which reached Europe through the Latin, Byzantine, and Arabic traditions.[48] The Latin tradition is both direct and indirect in its transmission of Platonism. The direct tradition took the form of a Latin translation of parts of Plato. Cicero and other classical and patristic writers had translated many important passages from Plato. The greatest direct source of Platonism for the Middle Ages was Chalcidius's commentary and translation of a part of the *Timaeus* (17a-53c3).[49] This translation of the *Timaeus* had a great influence on the Middle Ages, as the manuscripts in almost every mediaeval library show. Shorey says of it, "The shortest cut to the study of the philosophy of the early Middle Ages is to commit the *Timaeus* to memory. . . . The mediaeval writers paraphrased and glossed and quoted the *Timaeus* endlessly. . . . the *Timaeus* intoxicated the poetic, mystic, and imaginative minds of the early Middle Ages, who had little other high philosophy and poetry to feed their imagination."[50] Its doctrines of the divine Demiourgos, the creation of the world, the soul of the world, the intermediate spirits, and its four elements were creatively adapted by mediaeval thought. The analogy between the Demiourgos and the Christian God, the creation of the world as an image of the creator, and the teleological explanation of the universe furnished strong and natural ties between Platonism and Christianity. The theological use of the *Timaeus* made by mediaeval writers like Bernardus Silvestris in

[47] Klibansky, *The Continuity of the Platonic Tradition during the Middle Ages,* pp. 17-18; E. R. Dodds's edition of *Proclus, The Elements of Theology,* pp. xxix-xxx.

[48] The following discussion of the Latin, Byzantine, and Arabic traditions of Platonism in the Middle Ages is essentially based on Klibansky's excellent account. For the Arabic tradition, see also Richard Walzer, "Arab Transmission of Greek Thought to Medieval Europe," *Bulletin of the John Rylands Library* (Manchester), XXIX (1945), 160-183; Franz Rosenthal, "On the Knowledge of Plato's Philosophy in the Islamic World," *Islamic Culture,* XIV (1940), 387-422; A. S. Halkin, "Socrates in the Arab-Jewish Tradition," *Proceedings of the American Academy for Jewish Research,* XIV (1944), 38-60.

[49] Cf. B. W. Switalski, *Des Chalcidius Kommentar zu Platos Timaeus* (Münster, 1902); Klibansky, *The Continuity of the Platonic Tradition during the Middle Ages,* Plate 5 (all subsequent references to Klibansky, unless otherwise specified, are to this work).

[50] Shorey, *op. cit.,* pp. 105, 113.

his *De mundi universitate*[51] permeated the Middle Ages with a poetical and religious mysticism which influenced Dante, Petrarch, and Chaucer, all of whom Shelley read. Aside from the *Timaeus* the only other Latin translations of works of Plato were those of the *Meno* and *Phaedo* made by Henricus Aristippus.[52] Though less influential than the *Timaeus,* they were read by Roger Bacon, the Paris schoolmen, and Petrarch, and constitute a link in the introduction of Platonism into English literature.

While the direct tradition is somewhat limited, the indirect tradition is considerable. The indirect Latin tradition is divided into its pagan and Christian phases. The Middle Ages found in the pagan writers like Cicero, Seneca, Aulus Gellius, Apuleius, and Macrobius considerable Platonism which was supplemented by the Latin translations of Proclus and Chalcidius's commentary on the *Timaeus*. The knowledge of Plato from these sources varied in the degree of purity, ranging from direct references to Plato to the Neoplatonic interpretation of Plato's *Parmenides* by Proclus. The knowledge of Plato emanating from the Christian tradition is also extensive. Besides many reflections and comments on Plato in the Latin Fathers there were Latin translations of the Greek Fathers like Origen, Basil, Eustathius, and Gregory of Nyssa. The fusion of Christianity and Neoplatonism was fostered not only by Augustine's writings, but also by Hilduin's and Johannes Scotus's translation of the writings of Pseudo-Dionysius the Areopagite, whose works were based on Proclus. The Latin tradition of Platonism was further enriched by the Arabic and Byzantine traditions. The Arabic tradition acquired a knowledge of Plato and Neoplatonism through the Nestorians and Monophysites of the heterodox Syrian Christians. Versions of Plato's works were made in the Syriac, and these in turn were translated into Arabic. They included Hunaiṇ ibn Ishak's translations of the *Timaeus, Republic, Laws,* and the *Sophist,* of Olympiodorus, and later in the ninth century a translation of Galen's synopsis of Plato's Dialogues. This considerable body of Platonism was brought to Europe by the westward expansion of the Arabs in the tenth century. It entered through Spain and spread through Europe in the twelfth century.[53] The influence of the Platonic tradition on the Arabic philosophers of the Middle Ages

[51] *Ibid.,* p. 106.

[52] Valentin Rose, "Die Lücke im Diogenes Laërtius und der alte Übersetzer," *Hermes,* I (1866), 367-397; *Plato Latinus, Volumen I, Meno,* Interprete Henrico Aristippo, Edidit V. Kordeuter, Recognovit et Praefatione Instruxit, Carlotta Labowsky (London, 1940); cf. Klibansky, *op. cit.,* pp. 51, 29-30; for the MSS of the translation of the *Phaedo* and the *Meno,* see Haskins, *Studies in Mediaeval Science,*[2] pp. 166-167 nn. 41, 42, and Klibansky, *op. cit.,* pp. 29-31.

[53] Cf. Haskins, *op. cit.,* chaps. ix, xi, and bibliographical notes, pp. 366-367.

like al-Kindi, al-Farabi, and Avicenna in particular was in turn continued in the influence of these philosophers on the West. Through the Arabs the Platonic tradition also influenced Jewish philosophers like Isaac Israeli, Solomon ibn Gabirol, and Maimonides, whose works were also known in the West. The Latin translations of these Arabic and Jewish sources of Platonism contributed much to twelfth-century Renaissance in Europe. Thus the Arabic tradition brought to Europe a valuable and influential knowledge of Platonism.

A more important contribution to the Platonic tradition of the West comes from the Byzantine tradition, which can claim a continuous Platonic tradition from the Academy to the Renaissance in Europe. The one advantage which the Byzantine scholar had was that he could read Plato in the original language, which Gibbon described as giving "a soul to the objects of sense and a body to the abstractions of philosophy."[54] A steady stream of Platonic scholarship throughout the various stages of the Byzantine tradition assured a purity to the Platonism that entered the West from Byzantium. The points of contact included ambassadors to Byzantium and the arrival in Sicily of monks and other victims of the iconoclastic purge in Byzantium. The high point of a Platonic renascence in Byzantium came in the eleventh century under the leadership of Michael Psellus, who wrote commentaries on Plato and spread enthusiasm for the philosopher not only in Armenia but also in the West and particularly in Norman Sicily.[55] There Henricus Aristippus, archdeacon of Catania, who had been an ambassador to the court of Comnenus at Byzantium, translated, ca. 1156, the *Phaedo* and the *Meno* into Latin. These translations played a significant part in the spread of Platonism in the twelfth century. Aristippus dedicated his translation of the *Phaedo* to Robert of Crickdale, Prior of St. Frideswide's, Oxford, and the arrival of the *Meno* and *Phaedo* translations in England marked, as Burnet has pointed out, one of the ways by which Platonism entered England. Thus the Byzantine tradition emanating mostly from Psellus and his pupils

[54] Gibbon, *op. cit.*, VII, 114.

[55] Christian Zervos, *Un Philosophe néoplatonicien du XIe siècle: Michel Psellos* (Paris, 1919). For the history and culture of the Sicilian Norman Kingdom, see Evelyn Jamison, "The Sicilian Norman Kingdom in the Mind of Anglo-Norman Contemporaries," *Proceedings of the British Academy*, XXIV (1938), 237-285; L. T. White, Jr., *Latin Monasticism in Norman Sicily* (Cambridge, Mass., 1938), Introduction, chap. iii. For Henricus Aristippus and his translations of Plato, see *ibid.*, pp. 272-274; Klibansky, *op. cit.*, pp. 27-28; Haskins, *op. cit.*, pp. 292, 298, 344; C. H. Haskins and Dean P. Lockwood, "The Sicilian Translators of the Twelfth Century and the First Latin Version of Ptolemy's *Almagest*," *Harvard Studies in Classical Philology*, XXI (1910), 86-89; C. H. Haskins, *op. cit.*, pp. 165-171; Preface to *Meno*, Interprete Henrico Aristippo.

can be regarded as an important contribution to the Platonism of the Latin world.

The confluence of the Latin, Arabic, and Byzantine traditions of Platonism in Europe resulted in a considerable body of Platonism. An example of it is seen in the manuscripts of Nicholas of Cusa, which included the translations of Plato by Leonardo Bruni, Decembrio, Henricus Aristippus, the *Timaeus,* Macrobius on *Somnium Scipionis,* Apuleius, Proclus's *Elementatio Theologica, Theologia Platonis,* and three copies of Proclus's commentary on the *Parmenides.* As Klibansky writes:

. . . the mediaeval Platonic tradition as a whole is much too complex to be described as either Platonism, as was formerly, or Neoplatonism, as is now, the rule. The first view fails to recognize the difference which separates every form of mediaeval Platonism from Plato's own thought. The second, a reaction against the first, commits the opposite error. Starting from a preconceived idea of "mediaeval philosophy," regardless of the manifold and even conflicting trends of thought comprised in this abstraction, it soon finds a common denominator for all elements related in any way to so-called Platonic studies. Some of these, it is true, reflect a conception which seems to come near to Plotinus' theory of emanation. Just as often, we find a kind of Platonism which is neither the doctrine of Plato nor that of Plotinus or Proclus, but, based on Hellenistic thought, nourished by the religious experience, Christian, Jewish or Islamic, of later centuries, and intimately fused with teachings from Stoic and other philosophers, is, in fine, something new and individual, difficult to bring under a simple heading.[56]

This complexity which underlies mediaeval Platonism is in great part due to the creative use made of it by the minds of the Middle Ages. They contributed their own aesthetic, philosophic, and religious character to it, and the product of this synthesis eventually influenced Shelley through Albertus Magnus and through its influence on the writers whom Shelley read.

DANTE

Shelley's main points of contact with the Platonism of the Middle Ages are Dante, Petrarch, and Chaucer. In the account of the Platonic tradition in Shelley, Dante plays a most important role, for he personalized Platonic Love in the form of woman. Dante's poetry is concerned with the relation of Earth and Heaven. We recognize at once in Dante's thought the Platonic dualism: Earth is a shadow and Heaven is Reality, and man should devote his life to a purgation of the earthly and by a contemplation of the divine ascend to his true estate. But

---

[56] Klibansky, *op. cit.,* p. 36.

whereas in Platonism the ladder from this world of shadows to the world of Being is essentially a logical process, for Dante a woman is the medium linking man with the divine. The substitution of woman for logic, of a personality for dialectic, marks one of the most important changes in the history of Platonism. The conception of woman both as an immanent and as a transcendent force, as "light intellectual, replete with love,"[57] marks the point where Platonism becomes the most important source of poetic inspiration in European literature. In this respect Dante is the father of that aspect of Shelley's Platonism which looks upon woman as the intermediate spirit which links the two worlds. Poets in the succeeding generations use this symbol of Platonic Love in consonance with their character. Dante's Beatrice is different from Shelley's Cythna or Asia, but both poets find in woman a spiritual and intellectual symbol. Love for such a woman is an enlightening experience, a medium through which they see the Ideal. By infusing emotion, fantasy, and symbolism into the Platonic quest for the Ideal, Dante made Platonism one of the most abundant fountains of inspiration for European poetry.

Mediaeval Platonism is to be found in many places in the thought and poetry of Dante,[58] but he mostly uses it as atmosphere for the natural Platonism in his own soul and experience. The *Divine Comedy* is a Christianized and personalized Platonism. "It is," says De Sanctis, "the story of the soul in its human state, confused by the senses, which first despoils and purges itself, becoming freed from the flesh, and then is renewed, is once more made pure and divine."[59] It is a dramatization of the *Phaedo, Phaedrus,* and *Symposium* in the poetry of the particular. Beatrice is the spiritual and intellectual veil of the Divine, in the contemplation of which celestial intelligence Dante ascends from Purgatory to Paradiso. As an exemplar of every beauty and virtue Bea-

[57] *Paradiso*, XXX, 40.

[58] For Dante's Platonism, see Edward Moore, *Studies in Dante, First Series: Scripture and Classical Authors in Dante* (Oxford, 1896), pp. 156-164; Paget Toynbee, *Dante Dictionary* (Oxford, 1898), s.v. Plato, pp. 441-442; J. A. Symonds, "The Dantesque and Platonic Ideals of Love," in *The Key of Blue and Other Prose Essays* (London, 1893), pp. 55-86; Frédéric Ozanam, *Dante and Catholic Philosophy in the Thirteenth Century* (New York, 1897), pp. 280-301; Paride Chistoni, *La Seconda fase del pensiero dantesco: periodo degli studi sui classici e filosofi antichi e sugli espositore medioevali* (Livorno, 1903); Karl Vossler, *Mediæval Culture, An Introduction to Dante and His Times* (New York, 1920), I, 178-181; N. A. Robb, *Neoplatonism of the Italian Renaissance* (London, 1935), pp. 18-19.

[59] Francesco de Sanctis, *History of Italian Literature* (New York, 1931), I, 159; for the history of the fusion of Christian and Platonic Love, Agape as God's own love energizing in the human heart and Plato's heavenly Eros as upward movement of the soul in seeking the eternal, the true, and the Divine, see Anders Nygren, *Agape and Eros* (London, 1932-1939), 2 vols.; *Plato's Symposium*, ed. J. Sykoutres (Athens, 1934), pp. 230-246.

trice becomes a Platonic vision, Philosophy itself. In the *Divine Comedy* Dante dramatized a natural Platonic experience in his own soul, laid its scenery in Platonized Christianity, fused the divine love and the worship of Mary with spiritual Love, and created out of all this a poem which can legitimately be called one of the most important sources of Platonism in Shelley. The reading and admiration of Dante by Shelley[60] show that we must give an important place to Dante in the account of Shelley's Platonism.

PETRARCH

The Platonism of the Middle Ages also reached Shelley through his reading and admiration of Petrarch,[61] whose Platonism is natural, direct, and indirect.[62] Petrarch's direct acquaintance with Plato is to be seen in the care with which he read and annotated Chalcidius's translation of the *Timaeus*. It is probable that he also possessed Aristippus's Latin translations of the *Meno* and *Phaedo*. His love for Plato, whom he ranks as the first among philosophers, is also evident in the Greek manuscript, containing sixteen dialogues of Plato, found in Petrarch's library at Vaucluse, which was probably used as the text when Petrarch took Greek lessons from Barlaam. This knowledge of Plato was considerably supplemented by the Platonism which he absorbed in Latin writers like Cicero.

Petrarch followed in the tradition of Dante with respect to spiritual or, as it was later called, Platonic Love. Though Platonic Love as we know it in poetry and literature was strictly speaking the "invention" of Ficino, it was foreshadowed in a large degree by the spiritual love of Dante and Petrarch. But the relative difference in the capacities of the two poets to infuse the symbol of Platonic Love with their own experience and depth of imagination and thought makes Laura different from

[60] Adolph Droop, *Die Belesenheit Percy Bysshe Shelleys* (Weimar, 1906), pp. 147-149; White, *Shelley*, II, index, pp. xxi-xxii; Corrado Zaccheti, *Shelley e Dante* (Palermo, 1922); Oscar Kuhns, "Dante's Influence on Shelley," *MLN*, XIII (1898), 161-165; Thomas Medwin, *Journal of the Conversations of Lord Byron* (London, 1824), p. 161.

[61] For Shelley's reading of Petrarch, see Droop, *op. cit.*, pp. 149-150; White, *Shelley*, II, index, pp. lxxiv-lxxv; cf. Julian *Works*, VII, 224.

[62] For Petrarch's Platonism, see Pierre de Nolhac, *Pétrarque et l'humanisme*[2] (Paris, 1907), II, 132-134, 137-150; Giovanni Gentile, "I dialoghi di Platone posseduti dal Petrarca," *Rassegna critica della letteratura Italiana*, IX (1904), 193-219; Robb, *op. cit.*, pp. 17-30; Giuseppe Toffanin, *Storia Letteraria d'Italia, Il Cinquecento* (Milan, 1935), pp. 134-137, and bibliography cited on p. 147 nn. 17-18; R. V. Merrill, "Platonism in Petrarch's *Canzonieri*," *MP*, XXVII (1929-1930), 161-174, and *The Platonism of Joachim Du Bellay* (Chicago, 1925), pp. 121-123; *Bibliographie zum Nachleben der Antike*, Bibliothek Warburg (London, 1934), I, No. 871; De Sanctis, *op. cit.*, pp. 266-267, 273; Klibansky, *op. cit.*, pp. 28, 30, 32, 52; Alline, *op. cit.*, pp. 291-293.

Beatrice. Dante's Platonic Love is influenced by the higher divine love such as theologians like Bernardus Silvestris expressed. Petrarch's Platonic Love is more to be connected with the old Provençal and Tuscan lyrics, with the poets of the *dolce stil nuovo*. "Feeling," as De Sanctis says, "forbidden to be senses and forced to be reason, torn from the human heart, became a universal like the rest, an exterior fact, now symbolical, now scholastic, or, as they called it then, 'Platonic.' And the parent of feeling, which is love, was made into a philosophical fact, a uniting force, uniting the intellect and the act; its fruit was the Platonic lyrics from Guinicelli to Petrarch."[63] This love was influenced by the mediaeval code of courtly love wherein the relation of a knight to his lady was spiritualized into a code of service in which the lover, never equal to the beloved, was requited in ways and degrees sanctioned by usage and custom. It was a code which sublimated love into a love for the spirit, and in this respect it fused with Platonic Love, which had the same ideals.

Laura became the symbol of these forces which made of woman a spiritual being. Love for Petrarch is a force which leads to Heaven and gives glimpses of it only to those who can see woman as a veil of the spirit. This conception is expressed with the intensity of feeling and felicity of expression which are Petrarch's. He is close to Shelley in his expression of Platonic Love, and Laura is in many ways the counterpart of Shelley's women who are unearthly visions of Heaven. Shelley likewise pursues love with the anguish which characterizes Petrarch and differentiates the love of both poets from that of Dante, which is an intimation of the divine mystery. Petrarch as the model of Platonic Love became very influential in the spread of this doctrine in the love poetry of Europe.[64] As in the case of Dante, his influence reached Shelley directly through his reading of such important sources of poetic Platonism as the *Triumphs,* which, as Professor White has shown,[65] had a marked influence on the famous image of Shelley's *Adonais.*

CHAUCER

The third great mediaeval writer to serve as a source of Platonic influence on Shelley is Chaucer, who is referred to by Deschamps as "O

[63] De Sanctis, *op. cit.,* p. 292; for the Platonic treatment of Laura, see Merrill, *MP,* XXVII (1929-1930), 165-173. For the difference between the meaning of Platonic Love to these poets and to Ficino, see P. O. Kristeller, *The Philosophy of Marsilio Ficino* (New York, 1943), p. 287.

[64] See Pietro Borghesi, *Petrarch and His Influence on English Literature* (Bologna, 1906); P. N. Siegel, "The Petrarchan Sonneteers and Neo-Platonic Love," *SP,* XLII (1945), 164-182.

[65] White, *Shelley,* II, 294-295, 630-631.

Socrates, plain de philosophie." Chaucer may be considered the first great Platonic poet in English literature. He marks the high tide of a Platonism which had been coming into England from various sources. In the twelfth century, when the Normans held both England and Sicily, there came into England a significant amount of direct Platonism in the form of Aristippus's Latin translations of the *Phaedo* and *Meno;* copies of these versions are found in the mediaeval libraries of England. But considerably more Platonism came from Dante and Petrarch, from whom, Shelley says, "Chaucer caught the sacred inspiration." From French literature, in particular the *Roman de la Rose,* and from the Latin classics Chaucer enriched his knowledge of Platonism.[66] But probably the most influential factor in Chaucer's Platonism came to England from the influence of the School of Chartres, where Chalcidius's Latin translation of the *Timaeus* and Boethius were studied and discussed. These works became accessible to England through Englishmen like John of Salisbury, who formed an intellectual liaison between England and the School of Chartres.[67] Boethius's *Consolatio* had been previously translated by King Alfred, but the language of this translation was no longer understood by the people. Chaucer supplied the need of a new translation in English. The *Consolatio* influenced Chaucer profoundly, for in the very process of translation he assimilated some of the Platonism found in this work;[68] in turn this Platonism found its way into his own poetry. It is not pure Platonism, but rather mystical Neoplatonism with its atmosphere of magic, astrology, daemons, and witchcraft. The evidence of Platonism noted in Chaucer's poetry reveals the character of Platonism that might have influenced Shelley directly through his reading of Chaucer and indirectly through Chaucer's influence on the literature which Shelley read.

PLATONISM AND THE RENAISSANCE

Recent studies have shown that the period of the Renaissance, extending approximately from the middle of the fourteenth to the end of the sixteenth century, was in many respects a direct continuation of the Middle Ages. Ficino's interest in Platonic philosophy was first awakened

[66] For the Platonic tradition in Chaucer, see Karl Young, "Chaucer's Appeal to the Platonic Deity," *Speculum*, XIX (1944), 1-13; E. P. Hammond, *Chaucer, A Bibliographical Manual* (New York, 1908), p. 90; H. Schinnerl, *Die Belesenheit Chaucers in der Bibel und der Antiken Literatur* (Munich, 1923).

[67] See C. C. J. Webb, *John of Salisbury* (London, 1932), pp. 84-94, 157, 159-161; *Ioannis Saresberiensis Episcopi Carnotensis Metalogicon Libri III,* ed. C. C. J. Webb (Oxford, 1929), Prolegomena, xiii, and index, *s.v.* Plato; Jamison, *op. cit.,* pp. 272-273; G. R. Stephens, *The Knowledge of Greek in England in the Middle Ages* (Philadelphia, 1933).

[68] Cf. Patch, *op. cit.,* pp. 66-73.

by Augustine and other Latin Platonists; the central doctrines of Ficino's Platonism owe much to the basic ideas of Augustine and the Middle Ages.[69] Though the Platonism of the Renaissance is rooted in the Platonism of the Middle Ages, it increased in vigor and expression; it carried on the process of transmuting Platonism from a philosophy essentially logical and theological in character to Platonism as poetry.[70]

The Platonism of the Renaissance owed its quickening to the economic, diplomatic, and ecclesiastical contacts of Italy with Byzantium. Essential for the renascence of Platonism were Greek teachers and the Plato manuscripts of Bessarion, whose collection of Greek manuscripts numbered more than six hundred. As a by-product of attempts at

[69] Cf. W. W. Skeat, *The Complete Works of Geoffrey Chaucer* (Oxford, 1900), III, 340-341.

[70] For a selected bibliography of the Platonism of the Renaissance, see Marsilio Ficino, *Commentary on Plato's Symposium*, The Text and a Translation, with an Introduction by Sears Reynolds Jayne, *University of Missouri Studies*, V, xix, No. 1 (Columbia, Mo., 1944); Baldassare Castiglione, *Il Cortegiano*, trans. by Sir Thomas Hoby, as *The Book of the Courtier*, 1561, Reproduced with Introduction by Walter Raleigh (London, 1900), pp. lxvii-lxxvii, 342-365: the Doctrine of Love and Beauty; R. Rocholl, "Der Platonismus der Renaissancezeit," *Zeitschrift für Kirchengeschichte*, XIII (1892), 47-106; Gabriel Thomas, *Michel-Ange Poète. Étude sur l'expression de l'amour platonique dans la poésie italienne du moyen âge et de la Renaissance* (Paris, 1891); Luigi Ferri, "Il Platonismo di Marsilio Ficino" and "Platonismo di Ficino, dottrina dell' amore," in *La Filosofia delle scuole italiane*, XXIX (1884), 237 ff., 269 ff.; *Trattati d'amore del Cinquecento*, ed. Giuseppe Zonta (Bari, 1912); Jean Festugière, "La Philosophie de l'amour de Marsile Ficin et son influence sur la littérature française au XVIe siècle," *Revista da Universidade de Coimbra*, VIII (1922), 396-564; Lorenzo Savino, "Di alcuni trattati e trattatisti d'amore italiani della prima metà del secolo XVI," *Studi di Letteratura Italiana*, IX (1912), 223-435, X (1914), 1-342; Giuseppe Saitta, *La Filosofia di Marsilio Ficino* (Messina, 1923); Ludwig Mohler, *Die Wiederbelebung des Platons-studiums in der Zeit der Renaissance durch Kardinal Bessarion*, Vereinsg. Görres-Ges., 1921, pp. 41-48; Giovanni Semprini, *I platonici italiani* (Milan, 1926); Marian Heitzmann, "Études sur l'Académie platonicienne à Florence," *Bulletin International de l'Académie Polonaise de Sciences et Lettres, Classe de Philologie, Classe d'Histoire, et de Philosophie*, 1932, pp. 18-22, 1933, pp. 35 ff.; Bohdan Kieszkowski, *Studi sul Platonismo del rinascimento in Italia* (Florence, 1936); N. Ivanoff, "La Beauté dans la philosophie de Marsile Ficin et de Léon Hébreux," *Humanisme et Renaissance*, III (1936), 12-21; August Buck, *Der Platonismus in den Dichtungen Lorenzo de' Medicis* (Berlin, 1936); Giovanni Semprini, *La Filosofia di Pico della Mirandola* (Milan, 1936); Edouard F. Meylan, "L'Evolution de la notion d'amour platonique," *Humanisme et Renaissance*, V (1938), 418-442; Anders Nygren, *Agape and Eros* (London, 1939), II, 449-463; Erwin Panofsky, *Studies in Iconology* (New York, 1939), pp. 129-230, and bibliography cited on pp. 235-250; R. V. Merrill, "Eros and Anteros," *Speculum*, XIX (1944), 265-284; Ernst Cassirer, "Giovanni Pico della Mirandola," *Journal of the History of Ideas*, III (1942), 123-144, 319-346; P. O. Kristeller and J. H. Randall, Jr., "The Study of the Philosophies of the Renaissance," *Journal of the History of Ideas*, II (1941), 449-496; Shorey, *op. cit.*, pp. 118-145; Alline, *op. cit.*, pp. 281-315; Klibansky, *op. cit.*, pp. 29-32, 35-37, 42-47; Robb, *op. cit.*; Vittorio Rossi, *Il Quattrocento, storia letteraria d'Italia* (Milan, 1933), chaps. ii, vii; P. O. Kristeller, *The Philosophy of Marsilio Ficino* (New York, 1943) and "Augustine and the Early Renaissance," *Review of Religion*, VIII (1944), 352-357.

rapprochement between the Eastern and Western Churches there came to Italy Greeks like Chrysoloras, who stayed at Florence from 1396 to 1400 and taught Greek. With the arrival of many Byzantine Greeks after the fall of Constantinople in 1453, many towns followed Florence in its zeal for Greek; and the knowledge of Greek spread. Even the quarrels of Byzantium about Plato and Aristotle were transplanted to Italy and carried on by men like George Trapezuntios, Cardinal Bessarion, John Argyropoulos, and Theodore Gaza. Among these scholars, Gemistus Pletho, "the Proclus of Mistra,"[71] was directly influential in the establishment of the Platonic Academy in Florence. Pletho was sent to the Councils of Ferrara and Florence (1438-1439), where the union of the two Churches was discussed. This union fell through, but the union of Plato with the Western World succeeded. For Pletho enchanted Cosimo de' Medici and the Florentines, and as a result Cosimo founded the New Platonic Academy at Florence, under whose hierophant Ficino Plato was deified. The foundation for the communion of the Florentine Platonists was Ficino's cult of love and friendship, which was based on *amor divinus,* the love of the soul for God, and was sharply opposed to the vulgar concept of love.[72]

Shelley would have felt at home in the Platonic Academy at Florence. In this living community of friends, modeled after the Hellenistic schools of philosophy, the Plato enthusiasts gathered to commune through moral and intellectual discourse. They celebrated Plato's birthday, a revival of a practice of Plotinus, who sacrificed on the traditional birthdays of Plato and Socrates, giving afterwards a banquet at which every member of the circle who was able delivered an address. In their symposia they discussed Platonic Love, the world soul, the music of the spheres, transmigration, and other Platonic themes. Their Platonism, poetic and exuberant rather than scholarly, was joined by daemonology, astrology, Neoplatonic symbols, and forced equations between Christian and Platonic notions. But the greatest service which the Platonic Academy rendered was Ficino's translation of the complete works of Plato. This translation, which Shelley used as an aid in reading and translating Plato, was to the Europe of the succeeding centuries what Jowett's translation of Plato is to us. The translation of Ficino was accompanied by introductions to the various dialogues which often interpreted Plato Neoplatonically, allegorically, and mystically. The fanciful speeches delivered on Plato's birthday, which serve as the introduction to Ficino's

[71] Alline, *op. cit.,* p. 300.
[72] See Kristeller, *The Philosophy of Marsilio Ficino,* pp. 279 ff., and Arnaldo Della Torre, *Storia dell' Accademia Platonica di Firenze* (Florence, 1902).

translation of the *Symposium,* are an illustration of the Platonism which inevitably influenced the readers of Plato.

The character of the Platonism which emanated from the Academy requires a few words of comment because of its ultimate effect on Shelley. Platonic Love was singled out by the Florentine Academy as the very heart of Platonism. Though the concept of Platonic Love, expressive of idealistic tendencies in human nature, was anticipated by the spiritual love of Augustine and Dante, and was foreshadowed by poets of the *dolce stil nuovo* and Petrarch, it has been clearly shown by Professor Kristeller that Ficino is the "inventor" of Platonic Love in the Platonic tradition.[73] "One Soul," says Ficino, "exists in the bodies of several friends as the result of Platonic Love." This statement, which is the *fons et origo* of Shelley's doctrine in the *Epipsychidion,* marks the first appearance in the history of literature of the term "Platonic Love." In Ficino's philosophy Platonic Love meant something different from the vulgar conception of it found in later literature, a deformation for which Ficino was not responsible. For Ficino and his Platonic comrades Platonic Love had a precise meaning. It was, says Professor Kristeller, "intellectual love between friends; love which unites the members of the Academy into a community, which is based on the individual's love for God, and is called, with reference to Plato's *Symposium,* 'Platonic love'— that is, love conceived in the sense of Plato." Ficino's concept is a union of the Platonic *eros* and the Christian *agape;* it is the love of God "deflected toward persons and things by the reflected splendor of divine beauty and goodness in them."

Ficino colored the *Symposium* and the old poetry with a new conception of Platonic Love which grew in popularity and changed in meaning in the succeeding centuries. Platonic Love received such intense and vivid expression in his *De amore* and in the writings of his companions and followers that it became the most attractive and influential theme of the Platonic tradition. The concept found memorable expression in such lines of Michelangelo as

> The might of one fair face sublimes my love,

and

> One soul is in two bodies made eternal
> Uplifting both to heaven on equal wings.

It is found in the poetry of Lorenzo de' Medici, the *Canzone dell' amor divino* of Girolamo Benivieni, Pico della Mirandola's *Platonic Discourse*

---

[73] The following discussion of Platonic love is based on Professor Kristeller's excellent analysis of Ficino's conception of love (*The Philosophy of Marsilio Ficino,* pp. 286-288).

upon Love, the *Asolani* of Bembo, the *Dialoghi d'amore* of Leo Hebraeus, and Castiglione's *Il Cortegiano,* which became a handbook of Platonic Love on the Continent and in England.

Along with Platonic Love the *Timaeus* became a source of inspiration for the poetic mind which craves a personalized universe with a world soul, a universe in which the macrocosm is attuned to the microcosm of the poet's soul.[74] The *Timaeus* gave to the poet imagery from Plato's mythopoeic world which was capable of re-creative development. Finally by making Platonism intensely poetic and imaginative it furnished posterity with that appealing realm of poetry compounded of thought and emotion which was Shelley's natural realm.

PLATONISM IN THE SIXTEENTH AND SEVENTEENTH CENTURIES
ENGLISH LITERATURE: SPENSER

Shelley had a natural appreciation of the Renaissance which is expressed in various letters and essays. His direct contact with the Renaissance, however, was limited to Guicciardini, Ariosto, and Tasso, all of whom were influenced by Renaissance Platonism. Tasso in particular is full of Platonic imitations, and in Sophronia and Armida Shelley could find symbols of Platonic Love. The Renaissance, however, affected Shelley mostly through its influence on later European literature, from which emanates much of Shelley's Platonism. A survey of Shelley's reading shows that it includes most of the authors in all the centuries and all the countries which Renaissance Platonism had influenced. The most important tradition from which Shelley received the influence of indirect Platonism is English literature, at the head of which stands Spenser, one of Shelley's favorite authors.[75] His influence on Shelley extends both to metrical form and to poetic substance. His importance for Shelley's Platonism lies in the fact that Shelley read him before he had become deeply acquainted with Plato himself; his reading of Spenser at such a time helped wean him away from versified reform to poetic ideas. An account, therefore, of the sources and nature of Spenser's Platonism is important for an understanding of Shelley's Platonism.[76]

[74] Cf. Shorey, *op. cit.,* pp. 107-114; E. M. W. Tillyard, *The Elizabethan World Picture* (London, 1943), pp. 60-62, 80 ff.

[75] Cf. Droop, *op. cit.,* pp. 46-47; White, *Shelley,* II, index, pp. cxxxi-cxxxii; Traugott Böhme, *Spensers literarisches Nachleben bis zu Shelley,* Kap. VII, Abschnitt 5: "Spensers Einfluss auf Shelley" (Berlin, 1909); F. L. Jones, "Shelley and Spenser," *SP,* XXXIX (1942), 662-669.

[76] For a bibliography of Spenser's Platonism, see F. I. Carpenter, *A Reference Guide to Edmund Spenser* (Chicago, 1923), pp. 145-146, 184-187; D. F. Atkinson, *Edmund Spenser, A Bibliographical Supplement* (Baltimore, 1937), pp. 81-82; in particular see Mohinīmohana Bhaṭṭāchārya, *Platonic Ideas in Spenser* (Calcutta, 1935); A. E. Taylor, "Spenser's Knowl-

Spenser's translation of the *Axiochus* of Plato shows that he had some direct acquaintance with him. But for the most part the sources of Spenser's Platonism are to be found in Renaissance literature. In the sixteenth century many Englishmen visited Italy and brought back with them appreciation for its literature and the enthusiasm of its Academies and intellectual circles. Linacre, Colet, Grocyn, Elyot, Ascham, Erasmus, and More are the initiators in England of Renaissance Platonism.[77] Spenser's Platonism has many roots, but the most important is Ficino's *De amore,* to which many of Spenser's expressions and notions can be traced or in which they can be paralleled.[78] From Ficino, Castiglione, Tasso, and Pico della Mirandola, Spenser absorbed a Christianized Platonism, the doctrine of Platonic Love, and Neoplatonic symbols.

Spenser's Platonism essentially consists of what Milton has aptly phrased as

> . . . what surmounts the reach
> Of human sense, I shall delineate so,
> By lik'ning spiritual to corporal forms,
> As may express them best.[79]

Spenser, like Shelley, was a philosophical poet and made an eclectic and re-creative use of Platonic themes and imagery, fusing them with his own

---

edge of Plato," *MLR,* XIX (1924), 208-210; *The Works of Edmund Spenser,* A Variorum Edition, ed. Edwin Greenlaw, C. G. Osgood, F. M. Padelford (Baltimore, 1932), *Faerie Queene,* I, Appendix viii, "The Platonic Element," 501-505, and *The Minor Poems,* I, 508-570, 656-684; *The Axiochus of Plato,* translated by Edmund Spenser, ed. F. M. Padelford (Baltimore, 1934); the introductions in *The Fowre Hymnes,* ed. Lilian Winstanley (Cambridge, 1907); Rensselaer W. Lee, "Castiglione's Influence on Spenser's Early Hymns," *PQ,* VII (1928), 65-77; J. W. Bennett, "The Theme of Spenser's Fowre Hymnes," *SP,* XXVIII (1931), 18-57; *ibid.,* XXXII (1935), 131-157, cf. note 4; B. E. C. Davis, *Edmund Spenser* (Cambridge, 1933), chap. ix and index, *s.v.* Plato, Neoplatonism, Platonists; H. S. V. Jones, *A Spenser Handbook* (New York, 1930), pp. 357-370; Shorey, *op. cit.,* pp. 177-179; Dodds's edition of *Proclus, Elements of Theology* (Oxford, 1933), Introduction, pp. xxxii-xxxiii.

[77] For a bibliography of the introduction of Platonism to England, see R. Newald, "Nachleben der Antike (1920-1929)," *Jahresbericht über die Fortschritte der Klassischen Altertumswissenschaft,* CCXXXIII, 3 (1931), 78-80; Lewis Einstein, *The Italian Renaissance in England* (New York, 1902), pp. 1-53; Ingram Bywater, *Four Centuries of Learning in England* (Oxford, 1919); Friedrich Dannenberg, *Das Erbe Platons in England bis zur Bildung Lylys* (Berlin, 1932); Ernst Cassirer, *Die Platonische Renaissance in England und die Schule von Cambridge* (Leipzig and Berlin, 1932).

[78] Cf. J. S. Harrison, *Platonism in English Poetry of the Sixteenth and Seventeenth Centuries* (New York, 1903); Elizabeth Holmes, *Henry Vaughan and the Hermetic Philosophy* (Oxford, 1932); L. C. Martin, "Henry Vaughan and Hermes Trismegistus," *Review of English Studies,* XVIII (1942), 301-307; H. F. Thoma, "The Hermetic Strain in Seventeenth-century English Mysticism," *Summaries of Theses 1941, Harvard University* (Cambridge, Mass., 1945), pp. 344-347.

[79] Milton, *Paradise Lost,* V, 571-574.

conceptions. The Platonic character of the *Faerie Queene* is obvious; its theme, characters, and symbolism are steeped in Platonism. The Red Cross Knight represents Platonic idealism and Christian virtues, and Una represents Heavenly Beauty and Platonic Love. In the *Faerie Queene* our knight, who practices the Christian graces, ascends the Mount of Heavenly Contemplation, where, like the ideal lover of the *Symposium,* he sees the vision of Beauty; upon descending he sees Una with her black veil laid aside shining with "the blazing brightnesse of her beauties beame." The quest of Beauty and the One in the *Symposium* is here set forth with the romance of action, the imagery and language of poetry, and the symbolic embodiment of Platonic themes. The Red Cross Knight is the prototype of Shelleyan heroes; like the poet in *Alastor* he pursues the lovely Una, who is, as she appears to the knight half-revealed and half-concealed behind a veil, a symbol of Platonic Love. The Red Cross Knight's victory over Duessa and the Archimage, who try to lure him from his quest of holiness and beauty, symbolizes the Platonic victory of reason over passion. The poem abounds with poetic elaborations of Platonic thought; behind such personifications as "Mutabilitie" we find the Platonic doctrine of flux; the ladder of the *Symposium* is dramatized through a quest with Christian and Platonic values made vivid through men and women. As Spenser's poetry may not be understood without Platonism, so Shelley's poetry may not be completely understood without Spenser's *Faerie Queene,* which furnished Shelley with Platonic symbols and shaped his dramatic technique of symbolical incarnation.

Spenser expressed his Platonism in a more direct form in *Fowre Hymnes,* one of the best testaments of Platonism in English poetry. It is probable, as will be shown later,[80] that Shelley was influenced in the title of *Hymn to Intellectual Beauty* by a reading of Spenser's Platonic Hymns. If Shelley had not read Plato at all, he could have got the quintessence of Platonism from Spenser's Hymns. *An Hymne in Honour of Love* contains many direct references to the doctrines of the *Symposium:* that Eros was "begot of Plentie and Penurie," that Love tempers the elements of the universe, that mortals "multiply the likenesse of their Kynd," that man

> breathes a more immortall mynd,
> Not for lusts sake, but for eternitie,
> Seekes to enlarge his lasting progenie.[81]

The best of the *Symposium* is transmuted in lines like

[80] *Vide infra,* p. 196.
[81] *An Hymne in Honour of Love,* ll. 103-105.

> The flaming light of that celestiall fyre,
> Which kindleth loue in generous desyre,
> And makes him mount aboue the natiue might
> Of heauie earth, vp to the heauens hight.[82]

An Hymne in Honour of Beautie states and improvises further on the dualism of Earthly and Heavenly Beauty. Its statements of Platonism are pregnant with future influence:

> What time this worlds great workmaister did cast
> To make al things, such as we now behold,
> It seemes that he before his eyes had plast
> A goodly Paterne, to whose perfect mould
> He fashiond them as comely as he could;
> That now so faire and seemely they appeare,
> As nought may be amended any wheare.
>
> That wondrous Paterne wheresoere it bee,
> Whether in earth layd vp in secret store,
> Or else in heauen, that no man may it see
> With sinfull eyes, for feare it to deflore,
> Is perfect Beautie which all men adore,
> Whose face and feature doth so much excell
> All mortal sence, that none the same may tell.[83]

This poetic summary of the *Timaeus* is matched by other summaries of Platonic doctrines, for instance:

> That Beautie is not, as fond men misdeeme,
> An outward shew of things, that onely seeme[84]

and

> So euery spirit, as it is most pure,
> And hath in it the more of heauenly light,
> So it the fairer bodie doth procure
> To habit in, and it more fairely dight
> With chearefull grace and amiable sight.
> For of the soule the bodie forme doth take:
> For soule is forme, and doth the bodie make.[85]

This hymn is filled with various aspects of the doctrine of Platonic Love, such as the eternal nature of the "things immortall"; it states the difference between the two lovers in terms of light versus shadow; and finally

[82] *Ibid.*, ll. 186-189.
[83] *An Hymne in Honour of Beautie*, ll. 29-42.
[84] *Ibid.*, ll. 90-91.   [85] *Ibid.*, ll. 127-133.

the steps are indicated for the pursuit of Love. The hymn forms one of the best expressions of Renaissance Platonic Love.

The last two hymns, *An Hymne of Heavenly Love* and *An Hymne of Heavenly Beautie,* express Platonic themes like the hierarchical ascent to the highest reality, the Demiourgos of the *Timaeus,* and the contemplation of the Christian and Platonic values. For Spenser Platonism is a step in the attainment of Christian ends:

> Faire is the heauen, where happy soules haue place,
> In full enioyment of felicitie,
> Whence they doe still behold the glorious face
> Of the diuine eternall Maiestie;
> More faire is that, where those *Idees* on hie,
> Enraunged be, which *Plato* so admyred,
> And pure *Intelligences* from God inspyred.
>
> .   .   .   .
>
> Yet farre more faire be those bright *Cherubins,*
> Which all with golden wings ouerdight,
>
> .   .   .   .
>
> Yet fairer then they both, and much more bright,
> Be th' Angels and Archangels, which attend
> On Gods owne person, without rest or end.[86]

We find in these two hymns a fusion of Platonism, Neoplatonism, Christianity, and mysticism. The alchemy of the Renaissance mind fused them into a new entity which defies analytic separation. The praise of Sapience is in the spirit of Platonism; Beauty born in Heaven serves as the creative pattern for the world's creator; the contemplation of Heavenly Beauty involves the ascent of the soul through a Platonic and Christian hierarchy which is finally rewarded with the sight of wisdom, as in the *Symposium.* The exceptional poetic expression which these Platonic notions received in Spenser's poetry made them in turn a pattern of beauty which seemed to Shelley worthy of imitation, as his own Platonic hymn reveals.

SIR PHILIP SIDNEY

Another sixteenth-century figure from whom Shelley absorbed Platonism is Sir Philip Sidney.[87] The number of parallels noted between Sidney's *The Defence of Poesie* and Shelley's *A Defence of Poetry* indicates the care with which Shelley read Sidney.[88] It is to be noted that

[86] *An Hymne of Heavenly Beautie,* ll. 78-84, 92-93, 96-98.

[87] See Droop, *op. cit.,* p. 48; White, *Shelley,* II, index, p. cxxix; Irene Samuel, "The Influence of Plato on Sir Philip Sidney's *Defence of Poesy,*" *MLQ,* I (1940), 383-391.

[88] See *Peacock's Four Ages of Poetry, Shelley's Defence of Poetry,* ed. H. F. B. Brett-Smith (Oxford, 1923), Introduction, p. xx, and notes, *passim.* For a quotation from Sidney's *Defence of Poesie* in Shelley's Journal, see R. Glynn Grylls, *Mary Shelley,* p. 274.

Sidney's appraisal of Plato as a poet, despite his criticism of poetry, is re-echoed by Shelley, who maintains that "Plato was essentially a poet." Shelley's poetic theory is influenced by the small yet important indirect Platonism that is found in Sidney's *The Defence of Poesie*. It may not be farfetched to suppose that Sidney stimulated Shelley to read the *Ion*, whose views about poetry are woven in the fabric of *A Defence of Poetry*.

SHAKESPEARE

Though Shakespeare was a favorite author of Shelley,[89] he can be considered as only a minor source of Platonic influence on Shelley. There is no evidence that Shakespeare had read Plato or Ficino; his poetry and plays reflect only a Platonism that he absorbed as part of the literary atmosphere of his time or that was reflected in his English and Italian sources.[90] These sources would reflect in particular the Platonism of the *Timaeus*, the Platonism of Bernardus Silvestris's *De mundi universitate*, Alan of Lille's *Liber de planctu naturae*, and Jean de Meung's *Roman de la Rose*.[91] The Platonism of Shakespeare consists for the most part of Platonic notions like the macrocosm and microcosm, the Chain of Being reflected in Ulysses's famous speech on order in *Troilus and Cressida*, and images such as Lorenzo's discourse on the music of the spheres, which reflects a Pythagorean doctrine in Plato. The history of this notion is characteristic of other Platonic images in Shakespeare.[92] The sonnets, which Shelley read, reflect the doctrine of love as the desire for immortality found in *Symposium*, 208-209. In conjunction with similar Platonism flowing from other sources in Shelley's reading, this Platonism contributed to the shaping of Shelley's Platonism.

MILTON

Along with Spenser, Milton, whom Shelley greatly admired, stands out as another figure of great importance for Shelley's indirect Platonism.[93] In a study of Milton and Plato, Agar has shown that "As a

---

[89] See Droop, *op. cit.*, pp. 48-55; White, *Shelley*, II, index, pp. lxxxv, cxi; D. L. Clark, "Shelley and Shakespeare," *PMLA*, LIV (1939), 261-287; F. L. Jones, "Shelley and Shakespeare: A Supplement," *PMLA*, LIX (1944), 591-596.

[90] See E. M. W. Tillyard, *The Elizabethan World Picture*; Theodore Spencer, *Shakespeare and the Nature of Man* (New York, 1942); Walter F. Schirmer, "Chaucer, Shakespeare und die Antike," *Vorträge der Bibliothek Warburg*, IX (1930-1931; Leipzig and Berlin, 1932), 83-102; T. W. Baldwin, *William Shakspere's Small Latine & Lesse Greeke* (Urbana, 1944), Index, *s.v.* Plato.

[91] Cf. Burnet, *op. cit.*, pp. 163-168.

[92] *Ibid.*, pp. 265-276; cf. Tillyard, *op. cit.*, pp. 7-15, 37-47; J. H. Hanford, "A Platonic Passage in Shakespeare's *Troilus and Cressida*," *SP*, XIII (1916), 100-110; *Speculum, A Journal of Mediaeval Studies*, XIX (1944), 120 n. 2; Spencer, *op. cit.*, pp. 4-28; Shorey, *op. cit.*, pp. 180-182.

[93] See Droop, *op. cit.*, pp. 56-59; White, *Shelley*, II, index, pp. lxii, cx; Lane Cooper, "Dryden and Shelley on Milton," *MLN*, XXIII (1908), 93.

young man, Milton was much affected by Renaissance Platonism, but as he grew older he grew away from it. A probable reason for this change is that Milton became sufficiently interested in Plato to study him at first hand, disregarding the commentators and interpreters, and so becoming one of the first scholars in modern Europe to penetrate the mists of Neo-platonism and come face to face with the master."[94] This conclusion shows that the Platonism which Shelley found in Milton was both the Renaissance Neoplatonism and the direct Platonism of Plato's works. Milton absorbed from Italian Platonism and other sources the doctrines of Platonic Love, mystical Neoplatonism fused with Christian doctrines, daemonology, Trismegistic and Cabalistic Platonism. These doctrines are reflected in various poems, such as *Il Penseroso*:

> Where I may oft out-watch the *Bear*,
> With thrice great *Hermes*, or unsphear
> The spirit of *Plato* to unfold
> What Worlds, or what vast Regions hold
> The immortal mind that hath forsook
> Her mansion in this fleshly nook:
> And of those *Daemons* that are found
> In fire, air, flood, or under ground,
> Whose power hath a true consent
> With Planet, or with Element.[95]

As Milton grew older he turned to a direct study of Plato. A survey of Milton's writings by Agar shows that he "was familiar at least with the following works of Plato: *Republic, Timaeus, Phaedo, Symposium, Protagoras, Laws, Epistle VIII, Gorgias, Laches, Phaedrus, Critias* and that he very probably was familiar with the *Meno, Apology, Second Alcibiades*."[96] This wide acquaintance with Plato resulted in an influence on Milton which is extensive in content and depth. Agar's analysis

[94] Herbert Agar, *Milton and Plato* (Princeton, 1928), p. 23; cf. Edwin Greenlaw, " 'A Better Teacher than Aquinas,' " *SP*, XIV (1917), especially 206 ff., for a discussion of Milton's indebtedness to Spenser's Platonism, and "Spenser's Influence on *Paradise Lost*," *SP*, XVIII (1920), 320-359; E. C. Baldwin, "An Instance of Milton's Debt to the Greek Philosophers," *Classical Weekly*, XI (1918), 121-125, and "A Note on *Il Penseroso*," *MLN*, XXXIII (1918), 184-185, and "Milton and Plato's *Timaeus*," *PMLA*, XXXV (1920), 210-217; M. H. Nicolson, "The Spirit World of Milton and More," *SP*, XXII (1925), 433-452; R. B. Levinson, "Milton and Plato," *MLN*, XLVI (1931), 85-91; Camille Looten, "Milton et l'idée du poète," *Revue Anglo-Américaine*, IX (1931/2), 1-15; M. Y. Hughes, "Lydian Airs," *MLN*, XL (1925), 129-137; G. F. Sensabaugh, "Platonic Love and the Puritan Rebellion," *SP*, XXXVII (1940), 457-481; Irene Samuel, "Milton's References to Plato and Socrates," *SP*, XLI (1944), 50-64, and *Plato and Milton* (Ithaca, 1947).
[95] *Il Penseroso*, ll. 87-96.
[96] Agar, *op. cit.*, p. 1.

of Milton's Platonism shows that Milton's works reflect the following doctrines of Plato:

    a. Scepticism in regard to knowledge of the physical world and to the testimony of our senses.

    b. Confidence in our capacity to attain to knowledge of the moral world, this knowledge being reached by a species of intuition.

    c. The belief that virtue is knowledge, or understanding, or reason . . . , and that vice is ignorance.

    d. The tripartite division of the soul, and the doctrine that in a virtuous soul reason rules over the other two elements.

    e. The belief that the supreme virtue of the soul, or the state, or the universe, is a harmony which exists when each part fulfils its own function and does not interfere with any other part. With this may be included the analogy which Plato draws between the political state and the soul of the individual.

    f. The doctrine of ideas.

Among Plato's lesser doctrines reflected in Milton are:

    a. The creation of the world out of original formless matter (as given in the *Timaeus*).

    b. The application to the art of music of Plato's Puritan esthetics, and the consequent belief that some "modes" of music should be banished because they are morally harmful, while others should be encouraged because of the inspiration which they give.

Milton also makes use of the following myths, poetic fancies, and figures of speech in Plato,

    a. The comparison of the motion of the stars, or planets, to a dance.

    b. The sphere-music, as explained in the myth of Er.[97]

The influence of these doctrines on Milton, as set forth by Agar in the appendix, shows that in Milton Shelley found an almost complete compendium of Platonism. Few authors whom Shelley read show a more comprehensive knowledge or reflection of Platonism. The purity of Platonism which Shelley could absorb from Milton is reflected in the following lines, a direct transcription of *Phaedo,* 81c-d:

>   . . . but when lust
> By unchaste looks, loose gestures, and foul talk,
> But most by leud and lavish act of sin,
> Lets in defilement to the inward parts,
> The soul grows clotted by contagion,

[97] *Ibid.,* pp. 5-6.

Imbodies, and imbrutes, till she quite loose
The divine property of her first being.
Such are those thick and gloomy shadows damp,
Oft seen in Charnel vaults, and Sepulchers
Lingering, and sitting by a new made grave,
As loath to leave the Body that it lov'd,
And link't it self by carnal sensuality
To a degenerate and degraded state.[98]

Such lines as these make it difficult to know whether passages in Shelley which might reflect the same thought are derived from his reading of Plato or from indirect reflections in other literature. It would be a complex task to study the relative influence of direct versus indirect source, but the conclusion is obvious with Shelley, who was influenced both by direct and by indirect Platonism; sometimes the proportion of the one kind is greater than the other, sometimes one is absent, sometimes both are present. The reading of Milton in Shelley's non-Platonic as well as his Platonic period shows the difficulty of determining the nature of Plato's influence on Shelley. The importance of Milton for Shelley's Platonism is seen in the fact that Shelley could get a comprehensive view of Platonism in Milton's work and could find in it more of the substance and less of the shadow of Platonism.[99]

PARACELSUS

Shelley's love of philosophy led him into reading several important sixteenth- and seventeenth-century thinkers whose work is influenced by the Platonic tradition. In his letter to Godwin dated June 6, 1812, Shelley writes, "I . . . pored over the reveries of . . . Paracelsus."[100] The reading of Paracelsus in the earlier years of Shelley's creative period may constitute a potential source of Shelley's earlier Platonism. Paracelsus's Platonism is derivative from the Renaissance Platonism which had spread from Italy to Germany, where it had considerable influence on Trithemius, who was Paracelsus's teacher, and Cornelius Agrippa von Nettes-

[98] *Comus,* ll. 463-475.

[99] Though Spenser and Milton form the most important sources of indirect Platonism in the sixteenth and seventeenth centuries, Shelley's Platonism was also influenced to a lesser extent by other poets of the period. Though there is no direct reference to them in the Journal, Shelley may have been acquainted with poets like Donne, Drummond, and others who, as shown by Harrison's study, contain many strains of Platonism (see L. C. Martin, "Henry Vaughan and Hermes Trismegistus," *Review of English Studies,* XVIII [1942], 301-307). Shelley would have found in them variations of Platonic Love and other themes of the Platonic tradition.

[100] Julian *Works,* VIII, 331; see also Shelley's marking of a passage about Paracelsus in Bacon (D. L. Clark, "Shelley and Bacon," *PMLA,* XLVIII [1933], 540).

heim.[101]   Paracelsus's philosophy is an amalgam of many influences;[102] from his reading of Ficino, Agrippa, and Trithemius he absorbed much Platonism which appealed to him as a reaction against the Aristotelian dogmatism of the Middle Ages.   The Neoplatonic doctrine of emanation, which interrelates the One and the Many, is at the basis of Paracelsus's thought.   This accounts for the influence of the planets and the occult spirits on man's soul and body.   This doctrine with its supernatural and magical character was adapted to Paracelsus's medical, chemical, and theological ideas.   Such a philosophy would be attractive to Shelley, who, in the same letter to Godwin, confesses his early "fondness for natural magic and ghosts."   It may well be that Shelley found the doctrine of macrocosm and microcosm in Paracelsus or his influence on later works like Goethe's *Faust*.   "Although," says Erdmann, "the doctrine of the Macrocosm and Microcosm was of primitive antiquity, and had even lately been emphasized by Raymond of Sabunde, who had not remained unknown to Paracelsus, yet it is only since and by means of the latter that it was made the central point of the whole philosophy."[103] Miss Ebeling, who has worked out the Platonic influence of Paracelsus on Shelley, sees in Shelley's *Prometheus Unbound*, I, 195-202, the influence of the Evestrum of Paracelsus, which is in some ways analogous to Plato's Ideas and their relation to particulars.[104]   But since Shelley had been reading Plato at the time of the composition of *Prometheus Unbound*, the influence of Paracelsus on Shelley's Platonism may well be confined to the early years of Shelley's life.

MONTAIGNE

The next philosophical figure of importance for Shelley's indirect Platonism is Montaigne, whom Shelley read in 1816.   Mary's entry in the Journal for November 10, 1816, reads: "Shelley reads and finishes Montaigne, to his great sorrow."   Montaigne cannot be called a Platonist; he laughs at Platonic Love; and, as Villey points out, his originality consists in being a servant to none of the many authors and philos-

---

[101] J. M. Stillman, *Paracelsus* (Chicago, 1920), pp. 28-29.

[102] *Ibid.*, pp. 29-43; B. S. von Waltershausen, *Paracelsus am Eingang der deutschen Bildungsgeschichte* (Leipzig, 1936); bibliography listed in *Journal of the History of Ideas*, II (1944), 480-481.

[103] J. H. Erdmann, *A History of Philosophy* (London, 1893), I, 613; cf. G. P. Conger, *Theories of Macrocosms and Microcosms in the History of Philosophy* (New York, 1922); Rudolf Allers, "Microcosmus: From Anaximander to Paracelsus," *Traditio, Studies in Ancient and Mediaeval History, Thought, and Religion* (New York, 1944), II, 319-407; for the macrocosm and microcosm in Elizabethan literature, see Tillyard, *op. cit.*, pp. 60-91.

[104] Elizabeth Ebeling, "A Probable Paracelsian Element in Shelley," *SP*, XXXII (1935), 508-525.

ophies with which he came in contact. Montaigne's importance for Shelley's Platonism lies in the numerous quotations and references to direct Platonism. There are in Montaigne's *Essays* over 110 quotations from Plato: 29 come from the *Laws*, 22 from the *Republic*, 16 from the *Timaeus*, 6 from the *Gorgias*, 4 from the *Phaedo*, the remaining quotations being scattered among 14 other dialogues.[105] In Montaigne Shelley found a compendium of Platonic doctrines, some of which he already knew, others of which he met for the first time. Among these are the doctrine of the *Phaedo*, "Tota Philosophorum vita commentatio mortis est" (III, 12, I, 19); love as a desire for immortality (I, 20); philosophy as celestial music (I, 22). The twelfth essay of the second book is almost in itself an epitome of Platonism and ancient philosophy. In it Shelley could find the following doctrines of Plato: metempsychosis; the *Timaeus* with its doctrines on God, daemons, astronomy, and the notion of the microcosm; the nature of the soul as movement; the doctrine of reminiscence; catharsis; and the conception that knowledge is of the reason and not of the senses. In the third book Shelley could refresh his knowledge of Plato with respect to the doctrine that "love is an appetite of generation by the mediation of beauty" (III, 5), the dualism of mortal generation of body versus "a philosophical and spiritual breed and intelligence" (III, 5), and Plato's view of poetry as inspired madness (III, 9).

Besides giving Shelley direct factual acquaintance with Plato's doctrines, Montaigne's *Essays* served to focus his attention on the importance of Socrates.[106] Montaigne's interest in Plato centers mostly around the figure of Socrates. Montaigne found in Socrates "the master of masters" (III, 13), a portrait of the ideal philosopher, a man who is fearless of death, and a man who takes part in life without being corrupted by it. He translates the conclusion of the *Apology* and the picture of the retreat at Delium in the *Symposium* (III, 6, 12). The 59 references to Socrates show that Montaigne's influence on Shelley may have been in the direction of the importance of Socrates as a man and ethical thinker, a topic which receives considerable notice in eighteenth-century Platonism

---

[105] Pierre Villey, *Les Sources et l'evolution des essais de Montaigne* (Paris, 1908), p. 193; cf. Paul Hensel, "Montaigne und die Antike," *Vorträge der Bibliothek Warburg,* V (1925-1926; Leipzig and Berlin, 1928), 67-94; for a thematic summary of Plato quotations and references, see *The Essays of Michel De Montaigne*, translated and edited by Jacob Zeitler (New York, 1931), III, index, *s.v.* Plato *and* Socrates.

[106] For the importance of Socrates in French literature, see E. E. Rovillain, "Socrates in the French Literature, with a Few Other References," *Transactions of the Michigan Academy of Sciences, Arts, and Letters*, XVIII (1932), 539-550; cf. also Benno Böhm, *Sokrates in achtzehnten Jahrhundert: Studien zum Werdegange des modernen Persönlichkeits bewusstseins* (Leipzig, 1929).

and Shelley's writings. Read by Shelley in 1816, the year preceding his Platonic renascence, Montaigne must have acted as a stimulus to read Plato directly. Thus Montaigne's importance for Shelley's Platonism is that of a "carrier" of Platonism.

SPINOZA

Spinoza was a favorite of Shelley, and from time to time he busied himself with translating him.[107]   In December, 1812, Shelley had sent to Hookham for Spinoza, but it is evident from a later letter that Hookham could supply only the *Tractatus theologico-politicus* and *Opera posthuma*.[108]   There is hardly any Platonism in these; if we can be sure that Shelley confined himself to these works of Spinoza, we can dismiss Spinoza as a source of Shelley's Platonism. There is no reference in the Journal to a reading of the *Ethics*. If Shelley read this through, we have no mention of it. We may consider this work not so much as a source of the direct Platonic tradition but rather as a work containing many doctrines which ultimately go back to Plato. Professor Wolfson has shown that Spinoza's philosophy is essentially constructed out of traditional philosophy. "As for Spinoza," he says, "if we could cut up all the philosophic literature available to him into slips of paper, toss them up into the air, and let them fall back to the ground, then out of these scattered slips of paper we could reconstruct the *Ethics*."[109]   Many of these slips would come from Platonism,[110] such as the notion of macrocosm and microcosm, the gradations of reality, the intellectual love of God, and the notion of the "Transcendent Real." If Shelley did not meet such notions directly in his reading of the *Ethics*, he may have met them in philosophic literature which ultimately was affected by them in Spinoza.

BACON

Shelley, who was well read in English philosophy, can be expected to have been influenced by the Platonic tradition in it. At the head of the list stands Bacon, whom Shelley read with care, as the marginalia in his copy of Bacon's works show.[111]   His references to him as "Bacon's eagle spirit . . . leapt like lightning out of darkness" and "I had rather be damned with Plato and Lord Bacon" reveal his enthusiasm for this

[107] Droop, *op. cit.*, pp. 43-44; White, *Shelley*, II, index, p. cxxxii; cf. Sophie Bernthsen, *Der Spinozismus in Shelleys Weltanschauung* (Heidelberg, 1900).
[108] Julian *Works*, IX, 34.
[109] H. A. Wolfson, *The Philosophy of Spinoza* (Cambridge, Mass., 1934), I, 3.
[110] C. G. Gebhardt, "Spinoza und der Platonismus," *Chronicon Spinozanum*, I (1921), 178-234; Wolfson, *op. cit.*, index, *s.v.* Plato.
[111] Clark, *op. cit.* (*vide supra*, p. 111 n. 100), pp. 529-546.

philosopher.[112] Though Shelley couples Lord Bacon with Plato, Bacon is in no way a Platonist in temperament or thought. He quotes and alludes to essential features in Plato's thought, sometimes by way of criticism, at other times by way of illustration or information. On the whole Shelley was subjected to a presentation of many essential features of Platonism in his study of Bacon.[113] An illustration of the way in which Shelley absorbed the Platonic tradition from Bacon is seen in the following statement in Shelley's *Essay on Christianity:* "Every human mind has, what Bacon calls its 'Idola specus,' peculiar images which reside in the inner cave of thought. These constitute the essential and distinctive character of every human being."[114] In a note Shelley refers to the source: "Bacon Novum Organum App. 53—De aug. scient. Lib. V.c.4.," and has a marginal remark on the latter reference in his copy of Bacon's works. The "Idola specus," which Bacon got from the Myth of the Cave in *Republic,* 514 ff., becomes an important notion in Shelley's thought, as may be seen in variations of it in his poetry. In Bacon, Shelley also came in contact with Plato's theory of Ideas. Bacon contrasts the "Idols of the human mind" and the "Ideas of the divine," and criticizes the Platonic conception of "forms" as giving existence. In their place he gives his own theory of "forms," which have no existence apart from matter; he furthermore warns about any confusion between Plato's and his view of "forms."[115] But though Bacon is critical of Plato, Shelley could learn from him, if he did not already know, many characteristic doctrines of Plato. Bacon refers to Plato's "knowledge is but remembrance," to the division of the soul into "understanding, animosity, concupiscence," to the ancient doctrine of microcosmus, "which hath been fantastically strained by Paracelsus and the alchemists," to the similarity between Plato and his own logic of induction, to the difference between Sophists and Philosophers, and many other notions.[116] These instances of Platonism in an author whom Shelley took care to understand form a noteworthy source of Shelley's indirect Platonism.

THE CAMBRIDGE PLATONISTS: CUDWORTH

Though Shelley does not seem to have read any of the Cambridge

---

[112] *The Triumph of Life,* ll. 269-270; Julian *Works,* II, 174.

[113] Cf. F. H. Anderson, "Bacon on Platonism," *University of Toronto Quarterly,* XI (1941-42), 154-166; Emil Wolff, *Francis Bacons Verhältnis zu Platon* (Berlin, 1908).

[114] Julian *Works,* VI, 241; cf. Clark, *op. cit.,* p. 544, No. 57.

[115] *The Works of Francis Bacon,* Popular Edition, Based upon the Complete Edition of Spedding, Ellis, and Heath (Cambridge, Mass., 1877), I, *Novum Organum,* pp. 72, 83, 168; *Advancement of Learning,* pp. 219-220.

[116] *Ibid., Advancement of Learning,* pp. 88, 240-241; *Novum Organum,* pp. 138-139, 102.

Platonists,[117] he did read writers who were influenced by them. An instance of their influence on Shelley will illustrate the importance of the Cambridge Platonists as a source of Shelley's Platonism. In *Adonais* in describing Keats's soul after death, Shelley says:

> He is made one with Nature: . . .
>
> .   .   .   .
>
> He is a portion of the loveliness
> Which once he made more lovely: he doth bear
> His part, while the one Spirit's plastic stress
> Sweeps through the dull dense world, compelling there,
> All new successions to the forms they wear;
> Torturing th' unwilling dross that checks its flight
> To its own likeness, as each mass may bear. . . .[118]

This doctrine of a "plastic nature" is the form in which Cudworth, in his monumental treatise *The True Intellectual System of the Universe,* translated a doctrine which ultimately is derived from the *Timaeus.* In discussing the Platonic notion of the Chain of Being and the doctrine that nature is a subordinate instrument of Deity, Cudworth says, ". . . as God is inward to every thing, so nature acts immediately upon the matter, as an inward and living soul, or law in it."[119]   This plastic nature orders and disposes the heavens and the whole world; it penetrates and permeates nature down to its lowest plants and animals. "Every plant, herb, and pile of grass," he says, "hath a particular plastic life, or vegetable soul of its own."[120]   Here we have an ultimate source of Shelley's *Sensitive Plant,* which is an outworking of this notion. In describing the relation of plastic nature to Deity, Cudworth speaks of it as having "a certain dull and obscure idea of that which it stamps and prints upon matter."[121]   Though these verbal similarities between the *Adonais* and

---

[117] For the Cambridge Platonists, see H. von Stein, *Sieben Bücher zur Geschichte des Platonismus* (Göttingen, 1862-1875), III, 160 ff.; J. A. Stewart, "The Mythology and Metaphysics of the Cambridge Platonists," *The Myths of Plato* (London, 1905), pp. 475-519; K. J. Schmitz, *Cudworth und der Platonismus* (Giessen diss., 1919); F. J. Powicke, *The Cambridge Platonists* (London, 1926); Arthur Benson, "Henry More, the Platonist," *Contemporary Review,* LIV (1888), 393-407; *Henry More, Philosophical Poems,* edited with introduction and notes by Geoffrey Bullough (Manchester, 1931); Ernst Cassirer, *Die platonische Renaissance in England und die Schule von Cambridge* (Leipzig and Berlin, 1932); J. H. Muirhead, *The Platonic Tradition in Anglo-Saxon Philosophy* (London, 1931), pp. 25-71.

[118] *Adonais,* ll. 370, 379-385.

[119] Ralph Cudworth, *The True Intellectual System of the Universe* (London, 1845), I, 236; cf. Paul Janet, *Essai sur le Médiateur plastique de Cudworth* (Paris, 1860).

[120] *Ibid.,* p. 271; cf. Tillyard, *op. cit.,* pp. 23-27.

[121] Cudworth, *op. cit.,* p. 246.

Cudworth may point to this Cambridge Platonist as the source of this conception, there is no evidence at all that Shelley ever read Cudworth's treatise. But there are a number of definite ways by which Shelley assimilated this doctrine: it is found in Pope, Wordsworth, Coleridge, and Monboddo, all of whom Shelley did read.[122]

Cudworth's importance for Shelley's Platonism is also evident in his being the fountain of Platonism in England when the study of Plato himself was at a low ebb. As we have seen, the seventeenth, eighteenth, and early part of the nineteenth centuries were a period of neglect for Plato. During this time the influence of Platonism was carried on by second-hand sources: among these the Platonism of Cudworth is most important. An example of this is seen in Gibbon's *The Decline and Fall of the Roman Empire,* in which Gibbon acknowledges Cudworth's treatise as the source of his interpretation of Platonism.[123] The Cambridge Platonists therefore are the source of much of the Platonism in authors of the eighteenth and early nineteenth centuries found in Shelley's reading. It is important, therefore, to examine briefly the kind of Platonism that emanated from them. The conclusions of Miss Nicolson's unpublished dissertation as to the main points of difference between Cambridge Platonism and Renaissance and Alexandrian Platonism are:

1. Cambridge Platonism was less philosophical even than Renaissance or Neoplatonism. 2. Cambridge Platonism was less theoretical than the others, and also more sane. 3. Cambridge Platonism took some account of contemporary science. 4. In its final development, at least as expressed by More's *Grand Mystery of Godliness,* Cambridge Platonism advances from the idea of the One-ness of all religions to the conception of development in religion.[124]

These conclusions, however, are accompanied by a potpourri of a learned and mystical fusion of Plato with Egyptian philosophy and Jewish religion, with Neoplatonism, Christianized and Cabalistic Platonism,[125] as a survey of the index of references to Plato in Cudworth's treatise shows. Of the Cambridge Platonists, Henry More was the most spiritual and mystical, Cudworth the most learned and intellectual. More's *Psychozoia Platonica* and Cudworth's *The True Intellectual System of*

---

[122] Cf. J. W. Beach, *The Concept of Nature in Nineteenth-Century English Poetry* (New York, 1936), pp. 54-62.

[123] Gibbon, *op. cit.,* II, 336 n. 12.

[124] Agar, *op. cit.,* p. 29 n. 15.

[125] For the influence of the Cabala on Cudworth and the Cambridge Platonists, see A. E. Waite, *The Holy Kabbalah* (London, 1929), 470-485; for the fusion of Plato with Jewish religion, see John Burnet, *Early Greek Philosophy*[4] (London, 1930), pp. 16-17.

the Universe constitute the poetical and philosophical expression of this Platonism. A reading of Cudworth's treatise shows that Lord Monboddo's remark that Cudworth "is more learned in the whole of antient philosophy . . . than any modern author I know"[126] is quite true. Quotations from Plato and Neoplatonism strew his pages like rocks in the hills of New England. In the absence of any knowledge of Plato's text these quotations took the place of a modern source book.

But the value of Cudworth's treatise for Shelley lies not only in its valuable source material, but also in its aim to show the "absolute impossibility of all atheism." A contributing factor in Shelley's swing from atheism to theism is the case for theism put forth by Cudworth. In his attack on modern atheism Cudworth borrows Plato's fundamental conceptions and uses them with striking effect. Powicke writes:

The case against Materialism has seldom been put more cogently. His arguments are not new. They are as old as Plato. . . . Basing himself on Plato, his first position is that there is a Divine mind, the eternal home of Truth, the ultimate seat of the εἴδη, the "Intelligible Ideas." These have never been created. God did not make them, nor can He unmake or even change them. They are as eternal and necessary as Himself. Of these ideas, especially those specifically moral, reason has intuitive and certain perception. They are common to God and man; they are the truths or principles which neither rise nor set, but shine always with the same constant and benignant light.[127]

The literature which attracted Shelley to the idea of the divinity and immortality of the soul was influenced by Cudworth's re-creative use of Platonism. Thus Cudworth looms as an important shadow in the background of Shelley's Platonism.

SIR THOMAS BROWNE

The reading of Sir Thomas Browne's *Religio Medici* in 1815 contributed to the literature which persuaded Shelley to abandon materialism for Platonism as a philosophy of life. The Platonism in the *Religio Medici* is of two kinds: the intangible Platonism behind its Christian doctrines and its extensive references to Plato.[128] With respect to the first, Browne's doctrine of teleology, that "nature is the art of God" (I, 16), and the doctrine of the Chain of Being are essentially based on the theology of the *Timaeus*. It is evident in his account how inextricably woven are the Platonic and Christian doctrines, their fusion with Neo-

---

[126] Lord Monboddo, *Antient Metaphysics; or the Science of Universals* (Edinburgh, 1779-99), I, iii.
[127] Powicke, *op. cit.*, pp. 123, 127.
[128] Cf. Shorey, *op. cit.*, pp. 192-198.

platonism, and its particular emphasis on Hermes Trismegistus. In his reading of *Religio Medici* Shelley also came in contact with many important Platonic concepts like Plato's year (I, 6), Pythagoras and "the secret magick of numbers" (I, 12), Socrates and "the unity of God" (I, 26), Plato's opinion of "an universal and common spirit to the whole world" (I, 32), the doctrine of tutelary and guardian spirits (I, 33), Pythagorean transmigration and the "flesh, wherein the soul doth seem to be immured" (I, 37), the doctrine that "the soul is an harmony" (II, 9), "the musick of the sphears" (II, 9), God the geometrician (I, 16), and the attainment of immortality through procreation (I, 41). These references show with increasing evidence how it was possible for Shelley to absorb the essence of Platonism in periods when there is no evidence that he was reading Plato.

JOHN LOCKE

One remaining figure rounds out the influence of seventeenth-century Platonism on Shelley. John Locke, whom Shelley read and thought about throughout his life,[129] is an anti-Platonist if his attack on innate ideas is used as a criterion. But though Locke is not a Platonist on the surface, he has many points of contact with Plato. Shorey has pointed out some Platonic elements in him.

Locke's dialectic, his running fight against equivocation, his divisions and dichotomies, his conception of method, his comparison of mind to soft or hard wax—much that he says about power, pleasure and pain, the observation that the mind like the eye sees not itself, the comparison of intellectual inquiry to hunting, the observation that smells have no species, and several other touches, are Platonic.[130]

This kind of Platonism, however, is not the kind that Shelley used as material for poetry; it would mostly appear in Shelley's dialectical discussions with friends like Hogg. Locke therefore cannot be excluded from Shelley's oral Platonism, which could play an important part in our account of Shelley's Platonism if we had more than the few echoes of it in the testimony of his friends.

PLATONISM IN THE EIGHTEENTH CENTURY

POPE, DARWIN

If the literary historian were to plot the Platonic tradition in England, two peaks would stand out: the age of Spenser and Milton and the Romantic period. Even though the eighteenth century is marked by a

---

[129] See Droop, *op. cit.*, p. 97; White, *Shelley*, II, index, p. cx; Sen, *Studies in Shelley*, pp. 1-104.

[130] Shorey, *op. cit.*, p. 206.

wane in the direct influence of Platonism, it really marks the beginning of the Platonic renascence which attended the Romantic outburst in the nineteenth century. A study of the Platonic scholarship in eighteenth-century England[131] shows that there was a considerable activity in the translation of Plato, which extended from the complete translation of Plato's works to numerous translations and editions of the majority of Plato's Dialogues; it is this scholarship, as seen in the effect of Dacier's, Sydenham's, and Taylor's translations of Plato on Shelley, which contributed to the rise of Platonism in the Romantic period. The eighteenth century also marks the beginning of a reaction toward the antagonism to Plato which was fostered by the rise of anti-Platonic science and philosophy; it is in this background that we must view Shelley's revolt against the conventional attitude of disparagement toward Plato. Shelley's Platonism, like Romanticism itself, has its roots in the eighteenth century.

The indirect Platonism which Shelley absorbed from the writings of the eighteenth century was mostly the re-expression of the traditional Platonism which it inherited from previous centuries, but because it was the immediate intellectual antecedent of Shelley's milieu, it is of major importance in Shelley's Platonism. There is little Platonism in the poetry of the eighteenth century which can be said to have influenced Shelley in any great degree. Pope is not a Platonist of Spenser's or Milton's caliber, and temperamentally he is alien to Platonism, as the following lines indicate:

> Go, soar with Plato to th' empyreal sphere
> To the first good, first perfect and first fair;
> Or tread the mazy round his follow'rs trod;
> And quitting sense call imitating God.[132]

Pope's poetry, which Shelley read,[133] in general shows no direct knowledge of Plato but merely reflects traditional Platonism like the Chain of Being, the music of the spheres, the many-headed beast, plastic Nature, and other such Platonic allusions which Shelley had already met in other Platonic material.[134]

Perhaps of greater interest for Shelley's Platonism is Erasmus Darwin. Shelley asked his bookseller in 1812 for a copy of Darwin's *The Temple*

[131] F. B. Evans III, "Platonic Scholarship in Eighteenth-Century England," *MP*, XLI (1943), 103-110.

[132] *An Essay on Man*, II, 23-26; for Pope and Plato, see Austin Warren, *Alexander Pope as Critic and Humanist* (Princeton, 1929), pp. 187-188.

[133] Droop, *op. cit.*, p. 60.

[134] Tillyard, *op. cit.*, pp. 23-24; cf. *An Essay on Man*, I, 202, III, 9; *Imitations of Horace*, Book I, Epistle I, l. 121; see Shorey, *op. cit.*, pp. 208-210 for other instances.

of Nature, and in a letter to Hogg in 1811 he speaks of amusing himself with reading Darwin.[135]   His poetry contains a curious mixture of science and Platonism, like that also found in *Prometheus Unbound. Symposium,* 207-208, is reflected in

> And heaven-born STORGE weaves the social chain;
> Successive births her tender cares combine,
> And soft affections live along the line. . . .[136]

Platonic Love appears in lines like

> And learns ere long, the perfect form confess'd,
> IDEAL BEAUTY from its Mother's breast,

and

> With holy kisses wanders o'er her charms,
> And clasps the Beauty in Platonic arms.[137]

Such lines may have constituted rivulets of influence on Shelley's early Platonism.   In the other poets of the eighteenth century like Gray, Chatterton, Collins, and Burns, whom Shelley read, there are only minor echoes of the Platonic tradition, even though Gray himself was a competent Platonic scholar.[138]   The same is true with prose writers like Swift, Defoe, Addison, Sterne, the Earl of Chesterfield, and Scott, all of whom Shelley read.   Their Platonism consists of grace notes rather than Platonic themes.[139]

BERKELEY

It is mostly in the philosophic, social, and political thought of the eighteenth century that Shelley found important sources of Platonic influence.   From Berkeley, whom he read with care and whose influence on him was great,[140] Shelley absorbed an idealism which, combined with Plato's idealism, was of supreme importance in his philosophic conver-

[135] Julian *Works,* IX, 36; VIII, 135.

[136] Erasmus Darwin, *The Temple of Nature; or, The Origin of Society* (New York, 1804), Canto II, ll. 92-94.

[137] *Ibid.,* Canto III, ll. 175-176, 195-196; cf. Canto IV, l. 499.

[138] Cf. W. P. Jones, *Thomas Gray, Scholar* (Cambridge, Mass., 1937), pp. 66-69; T. M. Raysor, *Coleridge's Miscellaneous Criticism* (Cambridge, Mass., 1936), pp. 308-311; *Correspondence of Thomas Gray,* ed. Paget Toynbee and Leonard Whibley (Oxford, 1935), III, 1295.

[139] Cf. F. B. Evans III, "Platonic Scholarship in Eighteenth-Century England," *MP,* XLI (1943), 103-104.

[140] See Droop, *op. cit.,* pp. 98-99; White, *Shelley,* II, index, pp. vi, cviii; cf. G. S. Brett, "Shelley's Relation to Berkeley and Drummond," *Studies in English* by Members of University College, Toronto (Oxford, 1931), pp. 170-202; H. A. G. Liedtke, *Shelley-durch Berkeley und Drummond beeinflusst?* (Greifswald, 1933).

sion to idealism. In Berkeley, Shelley found a man with cognate Platonic elements; Berkeley's attack on matter, though epistemologically different from Plato's, only reinforced Plato's attack on the world of matter and conversely the belief in idealism. Furthermore, when he maintains in *Of the Principles of Human Knowledge* that the Divine Ideas are the archetype of our sensible ideas, his thought becomes tangent to Platonism. Berkeley, moreover, was derivatively influenced by Plato, who was his favorite author. A survey of the specific references to Plato in his works shows that Berkeley's thought is seen in a sharp focus only when related to its Platonic background.[141] Professor Wild in his study of Berkeley's thought has illustrated this by showing Berkeley's gradual evolution from the empiricism of Locke to Plato. "There was no stage," he says, "in Berkeley's intellectual career when he was not familiar with at least certain of the Platonic Dialogues, though his comprehension and appreciation of their significance developed hand-in-hand with the deepening of his thought. We must, in fact, think of Berkeley himself as a passage or movement—the passage from Locke to Plato."[142]

The influence of Plato is evident, not only in the form of Berkeley's dialogues, but in their content as well. Berkeley's conception of nature as a divine language, and of God as speaking to men by outward sensible systems, led him from sense to the transcendental and the Platonic "mental mode of reasoning." We hear the very voice of Plato in statements like "by the help of sensible things, as a scale or a ladder, ascend to moral and intelligible beauty."[143] "Indeed, the truth of the matter," says Professor Wild, "is that Berkeley's attempt to brush aside words and abstractions, in order to penetrate the 'veil' of language to the 'real,' led him on inevitably to the 'intellectual,' the 'world of ideas,' or as he preferred to call them in the *Dialogues,* 'archetypes.' Berkeley was forced by his love of the real, complete, or truly 'empirical' to the non-empirical, the 'archetypes,' and the transcendental."[144] Berkeley's influence on Shelley consists not only of this idealism but also of such details as Shelley's use of the dialogue form in *A Refutation of Deism* and his frequent

---

[141] For Berkeley's Platonism, see John Wild, *George Berkeley: A Study of His Life and Philosophy* (Cambridge, Mass., 1936), pp. 66-77, and references in index, p. 551; *Berkeley's Complete Works,* ed. A. C. Fraser (Oxford, 1901), 4 vols., IV, index, *s.v.* Plato, Platonism, Plotinus; *Berkeley and Percival Correspondence,* ed. Benjamin Rand (Cambridge, 1914), pp. 64, 68-69; D. S. Robinson, "The Platonic Model of Hylas and Philonous," *Philosophical Review,* XXIX (1920), 484-487; cf. Elizabeth Merrill, *The Dialogue in English Literature* (New York, 1911).

[142] Wild, *op. cit.,* p. 67.

[143] *Berkeley's Complete Works,* II, 132.

[144] Wild, *op. cit.,* p. 68.

use and elaboration of Berkeley's imagery of "the veil," which Shelley uses with the Platonic connotation of appearance and reality.

If Shelley had read Berkeley's *Siris* (and he probably had, for he possessed the whole of Berkeley's works, as we can see from his order to his bookseller, and furthermore Mrs. Shelley speaks of him as a follower of Berkeley, *ca.* 1817),[145] he would have found in Berkeley a Platonist of the first order. This little work is a remarkable *tour de force,* an eighteenth-century *Timaeus.* "It breathes," says Fraser, "the spirit of Plato and the Neoplatonists in the least Platonic generation of English history since the revival of letters, and it extracts this Platonic spirit from a thing of sense so commonplace as tar."[146] This Platonic treatise is, as its title indicates, a Chain or an account of the gradations of reality from tar water to God. Its thought and language are consciously Platonic:

Iamblichus . . . teacheth, what is also a received notion of the Pythagoreans and Platonics, that this is no chasm in nature, but a Chain or Scale of beings, rising by gentle uninterrupted gradations from the lowest to the highest, each nature being informed and perfected by the participation of a higher. . . . In this scale, each lower faculty is a step that leads to one above it. And the uppermost naturally leads to the Deity; which is rather the object of intellectual knowledge than even of the discursive faculty, not to mention the sensitive. There runs a Chain throughout the whole system of beings. In this Chain one link drags another. The meanest things are connected with the highest. The calamity therefore is neither strange nor much to be complained of, if a low sensual reader shall, from mere love of the animal life, find himself drawn on, surprised and betrayed, into some curiosity concerning the intellectual.[147]

In tracing the stages of the relationship of tar water to God, Berkeley not only gives an excellent epitome of Platonism and the Platonic tradition, but also makes use of its leading conceptions in formulating the stages of the ascent. One finds in it the basic conceptions of Platonism, such as Plato's theory of Ideas, the Platonic conceptions of the world of becoming and being, knowledge and opinion, the Cave of the *Republic,* the world soul of the *Timaeus,* the "οὐσία ὄντως οὖσα of Plato, which employeth mind alone," the mind clogged and borne downward by impressions of sense, God as a χωριστὸν εἶδος, and the "First Mover, invisible, incorporeal, unextended intellectual source of life and being."[148]

---

[145] Julian *Works,* IX, 36; Mrs. Shelley's note in *Essays, Letters from Abroad, Translations and Fragments* (1840): "Shelley was a disciple of the Immaterial Philosophy of Berkeley."

[146] *Berkeley's Complete Works,* III, 118.

[147] *Ibid.,* III, 256, 269-270.

[148] *Ibid.,* III, 285-286, 272, 270, 248, 257-259, 252, 268, 279, 266.

In it are also found many important quotations from Plato's dialogues like the comparison of the soul to the charioteer in *Phaedrus*, 246 ff.[149] Berkeley's praise of Plato gives us the keynote to his Platonism:

It might very well be thought serious trifling to tell my readers that the greatest men had ever a high esteem of Plato; whose writings are the touch-stone of a hasty and shallow mind; whose philosophy has been the admiration of ages. . . . Albeit in these days the depths of that old learning are rarely fathomed; and yet it were happy for these lands if our young nobility and gentry, instead of modern maxims, would imbibe the notions of the great men of antiquity. But, in these free-thinking times, many an empty head is shook at Aristotle and Plato, as well as at the Holy Scriptures. And the writings of those celebrated ancients are by most men treated on a foot with the dry and barbarous lucubrations of the schoolmen. It may be mostly presumed there are not many among us, even those who are called the better sort, who have more sense, virtue, and love of their country than Cicero, who in a Letter to Atticus could not forbear exclaiming, *O Socrates et Socratici viri! numquam vobis gratiam referam.* Would to God many of our countrymen had the same obligations to those Socratic writers! Certainly, where the people are well educated, the art of piloting a state is best learned from the writings of Plato.[150]

Such a tribute to Plato, as the *Siris* shows, is not rhetorical but the testament of the most Platonic of the eighteenth-century figures whom Shelley read and admired and from whom he could absorb not only the spirit but the entire alphabet of Platonism. Berkeley therefore must be ranked with Spenser and Milton as of the highest importance for Shelley's Platonism. Thus we see that although the Platonism of Berkeley had little effect on British philosophy, it is important for its influence on Blake, Coleridge, and Shelley, who blended the influence of Berkeley with that of Plato.[151] The philosophy of the eighteenth century, how-ever, followed the path of empiricism as laid out by Locke. In making sensation the basis of knowledge, eighteenth-century philosophy diverged from Platonism and its theory of Ideas. The Platonism that is found in this period is by way of a reaction to materialism. The quarrel had begun in the previous century. Hobbes's philosophy was provocative of charges of atheism by his opponents; Cudworth regarded his thought as the living exponent of the ancient atomic Epicureanism. This atheism was supplemented in the next century by the growth of materialism, which was a logical development of the empirical premises of Locke.

[149] *Ibid.*, III, 207.   [150] *Ibid.*, III, 283-284.
[151] See H. A. Hodges's chapter on British Philosophy in H. V. D. Dyson and John Butt, *Augustans and Romantics, 1689-1830* (London, 1940), pp. 115-116.

Berkeley's thought avoided the inevitable conclusion of these premises, and it was left to Hume to take the final step and lead the philosophy of the eighteenth century to an impasse of materialistic skepticism which fostered atheism. But such a premise and conclusion were not acceptable to the idealism in human nature. Philosophical opposition arose and found in Plato a storehouse of arguments and idealistic inspiration. We see the opposition starting with Cudworth, who opposes Hobbes by a Platonically based and inspired theism. Then followed Bishop Berkeley's idealism, which leaped over its empirical premises to reach God with the aid of Plato. Shaftesbury, alarmed at the premises of both Locke and Hobbes, like Cudworth, turned to Plato for philosophic aid. Shaftesbury's lack of rigorous and penetrating thought, however, led to a reaction. Mandeville, Berkeley, and others joined in polemic against him. Platonism once more rose with the philosophic reaction to Hume's skepticism. The "common-sense" school of Reid and Stewart, though not following the premises of Platonism, made an eclectic use of it by way of analogy, illustration, and parallel. The curve of Platonism rises higher with Lord Monboddo, a favorite of Shelley, who also set out to defend theism by a revival of Cudworth's Platonism. Thus the opposition to empiricism made considerable use of Platonism, and even when it did not adopt the premises of Platonic metaphysics it grafted Platonic elements on its own philosophy.

Shelley, being the child of eighteenth-century thought, partakes of both these points of view. His references to eighteenth-century philosophy, his reading list and book orders, his use of eighteenth-century terminology, his pronouncements on atheism, theism, and polytheism, show that he must be studied in the context of the eighteenth century as well as that of Romanticism. It can be shown that Shelley follows more or less the philosophical debates of the eighteenth century, allying himself now with one side, now with the other, and again partaking of both in unconscious contradiction. In his early thought he comes under the influence of eighteenth-century materialism and becomes an atheist; then, as his prose works show, he becomes a Deist with small excursions into polytheism. In this stage he absorbed the Platonism latent in the arguments of the Deists. Finally, finding materialism and logical Deism poetically and temperamentally unsatisfactory, he turns to Platonic idealism, passing through stages of alternate friendship and hostility to Christianity and culminating in a reconciliation of Plato and Christ in *Hellas*. This evolution in Shelley's thought must be studied in its philosophical milieu, and therefore it is essential to see the Platonic elements in the eighteenth century which influenced Shelley's ultimate conversion to Platonism.

SHAFTESBURY

Next to Berkeley, Shaftesbury looms up as an outstanding Platonist of the eighteenth century. Though there are no specific references to Shaftesbury in Shelley's reading, he was read by Mary, who often followed in the paths of Shelley's reading; Shelley, however, can hardly have missed his influence because Shaftesbury was an influential figure of major importance.[152] Shelley came in contact with Shaftesbury's thought in Lord Monboddo's *Of the Origin and Progress of Language,* which contains an analysis, summary, and enthusiastic appraisal of Shaftesbury's *The Moralists, A Philosophical Rhapsody,* to which Shaftesbury's reputation and influence as a Platonist are mostly due. Another important channel by which Shaftesbury's Platonism might have reached Shelley is Rousseau and Wieland; their novels, which Shelley read, are deeply influenced by Shaftesbury's Platonism. Furthermore, Shaftesbury's Platonism could reach Shelley even through his reading of Hume's *Essays,* which includes an essay, "The Platonist," setting forth some important conceptions of Plato derived from Shaftesbury.[153]

Shaftesbury's Platonism consists in the main of Platonic elaborations of the doctrine that order, harmony, and proportion in the universe beget a belief in Deism.[154] Shaftesbury's Neoplatonism is one of the important sources of Shelley's Platonism. In claiming that feeling is the chief criterion of judgment and that the aim of the artist is to recapture the divine beauty which emanates from Divinity, Shaftesbury set the stage for the development of Shelley's Platonism which makes feeling the dominant element in the search for divine beauty. Although Shaftesbury maintains with Plato that the pleasures of the mind are superior to those of the body, it is not reason but Platonic emotions that are the basis of his Platonism. The dithyrambic quality and the prose-poetry character of Shaftesbury's Platonism make it the forerunner of Romantic Platonism. In *The Moralists, A Philosophical Rhapsody,* Shaftesbury, like Ficino in

---

[152] *The Letters of Mary W. Shelley,* ed. F. L. Jones, I, 318; for Shaftesbury's Platonism, see Ernst Cassirer, "Shaftesbury und die Renaissance des Platonismus in England," *Vorträge der Bibliothek Warburg,* IX (1930-1931; Leipzig and Berlin, 1932), 136-155; H. F. Mueller, "Shaftesbury und Plotinos," *Berliner Philologische Wochenschrift,* XXXVIII (1918), 670-671; *MP,* XLI (1943), 104 n. 8.

[153] *Vide infra,* p. 614; also, *Essays, Moral, Political, and Literary,* by David Hume, ed. T. H. Green and T. H. Grose (London, 1907), I, 210-213, II, 221, 385-386; cf. Sen, *Studies in Shelley,* pp. 1-104.

[154] Anthony Ashley Cooper, Earl of Shaftesbury, *Characteristicks of Men, Manners, Opinions, Times*[3] (London, 1723), II, 75.

his *De amore,* gives way to a Platonic rhapsody. This dialogue is for the most part an improvisation on the *Symposium* and the *Timaeus.* Whatever of substance it has is Platonic, such as: Beauty and Good are one and the same; the orders of Beauty are (1) the dead Forms formed by Man or Nature, (2) the Forms which form, which have Intelligence, Action, and Operation, and (3) the Order of Beauty, the "Principle, Source, Fountain of all *Beauty.*"[155] It contains Platonic rhapsodies like "O Glorious *Nature!* supremely Fair, sovereignly Good! All-loving and All-lovely, All-divine! . . . whose Study brings such Wisdom, and whose Contemplation such Delight; . . . Thou impowering Deity, Supreme Creator! Thee I invoke . . . whilst thus inspir'd with Harmony of Thought, tho unconfin'd by Words, and in loose Numbers, I sing of Nature's Order in created Beings, and celebrate the Beautys which resolve in Thee, the Source and Principle of all Beauty and Perfection."[156] If we opened this dialogue at random we would find Platonic thought and expressions like this: ". . . whatever in Nature is beautiful or charming, is only the faint Shadow of that *First Beauty.* So that every *real Love* depending on the *Mind,* and being only *the Contemplation of Beauty,* either as it really is *in it-self,* or as it appears imperfectly in the Objects which strike the *Sense;* how can the rational Mind rest *here,* or be satisfy'd with the absurd *Enjoyment* which reaches the *Sense alone?*" He uses "Contemplation of the Ocean's *Beauty,*" pursuing "Shadow for Substance," "propagate that lovely Race of mental Children"—all direct echoes of the *Symposium.*[157] For Montesquieu the four greatest poets were Plato, Malebranche, Shaftesbury, and Montaigne. It is Shaftesbury the poet, through an indirect influence on writers whom Shelley read, who is important for Shelley's Platonism. If we were to explore, in Shaftesbury's own words, "the *interior Region* and *Recesses* of the *Mind,* the *hollow Caverns* of deep *Thought,* the private Seats of Fancy,"[158] we would find in Shelley's mind, not only such counterpart phrases as "Caverns of deep Thought," but also streams of poetic Platonism emanating from Shaftesbury.

THOMAS REID

Thomas Reid, whom Shelley read in 1811-12,[159] is important not only as a "carrier" of Platonism but as the leader of a revolt against the skeptical conclusions of Hume. He is not a Platonist, but in veering away from a philosophy which was subversive of morality and religion Reid

---

[155] *Ibid.,* II, 399, 406-408.   [156] *Ibid.,* II, 345.   [157] *Ibid.,* II, 395-396, 410.
[158] *Ibid.,* III, 211; for Shelley's phrase "inner cave of thought," *vide infra,* pp. 327-329.
[159] Julian *Works,* VIII, 331.

and the Scottish school of common sense were drawing closer to Platonism. In reading Thomas Reid's works Shelley came in contact with a considerable number of references to and expositions of Platonism. In discussing the nature of beauty Reid is almost a Platonist. He acknowledges that all the beauty which we perceive in the visible world is derived from mind. "This," he says, "was the opinion of the ancient philosophers . . . and it has been adopted by Lord Shaftesbury and Dr. Akenside among the moderns." Then he quotes Akenside's Platonic lines:

> Mind, mind alone, bear witness, earth and heav'n!
> The living fountains in itself contains
> Of beauteous and sublime. Here hand in hand
> Sit paramount the graces. Here enthron'd,
> Celestial Venus, with divinest airs,
> Invites the soul to never-fading joy.[160]

Even if Shelley's professed philosophy at this time was materialism, the poet in Shelley would be attracted to such reflections of Platonism. Besides this bit of idealism, Shelley would find in Reid a considerable analysis and exposition of Plato's leading concepts, such as Plato's Ideas, their relation to flux, and their character as model or exemplary causes. Shelley would also find in Reid a statement on the differences between Platonism and Neoplatonism, how Platonism was adopted by Christianity, how the body is the prison of the soul, which is celestial, how the soul is purified, how the senses give us no real knowledge, and how our knowledge is symbolized by "Plato's allegorical genius" in the Myth of the Cave.[161] These bits of Platonism imbedded in Reid contributed to the development of the Platonic tradition in Shelley at a time when Shelley was a latent Platonist.

DUGALD STEWART

Closely associated with Reid's common-sense school of philosophy is Dugald Stewart, whose *Outlines of Moral Philosophy* Shelley read and to which he refers in his writings. Shelley, who was keenly interested in the problem of punishment, would find in Stewart's treatise several significant Platonic explanations of punishment. Among the various theories concerning the origin of evil, Stewart lists the doctrine of Pre-

---

[160] *The Works of Thomas Reid*, Preface, Notes and Supplementary Dissertations by Sir William Hamilton (Edinburgh, 1863), I, 503; these lines come from Akenside's *The Pleasures of Imagination*, I, 481-486. For the Platonism in the poem, see A. O. Aldridge, "The Eclecticism of Mark Akenside's *The Pleasures of Imagination*," *Journal of the History of Ideas*, V (1944), 292-314.

[161] *Ibid.*, I, 264, 203, 225, 255, 262.

existence according to which "the evils we suffer at present are punishments and expiations of moral delinquencies committed in a former stage of our being."[162] Plato's view of evil and the goodness of God which Shelley noted, translated, and briefly commented on in his excerpts from the *Republic* is also noted by Stewart, who may have first called Shelley's attention to it.[163] If Shelley had read any other work of Stewart besides the *Outlines of Moral Philosophy*, he would have found a considerable storehouse of Platonism, as the index of the edition of his collected works shows.

LORD MONBODDO

Among the books which Shelley requested of his bookseller in December, 1812, was Lord Monboddo's *Of the Origin and Progress of Language*, which, along with Tooke's *Diversions of Purley*, stimulated Shelley's interest in the philosophy of language.[164] There is no doubt that Shelley read this treatise of Monboddo, for we have evidence of its influence on his prose.[165] The thesis of this treatise is that the progress of mankind from a state of nature, symbolized by Ouran-Outang, is the result of man's intellect. In the development of this thesis there is found a vast amount of Platonism. In it is found the phrase "Intellectual Beauty," which, along with other sources, constitutes the source for the title of Shelley's *Hymn to Intellectual Beauty*.[166] The treatise is filled with Platonic commentary. In his discussion of the origin and nature of ideas Monboddo has a good chapter on Plato's theory of Ideas; he discusses extensively the idea of τὸ καλόν and quotes the *Symposium*, 210-211, to illustrate its nature.[167] In the development and illustration of various aspects of his subject Monboddo makes considerable use of Plato's thought and language. Illustrative quotations come from many dialogues, and from them Shelley could absorb many important doctrines in the *Laws*, *Timaeus*, *Epinomis*, *Cratylus*, *Philebus*, *Sophist*, and *Phaedrus*. In his discussion of rhetoric is included an excellent analysis of Plato, "the greatest dialoguist of antient or modern times." Monboddo praises the artistry of the *Protagoras* and the *Gorgias* and summarizes the moral, political, and metaphysical concepts of Plato with a critical appraisal. This epitome of Platonism, to which is added a detailed and excellent analysis, summary, and exposition of Shaftesbury's

---

[162] *The Collected Works of Dugald Stewart*, ed. Sir William Hamilton (Edinburgh, 1854-1860), VI, 62.

[163] *Ibid.*, VI, 63.   [164] Julian *Works*, IX, 36.

[165] *Vide infra*, pp. 186-188.   [166] *Vide infra*, p. 197.

[167] Lord Monboddo, *Of the Origin and Progress of Language* (Edinburgh, 1774-1792), Vol. I, Book I, chap. viii.

important Platonic dialogue, the *Moralists,* makes Monboddo's treatise an important source of direct and indirect Platonism in Shelley.

In 1820 Shelley also read Lord Monboddo's *Antient Metaphysics,* which contains references, allusions, quotations, and commentaries on Plato's thought. Although Shelley was fairly well initiated into direct Platonism at this time, the reading of this treatise is important for its Platonic content. In the Introduction Monboddo writes, "What I propose in this Work is to revive antient Theism, particularly the Theism of Plato and Aristotle." His use of the Platonic tradition to combat atheism and modern philosophers who "make their system of Nature much too mechanical" is extensive. "The authors I have chiefly followed," he says, "are, Plato and Aristotle, together with the later philosophers of the Alexandrian School, such as Plotinus, Porphyry, Jamblichos, Ammonius Hermeias, and his scholars, Simplicius and Johannes Philoponus, the two best commentators upon Aristotle; likewise Proclus, who was thought to understand the philosophy of Plato so well, that he was dignified with the title of *his successor.*"[168] But his use of the Platonic tradition does not stop with the ancients; his use of Cudworth is such that his treatise may constitute one of several potential sources from which Shelley might have come in contact with Cudworth's doctrine of plastic nature, which figures prominently in the *Adonais.*[169] The fact that Shelley had been reading Monboddo's treatise less than a year before the composition of *Adonais* increases the importance of this treatise in the account of Shelley's indirect Platonism.[170]

The Platonic idealism and belief in the divinity and the immortality of the soul manifest in Shelley's compositions of 1820 and 1821 may have received some impetus from Monboddo's treatise. In Monboddo Shelley found a philosophy of theism which had its foundations in the Platonic conception that "Mind is the author of all the motion in the universe."[171] He follows Plato closely in his conception of the relation of mind to matter; he elaborates the Platonic conception of the soul as pervading and animating the whole universe, as a tripartite immaterial entity; he discusses the Platonic dichotomy of knowledge and opinion, the theory of ideas, the true status of sensation and flux, Plato's conception of immortality, reminiscence, and the Good. Yet not all the Platonism in this

---

[168] Monboddo, *Antient Metaphysics: or, the Science of Universals* (Edinburgh, 1779-1799), I, iii.

[169] *Ibid.,* I, 222-223.

[170] Entries for the reading of Monboddo's treatise occur on September 21-23, Oct. 1, 1820.

[171] Monboddo, *Antient Metaphysics,* I, ii.

treatise is pure; Monboddo is steeped in the later Platonic tradition with all its confusions, such as that the mystery of the Trinity and the doctrine of Ideas were known to the Egyptians, from whom Plato learned them. In it the macrocosm and microcosm are presented with Neoplatonic interpretations, many of which emanate from Cudworth. Thus we can see that Monboddo's treatises are important potential sources of Shelley's Platonism, Neoplatonism, and Theism.

ADAM SMITH, GILLIES, GIBBON

Although Monboddo is the last major figure in eighteenth-century England from whom Shelley absorbed Platonism through diffusion or derivation, other minor figures are worth noting. Among Shelley's books which Hogg mentions in his account of a visit to Shelley and Harriet in 1813 is Adam Smith's *Theory of Moral Sentiments.*[172] This work contains some rich veins of Platonism, such as the elaborate account of Plato's tripartite division of the soul and definition of justice.[173] Shelley's informational knowledge of Plato and the Platonic tradition could also have been increased by his reading of Gillies's *History of Greece* and Gibbon's *The Decline and Fall of the Roman Empire.*[174] Gillies's history would present Shelley with an excellent summary of Plato's life and thought which even today can stand as a model of *multum in parvo* exposition.[175] Here Shelley could find every important doctrine of Plato, pithily stated and related in a system which does no violence to Plato's thought. In it he could also find a forceful statement of the abuse of Platonism by "visionary fanatics who discovered, in the λóγος of Plato, the second person of the Trinity, recognised the Holy Spirit in his Soul of the World." Gibbon's history would give to Shelley a historical account of the decline and fall of Platonism,[176] of "the surviving sect of Platonists, whom Plato would have blushed to acknowledge" and who "extravagantly mingled a sublime theory with the practice and superstition of magic." His description of the Neoplatonists— Ammonius, Plotinus, Amelius, and Porphyry—is a masterful, though prejudiced, characterization of Neoplatonism. His account of Julian's Platonism is filled with Neoplatonic doctrines which, though despised by Gibbon's logical mind, could be, as some of Shelley's poems show, poetically acceptable as magical atmosphere. Scholars who probe through the Neoplatonic shadows of Shelley would do well to consider Gibbon's account of Julian's Platonism as a potential source.

[172] Hogg, *op. cit.,* II, 3.
[173] *The Works of Adam Smith* (London, 1812), I, 474-477.
[174] See Droop, *op. cit.,* pp. 101-102; White, *Shelley,* II, index, p. cix.
[175] John Gillies, *The History of Ancient Greece*[5] (London, 1809), III, 502-522.
[176] Gibbon, *op. cit.,* I, 392-393; II, 336-337; IV, 261-267.

An examination of Shelley's reading shows that it includes many great figures of French and German eighteenth-century literature and philosophy.[177] Shelley's catholic taste swept away any barriers that a foreign language might impose. His study of language shows that he learned foreign languages simply in order to become acquainted with the thought of its great figures. Shelley's reading in seventeenth-century French literature is negligible, consisting of Molière's *Georges Dandin* and Fénelon's *Aventures de Télémaque,* both of which are negative to the test of Platonism. But when we come to the eighteenth-century French literature, we find that we cannot understand Shelley's thought without it. A survey of Shelley's notes to *Queen Mab,* his letters, prose, and journal, reveal the extent and depth of the influence of French thought on Shelley. It is important, therefore, to examine the nature of the Platonism embodied in the French writers read by Shelley.

BARTHÉLEMY

In the month preceding Shelley's translation of the *Symposium* and extending through the period of its translation, Mary's Journal records in the daily entries Shelley's reading of Abbé Barthélemy's *The Travels of Anacharsis the Younger in Greece.* This eighteenth-century compendium of Greek civilization woven around the cultural odyssey of the younger Anacharsis constituted a very important source of Hellenism for France, England, and America in the eighteenth and nineteenth centuries. Read side by side with Aristophanes, it contributed to Shelley's intense Hellenism at Bagni di Lucca. Its influence on *A Discourse on the Manners of the Antient Greeks Relative to the Subject of Love* is apparent. This work constitutes an important source of Shelley's Platonism. The long chapter on Socrates[178] is not only encyclopedic in its information about his life and thought but is also well written. It presents a complete portrait of Socrates as found in Plato and Xenophon. One need not look elsewhere for the sources of Socrates in Shelley's writings after June, 1818; if we did not know that Shelley read both Plato and Xenophon, his knowledge of Socrates could be traced to this chapter in Barthélemy.

Barthélemy also devotes two long chapters to Plato which summarize the *Republic* and *Timaeus.*[179] The chapter on the *Republic* gives a readable and accurate account of the first seven books. All the important

---

[177] Droop, *op. cit.,* 123-145; White, *Shelley,* II, index.

[178] *Travels of Anacharsis the Younger,* by the Abbé Barthelemi, Translated from the French [by William Beaumont] in Four volumes (Philadelphia, 1804), III, chap. lxvii; for the Hellenism of Barthélemy, see Maurice Badolle, *L'Abbé Jean-Jacques Barthélemy et l'hellénisme en France dans la seconde moitié du XVIIIe s.* (Paris, 1926).

[179] *Ibid.,* III, chaps. liv, lix.

features of the *Republic* are presented here with such detail that again Shelley's knowledge of the *Republic* could be traced to this chapter, which may have stimulated his later reading of the *Republic* in the original. Barthélemy's romantic and dramatic presentation of the essence of the *Timaeus* must have made an impression on Shelley. Anacharsis and Plato visit Cape Sunium and are surveying the beautiful scenery of the promontory. "Plato," says Anacharsis, "on whom great and sublime objects had always made a strong impression, seemed to have fixed his whole attention on the gulfs which nature has excavated to receive the waters of the ocean." In the midst of this a storm arose, and they sought refuge in the temple crowning the promontory. The storm led to questions:

Why these seeming errors and revolutions in nature? Are they to be attributed to chance? . . . Are tempests excited and appeased by an intelligent cause? . . . From these enquiries we proceed to the existence of the gods, the reduction of chaos to form and order, and the origin of the universe. Wandering and lost in the mazes of these ideas, we conjured Plato to guide us to the truth. He was absorbed in profound meditation; it seemed as if the terrible and majestic voice of nature still resounded in his ears. At length, overcome by our entreaties, and the truths which he resolved in his labouring mind, he seated himself on a rustic seat, and having placed us by his side, began his discourse as follows:

Feeble mortals that we are! is it for us to penetrate the secrets of the Divinity; for us, the wisest of whom is to the Supreme Being only what an ape is to us? . . . If I were obliged to explain myself in the presence of the multitude concerning the first Author of all things, the origin of the universe, and the cause of evil, I should be compelled to speak in enigmas; but in these solitary places, where I am only heard by God and my friends, I shall have the satisfaction of rendering homage to truth.

The God which I declare unto you, is a God, single, immutable, and infinite, the centre of all perfections, and the inexhaustible source of intelligence and being. . . .[180]

Then follows a summary of the *Timaeus*. The presentation of the *Timaeus* in this romantic manner must have been attractive to Shelley. The reading of Barthélemy's travel tale is important for Shelley's Platonism, for in the absence of a direct reading, the influence of the *Republic*, the *Timaeus,* and the Socratic teachings on Shelley's writings after 1818 can be definitely traced to Barthélemy.

[180] *Ibid.*, III, 193-194.

Rousseau was one of Shelley's favorite authors, though his admiration for him, as shown in *The Triumph of Life*, was later qualified.[181] Shelley speaks of him "as the greatest man the world has produced since Milton" and refers to the "divine beauty of Rousseau's imagination," "the contemplation of whose imperishable creations had left no vacancy in my heart for mortal things." In speaking of the French language to a lady, he says, "If the great name of Rousseau did not redeem it, it would have been perhaps as well that you had remained entirely ignorant of it."[182] We have been accustomed to interpret this admiration for Rousseau as an indication of the influence of a philosophy which is diametrically opposed to Platonism. It will be clear, however, after an examination of the evidence that, although this may be the case, Shelley absorbed a significant amount of the Platonism which permeates Rousseau's work. It now remains to indicate the main outlines of this Platonism.

Rousseau, unlike most of the eighteenth-century thinkers, had a considerable direct acquaintance with and respect for Plato. As his writings reveal, he knew the *Republic* intimately, his knowledge of it extending from its leading ideas down to use of its minor similes. Besides the *Republic*, which is a cornerstone in Rousseau's thought, he read and made use in his writings of Plato's *Laws*, the *Statesman*, the *Phaedo*, *Apology*, *Symposium*, and a considerable amount of indirect Platonism emanating from Plutarch's *Moralia*, his favorite reading. Recent studies by Hendel and Vaughan show clearly the Platonic character of Rousseau's thought.[183]

The Platonic tradition in Rousseau centers for the most part on the social and educational thought of the *Republic* and Platonic Love. The importance of Plato in Rousseau's political thought has been shown by Vaughan,[184] who points out that Rousseau began as a pupil of Locke and in the crucial years of his growth became "the wholehearted disciple of Plato." Vaughan has shown how two traditions meet in the political theory of Rousseau. As the champion of individual liberty Rousseau is the heir of Locke; as the champion of the sovereignty of the state he is the heir of Plato. Rousseau was not successful in harmonizing these two

---

[181] See Droop, *op. cit.*, pp. 135-137; White, *Shelley*, II, index, pp. lxxxii-lxxxiii.

[182] Julian *Works*, VI, 124; IX, 176; X, 268; Scott, *Shelley at Oxford*, p. 53.

[183] Cf. C. W. Hendel, *Jean-Jacques Rousseau Moralist* (Oxford, 1934), which sets in relief the influence of "Socrate et le divin Plato" on Rousseau's thought. For a bibliography of Rousseau and Plato, see Albert Schinz, *État présent des travaux sur J. J. Rousseau* (Paris, New York, 1941), p. 377.

[184] C. E. Vaughan, *The Political Writings of Jean Jacques Rousseau* (Cambridge, 1915), I, 2-4.

strands in his thought, any more than Shelley, who also was torn between individual liberty and belief that some form of civil life is essential to the intellectual and moral life of man.

The influence of the *Republic* appears more specifically in Rousseau's *Émile,* which Shelley read and admired. Its importance is stated in the first few pages: "If you wish to know," writes Rousseau, "what is meant by public education, read Plato's *Republic.* Those who merely judge books by their titles take this for a treatise on politics, but it is the finest treatise on education ever written."[185] In his *Confessions,* which Shelley also read, Rousseau shows the extent of its influence on his actions. "In handing over my children to the State to educate . . . ," he says, "I thought that I was behaving like a citizen and a father, and considered myself a member of Plato's Republic."[186] Rousseau bases the education of Émile on many principles laid down in the *Republic.* Children, for example, are to be taught, as in Plato, through festivals, games, songs, and amusements; he insists on simple music and the avoidance of complicated Lydian music; moral stories and parables are to be used in the education of Émile, who is contrasted with "some young rascal from college, reading the fourth book of the *Aeneid,* or Tibullus or the *Banquet* of Plato." Exercise and hygienic living cannot be replaced by medicine, which he distrusts in the same way as Plato. Rousseau follows Plato not only in the education of Émile but also of Sophie, his destined wife, the education of both of whom is similar in many ways to that of Laon and Cythna in *Laon and Cythna.* Rousseau discusses Plato's education of women in the *Republic,* its doctrine of the same gymnastics for men and women, and the community of wives.[187]

In *Émile* Shelley would also have cause to admire the famous speech of the Savoyard priest, which is mostly Christianized Platonism. Some of its sentences are direct echoes of Plato, such as "when, freed from the illusions of the bodily senses, we behold with joy the supreme Being and the eternal truths which flow from him." The Platonic dualism in man's nature is described as raising man, on the one hand, "to the study of eternal truths, to the love of justice, and of true morality, to the regions of the world of thought, which the wise delight to contemplate," while on the other leading him "downwards to himself" and making him the "slave of his senses, of the passions which are their instruments, and thus opposed everything suggested to him by the former principle." In this speech the arguments for deism, for the immortality of the soul, and for

[185] *Émile or Education,* by J. J. Rousseau (Everyman's Library edition), p. 8.
[186] *Confessions,* by J. J. Rousseau (Everyman's Library edition), II, 9.
[187] *Émile,* pp. 71, 309, 326.

the use of corporeal images in ascending to God are all directly or ultimately derived from Plato and the Platonic tradition.[188]

Rousseau is also the source of romantic Platonic Love. "Return,"
says one of Rousseau's lovers, "to the depths of your soul: it is there that
you will always find again the source of that sacred fire which has inflamed us so often with the love of sublime virtues; it is there that you
will find that eternal image of true beauty whose contemplation fills us
with sacred enthusiasm and which our passions continually pollute without ever being able to efface."[189] This love, which Rousseau himself
tells us in a note is Platonic, is set in an atmosphere of romantic poetry.
Shelley, who thinks of Rousseau as essentially a poet,[190] would find
Rousseau's Platonic Love so close to his own heart that he could hardly
have escaped its influence. Rousseau transmits Platonic Love through
his own imagination and intense emotions and sets it against the background of nature.[191] Tears, sighs, ecstasies, and sentiments fill the Platonic and sensual loves of this *l'ame aimante*. We have Platonic moods
and reveries; Platonic Love becomes *l'amitie amoureuse* symbolized by
women who, as in Shelley's poems, not only console but educate. This
Platonic Love is made unforgettable by its association with the beauties
of nature—such as the first kiss of lovers in a grove which is then made
into a shrine—nature which joins in joys and sorrows and speaks as the
"voice of nature." This Platonic Love, suffused with sentiment, *sensi-
bilité,* subordinating reason to feeling, filled with individualism and
passion, and expressed with romantic feeling and enthusiasm, becomes
something new and different from the Platonic Love of the Middle
Ages and Renaissance. Rousseau's contributions to romantic Platonic
Love are such that we must seriously consider them as an important
influence on Shelley's romantic Platonism. A comparison of the romantic
Platonic Love in Rousseau and Shelley will reveal many similarities,
which arise not only from temperamental affinities but also because of
Shelley's absorption from Rousseau of a new language to express Platonic Love. This is perhaps consciously acknowledged by Shelley himself, who praises Rousseau as one who has "celebrated the dominion of
love, planting as it were trophies in the human mind of that sublimest
victory over sensuality."[192]

[188] *Ibid.,* pp. 246, 241, 238, 248.

[189] J. J. Rousseau, *La Nouvelle Héloïse* (Paris, 1852), p. 198; for other Platonic doctrines in this work, see pp. 325, 346.

[190] Julian *Works,* VII, 133 n. 1; cf. *ibid.,* p. 323.

[191] Cf. W. A. Nitze and E. P. Dargan, *A History of French Literature*[8] (New York,
1938), pp. 486-489.

[192] Julian *Works,* VII, 128.

FRENCH PHILOSOPHERS AND ENCYCLOPEDISTS

Shelley absorbed from his reading of eighteenth-century French thinkers a conception of Plato as a poetic dreamer. In his notes to *Queen Mab* he writes, "This belief, rolling through the lapse of ages, met with the reveries of Plato and the reasonings of Aristotle."[193] The phrase "reveries of Plato" is not Shelley's own but is an echo from French philosophy. The phrase and the sentiment expressed in this note are found in D'Holbach's *System of Nature*;[194] the phrase may also be found in Cabanis's *Rapports du physique et du moral de l'homme*, which Shelley cites in his notes on *Queen Mab*. In this work Cabanis speaks of *"les rêves de Platon, qui tendoient éminemment à l'enthousiasme,"*[195] a description which sums up a typical eighteenth-century conception of Plato. This conception of Plato as a dreamer has its roots in the Middle Ages and the Renaissance, but it comes into prominence in the eighteenth century. Bayle's *Dictionary*, a source of Platonism for many French thinkers, occasionally ridicules the dreams of the Platonists. Voltaire, who is full of this theme and whom Shelley read, says in *Plato's Dream:* "Plato was a great dreamer. . . . He dreamed that mankind were formerly double. . . . His republic was one of his principal dreams. . . . Dreams were at that time in great repute."[196] Though eighteenth-century rationalists may ridicule this Platonism, to the poetic mind it is the stuff of poetry, and Shelley's poetic outlook owes much to this eighteenth-century conception. It must be admitted that even when Shelley read Plato directly his view of Plato was influenced considerably by the tradition which viewed Plato as a poetic dreamer. Many of Shelley's Platonic poems, like *Alastor* and *Prince Athanase,* are nothing more than Platonic reveries, so congenial to Shelley's temperament.

In the preface to his translation of the *Symposium* Shelley, though he praises Plato's poetry and remarkable intuitions, remarks that his treatises are "stained by puerile sophisms"; furthermore, in his note *On a Passage in Crito,* Shelley gives "arguments which overturn the sophism placed in the mouth of Socrates by Plato."[197] The association of Plato

[193] Julian *Works*, I, 153.

[194] *System of Nature, or The Laws of the Moral and Physical World*, Translated from the French (Philadelphia, 1808), II, 115-117; for Shelley and D'Holbach, see Sen, *Studies in Shelley*, pp. 105-114.

[195] P. J. G. Cabanis, *Rapports du physique et du moral de l'homme*[2] (Paris, 1805), I, 33; cf. Julian *Works*, I, 143; I. J. Kapstein, "Shelley and Cabanis," *PMLA*, LII (1937), 238-243.

[196] *The Works of Voltaire*, Edition de la Pacification (Paris, London, New York, Chicago, 1901), IV, 42; the anti-Platonic tradition in eighteenth-century England (see *MP*, XLI [1943], 103, 106) was possibly influenced by the anti-Platonic tradition in France.

[197] Julian *Works*, VII, 161, 265; cf. "a sophism here," *Notes to Ion, infra,* p. 485.

with sophisms may be an echo of eighteenth-century French criticism of Plato. Though the eighteenth-century thinkers might tolerate Plato the poet, they had very little use for his "dazzling sophisms." Voltaire reflects a typical eighteenth-century attitude toward Plato when he says that "Plato wrote better than he reasoned."[198] In his article on Plato in the *Encyclopédie* Diderot says, "These dialogues so admired by the ancients are today insupportable"; Plato is for him obscure; it is the manner in which he says things rather than the things he says that is of importance.[199] Though Shelley does not share this attitude completely, we find echoes of it in his own work. In the instances in which he is subordinating Plato the thinker to Plato the poet he is reflecting the attitude of the eighteenth century which in embracing Locke's philosophy of sensation had very little sympathy for Plato the philosopher; it is *"l'eloquence, l'enthousiasme . . . les grâces"*[200] of Plato that are important.

Shelley absorbed considerable Platonism from these French eighteenth-century thinkers even though they are often antagonistic to Plato and the quality of their Platonism is impure. The French Encyclopedists, who play an important role in Shelley's early thought, are full of informational Platonism. "Gallica Encyclopedia non obliviscenda," which Shelley wrote in Claire Clairmont's diary for 1814, is only an echo of his enthusiasm for the French Encyclopedists, which he requested from his bookseller in 1812.[201] It is probable that Shelley read Diderot's article on Plato, which gives an excellent exposition of the life of Plato, a brief summary of his thought, and a history of the Platonic tradition as far as the Renaissance. Diderot's article on Plato, which Shorey appraises as "not half bad," is quite enthusiastic about Plato: "Il y a plus à profiter pour un homme de génie dans une page de cet auteur que dans mille volumes de critique."[202] In other articles in the *Encyclopédie* Shelley might have come across Diderot's article on *Nature plastique,* which is an exposition of Cudworth's Platonic conception. In Voltaire's *Dictionnaire philosophique,* which Shelley prescribed for Miss Westbrook in 1811,[203] he would have found a more unsympathetic account of Plato,[204] though it is rich in Platonic information, such as a summary

[198] See Shorey, *op. cit.,* p. 164; cf. Norton Nicholls's reminiscences of Thomas Gray in *Correspondence of Thomas Gray,* ed. Paget Toynbee and Leonard Whibley (Oxford, 1935), III, 1295: What Gray admired in Plato "was not his mystic doctrines which he did not pretend to understand, nor his sophistry, but his excellent sense, sublime morality, elegant style & the perfect dramatic propriety of his dialogues."
[199] *Oeuvres complètes de Diderot* (Paris, 1876), XVI, 317.
[200] *Ibid.,* p. 312.   [201] Julian *Works,* IX, 34.
[202] Diderot, *op. cit.,* XVI, 316.   [203] Julian *Works,* VIII, 93.
[204] *The Works of Voltaire,* XII, 197, 206, 207, 213.

of the *Timaeus*.[205] Of the other works of the Encyclopedists, D'Holbach's *System of Nature*, which Shelley calls "a work of uncommon powers" and wanted to translate,[206] is important for Shelley's early Platonism. Though this treatise contains an anti-Platonic bias, which is reflected in one of the notes to *Queen Mab*,[207] it is a treasure house of important Platonic doctrines.[208] It contains, for example, the doctrine of the harmony of the spheres found in *Queen Mab*, references to the Platonic views and arguments for the immortality of the soul, the notion that philosophy is "a meditation of death," the doctrine of the Universal Spirit, also found in *Queen Mab*, a reference to the ring of Gyges, and the influence of Plato on Christianity as reflected in such terms as "Spirits, intelligent, incorporeal substances, invisible powers, angels, daemons of mysterious virtues, supernatural effects, divine inspiration; innate ideas, etc." Such evidence is sufficient to impress on us the conclusion that Platonism flowed into Shelley's mind even in the most anti-Platonic of his sources, and at a time when Shelley had very little direct knowledge of Plato. The unique thing about the Platonism and anti-Platonism emanating from these French thinkers is that Shelley makes use of both: qua philosopher he uses their anti-Platonism in his notes and the versified philosophy of *Queen Mab;* qua poet he uses Platonic themes like the immortality of the soul, music of the spheres, and the world soul, side by side with his materialism. Thus the Platonism in the materialist philosophers is responsible for nourishing the poet with poetic material, while their anti-Platonic bias and materialistic thesis are responsible for Shelley's lukewarmness to Plato in the interval between his expulsion from Oxford and the Platonic renascence of 1817. That Shelley absorbed and utilized the Platonic tradition during this interval quite unconscious of the contradiction of its presence side by side with materialism is a testament to the power of Platonism.

WIELAND

The Hellenism in the German literature of the eighteenth century[209] is also of importance in the account of Shelley's Platonism. In reading Wieland, Winckelmann, Schlegel, and Goethe, Shelley came in contact

[205] *Ibid.*, XII, 205 ff.
[206] Julian *Works*, VIII, 331-332; IX, 20.
[207] *System of Nature*, II, 115-117, 205 n.
[208] *Ibid.*, I, 59, 70, 94, 206, 252, 259, 271-272; II, 33, 40, 63, 115-117.
[209] See Ernst Maass, *Goethe und die Antike* (Berlin, 1912); E. M. Butler, *The Tyranny of Greece over Germany* (Cambridge, 1935); Franz Schultz, *Klassik und Romantik der Deutschen*. I. Teil: *Die Grundlagen der klassisch-romantischen Literatur* (Stuttgart, 1935); Walther Rehm, *Griechentum und Goethezeit* (Leipzig, 1936); Humphrey Trevelyan, *Goethe and the Greeks* (Cambridge, 1941).

with a rich source of Hellenism. In Wieland especially Shelley found Platonism not so much in the form of Platonic information or philosophical doctrine as in Platonic romance and poetry. One of the main sources of the Platonism found in Shelley's poetry written in the interval of 1813 to 1815, a period in which direct Platonism is at a low ebb if not altogether absent, is Wieland's *Agathon* and *Peregrinus Proteus*. The circumstances in which Shelley came to read the *Agathon* combined with the Platonism in this romance to make an unusual impression on him. The poet was introduced to this highly romantic novel of Platonic Love in the Boinville circle, which he joined in July, 1813. Mrs. Boinville and her attractive, Platonic-minded daughter,[210] Cornelia Turner, offered to Shelley what Hogg has called "a paradise in Bracknell."

In writing of the Platonic atmosphere of this circle, Hogg, who visited Shelley at Bracknell, says:

Wieland's *Agathon* was the leading classic, the textbook, in that university; the work in which all who would graduate were to be examined, which it was necessary to master in order to obtain a degree, which all who ventured to contend for a prize must take up. *Agathon* was read, not in the original, for the German language was not cultivated or understood by the professors, but as *Histoire d'Agathon,* in the French translation of Citizen Pernay. . . . This book was immediately put into the hands of a neophyte. Shelley devoured it eagerly; he was fascinated with it, indeed.[211]

This book was then discussed by the circle with Cornelia Turner acting as the Diotima in the instruction of Platonic Love. The elucidation and expounding of Platonic Love in such discussions arising out of the reading of *Agathon* left their mark on Shelley. "The glowing young Platonic poet" says Hogg, "embraced the elegant and learned fiction with ardour, and accepted it with entire faith, as the testament of Platonic Love."[212] His ardor is further shown by the fact that Shelley appears to have reread this novel with Mary in 1814.

In view of the unusual and intense study of this Platonic novel, and of its association with Cornelia Turner, with whom Shelley fell in love at the time, we can expect some influence on Shelley. Professor White has pointed out the similarities between *Alastor* and *Agathon:*

[210] White, *Shelley*, I, 328-330; cf. Shelley's letter to Hogg from Bracknell, "I have felt myself translated to a paradise, which has nothing of mortality, but its transitoriness" (Julian *Works*, IX, 86); *Harriet and Mary*, ed. W. S. Scott (London, 1944), p. 39.

[211] Hogg, *op. cit.*, II, 144-145. The French translation which Shelley used was *Histoire d'Agathon,* traduction nouvelle et complete, faite, sur la dernière ed. des oeuvres . . . , par l'auteur de *Piétro d'Alby* et *Gianette* [F. D. Pernay], T, 1-3 (Paris: Mardan, 1801); cf. P. Groschwald, *Das Bild des klassischen Altertums im Wielands Agathon* (Giessen, 1914).

[212] Hogg, *op. cit.*, II, 145.

Agathon, like the young poet, is an intense idealist who has suffered persecution. His idealism does not lead him to his death, but in the end he concludes that it went beyond the bounds of true wisdom, though still preferable to materialism—which is Shelley's conclusion in his Preface. Psyche, Agathon's spiritual love, is a person rather than a spirit, but is obviously a personification of Platonic love. In a graphic vision Agathon sees her and follows her in vain, somewhat as Shelley's young poet follows his vision.[213]

Shelley's indebtedness to Wieland includes Platonic phrase as well. Professor White has also pointed out that Wieland's *Agathon* "contains passages on ideal beauty quite suggestive of Shelley's Intellectual Beauty. In the French translation read by Shelley the phrase 'Beauté Intellectuelle' occurs twice."[214]   Furthermore, Shelley's proposal of a *ménage à trois* to Harriet after his elopement with Mary may have been suggested by this novel, in which Agathon and his two former loves, one of a spiritual and the other of a sensual nature, are shown living together in the end in purely Platonic Love.[215]

The influence of this novel extends even further. It may be of interest to note in the *Agathon* a brother-and-sister parallel to the lovers in *Laon and Cythna*. In this novel Agathon, a Platonic idealist, meets Psyche, who, as the name signifies, is the embodiment of Platonic Love. Wieland skilfully has his lovers translate their Platonic Love into a brother-and-sister relationship. Agathon in relating the story of his love for Psyche says:

The name of friendship seemed now insufficient to express what we felt for each other, we agreed that the love which subsists between brother and sister, appeared to be the strongest, and the most pure of all the affections nature hath implanted in us. . . . Accordingly we commenced brother and sister, and continued this connection for some time, interchanging the innocent endearments warranted by those names, without any infringement, in our opinion at least, of the laws of virtue, which we had sworn to observe with the same fidelity, as those of love.[216]

Although the brother-sister motif was pretty much in the air at the time, as Byron's life and poems show, and there is the brother-sister emphasis in Shelley's own life, such as the relationship between Shelley and his sister Elizabeth and Elizabeth Hitchener, whom he called "sister of my soul," the parallel in *Agathon* may be considered as another pos-

[213] White, *Shelley*, I, 701.

[214] *Ibid.*, but *vide infra*, pp. 197-198.

[215] *Ibid.*, I, 349, 701.

[216] *The History of Agathon*, by C. M. Wieland, Translated from the German Original (London, 1773), II, 196-197.

sible source for the brother-and-sister relationship of the Platonic lovers in *Laon and Cythna.*

Besides these possible sources of influence, Shelley absorbed from his reading of the *Agathon* considerable Platonic atmosphere. The novel is a kaleidoscope of Platonism; a collection[217] made at random includes such Platonisms as the "mortification of passions," a picture of the soul based on the myth of the *Phaedrus,* references to Diotima, the Platonic doctrine of madness, the daemons, the *Timaeus,* "heavenly beauty inveloped in a terrestrial veil," and the harmony of the spheres, of the reality of which the Pythagorean sages had persuaded Agathon. The hero's initiation at Delphi into "the holy mystery of the philosophy of *Hermes,* and *Orpheus*" can constitute a major source of Shelley's Neoplatonism. Shelley need not have read Plotinus or other Neoplatonists; he could have absorbed the essence of Neoplatonism from such passages as

I insensibly wrought myself into an enthusiasm: according to the principles of my mysterious philosophy, I expatiated on intellectual love, the love which leads to the contemplation of essential excellence; the love which expands the spiritual wings of the soul, fills it with every virtue, and every perfection; and finally, by its connection with the origin and primary source of all goodness, loses it in an abyss of glory, tranquillity, and felicity, where it is entirely absorbed, and by being annihilated, becomes at the same time deified.[218]

The doctrine of emanation in Plotinus, with its "abyss of glory," the flight of the Lone to the Alone, is all here.

In Wieland's novel Shelley also found considerable Platonic atmosphere and phraseology. The descriptions of Platonic Love are many and varied, all Shelleyan in character:

the excellencies of her mind shone with so much brightness through this charming earthly veil . . . her looks seemed to cast a heavenly light on every object; and her breath to inspire all nature with the spirit of love; . . . the affection he had for this charming creature, was a sympathetic love, a harmony of the heart, a secret union, which cannot be described to those who have not experienced the same. This is, perhaps, the only kind of union, which if it could possibly become general, would be able to give us mortals, some ideas of the connection and happiness of heavenly spirits.[219]

Shelley must have found these too attractive to resist in describing his own loves. The importance of Wieland's *Agathon* for Shelley's Pla-

[217] *Ibid.,* I, 135-136; II, 13, 23, 28, 29, 36, 139, 147, 157-159.
[218] *Ibid.,* II, 178.
[219] *Ibid.,* II, 29 (cf. Shelley's similar use of the "veil" in Ellis's *Shelley Concordance* [*s.v.* veil]), pp. 32, 6.

tonism should not be underestimated. Wieland vitalized the traditional Platonic Love with a highly poetic and romantic Platonism which influenced Shelley's life, thought, and poetry in plot, themes, incidents, and atmosphere.

Wieland's *Peregrinus Proteus*, which appears in Shelley's reading for 1814,[220] is also important for Shelley's Platonism. Like *Agathon* it is permeated with a romantic kind of Platonic Love and Neoplatonism. Peregrinus Proteus is a Pythagorean philosopher, learned in Plato, Orpheus, and the Egyptian Hermes; in his grandfather's library he finds the works of Plato and in particular is attracted to Agathon's song of Love and to Socrates's and Diotima's speeches in the *Symposium*. In his travels Proteus visits Halicarnassus, where he meets Dioklea, the daughter of Apollonius of Tyana. We then have a typical Shelleyan love scene between Proteus and this Platonic priestess who plays melodies for her lover, ending in a hymn to Heavenly Aphrodite which fills his soul with holy feeling. Shelley also found in this novel considerable Neoplatonism with references to the doctrines of the Gnostics, Theurgic Magi, and the mysteries of Hermes Trismegistus.

The reading of *Peregrinus Proteus* and *Agathon* in 1814 marks them as significant sources for Platonic influence on poems like *Alastor* and *Laon and Cythna*. In these novels Shelley found rich Platonic possibilities; he found in their Platonic Love sources for plot, theme, phraseology, and romantic atmosphere. But their great value for Shelley's Platonism consists in the poet's coming in contact with sympathetic material which set on fire his own similar but latent Platonism. Wieland had shown what can be done in a novel with Platonic Love, what plots of adventure and magic and what characters symbolize it best. Shelley followed in Wieland's path, expressing in poetry the yearnings of his own heart for Ideal Beauty; he pursues it in the form of Platonic women who are counterparts of his own soul, who echo his love for poetry and freedom, and hatred of tyranny The cognate Platonism of Wieland and Shelley is seen in their lovers, who have much in common: their intellectual souls shine through the earthly veils of the body beautiful; they sigh, cry, and speak in Platonic rhetoric; they transcend the earthly in Platonic dream reveries. Wieland had shown Shelley the literary possibilities of Platonic Love, but Shelley followed the way in his own fashion.

In a letter from Italy dated April 30, 1818, Shelley writes to Hogg, "I am just reading a novel of Wieland's called 'Aristippus' which I think you would like." Later in the year when he was composing *A Discourse*

[220] White, *Shelley*, II, 540.

on the Manners of the Antient Greeks Relative to the Subject of Love he refers to Wieland as "a very tolerable Pagan" in his "delightful novels."[221] Anything attended with delight for Shelley is worth looking into for possibilities of Platonic influence. The abundant and attractive presentation of Platonism in this novel makes it significant for its possible influence on Shelley's Platonism. In the interval between his departure from England and his arrival at Bagni di Lucca, Shelley had read very little Greek and, as his Journal shows, included no Plato. We can never be sure whether his choice of Plato for translation in July of this year was due to the enthusiasm for Plato found in Wieland's *Aristippus,* which he was reading in the preceding months. The Platonism that Shelley found in *Aristippus* is of considerable magnitude.[222] Aristippus, who is on a visit to Athens, gives in a series of letters a comprehensive portrait of Socrates and Plato. In these letters we have a picture of the Athens in which Socrates lived; we see Socrates and Lais visiting the buildings going up on the Acropolis; we have a vivid picture of his life and discussions with friends and pupils. We have an extensive account of the daemon of Socrates, his irony, inductive reasoning, and definition; finally we have a picture of Socrates's last days with a recapitulation of the arguments about the immortality of the soul as presented in the *Phaedo.* In fact, without having read the *Phaedo,* Shelley could have got its essence from Wieland's novel.

The importance of *Aristippus* for Shelley's Platonism also lies in its restatement of Platonic notions found in the *Symposium* and the *Republic*.[223] Some prominent conceptions in the *Symposium* are attractively presented, such as Aphrodite Pandemos, "double-men," and the Idea of Beauty. Shelley found in this novel, as in Barthélemy's *Travels of Anacharsis,* a summary of the *Republic;* it is so extensive and attractive in presentation that, coupled with the summary in Barthélemy, which he read that summer, it may have stimulated Shelley to read the *Republic* in the original in the next year. To Shelley, who was more sensitive to Platonism presented in a poetic and artistic manner than to the factual and informational Platonism which characterizes so much of the Platonic tradition, Wieland's *Aristippus* attractively presented an intellectual and romantic Platonism.

WINCKELMANN, GOETHE, KANT

Though Wieland stands out as the most Platonic figure in eighteenth-

[221] Julian *Works,* VII, 227; cf. IX, 307.

[222] See *Wieland's Werke,* in Deutsche National-Litteratur edition, IV, 158-159, 134, 109-111, 61, 44, 246 ff.

[223] *Ibid.,* IV, 321, 336, 338-349; V, 199-320.

century German literature, there are several other major figures like Winckelmann and Goethe who may have affected Shelley's Platonism in a very minor way. Winckelmann's *History of Art*, which Shelley read, contains no tangible Platonism, but "noble simplicity and serene greatness." These characteristics of Greek art are the very expression in art of Platonic idealism; Shelley's description of the statues in the Florence galleries shows the influence of this idealism in art. Goethe's *Faust*, which Shelley read with Mr. Gisborne and in part translated, may have added to the Platonic coloration of Shelley's reading. Though Goethe had read the *Symposium, Phaedrus,* and the *Apology,* the Platonic elements in *Faust* are essentially Neoplatonic, like Faust's vision of the macrocosm, and spirit lore, both of which, as Goethe himself observes, were based on Neoplatonism, Hermetism, mysticism, and Cabalism, out of which he built "a world that looked strange enough" and therefore attractive to Shelley.[224]   Finally Kant, whom Shelley read in Born's translation,[225] is not derivatively dependent on Plato. His importance for Shelley's Platonism is that Shelley found in him a Platonic ally in his stress on reason and the categories of the mind.

PLATONISM IN SHELLEY'S CONTEMPORARIES

Though Shelley is the most outstanding Platonist in the Platonic renascence of the Romantic period, he is the recipient of a considerable amount of Platonic influence from his contemporaries who found in Plato a more vital philosophy after what Professor Whitehead has called "the narrow and efficient scheme of scientific concepts" of the preceding

---

[224] *Goethe's Faust*[3], ed. Calvin Thomas (Boston, New York, Chicago, 1912), Part I, Introduction, p. xxviii, note on p. 253. Cf. Elizabeth Ebeling, "A Probable Paracelsian Element in Shelley," *Studies in Philology*, XXXII (1935), 509-510. For Goethe and Shelley, see W. S. Scott, *Shelley at Oxford*, p. 64; P. M. Buck, Jr., "Goethe and Shelley," *University of Wisconsin Studies in Language and Literature*, XXXIV (1932), 84-100. For Goethe and Plato, see Ernst Cassirer, "Goethe und Platon," *Jahresbericht des Philologischen Vereins zu Berlin*, XLVIII (1922), 1-22; Arthur Liebert, "Goethes Platonismus," *Kant-Studien*, XXXVII (1932), 1-48; Ferdinand Günther, "Goethe und Platon," *Die Schonheit*, XVIII (1924), 3, 1-4; Franz Koch, *Goethe und Plotin* (Leipzig, 1925); Elizabeth Rotten, "Goethes Urphänomen und die platonische Idee," *Philosophische Arbeiten* (Giessen, 1913), VIII, 1; Georg Misch, "Goethe, Platon, Kant," *Logos*, V (1915), 276-289; Hermann Reuther, "Platons und Goethes Naturanschauung," *Neue Jahrbücher für Wissenschaft und Jugendbildung*, V (1929), 688-707; *A Bibliography of the Survival of the Classics*, The Warburg Institute, London, 1938, Nos. 1142, 1149.

[225] Cf. *Peter Bell the Third*, Part VI, ll. 61-67; Julian *Works*, IX, 34; the reading of Kant, as shown in the Journal entry for Sept. 1, 1821, shows that there is no foundation to the statement that Shelley "never got to know Kant though he resolved to study him," (René Wellek, *Immanuel Kant in England 1793-1838* [Princeton, 1931], p. 180); for Kant and Plato, see Ottomar Wichmann, *Platon und Kant* (Berlin, 1920); Misch, *op. cit.*; Paul Deussen, *Vedânta, Platon und Kant* (Vienna, 1917); O. Staeckel, *Der Begriff der Idee bei Kant im Verhältniss zu den Ideen bei Platon* (Rostock, 1869).

century. Before taking up the Platonism of the Romantic period, it is
well to consider the Platonic tradition in several older contemporaries
of Shelley who belong to the eighteenth century.

WILLIAM GODWIN

The figure most influential on Shelley's thought is William Godwin.[226] Godwin, like Rousseau and other eighteenth-century thinkers,
was influenced by the Platonic tradition and thus became for Shelley the
source of considerable Platonism. The indirect Platonic tradition influenced Godwin through Alexander Kippis, his tutor at Hoxton, his ration-
alist friend, Richard Price, and his reading of Shaftesbury. We have
an indication of Godwin's attraction to Plato in the character of Mandeville, who says, "I grew enraptured with the virtues and the elevated
minds of antiquity. . . . Socrates and Plato . . . became to me a sort of
gods." In Godwin's *Political Justice,* which became Shelley's philosophical gospel, we have some definite anti-Platonic philosophy in Godwin's premise that "all human knowledge is the result of perception";
Godwin devotes a chapter to refuting the Platonic conception of knowledge as innate or reminiscence. Yet, as has been shown by Professor Priestley in his study of the Platonism in *Political Justice,*[227] the fundamentals
of Godwin's thought are derived from the Platonic rather than the empirical tradition. His doctrine of rational progress, his insistence that politics
is an expression of rational morality, his belief in absolute and eternal
truth all rest ultimately on premises derived from the rationalism of the
Platonic tradition. That this influence was deliberate and conscious is
evident from the fact that Godwin had been reading Plato when his
Political Justice was being planned and started. Shelley also found in
this work many notions which are cognate with or ultimately derived
from the *Republic,* such as Godwin's own acknowledgment of Plato's
Republic as the ultimate source of his attack on property, the perfectibility
of man, the social-contract theory, the inutility of punishment, the equality
of sexes, and the abolition of marriage.[228] These doctrines predisposed
Shelley to the *Republic,* which he called the "greatest repository of important truths of all the works of Plato." A specific illustration of the

---

[226] Cf. Paul Elsner, *Percy Bysshe Shelleys Abhängigkeit von W. Godwins Political Justice* (Berlin, 1906); H. N. Brailsford, *Shelley, Godwin, and Their Circle* (London, 1913);
Amiyakumar Sen, "Godwin and Shelley," *Journal of the Department of Letters of the
University of Calcutta,* XX (1930), 1-123, and *Studies in Shelley* (Calcutta, 1936), pp.
115-242; Droop, *op. cit.,* pp. 104-108; White, *Shelley,* II, index, pp. xxxii-xxxiv.

[227] F. E. L. Priestley, "Platonism in William Godwin's *Political Justice,*" MLQ, IV
(1943), 63-69.

[228] William Godwin, *Enquiry concerning Political Justice*[2] (London, 1796), II, 452
n., 498 ff., 354 ff.; I, 93, 192, 180.

influence of this work on Shelley's Platonism may be seen in the history of the word "ante-natal," which Godwin coined for Plato's doctrine of reminiscence. Shelley became so fond of this Platonic term that he used it four times in his poetry.[229]

Shelley, however, found a more poetic Platonism in Godwin's novel *Mandeville,* which he enthusiastically acclaimed and reviewed. Godwin's picture of two Platonic lovers is but a sample of what caused Shelley's enthusiastic acclaim:

Theirs was not the hot, boiling and furious passion of youth, unacquainted with the refinements of sentiment, and undisciplined in the purest principles of morality and virtue. Their attachment was of the mind; they loved each other for qualities which appeared to them worthy of the most fervent admiration.

Beauty indeed came in for its share: the speaking eye, the ingenuous countenance, the features which corresponded to and fascinatingly expressed the emotions of the soul, and the gracefulness of motion and form, all served to bind and corroborate the feeling; but these held a subordinate place only, while the root of the attachment was nourished in the soul.[230]

Of further interest in this novel is the love of Mandeville for his sister Henrietta, which is symbolic of the Platonic lovers as halves of the same soul, physically incarnated on this earth in the love of a brother for his sister. Henrietta, whose religion is love, speaks in "divine discourses" with her brother, who refers to her as "thou dearest half of my soul," "my heavenly monitress," allusions to Diotima and Aristophanes's speech in the *Symposium.* Shelley was delighted with this Platonic scene, as his review shows: "Henrietta's first appearance to Mandeville at Mandeville House is an occurrence resplendent with the sunrise of life; . . . Henrietta seems at first to be all that a susceptible heart imagines in the object of its earliest passion. We scarcely can see her, she is so beautiful. There is a mist of dazzling loveliness which encircles her, and shuts out from the sight all that is mortal in her transcendent charms."[231] It is obvious that Shelley takes her as the symbol of Platonic Love. The Platonic Love between Mandeville and his sister was highly attractive to Shelley, who already had fashioned his lovers in *Laon and Cythna* in a parallel relationship.

DRUMMOND

Next to Godwin's *Political Justice* Sir William Drummond's *Aca-*

[229] *Political Justice,* I, 36, 367. Cf. *Epipsychidion,* l. 456, *Prince Athanase,* Part I, l. 91, *Peter Bell the Third,* Prol., l. 3, *Sensitive Plant,* l. 167; *vide infra,* p. 226.

[230] William Godwin, *Mandeville* (Philadelphia, 1818), II, 234.

[231] Julian *Works,* VI, 221-222.

demical Questions ranked high in Shelley's admiration, and therefore its Platonic contents are important for a study of Shelley's Platonism.[232] Shelley read this treatise as early as 1812 and refers to it in his notes to *Queen Mab.* In 1813 even Harriet read from it to Hogg; in 1815 when Shelley unpacked his books sent to him from Edinburgh he found the volume missing and wrote to Laing to see if he had mislaid it or added it by mistake to his own library. In the Preface to *Laon and Cythna* he calls it a "volume of very acute and powerful metaphysical criticism"; in *On Life* (1819) he writes, "Perhaps the most clear and vigorous statement of the intellectual system is to be found in Sir William Drummond's *Academical Questions.*" Finally Sir William Drummond himself, who was a friend of Godwin, called on the Shelleys on April 22, 1819.[233]

Drummond's treatise contributed much to the Platonic tradition in Shelley by the large body of Platonism which honeycombs its philosophical views. In discussing the nature of the soul, Drummond says, ". . . surely more sublime, was the Platonic doctrine, which taught the pre-existence of the immaterial soul, and according to which it was supposed, that the spiritual and incarnate effluence of universal mind, gradually awakes to reminiscence and intelligence, after its first slumber has passed in its corporeal prison."[234]   Here Shelley could find as early as 1812 the doctrine of the immortality of the soul presented in a Neoplatonic manner. Drummond's account of the soul is also of interest for Shelley's Platonic daemonology and Neoplatonism. "Mind," says Drummond, "is defined by Plato to be that which is self moved. Plato . . . appears to have believed, that it is contained in a material substance, which he considered as its proper organ. The later Platonists imagined, that the intellectual principle, when it quits the human body, immediately attaches itself to an aerial form, which becomes its vehicle."[235] Shelley could find in this conception of the soul as an "aerial form" suggestions for the various spirits in his poems. Furthermore, we have references in the *Adonais* to "Desires, and Adorations,/Wingèd Persua-

---

[232] Cf. G. S. Brett, "Shelley's Relation to Berkeley and Drummond," *Studies in English,* by Members of University College, Toronto (Oxford, 1931), pp. 170-202; H. A. G. Liedtke, *Shelley-durch Berkeley und Drummond beeinflusst?* (Greifswald, 1933); H. N. Fairchild, *The Romantic Quest* (New York, 1931), pp. 379-386, which deals with Drummond's influence on Shelley's transcendentalism.

[233] Julian *Works,* I, 242, 150-151; Hogg, *op. cit.,* II, 3; Julian *Works,* VI, 195; IX, 120; White, *Shelley,* II, 89. An echo of Drummond's visit with Shelley may be seen in *Peter Bell the Third,* Part VI, l. 75.

[234] *Academical Questions,* By the Right Honourable William Drummond (London, 1805), I, 26-27.

[235] *Ibid.,* I, 171, 173.

sions and veiled Destinies."[236] Though this passage shows the direct
influence of Moschus's lament for Bion, the root of this notion lies partly
in the Neoplatonic doctrine of Dionysius the Areopagite, whose work
On the Heavenly Hierarchy has had a great influence on the Platonic
tradition. Shelley found a reference to this doctrine in Drummond:

> Philosophers themselves have not disdained to employ under other names the
> useful machinery supplied by vulgar creeds. Genii, Daemons, and younger
> Gods, were beings whose existence was acknowledged by the Platonists;
> and the appellations only of these beings have been changed, by other sectaries
> who speak of Powers, Dominions, and Thrones. But the belief in the inter-
> ference of Deities and Daemons in human concerns, and in the order of
> nature, was gradually rejected, as the experience of men increased, and as their
> knowledge in physics extended.[237]

Yet Shelley, no less than Coleridge, made use of these doctrines in his
poetry. The importance of this summary statement of the doctrine in
Drummond lies in bringing to Shelley's notice at an early period in his
creative life a doctrine rich in poetic possibilities.

In a dialogue in this treatise between Hylus, Theophilus, and Eugenius we find a compendium of the philosophic views of the pre-
Socratics, Plato, Aristotle, and the subsequent schools of Greek philosophy. We find in Hylus's account several Platonic doctrines which may
have bearing on Shelley's Platonism. He refers to "the ancient dogma, of
the world's being a sentient and animated being (Κόσμος οὐσία ἔμψυχος
καὶ αἰσθητική),"[238] a doctrine which is found in *Queen Mab*. But of
greater significance for a possible source in Shelley is Hylus's discussion
of the doctrine of the One and Many. "Parmenides," he says, "by no
means understood the corporeal world, as Cudworth has truly observed,
when he spoke of ἓν τὸ πᾶν *One, that is all*, which he also called im-
moveable and indivisible."[239] In the passage which follows with its
long excerpt from Simplicius we find an excellent illustration of the
transmission of indirect Platonism. Through a series of refractions the
doctrine of the One and the Many could have reached Shelley through
an author whom he read and admired. Shelley came in contact with
the doctrine as early as 1812; it could have remained latent in his mind,
stimulated by other echoes of it and a possible rereading of Drummond's
treatise in 1819 as the result of Drummond's personal call on Shelley,

---

[236] *Adonais*, ll. 109-110; cf. Shorey, *op. cit.*, p. 41.

[237] Drummond, *op. cit.*, I, 176; cf. Dante's *Paradiso*, XXVIII, 121 ff.; Tillyard, *The
Elizabethan World Picture*, pp. 37-47.

[238] Drummond, *op. cit.*, I, 237.   [239] *Ibid.*, I, 241.

until it found poetic expression in *Adonais*. This passage reveals at the same time how Platonism and Neoplatonism are inextricably fused in the Platonic tradition, and how once more Shelley could absorb the essence of Neoplatonism without being a student of the direct sources of Neoplatonism.

Shelley also found many other Platonic doctrines in this treatise, such as "objects of sense are in a perpetual state of change and progression."[240] An example of their use by Shelley is found in *On the Devil and Devils*. He speaks of "The refined speculations respecting the existence of external objects, by which the idea of matter is suggested, to which Plato has the merit of first having directed the attention of the thinking part of mankind. . . ."[241] The source of this statement can be found in the first sentence of the fourth chapter, where Drummond writes: "Plato, in speaking of the primary matter, from which modern philosophers have borrowed their doctrine concerning material substance, observes, *that it is a question dubiously to be understood, and difficult to be comprehended.*"[242]

Shelley's Platonism could have been enriched by this treatise not only by the magnitude of direct Platonism but also by considerable indirect Platonism in modern authors. He did not, as far as we know, read Abraham Tucker's *Light of Nature Pursued*, which is veined with Platonism.[243] Drummond reflects the Platonism in this treatise through a summary and through quotations such as "our being pent up in walls of flesh which cut off our communications with the blessed spirits, and shut us out from all participation in their lights and their joys."[244] Shelley could also find refractions of the Platonic tradition in Drummond's account of Leibniz's doctrine of pre-established harmony and monads, in "the celebrated doctrine of metempsychosis," in a long quotation from Sextus Empiricus on Pythagoras, and in such echoes of the *Republic* as "The supreme being cannot consistently be supposed to be the author of any thing, which is not good."[245] Finally in Drummond's account of Kant, Shelley could find Kant's passage on Plato poetically attractive: "sic quondam Plato, relicto mundo sensibili, quo tam arctis inclusam carceribus intelligentiam videbat, idearum tanquam pinnis in inani intelligentiae purae spatio periclitabatur; velut columba levis quae libero volatu, quem reluctantem sentit, aëra secans, longe secum actum

---

[240] *Ibid.*, I, 262; cf. *ibid.*, I, 90. [241] Julian *Works*, VII, 88.
[242] Drummond, *op. cit.*, I, 41. [243] Cf. Shorey, *op. cit.*, p. 215.
[244] Drummond, *op. cit.*, I, 313.
[245] *Ibid.*, I, 321 ff., 330-332, 347, 350; for Platonism in Leibniz, see Joseph Politella, *Platonism, Aristotelianism, and Cabalism in the Philosophy of Leibniz* (Philadelphia, 1938).

iri praeclarius in spatio ab omni aere vacuo existimet."[246] Shelley could hardly fail to notice the Platonic affinities of this philosopher, of whom Drummond said, ". . . he quits the prisons of experience; he studies the architecture of pure reason; he sees visions, traverses and measures the island of intelligence."[247] It was possibly Drummond's enthusiasm that made Shelley send in 1812 for a Latin translation of Kant.[248] Drummond may be looked upon as one of the sources of Shelley's Platonism; he served as a magnet to draw Shelley away from materialism to Plato, and it may well be that the ubiquitous presence of Platonism in this treatise was an incentive for Shelley to read Plato directly. It is a case of being attracted to the beauty of the original through its suggestive shadows in Drummond and other Platonic thinkers.

ROBERT FORSYTH

A minor philosopher from whom Shelley may have gleaned Platonism is Robert Forsyth, whose *Principles of Moral Science* he probably read, for in the preface to *Prometheus Unbound* he says, "I have what a Scotch philosopher characteristically terms, 'a passion for reforming the world'; what passion incited him to write and publish his book, he omits to explain."[249] Besides finding this phrase used as the title of the sixteenth chapter, Shelley would have met with some essential elements of Platonism in this treatise. He would find in it Plato's doctrine of the three parts of the soul stated and explained; he would meet once more with the Platonic conception of "certain uncreated essences of things, which existed from all eternity in the Divine Mind, and that these essences are the objects of thought"; he would find the Platonic doctrine of imitation of God; and finally in the Platonic myth, "Vision of Hystaspes," he would find, besides a Platonic revery, another instance of the phrase "Intellectual Beauty."[250] These rivulets of Platonism poured into the ever-increasing stream of Shelley's indirect Platonism.[251]

SYDNEY OWENSON

Another of the minor contemporary figures who influenced Shelley's Platonism is Sydney Owenson (Lady Morgan), whose novel *The Missionary* (1811) Shelley read and admired. Professor White has pointed

---

[246] Drummond, *op. cit.,* I, 369-370 (Born's translation).

[247] *Ibid.,* pp. 380-381.　　　　　[248] Julian *Works,* IX, 34.

[249] *Ibid.,* II, 174; cf. H. B. Forman, *The Shelley Notebooks* (St. Louis, Boston, 1911) I, 10.

[250] Robert Forsyth, *The Principles of Moral Science* (Edinburgh, 1805), pp. 48, 50, 119, 435, 513-514.

[251] For some additional Platonic influence in another minor figure, George Ensor, see White, *Shelley,* I, 624-626.

out the possible influence of this novel on *Alastor*. This tale, like *Alastor*, "is the story of a priest who tries to lead a life of isolated high idealism, who forsakes this way of life to follow Ideal Beauty in the form of a beautiful priestess ('the divine Luxima,' as Shelley called her), and thereby comes to ruin."[252] This novel, along with those of Wieland, Rousseau, and Godwin, must have added to the attractiveness of Platonic Love and Ideal Beauty as a theme for poetry. Shelley was excited by it as he was with the novels of Wieland and Godwin. He writes to Hogg: "Luxima, the Indian, is an angel. What a pity that we cannot incorporate these creations of fancy; the very thoughts of them thrill the soul! Since I have read this book, I have read no other."[253] Such ecstasy is only another testimony to Shelley's sensitivity to romantic presentation of Platonic women and Ideal Beauty.

SOUTHEY

Shelley's imagination relished not only this Indian tale but also Southey's *Curse of Kehama*, which he described to Elizabeth Hitchener in 1811 as "my most favourite poem."[254] The influence of this Indian tale on *Queen Mab* has been noted.[255] It remains now to point out several passages of possible significance for Shelley's Platonism. In its Hindu background there are many elements in common with the Platonic tradition, such as the transmigration of souls, the Good and Evil Spirits which find analogy in the *Timaeus* and *Laws,* the symbolism of Light and Darkness, and the Charioteer ascending the empyrean, which are also found in Plato.[256] These cognate, if not derivative, elements of Platonism are also found in variant forms in Shelley's poetry. The poem also contains many passages which served to suggest Platonism as a theme of poetry for Shelley. The essence of Platonic Love finds one more echo in the following lines, which Shelley quoted to Elizabeth Hitchener in a letter dated November 26, 1811:

> They sin who tell us Love can die.
> With life all other passions fly,
> All others are but vanity.
> In Heaven Ambition cannot dwell,
> Nor Avarice in the vaults of Hell;
> Earthly these passions of the Earth,

---

[252] *Ibid.,* I, 700.

[253] Julian *Works,* VIII, 117; cf. *ibid.,* VIII, 112.

[254] *Ibid.,* VIII, 103.

[255] Peck, *op. cit.,* I, 303-324.

[256] *Kehama,* XXII, 3, 14; *The Poetical Works of Robert Southey* (London, 1838), VIII, 217, 235-236 nn.

> They perish where they have their birth;
> But Love is indestructible.
> Its holy flame for ever burneth,
> From Heaven it came, to Heaven returneth;
> Too oft on Earth a troubled guest,
> At times deceived, at times opprest,
> It here is tried and purified,
> Then hath in Heaven its perfect rest.[257]

A Platonic conception of the soul is also found in

> The immortal Powers, who see
> Through the poor wrappings of mortality,
> Behold the soul, the beautiful soul, within,
> Exempt from age and waiting maladies,
> And undeform'd, while pure and free from sin.[258]

A Platonic maid is sketched and, as T. E. Lawrence says of Homer's
Nausicaä, "then fades unused" in lines like

> Sure if the mortal Maiden had not fed
> On heavenly food, and long been strengthened
> With heavenly converse for such end vouchsafed,
> Her human heart had fail'd, and she had died
> Beneath the horrors of this aweful hour.
> But Heaven supplied a power
> Beyond her earthly nature, to the measure
> Of need infusing strength.[259]

These examples show that there is in Southey a quantity of Platonism
great enough to make him a potential source of Platonic influence on
Shelley's early poems like *Queen Mab*. Platonic imagery like "the Veil
of Separation," the Demon Minister, and

> The many-coloured domes
> Yet wore one dusky hue

show possible Platonic influence of great value.[260] Shelley may have
stored this last image in his subconscious mind, where it stayed until
the composition of *Adonais*, when, fertilized by Petrarch's *Triumphs* and
instances of the dome imagery in Romantic poetry, it came out of the
alembic of his mind as a phrase symbolic of the Platonic One and

[257] *Kehama*, X, 10.
[258] *Ibid.*, XIX, 3; cf. XXI, 6, and *Poetical Works*, VIII, 223-224 nn.
[259] *Kehama*, XXIII, 8.
[260] *Thalaba*, III, 11; II, 14; V, 9.

Many.[261] Shelley's possible transmutation of this phrase into Platonic imagery is an example of his power to reshape his sources of ideas and phrases.

In the *Biographia Literaria* Coleridge, in speaking of his education, says, ". . . no models of past times, however perfect, can have the same vivid effect on the youthful mind, as the productions of contemporary genius." As Shelley shows in the preface to *Prometheus Unbound,* he derives from the latter to no less extent than the former:

It is impossible that any one who inhabits the same age with such writers as those who stand in the foremost rank of our own, can conscientiously assure himself that his language and tone of thought may not have been modified by the study of the production of those extraordinary intellects. . . . There is a similarity between Homer and Hesiod, between Aeschylus and Euripides, between Virgil and Horace, between Dante and Petrarch, between Shakespeare and Fletcher, between Dryden and Pope; each age has a generic resemblance under which their distinctions are arranged. If this similarity be the result of imitation, I am willing to confess that I have imitated.

The generic resemblance between Shelley, Coleridge, and Wordsworth has been expressed by grouping them as Romantic poets. But there is also another generic resemblance to be noted. This is the generic resemblance of their Platonism. Among the contemporaries of Shelley, Coleridge and Wordsworth are therefore of prime importance for Shelley's Platonism. Shelley read and admired the poetry of these older contemporaries, and from them he received considerable poetic Platonism.

A study of the origins of the Romantic period shows a revolt from what Whitehead has called the "materialistic mechanism of science"; it was a revolt of "the aesthetic intuitions of mankind," most vividly expressed in the poetry of the Romantic poets, against a philosophy of materialism.[262] As the Renaissance found in Platonism a more satisfying philosophy than scholasticism, so Romanticism found in Platonism a philosophy more expressive of its spirit than the materialistic mechanism of eighteenth-century science and philosophy. Platonism has always been the most satisfying of the philosophies for religious, moral, and poetic minds. The Romantic poets, with the exception of Coleridge, were not

---

[261] Cf. Dante, *Paradiso,* XXIX, 142 ff.; for a definitive study of the symbolism of the dome in Romantic poetry, see G. Wilson Knight, *The Starlit Dome* (London, 1941); cf. also White, *Shelley,* II, 294, 630-631; Karl Lehman, "The Dome of Heaven," *Art Bulletin,* XXVII (1945), 1-27.

[262] A. N. Whitehead, *Science and the Modern World* (New York, 1925), pp. 105-133; cf. J. H. Randall, Jr., *The Making of the Modern Mind*[2] (Boston, New York, 1940), pp. 417-421.

original philosophers; they gravitated therefore to Platonism as the philosophy most compatible with their intuitions. They found in it elements capable of poetic re-creation, such as the cosmology of the Platonic tradition, its dramatis personae of spirits between man and nature and between man and god, its pantheism, transcendentalism, and the world soul immanent in the world of nature, speaking to the sensitive poet, the hierophant of society, appearing to him as

> Ye Presences of Nature in the sky
> And on the earth! Ye Visions of the hills!
> And Souls of lonely places![263]

Romanticism, by adding to this derivative and cognate Platonism its own essential characteristics, created a Platonism in its own image; it was an eclectic Platonism adapted to the needs of a new poetic creed.[264] In the Platonism of his Romantic contemporaries Shelley found a philosophy already molded for the romantic mind. The development which he gave to it is only the "specific distinction" of a generic resemblance of Romantic Platonism.

COLERIDGE

Coleridge is the hierophant of Romantic Platonism; his *Biographia Literaria* and poems, which Shelley read, are important sources of Shelley's Platonism. In the *Biographia Literaria* Coleridge gives a brief account of his early study of Platonism which is an index of all his Platonism. "The early study," he says, "of Plato and of Plotinus, with the commentaries and the THEOLOGIA PLATONICA of the illustrious Florentine [Ficino]; of Proclus, and Gemistius Pletho . . . had all contributed to prepare my mind for the reception and welcoming of the *Cogito quia Sum, et Sum quia Cogito*."[265] We find considerable evidence for this statement. In the notebook of Coleridge, Professor Lowes has noted that there "stand, among other entries, excerpts from the Greek text of the *Phaedo* and the *Republic*: a phrase which contains the core of the Platonic doctrine of pre-existence, and the beginning of the great Parable of the Cave. And the passage from the *Republic* is slipped in between a reference to Aristotle's *Metaphysics* and a direct quotation from it. And the citation from the *Phaedo* and the reference to the *Metaphysics* are separated by a sentence from Plotinus."[266] The effect of this philosophy is further seen in

[263] *The Prelude*, I, 464-466.

[264] See H. N. Fairchild, "The Romantic Movement in England," in "Romanticism: A Symposium," *PMLA*, LV (1940), 20, 22.

[265] *The Complete Works of Samuel Taylor Coleridge*, ed. William Greenough Shedd (New York, 1853), III, 249.

[266] J. L. Lowes, *The Road to Xanadu* (Boston and New York, 1927), p. 29.

his letter to Thelwall dated December 31, 1796: "I love Plato, his dear, *gorgeous* nonsense."[267]   In another letter written on November 19, 1796, we get a clear picture of the heavy doses of Neoplatonism that he was taking: "Metaphysics and poetry and 'facts of mind,' that is, accounts of all the strange phantasms that ever possessed 'your philosophy'; dreamers, from Thoth the Egyptian to Taylor the English Pagan, are my darling studies.   In short, . . . I am almost always reading."[268]   His "darling studies" are illustrated in a postscript to this letter which is, as Lowes calls it, "a bead-roll of Coleridge's 'dreamers.'"   Coleridge asks Thelwall to buy for him, from booksellers' catalogues, "Iamblichus, Proclus, Prophyrius, etc., one shilling and sixpence, one little volume," and Juliani Opera, Iamblichus de Mysteriis, Sidonius Apollinaris, and Ficino's translation of Plotinus.[269]   Furthermore, in a memorandum of 1807 we find him going to Cuthill's shop to "hunt for Proclus."[270] Charles Lamb, who in 1796 and 1814 received "pressing instructions from Coleridge to pick up Plutarch and Porphyry and Proclus," gives us a picture of Coleridge at Christ's Hospital as "the young Mirandula . . . unfolding in [his] deep and sweet intonations the mysteries of Iamblichus or Plotinus."[271]   The list of Coleridge's readings is significant of the close affinities of the Romantic mind to Neoplatonism. Coleridge knew both Plato and Neoplatonism, but he found the latter more congenial.   Its dreams and "dreamers," which include Thomas Taylor, also read by Shelley, supplied the poet with Neoplatonic material. We have no evidence for Shelley's reading of any of the Neoplatonic writers who figure in Coleridge's list of reading; yet there is a considerable amount of Neoplatonism in Shelley.   A great deal of this reached Shelley through the Platonic tradition in his readings, but a more concentrated and attractive amount reached him through his reading of Coleridge's *Biographia Literaria* and poems which reflect Neoplatonism.[272]

Shelley read the *Biographia Literaria* in 1817, at the threshold of his great creative period. A survey, therefore, of the quality and variety of the Platonism in this book may show us the possible sources of some of Shelley's Platonism.   There is no definite development of a Platonic thesis in *Biographia Literaria,* but it contains many Platonic notions of interest for Shelley's Platonism.   Suggestive as a possible source of

---

[267] *Letters of Coleridge,* ed. E. H. Coleridge (London, 1895), I, 211.
[268] *Ibid.,* I, 181.   [269] Lowes, *op. cit.,* p. 231.
[270] *Ibid.,* p. 232.   [271] *Ibid.,* p. 232.
[272] Droop, *op. cit.,* pp. 70-72; White, *Shelley,* II, index, p. xix.

Shelley's expression of "one Spirit's plastic stress" in *Adonais* is Coleridge's Neoplatonic doctrine of the imagination as a plastic power which he calls "esemplastic," a word which he coined from εἰς ἓν πλάττειν, "to shape into one."[273]   This philosophic imagination, which he later defines in a Plotinian way as "a repetition in the finite mind of the eternal act of creation in the infinite I AM,"[274] takes the place of dialectic or λόγος in the Platonism of both Coleridge and Shelley; the home which Coleridge has prepared for this imagination is a philosophical mysticism where "substances were thinned away into shadows, while everywhere shadows were deepened into substances."[275]   This philosophic imagination is akin to the intuitive knowledge which, says Coleridge (quoting Plotinus), "we ought not to pursue with a view of detecting its secret source, but to watch in quiet till it suddenly shines upon us; preparing ourselves for the blessed spectacle as the eye waits patiently for the rising sun."[276]   Shelleyan Platonism has much in common with the character of this philosophic imagination.   The realm in which this philosophic imagination of Coleridge plays is the entire keyboard of the Platonic tradition.   Everywhere in his treatise Coleridge gives reflections of his vast and varied reading in Plato and Neoplatonism. In a learned footnote he gives a history of the word *idea,* the origin of the word, then its adoption by Plato, whose Ideas he describes as "mysterious powers, living, seminal, formative, and exempt from time."[277] The adjective *mysterious* at once clothes them with the magic veil of poetry, and they mean to the poet something more than the logically grasped essence of Plato.   This atmosphere of Platonism pervades other Platonic doctrines.   Pythagoras with his number and Plato by his geometric discipline and symbols free us from the bondage of the sensuous and help us see the invisible things which are not the object of vision. This education of the soul through the *"body celestial* instead of *the body terrestrial"*[278] is set in an atmosphere of "mysterious hieroglyphics" (a characteristic phrase of Shelley) and in the philosophic setting of Plotinian emanation where not a single act or thought is "lost from that living chain of causes, with all the links of which, conscious or unconscious, the free will, our only absolute Self, is co-extensive and co-present."[279]   Coleridge, even in his metaphysical abstractions, manages occasionally to interject poetical mysticism that could not fail to attract

[273] *Coleridge's Works,* III, 272, 356 ff.; cf. P. L. Carver, "The Evolution of the Term 'Esemplastic,' " *MLR,* XXIV (1929), 329-331.

[274] *Coleridge's Works,* III, 363.   [275] *Ibid.,* III, 361.

[276] *Ibid.,* III, 328.   [277] *Ibid.,* III, 213.

[278] *Ibid.,* III, 230.   [279] *Ibid.,* III, 231.

Shelley's mental eye, which was sensitive to such philosophical statements. "It is profanation," says Coleridge, "to speak of these mysteries [and here he quotes in the Greek and translates the following passage from Plotinus:] 'to those to whose imagination it has never been presented, how beautiful is the countenance of justice and wisdom; and that neither the morning nor the evening star are so fair. For in order to direct the view aright, it behooves that the beholder should have made himself congenerous and similar to the object beheld. Never could the eye have beheld the sun, had not its own essence been soli-form' (i.e. *pre-configured to light by a similarity of essence with that of light*) 'neither can a soul not beautiful attain to an intuition of beauty.' "[280]

In the *Biographia Literaria* Shelley had another opportunity to become acquainted with an important Platonic doctrine found in the *Adonais*. The deeper we go into the nature of things, Coleridge points out, the more truth we discover in the doctrines of "the harmonies or numbers, the prototypes and ideas, to which the Pythagoreans and Platonists reduced all things; the *ONE* and *ALL* of Parmenides and Plotinus, without Spinozism." This doctrine is amplified in a note where Coleridge cites and comments upon three lines of Synesius's Third Hymn, which he had translated along with the rest before his fifteenth year:

Ἐν καὶ Πάντα (taken by itself) is *Spinozism*
Ἐν δ' Ἀπάντων—a mere *Anima Mundi*
Ἐν τε πρὸ πάντων—is mechanical Theism.

But unite all three, and the result is the Theism of St. Paul and Christianity.[281]

In the Platonic potpourri of this work Shelley would meet with other Platonisms, such as the example of the ignorant slave boy in the *Meno*, the doctrine of Γνῶθι σεαυτόν. Here Plato is considered to be a poet writing in prose, a view which Shelley shared. Transcendental Idealism, a cognate of the Platonic tradition in German philosophy, is analyzed and discussed.[282] In Coleridge, Shelley found a philosopher who was so steeped in Platonism that he intended to develop a Logosophia or "Dynamic Philosophy," which is "no other than the system of Pythagoras and of Plato revived and purified from impure mixtures."[283] The *Bio-*

---

[280] *Ibid.*, III, 231.

[281] *Ibid.*, III, 331 (accents as in the 1853 edition); for the history of the Platonic formula ἓν τὸ πᾶν in the Neoplatonic and Hermetic writings, see Eduard Norden, *Agnostos Theos* (Leipzig, 1913), pp. 248-250.

[282] *Coleridge's Works*, III, 334, 353, 373, 266.

[283] *Ibid.*, p. 342.

graphia Literaria may be rightly viewed as one of the most richly veined mines of Shelley's Platonism and Neoplatonism.

Coleridge, moreover, transmuted a considerable amount of this Platonism into his poetry. Shelley was fond of Coleridge's poetry, and Peacock says that he devotedly admired Coleridge, who had great influence on his style and imagination. He ordered Coleridge's poems in December, 1812. The Journal attests that he read the *Ancient Mariner* on September 15 and October 5, 1814, and that he read it again on February 22, 1821; Coleridge's Poems appear among the volumes read by Shelley in 1815; in 1816 he read *Christabel,* and on July 13, 1817, he placed an immediate order with his bookseller for *Sibylline Leaves.* It is natural, therefore, that Shelley, through this reading, should have come in contact with the Platonism in these poems. The extent to which the poems of Coleridge influenced Shelley in a tangible way has been pointed out by Bradley.[284] It remains to point out some important instances which may have affected Shelley's Platonism.

In *The Rime of the Ancient Mariner,* which Shelley admired, Coleridge says in a gloss: "A Spirit had followed them; one of the invisible inhabitants of this planet, neither departed souls nor angels; concerning whom the learned Jew, Josephus, and the Platonic Constantinopolitan, Michael Psellus, may be consulted. They are very numerous, and there is no climate or element without one or more."[285] Professor Lowes has penetratingly traced the Neoplatonic source of this Daemon in Coleridge's readings to a volume edited by Ficino which contained Iamblichus's *De mysteriis Aegyptiorum, Chaldaeorum, Assyriorum;* Proclus's *In Platonicum Alcibiadem de anima, atque daemone;* Porphyrius's *De divinis atque daemonibus;* Psellus's *De daemonibus;* and the *Pimander* and *Asclepius* of Hermes Trismegistus.[286] The Neoplatonic development of the intermediaries between gods and men spread from philosophy and religion to poetry, finally shaping up as Coleridge's Daemon.[287] Shelley also makes considerable use of the daemon of Greek philosophy. He revised part of *Queen Mab* and later published it under the title *The Daemon of the World;* in *Alastor, or the Spirit of Solitude* the Spirit of Solitude is in the same Platonic tradition; the *Prometheus Unbound* is filled with such spirits as Demogorgon, the Spirit of the Earth, the Moon, and Hours. It cannot be claimed that Shelley derived all this from Coleridge,

[284] A. C. Bradley, "Coleridge-Echoes in Shelley's Poems," *A Miscellany* (New York, 1929), pp. 171-176.
[285] *The Rime of the Ancient Mariner,* gloss to ll. 131-138.
[286] Lowes, *op. cit.,* pp. 234-241.
[287] For daemonology, see references cited *supra,* p. 186.

for daemonology forms part of the Platonic tradition in every age, but it may be said that Shelley found in Coleridge an appealing use of the Neoplatonic daemon.

Of interest for a possible source of "the Spirit's plastic stress" in *Adonais* is the *Sonnet to Rev. W. L. Bowles*. In the second version of it Coleridge describes "a strange mysterious Pleasure" brooding over mind

> As the great SPIRIT erst with plastic sweep
> Mov'd in the darkness of the unform'd deep.

Here and in *The Eolian Harp*:

> And what if all of animated nature
> Be but organic Harps diversely fram'd,
> That tremble into thought, as o'er them sweeps
> Plastic and vast, one intellectual breeze,
> At once the Soul of each, and God of all?[288]

we have a Neoplatonic echo of Cudworth's theory of plastic Nature. Though we have seen that this theme is found in various places in Shelley's reading, he would more likely have been influenced by such a poetic version as is found in Coleridge's and Wordsworth's poetry.

The outstanding Platonic poem in Coleridge is *Religious Musings;* it contains both general Platonism, such as nature which

> Imaged the supreme beauty uncreate,

and derivative Neoplatonism like

> . . . Holy with power
> He on the thought-benighted Sceptic beamed
> Manifest Godhead, melting into day
> What floating mists of dark idolatry
> Broke and misshaped the omnipresent Sire.

Coleridge himself points out in a footnote that these lines are derived from "Damas. De Myst. Aegypt. Τὸ Νοητὸν διῃρήκασιν εἰς πολλῶν Θεῶν ἰδιότητας *(Men have split up the Intelligible One into the peculiar attributes of Gods many)*."[289]

This poem is filled with Christianized Platonism which is reflected in lines like

> And blest are they,
> Who in this fleshly World . . .

---

[288] *The Eolian Harp*, ll. 44-48; cf. *Religious Musings*, ll. 246-247, 402-407, for a similar poetic conception.

[289] *Religious Musings*, ll. 21, 29-33.

Adore with steadfast unpresuming gaze
Him Nature's essence, mind, and energy!
And gazing, trembling, patiently ascend
Treading beneath their feet all visible things
As steps, that upward to their Father's throne
Lead gradual—else nor glorified nor loved.
They nor contempt embosom nor revenge:
For they dare know of what may seem deform
The Supreme Fair sole operant: in whose sight
All things are pure, his strong controlling love
Alike from all educing perfect good.[290]

In another section of the poem we have a poetic transcription of the Platonic use of the sensory world as an aid in the ascent of the soul to a life of contemplation. Coleridge speaks of

. . . the inventive arts, that nursed the soul
To forms of beauty, and by sensual wants
Unsensualized the mind, which in the means
Learnt to forget the grossness of the end,
But pleasured with its own activity.[291]

After telling the Soul that

Life is a vision shadowy of Truth[292]

Coleridge invokes the Neoplatonic

Contemplant Spirits! ye that hover o'er
With untired gaze the immeasurable fount
Ebullient with creative Deity!
And ye of plastic power, that interfused
Roll through the grosser and material mass
In organizing surge! Holies of God!
(And what if Monads of the infinite mind?)
I haply journeying my immortal course
Shall sometime join with your mystic choir![293]

Finally the poem ends with Coleridge's desire to soar aloft to a Platonic world and

. . . breathe the empyreal air
Of Love, omnific, omnipresent Love.[294]

[290] *Ibid.*, ll. 45-58; cf. ll. 105-110.
[291] *Ibid.*, ll. 208-212.
[292] *Ibid.*, ll. 396.
[293] *Ibid.*, ll. 402-410.
[294] *Ibid.*, ll. 414-415.

If Coleridge did nothing else for Shelley in this poem, he showed him how Platonism makes good philosophic poetry.

Another important Platonic poem is *The Destiny of Nations,* which Shelley read in *Sibylline Leaves,* ordered in 1817. Coleridge here defines Freedom as the use of the power which God gave.

> . . . him First, him Last to view
> Through meaner powers and secondary things
> Effulgent, as through clouds that veil his blaze.
> For all that meets the bodily sense I deem
> Symbolical, one mighty alphabet
> For infant minds; and we in this low world
> Placed with our backs to bright Reality,
> That we may learn with young unwounded ken
> The substance from its shadow. Infinite Love,
> Whose latence is the plenitude of All,
> Thou with retracted beams, and self-eclipse
> Veiling, revealest thine eternal Sun.
>
> But some there are who deem themselves most free
> When they within this gross and visible sphere
> Chain down the wingéd thought, scoffing ascent. . . .[295]

In these lines Coleridge transmutes into good poetry the Myth of the Cave and the philosophic doctrine of the fifth, sixth, and seventh books of the *Republic,* which, as his notebook shows, he had read.

All these direct[296] and indirect echoes of Plato and the Platonic tradition show that Shelley found in Coleridge's prose and poetry the essence of Platonism. There are, as has been shown, some parallels between Shelley and Coleridge's Platonic passages; it may be that Coleridge influenced Shelley directly. But if that is not demonstrable, and it cannot be, we may include Coleridge as a source in which Shelley could find inspiration for Platonic poetry.

WORDSWORTH

Wordsworth, in an even greater degree than Coleridge, is an outstanding proof of Shelley's belief that a writer is profoundly influenced by the foremost poets of his age. Scholars have traced the influence of Wordsworth on Shelley's thought and style, have shown that such poems as *Alastor, Mont Blanc,* and others are full of Wordsworthian echoes

---

[295] *The Destiny of Nations,* ll. 15-29; cf. *This Lime-Tree Bower My Prison,* ll. 40-43, and *Frost at Midnight,* ll. 58-64.

[296] See also *Sonnet: Composed on a Journey Homeward; the Author having received Intelligence of the Birth of a Son, Sept. 20, 1796.*

in both ideas and phraseology.[297]   This influence is to be connected with Shelley's reading and admiration of the poet.[298]   Shelley's interest in Wordsworth is first reflected in an order to his bookseller in December, 1812, for "Wordsworth's Poems, 4 vols." No doubt these volumes were the *Lyrical Ballads* and *Poems* (1807), each issued in two volumes and comprising the poetry of Wordsworth's best decade, 1797 to 1807.[299] Wordsworth's poems are found in Shelley's reading for 1815;[300] immediately following the publication of *The Excursion* in August, 1814, we find Shelley reading it with Mary in September, 1814; this poem also appears on Shelley's list of reading for 1815.   The immediate effect of this reading of Wordsworth is seen in reflections of Shelley's enthusiasm by Byron, who said that Shelley "dosed" him with Wordsworth; and by Peacock, who records a conversation about Wordsworth's poetry.[301] The importance of Wordsworth for Shelley's Platonism is considerable; Wordsworth forms a part of a large group of influences working to draw Shelley away from materialistic thinking to a Platonic philosophy of idealism and immortality of the soul; he is a "carrier" of Platonism; and finally, in his poetry Shelley found how Platonism is excellent material for poetic thought.

Wordsworth, next to Spenser, Milton, and Coleridge, is one of the great Platonic poets in English poetry.   Like Shelley, he is a direct, indirect, and natural Platonist.   Wordsworth's knowledge of Plato must date from his school days at Hawkshead, where in a poetic school exercise he speaks of Education emerging from Academus's grove.   It is not known specifically whether Wordsworth read Plato while at Cambridge, but, as Professor Cooper points out, he could hardly "have escaped the chief traditional influence in a literary way at Cambridge, the home of Platonic and Neoplatonic studies."[302]   Wordsworth, who called himself a discursive reader, included Plato among his reading, as the catalogue of the Rydal Mount Library shows.   It contained Thomas Taylor's translation of *The Cratylus, Phaedo, Parmenides,* and *Timaeus* (Ox-

[297] Cf. Walter Graham, "Wordsworth and Shelley," *Notes and Queries,* Eleventh Series, XI (1915), 83-84; Paul Mueschke and E. L. Griggs, "Wordsworth as the Prototype of the Poet in Shelley's *Alastor*," *PMLA*, XLIX (1934), 229-245; White, *Shelley,* I, 702 n. 25.

[298] Droop, *op. cit.,* pp. 65-69; White, *Shelley,* II, index, pp. cxlvi-cxlvii.

[299] See C. H. Patton, *The Amherst Wordsworth Collection* (Amherst College Library, Amherst, Mass., 1936), pp. 3-5.

[300] This reading may be in the 1815 edition of these poems; see Patton, *op. cit.,* p. 8.

[301] Thomas Medwin, *Journal of the Conversations of Lord Byron: Noted During a Residence with his Lordship at Pisa in the Years 1821 and 1822* (London, 1824), p. 192; Peacock, *op. cit.,* II, 328-329.

[302] Lane Cooper, "Wordsworth's Knowledge of Plato," *MLN,* XXXIII (1918), 498-499.

ford, 1793), and *Platonis Dialogi V, ex recens.* Forster (Oxford, 1752).[303] The direct references to Plato in his poetry and prose show that Wordsworth's Platonism is grounded in some direct knowledge of Plato.[304]

Wordsworth was also influenced by the indirect Platonic tradition through his extensive reading. One of the sources of his indirect Platonism is Cudworth's *The True Intellectual System of the Universe,* which appears in the Rydal Mount Catalogue;[305] from it Wordsworth possibly got the Platonic notion of Nature as a Plastic Power which is reflected in *The Prelude,* II, 362, XI, 138. Likewise Shaftesbury's *Characteristics,* which also was in his library,[306] may account for additional Platonic influence. Furthermore, his reading of Chaucer, Spenser, Sidney, Milton, Vaughan, Bacon, and Berkeley made him subject to all the great Platonic tradition found in these poets and philosophers.[307] But Wordsworth's Platonism was mostly influenced by his friend Coleridge. Wordsworth's dependence on Coleridge for intellectual ideas is so strong that we need not look elsewhere for the source of his Platonism. He acknowledges Coleridge along with his sister Dorothy as "the two beings to whom my intellect is most indebted."[308] He constantly pays tribute to Coleridge's fertilizing mind.[309] He writes to Beaumont: "Should Coleridge return so that I might have some conversation with him on the subject [i.e., *The Recluse*], I should go on swimmingly."[310] Knowing how steeped Coleridge was in Neoplatonism, we can infer the degree of Neoplatonic influence on Wordsworth. This influence from Coleridge is evident in the *Ode on Intimations of Immortality,* which is one of the finest expressions of the Platonic tradition in English poetry. In a study

[303] "Sale Catalogue of the Library at Rydal Mount," *Transactions of Wordsworth Society,* VI (1884), 234, Nos. 408, 409; cf. E. A. White, "Wordsworth's Knowledge of Plato," *MLN,* XXXIII (1918), 246-248.

[304] Cf. Kurt Lienemann, *Die Belesenheit von W. Wordsworth* (Berlin, 1908), pp. 213-214; J. H. Shorthouse, "On the Platonism of Wordsworth," *Transactions of the Wordsworth Society,* VI (1884), 119-131 ff.; James Adam, *The Vitality of Platonism* (Cambridge, 1911), pp. 4 ff.; M. M. Rader, "Presiding Ideas in Wordsworth's Poetry," *University of Washington Publications in Language and Literature,* VIII (1931), 196-197, 199-200; H. E. Cookson, "Wordsworth and Plato," *Times Literary Supplement,* Nov. 25, 1926, p. 888. For clear echoes of the Platonic tradition in Wordsworth's poems which Shelley read, see the notion of the music of the spheres in *Peter Bell,* l. 83; for divine love and intellectual soul, see *The Excursion,* IV, 1274; for the Platonic *scala naturae,* see *The Excursion,* IV, 342-343; for Plato's theory of ideas, see *Miscellaneous Sonnets,* XXV, 8, *The Excursion,* IV, 1230-1234.

[305] *Rydal Mount Catalogue,* p. 219, No. 220.

[306] *Ibid.,* p. 236, No. 430.   [307] Cf. Lienemann, *op. cit.*

[308] E. C. Batho, *The Later Wordsworth* (Cambridge, 1933), p. 367.

[309] *Ibid.,* p. 368.

[310] *Letters of the Wordsworth Family from 1787 to 1855,* collected and edited by William Knight (Boston and London, 1907), I, 196.

of this ode, Rea has shown how sections V-VIII, which express Neoplatonically the doctrine of pre-existence, were the result of conversations with Coleridge, who expressed the same thought in his sonnet on the birth of his son.[311] Rea goes so far as to trace the doctrine to Coleridge's copy of Ficino's edition of the Neoplatonists, which, he believes, was probably in one of the sacks full of books which Coleridge brought with him when he visited Wordsworth on June 10, 1802.[312] On the other hand Pierce has pointed out parallels between the ode and Thomas Taylor's notes in his translation of Plato.[313] Whatever be the medium through which this doctrine reached Wordsworth, the ultimate source of it is Plato, though its use here does not derive directly from Plato. Whereas Plato relates the doctrine of reminiscence with the epistemology of the theory of Ideas, Wordsworth uses it as a philosophical explanation of the dejection caused by the loss of the imagination-stirring and holy experiences of childhood.[314] Wordsworth shows in this poem the adaptability of Platonism to the non-Platonic experiences and problems of individual poets. It reveals the assimilative rather than the imitative use of Platonic doctrines. In this ode and other poems Shelley could find some poetically attractive doctrines of Platonism.

But besides the direct and indirect Platonism in Wordsworth's poetry there is a greater amount of natural Platonism. Wordsworth is, along with Shelley, one of the great exemplars of natural Platonism. He possessed, according to Coleridge, a "weight and sanity of the Thoughts and Sentiments,—won, not from books; but from the poet's own meditative observation. They are *fresh* and have the dew upon them."[315] Wordsworth has in himself natural affinities to Plato which find expression in lines like

> Authentic tidings of invisible things;
> Of ebb and flow, and ever-during power;
> And central peace, subsisting at the heart
> Of endless agitation.[316]

[311] J. D. Rea, "Coleridge's Intimations of Immortality from Proclus," *MP*, XXVI (1928-1929), 201-213; cf. Herbert Hartman, "The 'Intimations' of Wordsworth's Ode," *Review of English Studies*, VI (1931), 129-148; E. C. Baldwin, "Wordsworth and Hermes Trismegistus," *PMLA*, XXXIII (1918), 235-243.

[312] *Ibid.*, p. 207.

[313] F. E. Pierce, "Wordsworth and Thomas Taylor," *PQ*, VII (1928), 60-64; cf. F. B. Evans III, "Thomas Taylor, Platonist," *PMLA*, LV (1940), 1075.

[314] Cf. H. W. Garrod, *Wordsworth* (Oxford, 1923), pp. 117-118; Rea, *op. cit.*, pp. 203-206; N. P. Stallknecht, "The Doctrine of Coleridge's *Dejection* and Its Relation to Wordsworth's Philosophy," *PMLA*, XLIX (1934), 196-207.

[315] *Coleridge's Works*, III, 487.

[316] *The Excursion*, IV, 1144-1147; cf. *ibid.*, IV, 1234, and Shorthouse, *op. cit.*, pp. 126-128.

Stewart has shown how Wordsworth's poetry is essentially the Platonic "mood of one who has a curious eye for the endless variety of this visible and temporal world and a fine sense of its beauties, yet is haunted by the presence of an invisible and eternal world behind, or, when the mood is most pressing, within, the visible and temporal world, and sustaining both it and himself—a world not perceived as external to himself, but inwardly lived by him, as that with which, at moments of ecstasy, or even habitually, he is become one."[317] This personal Platonism finds many and varied expressions such as

> . . . that blessed mood,
> In which the burden of the mystery,
> In which the heavy and weary weight
> Of all this unintelligible world,
> Is lightened;—that serene and blessed mood,
> In which the affections gently lead us on,—
> Until, the breath of this corporeal frame
> And even the motion of our human blood
> Almost suspended, we are laid asleep
> In body, and become a living soul:
> While with an eye made quiet by the power
> Of harmony, and the deep power of joy,
> We see into the life of things.[318]

Wordsworth finds the Soul of the World, circulating from link to link in the world of nature where

> . . . the light of sense
> Goes out, but with a flash that has revealed
> The invisible world. . . .[319]

Though he possesses what Garrod has called the sense that "always points us beyond sense,"[320] his transition between the two realms is not intellectual, nor would Plato approve of the substitution of affection and imagination for reason. But this is a mode of insight more natural to the poet than the philosopher.

The impact of this Platonism on Shelley's poetry written in 1814 and

[317] J. A. Stewart, "Platonism in English Poetry," *English Literature and the Classics* (Oxford, 1912), p. 26.

[318] *Lines Composed a Few Miles above Tintern Abbey*, ll. 37-49.

[319] *The Prelude*, VI, 600-602; cf. *The Excursion*, IX, 1-15; for other passages of natural Platonism, see Shorthouse, *op. cit.*; Stewart, *op. cit.*; G. M. Harper, *William Wordsworth, His Life, Works, and Influence* (London, 1923), II, 223.

[320] Garrod, *op. cit.*, pp. 109-110.

1815 cannot be specifically determined, but we see a sample of it in a derivative parallel.   In *Alastor* Shelley writes:

> . . . Whither have fled
> The hues of heaven that canopied this bower
> Of yesternight?

This must be related to Wordsworth's *Ode. Intimations of Immortality from Recollections of Early Childhood:*

> Whither is fled the visionary gleam?
> Where is it now, the glory and the dream?[321]

It is not Plato's *Phaedo* but Wordsworth's re-creative use of it that is the source of these lines of Shelley.   We see another tangible instance of Wordsworth's influence on Shelley's Platonism in the story which Hogg tells of Shelley's rushing up to a woman with a child in her arms in the middle of Magdalen Bridge and asking, "Will your baby tell us anything about pre-existence, Madam?"[322]   Though Shelley had been reading the *Phaedo* at this time, he was interpreting one of its doctrines through Wordsworth's adaptation of the theory of reminiscence to infancy.   But the influence of Wordsworth on Shelley's Platonism lies not so much in tangible borrowing as the awaking of a cognate Platonism in Shelley's soul upon hearing the lark of Wordsworth's Platonism.

PEACOCK

Finally one other contemporary of Shelley's looms up as a figure of importance for Shelley's Platonism.   Peacock, as we have seen,[323] was largely responsible for bringing Shelley back to the Platonic pastures; moreover, he influenced Shelley through the presence of the Platonic tradition in his poems and novels, which Shelley read and admired.   The Platonism in Peacock's works centers mostly on Platonic Love.   The Platonism in *Rhododaphne* offered to Shelley another example of the poetic possibilities of Platonism.   Like Spenser, Wieland, and others, Peacock took Platonic themes out of their Platonic context of philosophy and fashioned romantic Neoplatonic works of art which perhaps affected Shelley much more profoundly than a direct reading of Plato. Such Platonism, which was made more vivid by Peacock's friendship with Shelley, makes Peacock the final link in the Platonic chain of

[321] Cf. Mueschke and Griggs, *op. cit.,* p. 236.
[322] Cf. Hogg, *op. cit.,* I, 147-148; *supra,* pp. 36-37.
[323] *Vide supra,* pp. 38-40, 46-54.

influence which starts from Plato's own successors and extends down to Shelley's own contemporaries. Now that this long story of the indirect Platonic tradition is ended, there is no better statement of its significance for Shelley's Platonism than Shelley's own dictum: "Poets, the best of them are a very camaeleonic race; they take the colour not only of what they feed on, but of the very leaves under which they pass."[324]

[324] Julian *Works*, X, 283; see "An Exhortation" (Julian *Works*, II, 293-294) and *Prometheus Unbound*, IV, 483-484, for similar thoughts.

Part II

THE
PLATONISM OF SHELLEY'S WRITINGS

*Commentary on the Platonism
of Shelley's Poetry and
Prose*

The Platonism of Shelley's Poetry

TWO METHODS present themselves for the study of Shelley's Platonism. One studies Shelley's Platonism under such categories as Platonic Love, Beauty, Goodness, Immortality, Theory of Ideas, Politics and Society, Art, etc. This method, as employed by detailed studies of Shelley's Platonism,[1] often tends to sever the organic relationship of Shelley's thoughts. Any study of Shelley's Platonism which emphasizes system through the abstraction of concepts from their setting in poetry does injustice to the poet. Shelley's ideas on immortality, for example, are protean; they follow no strict chronological evolution, admit of inconsistency, and cannot be explained by any one rigid concept.

The other method emphasizes the organic relation of Shelley's ideas to the immediate past or present which was influencing Shelley's mind and compositions. This method is chosen for the study of Shelley's Platonism in this book. The manifestation of Platonism in Shelley's poetry and prose is examined, wherever possible, with respect to all its Platonic facets. A passage, for example, may be a complex amalgam of Platonic Love, Beauty, Immortality, and Cosmology; to isolate these categories is to distort the complexity of Shelley's Platonic imagination. Finally, the chronological method, which has been set on a firmer foundation through a more precise dating of Shelley's prose,[2] is related to the account of the natural, direct, and indirect Platonism of Shelley. The text and punctuation of Shelley's poetry, prose, and letters are those of the Julian edition. Some errors in the Julian edition are silently corrected in the text.

The ensuing commentary on the Platonism of Shelley's writings takes the following form. First, the readings of Shelley in the direct and indirect Platonic tradition are recorded chronologically so that the reader may see the immediate sources of influence on Shelley's composition. Then there follow the quotation, the reference, and the Platonic com-

---

[1] See Helene Richter, "Zu Shelleys philosophische Weltanschauung," *Englische Studien,* XXX (1902), 224-265, 383-435; Lilian Winstanley, "Platonism in Shelley," *Essays and Studies by Members of the English Association,* IV (1913), 72-100; Amiyakumar Sen, "Platonism in Shelley," *Journal of the Department of Letters,* Calcutta University, XV (1927), 13-60.

[2] See J. A. Notopoulos, "The Dating of Shelley's Prose," *PMLA,* LVIII (1943), 477-498.

mentary on the passage. In the case of major Platonic works an opportunity is provided in the introductions to discuss more comprehensively the nature of Shelley's Platonism as manifested in this work and in other related writings of Shelley. The reader will readily find the commentary to specific passages in Shelley's writings by consulting the index.

SHELLEY'S READING IN PLATO AND THE PLATONIC TRADITION, 1810-1811

DIRECT PLATONISM: *The Symposium* (1808-1810 at Eton with Dr. Lind); *Alcibiades I* and *II, Theages, Euthyphro, Apology, Crito, Phaedo, Laches, Protagoras, The Rivals, Republic; Parmenides?, Cratylus?, Timaeus?, Symposium?, Ion?* (read in Dacier's, Taylor's, and Sydenham's translations at Oxford in 1810-1811); analysis or quotation from the *Timaeus, Laws, Republic, Epistles,* and *Symposium* in Dacier's Introduction.

INDIRECT PLATONISM: Lucretius, Albertus Magnus, and Paracelsus (1804-1810?); Southey, *Curse of Kehama* (———-1810?); Dacier's and Taylor's Introduction and Notes to their translations of Plato (1810-1811); Godwin's *Political Justice* (1810-1811); Pope (1811?), Locke (1810-1811), Berkeley (1811-1812), Thomas Reid (1811-1812), Erasmus Darwin (July, 1811); Southey, *Curse of Kehama* (June, 1811), Lady Morgan, *The Missionary* (1811), Ensor, *National Education* (1811), Rousseau, *Confessions* (1811).

PLATONISM IN SHELLEY'S POETRY WRITTEN IN 1811-1812

Original Poetry by Victor and Cazire
January, 1810

Your writings may then with old Socrates vie,
May on the same shelf with Demosthenes lie,
May as Junius be sharp, or as Plato be sage . . . .
(I, 33-35)

If this poem was written by Shelley (Victor), we have here the first mention of Plato in Shelley. If written earlier than Shelley's matriculation at Oxford, the reference is a reflection of the reading of the *Symposium* at Eton with Dr. Lind, or may be a rhetorical echo of the Platonic tradition.

Posthumous Fragments of Margaret Nicholson: Fragment, Supposed to be an Epithalamium of Francis Ravaillac and Charlotte Cordé
1809-1810

> My form upborne by viewless aether rode,
>   And spurn'd the lessening realms of earthly night.
> What heavenly notes burst on my ravish'd ears,
>   What beauteous spirits met my dazzled eye!
> Hark! louder swells the music of the spheres . . . .
>   (Ll. 26-30)

Though Shelley could find the notion of the heavenly music produced by the spheres in *Republic,* 616d-617c, it is probable that this notion reached him through the Platonic tradition, where it figures prominently (for the classical conception of the music of the spheres, see Carl v. Jan, "Die Harmonie der Sphären," *Philologus,* LII [1898], 13-37; for references and a discussion of the music of the spheres in the Platonic tradition, see E. M. W. Tillyard, *The Elizabethan World Picture* [London, 1943], pp. 38-47, 94-99; Milton, *Arcades,* ll. 62-73, and *De sphaerarum concentu* [*The Works of John Milton,* New York, 1936, XII, 148-156]; Dryden, *A Song for Saint Cecilia's Day,* ll. 56-57; Pope, *An Essay on Man,* I, 201-202; Leo Spitzer, "Classical and Christian Ideas of World Harmony," *Traditio,* II [1944], 409-464, III [1945], 307-364; Rudolf Allers, "Microcosmus," *Traditio,* II [1944], 374-378).

> Congenial minds will seek their kindred soul,
>   E'en though the tide of time has roll'd between;
> They mock weak matter's impotent control,
>   And seek of endless life the eternal scene.
>   (Ll. 42-45)

This is the first appearance in Shelley's poetry of the poet's Platonic faith in something permanent amid the transient. It is an expression of natural Platonism possibly blended with a remote echo from the *Symposium,* in particular its doctrine of the union of kindred souls seeking immortality. The essence of these lines is also found in a letter to Elizabeth Hitchener, dated November 24, 1811 (Julian *Works,* VIII, 202; cf. commentary *infra,* pp. 358-359).

SHELLEY'S READING IN PLATO AND THE PLATONIC TRADITION, 1812-1813

DIRECT PLATONISM: ?

INDIRECT PLATONISM: Milton's prose works (1812?), Thomas Gray (1812?), Gibbon, *The Decline and Fall of the Roman Empire* (1812), the

Encyclopedists (1812-1813), D'Holbach, *Système de la Nature* (May-June, 1812), Sir William Drummond, *Academical Questions* (1812-1813), Godwin, *Political Justice* (1812), Cicero's Philosophical Essays (1813), Polybius (1813-?), Plutarch (1813), Petrarch (1813-?), Spinoza (1813-?), Berkeley (1813), Adam Smith, *Theory of Moral Sentiments* (1813-?), Dugald Stewart, *Outlines of Moral Philosophy* (1813-1814), Erasmus Darwin, *Temple of Nature, Zoönomia* (1813?), Kant (1813-?), Cabanis, *Rapports du physique et du moral de l'homme* (1812-1813), Lord Monboddo, *Of the Origin and Progress of Language* (1813-?)

To Ireland

1812

> Thou art a conqueror, Time! All things give way
> Before thee but the 'fixed virtuous will';
> The sacred sympathy of soul which was
> When thou wert not, which *shall be* when thou perishest.
>
> (Ll. 22-25)

This is the first appearance in Shelley's poetry of the immortality of the soul. It is the expression of natural Platonism rather than the doctrine of the *Phaedo*.

The Retrospect: Cwm Elan

1812

> And early I had learned to scorn
> The chains of clay that bound a soul
> Panting to seize the wings of morn,
> And where its vital fires were born
> To soar, and spur the cold control
> Which the vile slaves of earthly night
> Would twine around its struggling flight.
>
> (Ll. 57-63)

These lines aptly illustrate the effect of the reading of the *Phaedo* at Oxford (see Hogg, *op. cit.*, I, 73). Shelley here makes a tangible use of its doctrine of the body's being the earthly prison of the soul (*Cratylus,* 400b-c, *Phaedo,* 62b, 67d, 82e; see Burnet's edition of the *Phaedo,* notes, pp. 22-23; cf. Plotinus, *Enneads,* IV, viii, 1, 3, 4).

Queen Mab

August, 1812—February 19, 1813

Shelley's mind, at the time of the composition of *Queen Mab,* was steeped in the Platonism which he had read at Oxford and in radical philosophy and literature. Although, as has been shown in Chapter IV, the radical philosophers whom Shelley read are themselves considerably influenced by the Platonic tradition and some of the Platonism in the poem had been refracted through these thinkers, the presence of Platonism in this poem side by side with the materialistic philosophy of the eighteenth century reveals Shelley's paratactic mind, with its capacity to see things separately, to gravitate to two different systems of philosophy without being aware of the contradictions. (For a parallel to Shelley's capacity for viewing things separately, see B. E. Perry, "The Early Greek Capacity for Viewing Things Separately," *Transactions of the American Philological Association,* LXVIII [1937], 403-427.) For example, the *Phaedo,* with its doctrine of the immortality of the soul, and Godwin's *Political Justice,* with its premise that "all human knowledge is the result of perception," are poor bedfellows, yet both strains are found in *Queen Mab* (I, 148-156, and "The senses are the sources of all knowledge to the mind," note to *Queen Mab,* VII, 13). It is evident that Platonism satisfied Shelley the idealist and the poet, whereas the radical literature of the eighteenth century satisfied Shelley the reformer and practical idealist, who was warring against the evils of religion and society which had led to the degeneration of man's pristine natural goodness. This strain persists throughout Shelley's life. Qua philosopher Shelley can find no basis for a belief in the immortality of the soul; qua poet he is often led to attach himself to immortality. In a note to *Hellas* we find Shelley's own answer to this dilemma:

That there is a true solution of the riddle, and that in our present state that solution is unattainable by us, are propositions which may be regarded as equally certain; meanwhile, as it is the province of the poet to attach himself to those ideas which exalt and ennoble humanity, let him be permitted to have conjectured the condition of that futurity towards which we are all impelled by an inextinguishable thirst for immortality. Until better arguments can be produced than sophisms which disgrace the cause, this desire itself must remain the strongest and the only presumption that eternity is the inheritance of every thinking being.

This forms the best commentary on the Platonism which is found independent of, in combination with, and side by side with, materialism in *Queen Mab,* a poem in which the unity, if any, is aesthetic rather than logical.

Although many of the ideas of the poem can be traced to the direct influence of eighteenth-century radicalism, the ultimate source of many of these ideas goes back to Platonism itself. For example, the main thesis of the poem is that the spirit of Nature and of life is Necessity, a force which permeates the universe; yet this conception is a fusion of two Platonic conceptions, Necessity and the World Soul. In the *Republic* (616c-617c) Necessity is the mother of the Fates; the orbits of the universe turn on the spindle of Necessity. In the *Timaeus* (48a), "Mind, the ruling power, persuaded necessity to bring the greater part of created things to perfection." In the *Laws* (741a, 818b) not even God can fight against Necessity ("He [God] is also subjected to the dominion of an immutable necessity," note on Necessity in *Queen Mab,* VI, 198).[3] The other basic conception in *Queen Mab,* the Spirit of Nature, "a pervading Spirit co-eternal with the Universe" (see note VII) is the poetic foster child of a philosophic conception which ultimately stems from the *Timaeus.*[4] In discussing the creation of the world in the *Timaeus* (30b), Plato says:

. . . the creator, reflecting on the things which are by nature visible, found that no unintelligent creature taken as a whole was fairer than the intelligent taken as a whole; and that intelligence could not be present in anything which was devoid of soul. For which reason, when he was framing the universe, he put intelligence in soul, and soul in body, that he might be the creator of a work which was by nature fairest and best. Wherefore, using the language of probability, we may say that the world became a living creature truly endowed with soul and intelligence by the providence of God.

This conception of the universe as a sentient organism is one of the most influential contributions of Plato to the poetic mind, for its ultimate re-expression in poetry as the Spirit of Nature gives the poet's soul an appropriate realm for the exercise of imagination. It makes possible a

---

[3] For a study of Necessity in Plato, see Wilhelm Gundel, *Beiträge zur Entwickelungsgeschichte der Begriffe Ananke und Heimarmene* (Giessen, 1914); Jacques Chevalier, *La Notion du nécessaire chez Aristote et chez ses prédécesseurs* (Paris, 1915); W. C. Greene, *Moira: Fate, Good, and Evil in Greek Thought* (Cambridge, Mass., 1944), pp. 302 ff.

[4] For an account of the World Soul in Plato and the Platonic tradition, see F. M. Cornford, *Plato's Cosmology* (London, 1937), pp. 58-137; Pierre Thévenaz, *L'Ame du monde, le devenir et la matière chez Plutarque* (Paris, 1938); Joseph Moreau, *L'Ame du monde de Platon aux Stoiciens* (Paris, 1939); Friedrich Solmsen, *Plato's Theology* (Ithaca, 1942), pp. 177-195 (and especially bibliography listed in n. 27); Rudolf Allers, "Microcosmus," *Traditio,* II (1944), 352 ff.; Hugo Perls, *Platon, sa conception du kosmos* (New York, 1945).

union between the poet's soul and the soul of nature. This relationship, which is the theme of much of Shelley's poetry, was ultimately made possible by the development of certain suggestions found in the *Timaeus*. Plato himself did not explicitly develop the conception of microcosm and macrocosm which makes it possible for the poet to commune with the spirit of Nature. Yet the nucleus of this conception is found in Plato's statement that the world is a perfect animal in unity (*Timaeus*, 30d) and that the structure of man's head is an imitation of the spherical form of the universe (*Timaeus*, 44d). Aristotle carries this notion further by referring to animals as the "small world" μιϰρῷ ϰόσμῳ and to the universe as the "great world" (μεγάλῳ) (*Physics*, VIII, 2, 252b, 26-27). Plotinus contributes to the crystallization of this notion by calling animals microcosms (μορφοῦσι τὰ ζῷα οἷον μιϰρούς τινας ϰόσμους, *Enneads*, IV, iii, 10) and making the human souls detachments of the world soul. This idea was taken up in medieval thought and finds considerable expression in Paracelsus (*vide supra*, p. 112), whom Shelley read at Eton. This conception is finally applied to the soul of man, which becomes a microcosm of the soul of the world; it becomes a favorite doctrine in religion and poetry, which seek to relate the soul of man with God and Nature (Tillyard, *The Elizabethan World Picture*, pp. 42, 60-62). It finds a direct echo in Shelley's statement: "Religion is the perception of the relation in which we stand to the principle of the universe. But if the principle of the universe be not an organic being, the model and prototype of man, the relation between it and human beings is absolutely none" (note on *Queen Mab*, VI, 198). The immortality of the soul is a necessary concomitant of this concept; if the world soul is eternal, the soul of man which is a miniature of it must also be eternal. This accounts for the immortality of the soul in *Queen Mab*, which is set in the context of a universe which is alive and sentient, one which can sympathize with man, one which the poet can come to know if he is able to read and interpret the divine visual language and moods of nature (*vide supra*, p. 21). In all this Shelley is the unconcious heir of Plato, whose *Timaeus* is the ultimate source of poetic pantheism, which is one of the basic moods of Romantic poetry. Although Shelley might have read the *Timaeus* at Oxford in translation and knew at least its essential features from Dacier's Introduction, he inherited these Platonic notions from the influence of the Platonic tradition in the philosophic and poetic atmosphere in which he was born. One example may be quoted to show Shelley's contact with this Platonism. Sir William Drummond's *Academical Questions*, which Shelley quotes in his notes to *Queen Mab*, contains a reference to "the ancient dogma of the world's being a sentient and animated being (Κόσμος οὐσία ἔμψυχος καὶ αἰσθητική)" (*Academical Questions*, p. 237). It is from such seeds that Shelley's Platonism in this poem grew.

Hogg, who was Shelley's fellow-Platonist at Oxford, says of this poem, "*Queen Mab* is the production of a Platonist incontestably; and if the great master of the academy were to read it, he would at once acknowledge the author for a disciple—for a favoured and a favourite one." This judgment has some foundation; the Platonism of *Queen Mab* is filled with what Mary calls in her notes to the poem "unworldliness"; the poem is something of a Platonic revery or myth wherein the disembodied soul of sleeping Ianthe ascends to the ideal world and is instructed by Queen Mab on the significance of her vision. The natural Platonism of Shelley is evident in this flight of the soul from the body to ascend to the heights of clearer vision. This common denominator with the *Phaedo* and with the Christian conception of immortality is constantly repeated in passages which proclaim the immortality of the soul. The direct Platonism in the poem comes from reminiscences of thought and phrase, mostly from the *Phaedo*, while the indirect Platonism is reflected in such themes as the music of the spheres and reference to the "reveries of Plato."

> Sudden arose
> Ianthe's Soul; it stood
> All beautiful in naked purity,
> The perfect semblance of its bodily frame.
> Instinct with inexpressible beauty and grace,
> Each stain of earthliness
> Had passed away, it reassumed
> Its native dignity, and stood
> Immortal amid ruin.
>
> (I, 130-138)

The Platonism of these lines is transparent in the beautiful purity of the soul severed from "the stains of earthliness," which is a poetic echo of *Phaedo,* 81b. There, of course, the soul of the philosopher is freed from the bonds of the body by a practice of philosophy; its emphasis on dialectic and the pursuit of ideal forms is vastly different from this romantic natural Platonism of Shelley. This disembodied, pure, unearthly condition of the soul is Platonic in language as well as conception.

Upon the couch the body lay
Wrapped in the depth of slumber:
Its features were fixed and meaningless,
 Yet animal life was there,
And every organ yet performed
Its natural functions: 'twas a sight
Of wonder to behold the body and soul.
The self-same lineaments, the same
Marks of identity were there:
Yet, oh how different! One aspires to Heaven,
Pants for its sempiternal heritage,
And ever changing, ever rising still,
 Wantons in endless being.
The other, for a time the unwilling sport
Of circumstance and passion, struggles on;
Fleets through its sad duration rapidly;
Then, like an useless and worn-out machine,
 Rots, perishes, and passes.

(I, 139-156)

The contrast of the soul longing for the "sempiternal heritage" of Heaven while the body "rots, perishes, and passes" is a poetic transcription of *Phaedo,* 80b. This passage, which develops the theme of lines 130-138, is one of the clearest expressions of Platonism in *Queen Mab.* The Platonism of the *Phaedo,* however, is mingled with another conception whose ultimate source can be traced to Pindar. In *Queen Mab* the soul leaves the body wrapped in slumber and ventures forth on its vision of the world. Of pointed interest for this conception is a fragment of Pindar which Shelley might have read in one of Plutarch's essays (see Shelley's excerpts from Plutarch's essay in the notes to *Queen Mab*): "And, while the body of all men is subject to over-mastering death, an image of life remaineth alive, for it alone cometh from the gods. But it sleepeth, while the limbs are active; yet, to them that sleep, in many a dream it giveth presage of a decision of things delightful or doleful" (*Pindar* [quoted by Plutarch, *Consolatio ad Apollonium,* 35], fragment 131, Loeb Classical Library). The similarity between Shelley's "the perfect semblance of its bodily frame" (l. 133) and Pindar's "image of life," between Ianthe's soul which leaves the body wrapped in the depth of slumber and Pindar's "the soul sleeps while the limbs are active," points to a fusion of the conception of the *Phaedo* with a conception which ultimately goes back to Pindar. (For the notion of the "Sleeping Soul" in the Platonic tradition, see Plotinus, *Enneads,* III, vi, 6; R. E.

Witt, *Albinus and the History of Middle Platonism* [Cambridge, 1937], pp. 131-132.)

> And it is yet permitted me, to rend
> The veil of mortal frailty, that the spirit,
> Clothed in its changeless purity, may know
> How soonest to accomplish the great end
> For which it hath its being, and may taste
> That peace, which in the end all life will share.
>
> .   .   .   .
>
> The chains of earth's immurement
>   Fell from Ianthe's spirit . . . .
>   (I, 180-185, 188-189)

These lines are a variant development of the Platonism in the above passages. "Chains of earth's immurement" is a poetic variation of *Phaedo*, 62b, 82e; here also appears for the first time in Shelley the Platonic image of life as a veil. It is a favorite image of Shelley and seems to be an echo of the Platonic tradition rather than the *Phaedo* itself (cf. Spenser's and Berkeley's use of the veil; *vide supra*, pp. 105, 123. For other uses of the veil, see *Adonais*, ll. 72, 493; *Sonnet*, "Lift not the painted veil"; *Prometheus Unbound*, II, iii, 59, III, iii, 62, 113, III, iv, 190, IV, 58; *Ginevra*, l. 122; *Cenci*, V, i, 78; *Ode to Liberty*, l. 86; *Epipsychidion*, ll. 22, 26, 244. For the figure of life as a veil, see N. I. White, *The Best of Shelley* [New York, 1932], p. 471; A. T. Strong, *Three Studies in Shelley* [Oxford, 1921], pp. 70-80).

> Spirit of Nature! here!
> In this interminable wilderness
> Of worlds, at whose immensity
>   Even soaring fancy staggers,
>   Here is thy fitting temple!
>   Yet not the lightest leaf
> That quivers to the passing breeze
>   Is less instinct with thee:
>   Yet not the meanest worm
> That lurks in graves and fattens on the dead
> Less shares thy eternal breath.
>   Spirit of Nature! thou,
> Imperishable as this scene,
>   Here is thy fitting temple!
>   (I, 264-277)

For the relation of Shelley's Spirit of Nature to Plato's World Soul,

see introductory remarks to the Platonism of *Queen Mab, supra,* pages
176-177. See also A. E. Taylor, *A Commentary on Plato's Timaeus* (Oxford, 1928), pages 106 ff., and Plotinus's elaboration of this doctrine, "The
soul is of so far-reaching a nature—a thing unbounded—as to embrace the
entire body of the All in one extension; so far as the universe extends,
there soul is; and if the universe had no existence, the extent of Soul
would be the same; it is eternally what it is" (Plotinus, *Enneads,* IV,
iii, 9, MacKenna's translation).

> Below lay stretched the universe!
> There, far as the remotest line
>   That bounds imagination's flight,
>   Countless and unending orbs
>   In mazy motion intermingled,
>   Yet still fulfilled immutably
>   Eternal nature's law.
>   Above, below, around
>   The circling systems formed
>   A wilderness of harmony;
>   Each with undeviating aim,
> In eloquent silence, through the depths of space
> Pursued its wondrous way.
>   (II, 70-82)

These lines are an expression of Shelley's own cosmic imagination
with a distant echo, perhaps, of the Platonic cosmology in *Republic,*
616c-617c, or such sources as Psalm 19 and Addison's *Ode:* "What though,
in solemn Silence, all/Move round the dark terrestrial Ball?"

> Worthy a soul that claims
> Its kindred with eternity.
>   (II, 209-210)

See remarks on I, 130-138, 139-156 *supra,* pp. 178-180.

> Spirit of Nature! thou
> Life of interminable multitudes;
>   Soul of those mighty spheres
> Whose changeless paths thro' Heaven's deep silence lie;
>   Soul of that smallest being,
>   The dwelling of whose life
>   Is one faint April sun-gleam . . . .
>   (III, 226-232)

See remarks on Shelley's Spirit of Nature and Plato's World Soul
(commentary on I, 264-277), *supra,* pp. 180-181.

> and life's smallest chord
> Strung to unchanging unison . . .
>
> (IV, 91-92)

This is perhaps a reflection in the Platonic tradition of "the concord
of a single harmony," *Republic,* 617b.

> whilst specious names,
> Learned in soft childhood's unsuspecting hour,
> Serve as the sophisms with which manhood dims
> Bright reason's ray . . .
>
> (IV, 112-115)

See Plato's similar views in *Republic,* 377 ff.

> Throughout this varied and eternal world
> Soul is the only element, the block
> That for uncounted ages has remained.
> The moveless pillar of a mountain's weight
> Is active living spirit. Every grain
> Is sentient both in unity and part,
> And the minutest atom comprehends
> A world of loves and hatreds; these beget
> Evil and good: hence truth and falsehood spring;
> Hence will, and thought and action, all the germs
> Of pain or pleasure, sympathy or hate,
> That variegate the eternal universe.
> Soul is not more polluted than the beams
> Of heaven's pure orb, ere round their rapid lines
> The taint of earth-born atmospheres arise.
>
> (IV, 139-153)

These lines are an important expression of Shelley's Platonism at
this time. For the inevitable association of a belief in immortality and
the World Soul, see introductory remarks to *Queen Mab* (*supra,* p. 177).
The Platonism in this passage consists of a Lucretian-tinged notion of
the World Soul, the immortality of the soul, and its pollution by the corporeal. The comparison of the soul and mortality by means of the
imagery of the sun and "the taint of earth-born atmospheres" is a
felicitous natural Platonic image. For the use of light in Neoplatonic
thought, see E. R. Goodenough, *By Light, Light* (New Haven, 1936).

> Thus do the generations of the earth
> Go to the grave, and issue from the womb,
> Surviving still the imperishable change
> That renovates the world . . . .
>
> (V, 1-4)

Shelley conceives of the alternation of life and death as Plato does in *Symposium*, 207d, and *Phaedo*, 70c-72e. It is doubtful whether Shelley had these passages in mind. The lines are rather the expression of a phenomenon of nature which both Plato and Shelley observed and expressed cognately.

> The weight that drags to earth his towering hopes . . .
>
> (V, 83)

A Platonic phrase which finds analogy or possibly derivation from *Phaedrus*, 248c, *Phaedo*, 80e, 81cd, *Republic*, 515c.

> Nature, impartial in munificence,
> Has gifted man with all-subduing will.
> Matter, with all its transitory shapes,
> Lies subjected and plastic at his feet.
>
> (V, 132-135)

In endowing man with will and power over matter, Shelley agrees with Plato's general belief expressed particularly in *Republic,* 617e, and *Laws,* 897a-b. This passage is also interesting for its Platonic conception of a plastic nature, which later finds re-expression in *Adonais*, ll. 379-385. As has been shown in Chapter IV (*vide supra*, p. 116), this conception of plastic nature is ultimately derived from the *Timaeus.* Cudworth's elaboration of this doctrine into Plastic Nature influenced Pope, Coleridge, Wordsworth, and Shelley. Though Cudworth does not appear in Shelley's reading, the doctrine reached Shelley through his reading of these poets and possibly his reading of Lord Monboddo's *Antient Metaphysics.*

> 'How sweet a scene will earth become!
> Of purest spirits, a pure dwelling-place,
> Symphonious with the planetary spheres . . . .
>
> (VI, 39-41)

For an allusion to the Platonic music of the spheres, *vide supra,* page 173.

> Soul of the Universe! eternal spring
> Of life and death, of happiness and woe,
> Of all that chequers the phantasmal scene
> That floats before our eyes in wavering light,
> Which gleams but on the darkness of our prison,
>   Whose chains and massy walls
>   We feel but cannot see.
>
> 'Spirit of Nature! all-sufficing Power,
> Necessity! thou mother of the world!
>   (VI, 190-198)

For the Platonic conceptions of the Soul of the Universe and Necessity here and in VI, 146-164, 214-219, 225-238, see commentary *supra*, pages 176-178; in lines 192-195 Shelley echoes the feeling and language of the myth of the Cave in *Republic,* 514 ff. The phrases "phantasmal," "light, which gleams," "on the darkness of our prison" show that Shelley possibly had the *Republic* in mind, or they may equally be echoes of the Platonic cave in literature influenced by the Platonic tradition.

>   And all its pulses beat
>   Symphonious to the planetary spheres:
>   Then dulcet music swelled
>   Concordant with the life-strings of the soul . . . .
>   (VIII, 17-20)

For the Platonic notion of the music of the spheres, *vide supra*, page 173.

>   O human Spirit! spur thee to the goal
>   Where virtue fixes universal peace,
>   And, midst the ebb and flow of human things,
>   Show somewhat stable, somewhat certain still,
>   A lighthouse o'er the wild of dreary waves.
>   (VIII, 53-57)

These lines are an expression of the natural Platonic conception of the dualism of permanence and change. The last line is another of Shelley's natural Platonic images.

>   All things are recreated, and the flame
>   Of consentaneous love inspires all life . . . .
>   (VIII, 107-108)

The spirit of nature is thought of here in terms of cosmic love, a conception which has some affinities with the *Symposium*.

Yet, human Spirit, bravely hold thy course,
Let virtue teach thee firmly to pursue
The gradual paths of an aspiring change:
For birth and life and death, and that strange state
Before the naked soul has found its home,
All tend to perfect happiness, and urge
The restless wheels of being on their way,
Whose flashing spokes, instinct with infinite life,
Bicker and burn to gain their destined goal:
For birth but wakes the spirit to the sense
Of outward shows, whose unexperienced shape
New modes of passion to its frame may lend;

Life is its state of action, and the store
Of all events is aggregated there
That variegate the eternal universe;
Death is a gate of dreariness and gloom,
That leads to azure isles and beaming skies,
And happy regions of eternal hope.

(IX, 146-163)

This is the most important Platonic passage in *Queen Mab*. It knits together the threads of natural, direct, and indirect Platonism. In Shelley's belief of a spiritual universe, in his exhortation to the soul to pursue through virtue "the gradual paths of an aspiring change," we have an expression of natural Platonism. The passage is also permeated with direct echoes from the *Phaedo;* a knowledge of the *Phaedo* is revealed in "birth but wakes the spirit to the sense of outward shows" and in the theme of lines 149-150, 161-163. The indirect Platonic tradition is shown in the image of the chariot (IX, 227) ascending to its goal (cf. *Phaedrus,* 246 ff.), in the "outward show" of the material world, and the Platonic symbolism of light and darkness.

This belief, rolling through the lapse of ages, met with the reveries of Plato and the reasonings of Aristotle, and acquired force and extent, until the divinity of Jesus became a dogma, which to dispute was death, which to doubt was infamy.

(Notes on *Queen Mab*, VII, 135-136)

For the influence of the Platonic tradition on this statement, *vide supra*, page 137.

The Daemon of the World
1812-1815

This poem, which is a revision of Sections I, II, VIII, and IX of *Queen Mab,* contains little Platonism not already noted in *Queen Mab.* The title of the poem, however, has a Platonic significance. Love in the *Symposium* is conceived of as a *daemon,* an intermediary spirit between gods and men (cf. *Laws,* 903b; *Epinomis,* 984d ff.). Platonic demonology was developed by Neoplatonism (see Plotinus, *Enneads,* III, iv) and is one of the most influential conceptions of Platonism. (For Platonic demonology, see F. A. Ukert, "Über Dämonen, Heroen, und Genien," *Abhandlungen der Philologisch—Historischen Classe der Königlich Sächsischen Gesellschaft der Wissenschaften* [Leipzig, 1850], I, 137-219; J. A. Hild, *Étude sur les démons dans la littérature et la religion des grecs* [Paris, 1881]; Richard Heinze, *Xenokrates* [Leipzig, 1892], pp. 78-123; Léon Robin, *Théorie platonicienne de l'amour* [Paris, 1933], pp. 129-138; A. D. Nock, *Sallustius, Concerning the Gods of the Universe* [Cambridge, 1926], pp. xxxix-lxxviii; *Proclus, the Elements of Theology,* A Revised Text with Translation, Introduction and Commentary by E. R. Dodds [Oxford, 1933], pp. 294-296; *Harvard Theological Review,* XXXVI [1943], 263-264.) This notion might have reached Shelley through any one of its multitudinous appearances in the literature and thought of Europe. (For Love as a daemon or intermediary spirit in Shelley's doctrine of Love, see Floyd Stovall, "Shelley's Doctrine of Love," *PMLA,* XLV [1930], 293.)

> Where the vast snake Eternity
> In charmèd sleep doth ever lie.
>
> (I, 100-101)

The serpent symbolism also appears in *Laon and Cythna* (IV, 32-33); *Prometheus Unbound,* IV, 565-567; *On the Devil and Devils*

(Julian *Works,* VII, 103); and in a fragment of *A Defence of Poetry* (see *Shelley's Prose in the Bodleian Manuscripts,* ed. A. H. Koszul [London, 1910], p. 122).

Among Shelley's sources of this image are Count Volney's *Les Ruines* (see *PMLA,* LVI [1941], 203) and Lord Monboddo's *Of the Origin and Progress of Language* [Edinburgh, 1774-1792], which Shelley ordered from his bookseller on December 24, 1812. In discussing Egyptian hieroglyphics Lord Monboddo says, "There are many other symbols of the same kind . . . which we find in other antient authors; such as, a serpent in a circle to denote eternity" (II, 249).

The symbol to which Shelley has reference is the δράκων οὐροβόρος, the tail-eating serpent whose figure, without beginning or end, signifies eternity. The *locus classicus* of the symbol in ancient authors is to be found in the *Hieroglyphica* of Horapollo (fourth century A.D.?): Αἰῶνα γράψαι βουλόμενοι, ὄφιν ζωγραφοῦσιν, ἔχοντα τὴν οὐρὰν ὑπὸ τὸ λοιπὸν σῶμα κρυπτομένην and also Κόσμον βουλόμενοι γράψαι, ὄφιν ζωγραφοῦσι τὴν ἑαυτοῦ ἐσθίοντα οὐράν (*Hori Apollinis Hieroglyphica,* ed. Francesco Sbordone [Naples, 1940], I, 1, 1, 2; see commentary, pp. 2-6). The symbol appears on a Mithraic monument, in Egyptian magical papyri, and in Gnostic inscriptions and becomes prominent in the alchemical treatises of the Hermetic writings ascribed to Hermes Trismegistus, the Egyptian Thoth, from whom, it was believed, all Greek philosophy was derived. These Hermetic writings embodied many Neoplatonic notions which found symbolical expression in the magical, astrological, and chemical writings. The influence of Plato on this literature is so great that it is manifest in almost every page. (See Walter Scott, *Hermetica* [Oxford, 1924], I, Introduction, pp. 9 ff.; A. J. Hopkins, *Alchemy, Child of Greek Philosophy* [New York, 1934], pp. 12-88; Martin P. Nilsson, "Problems of the History of Greek Religion in the Hellenistic and Roman Age," *Harvard Theological Review,* XXXVI [1943], 270-271; A.-J. Festugière, *La Révélation d'Hermès Trismégiste. I. L'Astrologie et les Sciences Occultes* [Paris, 1944]; A. D. Nock and A.-J. Festugière, *Corpus Hermeticum* [Paris, 1945].) The tail-eating serpent became in Hermetic literature a symbol of the Platonic formula ἓν τὸ πᾶν which appears in Shelley's *Adonais* as "The One Remains, the many change and pass." (Cf. *Collection des anciens alchimistes grecs,* ed. Marcellin Berthelot [Paris, 1888], I, 132-133; the illustration comes from Codex Marcianus no. 299, fol. 188 verso, Xth century A.D.; for the syncretism of this Platonic doctrine with Hermetic writings and symbolism, see Eduard Norden, *Agnostos Theos* [Leipzig, 1913], pp. 248-250.) This, along with some other Neoplatonic images, entered the Platonic tradition and reached Shelley through his reading. Shelley's fondness for this Neoplatonic symbol shows specifically how the Platonic tradition furnished symbolic elements for the alchemy of Shelley's imagination.

For some other sources, discussions, and illustrations of the δράκων οὐροβόρος see *Servius Ad Aen.*, 5, 85; Capitolinus, *Antoninus Pius*, 9, 4; Martianus Capella, I, 70; Suidas, *s.v.* πολύποδος δίκην; possibly (by emendation) Nicander, *Theriaca*, 826; Epiphanius, *Adversus Haereses*, 1, 2, 30, 26 (*Patrologia Graeca*, 41, 449D); 1, 2, 22, 2 (*ibid.*, p. 297A); Eitrem in *Papyri Osloenses*, I, 81, and works cited; Marian Harmon in *Studies in Honor of W. A. Oldfather* (Urbana, 1943), page 67 note 35; Campbell Bonner in *Hesperia*, XIII (1944), 35 (I owe the above references to the courtesy of Professor A. S. Pease); Macrobius, *Saturnalia*, I, 9, 12; Lydus, *De mensibus*, 3, 4: *Imagines deorum, qui ab antiquis colebantur . . . olim a Vicentio Chartario . . . collectae, atque Italica lingua expositae: nunc vero . . . Latino sermone ab Antonio Verderio expressae . . .* (Lugduni, 1581), pages 18-21; John Ruskin, *Fors Clavigera*, Letter 23 (October 24, 1872), *The Works of John Ruskin* (London, 1907), XXVII, 405; Franz Cumont, "Masque de Jupiter sur un aigle éployé, bronze du Musée de Bruxelles," *Festschrift für Otto Benndorf* (Wien, 1898), pages 291-295; Franz Valery Marie Cumont, *Textes et monuments figurés relatifs aux mystères de Mithra* (Bruxelles, 1899, 1896), No. 25; *Collection des anciens alchimistes grecs*, I, Introduction, 9, 130, 132, 137, 159, 196, II, 21-23, 80; Scott, *Hermetica*, IV, 147; *Papyri Graecae Magicae*, edited by Karl Preisendanz (Berlin, 1931), II, Tafel I; J. H. Iliffe, "A Neolithic Celt with Gnostic Inscriptions at Toronto," *American Journal of Archaeology*, XXXV (1931), 304 note 5; Arthur Darby Nock, "A Vision of Mandulis Aion," *Harvard Theological Review*, XXVII (1934), 88 note 117; *Time*, February 12, 1945, page 8; Robert Frost, *A Masque of Reason* (New York, 1945), page 17.

> return,
> Surpassing Spirit, to that world, where thou
> Art destined an eternal war to wage
> With tyranny and falsehood, and uproot
> The Germs of misery from the human heart.
> (II, 572-576)

The spirit, after seeing perfection and the light of truth, must, like the philosopher in *Republic,* 540, return to the world and liberate it from error and oppression.

Shelley's Reading in Plato and the Platonic Tradition, 1814-1815

Direct Platonism:?

Indirect Platonism: Cicero, *Collectanea* (1814; October 14, 1814); Cicero, *Paradoxa* (October 14, 1814); Diogenes Laertius (1814; December 4, 1814); Dante (1814); Godwin, *Political Justice* (1814; October 7, 1814); Goethe (1814); Wieland, *Peregrinus Proteus* (1814; November 24-26, 1814), *Agathon* (1814); Southey, *Curse of Kehama* (1814-1815; September 17, 1814); *Thalaba* (1814; September 20-24, 1814); Coleridge, *Rime of the Ancient Mariner* (1814; September 15, October 5, 1814), *Poems* (1815); Wordsworth, *The Excursion* (1814; September 14, 1814), *Poems* (1815); Cicero's philosophic dialogues (1815); Virgil (1815); Seneca's works (1815; February 13, April 18, May 4-5, 10-11, 1815); Augustine, *Confessions* (1815); Bacon, *Novum Organum* (1815); Spenser, *Faerie Queene* (November 29, December 2, 1814; 1815); Shakespeare's plays (1815); Sir Thomas Browne, *Religio Medici* (March 14, 1815); Milton, *Paradise Lost, Paradise Regained, Areopagitica, Lycidas, Comus* (1815); Locke, *Essay on Human Understanding* (1815); Gibbon, *Decline and Fall* (1815); Rousseau, *Rêveries d'un promeneur solitaire* (1815).

Platonism in Shelley's Poetry Written in 1814-1815

Alastor

Autumn of 1815

Alastor marks the beginning of a kind of Platonic poetry which Shelley continued to write the rest of his life. It sets the Platonic pattern which other poems like *Laon and Cythna, Prince Athanase,* and *Epipsychidion* follow with variation. The Platonism in these poems is essentially rooted in the natural Platonism of the poetic mind, which, as Shelley himself states, seeks in a mortal image the likeness of the eternal. The Platonism in these poems is a dramatization of this Platonic quest; in Shelley it takes the form of the central character of the poem, who is usually Shelley's *alter ego.* Although the dramatization shapes up differently in each of these poems, the hero is a reflection of the natural Platonism in Shelley's own soul, which manifested itself in his life as a continuous search on this earth for a physical counterpart of an ideal beauty. The sphere wherein ideal beauty manifests itself for Shelley is (1) nature, which is a veil of ideal beauty, a realm in which "some spirit of great intelligence and power" invests the visible world with beauty; and (2) woman, who is for the poet the prototype on earth of his own

natural platonism?
is this a schism in the 2 voices

Platonic soul, a veiled maid, as in *Alastor,* "whose voice was like the voice of his own soul." Shelley's natural Platonism is largely preoccupied with these two manifestations of Ideal Beauty on this earth (*vide supra,* pp. 17-21).

It is important to realize the significant and basic differences between Shelley's and Plato's natural Platonism. Shelley's natural Platonism is determined by his nature, temperament, and experiences. Whereas Plato seeks a completely intellectualized and unsensualized idea, Shelley seeks a "veiled maid" who incarnates Ideal Beauty. The symbolic incarnation of ideal love and beauty in the form of beautiful women in contrast to Plato's completely intellectual otherworldliness is the identity-in-difference between Plato and Shelley. Our poet is not a dialectician, but a poet who, even though he searches for truth and "the fountain of divine philosophy," is always in love with earthly forms which he, to his sorrow, often confuses with the ideal; he follows the Platonic gleam in his own romantic and image-clinging way. Shelley's expression of Platonism is the poet's way, which Milton has described as

> what surmounts the reach
> Of human sense, I shall delineate so,
> By lik'ning spiritual to corporal forms
> As may express them best . . . .
>   (*Paradise Lost,* V, 571-574)

Alastor is the first of Shelley's poems which expresses natural Platonism as the search on earth for a Platonic soul-mate, who is the physical counterpart of Ideal Beauty. It is the Platonic leitmotif which is to appear in *Laon and Cythna, Prince Athanase, Epipsychidion,* and other poems.

This basic mood of natural Platonism was articulately shaped and influenced by the Platonic tradition. Starting with Dante, philosophic poetry had made woman an immanent and transcendent symbol, a veiled intermediary between the ideal and earthly world; it had developed the symbolism of the "veil," had endowed it with much of the poetic coloration and atmosphere. Shelley was greatly influenced by its expressions in the Platonic tradition. As we have seen in the account of the Platonic tradition in Shelley's reading (*vide supra,* pp. 95-97, 105, 136, 139-144, 151-152), Wieland's *Agathon* and *Peregrinus Proteus,* Spenser's *Faerie Queene,* Rousseau, Petrarch, and Lady Morgan's *The Missionary,* which Shelley had been reading shortly before the composition of *Alastor,* are of major importance for Shelley's Platonism. In particu-

lar Wieland's *Agathon* (*vide supra,* pp. 140-143) influenced and shaped
the Platonism of Shelley's *Alastor;* this is evident not only in the similarity of the poet in *Alastor* to Agathon, a Platonic idealist who loves
Psyche, the embodiment of Platonic love, but also in such phrases as
"heavenly beauty enveloped in a terrestrial veil," which finds a counterpart in the vision of a veiled maid in *Alastor.* Shelley's attraction to
Platonic Love as expressed in the Platonic tradition is so great that even
when in 1817 he read the *Symposium* itself, he shaped its transmutation
in *Prince Athanase* largely on the basis of traditional Platonism (*vide
supra,* pp. 48-54). Thus it is evident that the natural Platonism in
Alastor is deeply influenced by the Platonic tradition.

The poem entitled *Alastor* may be considered as allegorical of one of the
most interesting situations of the human mind. It represents a youth of un-
corrupted feelings and adventurous genius led forth by an imagination inflamed and purified through familiarity with all that is excellent and majestic,
to the contemplation of the universe. He drinks deep of the fountains of
knowledge, and is still insatiate. The magnificence and beauty of the external
world sinks profoundly into the frame of his conceptions, and affords to their
modifications a variety not to be exhausted. So long as it is possible for his
desires to point towards objects thus infinite and unmeasured, he is joyous,
and tranquil, and self-possessed. But the period arrives when these objects
cease to suffice. His mind is at length suddenly awakened and thirsts for
intercourse with an intelligence similar to itself. He images to himself the
Being whom he loves. Conversant with speculations of the sublimest and
most perfect natures, the vision in which he embodies his own imaginations
unites all of wonderful, or wise, or beautiful, which the poet, the philosopher,
or the lover could depicture. The intellectual faculties, the imagination, the
functions of sense, have their respective requisitions on the sympathy of corresponding powers in other human beings. The Poet is represented as uniting
these requisitions, and attaching them to a single image. He seeks in vain
for a prototype of his conception. Blasted by his disappointment, he descends
to an untimely grave.

(Preface)

In this statement Shelley delineates the stages in the search for Ideal
Beauty: first, the beauty of the external world impresses and permeates
the poet's mind; then the mind of the poet suddenly awakens and
"thirsts for intercourse with an intelligence similar to itself" (see *Symposium* and *Phaedrus* for a similar view); the approach is through
imagery (compare the use of imagery in the philosopher's quest in
Republic, 510d-e); the vision embodies the wisdom and beauty which

the philosopher, the poet, and the lover seek; it is the quest for unity in multiplicity; finally the failure to find the "prototype of his conception" on this earth is the very conclusion of Platonism itself, as Shelley later acknowledges in a letter to Gisborne (*vide infra,* p. 276). Shelley, with a mythopoeic talent comparable to that of Plato, writes an allegory to express the birth and experiences of the Platonic mood in the poet. Though the motto to the poem comes from Augustine (*Confessions,* Book III, chap. i), Shelley's interpretation of *amans amare* is essentially Platonic.

> Mother of this unfathomable world!
> Favour my solemn song, for I have loved
> Thee ever, and thee only; I have watched
> Thy shadow, and the darkness of thy steps,
> And my heart ever gazes on the depth
> Of thy deep mysteries.
>
> (Ll. 18-23)

In these lines Shelley makes use of Plato's favorite image of shadow versus the original (see *Republic,* 510e). These lines foreshadow the greater development of this symbolism in *Hymn to Intellectual Beauty* (*vide infra,* p. 204).

> By solemn vision and bright silver dream,
> His infancy was nurtured. Every sight
> And sound from the vast earth and ambient air,
> Sent to his heart its choicest impulses.
> The fountains of divine philosophy
> Fled not his thirsting lips, and all of great,
> Or good, or lovely, which the sacred past
> In truth or fable consecrates, he felt
> And knew.
>
> (Ll. 67-75)

The nature of infancy is conceived here in a Wordsworthian Neoplatonism (*vide supra,* pp. 164-165); the education in the "good, or lovely" of divine philosophy is partly, as his own readings show, autobiographic of Shelley's philosophical interest in Plato and other philosophers.

> . . . but ever gazed
> And gazed, till meaning on his vacant mind
> Flashed like strong inspiration, and he saw
> The thrilling secrets of the birth of time.
>
> (Ll. 125-128)

The language in these lines is analogous to Plato's expression in *Letter* VII, 341c.

> He dreamed a veilèd maid
> Sate near him, talking in low solemn tones.
> Her voice was like the voice of his own soul
> Heard in the calm of thought . . . .
> (Ll. 151-154)

For the Platonic elements in these lines, see commentary on the Platonism of *Alastor, supra,* pages 189-191.

> Knowledge and truth and virtue were her theme,
> And lofty hopes of divine liberty,
> Thoughts the most dear to him, and poesy,
> Himself a poet.
> (Ll. 158-161)

Shelley's Platonic women are the intellectual counterpart of his own soul and its characteristics.

> Her glowing limbs beneath the sinuous veil . . .
> (L. 176)

The veil is another characteristic of Shelley's Platonic women; its Platonic connotation of philosophical half-revealing and half-concealing is not always present, as this instance shows.

> Does the dark gate of death
> Conduct to thy mysterious paradise,
> O Sleep? Does the bright arch of rainbow clouds . . .
> (Ll. 211-213)

For an analogous statement, see Plato's *Apology,* 40c-41c.

> O stream!
> Whose source is inaccessibly profound,
> Whither do thy mysterious waters tend?
> Thou imagest my life. Thy darksome stillness,
> Thy dazzling waves, thy loud and hollow gulfs,
> Thy searchless fountain, and invisible course
> Have each their type in me: And the wide sky,
> And measureless ocean may declare as soon
> What oozy cavern or what wandering cloud
> Contains thy waters, as the universe

Tell where these living thoughts reside, when stretched
Upon thy flowers my bloodless limbs shall waste
I' the passing wind!

(Ll. 502-514)

Grabo (*The Magic Plant,* pp. 176-178) sees in the boat (see ll. 299 ff.) and stream Neoplatonic symbols of the soul and its voyage through life. That Shelley was conscious of any Neoplatonic symbolism in these lines seems doubtful. W. B. Yeats in his study of Shelley's symbolism has pointed out that the symbol of the stream was inspired by Shelley's sailing on rivers and streams in an open boat. In his preface to *Laon and Cythna* Shelley lists among the things that helped to make him a poet sailing down mighty rivers and streams. Shelley was a natural Platonic symbolist, and one can even go so far as to read in these lines an analogous expression of the Neoplatonic relation of the microcosm and macrocosm. A simpler expression of the same thought appears in *Adonais,* line 370: "He is made one with Nature," where a portion of the Eternal goes back to its ultimate source, even as in Plotinus's philosophy of emanation (see commentary on these lines of the *Adonais, infra,* p. 296). For the boat and stream as a symbol, see W. B. Yeats, *Ideas of Good and Evil²* (London, 1903), pages 115 ff.; A. T. Strong, *Three Studies in Shelley* (Oxford, 1921), pages 89-105; G. Wilson Knight, *The Starlit Dome* (London, 1941), pages 186-187, 228-230.

To—
Δάϰϱυσι διοίσω πότμον ἄποτμον
1815

Ah! wherefore didst thou build thine hope
On the false earth's inconstancy?

(Ll. 19-20)

A natural Platonic realization of the inconstancy of the relative world. (The Greek comes from Euripides's *Hippolytus,* line 1144. Since "some plays of Euripides" are recorded in Shelley's reading for 1815, the poem should be dated in 1815.)

Mutability

Late 1815 or early 1816

We are as clouds that veil the midnight moon;
   How restlessly they speed, and gleam, and quiver,
Streaking the darkness radiantly!—yet soon
   Night closes round, and they are lost for ever:

Or like forgotten lyres, whose dissonant strings
   Give various response to each varying blast,
To whose frail frame no second motion brings
   One mood or modulation like the last.

We rest.—A dream has power to poison sleep;
   We rise.—One wandering thought pollutes the day;
We feel, conceive or reason, laugh or weep;
   Embrace fond woe, or cast our cares away:

It is the same!—For, be it joy or sorrow,
   The path of its departure still is free:
Man's yesterday may ne'er be like his morrow;
   Nought may endure but Mutability.

The title of the poem is an echo of the Platonic tradition in Spenser. Shelley possibly found it in his reading in 1815 of Spenser's *Faerie Queene: Booke VII, Two Cantos of Mutabilitie* (see C. H. Whitman, *A Subject-Index to the Poems of Edmund Spenser* [New Haven, 1918], *s.v.* Mutabilitie). The two cantos on *Mutabilitie* are an allegorical dramatization of the Platonic dualism of Eternity versus Change. Compare

But stedfast rest of all things firmely stayd
Upon the pillours of Eternity,
That is contrayr to *Mutabilitie:*
For, all that moueth, doth in *Change* delight . . . .
            (Canto VIII)

(For the Platonism in this poem, see H.S.V. Jones, *A Spenser Handbook* [New York, 1930], pp. 305-308.) The experience described here is Shelley's consciousness of the Heraclitean flux which characterizes the earthly and human experiences in contrast to the permanence of the ideal and divine realm. In this poem Shelley expresses only the lower realm; in his later poems he contrasts the two worlds. In the first line of the poem we have the Platonic image of life as a veil which half-reveals and half-conceals the ideal world of permanence. For the part which Mutability plays in Shelley's philosophy, see White, *The Best of Shelley,* pages 470-471.

Shelley's Reading in Plato and the Platonic Tradition in 1816

direct platonism: ?

indirect platonism: Lucretius (1816; July 28, 29, 1816); Lucian (1816;

September 29, October 21-22, November 10-14, 1816); Milton's *Paradise Lost* (1816; November 15-22, 1816); Montaigne's essays (1816; September 24, October 18-27, 29-30, November 2-5, 7-10, 1816); Gibbon, *The Decline and Fall of the Roman Empire* (1816; November 25-26, 28-30, December 1, 3-4, 1816); Locke (November 15-23, December 5, 1816); Rousseau, *Émile* (1816; September 22, 1816), *Julie, ou la Nouvelle Héloïse* (1816); Godwin, *Political Justice* (1816; November 29-31, December 1, 1816); Coleridge, *Lay Sermon* (1816); Peacock, *Headlong Hall* (1816).

PLATONISM IN SHELLEY'S POETRY WRITTEN IN 1816

Hymn to Intellectual Beauty

June 30, 1816

It will be shown that the experience described in Shelley's *Hymn to Intellectual Beauty* is personal and not derivative from Plato. The derivative Platonic element in the poem appears more in the title, which reveals Shelley's awareness of the affinity of his experience with Platonism. There is no evidence in Shelley's letters or Journal that he had been reading Plato shortly before or at the time of the composition of the poem. It is probable that a reading of Spenser's Platonic Hymns suggested to Shelley the title of his poem. We have a specific entry in the Journal for Mary Shelley's reading of Spenser's Platonic Hymns on September 1, 1818. As Mary's reading is often a reflection of Shelley's previous reading, it is likely that Shelley, too, read Spenser's Platonic Hymns. He ordered Spenser's works in December, 1812, and Spenser appears in his reading for 1815. It is very likely that Shelley had read Spenser's *An Hymne of Heavenly Beautie*, for the title of his own poem is, with the substitution of the adjective "Intellectual" for "Heavenly," the same as Spenser's title.

Yet even Shelley's substitution is derived from the Platonic tradition rather than Plato himself. The phrase "Intellectual Beauty," which is synonymous with the essence of Platonism, is not found anywhere in Plato's Dialogues. It was evidently coined by Plotinus and first appears in *Enneads,* V, viii, which is entitled Περὶ τοῦ νοητοῦ κάλλους, *Concerning Intellectual Beauty*. Plotinus and the other Neoplatonists do not appear in Shelley's reading. It can be shown, however, that Shelley found the phrase "Intellectual Beauty" floating in the Platonic and Neoplatonic tradition. The phrase was so attractively presented in

Shelley's reading that we need not assume a hypothetical reading of Neoplatonic literature.[5] The following instances found in books which Shelley read prior to the composition of the *Hymn to Intellectual Beauty* in the summer of 1816 are sufficient in number and attractiveness to influence Shelley's choice of the title for a poem embodying a personal Platonic experience.

Among the books which Shelley ordered from Clio Rickman on December 24, 1812, was Lord Monboddo's *Of the Origin and Progress of Language*. It is very probable, as Professor White suggests, that Shelley received most of the books in the list and read them at Tanyrallt. In discussing the Pythagorean music of the spheres Monboddo says: "If it be objected, that this intellectual music of the Pythagoreans is as difficult to be conceived as Plato's intellectual beauty, I answer, that I myself have known a man who understood it perfectly" (I, 105-106). This passage shows that Plotinus's phrase had become a commonplace Platonic formula.

Furthermore, Shelley read in 1813, and appears to have reread in 1814, Wieland's *Agathon* in Pernay's French translation.[6] This work, as Professor White has shown, had considerable influence on Shelley (*vide supra*, pp. 140-143). Professor White points out that the phrase "Beauté Intellectuelle" occurs twice in this novel. It actually appears three times, in contexts which must have been very attractive to Shelley:

1. When Danae is trying, at the instigation of the sophist Hippias, to seduce Agathon, the Platonic idealist, she knows very well "that no passions were excited by intellectual beauty" (*Agathon,* II, 4).

2. Cleonissa, who is a pupil of Plato at the court of Dionysius, is described by Wieland as one who "kept up the reputation of being a living instance of this Platonic maxim, that external beauty is the reflection of the intellectual beauty of the soul" (IV, 48-49).

3. The last instance of the phrase in the novel is found in a description of Agathon: "Enraptured with the idea of virtue, he imagined not

---

[5] See Carl Grabo, *The Magic Plant* (Chapel Hill, N. C., 1936), p. 248; for the opposite view, which the writer shares, see White, *Shelley,* II, 597. The phrase "Intellectual Beauty" is not found in Thomas Taylor's translation of Plato. The closest parallel is "intelligible beauty"; see *The Works of Plato* (London, 1804), V, 719.

[6] *Histoire d'Agathon,* traduction nouvelle et complète, faite sur la dernière éd. des oeuvres . . . par l'auteur de Piétro d'Alby et Gianette [F. D. Pernay], T. 1-3 (Paris: Maradan, 1801). See T. J. Hogg, *The Life of Shelley,* ed. Humbert Wolfe (London, 1933), II, 144-145. After an extensive search the writer was unable to locate a copy of Pernay's French translation. The English translation used here is C. M. Wieland, *The History of Agathon,* translated from the German original (London, 1773).

that his soul could ever find attractions in what was directly contrary to his intellectual beauty" (III, 78).

Besides this phrase we find in the novel two instances of a variation in the phrase "intellectual love" (II, 28, 178).

In the Preface to *Prometheus Unbound* Shelley refers to "a passion for reforming the World." The Draft Preface in *Shelley's Notebooks*[7] shows that Shelley had read Robert Forsyth's *The Principles of Moral Science* and found the phrase used as the title of Chapter XVI.[8] It is not known when Shelley read this work. If he read it before the summer of 1816, he would have found another instance of the phrase. In the "vision of Hystaspes," modeled after a Platonic myth, men are described as engaged in ideal contemplation: "continually discovering new and deep treasures of reason and truth; and unknown regions of moral and intellectual beauty and excellence are continually rising to their view" (*The Principles of Moral Science*, pp. 513-514).

These examples in Shelley's reading do not exhaust all the possibilities of his contact with the phrase. Shelley was a prodigious reader (see White, *Shelley*, II, index, pp. cviii-cxii), and many of the authors he read were affected by the Platonic tradition. These examples show that Plotinus's phrase had already become in European literature a leitmotif of Platonism. It may have taken only one attractive instance, as in Wieland's *Agathon*, to have Shelley store the phrase in his memory. Then, held in suspension, it was evoked in the creative process, grafted to Spenser's title *An Hymne of Heavenly Beautie*, and thus became *le mot juste* for the expression of the Platonic experience described in the poem.

In order to understand the Platonism of the poem one must have a clear notion of Plato's conception of Ideal Beauty, which is essentially expressed in two important passages in the *Phaedrus* and the *Symposium*. In the *Phaedrus* (249d-252a) Plato remarks:

"Thus far I have been speaking of the fourth and last kind of madness, which is imputed to him who, when he sees the beauty of earth, is transported with the recollection of the true beauty; he would like to fly away, but he cannot; he is like a bird fluttering and looking upward and careless of the world below; and he is therefore thought to be mad. And I have shown this of all inspirations to be the noblest and highest and the offspring of the highest to him who has or shares in it, and that he who loves the beautiful is called a lover because he partakes of it. . . .

[7] H. B. Forman, *The Shelley Notebooks* (St. Louis, Boston, 1911), I, 10.
[8] Robert Forsyth, *The Principles of Moral Science* (Edinburgh, 1805), p. 283.

"But of beauty, I repeat again that we saw her there shining in company with the celestial forms; and coming to earth we find her here too, shining in clearness through the clearest aperture of sense. For sight is the most piercing of our bodily senses; though not by that is wisdom seen; her loveliness would have been transporting if there had been a visible image of her, and the other ideas, if they had visible counterparts, would be equally lovely. But this is the privilege of beauty, that being the loveliest she is also the most palpable to sight. Now he who is not newly initiated or who has become corrupted, does not easily rise out of this world to the sight of true beauty in the other; he looks only at her earthly namesake, and instead of being awed at the sight of her, he is given over to pleasure, and like a brutish beast he rushes on to enjoy and beget; he consorts with wantonness, and is not afraid or ashamed of pursuing pleasure in violation of nature. But he whose initiation is recent, and who has been the spectator of many glories in the other world, is amazed when he sees any one having a god-like face or form, which is the expression of divine beauty; and at first a shudder runs through him, and again the old awe steals over him; then looking upon the face of his beloved as of a god he reverences him, and if he were not afraid of being thought a downright madman, he would sacrifice to his beloved as to the image of a god; then while he gazes on him there is a sort of reaction, and the shudder passes into an unusual heat and perspiration; for, as he receives the effluence of beauty through the eyes, the wing moistens and he warms. And as he warms, the parts out of which the wing grew, and which had been hitherto closed and rigid, and had prevented the wing from shooting forth, are melted, and as nourishment streams upon him, the lower end of the wings begins to swell and grow from the root upwards; and the growth extends under the whole soul—for once the whole was winged. During this process the whole soul is all in a state of ebullition and effervescence,—which may be compared to the irritation and uneasiness in the gums at the time of cutting teeth,—bubbles up, and has a feeling of uneasiness and tickling; but when in like manner the soul is beginning to grow wings, the beauty of the beloved meets her eye and she receives the sensible warm motion of particles which flow towards her, therefore called emotion (ἵμερος), and is refreshed and warmed by them, and then she ceases from her pain with joy. But when she is parted from her beloved and her moisture fails, then the orifices of the passage out of which the wing shoots dry up and close, and intercept the germ of the wing; which, being shut up with the emotion, throbbing as with the pulsations of an artery, pricks the aperture which is nearest, until at length the entire soul is pierced and maddened and pained and at the recollection of beauty is again delighted. And from both of them together the soul is oppressed at the strangeness of her condition, and is in a great strait and excitement, and in her madness can neither sleep by night nor abide in her place by day. And wherever she thinks that she will behold the beautiful one, thither in her desire she runs. And when she has seen him, and bathed her-self in the waters of beauty, her constraint is loosened, and she is refreshed, and has no more pangs and pains; and this is the sweetest of all pleasures at the time, and is the reason why the soul of the lover will never forsake his beautiful one, whom he esteems above all . . . ."

In the *Symposium* (210a-211d) Plato gives a more philosophically substantial account of the same conception:

"These are the lesser mysteries of love, into which even you, Socrates, may enter; to the greater and more hidden ones which are the crown of these, and to which, if you pursue them in a right spirit, they will lead, I know not whether you will be able to attain. But I will do my utmost to inform you, and do you follow if you can. For he who would proceed aright in this matter should begin in youth to visit beautiful forms; and first, if he be guided by his instructor aright, to love one such form only—out of that he should create fair thoughts; and soon he will of himself perceive that the beauty of one form is akin to the beauty of another; and then if beauty of form in general is his pursuit, how foolish would he be not to recognize that the beauty in every form is one and the same! And when he perceives this he will abate his violent love of the one, which he will despise and deem a small thing, and will become a lover of all beautiful forms; in the next stage he will consider that the beauty of the mind is more honourable than the beauty of the outward form. So that if a virtuous soul have but a little comeliness, he will be content to love and tend him, and will search out and bring to the birth thoughts which may improve the young, until he is com-pelled to contemplate and see the beauty of institutions and laws, and to understand that the beauty of them all is of one family, and that personal beauty is a trifle; and after laws and institutions he will go on to the sciences, that he may see their beauty, being not like a servant in love with the beauty of one youth or man or institution, himself a slave mean and narrow-minded, but drawing towards and contemplating the vast sea of beauty, he will create many fair and noble thoughts and notions in boundless love of wisdom; until on that shore he grows and waxes strong, and at last the vision is re-vealed to him of a single science, which is the science of beauty everywhere. To this I will proceed; please to give me your very best attention:

"He who has been instructed thus far in the things of love, and who has learned to see the beautiful in due order and succession, when he comes toward the end will suddenly perceive a nature of wondrous beauty (and this, Socrates, is the final cause of all our former toils)—a nature which in the first place is everlasting, not growing and decaying, or waxing and waning; secondly, not fair in one point of view and foul in another, or at one time or in one relation or at one place fair, at another time or in another relation or at another place foul, as if fair to some and foul to others, or in the likeness of a face or hands or any other part of the bodily frame, or in any form of speech or knowledge, or existing in any other being, as for example, in an animal, or in heaven, or in earth, or in any other place; but beauty absolute, separate, simple, and everlasting, which without diminution and without increase, or any change, is imparted to the ever-growing and perishing beauties of all other things. He who from these ascending under the influence of true love, begins to perceive that beauty, is not far from the end. And the true order of going, or being led by another, to the things of love, is to begin from the beauties of earth and mount upwards for the sake of that other beauty, using these as steps only, and from one going on to two, and from two to all fair forms, and from fair forms to fair practices, and from fair practices to fair notions, until from fair notions he arrives at the notion of absolute beauty, and at last knows what the essence of beauty is. . . ."

If we read the *Hymn to Intellectual Beauty* in the light of these passages, it is apparent at once that Shelley's poem is not directly derived from Plato. In the first place the poem is not the result of a reading of Plato, as *Prince Athanase* was; it was written when Shelley was deeply stirred by the scenic beauty of Switzerland, which agitated him "even to tears." In the second place Shelley had experienced this visitation of Ideal Beauty since childhood (see the fifth and sixth stanzas). The poem is a testament of the natural Platonism in Shelley's own soul. A corroboration of this is seen in Wordsworth's *The Prelude*, which, although not yet published, describes a similar awareness of an immanent transcendent Beauty. As Shelley grew older and pursued this Beauty with "studious zeal," he found in Plato's pages a similar experience, and in shaping the articulation of his own native experience he gave it a Platonic title. That this was the case is apparent in Shelley's translation of the *Symposium* in 1818. As we have seen, the phrase "Intellectual Beauty" is not found in Plato; yet in his translation of the *Symposium* Shelley translated Plato's phrase ἀλλ' ἐπὶ τὸ πολὺ πέλαγος τετραμμένος τοῦ καλοῦ (210d) as "would turn towards the wide ocean of intellectual beauty." The interpolation of the word *intellectual* shows that Shelley definitely associated his own experience with that of Plato. Thus it is evident that the Platonism of the *Hymn* is a natural Platonism which had haunted Shelley since childhood; at the time of the composition of the *Hymn* Shelley realized its Platonic affinities and gave it a Platonic title which he had found in the Platonic tradition rather than in Plato himself.

For a better understanding of the *Hymn* it is well to compare and contrast Shelley's conception of Intellectual Beauty with Plato's Ideal

Beauty. The kinship of these two conceptions consists in identity-in-difference. Both reveal a fundamental kinship in that they are expressions of the natural Platonism of a mind which sees an immanent and transcendent relation between the intellectual and relative world (*vide supra*, p. 18). Both conceptions make use of the imagery of shadow and original to express this relationship. Shelley's conception of Beauty is more akin to that in the *Phaedrus* than that in the *Symposium*. The lovers in the *Hymn* and the *Phaedrus* have much in common. Shelley's lover is desolate in a vale of tears; he shrieks and clasps his hands in ecstasy when the shadow of Beauty falls on him. Plato's lover is pierced, maddened, and pained in his soul; he is "like a bird fluttering and looking upward and careless of the world below"; at the sight of beauty "first a shudder runs through him, and again the old awe steals over him"; his "soul is all in a state of ebullition and effervescence" and like Shelley's lover is refreshed after communion with Beauty, "and has no more pangs and pains." A comparison of Shelley's conception with that in the *Symposium* shows the one fundamental difference between Shelley's lover and Plato's lover: Shelley's lover is constantly seeking the shadow of Beauty on this earth; Plato's lover starts with the shadow of Beauty on the earth and immediately transcends it in a dialectical pursuit of its shadows in morals and sciences. Though it is titled *Intellectual Beauty,* Shelley's poem is emotional and mystic rather than intellectual and objective, as is Plato's conception. In Plato we have a progressive ascent from particular beauties to Beauty, each step attained by the use of reason alone, with only the suggestion of the senses in the preliminary stage; in Shelley we have an imaginative leap with little distinction between emotion and idea. Shelley's approach is purely aesthetic, whereas Plato's is ethical, logical, and metaphysical as well. Shelley's is biographical, and Plato's is objective and universal; the poet's joy and sorrows find intense romantic expression, whereas the philosopher's revelation has the calm soaring, bursting to white heat of ineffable emotion only when the ultimate "ocean of Beauty" is reached. A realization of these differences will serve to clarify the difference between the Platonic experiences of the poet and the philosopher. Yet even here the difference verges on similarity, for Shelley's lover, after the visitation of Beauty in childhood, outwatches the envious night with studious zeal (ll. 65-67). Shelley's lines appear to be a compressed version of Milton's lines in *Il Penseroso:*

> Where I may oft out-watch the *Bear,*
> With thrice great *Hermes,* or unsphear

> The spirit of *Plato* to unfold
> What Worlds, or what vast Regions hold
> The immortal mind that hath forsook
> Her mansion in this fleshly nook.

Since Shelley had been reading Milton in 1815 and 1816, this may well be the case. If so, then Shelley's outwatching the night with studious zeal might well mean a pursuit of Intellectual Beauty through the study of Plato and other Platonic writers which he had been reading since his Oxford days; if we finally associate these lines with Shelley's intention in the preface to *Prometheus Unbound* to "familiarize the highly refined imagination . . . with beautiful idealisms of moral excellence," we can see that Shelley's pursuit of Intellectual Beauty possesses much in common even with Plato's conception in the *Symposium*.

And in their broader aspects there is a considerable philosophical analogy between Shelley's and Plato's conceptions. Both Shelley and Plato show an evolution from Necessity to a personalized Power governing the world. Professor White has traced Shelley's evolution from a dispassionate and mechanical Necessity in *Queen Mab* to Intellectual Beauty, which finally coalesces with the idea of Love to supplant Necessity, now become an almost forgotten overlord (see *The Best of Shelley*, p. 474; *Shelley*, I, 362-363). The stages in this evolution are quite marked; in *The Assassins* in describing the valley Shelley says, "No spectator could have refused to believe that some spirit of great intelligence and power had hallowed these wild and beautiful solitudes to a deep and solemn mystery." The spirit of great intelligence reappears in the preface to *Alastor* as "that Power which strikes the luminaries of the world with sudden darkness and extinction, by awakening them to too exquisite a perception of its influences." The beauty of nature in Switzerland deepened Shelley's awareness of "the inconstant summer of delight which invests this visible world" (Preface to *A History of Six Weeks' Tour*). In the *Hymn to Intellectual Beauty* the often-experienced intuition of an immanent and transcendent Beauty is articulately expressed as a Power whose shadow visits Shelley and the world too infrequently, a power which is intellectual in the sense that it is unseen, or seen only by the eye of the mind as it lives in the world of Beauty. This evolution from a detached Necessity to a Power to which man's spirit is attuned is matched by an analogous evolution in Plato's own thought. In the *Republic* (616c-617d) the universe turns on the spindle of Necessity, which is the mother of the Fates; like Shelley's Necessity, it becomes a forgotten overlord in the development of Plato's thought. It is kept in the background, while Ideal Beauty in the *Symposium* and *Phaedrus* appears to man as a shadow in the physical world which becomes a stepping stone to the apprehension of intelligible Beauty. In the *Sophist* (247e) this Reality appears as Power, and in the *Timaeus* the ultimate cause is shown as an almost personalized God who fills the universe with a world soul that manifests itself in the imperfect Beauty of the relative world. This analogous development in both Shelley and Plato is indicative of a natural Platonism which found in Necessity a traditional conception not satisfying to the poetic and philosophic mind. Thus in this account of the Platonism of the poem it is evident that its greatness lies in its natural, direct, and indirect Platonisms, which upon analysis are distinguishable but in the poem form a perfect fusion.

> The awful shadow of some unseen Power
> Floats tho' unseen among us; visiting
> This various world with as inconstant wing . . .
> (Ll. 1-3)

The statement of the relation of the two realms as one of shadow and original is deeply indebted to the Platonic tradition which ultimately stems from the *Republic* (510e ff.), where the world of Becoming is related to that of Being as a shadow is to its original. The imagery was taken over by Neoplatonism (see *Enneads*, I, ii, 1; III, vi, 7; III, viii, 1; IV, iii, 12; IV, iii, 13), and from there it permeated European thought, becoming a favorite philosophical, religious, and poetical idiom. It became a favorite with Shelley (see *Epipsychidion*, ll. 116, 137, 268; *Prometheus Unbound*, II, iii, 13; O. W. Firkins, *Power and Elusiveness in Shelley*, pp. 156 ff.). Thus this Platonic imagery became such a commonplace in literature that it cannot be classed as a conscious borrowing from Plato.

> Spirit of BEAUTY, that dost consecrate
> With thine own hues all thou dost shine upon
> Of human thought or form,—where art thou gone?
> (Ll. 13-15)

These lines are a very close parallel to Plato's conception of Beauty, even to the extent that the object is consecrated by the visitation of Beauty (see J. A. Notopoulos, "φαντάσματα θεῖα (*Republic* 532c)," *Classical Philology*, XXXIII [1938], 99-100). Even in his use of "illume" (l. 68) Shelley is akin to Plato, who speaks of the Good in the *Republic*

in terms of light (see J. A. Notopoulos, "The Symbolism of the Sun
and Light in the *Republic* of Plato," *Classical Philology*, XXXIX [1944],
163-172, 223-240,; for a study of light in Shelley, see Firkins, *Power and
Elusiveness in Shelley*, pp. 110-118).

> Why dost thou pass away and leave our state,
> This dim vast vale of tears, vacant and desolate?
>   Ask why the sunlight not forever
>   Weaves rainbows o'er yon mountain-river,
> Why aught should fail and fade that once is shown,
>   Why fear and dream and death and birth
>   Cast on the daylight of this earth
>   Such gloom, why man has such a scope
> For love and hate, despondency and hope?
>   (Ll. 16-24)

Shelley's lament for mutability is in sharp contrast to the Platonic
belief that it is not worth the Shelleyan tears (cf. Plato's general attitude
in the *Phaedo*).

> Thy light alone, like mist o'er mountains driven,
>   Or music by the night-wind sent
>   Thro' strings of some still instrument,
>   Or moonlight on a midnight stream,
> Gives grace and truth to life's unquiet dream.
>   (Ll. 32-36)

Shelley is in harmony with Plato in his belief that the ideal world
is what gives "grace and truth to life's unquiet dream." Whatever of
truth or beauty there is in the relative world is derivative from the ideal
world (see *Phaedo*, 100d, *Symposium*, 212). Again the use of "light"
(l. 32) is common to both poet and philosopher.

> Man were immortal and omnipotent,
> Didst thou, unknown and awful as thou art,
> Keep with thy glorious train firm state within his heart.
>   (Ll. 39-41)

The association of immortality with the Spirit of Beauty is another
Platonic belief (see *Symposium*, 209). Also in the *Hymn* (ll. 47-48)
the vanishing of Beauty takes with it the hope of immortality which
makes man fearless of death (cf. *Phaedo*, 107c).

> Sudden, thy shadow fell on me;
> I shrieked, and clasped my hands in extacy!
> I vowed that I would dedicate my powers
> To thee and thine: have I not kept the vow?
>
> (Ll. 59-62)

The conversion in the *Hymn* is aesthetic only, whereas in Plato it is the conversion of the entire soul (see *Republic,* 518, and *Apology,* 21 ff., for a conversion which had a profound effect on Socrates's life. For philosophic conversion, see A. D. Nock, *Conversion* [Oxford, 1933], pp. 164-186).

Mont Blanc
July 23, 1816

This poem is the result of "extatic wonder, not unallied to madness" (letter to Peacock, July 22, 1816); it is an illustration of the madness of the soul in the presence of Beauty which Plato attributes to the poet and lover (see *Phaedrus,* 245b, 250-251). The poem is an amalgam of the natural Platonism which is often aroused in the presence of physical beauty and Platonic concepts which aid Shelley in giving a metaphysical interpretation of the phenomena of nature. Nature is used by Shelley, as by Plato and Berkeley, as the symbol of the inner world of thought, the physical manifestation of

> The secret Strength of things
> Which governs thought, and to the infinite dome
> Of heaven is as a law.

The natural Platonism of the poem centers on the relation of the eternal and the passing. Shelley, like Plato, has a great talent for symbolism; as Plato used the Sun and the Cave to describe the realm of the eternal and the passing, so Shelley uses Mont Blanc and the river Arve to symbolize Power and the temporal world. External nature is conceived of as a stream (the Arve) which symbolizes flux. The relation of Mont Blanc and the Arve is symbolic of the immanent and transcendent relation of Intellectual Beauty (cf. Power as Intellectual Beauty in Shelley's *Hymn*); the streams that finally meet to form one majestic river emanate from the ice gulfs of Mont Blanc, yet though

> Power in likeness of the Arve comes down
> From the ice gulphs that gird his secret throne,

Power itself, like Mont Blanc, is transcendent:

> Power dwells apart in its tranquillity,
> Remote, serene, and inaccessible . . . .

Shelley's genius as a natural Platonic symbolist is evident in his use of a mountain and a stream which has its source in this mountain to symbolize the transcendent yet immanent character of Platonic Reality. Mont Blanc is symbolic of Power, "the secret strength" which governs thought and is the law to the universe; the various streams that flow from the mountain forming one majestic river are symbolic of the temporal experiences that flow through the human mind. The use of a stream for a symbol is as old as Heraclitus (see fragments 41-42), who uses it as a symbol of change; it is a favorite natural metaphysical symbol, as may be seen from its use by Coleridge in *Kubla Khan* (see Knight, *The Starlit Dome*, pp. 101 ff.) and by Robert Frost in *West Running Brook*. In equating Mont Blanc and the Arve with mind and experience, Shelley makes a slight but significant change; the ravine is a passive recipient of the Arve, whereas for Shelley the mind through which the stream flows is, like Plato's conception of the soul (*Phaedrus*, 245e), an active agent. The mind is endowed with a power which it derives from "secret springs"; though not developed, the "springs" are, as will be shown later, symbolic of a power emanating from the mind's immortal and divine heritage. The fusion of the stream of the external universe with the stream of the soul may be interpreted as a Platonic conception of the mind in contrast to the Lockean conception; it marks a turning point from materialism to immaterialism. The fusion of the two streams may further be interpreted either as the Platonic macrocosm and microcosm or, in the light of the *Timaeus*, as the world which is created by the imposition of divine form and values on the relative world. Perhaps this is why Shelley describes the stream as "with a sound but half its own." The result, therefore, of the fusion is an animate cosmos, a manifestation of the world soul which figures prominently in Shelley's conception of the universe.

In the second stanza of the poem Shelley develops the Platonic theme paratactically. Like Pindar, he leaps from symbol to symbol with slight formal transition. The imagery of the poem is itself in flux; it becomes the moving and kaleidoscopic image of Eternity, which remains the same. There is a technique of transposition in the symbols in this stanza. The Ravine of Arve is like the receptacle of the *Timaeus* (50c) on which the pattern of God is imposed; "Power" (l. 16), like the stream of Arve, is the visitation or imposition of the ideal world upon the "receptacle" of nature. Thus nature is pervaded with the "ceaseless motion" of the divine. In all this we can see a technique of transposition: the stream of Arve is no longer the symbol of flux, but that of "Power" pervading the passive Ravine of Arve, which is the symbol of the relative world. Shelley has selected the stream in the second stanza, not for its mutability, but for its "ceaseless motion," the "lightning" of its visitation, its power, life, and vitality. There is nothing static in Shelley's symbols; they partake of the rapid, constantly shifting movements of his imagination.

As he proceeds in the second stanza Shelley shifts the focus to another Platonic symbol. Mind is to the influence that visits it as the Ravine is to the stream of Arve. It is the theme of image and original which was developed in the *Hymn to Intellectual Beauty*. The essential difference between "mind" in line 37 and "mind" in line 2 is that of the mind of the poet, passive because he is in "a trance sublime" as the result of the spectacle before him, and mind in general capable of acting. With this exception there is a common denominator to the first and second Platonic symbols.

The natural Platonism of the relation of thought and nature is developed in lines 37-47 by means of traditional Platonic imagery. The mind, in intercourse with the "clear universe of things around," ventures on the wings of thought to the "cave of the witch Poesy,"

> Seeking among the shadows that pass by
> Ghosts of all things that are, some shade of thee,
> Some phantom, some faint image . . . .

These are a felicitous transcription of Plato's doctrine that the temporal world is but a shadow of the Ideas, "the essences that are." The conception is developed in the *Republic* (507b), and Shelley's language here points to direct knowledge of this doctrine and the symbolism which Plato uses to express it. Though Shelley may have known of this doctrine through an earlier reading of the *Republic*, he probably was refreshed in his reminiscence of it by Bacon's *idola specus,* to which Shelley refers in his *Essay on Christianity,* written shortly after this poem (*vide infra,* pp. 327-328). It forms an excellent illustration of Shelley's natural Platonism refracted through direct and indirect Platonism. This Platonic doctrine is one of the dominant themes in Shelley's Platonism.

In the third stanza we have allusions to Platonic themes like the pre-existence of the soul and whether death is a sleep. The visitation of "gleams of a remoter world" is attributed by Shelley to unnamed sources. It might refer to Wordsworth's *Ode on Intimations of Immortality* or to the doctrine of the *Phaedo,* which he passionately embraced at Oxford. It is these gleams from another world that must be the "secret springs" of the soul in line 5. From this realm comes the "unknown omnipotence" which unfurls the "veil of life and death"; one is enabled to see Mont Blanc as the symbol of the ideal world, apart in its tranquillity, a mountain which is symbolic of the Neoplatonic doctrine of emanation, teaching mankind, and before whose grandeur and majesty the spirit of the poet fails, as in the *Hymn to Intellectual Beauty.*

Here again Shelley's paratactic technique in the use of symbols is manifest; to express the ideal world he uses stream versus mountain, ravine versus stream, shadows versus things that are; and in a sweeping feeling of exaltation he finds in Mont Blanc the loftiest symbol to express the eternity of Being in Platonic philosophy. The Platonism of this poem consists of a series of images from nature, transposed with Aeschylus's or Pindar's paratactic genius, to symbolize the natural Platonism of earthly and ideal. Just as Plato uses the sun as the image of the Good, so Shelley uses a mountain as the most permanent, abiding, enduring, majestic, and immanent-transcendent phenomenon in nature to symbolize the highest Beauty.

> The everlasting universe of things
> Flows through the mind, and rolls its rapid waves,
> Now dark—now glittering—now reflecting gloom—
> Now lending splendour, where from secret springs
> The source of human thought its tribute brings
> Of waters,—with a sound but half its own . . . .
>
> (Ll. 1-6)

For the Platonism in these lines, see introductory remarks *supra,* pages 206-208. The relation of nature to mind is conceived somewhat in Platonic epistemology; the relative world is characterized by flux, unstable reflections of light and darkness, while the mind contributes to experience from its own sources which are in the divine nature of the soul (cf. ll. 49-50).

> Thus thou, Ravine of Arve—dark, deep Ravine—
> Thou many-coloured, many-voiced vale,
> Over whose pines, and crags, and caverns sail
> Fast cloud-shadows, and sunbeams: awful scene,
> Where Power in likeness of the Arve comes down
> From the ice gulphs that gird his secret throne,
> Bursting thro' these dark mountains like the flame

> Of lightning thro' the tempest; thou dost lie,—
> Thy giant brood of pines around thee clinging,
> Children of elder time, in whose devotion
> The chainless winds still come and ever came
> To drink their odours, and their mighty swinging
> To hear—an old and solemn harmony;
> Thine earthly rainbows stretched across the sweep
> Of the ethereal waterfall, whose veil
> Robes some unsculptured image; the strange sleep
> Which when the voices of the desert fail
> Wraps all in its own deep eternity;
> Thy caverns echoing to the Arve's commotion,
> A loud, lone sound no other sound can tame;
> Thou art pervaded with that ceaseless motion,
> Thou art the path of that unresting sound . . . .
>
> 　　　　　　　　　　　(Ll. 12-33)

The relation of the Ravine of Arve to the river Arve is that of image and original which for Shelley is a "Power," or the ideal world.

> Dizzy Ravine! and when I gaze on thee
> I seem as in a trance sublime and strange
> To muse on my own separate phantasy,
> My own, my human mind, which passively
> Now renders and receives fast influencings,
> Holding an unremitting interchange
> With the clear universe of things around . . . .
>
> 　　　　　　　　　　　(Ll. 34-40)

The mind is conceived somewhat like the prisoner in the cave of the *Republic* passively receiving images.

> In the still cave of the witch Poesy,
> Seeking among the shadows that pass by
> Ghosts of all things that are, some shade of thee,
> Some phantom, some faint image; till the breast
> From which they fled recalls them, thou art there!
>
> 　　　　　　　　　　　(Ll. 44-48)

These lines are one of the most Platonic echoes in Shelley (see introduction, *supra,* pp. 208-209). W. B. Yeats points out the association of the cave and the stream in many of Shelley's poems. He surmises that Shelley "may have seen some cave that was the bed of a rivulet by some river side, or have followed some mountain stream to its source in a cave. . . . But so good a Platonist as Shelley could hardly have thought of any cave as a symbol, without thinking of Plato's cave that was the world" (*Ideas of Good and Evil*, pp. 115, 117-118). For the cave as a symbol in the poetry of Coleridge and Shelley, see Knight, *The Starlit Dome*, pages 99-100, 186, 192, 214-215.

> Some say that gleams of a remoter world
> Visit the soul in sleep,—that death is slumber,
> And that its shapes the busy thoughts outnumber
> Of those who wake and live.—I look on high;
> Has some unknown omnipotence unfurled
> The veil of life and death? or do I lie
> In dream, and does the mightier world of sleep
> Spread far around and inaccessibly
> Its circles?
>
> (Ll. 49-57)

Shelley here touches upon, without developing, such Platonic themes as the immortality of the soul and death as a sleep (see introduction, *supra,* pp. 208-209).

> Power dwells apart in its tranquillity,
> Remote, serene, and inaccessible . . . .
>
> (Ll. 96-97)

Mutability is contrasted with transcendent Power, whose visible symbol is Mont Blanc (see Knight, *The Starlit Dome*, p. 104).

> The secret Strength of things
> Which governs thought, and to the infinite dome
> Of heaven is as a law, inhabits thee!
> And what were thou, and earth, and stars, and sea,
> If to the human mind's imaginings
> Silence and solitude were vacancy?
>
> (Ll. 139-144)

For the spiritual essence of Power, see introduction, *supra,* pages 206-207. These lines reveal a modification of the doctrine of Necessity by Intellectual Beauty (see White, *The Best of Shelley*, pp. xliv, 475).

SHELLEY'S READING IN PLATO AND THE PLATONIC TRADITION, 1817

DIRECT PLATONISM: February 23, 1817: "Several of the works of Plato"; *Menexenus, Symposium* (1817; August 13, 1817); *Phaedrus* (part; 1817).

INDIRECT PLATONISM: Apuleius, *Story of Psyche* (1817; May 9, 1817); Spenser, *Faerie Queene* (1817; April 13, 14, 23, 24, 25, 29, May 9, 13, 15, 19-21, June 5-6, 14, July 8, 10, 11, 22, 1817); Berkeley (1817; December 12-14, 1817); Hume, *Essays* (1817); Gibbon, *Decline and Fall* (1817; August 5, 9, 13, 17, December 24-31, 1817); Godwin, *Political Justice* (1817; November 29, December 1, 1817); Godwin, *Mandeville* (1817; December 2, 1817); Robert Forsyth, *Principles of Moral Science* (1817-1818?); Rousseau, *Discours sur les sciences et les arts* (December, 1817-1818); Coleridge, *Biographia Literaria* (1817; December 8, 1817); Peacock, *Melincourt* (1817); Peacock, *Rhododaphne* (November 28?, 1817).

PLATONISM IN SHELLEY'S POETRY WRITTEN IN 1817

To Constantia, Singing

1817

> The cope of Heaven seems rent and cloven
>   By the enchantment of thy strain,
> And o'er my shoulders wings are woven
> To follow its sublime career
> Beyond the mighty moons that wane
>   Upon the verge of Nature's utmost sphere
>   Till the world's shadowy walls are past and disappear.

(Ll. 27-33)

The sprouting of wings on the shoulders and the ascent to "Nature's utmost sphere" where "the world's shadowy walls are past and disappear" is an echo of the *Phaedrus* (249d-251). Inasmuch as Shelley refers to the *Phaedrus* in his review of Peacock's *Rhododaphne*, it is probable that Shelley is echoing the language of the *Phaedrus*. Cf. Horace, *Odes*, 2, 20.

Fragment: Igniculus Desiderii

1817

> To thirst and find no fill—to [wail] and wander
> With short unsteady steps—to pause and ponder—
> To feel the blood run through the veins and tingle
> Where busy thought and blind sensation mingle;
> To nurse the image of unfelt caresses
> Till [dizzy] imagination just possesses
> The half created shadow, then all the night
> Sick . . .

(Ll. 1-8)

A romantic illustration of love described in *Symposium*, 200. The title comes from Cicero's *Epp. ad Familiares*, XV, 20, 2.

Fragment: Amor Aeternus
1817

> Wealth and dominion fade into the mass
>   Of the great sea of human right and wrong
> When once from our possession they must pass;
>   But love, though misdirected, is among
> The things which are immortal, and surpass
>   All that frail stuff which will be—or which was.

(Ll. 1-6)

A Platonic affirmation and yearning of the eternal amid the flux. Possibly an echo of the reading of the *Symposium*.

Laon and Cythna
March 15 ?—Sept. 23, 1817

In the preface to this poem Shelley says:

The poetry of ancient Greece and Rome, and modern Italy, and our own country, has been to me, like external nature, a passion and an enjoyment. Such are the sources from which the materials for the imagery of my Poem have been drawn. I have considered Poetry in its most comprehensive sense; and have read the Poets and the Historians, and Metaphysicians whose writings have been accessible to me, and have looked upon the beautiful and majestic scenery of the earth as common sources of those elements which it is the province of the Poet to embody and combine.

These remarks are significant for the study of the Platonism of the poem, which is poorly assimilated with its revolutionary character; they reveal a conscious effort on Shelley's part to single out the sources of his poetry. Of the sources which he mentions, the beautiful scenery of nature is the source of considerable natural Platonism in the poem. The possibilities of direct Platonism in the poem are many, for Shelley read in 1817 several works of Plato, including the *Symposium* and part of the *Phaedrus*, and his friends and companions frequently mention his reading of Plato at Marlow. Finally, the extensive reading in indirect Platonism, such as Apuleius's *Story of Psyche*, Spenser's *Faerie Queene*, Berkeley, Peacock's *Melincourt*, and Coleridge's *Biographia Literaria*, accounts for much of the indirect Platonism of the poem. The three levels of Platonism are all present in the poem; though subordinated to its revolutionary gospel, they contribute to its inorganic beauty and reveal the more prominent part Platonism was beginning to play in Shelley's philosophy.

The characters of the poem are Platonic symbols: Laon is a philosopher, an idealist, a Platonic lover; Cythna, even though an idealization of Mary, is a Platonic soul mate. Here as in *Alastor* (*vide supra,* pp. 190-191) Shelley incarnates his ideal values in the form of beautiful, Platonic, veiled maids, and heroes who are a counterpart of Shelley's own mind and aspirations. The influence of Wieland's *Agathon* is visible in the shaping of the lovers; Laon and Cythna have much in common with Agathon and Psyche. Shelley made the lovers brother and sister; it may be of interest to note in Wieland's *Agathon* a brother-sister parallel. In this novel Agathon, a Platonic idealist, meets Psyche, who, as the name signifies, is the embodiment of Platonic love. Wieland skilfully has his lovers translate their Platonic love into a brother-sister relationship. This incident in the novel, in combination with the speech of Aristophanes in the *Symposium,* suggested or strengthened Shelley's resolution (*vide supra,* pp. 141-142) to make Laon and Cythna brother and sister, a Platonic counterpart of the male and female union of the pristine soul before its division by Apollo.

> I have sought to enlist the harmony of metrical language . . . in the cause of a liberal and comprehensive morality.
>
> (Preface, Julian *Works,* I, 239)

Shelley's view of poetry here is somewhat analogous to the *Republic,* 398a.

> Love is celebrated every where as the sole law which should govern the moral world.
>
> (Preface, *ibid.,* I, 247)

A Platonic conviction which may be the result of Shelley's reading of the *Symposium,* this statement marks the appearance of the Platonic doctrine of Love which is to fuse with Shelley's conception of Intellectual Beauty.

> . . . can look from our tranquillity
> Like lamps into the world's tempestuous night,—
> Two tranquil stars, while clouds are passing by
> Which wrap them from the foundering seaman's sight,
> That burn from year to year with unextinguished light.
>
> (Dedication, ll. 122-126)

This simile expresses the natural Platonism of permanence and change.

> There was a Woman, beautiful as morning,
>> Sitting beneath the rocks, upon the sand
> Of the waste sea—fair as one flower adorning
>> An icy wilderness—each delicate hand
>> Lay crossed upon her bosom, and the band
> Of her dark hair had fall'n, and so she sate
>> Looking upon the waves; on the bare strand
> Upon the sea-mark a small boat did wait,
> Fair as herself, like Love by Hope left desolate.
>> (Canto I, ll. 136-144)

The imagery of the woman and the boat is, according to Grabo (*The Magic Plant,* p. 209), Neoplatonic; it represents "the vehicle of the soul or of the gods and goddesses." If considered, however, in the scenic context of the water scene and imagery which inspired so many descriptions in the poem (see Yeats, *Ideas of Good and Evil,* p. 115; Strong, *Three Studies in Shelley,* pp. 89 f.), this imagery may not be Neoplatonic at all, or so only by coincidence with Plotinus, *Enneads,* III, iv, 6. For a discussion of this passage, *vide infra,* pages 250-251.

> Then Greece arose, and to its bards and sages,
>> In dream, the golden-pinioned Genii came,
> Even where they slept amid the night of ages
>> Steeping their hearts in the divinest flame
>> Which thy breath kindled, Power of holiest name!
> And oft in cycles since, when darkness gave
>> New weapons to thy foe, their sunlike fame
> Upon the combat shone—a light to save,
> Like Paradise spread forth beyond the shadowy grave.
>> (I, 280-288)

Shelley's tribute to Greece here reflects also his tribute to Plato, whom he had been reading at the time of the composition.

> We came to a vast hall, whose glorious roof
>> Was diamond, which had drank the lightning's sheen
> In darkness, and now poured it thro' the woof
>> Of spell-inwoven clouds hung there to screen
>> Its blinding splendour—thro' such veil was seen
> That work of subtlest power, divine and rare;
>> Orb above orb, with starry shapes between,

And horned moons, and meteors strange and fair,
On night-black columns poised—one hollow hemisphere!
                    (I, 460-468)
These lines contain natural Platonic imagery tangent to Plato's theme
of appearance and reality.

Beneath, there sate on many a sapphire throne,
  The Great, who had departed from mankind,
A mighty Senate . . . .
                    (I, 478-480)
The mighty Senate of the Great is analogous to Socrates's conception
in *Apology*, 41; for a different interpretation, see Grabo, *The Magic Plant,*
pages 210-211.

The starlight smile of children, the sweet looks
  Of women, the fair breast from which I fed,
The murmur of the unreposing brooks,
  And the green light which shifting overhead,
  Some tangled bower of vines around me shed,
The shells on the sea-sand, and the wild flowers,
  The lamp-light thro' the rafters cheerly spread,
And on the twining flax—in life's young hours
These sights and sounds did nurse my spirit's folded powers.
                    (II, 1-9)
The objects described here constitute the first stage in the ascent
described in the *Symposium*, 210-211 (see also *Republic*, 401).

With deathless minds, which leave where they have past
  A path of light, my soul communion knew;
Till from that glorious intercourse, at last,
  As from a mine of magic store, I drew
  Words which were weapons . . . .
                    (II, 172-176)
If Plato is one of these deathless minds, we have here Shelley's own
words of appraisal.

She moved upon this earth a shape of brightness,
  A power, that from its objects scarcely drew
One impulse of her being—in her lightness
  Most like some radiant cloud of morning dew
  Which wanders thro' the waste air's pathless blue.

> To nourish some far desert: she did seem
> Beside me, gathering beauty as she grew,
> Like the bright shade of some immortal dream
> Which walks, when tempest sleeps, the wave of life's dark stream.
> (II, 199-207)

The description of Cythna is in terms of the Platonic theory of Beauty and Love; Cythna is the image of immortal beauty and casts light on the dark stream of life. Shelley's symbolizing Ideal Beauty by a beautiful woman is characteristic of his Platonism.

> In me, communion with this purest being
> Kindled intenser zeal, and made me wise
> In knowledge, which in her's mine own mind seeing,
> Left in the human world few mysteries . . . .
> (II, 280-283)

Communion with beauty leads to wisdom in the ladder of the *Symposium* (210-211); Cythna was to Laon what Diotima was to Socrates in the *Symposium*.

> Till free and equal man and woman greet.
> (II, 329)

The theme of the equality of women (see also IV, 181-182) is analogous to the *Republic*, 540c; the equality of sexes was preached by Mary Wollstonecraft in England (see Brailsford, *Shelley, Godwin, and Their Circle*, p. 30).

> He struck my chains, and gently spake and smiled:
> As they were loosened by that Hermit old . . . .
> (III, 253-254)

The Hermit is Dr. Lind, who befriended Shelley at Eton and probably introduced him to Plato (*vide supra*, p. 30, and Mary's note on *Laon and Cythna*). He is the incarnation of Philosophy.

> From sleep, as many-coloured as the snake
> That girds eternity?
> (IV, 32-33)

For commentary, *vide supra*, pages 186-188.

> That hoary man had spent his livelong age
> In converse with the dead, who leave the stamp
> Of ever-burning thoughts on many a page,

When they are gone into the senseless damp
Of graves;—his spirit thus became a lamp
Of splendour, like to those on which it fed . . . .

(IV, 64-69)

See *Prince Athanase*, Fragment 3, lines 60-66, where these lines find a parallel in the reading of the *Symposium*. They illustrate Shelley's own reaction to Plato and other great minds who molded his own (cf. "The mind becomes that which it contemplates," *Prince Athanase*, Fragment 2, line 15).

O Spirit vast and deep as Night and Heaven!
Mother and soul of all to which is given
The light of life, the loveliness of being,
    Lo! thou dost re-ascend the human heart,
    Thy throne of power, almighty as thou wert,
In dreams of Poets old grown pale by seeing
    The shade of thee . . . .

(V, 478-484)

The invocation to Wisdom is permeated with Platonic feeling and idiom; here Wisdom is associated with Intellectual Beauty, which permeates life as light and loveliness.

Our toil from thought all glorious forms shall cull,
To make this Earth, our home, more beautiful . . . .

(V, 534-535)

"Forms" here may be a literal translation of Platonic εἴδη, whose intellectual vision makes the Earth more beautiful.

Louder and louder from the utmost Ocean
Of universal life, attuning its commotion.

(VI, 260-261)

The Ocean of universal life may be a Platonic or a Neoplatonic image (see *Symposium*, 210d).

To the pure all things are pure!

(VI, 262)

This comes directly from the *Epistle of Paul to Titus*, 1:15, which is also an Orphic doctrine found in *Phaedo*, 67b, 69c, *Sophist*, 227c. For Orphism and Paul, see A. Faux, "L'Orphisme et Saint Paul," *Revue d'Histoire Ecclésiastique*, XXVII (1931), 245-292, 751-791.

> Two disunited spirits when they leap
> In union from this earth's obscure and fading sleep.
>
> (VI, 305-306)

In these lines Shelley fuses two Platonic notions. The union of two disunited spirits into one is analogous to or an echo of Aristophanes's conception of love in *Symposium*, 191d.

> What is the strong controul
> Which leads the heart that dizzy steep to climb,
> Where far over the world those vapours roll,
> Which blend two restless frames in one reposing soul?
>
> (VI, 321-324)

A Shelleyan version of Platonic love which combines the notion of transcendence (see *Phaedrus*, 246a ff., and *Symposium*, 210-211) with the conception of love as expressed by Aristophanes in the *Symposium*, 191d.

> It is the shadow which doth float unseen,
> But not unfelt, o'er blind mortality . . . .
>
> (VI, 325-326)

This is one of the most epigrammatic expressions of the Platonic conception of Intellectual Beauty as described in the *Symposium*, 210-211, and Shelley's *Hymn to Intellectual Beauty* (*vide supra*, p. 204). It is both natural and direct Platonism refracted through Shelley's romantic temperament. The lines are permeated with Platonic connotations such as the shadow of the divine which infrequently visits blind mortality (see *Republic*, 514 ff.).

> Where like a Spirit in fleshly chains she lay . . .
>
> (VII, 53)

The image of a spirit in fleshly chains is ultimately derived from *Phaedo*, 67d.

> By intercourse of mutual imagery . . .
>
> (VII, 259)

This phrase aptly characterizes Shelley's and Plato's natural talent in using similar images for the expression of their thought.

> One mind, the type of all, the moveless wave
> Whose calm reflects all moving things that are . . .
>
> (VII, 275-276)

The description of mind here is in terms of Platonism; this line is the germ which is later to find full Platonic expression in *Adonais*, lines 460-463 (*vide infra*, pp. 298-301).

> "All is not lost! There is some recompense
> For hope whose fountain can be thus profound . . . ."
>
> (VII, 316-317)

Grabo sees in the fountain a Neoplatonic image (*The Magic Plant,* p. 219).

> "What is that God? Some moon-struck sophist stood
> Watching the shade from his own soul upthrown
> Fill Heaven and darken Earth, and in such mood
> The Form he saw and worshipped was his own,
> His likeness in the world's vast mirror shown . . . .
>
> (VIII, 46-50)

These lines may be a Shelleyan elaboration of the Sophistic doctrine of Protagoras that man is the measure of all things. The preoccupation of sophists with shadows is a Platonic theme (see *Sophist,* 233c, 254a).

> "Alas, what strength? Opinion is more frail
> Than yon dim cloud now fading on the moon
> Even while we gaze, though it awhile avail
> To hide the orb of truth—
>
> (VIII, 73-76)

Shelley conceives of Opinion in the same epistemological way as Plato (see *Republic,* 479d-e).

> Look on your mind—it is the book of fate—
>
> (VIII, 174)

The notion that mind is a man's fate is analogous to *Republic,* 617e, where the soul chooses its own fate to which it is irrevocably bound.

> For, with strong speech I tore the veil that hid
> Nature, and Truth, and Liberty, and Love,—
>
> (IX, 55-56)

Another instance of Shelley's use of the Platonic image of the veil (*vide supra,* p. 180).

> One comes behind,
> Who aye the future to the past will bind—

> Necessity, whose sightless strength for ever
> Evil with evil, good with good, must wind
> In bands of union, which no power may sever . . . .
> (IX, 239-243)

This marks the last appearance of Necessity in Shelley's philosophy; from now on it is supplanted by Platonic idealism (see White, *The Best of Shelley*, p. 475).

> Our many thoughts and deeds, our life and love,
> Our happiness, and all that we have been,
> Immortally must live, and burn and move,
> When we shall be no more . . . .
> (IX, 263-266)

These lines are tangent to Plato's notion of the immortality of the soul; like Plato, Shelley seems to rule out personal immortality, which is a characteristic of Christian immortality.

> 'Fair star of life and love,' I cried, 'my soul's delight,
> Why lookest thou on the crystalline skies?
> O, that my spirit were yon Heaven of night,
> Which gazes on thee with its thousand eyes!'
> She turned to me and smiled—that smile was Paradise!
> (IX, 321-325)

These lines are Shelley's translation of Plato's epigram, *Anthologia Palatina*, VII, 669. Shelley found this epigram in Apuleius's *Apologia*, which he read in 1816. He made another version of this epigram in 1817 (*vide infra*, pp. 508-509). The translation reflects Shelley's interest in Plato the poet.

> . . . or do indeed
> All living things a common nature own,
> And thought erect an universal throne,
> Where many shapes one tribute ever bear?
> (X, 3-6)

Shelley approaches here vaguely the Platonic conception of the one and the many (cf. *Philebus*, 15 ff.).

> . . . all mortal things are cold
> And senseless then; if aught survive, I deem
> It must be love and joy, for they immortal seem.
> (XI, 151-153)

Another expression in Shelley of the Platonic dualism of transience and the immortality of Platonic Love.

> Then suddenly I stood, a wingèd Thought,
>   Before the immortal Senate, and the seat . . .
>   (XII, 271-272)

Compare commentary on Canto I, 478-480, *supra*, p. 216.

> The better Genius of this world's estate.
>   (XII, 275)

This conception is perhaps derived from Plato's notion of good and evil in the universe (see *Laws*, 896c ff.; in the *Symposium*, 203a, Love is described as a beneficial Daemon; see also *Timaeus*, 41 ff., 90a, and *Statesman*, 271e; Plotinus, *Enneads*, III, iv).

> That virtue, tho' obscured on Earth, not less
> Survives all mortal change in lasting loveliness.
>   (XII, 332-333)

In these lines Shelley has compressed the Platonism of the temporal versus the eternal. For Shelley virtue, like the Platonic forms, is obscured in the temporal world and survives in the world of Platonic immortality. Shelley here has combined the doctrines of the *Phaedo* and *Symposium*, immortality and Beauty. Like Canto VI, 325-326, these lines are one of the most felicitous of Shelley's Platonic expressions.

> The stream became, and fast and faster bare
> The spirit-wingèd boat, steadily speeding there.
>   (XII, 341-342)

The symbolism of the boat and the soul may have some connection with that of the soul and its voyage through the relative world (cf. Plotinus, *Enneads*, III, iv, 6; and commentary, *Laon and Cythna*, I, 136-144, *supra*, p. 215).

> Which four great cataracts from four vales . . .
>   (XII, 358)

Grabo (*The Magic Plant*, p. 224) interprets these as Neoplatonic symbols; the four cataracts may ultimately be symbols derived from *Timaeus*, 39e ff., where Plato discusses the four orders of intellect, the gods; or they might be symbolic of the four elements in nature—earth, air, fire, and water, the materials out of which the Creator in the *Timaeus* creates the universe.

Lines from Rejected Stanzas

Probably written for the First Canto (*Shelley, Verse and Prose,* edited
by Sir John C. E. Shelley-Rolls and Roger Ingpen, pp. 18-20).

> There is a Power whose passive instrument
> Our nature is—a Spirit that with motion,
> Invisible and swift, its breath hath sent
> Amongst us, like the wind on the wide Ocean
> Around whose path the tumult and commotion
> Throng fast—deep calm doth follow, and precedeth.
> This Spirit, claimed by some remote devotion,
> Our choice or will demandeth not nor heedeth,
> But for its hymns doth touch the human souls it needeth.
>
> (Ll. 19-27)

This stanza reveals the natural Platonism of a transcendent power,
Love or Beauty, which like the Power in the *Hymn to Intellectual Beauty*
visits the world and leaves its imprint or shadow.

> The lamps of mind which make this night of earth
> So beautiful were kindled thus of yore—
> All streams of mortal hope whence drew their birth,
> The lyres of antient song which evermore
> Thro' silent years their mighty music pour,
> Have thus been fed with sweetness; mighty lyres
> Whose sounds awaken thoughts that sleep no more
> When that immortal Spirit which respires
> In visioned rest has breathed upon the silent wires.
>
> (Ll. 37-45)

A variant expression of Shelley's tribute to classical literature (cf. I,
280-288) and its association with the immortal Spirit.

Rosalind and Helen

Begun in the summer of 1817, laid aside at the end of September, and
finished by August 14, 1818

There is not much Platonism to be found in this poem, even though
Shelley had been reading Plato at the time of its composition. As Shelley says in the advertisement, "It is in no degree calculated to excite
profound meditation." Yet the influence of Plato is apparent in the
philosophic Lionel, who is a reflection of Shelley.

> And subtile mists of sense and thought . . .
>
> (L. 809)

An apt phrase characterizing some of Shelley's romantic Platonism (cf. l. 1014).

> We lay, till new emotions came,
> Which seemed to make each mortal frame
> One soul of interwoven flame,
> A life in life, a second birth,
> In worlds diviner far than earth,
> Which, like two strains of harmony
> That mingle in the silent sky,
> Then slowly disunite, past by
> And left the tenderness of tears,
> A soft oblivion of all fears,
> A sweet sleep . . . .
>
> (Ll. 977-987)

These lines reveal a fusion of two Platonic strains, immortality and the union of two parts of the same soul into one soul again (see commentary on *Laon and Cythna,* VI, 305-306, *supra,* p. 219).

Prince Athanase

"Part I of this poem is dated by Mrs. Shelley, 'December, 1817,' and the remainder 'Marlow, 1817.' The verses were probably rehandled in Italy during the following year" (Hutchinson).

As has been shown above (pp. 51-54), this poem is another example of Shelley's direct Platonism refracted through indirect Platonism. Even though Shelley had just read Plato's *Symposium,* the poem shows the direct influence of the poetically attractive account of Earthly and Heavenly Love in Peacock's *Rhododaphne.* Despite Mary's claim that the poem "was a good deal modelled on Alastor," the poem is so closely parallel to *Rhododaphne* in plot, in its themes of Earthly and Heavenly Love, "intellectual soul," and its incarnation of Platonic abstractions in the form of women, that it is evident that Shelley composed the poem after an enthusiastic reading of *Rhododaphne.* As has been shown above (p. 51), Shelley started the poem on December 5, immediately after the reading of *Rhododaphne* (*ca.* Nov. 28), which he read aloud, had Mary transcribe, and later enthusiastically reviewed. The close intellectual companionship and similar readings of Shelley and Peacock at this time show that Peacock as much as Plato influenced the Platonism of this poem; it may be possible that Shelley left it unfinished because of his awareness of the inability of his own composition to achieve the perfection which he imputed to *Rhododaphne* and his awareness of its too close similarity to Peacock's poem.

The title of the first sketch of the poem, derived from the *Symposium* (180c-181) and from Peacock's *Rhododaphne*, and the dramatic story planned to illustrate this poetically attractive doctrine of the *Symposium* mark the first and significant manifestation of direct Platonism in Shelley. After a reading of the *Symposium*, Shelley re-expressed the natural Platonism of *Alastor* in the framework and inspiration of direct and indirect Platonism. Shelley now becomes more and more conscious of the natural Platonism in his own mind as a result of his contact with Plato and Peacock. This poem, however, reveals again Shelley's romantic predisposition to change the intellectual and logical nature of Plato's philosophy into its symbolic apprehension through a woman. As in *Alastor*, the One in this poem is a woman, not a philosophical essence. The characters of the poem are unmistakably a Platonic philosopher and a woman who is the symbol of a Platonic Psyche. This poem is an exalted example of a romantic reshaping of direct Platonism.

As in the case of *Adonais* and *Epipsychidion*, Shelley uses a title which is significantly associated with the root of the word in Greek. Here he used *Athanase*, the French name of Athanasius, which comes from the root ἀθάνατ—deathless. What led him to change the title from the first sketch of the poem is not known. Perhaps he wanted to make the philosopher the central character of the tale and changed the title to suit his purpose.

> —Philosophy's accepted guest.
> (Part I, l. 15)

The central character of the tale, like Lionel in *Rosalind and Helen* and Laon in *Laon and Cythna*, is a philosopher. Though differing in many ways from the Platonic philosopher, Athanase shares many characteristics with Plato's ideal philosopher.

> Or that loved good more for itself alone . . .
> (I, 17)

The love of ideal values for their own sake is a Platonic characteristic.

> His soul had wedded Wisdom, and her dower
> Is love and justice . . . .
> (I, 31-32)

Additional characteristics of a Platonic philosopher.

> Pitying the tumult of their dark estate.—
>
> (I, 34)

The condition of the multitude is, like Plato's description in *Republic*, 514 ff., one of darkness.

> Some said that he was mad, others believed
>
> That memories of an antenatal life
> Made this, where now he dwelt, a penal hell . . . .
>
> (I, 90-92)

These characterizations refer to the "madness" in the *Phaedrus* (245) and the central doctrine of the *Phaedo* (72e-73a), where memories of an antenatal life make the philosopher despise the earthly imprisonment. The *Oxford English Dictionary* cites *Prince Athanase* as the first appearance of the word *antenatal* in the English language; it is evident, however, that Shelley did not coin this word to express Plato's doctrine of reminiscence, but found it in his reading of Godwin's *Political Justice*, which he had been reading on November 29 and 30 and December 1, only a few days before the composition of the poem (*ca.* December 5). In this work (I, 36) Godwin uses the word *antenatal* for Plato's theory of reminiscence (*vide supra*, p. 147). It is of interest to note Shelley's independence of mind in this instance, for whereas Godwin denounces this doctrine, Shelley here endows others with this Platonic belief.

> On souls like his which owned no higher law
> Than love; love calm, steadfast, invincible . . .
>
> (I, 95-96)

For the philosopher's preoccupation with love, see *Symposium*, 204b.

> . . . he to and fro
> Questioned and canvassed it with subtlest wit . . . .
>
> (I, 115-116)

The philosopher's skill in dialectic is drawn from Shelley's reading of Plato.

> Fragments of a continuation of *Prince Athanase:*
>
> Prince Athanase had one belovèd friend,
> An old, old man, with hair of silver white,
> And lips where heavenly smiles would hang and blend
>
> With his wise words; and eyes whose arrowy light
> Shone like the reflex of a thousand minds.
>
> (Fragment 2, ll. 1-5)

An idealized account of Dr. Lind, who befriended Shelley at Eton and with whom he probably read the *Symposium* (see *Laon and Cythna,* III, 253-254). Shelley has also added to the portrait of this philosopher certain features from Diotima, who in the *Symposium* is the philosophic tutor of Socrates.

'The mind becomes that which it contemplates'—
(Fragment 2, l. 15)

This line is an adaptation of a sentence in Paine's *The Rights of Man:* "It is the faculty of the human mind to become what it contemplates, and to act in unison with its object (*The Political Works of Thomas Paine* [New York, 1830], II, 111). Claire Clairmont also notes this sentence in her Diary for Wednesday, February 9, 1820. Inasmuch as the Journal shows that Shelley had been reading *The Rights of Man* on December 5, it is evident that we have a *terminus post quem* for the date of the composition. For the Platonic doctrine in this line, see *Republic,* 401b-402d. See also *Marenghi,* l. 135 (and *Prometheus Unbound,* I, 450).

> Thus thro' his age, dark, cold, and temptest-tossed,
> Shone truth upon Zonoras; and he filled
> From fountains pure, nigh overgrown and lost,
>
> The spirit of Prince Athanase, a child,
> With soul-sustaining songs of antient lore
> And philosophic wisdom, clear and mild.
>
> And sweet and subtle talk they evermore,
> The pupil and the master, shared; until,
> Sharing that undiminishable store,
>
> The youth, as shadows on a grassy hill
> Outrun the [winds] that chase [them], soon outran
> His teacher, and did teach with native skill
>
> Strange truths and new to that experienced man;
> Still they were friends, as few have ever been
> Who mark the extremes of life's discordant span.
> (Fragment 3, ll. 4-18)

This account of the philosophical association of Zonoras is patterned in part on the picture of Socrates and his pupils, and in particular Plato, who "outran his teacher."

And, with a soft and equal pressure, prest
That cold lean hand:—"Dost thou remember yet
When the curved moon then lingering in the west

"Paused, in yon waves her mighty horns to wet,
How in those beams we walked, half resting on the sea?
'Tis just one year—sure thou dost not forget?

"Plato's words of light in thee and me
Lingered like moonlight in the moonless east,
For we had just then read—thy memory

"Is faithful now—the Story of the Feast;
And Agathon and Diotima seemed
From death and [dark]   released,

"To talk [with us of all they knew or dreamed]
Of love divine . . . .
                              (Fragment 3, ll. 55-68)

These lines refer to the reading of the *Symposium* with Dr. Lind at
Eton (*vide supra*, p. 30) and again to his reading of it in 1817. The
impression which the dialogue made on Shelley was so tremendous that
its reading became a turning point in his poetry and philosophical outlook (*vide supra*, pp. 47-48). The reference to the speeches of Agathon
and Diotima is repeated in *Epipsychidion*, Fragments, ll. 101-108; with the
speech of Agathon, compare Shelley's reference to it in his letter to
Godwin dated December 7, 1817 (*Works*, IX, 260), and his *Note on the
Banquet of Plato*, where he jots down a memorandum for a poem on
this subject.

How many a one, though none be near to love,

Loves then the shade of his own soul, half seen
In any mirror—
                              (Fragment 4, ll. 12-14)

An analogy to the mental state of "conjecture" (εἰκασία) in *Republic*, 510d.

How many a spirit then puts on the pinions
Of fancy, and outstrips the lagging blast,
And his own [steps]—and over wide dominions

Sweeps in his dream-drawn chariot, far and fast,
Exalting while the wide world shrinks below,
When winter and despondency are past.
                              (Fragment 4, ll. 16-21)

These lines may contain an allusion to the wings of the soul, the chariot and the ascent to the empyrean (*Phaedrus,* 256a ff.). For Shelley's reading of the *Phaedrus* in 1817, *vide supra,* pages 46-47.

> Thou art the wine whose drunkenness is all
> We can desire [O Love!] and happy souls,
> Ere from thy vine the leaves of Autumn fall,
>
> Catch thee, and feed from their o'erflowing bowls
> Thousands who thirst for thine ambrosial dew;—
> Thou art the radiance which where ocean rolls
>
> Investeth it; and when the heavens are blue
> Thou fillest them; and when the earth is fair
> The shadow of thy moving wings imbue
>
> Its deserts and its mountains, till they wear
> Beauty [like] some light robe;—thou ever soarest
> Among the towers of men, and as soft air
>
> In Spring, which moves the unawakened forest,
> Clothing with leaves its branches bare and bleak,
> Thou floatest among men. . . .
>
> (Fragment 5, ll. 1-15)

This invocation to Love is filled with many echoes from Agathon's speech in praise of love (*Symposium,* 197c-e). For the impression of Agathon's speech on Shelley, see Fragment 3, lines 55-67.

SHELLEY'S READING IN PLATO AND THE PLATONIC TRADITION, 1818

DIRECT PLATONISM: Translation of *Symposium* (July 9-10, 12-17, 20, 1818); *Phaedrus* (part; August 4-5, 1818); *Republic* (part; October 20, November 7, 9, 1818); translation of *Menexenus* (part).

INDIRECT PLATONISM: Xenophon's *Memorabilia* (July 13-17, 1818); Virgil, *Aeneid,* VI, (January 6, 24, 1818); Lucian's works (1818; August 16, 1818); Dante (1818; April 19, 1818, finishes *Purgatorio;* April 22, 1818, reads *Paradiso*); Gibbon, *Decline and Fall* (1818; January 1-2, June 18, 20-21, 1818); Winckelmann, *History of Art* (December 24, 27-29, 31, 1818; January 2, 3, March 14, 1819); Barthélemy, *Travels of Anacharsis the Younger* (1818; June 22-30, July 2, 5, 6, 1818); Wieland, *Aristippus* (April, May 2, 1818).

PLATONISM IN SHELLEY'S POETRY WRITTEN IN 1818

Lines Written Among the Euganean Hills
October, 1818

> Interpenetrated lie
> By the glory of the sky:
> Be it love, light, harmony,
> Odour, or the soul of all
> Which from heaven like dew doth fall,
> Or the mind which feeds this verse
> Peopling the lone universe.
>
> (Ll. 313-319)

The natural Platonism of these lines consists in the permeation of nature and man by such values of the ideal world as love, harmony, and soul.

Stanzas, Written in Dejection, Near Naples
December, 1818

> Nor that content surpassing wealth
> The sage in meditation found . . . .
>
> (Ll. 21-22)

This sentiment is also found to be the ideal of the philosopher in Socrates's prayer at the end of the *Phaedrus* and in *Apology, 30b.*

Marenghi
Winter of 1818

> Till his mind grew like that it contemplated.
>
> (L. 135)

See commentary on *Prince Athanase,* Fragment 2, line 15 (*supra,* p. 227).

Sonnet
1818

> Lift not the painted veil which those who live
> Call Life: though unreal shapes be pictured there,
> And it but mimic all we would believe
> With colours idly spread . . . .
>
> (Ll. 1-4)

This Platonic veil is a symbol of the world of mutability in contrast to the reality of the ideal world; see commentary on *Mutability* (*supra,* pp. 194-195), on *Queen* Mab, I, 181 (*supra,* p. 180), and on *Prometheus Unbound,* III, iii, 113 (*infra,* p. 256). The "unreal shapes of life are the counterpart of the shadows of the Cave of the *Republic,* 514 ff. The same sentiment is expressed almost in identical phraseology in *Prometheus Unbound,* III, iii, 113.

Julian and Maddalo
Autumn of 1818

". . . it is our will
That thus enchains us to permitted ill.—
We might be otherwise—we might be all
We dream of happy, high, majestical.
Where is the love, beauty and truth we seek,
But in our mind? and if we were not weak,
Should we be less in deed than in desire?"
"Aye if we were not weak,—and we aspire
How vainly to be strong!" said Maddalo:
"You talk Utopia."
            "It remains to know,"
I then rejoined, "and those who try may find
How strong the chains are which our spirit bind;
Brittle perchance as straw . . . We are assured
Much may be conquered, much may be endured,
Of what degrades and crushes us. We know
That we have power over ourselves to do
And suffer—what, we know not till we try;
But something nobler than to live and die—
So taught those kings of old philosophy
Who reigned before Religion made men blind;
And those who suffer with their suffering kind
Yet feel their faith, religion."

(Ll. 170-191)

These lines reveal a considerable swing of the pendulum toward Platonism. The freedom of the will, expressed by Julian in answer to Maddalo, is similar to that expressed by Plato in *Republic,* 617e. It is doubtful that this passage emanates from Plato; it is rather a general point of view which is tangent to the Platonic conception. This philosophy which Shelley attributes to "those kings of old philosophy" includes, no doubt, that of Plato, whom he had been reading. Though he does not name him, his presence is felt in the lines. The devotion of the mind to "love, beauty, and truth" (l. 174) is definitely a Platonic idea; furthermore, the pursuit of "a soul of goodness" (l. 204) finds an echo in *Apology*, 30b. Julian, the philosopher, is the projection of Shelley, whose reading of Plato strengthened him in his belief of "the power of man over his own mind" (Preface). In general the idealism of Julian is rooted in that of Plato.

> ". . . as when a boy
> I did devote to justice and to love
> My nature, worthless now! . . .
> "I must remove
> A veil from my pent mind. 'Tis torn aside! . . ."
> (Ll. 380-384)

Another echo of Shelley's early dedication to Intellectual Beauty which is now beginning to merge with Platonic Love.

SHELLEY'S READING IN PLATO AND THE PLATONIC TRADITION, 1819

DIRECT PLATONISM: *Republic* (part; October 9, 10, 24, 28, November 2, 6, 7, 8, 9, 1819); *Statesman* ? (1819 ?).

INDIRECT PLATONISM: Spenser (October 20, 1819); Lucretius (1819; March 15, 16, 22, 1819).

PLATONISM IN SHELLEY'S POETRY WRITTEN IN 1819

Prometheus Unbound

Act I, September 5—October 8, 1818; Acts II, III, March—April 6, 1819; Act IV, close of 1819

Prometheus Unbound marks the fruition of the development of Shelley's Platonism. In this poem Platonism supplants the poetically unsatisfying eighteenth-century materialistic philosophy. The Platonism consists not only of Shelley's Platonic philosophy of Reality, but also of a more mature development of his natural Platonism, a deeper penetration of direct and indirect Platonism into Shelley's thought and expression. In the Preface, where Shelley states his *ars poetica,* we find a conscious analysis of the sources of the poem. Shelley is keenly aware of the natural Platonism which is stirred by the beauty of nature. As in the *Phaedrus,* the sight of beauty stirs the soul with excitement and the soul begins to sprout wings, so that "The bright blue sky of Rome, and the effect of the vigorous awakening spring in that divinest climate, and the new life with which it drenches the spirits even to intoxication, were the inspiration of this drama." This stimulus may be the source of much of the natural Platonism in the poem, which consists of the intuitive and natural quest for the spirit of Beauty in the various manifestations of nature.

But the natural Platonism of the poem is much more than this. Shelley shares many points of view with Plato. In the *Symposium* (209a) Plato says that the poets should conceive what is proper for the soul to conceive or contain, namely, wisdom and virtue; in the *Republic* the only poetry that is allowed in the ideal state is that which has as its theme moral virtues. In the preface to *Prometheus Unbound* Shelley says that his purpose in writing the poem has been "simply to familiarize the highly refined imagination of the more select classes of poetical readers with beautiful idealisms of moral excellence." The use of philosophical poetry as a means to moral regeneration rather than as an end in itself is analogous to Plato's use of poetical philosophy to achieve the same end.

Furthermore, Shelley's imagination and mythopoeic talent have much in common with Plato's similar talents as shown in his various myths. Shelley, like Plato, resorts to poetic myths to illustrate vividly a philosophical abstraction or principle, and to furnish emotional stimulation for the awakening of the latent idealism in man's soul. In achieving this purpose Shelley reveals some remarkably similar, though not essentially derivative, elements. Shelley mingles science and poetry as Plato does in his myth in the *Phaedo* and the *Republic,* and as the entire *Timaeus* shows; both the *Prometheus Unbound* and the myths of Plato are a result of the cosmic imagination which makes the soul of man at home in the universe. Symbolism plays an important part in both Plato's and Shelley's attempts to make their philosophic aims more vivid and inspiring for their readers. Shelley shares or perhaps derived from his reading of the sixth and seventh books of the *Republic* the view that "the deep truth is imageless" (*Prometheus Unbound,* II, iv, 116). Yet Shelley's and Plato's insight into the nature of Being is characterized by a frequent use of symbolism. For a full understanding of Shelley's natural Platonic symbolism and the metaphysical background of the Demogorgon's reply and her inability to account for the source of evil, we must go to Plato. The ideal method of the Platonic philosopher is dialectic that proceeds without the aid of symbols; but often when direct knowledge is not possible, the philosopher, like the poet, proceeds with the aid of symbolism, which is inherent in the very nature of thought. Language itself is symbolic; when insight grasps meaning it expresses it through the written word, which is an image of thought (see *Phaedrus,* 276a). The dependence of thought on imagery is the state of mind described in the third segment of the Divided Line in *Republic,* 510d. Understanding (διάνοια) proceeds to knowledge with the aid of symbols, and consequently is inferior to knowledge (νόησις), which proceeds by the grasp of the first principles themselves. In speaking of the mathematicians who "dream about Being" and the mathematical procedure of διάνοια, Plato says:

. . . they further make use of the visible forms and talk about them, though they are not thinking of them but of those things of which they are a likeness, pursuing their inquiry for the sake of the square as such and the diagonal as such, and not for the sake of the image of it which they draw. And so in all cases. The very things which they mould and draw . . . these things they treat in their turn as only images, but what they really seek is to get sight of those realities which can be seen only by the mind.

If we substitute for mathematical symbolism in this passage the symbolism of the world of nature, poetry, art, and the sciences, we will find the key to Plato's and Shelley's use of symbolism.

The use of symbolism is necessitated by the very nature of deep truth which is "imageless." Absolute knowledge, according to Plato, is possible only to God and to the men to whom he chooses to reveal it (see *Timaeus,* 53d). In the *Timaeus,* where Plato fully explains the need of myth, he says "to put these speculations to an experimental test would be to ignore the difference between humanity and deity, which lies in this, that though God has in their fulness all the knowledge and all the power required to blend multitude into unity and dissolve again into multitude, no son of man has now, nor ever will have, the competence for either task" (*Timaeus,* 68d, A. E. Taylor's translation). Failing to attain the perfection of direct knowledge, the only recourse left to man is what Plato calls in the *Phaedo* "the second voyage," the resort to hypotheses and images of truth. The substitution of probability for absolute knowledge, of symbolism for imageless truth, of "dreaming" about Being for direct knowledge of it, is the honest confession of a philosopher who knows the status of human knowledge. Symbolism in both Plato and Shelley is therefore not merely the expression of a poet who gets the better of the philosopher, but the result of the limitations of the human mind and its compromise with probability. As Plato puts it, if unable to see the sun directly, it is wise for one to see it first through its reflections in the world of nature. Symbolism is therefore part of the method and technique of the philosopher and the poet.

Symbolism in both Plato and Shelley is of two kinds, natural and artificial. Natural symbolism is essentially concerned with the use of pure sense perceptions in the character of symbols. The artificial is concerned with the imaginative and arbitrary use of common symbols in an uncommon and novel way; the plastic imagination in this case uses symbols as arbitrarily as a mathematician. The more these symbols are used out of their traditional context and the more uncommon they are, the more obscure they become to the mind which is conservative and rooted in the traditional context of images. But the poet and philosopher, like Plato's geometric god, are constantly creating new images to get a closer approximation to truth; the deeper and fresher the symbol, the more obscure it is likely to become, and the obscurity in this case may be only the result of the lack of exploration by the mind. Because Shelley tried to plunge deeper into metaphysical reality in this poem, the greater is his use of images which try to express his cognate Platonic insights. Shelley's natural and artificial symbolism is partly rooted in Plato's imagery, but for the most part it is original imagery created to express his natural Platonic intuition concerning the transient and eternal. An example will make this natural Platonic imagery of Shelley clearer. He introduced for the first time into English poetry the distinction between characters and their "phantasms." Though Shelley gives an explanation of his use of phantasms in his references to Magus Zoroaster (*Prometheus Unbound,* I, 191-203), the imagery is ultimately a mythopoeic or Neoplatonic derivative from the Platonic imagery of original and image projected from the inert world of nature to the dramatic world of men and their ideas. Shelley himself is aware of this re-creative use of imagery. "The imagery," he says, "which I have employed will be found, in many instances, to have been drawn from the operations of the human mind." As will be shown in the detailed analysis of this poem, these operations of the human mind which are the source of much of his imagery are the operations of a Platonic mind which views this earthly world as the veil of transcendent Reality.

In the *Prometheus Unbound* Shelley also shares both cognately and derivatively many of Plato's own views about the problem of evil (see C. M. Chilcott, "The Platonic Theory of Evil," *Classical Quarterly,* XVII [1923], 27-31). There is no consistent point of view or explanation of evil either in the poet or in the philosopher, but both reveal even in their contradictions a natural Platonism which is significant. For Shelley evil is "a loathsome mask" which falls from reality "veil by veil." In the *Laws* (903c) Plato suggests that evil is only in the appearance of things which fades once we perceive the whole of Reality. For Shelley evil belongs to the realm of the passing; when Asia asks Demogorgon about the ultimate origin of Evil, Demogorgon replies that it is involved with Fate, Time, Occasion, Chance, and Change, to which all except Love are slaves. Plato would endorse this statement, for he believed that evil, having its seat in the passions of the soul, is of the world of appearance, whereas Love is an aspiration for the immortal and is not subject to Mutability. Thus Shelley and Plato agree that evil belongs to the realm of appearance and not to that of Reality. Shelley, furthermore, believes that evil is not inherent but accidental. This is also one of Plato's beliefs; in the *Republic* (379 ff.) he says that God is not the cause of all things but only of the good and that we must look for the cause of evil in other things and not God. Since evil is not inherent in the nature of God, Plato relegates it to the realm of the accidental, saying in the *Timaeus* that it is due to the receptacle. Shelley, who had been reading the *Republic* at the time of the composition of the poem and, in his translation of the fragments of the *Republic*, had taken special note of this view of Plato (see Fragment VII, *infra*, p. 496), may have been directly influenced by it. Furthermore, Shelley believes that evil can be overcome by the exercise of the will (*Prometheus Unbound*, I, 273-274), while Plato believes that it can be overcome by the mastery in the soul of the rational element. Yet Shelley contradicts himself, even as Plato does, with respect to evil. In *Prometheus Unbound*, I, 294, Shelley states that evil and good are infinite as the universe, and in *Prometheus Unbound*, II, iv, 101, Asia calls evil "the immedicable plague." This dualism is also shared with Plato, who says in the *Theaetetus* (176a) that "it is impossible that evil should be done away with, for there must always be something opposed to the good." In the *Statesman* (272-274) evil is the result of the absence of God from the world, and, as a result of the world's being given over to earthly desires, it returns to its primeval disorder (*vide infra*, pp. 251-253). This systole and diastole of evil and good is analogous to Shelley's symbolic representation of these two forces in the form of the eagle and the snake (see *Laon and Cythna*). This is matched by Plato's belief expressed in the *Laws* that there are two separate divinities, the one which causes evil and the other good in the world. These *points d'appui* between Shelley's and Plato's theories as to evil show that Shelley's natural

Platonism includes more than Intellectual Beauty as its great common denominator, and that Plato, no less than Shelley and other philosophers and theologians, finally retreats to a dualistic conception of good and evil.

Shelley's developing natural Platonism reaches its final form in *Prometheus Unbound*. Although the seed of it was latent in Shelley's own soul, it took experience and the reading of Berkeley and Plato to shape its final expression. Continuous disappointments and frustrations in his own life and in experiments like the French Revolution had shown Shelley that ideal perfection is not of this world; the undermining of his confidence and faith in the temporal world inevitably led to an undermining of his confidence in an eighteenth-century radical, rationalistic, and mechanistic conception of reality. For this reason Necessity with its denial of the freedom of the will gives way to the idealistic element in his soul. Shelley had felt its presence since childhood, as he tells us in the *Hymn to Intellectual Beauty*, but its development was slow. With *Alastor* it begins to become more articulate in its expression. The *Hymn to Intellectual Beauty*, as we have seen, reveals Shelley's maturing apprehension of the ideal realm where the human soul is supremely happy. In the contemplation of the essence of Intellectual Beauty, whose shadow in the world of nature leaves him unhappy, Shelley discovers, like Plato's lover in the *Phaedrus*, the world of mind where man is unconquered by the world of evil and tyranny. As compared to that ideal world which is found in the mind of man, this world is only a veil, a phantom. Even though he was not happy in this world unless he was beholding its shadow, Shelley found a new joy at the prospect of the regeneration of man through living in the realm of the ideal, through grounding his hopes of reform, not on external revolution, but, as Plato himself does, on the lasting revolution that comes about by the conversion of man's soul and mind from the shadows of the cave to the eternal and abiding values of the mind. Once this inward revolution of the soul to ideal Reality takes place, then the regeneration of man and society can start. In this respect he is at one with Plato. Shelley saw that if he could stir the deep impulses which lay latent in the soul of man, if mankind could realize that the mind of man which is nurtured on Platonic values and truths is invincible if it possesses freedom of the will assured by the philosophy of idealism, then and then only could man reshape the world closer to his heart's desire. Shelley saw that once he could awaken these potent forces which can be evoked and nourished by a philosophy of idealism, then they would overcome evil as spring does winter or as the West

Wind, which brings about a vernal rebirth. The poem is an evangelistic hymn to stir the beautiful idealisms in the soul essential for the overcoming of earthly evil. Shelley, like the Greeks, believed that poetry should teach through aesthetic entertainment, a propaedeutic role which Plato assigns to poetry in his ideal state. A comparison of *Prometheus Unbound* with the *Republic,* which Shelley was reading at the time of its composition, shows that this masterpiece of Plato helped to shape and express this new conversion in Shelley's own soul. Plato became his guide, as Shelley admits in the Preface. "Should I live," he says, "to accomplish what I purpose, that is, produce a systematical history of what appear to me to be the genuine elements of human society, let not the advocates of injustice and superstition flatter themselves that I should take Aeschylus rather than Plato as my model." Even though he does not write a systematic history of the Platonic regeneration of man in this poem, the metaphysical basis of Plato's reform of society is reflected in *Prometheus Unbound;* the philosophy of Reality and Shelley's passion to reform the world center on the Platonic faith that life and the world are but unreal shadows of an intellectual reality, the pursuit of whose inconstantly apprehended shadow forms the only real hope of man's moral, political, and spiritual salvation.

Though the *Republic* had shaped the expression of Shelley's philosophy of idealism, the reading and translation of the *Symposium,* in the few months before the beginning of the composition of the poem, shaped the expression of the same metaphysical conception of Reality in terms of Beauty, for the *Symposium* is but the expression of the metaphysical basis of the *Republic* in terms of Love and Beauty. The *Republic* appealed to Shelley the reformer, whereas the *Symposium* appealed to Shelley the poet and lover; Shelley manifests both of these sides of his nature in the *Prometheus Unbound.* The influence of the *Symposium* is seen in the fact that Shelley's Intellectual Beauty is beginning to merge with his doctrine of Love. In the poem Asia is the "Lamp of Earth," "the light of life," "the Life of Life," "the shadow of beauty unbeheld." These phrases show that Shelley plastically shapes the basic doctrine of Platonism to suit his moods and the needs of his imagination. Even as Plato equates Beauty and Truth, the Beautiful and the Good, so Shelley equates Intellectual Beauty and Love. The words "shadow of beauty unbeheld" show that Shelley is but reshaping with some modification the essence of the *Hymn to Intellectual Beauty* into Platonic Love; furthermore, in reshaping it he is also interpolating from the *Symposium* and the Platonic tradition; he borrows from the *Symposium* the poetic ecstasy and fervor of Agathon's speech and fuses it, not with Plato's doctrine of Ideal Love as expressed in his own words in the *Symposium,* but rather with the shaping of this Platonic Love by the Platonic tradition in the form of a woman, which is the most poetic representation of Platonic Beauty in the world of earthly symbols. The choice of woman as the most apt and living symbol of Platonic Beauty and Love shows that the Platonism of the *Symposium* is refracted in this poem through Shelley's own poetic nature, which sees abstractions through concrete symbols, and through the Platonic tradition, where it finds expression in Dante, in Spenser, and in Wieland, all of whom influenced Shelley. Thus we see that when Mary says, "Shelley loved to idealize the real—to gift the mechanism of the material universe with a soul and a voice,"[9] the soul and voice of this idealism is that of Plato's *Symposium* and *Republic* which enriched Shelley's natural Platonism with concept, imagery, and artistically expressed and poetically nourishing philosophy of reality.

The *Prometheus Unbound* is unique for its clear expression of direct Platonism. Many of the great Platonic passages in the poem are a poetic transcription of the *Symposium.* A few months prior to the commencement of the first act, Shelley had translated the *Symposium* and had thus steeped himself in its thought and expression. The translation further served to crystallize the expression of Shelley's own natural Platonic quest for love and beauty. Shelley was the kind of poet who is influenced profoundly by whatever moves him. An examination of the letters he wrote at the time of the translation, the Preface to the *Banquet,* and his essay on the *Manners of the Antients* reveals the extent that Plato permeated his thought and expression. In the Preface to the poem Shelley gives formal expression to the profound influence that Plato, who, though not singled out by name, is included among the ancients, had in the creation of the poem. Plato's mind becomes for Shelley "the mirror upon which all forms are reflected, and in which they compose one form." Plato, who was now beginning to be for Shelley the ideal poet-philosopher, the model in writing the history of the genuine elements of human society, with whom he would rather be damned than go to Heaven with Paley and Malthus, and whom he read, translated, and understood by "the uncommunicated lightning" of his mind, is the direct source and inspiration of much of the best in the poem.

[9] Cf. Mary's letter to Edward Bulwer, March, 1838: "I think that in this play you have done as Shelley used to exhort Lord Byron to do—left the beaten road of old romance, so worn by modern dramatists, and *idealised the present"* (*The Letters of Mary W. Shelley,* ed. F. L. Jones, II, 124).

Finally, in the poem there is much evidence of indirect Platonism which emanated from his reading of such writers as Dante, Milton, Spenser, Berkeley, Wieland, Coleridge, and Barthélemy, all of whom Shelley had been reading before and during the composition of the poem. Berkeley in particular is important for Shelley's conversion to idealism; Dante, Spenser, and Wieland are important for the Platonic conception of Asia; Coleridge and Wieland for sources of Neoplatonism; and Barthélemy's summary of the *Timaeus* is important for the scientific and cosmological echoes of this work in the poem. Shelley fused in the alchemy of his poetry all three sources of his Platonism: natural, direct, and indirect. Sometimes these sources stand out individually; sometimes they are mingled as rivulets in the greater stream of his own individual creation, in which case it is difficult to note anything except the general Platonic character of the lines.

> Monarch of Gods and Daemons, and all Spirits
> But One, who throng those bright and rolling worlds . . .
> (Act I, ll. 1-2)

Literally here the One refers to Prometheus. According to Grabo (see *Prometheus Unbound: An Interpretation* [Chapel Hill, N. C., 1935], pp. 68, 90-91, 139), Prometheus and Asia are but portions of the One, struggling in the world of illusion and returning to it. If this be the right interpretation, the One, which is the central conception in the philosophy of Plotinus, is the source of the emanations and irradiations such as Divine Thought, and is the object of all aspiration. It underlies the world of flux and illusion, and everything that emanates from it returns to it (cf. references in Plotinus, "Index Analytique des Matières," *Enneads,* edited and translated by Émile Bréhier [Paris, 1938], VI, 293-294). In view of Mrs. Shelley's statement that a full comprehension of Shelley's meaning requires "a mind as subtle and as penetrating as his own" and the fact that Shelley's prodigious reading put him in contact with imagery and thoughts which may escape scholarly analysis, it is tempting to follow Grabo in his Neoplatonic interpretation of this poem. In our account of the Platonic tradition in Shelley's reading we have seen that, although Shelley did not read the Neoplatonists themselves, he found much Neoplatonism in his reading of Coleridge's *Biographia Literaria,* where this doctrine of the One appears (*vide supra,* p. 158), in Wieland's novels, in Berkeley's *Siris,* in Spenser, and in Dante. Yet a word of caution is needed in venturing on a Neoplatonic interpretation where the substance of Plato is thinned to shadows and shadows deepened to substance. In view of Shelley's own natural mythopoeic and symbolic talent it is difficult to differentiate between his own creation and derivation from the Platonic tradition. A natural creation of Shelley's own thought or symbolic mind can easily lead us to mistake it for a Neoplatonic derivation, especially if we can find in Neoplatonism any remote or cognate parallels. In discussing the sources of Shelley's poetry we must never forget the complexity of Shelley's mind and life; we must always keep before us the warning that no single idea or source should be regarded as basic or decisive. In his article *"Prometheus Unbound, or Every Man His Own Allegorist"* (*PMLA*, XL [1925], 172-184) Professor White has given a salutary warning about reading too much into the symbolism and allegory of the poem.

Of the attempts made to understand the symbolism, that of Professor Grabo goes furthest in penetrating the obscurities of the poem. It is essential, however, in literary criticism to ask the right questions even if they cannot be satisfactorily answered. The same question may be asked about Shelley's Neoplatonism as is asked about his Platonism. May we not also differentiate between a natural and a direct or indirect Neoplatonism (cf. *supra* pp. 25-26)? It cannot be doubted that much Neoplatonism, as we have seen, reached Shelley as part of the indirect tradition which has permeated European thought. It is inferred that he read and knew something of direct Neoplatonism from his acquaintance with Thomas Taylor. But it is open to serious doubt whether the poem is so largely Neoplatonic in character or that Shelley was so conscious of the Neoplatonic explanation as Professor Grabo thinks. There is no reading of Plotinus in the Journal of Mary and Shelley at this time, or any other period; yet there is considerable reading and translation of Plato shortly before the composition of *Prometheus Unbound*. If anything, Platonism should be the character of the poem. But it is in the alchemy of Shelley's mind, in its fusion of Platonic notions with his own "operations of the human mind," that there results a quality of poetry which, because of its general resemblance to Neoplatonism, is called Neoplatonic. Shelley's romantic improvisation on Platonic themes (cf. *infra*, pp. 335-336) is more akin to Neoplatonism than Platonism, and it is in the unawareness of this that Professor Grabo's interpretation suffers.

> I am the Earth,
> Thy mother; she within whose stony veins,
> To the last fibre of the loftiest tree

Whose thin leaves trembled in the frozen air,
Joy ran, as blood within a living frame,
When thou didst from her bosom, like a cloud . . .

(I, 152-157)

The conception of Earth as a living organism finds analogy in *Timaeus,* 34 ff. (see commentary on *Queen Mab,* Introduction, and I, 264-267, pp. 176-178, 180-181, *supra*).

For know there are two worlds of life and death:
One that which thou beholdest; but the other
Is underneath the grave, where do inhabit
The shadows of all forms that think and live
Till death unite them and they part no more . . .

(I, 195-199)

These lines refer to two Platonic notions: (1) the eternal versus the relative world, and (2) the immortality of the soul. The two notions are complementary in Shelley as in Plato. Shelley not only fuses these Platonic conceptions but also makes the habitation of the eternal beneath the grave a symbol of nether instead of upper transcendence, a conception probably inspired by the subterranean locus of Elysium, a word which Shelley used frequently. The phrase "shadows of all forms" is almost a Platonic formula for the shadowy manifestation of Platonic forms (εἴδη) in the relative world. Professor Grabo takes these lines to be influenced by Porphyry (*Prometheus Unbound: An Interpretation,* pp. 24-27); and Miss Ebeling, as influenced by Paracelsus's doctrine of Evestra (*SP,* XXXII [1935], 517-518). It is not necessary, however, to go beyond the *Symposium* and *Phaedo,* where both doctrines are set forth (*vide supra,* p. 112).

Phantasm of Jupiter, arise, appear!

(I, 221)

For this Platonic image, see White, *The Best of Shelley,* page 484, and commentary on the Platonism of this poem (*supra,* p. 235). The "Phantasm of Jupiter" is Shelley's own development of the Platonic notion of shadow versus original (cf. *supra,* p. 204), which has already appeared in lines 195-199. Shelley here dramatizes the two Platonic realms by taking Platonic imagery and adapting it to suit the needs of his dramatic imagination.

Methinks I grow like what I contemplate . . . .

(I, 450)

This conception, which is tangent to *Republic,* 401-402a, has already been expressed in *Prince Athanase,* Fragment 2, line 15, and *Marenghi,* line 135 (*vide supra,* p. 227).

> Yet am I king over myself, and rule
> The torturing and conflicting throngs within . . . .
> (I, 492-493)

Plato would have been delighted with this sentiment, which finds a parallel in *Republic,* 440b ff., and *Phaedrus,* 253d ff.

> In young spirits, sense-enchanted . . .
> (I, 511)

A condition of the dwellers of the cave, *Republic,* 514 ff.

> The wise want love; and those who love want wisdom . . . .
> (I, 627)

This line is perhaps a direct allusion to the *Symposium,* 200e, where love is defined as a love for what it does not possess.

> This was the shadow of the truth I saw.
> (I, 655)

This line is a Platonic formula for the myth of the Cave in the *Republic,* 514 ff. The doctrine appears as a Platonic leitmotif in this poem.

> Whose homes are the dim caves of human thought . . .
> (I, 659)

The cave of human thought is a favorite Platonic symbol of Shelley; compare *Mont Blanc,* line 44, and Shelley's comment on an image of Sophocles which Mary cites in her Note on *Prometheus Unbound* (*vide supra,* pp. 210-211, and *infra,* pp. 327-329).

> *Fourth Spirit*
> On a poet's lips I slept
> Dreaming like a love-adept
> In the sound his breathing kept;
> Nor seeks nor finds he mortal blisses,
> But feeds on the aerial kisses
> Of shapes that haunt thought's wildernesses.
> He will watch from dawn to gloom
> The lake-reflected sun illume

> The yellow bees in the ivy-bloom,
> Nor heed nor see, what things they be;
> But from these create he can
> Forms more real than living man,
> Nuslings of immortality!
> One of these awakened me,
> And I sped to succour thee.
>
>   (I, 737-751)

There is a remarkable similarity between the spirit of these lines and Agathon's speech in the *Symposium*. Likewise there is a similarity between lines 745-749 and Shelley's translation of a passage from the *Ion:* "They tell us that these souls, flying like bees from flower to flower, and wandering over the gardens and the meadows and the honey-flowing fountains of the Muses, return to us laden with sweetness of melody; *and arrayed as they are in the plumes of rapid imagination,* they speak truth." As Shelley had not read the *Ion* until 1821, it cannot be maintained that there is a direct influence. On the contrary, this passage in *Prometheus Unbound* seems to be the sort of inspiration that is responsible for the interpolation of the italicized phrase, which is not in Plato's text. In this respect we have here a tangent image emanating independently in the mind of the poet.

The phrase "Forms more real than living man, Nurslings of immortality" (ll. 748-749; cf. *infra,* p. 337) refers, of course, to the immortal creations of poetry, but the words also have the connotation of the Platonic forms (εἴδη), to which Shelley refers in Act III, scene iii, line 51.

> Ah, sister! Desolation is a delicate thing:
> It walks not on the earth, it floats not on the air,
> But treads with lulling footstep, and fans with silent wing
> The tender hopes which in their hearts the best
>   and gentlest bear . . . .
>
>   (I, 772-775)

These lines are a direct transcription of a passage in Agathon's speech in the *Symposium,* 195d, which Shelley had translated only a few months before the composition of these lines. The passage reads: "For Homer says, that the Goddess Calamity is delicate, and that her feet are tender. 'Her feet are soft,' he says, 'for she treads not upon the ground, but makes her path upon the heads of men.' He gives as an evidence of her tenderness, that she walks not upon that which is hard, but that which is soft. The same evidence is sufficient to make manifest the tenderness of Love" (Shelley's translation). Just as Agathon substituted Love for Calamity, so Shelley reverts to Homer's conception and substitutes Desolation. Shelley's interest in the speech of Agathon is reflected not only in his reference to it in *Prince Athanase,* Fragment 3, lines 60-68, but also in *Epipsychidion,* Fragments, lines 101-108, in a reference to it in a letter to Godwin (Julian *Works,* IX, 260), and finally in his *Note on the Banquet of Plato,* where he writes, "The wonderful description of Love in Plato, *Sympos.* p. 214—particularly l. 8—*l. ultima, et passim,* 218," referring to this passage (cf. *infra,* p. 461).

> . . . the azure night
> Grew radiant with the glory of that form
> Which lives unchanged within. . . .
> (II, i, 63-65)

The form which lives unchanged within is another of Shelley's felicitous phrases with an aura of Platonic connotation.

> Or when some star of many a one
> That climbs and wanders thro' steep night,
> Has found the cleft thro' which alone
> Beams fall from high those depths upon
> Ere it is borne away, away,
> By the swift Heavens that cannot stay,
> It scatters drops of golden light.
> Like lines of rain that ne'er unite:
> And the gloom divine is all around . . . .
> (II, ii, 14-22)

These lines are imbued with natural Platonic imagery expressive of the fleeting disappearance of the shadow of beauty in the world of nature.

> Hither the sound has borne us—to the realm
> Of Demogorgon . . . .
> (II, iii, 1-2)

The Demogorgon is not found in ancient mythology. It enters English literature through Boccaccio's *Genealogia deorum.* In his study of the sources of this conception in Boccaccio, Castelain concludes that Demogorgon is a scribe's error for Plato's *Demiourgon* (δημιουργόν), the Demiourgos of the *Timaeus* (Maurice Castelain, "Démogorgon ou le barbarisme déifié," *Bulletin de l'Association Guillaume Budé,* No. 36 [1932], pp. 22-39; Carlo Landi, *Démogorgone. Con saggio di nuova edizione delle genealogie deorum gentilium del Boccaccio e silloge dei frammente di Teodonzio* [Palermo, 1930]).

The Demogorgon, like Asia, is another of Shelley's dramatis personae which admit of Platonic or Neoplatonic interpretation. The word *Demogorgon* appears in the correspondence of Peacock and Hogg in 1817-1818, and it is not unlikely that it was shared with Shelley, their fellow-Athenian (see *The Athenians,* pp. 39, 45). It has been widely interpreted as Eternity (Salt, *A Shelley Primer,* p. 63), whose "mighty law" is the renascence of the human spirit symbolized by the spring (White, *Shelley,* II, 116). Professor Grabo (*The Magic Plant,* p. 280) interprets it as fate or necessity, which is related to the story in the following way: "By casting out hate Prometheus has identified himself with the ruling power of the universe which is Love, and Love commands Destiny or Fate, which is Demogorgon"; then Professor Grabo identifies this philosophy of Shelley with Neoplatonism, "in which the One is thought of as triune, the mysterious all-perfect source of life and energy, the creative brain, and the executive will" (*The Magic Plant,* p. 280). Another Platonic interpretation of Demogorgon is that "he stands for the mysterious reality, the eternal order, behind and above the temporal world, and he is something like Greek fate, with a strong coloring of Shelleyan 'necessity' " (Bush, *Mythology and the Romantic Tradition in English Poetry,* p. 146; see *ibid.,* note 40, for other interpretations of Demogorgon). In all these interpretations Demogorgon is tangent to various Platonic and Neoplatonic forces or powers without being definitely or precisely identified with any one in particular. It is characteristic of Shelley to use symbols or abstractions in a half-revealing and half-concealing manner, even as these symbols and abstractions are often used in Aeschylean, Pindaric, and Platonic thought and in particular in myths of Plato. To expect precise identification in Shelley's symbols and abstractions is to disregard the fact that symbols often in the flux of his imagination become protean and plastic. The difficulty is further increased by the fact that Shelley takes traditional symbols and infuses them with a meaning all his own; this being the case, it is impossible to identify these symbols with a traditional conception of philosophy which no longer fits Shelley's new and re-creative conception of it.

> How glorious art thou, Earth! And if thou be
> The shadow of some spirit lovelier still,
> Though evil stain its work, and it should be
> Like its creation, weak yet beautiful,
> I could fall down and worship that and thee.
>
> (II, iii, 12-16)

An outburst of Platonic feeling which views the earth as the shadow of some lovelier spirit. As the *Hymn to Intellectual Beauty* shows,
it is a Power conceived in terms of Plato's intellectual Beauty. Though
the earth is stained by the evil of partaking of the eternal Beauty, it
acquires a derivative Beauty which is not its own (*vide infra*, p. 300).

> Down, down!
> Through the shade of sleep,
> Through the cloudy strife
> Of Death and of Life;
> Through the veil and the bar
> Of things which seem and are . . . .
> (II, iii, 55-60)

These melodious lines, which make lyrical use of the Platonic theme
of appearance and reality and immortality, constitute one of the most
perfect Platonic lyrics in English poetry.

> Who reigns? There was the Heaven and Earth at first,
> And Light and Love; then Saturn . . . .
> (II, iv, 32-33)

For Love as one of the eldest gods, see *Symposium*, 178b-c.

> And mad disquietudes, and shadows idle
> Of unreal good . . .
> (II, iv, 56-57)

"Shadows idle of unreal good" seems to be an echo of the myth of
the Cave in *Republic*, 514 ff.

> . . . and Love he sent to bind
> The disunited tendrils of that vine
> Which bears the wine of life, the human heart . . . .
> (II, iv, 63-65)

Similarly, Plato conceives of mutual love as "that reconciler and bond
of union of their original nature, which seeks to make two, one, and to
heal the divided nature of man" (*Symposium*, 191d, Shelley's translation).

> Evil, the immedicable plague . . .
> (II, iv, 101)

For Plato's similar view, see *Theaetetus*, 176a, and commentary *supra*,
pages 235-237.

... the deep truth is imageless ....
(II, iv, 116)

For the important Platonic metaphysical background of this line, see commentary *supra*, pages 233-235, and *Republic*, 511, 516b.

What to bid speak
Fate, Time, Occasion, Chance and Change? To these
All things are subject but eternal Love.
(II, iv, 118-120)

The eternal Love is the Love described in Plato's *Symposium*, 197c-d, 210-211; this ideal eternal Love is contrasted with the realm of mutability, which is subject to the forces listed in line 119. For the relation of these lines to evil, see commentary *supra*, pages 235-237.

How thou art changed! I dare not look on thee;
I feel but see thee not. I scarce endure
The radiance of thy beauty. Some good change
Is working in the elements, which suffer
Thy presence thus unveiled. . . .
.   .   .   .
. . . love, like the atmosphere
Of the sun's fire filling the living world,
Burst from thee, and illumined earth and heaven
And the deep ocean and the sunless caves
And all that dwells within them; till grief cast
Eclipse upon the soul from which it came:
Such art thou now; nor is it I alone,
Thy sister, thy companion, thine own chosen one,
But the whole world which seeks thy sympathy.
Hearest thou not sounds i' the air which speak the love
Of all articulate beings? Feelest thou not
The inanimate winds enamoured of thee? List!
(II, v, 16-20, 26-37)

Asia is another of Shelley's dramatis personae who are symbolic incarnations of Platonic conceptions. In this drama Asia is symbolic of the ideal Love and Beauty which permeate the world. She is so transcendently beautiful that Panthea can scarcely endure the radiance of her beauty, even as the prisoner in the *Republic* when released from the cave can scarcely endure the radiance of the Sun. Like Spenser's Una, Asia is seen through a veil, so beautiful is she. (For a Dantean parallel, see Oscar Kuhns, "Dante's Influence on Shelley," *MLN*, XIII [1898], 164). Asia, like Plato's Sun, fills the whole world with light, and all of nature seeks her sympathy. In these lines Shelley stresses the immanent rather than the transcendent nature of Beauty. This is in consonance with his conception of Platonic Love, which is filled with Shelleyan sympathy, a force which Shelley interpolates in his reshaping of the Ideal Love of the *Symposium*. These lines also show that Shelley is using Platonic Love synonymously with Beauty.

> Life of Life! thy lips enkindle
>   With their love the breath between them;
> And thy smiles before they dwindle
>   Make the cold air fire; then screen them
> In those looks, where whoso gazes
> Faints, entangled in their mazes.
>
> Child of Light! thy limbs are burning
>   Thro' the vest which seems to hide them;
> As the radiant lines of morning
>   Thro' the clouds ere they divide them;
> And this atmosphere divinest
> Shrouds thee whereso'er thou shinest.
>
> Fair are others; none beholds thee,
>   But thy voice sounds low and tender
> Like the fairest, for it folds thee
>   From the sight, that liquid splendour,
> And all feel, yet see thee never,
> As I feel now, lost for ever!
>
> Lamp of Earth! where'er thou movest
>   Its dim shapes are clad with brightness,
> And the souls of whom thou lovest
>   Walk upon the winds with lightness,
> Till they fail, as I am failing,
> Dizzy, lost, yet unbewailing!

(II, v, 48-71)

For the influence of the *Symposium* on these lines and for Shelley's ideal philosophy and equation of Love with Intellectual Beauty, see commentary *supra,* pages 238-239. The lyric is full of Platonic nuances, images, and ideas. Asia, like Beauty, is felt but not seen; as in Plato the Sun gives light and truth to the world (*Republic,* 508-509), so Asia is the Lamp of the Earth which endows all the earthly objects with brightness of beauty. The stress on emanation rather than transcendence makes Shelley's conception closer to Plotinian emanation than Plato's conception in the *Symposium*. Asia's veil is an accoutrement of Platonic women (cf. Spenser's Una and Wieland's Psyche, *supra*, pp. 105, 142).

Asia

My soul is an enchanted boat,
Which, like a sleeping swan, doth float
Upon the silver waves of thy sweet singing;
And thine doth like an angel sit
Beside the helm conducting it,
Whilst all the winds with melody are ringing.
It seems to float ever, for ever,
Upon that many-winding river,
Between mountains, woods, abysses,
A paradise of wildernesses!
Till, like one in slumber bound,
Borne to the ocean, I float down, around,
Into a sea profound, of ever-spreading sound . . . .
(II, v, 72-84)

Oscar Kuhns considers this passage as influenced by Dante (*MLN*, XIII [1898], 164-165). Apropos of Dantean influence we must keep in mind a statement of Mary in a letter to Leigh Hunt written in 1846: "Can any thing be so wondrously poetical as the approach of the boat with souls from earth to Purgatory—Shelley's most favourite passage" (*Letters of Mary W. Shelley*, ed. F. L. Jones, II, 283). The imagery of the boat and the stream could also come from Shelley's fondness for sailing down streams (cf. W. B. Yeats, *Ideas of Good and Evil*, pp. 115 ff.). It is also a common symbol in Romantic poetry. Professor G. Wilson Knight has pointed out the parallelism between Shelley's voyages and Coleridge's in *Kubla Khan* and the *Ancient Mariner* (*The Starlit Dome*, pp. 186-189, 192, 228-229).

Grabo asserts that the symbolism here is derived from Neoplatonism: the sea is symbolic of ultimate being, the streams leading to the sea bear the souls as in a boat (*Prometheus Unbound*, p. 89). The lyric is capable of such an interpretation on the basis of the return of the soul to the One from whence it emanated. Plato had already used the word *ocean* for the ultimate unity of Beauty (*Symposium*, 210d), and Plotinus uses the symbolism of the boat for the soul in the following passage: "If the Soul returns to this Sphere it finds itself under the same Spirit or a new, according to the life it is to live. With this Spirit it embarks in the skiff of the universe: the 'spindle of Necessity' then takes control and appoints the seat for the voyage, the seat of the lot in life" (Plotinus,

Enneads, III, iv, 6, Mackenna's translation). Whether Shelley's symbolism is derivatively rooted in the metaphysics of this passage is a moot point. Grabo maintains that Shelley is making a conscious use of this Neoplatonic symbolism, but the absence of any metaphysical overtones leads one to think that the symbolism is emotional and poetically cognate rather than metaphysically derivative from Neoplatonism. W. M. Rossetti, who speaks of the "ideal charm" and "supersensual meander" of this passage, says, "The meaning of the lyric . . . is that the soul, transported into idealism by melody, muses upon indefinable possibilities of existence praenatal and praeterlethal—the world of spirit before birth and after death" (*The Shelley Society's Papers,* First Series, No. 1, Part I [London, 1888], p. 156).

> But, by the instinct of sweet music driven;
> Till through Elysian garden islets
>   By thee, most beautiful of pilots,
>   Where never mortal pinnace glided,
>   The boat of my desire is guided;
> Realms where the air we breathe is love,
> Which in the winds and on the waves doth move,
> Harmonizing this earth with what we feel above.
>   (II, v, 90-97)

In these lines we have echoes of Agathon's speech in the *Symposium:* "Love . . . our most excellent pilot," and "Love is the divinity who creates peace among men, and calm upon the sea. . . ." The harmonizing of this earth with what we feel above is capable of Platonic exploitation if we remember that for Plato the relative world should try to imitate the divine world as much as possible.

> We have passed Age's icy caves,
> And Manhood's dark and tossing waves,
> And Youth's smooth ocean, smiling to betray;
>   Beyond the glassy gulphs we flee
>   Of shadow-peopled Infancy,
> Through Death and Birth, to a diviner day . . . .
>   (II, v, 98-103)

The retrograde return from Age to Infancy and then to Death, a basic feature of Shelley's thought (see Knight, *The Starlit Dome,* pp. 187, 196-197, 208-209), has been interpreted by Mr. E. M. W. Tillyard as a direct allusion to Plato's *Statesman,* 270d, e. He interprets these lines as a sailing back of the souls of Asia and Prometheus "through the golden or Saturnian order, where time still rules, to the 'diviner day' or timeless realm of 'Light of Love' (*Times Literary Supplement*, September 29, 1932, p. 691). Mr. George Sampson points out in his reply to Mr. Tillyard's note (*Times Literary Supplement*, October 20, 1932, p. 762) that these lines in the poem can be explained in other ways:

Shelley is doing precisely what Wordsworth did in the "Intimations" Ode, but (as demanded by the situation) in the reverse order. . . . Shelley, writing perhaps as a Platonist, but certainly as an eager Perfectionist, makes Age remotest from Heaven (as he conceived it), and traces the course of the soul back through Manhood, Youth and Infancy to the "diviner day" which is lost by Birth and can regain only by Death— *i.e.* by leaving Jupiter's world with its tortures, and passing into the new Heaven and Earth described later in the poem.

This return to a "diviner day," to the pre-existence of the soul, and the withdrawal from the world of Becoming is a characteristic Platonic theme, though the expression of it shows affinities with the Neoplatonism of Wordsworth's *Ode* (*vide supra*, pp. 164-165).

In this connection it is well to discuss the influence of Plato's *Statesman* on Shelley's *Prometheus Unbound* as pointed out by Miss Winstanley, who writes:

The correspondence between Plato's *Statesman* and *Prometheus Unbound* is, in many respects, very close. Shelley has availed himself of Plato's myth for a considerable part of the framework of his drama. . . . The age of Cronos corresponds to the age of Saturn in *Prometheus Unbound* (Act II, Sc. 4). According to Plato's myth there comes, however, a change. . . . This convulsion which ends the reign of Saturn is several times alluded to by Shelley. (Act IV, 1. 316, Act IV, 1. 295). . . . This time of darkness and gloom [i.e. when the world is left to itself] corresponds, of course, to the age of Jupiter as given by Shelley, which steadily deteriorates till the good of the world seems well nigh lost. (*Prometheus Unbound*, Act II, Sc. 4; *Ibid.* Act I, ll. 170-80) In Plato's myth these times of gloom are succeeded by times of guidance when God will again seat himself at the helm. . . . It is such a "reversal" which is described in Act III of *Prometheus Unbound*, the animals are at peace with one another. . . . Men are free from hate. . . . ("Platonism in Shelley," *Essays and Studies by Members of the English Association*, IV [1913], 98-100)

Mr. Tillyard corroborates Miss Winstanley's account by pointing out that *Prometheus Unbound*, II, v, 98-103, is explained by a direct allusion to Plato's *Statesman*.

The correspondence between these episodes in *Prometheus Unbound* and Plato's *Statesman* can be accounted for, however, in terms of Shelley's contact with the Platonic tradition rather than with the *Statesman* itself. A comparison of the passage in *Prometheus Unbound* with the *Statesman* shows no direct knowledge; though Shelley had been reading Plato at the time of the composition, this reading, as the Journal shows, was confined to the *Republic;* nor is there evidence of the reading of the *Statesman* previous to this. Yet Shelley could have absorbed the notion of the different ages through his reading of Hesiod's *Works and Days* (ll. 109-201) in 1815 and Virgil's *Fourth Eclogue.* The influence of *Eclogue VI,* 31-42, is seen in *Prometheus Unbound,* II, ii, 91 (cf. Woodberry, *Shelley's Complete Poetical Works,* p. 624, note on *Prometheus Unbound,* II, ii, 91). It can be shown with equal plausibility that Shelley absorbed the doctrine from Virgil's *Fourth Eclogue,* which has, as Professor Rose points out, Plato's *Statesman,* 268d ff., for its source. (See "Some Neglected Points in the Fourth Eclogue," *Classical Quarterly,* XVIII [1924], 113-118; *The Eclogues of Vergil* [Berkeley and Los Angeles, 1942], pp. 183-186.) Shelley reflects this same Virgilian source in the chorus *of Hellas:*

> The world's great age begins anew,
> The golden years return . . . .

which, as Shelley himself points out in his note on line 1060 of *Hellas,* is derived from Virgil's *Fourth Eclogue:*

> magnus ab integro saeclorum nascitur ordo
> iam redit et Virgo, redeunt Saturnia regna . . . .

Thus the complexity of the various sources of Shelley's ideas should caution us to regard no single source as basic or decisive. Though the influence of Plato in these scenes is apparent, yet the influence may have reached Shelley indirectly through the Platonic tradition.

The presence of the "Island of Atlantis" in scene ii of Act III reflects Shelley's knowledge of it through a reading of Plato's *Critias,* which was included in the tenth volume of the Bipont edition which Shelley took with him to Italy.

> Asia, thou light of life,
> Shadow of beauty unbeheld . . . .
> (III, iii, 6-7)

For the conception of Asia in terms of Platonic concepts and phrases, see commentary *supra,* pages 248-250. Asia marks the fusion in Shelley of the concepts of Intellectual Beauty and Platonic Love. The phrase "shadow of beauty unbeheld" is one of Shelley's most Platonic lines and forms the basic common denominator between Shelley and Plato.

> Where we will sit and talk of time and change,
> As the world ebbs and flows, ourselves unchanged.
> What can hide man from mutability?
>
> (III, iii, 23-25)

The immutability of Prometheus and Asia amid the world of flux is a Platonic doctrine applied from the character and nature of Plato's Ideas to Shelley's dramatis personae. For Shelley's philosophic doctrine of Mutability, see pages 194-195, *supra.*

> Weave harmonies divine, yet ever new,
> From difference sweet where discord cannot be . . . .
>
> (III, iii, 38-39)

Compare *Symposium,* 187b: ". . . from sounds which first differed, like the grave and the acute, and which afterwards agreed, harmony was produced according to musical art" (Shelley's translation).

> And lovely apparitions,—dim at first,
> Then radiant, as the mind, arising bright
> From the embrace of beauty (whence the forms
> Of which these are the phantoms) casts on them
> The gathered rays which are reality,
> Shall visit us, the progeny immortal
> Of Painting, Sculpture, and rapt Poesy,
> And arts, tho' unimagined, yet to be.
>
> (III, iii, 49-56)

These lines constitute one of the best examples in Shelley of the direct influence of Plato and Shelley's power of transmuting Platonic metaphysics into poetry (see also I, 748). The lines are a direct transcription of the *Symposium,* 209-212, and set forth the various stages in the ascent to Ideal Beauty from the relative world. The "lovely apparitions," the "phantoms," are the shadows of Ideal Beauty, the Platonic εἴδη, which Shelley here translates literally as "forms." In expressing this Platonic doctrine Shelley also enlists the Platonic contrast of dimness and light for the degree of reality embodied in physical and ideal Beauty. The mind nurtured on beauty focuses on the dim objects a bright light, and they are seen as the Platonic forms of Reality. The intellectual character of this Beauty is seen in Shelley's emphasis on mind, which grasps the beauty of the forms. In this passage the Platonic metaphysics of appearance and reality is developed through Plato's own imagery. Furthermore, Shelley echoes in these lines Plato's view stated in the *Symposium,* 209c, that the arts are the immortal progeny of Love. This poetic transcription of the Platonic theory of Beauty may be compared to Robert Bridges's great passage in *The Testament of Beauty,* I, 670-691, and W. B. Yeats's

> Plato thought nature but a spume that plays
> Upon a ghostly paradigm of things.
> *(Among School Children,* vi)

These passages constitute the clearest re-expression of Plato's philosophy in English poetry. If we analyze Shelley's language we can see how much Shelley owes to Plato:

1. "Lovely apparitions" "dim at first," "the phantoms" are poetic references or translations from the *Symposium* of καλὰ σώματα (210a6), εἴδωλα ἀρετῆς (212a4), φαντασθήσεται (211a5); and from the *Republic* of σκότους ἀνάπλεως (516e5), πρῶτον μὲν τὰς σκιὰς ἂν ῥᾷστα καθορῷ (516a6).

2. "Radiant," "rising bright from the embrace of beauty," "forms," "reality," "progeny immortal" are poetic references to οὗτος περιιὼν τὸ καλὸν ἐν ᾧ ἂν γεννήσειεν (*Symposium,* 209b2), ἁπτόμενος γὰρ οἶμαι τοῦ καλοῦ (209c2), καλλιόνων καὶ ἀθανατωτέρων παίδων κεκοινωνηκότες (209c6-7), καθαρόν (211e1), μόνῳ θεατὴ νῷ (*Phaedrus,* 247c7), κάλλος . . . ἰδεῖν λαμπρόν (*Phaedrus,* 250b5-6), ἐν αὐγῇ καθαρᾷ (*Phaedrus,* 250c4), τούτοις μὲν ὡς εἰκόσιν αὖ χρώμενοι (*Republic,* 510e3), τελευτᾷ εἰς εἴδη (*Republic,* 511c2). Out of all these phrases and conceptions Shelley has woven a new fabric of his own which is a poetic summary of his reading of the *Symposium,* the *Phaedrus,* and the *Republic.* The passage is one of the best illustrations in English poetry of how Platonism directly affects the poetic mind.

> The wandering voices and the shadows these
> Of all that man becomes, the mediators
> Of that best worship love, by him and us
> Given and returned . . . .
> (III, iii, 57-60)

As in lines 54-56 Shelley conceives of the arts as progeny immortal, a reflection of the *Symposium,* 209c, so in these lines Shelley fuses Art with the conception of Eros as an intermediary spirit (cf. *Symposium,*

202e). Likewise Shelley alludes to his favorite doctrine, the "mind becomes that which it contemplates" (cf. commentary on *Prince Athanase*,
Fragment 2, l. 15, *supra*, p. 227).

> . . . swift shapes and sounds, which grow
> More fair and soft as man grows wise and kind,
> And, veil by veil, evil and error fall . . .
> (III, iii, 60-62)

For Shelley's ascription of evil to Appearance rather than Reality, see
commentary *supra*, pages 235-237.

> Death is the veil which those who live call life:
> They sleep, and it is lifted . . . .
> (III, iii, 113-114)

This Platonic view of immortality is expressed with slight variation
in the *Sonnet* "Lift not the painted veil"; see commentary *supra*, pages
230-231.

> there the emulous youths
> Bore to thy honour thro' the divine gloom
> The lamp which was thine emblem; even as those
> Who bear the untransmitted torch of hope
> Into the grave, across the night of life,
> As thou hast borne it most triumphantly
> To this far goal of Time. Depart, farewell.
> (III, iii, 168-174)

An allusion here is made to the transmission of the torch of life (cf.
Plato's *Laws*, 776b; *Republic*, 328a; Lucretius, II, 79).

> It is the delicate spirit
> That guides the earth through heaven. From afar
> The populous constellations call that light
> The loveliest of the planets . . . .
> (III, iv, 6-9)

Miss Winstanley sees in these lines the influence of the *Timaeus*, 41e,
in which is set forth the conception that the planets, including the earth,
are inspired by "souls" or spirits.

> As if the sense of love dissolved in them
> Had folded itself round the spherèd world.
> (III, iv, 102-103)

Compare *Symposium*, 196a: "For if he [Love] were otherwise [than liquid], he could not, as he does, fold himself around everything" (Shelley's translation).

> The painted veil, by those who were, called life,
> Which mimicked, as with colours idly spread,
> All men believed or hoped, is torn aside . . . .
>
> (III, iv, 190-192)

For this Platonic doctrine of the nature of the relative world and the imagery of the veil, see commentary on the *Sonnet* "Lift not the painted veil," *supra*, pages 230-231. In connection with the phrase "painted . . . colours idly spread," compare *Symposium*, 211e: ". . . the supreme beauty itself, simple, pure, uncontaminated with the intermixture of human flesh and colours, and all other idle and unreal shapes attendant on mortality" (Shelley's translation).

> The loathsome mask has fallen, the Man remains
> Sceptreless, free, uncircumscribed, but man
> Equal, unclassed, tribeless, and nationless,
> Exempt from awe, worship, degree, the king
> Over himself; just, gentle, wise . . . .
>
> (III, iv, 193-197)

For Shelley's conception of evil as an accident of the relative world, see commentary *supra*, pages 235-237. Miss Winstanley sees in these lines a parallel to the myth in the *Statesman* of Plato in which gloom gives way to God's guidance. Compare commentary on *Prometheus Unbound*, II, v, 98-103, *supra*, pages 251-253. Perhaps Shelley is echoing here the conception of primitive man found in Rousseau and Lucretius. Line 193 is an echo of "eripitur persona, manet res," *De Rerum Natura*, III, 58. As Barker points out in *Greek Political Theory*[2] (London, 1925), page 255, the condition described here by Shelley would be found only in the anarchism of Plato's description of democracy.

> Nor yet exempt, though ruling them like slaves,
> From chance, and death, and mutability,
> The clogs of that which else might oversoar
> The loftiest star of unascended heaven,
> Pinnacled dim in the intense inane.
>
> (III, iv, 200-204)

The picture of man here is filled with Platonic echoes from the *Phaedo,* where man, though subject to death and mutability, masters

them through the philosophic exercise of reason and living on the plane
of the pure and divine, as much as is in his power. If it were not for the
"clogs" of the earthly, the philosopher would be next to the gods, a condition which Shelley also ascribes to man.

> We bear Time to his tomb in eternity . . . .
>
> (IV, 14)

This line is a felicitous rendering of the core of natural and direct
Platonism.

> The voice of the Spirits of Air and of Earth
>   Have drawn back the figured curtain of sleep,
> Which covered our being and darkened our birth
>   In the deep.
>
> (IV, 57-59)

Another of the many references to the Platonic immortality of the
soul in Shelley; "the figured curtain" is a variant of the "painted veil"
(cf. *Prometheus Unbound*, III, v, 190).

> And your eyes are as love which is veilèd not?
>
> (IV, 92)

For Shelley's conception of a Platonically veiled love, see commentary
on Asia, *Prometheus Unbound*, III, v, 48-71, *supra*, pages 249-250.

> And from the other opening in the wood
> Rushes, with loud and whirlwind harmony,
> A sphere, which is as many thousand spheres,
> Solid as crystal, yet through all its mass
> Flow, as through empty space, music and light:
> Ten thousand orbs involving and involved,
> Purple and azure, white and green and golden,
> Sphere within sphere; and every space between
> Peopled with unimaginable shapes,
> Such as ghosts dream dwell in the lampless deep,
> Yet each inter-transpicuous, and they whirl
> Over each other with a thousand motions,
> Upon a thousand sightless axles spinning,
> And with the force of self-destroying swiftness,
> Intensely, slowly, solemnly, roll on,
> Kindling with mingled sounds, and many tones,
> Intelligible words and music wild.
>
> (IV, 236-252)

The Platonic music of the spheres is fused here with Shelley's scientific poetry (see commentary on the music of the spheres, *supra*, p. 173). The songs of the Earth and the Moon (ll. 319 ff.) are possibly a development of the notion of the music of the. spheres in *Republic*, 616 ff. There Plato pictures the heavenly music which the spheres produce as they revolve on their axis. Plato, moreover, pictures the music as issuing from the siren on each sphere. Coleridge in his *Ode to the Departing Year*, which Shelley read and which influenced his conception of the Spirit of the Earth in *Prometheus Unbound,* makes striking use of the doctrine. In a note on the fourth stanza of this ode Coleridge writes: "The first Antistrophe describes the Image of the Departing Year, as in a vision; and concludes with introducing the Planetary Angel of the Earth preparing to address the Supreme Being." Shelley no doubt took up this Platonic notion which he found in Coleridge; he pictures the Earth and Moon as singing each in its respective sphere, a notion which also might be influenced by the antiphonal structure of Greek choral lyrics. The songs which they sang are permeated with Platonic sentiments as well as the scientific ideas which Grabo has pointed out.

> It interpenetrates my granite mass,
> Through tangled roots and trodden clay doth pass,
> Into the utmost leaves and delicatest flowers;
> Upon the winds, among the clouds 'tis spread,
> It wakes a life in the forgotten dead,
> They breathe a spirit up from their obscurest bowers.
>
> (IV, 370-375)

The interpretation of love throughout the earth is consonant with Plato's notion of a spirited universe as set forth in the *Timaeus*, 34 ff., and in Eryximachus's speech in the *Symposium,* 185e-188e, where the effect of love is visible in every aspect of the universe.

> Man, oh, not men! a chain of linked thought,
> Of love and might to be divided not,
> Compelling the elements with adamantine stress;
> As the sun rules, even with a tyrant's gaze,
> The unquiet republic of the maze
> Of planets, struggling fierce towards heaven's free wilderness.
>
> (IV, 394-399)

There is perhaps in line 395 an allusion to Aristophanes's speech in the *Symposium*, 192d-e; in line 396 we have a foreshadowing of the Platonic doctrine of *Adonais,* lines 379-387. In Shelley's MS notebook lines 398-399 appear as

> . . . the unquiet Republic of the maze
> Of worlds struggling to seek Heaven's keepless wilderness.
>
> (H. B. Forman, *Notebook of P. B. Shelley*, I, 55)

In this line Shelley possibly has a reference either to an astronomical centrifugal force or to Plato's *Republic*, transferring from society to cosmology the problem of creating harmony in the maze of spheres.

> Man, one harmonious soul of many a soul,
> Whose nature is its own divine controul . . .
>
> (IV, 400-401)

The thought here is Plato's harmony of the elements in the soul, which is discussed in the *Republic*, 433a, and illustrated in the myth of the *Phaedrus*, 253-254.

> . . . a tempest-wingèd ship, whose helm
> Love rules, through waves which dare not overwhelm,
> Forcing life's wildest shores to own its sovereign sway.
>
> (IV, 409-411)

We find a comparison of Love to a pilot in Agathon's speech, *Symposium*, 197e, which Shelley translated as, Love "the abolisher of all evil; our most excellent pilot, defence, saviour and guardian in labour and in fear."

> Thou art speeding round the sun,
> Brightest world of many a one;
> Green and azure sphere which shinest
> With a light which is divinest
> Among all the lamps of Heaven
> To whom life and light is given;
> I, thy crystal paramour,
> Borne beside thee by a power
> Like the polar Paradise,
> Magnet-like, of lovers' eyes;
> I, a most enamoured maiden,
> Whose weak brain is overladen
> With the pleasure of her love,
> Maniac-like around thee move
> Gazing, an insatiate bride,
> On thy form from every side
> Like a Maenad, round the cup
> Which Agave lifted up
> In the weird Cadmaean forest.

Brother, whereso'er thou soarest
I must hurry, whirl and follow
Through the heavens wide and hollow,
Sheltered by the warm embrace
Of thy soul from hungry space,
Drinking from thy sense and sight
Beauty, majesty, and might,
As a lover or a cameleon
Grows like what it looks upon,
As a violet's gentle eye
Gazes on the azure sky
Until its hue grows like what it beholds
As a grey and watery mist
Glows like solid amethyst
Athwart the western mountain it enfolds,
When the sunset sleeps
Upon its snow.

(IV, 457-492)

The Platonism in these lines is interpreted by Miss Winstanley as follows: "In the fourth act of *Prometheus Unbound*, Shelley, in the most magical way, blends his Platonism with the ideas of modern astronomy. In the *Timaeus* the law of gravitation is explained by Plato as being not only an attraction of lesser bodies to greater, but as having a magnetic power. Shelley avails himself of this idea: the Moon and the Earth he represents as living spirits, and the force of gravity which binds them together as the magnetic attraction of their love" (*Platonism in Shelley*, p. 87). For a more subtle study of the mixture of Platonism and Science, see Carl Grabo, *Prometheus Unbound, An Interpretation*. The theme of the song is a Platonic interpretation of physical science. Shelley's imagery, as has been shown, "presents mental phenomena in terms of the physical, physical phenomena in the terms of the mental, and even fuses matter and spirit in the same image" (White, *Shelley*, II, 130). These lines are an illustration of the second class in which Shelley presents scientific phenomena in terms of Platonic mental concepts. Shelley pictures astronomical phenomena in terms of Platonic concepts and emotions, such as a spirit governing each planet (see *Timaeus*, 41); male and female parts of the soul trying to merge (see Aristophanes's speech in the *Symposium*); and the Platonic theme of the mind becoming that which it contemplates (see *Prince Athanase*, Fragment 2, line 15), presented here in terms of the simile of a chameleon growing in its hue like that which it contemplates (see also *An Exhortation* and Shelley's letter to John and

Maria Gisborne, July 13, 1821 [Julian *Works*, X, 283]). For a variant expression of this theme, see *Variation of the Song of the Moon*, which is an early draft of Act IV, lines 485 ff. (Julian *Works*, II, 267 = III, 300).

> *Demogorgon.*
> Ye happy dead, whom beams of brightest verse
>   Are clouds to hide, not colours to pourtray,
> Whether your nature is that universe
>   Which once ye saw and suffered—
>
> *A Voice from Beneath.*
>   Or as they
> Whom we have left, we change and pass away.
> *Demogorgon.*
> Ye elemental Genii, who have homes
>   From man's high mind even to the central stone
> Of sullen lead . . . .
>
> (IV, 534-541)

The dead are conceived here in terms of Platonic immortality, and the elemental Genii are conceived as portions of the World Soul extending from man's mind down to the lowest grade of physical nature.

> And if with infirm hand, Eternity,
> Mother of many acts and hours, should free
> The serpent that would clasp her with his length . . .
>
> (IV, 565-567)

For commentary, see pages 186-188, above.

The Cenci
May 4–August 8, 1819

> I rarely kill the body, which preserves,
> Like a strong prison, the soul within my power . . . .
>
> (I, i, 114-115)

The body as the prison of the soul is an echo of *Phaedo*, 62b, 67d, 82e.

> I see, as from a tower, the end of all . . . .
>
> (II, ii, 147)

Compare *Republic*, 445c: "I can see as it were from a watchtower, now that we have ascended to this lofty stage in the argument." For the tower as a symbol in Shelley's poetry, see W. B. Yeats, *Ideas of Good and Evil*, pages 126-127.

No, I am dead! These putrefying limbs
Shut round and sepulchre the panting soul
Which would burst forth into the wandering air!
(III, i, 26-28)

Another example of the Platonic metaphor which Shelley uses in Act I, scene i, 114-115 (*vide supra*, p. 262).

I do not feel as if I were a man,
But like a fiend appointed to chastise
The offences of some unremembered world.
(IV, i, 160-162)

The "unremembered world" is an allusion to Plato's doctrine of the pre-existence of the soul in *Phaedo*, 72e-77a; *Meno*, 81 ff.

Peter Bell the Third
October, 1819

First, the antenatal Peter . . .
(Prologue, l. 3)

For the Platonic conception and the history of the word *antenatal* in Shelley, see commentary on *Prince Athanase*, I, 91 (*supra*, p. 226).

And these obscure remembrances . . .
(Part V, l. 46)

The phrase is an echo of the obscure recollections of a pre-existent life (cf. *Phaedo*, 72e-77a; *Meno*, 81 ff.).

[1] A famous river in the new Atlantis of the Dynastophylic Pantisocratists.
(VI, 126 n.)

A reference to Plato's lost continent (see *Timaeus*, 25a; *Critias*, 108e) in Southey's and Coleridge's Platonic Utopia which was to be founded on the banks of the Susquehanna (see J. R. MacGillivray, "The Pantisocracy Scheme and Its Immediate Background," *Studies in English by Members of University College, Toronto* [London, 1931], pp. 131-169).

Song of the Men of England
1819

Wherefore, Bees of England, forge
Many a weapon, chain, and scourge,

That these stingless drones may spoil
The forced produce of your toil?
                            (III, 9-12)

The image here is ultimately derived from Plato's *Republic,* 552c: "Shall we, then, say of him that as the drone springs up in the cell, a pest of the hive, so such a man grows up in his home, a pest of the state?" (see Paul Shorey, *Plato's Republic* [Loeb Classical Library], II, 268-269, where this instance is cited).

Ode to Heaven
December, 1819

Heaven! for thou art the abode
  Of that power which is the glass
Wherein man his nature sees.
                            (Ll. 20-22)

The affinities of man to the Divine, and the whole mood of the poem are natural Platonism. In these lines we have a foreshadowing of the Platonic imagery of *Adonais,* line 462.

Thou art but the mind's first chamber,
Round which its young fancies clamber,
  Like weak insects in a cave,
Lighted up by stalactites;
  But the portal of the grave,
Where a world of new delights
  Will make thy best glories seem
  But a dim and noonday gleam
  From the shadow of a dream!
                            (Ll. 28-36)

The lines are the expression of the natural Platonism in Shelley's mind which verges on Platonic immortality and its theme that this world is but "the shadow of a dream" of the ideal world.

Love's Philosophy
September-December, 1819

The fountains mingle with the river,
  And the rivers with the ocean;
The winds of Heaven mix for ever
  With a sweet emotion;

Nothing in the world is single;
All things by a law divine
In one another's being mingle—
Why not I with thine?

(Ll. 1-8)

Shelley's idea of universal love finds analogous though nonromantic expression in the conception of love in the *Symposium*, 186-188, 191d.

Ye Gentle Visitations of Calm Thought
1819

Ye gentle visitations of calm thought,
Moods like the memories of a happier earth—
Which come arrayed in thoughts of little worth,
Like stars in clouds by the weak winds inwrought,
But that the clouds depart and stars remain
While they remain, and ye alas! depart—
Leaving these garments from the naked heart
Which the next hour with its frozen rain . . .

A reflection of the theme of mutability and ideal permanence in Shelley's natural Platonism. (The complete text of this fragment, which differs from the 1839 edition, is that of the manuscript [*MS Shelley adds. e. 8*, p. 145] which also contains the first draft of Shelley's translation of Plato's epigram, *To Stella*).

SHELLEY'S READING IN PLATO AND THE PLATONIC TRADITION, 1820

DIRECT PLATONISM: Read Plato (February 14, 16-17, 19, 1820); *Phaedrus* (finished on May 2, 1820); *Phaedo* (1820; May 9, 1820); *Republic* (1820; September 4, 9, 1820).

INDIRECT PLATONISM: Lucretius (1820; June 28-30, July 3-6, 8, 1820); Spinoza (1820; January 5, 8-9, 12, 15-16, 23, March 17, 21-22, 26-31, April 1-2, 4-8, 23, June 3, 1820); Locke (1820); Lord Monboddo, *Antient Metaphysics* (September 21, 22, 23, October 1, 1820); Gillies, *Greece* (September 23, October 1, 1820); Godwin, *Political Justice* (1820; March 22, 26, April 1, 4).

PLATONISM IN SHELLEY'S POETRY WRITTEN IN 1820

The Sensitive Plant
March, 1820

This poem is an interesting amalgam of direct and indirect Platonism. The nature and character of the sensitive plant *(Mimosa pudica)* is given a Platonic interpretation. The basic idea of a sensitive plant is rooted in the conception of a Plastic Nature which emanates from Plato's *Timaeus*. Plotinus, arguing against Aristotle (*Eth. Nic.*, 1176a34, 1178b11), by attributing a happy life to the plants lays the foundation for Shelley's poem (*Enneads*, I, iv, 1-3). Cudworth's development of this idea in his *The True Intellectual System of the Universe* is of interest for Shelley's poem. Cudworth's Plastic Nature orders and disposes the heavens and the whole world, penetrating and permeating even the lowest animals and plants; every plant, herb, blade of grass, he says, "hath a particular plastic life, a vegetable soul of its own." Shelley takes this traditional Platonism and reshapes it so as to express his philosophy of idealism, which received full expression with his reading of Plato. The poem is another in the series of poems in which Shelley pursues Platonic Beauty. The plant in the poem is symbolic of Shelley; the Lady of the garden, of Love or Intellectual Beauty. The poem expresses Shelley's new Platonic philosophy (see commentary on *Prometheus Unbound, supra*, p. 237) of Ideal Reality versus the shadowy world of appearance. This philosophy is expressed in terms of the direct Platonism of the *Symposium* and the *Phaedrus* which filled Shelley's thoughts at this time. Parts of the poem are direct echoes of the *Symposium*. The Platonism of the poem is largely an illustration of *Symposium*, 201b: "Love wants and does not possess beauty. . . . Love is that which thirsts for the beautiful." In the poem Love is symbolized by the Sensitive Plant, and Ideal Beauty by the Lady in the garden.

> Like the Spirit of Love felt every where . . .
> (Part First, l. 6)

The universal presence of love finds a counterpart in Eryximachus's and Agathon's speeches in the *Symposium*, 186-188, 195-198.

> For the Sensitive Plant has no bright flower;
> Radiance and odour are not its dower;
> It loves, even like Love, its deep heart is full,
> It desires what it has not, the beautiful!
> (Part First, ll. 74-77)

These lines are another outstanding example of the direct influence of the *Symposium* on Shelley's poetry. They are almost a direct transcription of *Symposium*, 201b: "'It is conceded, then, that Love loves that which he wants but possesses not?' 'Yes, certainly.' 'But Love wants and does not possess beauty?' 'Indeed it must necessarily follow . . .

Love is that which thirsts for the beautiful.' " Shelley was hauntingly attracted to this conception, as its first appearance in his review of Peacock's *Rhododaphne* shows: "Plato says, with profound allegory, that Love is not itself beautiful, but seeks the possession of beauty; this idea seems embodied in the deformed dwarf who bids, with a voice as from a trumpet, Anthemion enter" (Julian *Works,* VI, 275). *The Sensitive Plant* is Shelley's own poetic allegory embodying this philosophic doctrine of Plato.

> A Lady, the wonder of her kind,
> Whose form was upborne by a lovely mind,
> Which, dilating, had moulded her mien and motion
> Like a sea-flower unfolded beneath the ocean . . .
> (Part Second, ll. 119-122)

The Lady of the Garden is another example of Shelley's women who symbolize Platonic values. The stress on the mind as the source of beauty and the dependence of the body upon the soul for its derivative beauty is a Platonic doctrine, as may be seen in *Republic,* 403d: "My belief is, not that a good body will by its own excellence, make the soul good; but on the contrary that a good soul will by *its* excellence render the body as perfect as it can be." Shelley may have got this conception from the *Republic* itself, which he was reading in 1819 and 1820, or from the indirect Platonic tradition, where it appears in Spenser's *An Hymne in Honour of Beautie:* "For of the soule the bodie forme doth take:/ For soule is forme, and doth the bodie make."

> And many an antenatal tomb,
> Where butterflies dream of the life to come . . .
> (Part Second, ll. 167-168)

For the Platonic conception of immortality and Shelley's use of the word *antenatal,* see the commentary on *Prince Athanase,* line 91, page 226, *supra.*

> . . . but in this life
> Of error, ignorance, and strife,
> Where nothing is, but all things seem,
> And we the shadows of the dream,
>
> It is a modest creed, and yet
> Pleasant if one considers it,
> To own that death itself must be,
> Like all the rest, a mockery.

That garden sweet, that lady fair,
And all sweet shapes and odours there,
In truth have never pass'd away:
'Tis we, 'tis ours, are changed! not they,

For love, and beauty, and delight,
There is no death nor change; their might
Exceeds our organs, which endure
No light, being themselves obscure.

(Conclusion, ll. 9-24)

These lines constitute one of Shelley's finest expressions of Platonic faith and idealism, a philosophy which had supplanted his earlier philosophy of Necessity and eighteenth-century philosophic materialism. Here is an expansion of the Platonic immortality and metaphysical philosophy expressed in *Prometheus Unbound*, III, iii, 113-114 (see commentary *supra*, p. 237):

Death is the veil which those who live call life:
They sleep, and it is lifted.

and Shelley's *Sonnet:*

Lift not the painted veil which those who live
Call Life; though unreal shapes be pictured there ...

These lines in *The Sensitive Plant* are direct echoes of the *Phaedo, Symposium, Phaedrus,* and *Republic;* they weave together Plato's conception of the immortality of the soul and the contrast of the ideal and relative worlds. The contrast between our transience and the immortality of Platonic love and beauty, symbolized by the garden and the Lady, is set in the context of Plato's doctrine of the inability of our senses to grasp Intellectual Beauty. Lines 22-24 make it clear that Shelley is thinking of Intellectual Beauty; they also express a Platonic doctrine which is found in *Republic*, 508b, where it is stated that our organ of sight is by itself obscure, unable to perceive the Sun, unless it receives "the power which it possesses as an influx, as it were, dispensed from the sun." This doctrine is taken up by Plotinus, who says, "Never did eye see the sun unless it had first become sunlike, and never can the soul have vision of the First Beauty unless itself be beautiful" (*Enneads,* I, 6, 9), and finally by Goethe, who in *Entwurf einer Farbenlehre* expresses it as:

Wär' nicht das Auge sonnenhaft,
Wie Könnten wir das Licht erblicken?

> Lebt' nicht in uns des Gottes eigne Kraft,
> Wie Könnt' uns Göttliches entzücken?

Furthermore, Shelley's statement that our organs "endure no light" is also an echo from the *Republic*. In the myth of the Cave in the *Republic* the prisoner when released from the cave is unable "to lift up his eyes to the light, and in doing all this felt pain and, because of the dazzle and glitter of the light, was unable to discern the objects whose shadows he formerly saw" (515c). The *Republic,* which Shelley was reading in 1819 and 1820, thus is the source of these metaphysical subtleties of Shelley's lines.

Ode to Liberty
Early 1820

> Athens, diviner yet,
> Gleamed with its crest of columns, on the will
> Of man, as on a mount of diamond, set;
>
> For thou wert, and thine all-creative skill
> Peopled with forms that mock the eternal dead
> In marble immortality, that hill
> Which was thine earliest throne and latest oracle.
>
> Within the surface of Time's fleeting river
> Its wrinkled image lies, as then it lay
> Immovably unquiet, and for ever
> It trembles, but it cannot pass away!
> (Ll. 69-79)

A praise of Athens in terms of a Platonically expressed immortality.

> . . . and Art, which cannot die,
> With divine wand traced on our earthly home
> Fit imagery to pave heaven's everlasting dome.
> (Ll. 133-135)

As Plato enjoins man to imitate the divine in this world, so for Shelley the function of Art is to give shadows of the Divine on this earth.

> Art, an ardent intercessor,
> Driving on fiery wings to Nature's throne . . .
> (Ll. 249-250)

This notion is ultimately derived from the *Symposium,* 202e, where Eros is an intercessor from men to the Gods, and the *Phaedrus,* 246 ff., where the soul of the lover sprouts wings at the sight of Beauty and ventures on its heavenward quest. Shelley may be directly influenced here, however, by the Spirit of the Earth in Coleridge's *Ode to the Departing Year,* where the Spirit of the Earth is an intercessor before the gods (see ll. 70-73).

Letter to Maria Gisborne
July 1, 1820

> . . . and how we spun
> A shroud of talk to hide us from the sun
> Of this familiar life, which seems to be
> But is not:—or is but quaint mockery
> Of all we would believe, and sadly blame
> The jarring and inexplicable frame
> Of this wrong world . . .
>
> (Ll. 154-160)

These lines are a variant expression with direct verbal echoes of Shelley's similar statement of the Platonic philosophy in *The Sensitive Plant,* Conclusion, ll. 9-24 (for commentary on these lines, *vide supra,* pp. 267-269).

The Cloud
1820

The Platonism in this poem consists in the interpretation of the cloud as a natural Platonic symbol of the one and the many, a symbol of the change of that which cannot die. Though Shelley definitely is not thinking of Plato, the poem is an expression of the natural Platonism of a "being" which remains unchanged through every change. Shelley in this poem uses the cloud as the symbol of scientific growth and destruction, but at the same time the cloud may also be used as a symbol of Shelley's Platonic philosophy.

> I change, but I cannot die.
>
> (L. 76)

An epigrammatic statement of the natural Platonism in the heart of the poet and the philosopher.

To a Skylark
June 22, 1820

This poem, like *The Cloud,* may be interpreted as a natural Platonic symbol of the upward, ethereal, and incorporeal transcendence of the soul away from mortality to the heavens of Platonic purity. In both poems Shelley has written poetry capable of being interpreted as natural Platonism.

The Witch of Atlas
August 14-16, 1820

Inasmuch as Shelley read the *Phaedrus* a few months before the composition of this poem, it is natural to see in the Witch another of Shelley's incarnations of Intellectual Beauty or Love. A comparison of her description in this poem with that of Asia in *Prometheus Unbound* shows clearly the identification of the Witch with Platonic values. The same characteristics appear here as in the description of Asia: the veil is the Platonic counterpart of seeing the Sun in its images on water if one is unable to see it directly, as was the case with the prisoner released from the cave of the *Republic;* her beauty is described in terms of the Platonic light and the shadows of the earthly world. Here, too, is the Platonic philosophy of the unreality of the relative world, which links the poem to Shelley's Platonic philosophy. Yet this incarnation of Intellectual Beauty and Love differs from Shelley's other Platonic women; as Professor White shows, "the Witch is clearly Shelley's one and only goddess, Intellectual Beauty, transparently veiled in the cloudy semi-mischievous magic of *Ricciardetto*," an epic romance of Nicollò Forte-guerri which Shelley and Mary were reading aloud up to about three weeks from the time of the composition of *The Witch of Atlas* (White, *Shelley,* II, 219). Professor White's evidence clearly shows that Shelley was refracting Intellectual Beauty through the playful lightness of this work rather than, as Professor Grabo has argued in *The Meaning of "The Witch of Atlas"* (Chapel Hill, N. C., 1935), through the complex machinery and symbolism of Neoplatonic writers whom Shelley had not read (see White, *Shelley,* II, 597).

> If you unveil my Witch, no priest nor primate
> Can shrive you of that sin,—if sin there be
> In love, when it becomes idolatry.
> ("To Mary," ll. 46-48)

These lines are interpreted by Professor White as meaning that it is deadly to attempt to unveil Intellectual Beauty (*Shelley,* II, 218-219). In this Shelley is using a Platonic conception in an un-Platonic way, for Plato enjoins the philosopher in the *Republic,* 511, and the *Symposium,* 211, to see Beauty without the veil of imagery or hypotheses.

> For she was beautiful: her beauty made
>> The bright world dim, and everything beside
> Seemed like the fleeting image of a shade:
>> No thought of living spirit could abide,
> Which to her looks had ever been betrayed,
>> On any object in the world so wide,
>> On any hope within the circling skies,
> But on her form, and in her inmost eyes.
>
> (Ll. 89-96)

This description of the Witch is a variation of that of Asia in *Prometheus Unbound*. The Witch is described in terms of the transcendent Beauty of the Ideal World which is so shiningly beautiful that all earthly beauty is but a shadow in comparison with it (see commentary *supra*, pp. 248-250).

> Which when the lady knew, she took her spindle
>> And twined three threads of fleecy mist, and three
> Long lines of light, such as the dawn may kindle
>> The clouds and waves and mountains with, and she
> As many star-beams, ere their lamps could dwindle
>> In the belated moon, wound skilfully;
> And with these threads a subtle veil she wove—
> A shadow for the splendour of her love.
>
> (Ll. 97-104)

Shelley at the time of the composition of this poem was engaged in reading the last few books of Plato's *Republic*. It is possible that he may have got the idea for the spindle and the long lines of light from *Republic,* 616b-c, which reads:

. . . and they came in four days to a spot whence they discerned, extended from above throughout the heaven and the earth, a straight light like a pillar, most nearly resembling the rainbow, but brighter and purer. To this they came after going forward a day's journey, and they saw there at the middle of the light the extremities of its fastenings stretched from heaven. . . . And from the extremities were stretched the spindle of Necessity, through which all the orbits turned. Its staff and its hook were made of adamant, and the whorl of these and other kinds was commingled.

If this is the case, Shelley took this spindle and its lines of light and used it for the weaving of a veil as the "shadow for the splendor of the Witch's love." The veil, as we have seen (*vide supra,* pp. 248-250), is a Platonic accoutrement for perceiving the insupportable beauty of the Witch. It is possible that Shelley may also have had in mind here the *Phaedo,* which he had just finished reading; in this work Plato refers to the weaver weaving a coat for the body (*Phaedo,* 87).

> Then by strange art she kneaded fire and snow
>   Together, tempering the repugnant mass
> With liquid love—all things together grow
>   Through which the harmony of love can pass . . . .
>
>   (Ll. 273-276)

For an analogy to this conception, see *Symposium,* 188. These lines show that the Witch has the power of Plastic Nature to compel the repugnant mass to her creative will. With this conception, compare Cudworth's theory discussed on pages 116-117, *supra.* These lines foreshadow the greater development of this conception in the *Adonais.*

> Fit to have borne it to the seventh sphere.
>
>   (L. 290)

Perhaps Shelley borrowed this notion from the *Republic,* which appears in his reading about the time of the composition of the poem. Plato tells us, ". . . and that of the greatest [whorls] was spangled, that of the seventh brightest, that of the eighth took its colour from the seventh, which shone upon it" (616e).

> But she in the calm depths her way could take
> Where in bright bowers immortal forms abide
> Beneath the weltering of the restless tide.
>
>   (Ll. 502-504)

These lines are another instance of Shelley's various improvisations on the Platonic theme of the relative versus the ideal world.

Ode to Naples
August 17-25, 1820

> Great Spirit, deepest Love!
>   Which rulest and dost move
> All things which live and are, within the Italian shore;
>   Who spreadest Heaven around it,
>   Whose woods, rocks, waves, surround it;
> Who sittest in thy star, o'er Ocean's western floor;
> Spirit of beauty!
>
>   (Ll. 149-155)

This invocation to Love and Beauty is permeated with Platonic feeling; compare the similar Platonic invocation in *The Coliseum* (Julian *Works*, VI, 304).

Hymn of Apollo
1820

I am the eye with which the Universe
    Beholds itself and knows itself divine . . . .
(Ll. 31-32)

These lines carry an aura of the feeling and thought of Plato about the sun (see *Republic*, 505 ff.).

An Allegory
1820

A portal as of shadowy adamant
    Stands yawning on the highway of the life
Which we all tread, a cavern huge and gaunt;
    Around it rages an unceasing strife
Of shadows . . . .
(Ll. 1-5)

In the use of the cave and the shadows in this allegorical poem Shelley may be giving a variant of his philosophy of the illusory nature of the relative world which is symbolized by Plato himself through the cave and shadows (*Republic*, 514 ff.). W. B. Yeats in his study of the cave of the *Witch of Atlas* compares it to Porphyry's allegorical interpretation of the cave where the Phaeacian boat left Odysseus (*Ideas of Good and Evil*, pp. 118-125).

Fiordispina
1820

Who knows whether the loving game is played,
When, once of mortal [vesture] disarrayed,
The naked soul goes wandering here and there
Through the wide deserts of Elysian air?
(Ll. 78-81)

Since Shelley read and translated part of the *Phaedo* in 1820, these lines are probably a direct echo of *Phaedo*, 62b, 67d, 82 ff., 110c ff., describing the soul's leaving its mortal vesture, and the fields of Elysium, where the purified soul dwells. Compare Shelley's similar statement: "The beauty of the internal nature cannot be so far concealed by its accidental vesture" (Julian *Works*, VII, 117).

Shelley's Reading in Plato and the Platonic Tradition, 1821

DIRECT PLATONISM: "Read Plato" (April 19, 1821); *Ion* (1821); *Crito* (1821?); *Laws* (1821?); *Gorgias* (1821); *Apology?* (1821?); *Timaeus?* (1821?).

INDIRECT PLATONISM: Dante, *Vita Nuova* (January 31, 1821); Sidney, *Defence of Poesie;* Spinoza (November 15, 1821); Kant (Sept. 1, 1821); Goethe, *Faust* (winter, 1821-1822).

Platonism in Shelley's Poems Written in 1821

Epipsychidion

Composed in the first two weeks of February, 1821

Nowhere is the complex nature of Shelley's Platonism more manifest than in this poem, which is synonymous with Platonism. The poem is a complex fusion of Shelley's natural, direct, and indirect Platonism. The root of the natural Platonism in this poem is an innate and passionate desire in Shelley for personal sympathy. In his essay *On Love* Shelley wrote, "There is something within us which, from the instant that we live, more and more thirsts after its likeness." From Shelley's early childhood this instinctive search for his counterpart led to Intellectual Beauty and Love. Professor White has aptly pointed out the basic relation of Shelley's craving for personal sympathy to his Intellectual Beauty and Love:

Whoever reads such poems as *Alastor,* the "Hymn to Intellectual Beauty," and "Julian and Maddalo" (not to mention certain passages in Shelley's letters) will realize that Intellectual Beauty, or universal sympathy, was closely related with Shelley to an intense desire for personal sympathy. It is quite possible that Shelley's almost preternatural sensitiveness and desire for sympathy are the original bases not only for his occasional self-pity, but also for his devotion to Freedom and to Intellectual Beauty. (*Shelley,* II, 254)

The complex character of Shelley's natural Platonism is seen in the fact that Shelley has added to Platonism sympathy, a personal element which Plato would have denounced as the negation of Platonism itself. It is in this respect that Shelley's Platonism is more un-Platonic and forms the grounds for its characterization as pseudo-Platonism. Yet it is a fact that the natural Platonism of this poem is a fusion of personal sympathy with Shelley's quest since childhood for Intellectual Beauty. Shelley had found the answer to his search for a creature who would embody this fusion of Platonic Beauty and sympathy. He found it in Emilia Viviani, the Platonic counterpart of his soul. Emilia furnishes the personal and historical occasion for releasing from Shelley's soul the pent-up mood of sympathy voiced in terms of Platonic Love and Beauty. As we have seen before, it is a characteristic of Shelley to symbolize the concrete through the operations of the mind itself, to transmute the personal through the universal, to express his love of the individual most fully by raising it to Platonic universality, to enjoy a personal and physical element by refracting it through the natural Platonism in his soul which found felicitous expression and articulation in Plato's philosophy. Thus the Platonism of *Epipsychidion* consists of the refraction of Shelley's sympathy and Platonic affinities with Emilia through Plato's philosophy and Dante's and Petrarch's poetic transmutation of Plato's Intellectual Beauty and Love.

Emilia forms the climax of a long list of Shelley's attempts to grasp Intellectual Beauty and Love in his own life and in his poetry. The quest for the ideal runs in a parallel search in his own life and in his poetry; in this respect Shelley's life and thought are at one. Yet like Plato's lover in the *Phaedrus*, Shelley could not ascend completely to the Platonic heaven; his efforts are strewn with failures in his own life and poems. "I think," he writes to Gisborne, "one is always in love with something or other; the error, and I confess it is not easy for spirits cased in flesh and blood to avoid it, consists in seeking in a mortal image the likeness of what is perhaps eternal" (Julian *Works*, X, 401). In the *Epipsychidion* Shelley finally reaches the summit of his Platonic experiences, and in the poem there meet the two efforts to find Platonic beauty in the world of flesh and blood and in the world of the mind. In Emilia, Shelley found fused both the earthly symbol he had been looking for with various degrees of failure from his earliest love on, and the Intellectual Beauty he had been seeking in the realm of mind from childhood on, as the *Hymn* shows. The great intensity of Platonism in this poem reflects Shelley's joy in finding Intellectual Beauty on this earth; that is why *Epipsychidion* is the most Platonic of his poems in intensity, Platonic emotion, joy, and ecstasy. That is why he calls the poem, in a letter to Gisborne, "a mystery," one in which he reveals his initiation into the mysteries of Platonic love and the exultation of one who has at last seen through this experience; he has completely transcended the earthly, as the letter to Gisborne further reveals: "As to real flesh and blood," he writes, "you know that I do not deal in those articles; you might as well go to a ginshop for a leg of mutton as expect any thing human or earthly from me" (Julian *Works*, X, 333). The *Epipsychidion* is "an idealized history" of his Platonic life and feelings. To give full and satisfactory expression to this idealized history and Platonic joy at finding Intellectual Beauty on this earth, Shelley enlists the aid of Plato. His mind came to the poem fresh from his reading of the *Phaedrus, Phaedo,* and *Republic* in the preceding year. The concrete experience of meeting Emilia suddenly evoked the haunting beauty of the *Symposium,* which he had made all the more his own through translation; its thought, phrases, and imagery suddenly caught on fire in Shelley's mind; and his soul, arising fresh from the embrace of Platonic Beauty in the *Symposium, Phaedrus, Phaedo,* and *Republic,* cast on Emilia the gathered rays of Platonic reality. She became the mirror in Shelley's mind upon which all of the Platonic forms, concepts, images, metaphors, and similes were reflected, and in which they composed one form.

The relation of direct and indirect Platonism in expressing Shelley's natural Platonism calls for a word of comment. Shelley's poetic experience is both cognate and derivative from Plato's *Phaedrus* and *Symposium.* Both of these dialogues reveal the Platonic mood of the human soul, how it perceives in the phenomena of the physical world reminders or shadows of an ideal reality which transcends the phenomena in beauty, completeness, and degree of being. Plato has expressed this experience and search for the ideal in two ways: in the *Symposium* as theory, and in the *Phaedrus* as a myth which dramatizes the birth of the mood, the occasion, and the ascent to the ideal. In the latter dialogue Plato is a mythopoeic artist who has dramatized the theory through a myth, an allegory. Poetry is more akin to the method of the *Phaedrus,* the dramatization of theories and ideas. Dante is also in this tradition. He shares with Plato the same predisposition of soul which finds in the manifestations of earthly beauty the ladder to the divine and eternal. He is a poet and therefore dramatizes a fact out of his own experience and makes Beatrice the incarnation and the occasion for the ascent to the ideal and divine world, following the method of the *Phaedrus,* which is the way of art. Shelley, endowed with a similar Platonic mood of the human soul, dramatizes in the poem the incarnation of the ideal through Emilia, who leads him away from the world of flesh and blood to Plato's world. Shelley not only shared the natural Platonic mood of Plato and Dante, but he also read their works, which describe and dramatize this experience. He borrowed from both certain imagery, certain modes of expression, and absorbed from them a traditional language of simile and metaphor, of denotation and overtone, a language already molded to express beautifully the native beauty of the Platonic experience of the soul. From his reading of the *Phaedrus* and *Symposium* Shelley absorbed a conscious shaping and expression of the Platonic mood. In Dante he found a kindred soul, and in his *Divine Comedy* and *Vita Nuova* (the latter he was reading aloud to Mary just before the composition of the poem) Shelley found Beatrice a beautiful shadow of Divine Love. Dante differs from Plato in not spurning the symbol because it is a shadow, but loving it as a poet does. Shelley therefore absorbed from Dante considerable technique and symbolism in portraying woman as the shadow of beauty and Heaven. In *A Defence of Poetry* Shelley expresses his kinship with Dante's method of approaching the ideal world. He refers to "His apotheosis of Beatrice in Paradise, and the gradations of his own love and her loveliness, by which as by steps he feigns himself to have ascended to the throne of the Supreme Cause" (Julian *Works,* VII, 128). The *Epipsychidion* fuses the *Symposium,* the *Phaedrus,* and the Dantean as well as Petrarchan Platonism. The vision is his own nautral Platonism; but the symbol of language, thought, emotion and the dramatic technique are those of Plato, who first gave expression to this mood of human nature, and of Dante, who shaped it closer to man's desire by making *woman* incarnate, the most embracing and appealing of all of nature's phenomena and symbols, represent and foreshadow the ideal Reality of Heaven. These direct and traditional Platonic symbols modulate with variety the eternal fascination of Platonic idealism.

Thus Plato became for Shelley an inspiriting influence which molded, shaped, and helped give expression to his own poetic nature. In the *Epipsychidion* we have the high-water mark of Shelley's Platonism. It is a misnomer to call the poem Platonic if by that word is meant strictly Plato's own calm and philosophically serene expression. The poem is a hybrid, reflecting Shelley's own craving for sympathy and his use of Platonic themes in a manner which Plato would not approve or sanction as orthodox Platonism. To understand the Platonism of this poem, therefore, we must not indulge in a critical battle over whether its Platonism is of the "Shibboleth" or "Sibboleth" kind. We must understand that Shelley first of all expresses his own soul and not Plato's, and secondly that in expressing it he finds a cognate philosophy in Plato, whose thought and symbols he borrows and transmutes in expressing his own soul.

Title of the Poem

An examination of the title of the poem in the context of Shelley's other writings shows that it too is natural Platonism consciously baptized with a Platonic name. One of the most characteristic of Shelley's expressions is what may be called, for lack of a better name, the Platonic partitive genitive; it briefly consists of such phrases as "soul of my soul," "soul out of my soul," "Life of Life," "world within a world." A study of such phrases shows that "the soul of my soul," which is the basic meaning of *Epipsychidion,* is, as Professor White has shown, present in Shelley's earliest writings. It first occurs in a letter to Godwin, dated January 10, 1812, wherein he says "the sublime interest of poetry, . . . the proselytism of the world, . . . were to me soul of my soul." Shelley also uses this phrase with slight variation to describe one of his earliest Platonic soul mates, Elizabeth Hitchener, to whom he writes, "I profess you are the sister of my soul, its dearest sister, and I think the component parts of that soul must undergo complete dissolution before its sympathies can perish" (Letter, Oct. 15?, 1811 [Julian *Works,* VIII, 157]). She in turn reciprocates by addressing him as "Brother of my soul" (Peck, *Life of Shelley,* II, 326). This notion in Shelley was next enriched by his reading of Wieland's *Agathon,* wherein Agathon (the Platonic philosopher) and Psyche (Platonic Beauty) translate their love into a brother-and-sister relationship (*vide supra,* pp. 141-142). Shelley's own conception now becomes tangent to that of the Platonic tradition, which symbolizes the Platonic conception of love as two parts of an original soul. It marks the rise in Shelley's consciousness of the affinity of his own feeling to that of Plato. This basic conception is next found in *Prometheus Unbound* as "Life of my Life," which is a variant expression/ of "soul of my soul," "world within a world," or "being within our being," and which is a translation of the Platonic conception of the macrocosm and microcosm. Shelley's essay *On Love,* which was greatly influenced by Plato's *Symposium,* contains the next expression of this notion in the form of "a soul within our own soul." Finally it appears in the *Epipsychidion* itself as "this soul out of my soul" (l. 238) and as "I am a part of *thee*" (l. 53).

In the title Shelley gave to the poem we have an illustration of what Mary calls his imitation of Greek imagery by gifting "it with that originality of form and colouring which sprung from his own genius." Likewise to understand Shelley's choice of title we must keep in mind Mary's statement about the *Prometheus Unbound:* "It requires a mind as subtle and penetrating as his own to understand [its] mystic meanings." An attempt will be made to follow the convolutions of Shelley's mind in shaping the title of the poem. Shelley was aware of the formal affinities of his own theme and emotions to Platonism. In coining a Greek title for the poem he was thereby consciously and deliberately baptizing the "soul of his soul" with its equivalent in Platonic language. As we have seen, Shelley refracted his own individual feeling of love through Plato's language and imagery. Shelley was only extending this process to the title of the poem by formally shaping out of Platonic words a new name to translate the "soul of his soul." His conscious effort to Platonize the title of the poem is seen in the root meaning of *psyche,* which is a transliteration of the Platonic soul, ψυχή. Psyche, however, had to be reshaped to express certain characteristics of Shelley's conception of the lover's soul. The lover's soul for Shelley is not one but two in one, a conception which is rooted in Aristophanes's picture of the lovers in the *Symposium* as two incomplete parts of a pristine whole, which, after being separated by Apollo, have been forever seeking their counterpart soul mates. In his essay *On Love* Shelley states this partitive quality of the lover's soul: "We dimly see within our intellectual nature a miniature as it were of our entire self," and then in the next few lines he restates this conception by referring to it as "a soul within our soul." To express the partitive quality of the soul, the "miniature soul within the soul," Shelley felicitously uses the diminutive form of ψυχή, which is formed in Greek by adding to the noun the suffix -ιδιον (cf. τὸ ψυχίδιον, Lucian, Πλοῖον ἢ Εὐχαί, 26; Shelley read Lucian in 1816 and 1818); the diminutive in the Greek also includes the connotation of endearment and affection (cf. πατήρ, "father"; πατρίδιον, "daddy"). This was not the first attempt in the Platonic tradition to express affectionately the miniature of the Platonic soul. Wieland in his *Agathon,* which Shelley read in 1814, uses *Psycharion* (*Agathon, Wielands Werke,* ed. Jacobi, III, 107, l. 3) to mean "Kleine Psyche." Shelley may or may not have had this instance in his mind when he was coining the Platonic title of the poem. Possibly Shelley used Lucian's word *psychidion* to express affectionately the diminutive of the Platonic ψυχή. There still remains the question of what Shelley intended by the prefix *epi.* The prepositional compound ἐπί in Greek has a wide variety of flexible meanings; it basically means "on, upon, being upon or supported upon a surface or point" (Liddell and Scott, *A Greek-English Lexicon*[9]). This meaning then radiates into a variety of meanings denoting, in a pregnant sense, the goal of motion; before, in the presence of; of occasions, in dependence upon; to or towards; object or purpose for which one goes; motive for, etc. One can ingeniously play with any of these meanings and read much into Shelley's title. It is likely, however, that Shelley is using the preposition *epi* in its traditional association with poetry such as we see in *epinicion, epithalamium,* meaning a song in honor of a victory or on the occasion of a marriage. This probability increases when we realize how the influence of Dante's *Vita Nuova* on Shelley is shown "in the fact and manner of sending a song to deliver messages of love" (White, *The Best of Shelley,* p. 503). Like an epinicion or an epithalamium, the poem is a song to or in honor of the little soul of his own soul. That Shelley intended this meaning for *epi* is seen in the words which immediately follow the title, "Verses addressed to the noble and unfortunate lady, Emilia V—," and in the opening lines: "In my heart's temple I suspend to thee/These votive wreaths of withered memory."

> Till those bright plumes of thought, in which arrayed
> It over-soared this low and worldly shade . . .
> (Ll. 15-16)

The imagery and thought here are suggestive of *Phaedrus,* 246 ff., a dialogue which Shelley read in 1820. In his translation of the *Ion* shortly after the composition of this poem, Shelley interpolated a variation of this phrase: "arrayed as they [i.e., the Muses] are in the plumes of rapid imagination" (*vide infra,* p. 473).

> Seraph of Heaven! too gentle to be human,
> Veiling beneath that radiant form of Woman
> All that is insupportable in thee
> Of light, and love, and immortality!
> Sweet Benediction in the eternal Curse!
> Veiled Glory of this lampless Universe!
> Thou Moon beyond the clouds! Thou living Form
> Among the Dead! Thou Star above the Storm!
> Thou Wonder, and thou Beauty, and thou Terror!
> Thou Harmony of Nature's art! Thou Mirror
> In whom, as in the splendour of the Sun,
> All shapes look glorious which thou gazest on!
> (Ll. 21-32)

This Platonic rhapsody crystallizes the essence of Shelley's Platonic idealization of woman. In these lines Shelley expresses with greater emotional intensity the same Platonic qualities and philosophy which he used in the case of Asia (for commentary, *vide supra,* pp. 248-250). Emilia is a Platonic theophany on earth; she is the earthly vision of Platonic Beauty, Love, and Immortality. She is so divinely radiant that she can be seen only through a veil which half reveals and half conceals the eternal archetype. As in the *Republic* the sun is insupportable to the earthly vision except through its refractions in earthy surfaces, thus her Beauty is so insupportable that she can be seen only through a veil. We have an illustration of Shelley's meaning in lines 199-200, where he speaks of meeting a Being (Intellectual Beauty):

> robed in such exceeding glory,
> That I beheld her not . . . .

W. M. Rossetti, in answering a query as to the meaning of the word *insupportable* in this passage, replied, "The glory and intensity of light, love, and immortality, inherent in the nature of a seraph, would be 'insupportable' to the inferior nature and faculty of human beings: to human beings they would be awful, overwhelming, and inappreciable" (*The Shelley Society's Papers*, First Series, No. 2, *Note-Book of the Shelley Society* [London, 1888], Part I, p. 47; cf. Dante's *Paradiso*, XXVIII, 16-18). The veil is the symbol in poetic tradition for the image in Plato, and their function is the same: namely, a convenience to mortals for grasping the divinely perfect, which in its pure essence is imageless. Thus Emilia is the earthly symbol through which Intellectual Beauty reveals itself to Shelley.

In lines 26-32 Shelley improvises on the Platonic theme as stated in lines 22-24, evoking further Platonic feeling. "Veiled Glory of this lampless Universe" is the repetition of the main Platonic theme by means of Platonic imagery; the Platonic veil is transposed to the metaphor of light and darkness, which are Platonic images for Reality and Appearance. "Moon beyond the clouds" and "Star above the Storm" are Shelley's own images expressing the relation of the ideal and the relative. All these and the succeeding images express Platonic Beauty, which, as Plato says in *Phaedrus*, 249e, is the only one of the Platonic ideas which is most clearly evident on earth.

> Would we two had been twins of the same mother!
> Or, that the name my heart lent to another
> Could be a sister's bond for her and thee,
> Blending two beams of one eternity!
> Yet were one lawful and the other true,
> These names, though dear, could paint not, as is due,
> How beyond refuge I am thine. Ah me!
> I am not thine: I am a part of *thee*.
>
> (Ll. 45-52)

For the affinity of these lines to the Platonic conception of love as two parts of a once perfect and whole soul, compare commentary on pages 279-280, *supra*.

> Or, like a dying swan who soars and sings . . .
> (L. 54)

The image of the dying swan is ultimately or directly derived from the *Phaedo*, 84e-85a.

> A Star
> Which moves not in the moving Heavens, alone?
> (Ll. 60-61)

A natural Platonic image expressive of the absolute and the temporal.

> Of planetary music heard in trance . . .
> (L. 86)

For the music of the spheres, see page 173, *supra*.

> Beauty furled
> Which penetrates and clasps and fills the world . . .
> (Ll. 102-103)

Platonic Beauty is presented here in its immanent character, a conception which is derivative from the world soul of the *Timaeus* and *Symposium*, 210 (cf. *Adonais*, lines 379-387) .

> See where she stands! a mortal shape indued
> With love and life and light and deity,
> And motion which may change but cannot die;
> An image of some bright Eternity . . . .
> (Ll. 112-115)

These lines are a variant expression of the Platonism in lines 21-32 (cf. commentary *supra*, pp. 281-282).

> Spouse! Sister! Angel! Pilot of the Fate
> Whose course has been so starless! O too late
> Belovèd! O too soon adored, by me!
> For in the fields of Immortality
> My spirit should at first have worshipped thine,
> A divine presence in a place divine;
> Or should have moved beside it on this earth,
> A shadow of that substance, from its birth . . . .
> (Ll. 130-137)

The Platonism in these lines lies in the association of Emilia with the immortality of the *Phaedo*, which was fresh in Shelley's mind as the result of the reading and partial translation of it in 1820. Shelley immortalizes his love by wishing he had known her in the Platonic world of pre-existence and thus makes his love timeless and transcendent of earthly qualities. In the field of immortality Shelley would have worshiped her spirit to the extent of becoming the shadow of its substance in this world. Here Shelley makes their love a unity in which she is the substance and he but its shadow; this conception is bound up with the "soul of my soul" character of their love, which is the theme of the poem.

> We—are we not formed, as notes of music are,
> For one another, though dissimilar;
> Such difference without discord, as can make
> Those sweetest sounds, in which all spirits shake,
> As trembling leaves in a continuous air?
> (Ll. 142-146)

Perhaps Shelley is alluding to the following statement of Eryximachus in the *Symposium*, 187a-b: "It is great absurdity to say that an harmony differs, and can exist between things whilst they are dissimilar; but probably he meant that from sounds which first differed, like the grave and the acute, and which afterwards agreed, harmony was produced" (Shelley's translation).

> I never was attached to that great sect,
> Whose doctrine is, that each one should select
> Out of the crowd a mistress or a friend,
> And all the rest, though fair and wise, commend
> To cold oblivion, though it is in the code
> Of modern morals, and the beaten road
> Which those poor slaves with weary footsteps tread,
> Who travel to their home among the dead
> By the broad highway of the world, and so
> With one chained friend, perhaps a jealous foe,
> The dreariest and the longest journey go.
> (Ll. 149-159)

In claiming these lines to be Platonic one must keep in mind the sound interpretation of them by Professor White, who says:

To take these declarations as a repetition of the anti-matrimonial thesis of *Queen Mab* is easy, but fallacious. . . . It is the old position applied to ideal instead of physical love, and describes no more than the situation in which

Shelley was living as he wrote. He was simply asserting a belief that to love Mary for her qualities and to love Emilia with a different kind of love for totally different qualities did not detract from either love. (*Shelley*, II, 260)

These lines have been associated with Plato's doctrine expressed in the *Symposium*, 210a-b:

He who aspires to love rightly, ought from his earliest youth to seek an intercourse with beautiful forms, and first to make a single form the object of his love, and therein to generate intellectual excellencies. He ought, then, to consider that beauty in whatever form it resides is the brother of that beauty which subsists in another form; and if he ought to pursue that which is beautiful in form, it would be absurd to imagine that beauty is not one and the same thing in all forms, and would therefore remit much of his ardent preference towards one, through his perception of the multitude of claims upon his love. (Shelley's translation)

If Shelley, however, is applying his lines to ideal instead of physical love, then Plato's doctrine quite rightly cannot be abstracted from its context to justify Shelley's antimatrimonial view expressed in *Queen Mab* and his own conduct with respect to Harriet. The poem, as Professor White insists, is an idealized history of Shelley's feelings; and it is only natural that Shelley should not be considered here as converting Plato into an *advocatus Diaboli*. If this is the case, then Plato's conception has no connection with Shelley's thought here; the great sect is not Plato but ordinary morality, "the code of modern morals." Shelley defends his unwillingness to be circumscribed in his pursuit of Emilia, who is Intellectual Beauty on this earth, by referring in lines 169-173 to Plato's view.

> True Love in this differs from gold and clay,
> That to divide is not to take away.
> (Ll. 160-161)

The source of this sentiment is the Neoplatonic doctrine of emanation that "in giving rise to the effect the cause remains undiminished and unaltered" (cf. E. R. Dodds's edition of Proclus's *Elements of Theology* [Oxford, 1933], proposition 26-27, p. 214, where are cited the sources of and parallels to this doctrine, including Bridges's: "Immortal happiness . . . a gift / Whose wealth is amplified by spending"). Yet, as Dodds states, this doctrine is covered by the *Symposium*, 211b, where Socrates asserts that the participation of an idea does not alter or diminish it. It is also possible, as Kuhns points out, that Shelley was directly influenced by Dante here (*MLN,* XIII [1898], 163). The phrase "true love" here, as Professor White points out, is used by Shelley to mean "ideal love," being an echo of Emilia's essay wherein she describes ideal love as true love (*Shelley,* II, 260).

> Love is like understanding that grows bright,
> Gazing on many truths . . . .
> (Ll. 162-163)

Here Shelley identified Love with Intellectual Beauty, which is essentially philosophic in character.

> Narrow
> The heart that loves, the brain that contemplates,
> The life that wears, the spirit that creates
> One object, and one form, and builds thereby
> A sepulchre for its eternity.
> (Ll. 169-173)

These lines are a direct echo of the philosophic principle stated in the *Symposium,* 210a-b (see commentary on ll. 149-159, *supra,* pp. 284-285). Shelley applies them to ideal love, which is not embodied solely by Mary (see White, *Shelley,* II, 260, 266). For Mary's view of "Shelley's Italian platonics," see *The Letters of Mary W. Shelley,* ed. F. L. Jones, I, 161.

> There was a Being whom my spirit oft
> Met on its visioned wanderings, far aloft,
> In the clear golden prime of my youth's dawn,
> Upon the fairy isles of sunny lawn,
> Amid the enchanted mountains, and the caves
> Of divine sleep, and on the air-like waves
> Of wonder-level dream, whose tremulous floor
> Paved her light steps;—on an imagined shore,
> Under the grey beak of some promontory
> She met me, robed in such exceeding glory,
> That I beheld her not. In solitudes
> Her voice came to me through the whispering woods,
> And from the fountains, and the odours deep
> Of flowers, which, like lips murmuring in their sleep
> Of the sweet kisses which had lulled them there,
> Breathed but of *her* to the enamoured air;
> And from the breezes whether low or loud,
> And from the rain of every passing cloud,
> And from the singing of the summer-birds,

And from all sounds, all silence. In the words
Of antique verse and high romance,—in form,
Sound, colour—in whatever checks that Storm
Which with the shattered present chokes the past;
And in that best philosophy, whose taste
Makes this cold common hell, our life, a doom
As glorious as a fiery martyrdom;
Her Spirit was the harmony of truth.

(Ll. 190-216)

In these lines we have an autobiographical account of Shelley's natural Platonism. The "Being" in line 190 is the Intellectual Beauty of Shelley's *Hymn* presented in a highly romantic mood (see White, *Shelley*, II, 261). This identification is partly seen in lines 199-200, where Shelley is referring, of course, to the insupportable light (cf. ll. 22-24) of Platonic Beauty and Love, which is always seen in the case of Shelley's Platonic women through the Platonic veil (see commentary *supra*, pp. 248-250). Furthermore, the taste for the philosophy (ll. 213-216) which makes this earthly life a miserable martyrdom is that of Plato, and in particular that as expressed in the *Phaedo*. Finally the intellectual character of this Being is seen in line 216, which refers to its association with truth.

Whither 'twas fled, this soul out of my soul . . .

(L. 238)

Compare commentary on the title of the poem, *supra*, pages 278-281.

That world within this Chaos, mine and me,
Of which she was the veiled Divinity . . .

(Ll. 243-244)

Compare commentary on lines 21-32, *supra*, pages 281-282.

In many mortal forms I rashly sought
The shadow of that idol of my thought.

(Ll. 267-268)

With these lines compare Shelley's statement to John Gisborne, quoted *supra*, pages 276-277. "The shadow of that idol of my thought" (cf. *With a Guitar, to Jane*, l. 43, and "inmost idol of my error," Julian *Works*, X, 243) is a direct echo from Plato's myth of the Cave (*Republic*, 514 ff.), where the idols carried by passing men cast their shadows on the wall in front of the prisoners. In lines 216-320 Shelley gives a biographical account of this trial-and-error quest for Platonic Beauty. The association of "One, whose voice was venomed melody" (l. 256) may be, as Professor White suggests (*Shelley,* II, 262), Venus Pandemos as opposed to Venus Urania.

> I knew it was the Vision veiled from me
> So many years—that it was Emily . . . .
> (Ll. 343-344)

Shelley finds in Emily the Intellectual Beauty and Love at the end of his quest for the ideal among earthly forms, even as in the *Symposium* Beauty itself is the final stage of a long and arduous search. Shelley speaks here of seeing Emily directly without the veil, which corresponds with the imageless character of Beauty itself.

> To whatsoe'er of dull mortality
> Is mine, remain a vestal sister still . . . .
> (Ll. 389-390)

In the first line Shelley refers to his mortal self in the language of the *Phaedo* (cf. "dull dense world," *Adonais,* l. 382). The conception of Emilia as "a vestal sister" is to be understood as an expression of Shelley's own tendency to call his loves sisters of his soul (*vide supra,* p. 279).

> An atom of th' Eternal . . .
> (L. 479)

A Neoplatonic conception of the soul as an emanation from the One (cf. pp. 86-88, *supra*).

> We shall become the same, we shall be one
> Spirit within two frames, oh! wherefore two?
> One passion in twin-hearts, which grows and grew,
> 'Till like two meteors of expanding flame,
> Those spheres instinct with it become the same,
> Touch, mingle, are transfigured; ever still
> Burning, yet ever inconsumable:
> In one another's substance finding food,
> Like flames too pure and light and unimbued
> To nourish their bright lives with baser prey,
> Which point to Heaven and cannot pass away:
> One hope within two wills, one will beneath
> Two overshadowing minds, one life, one death,
> One Heaven, one Hell, one immortality,
> And one annihilation . . . .
> (Ll. 573-587)

The finale of the poem is a mixture of Shelley's own romantic emotions with Plato's conception of love as the union of complementary parts of the soul: as his ecstasy arises this love assumes Platonic wings; it transcends the earthly "like flames too pure and light" to nourish their lives with baser food; it points to a Heaven of immortality where they cannot pass away.

> The winged words on which my soul would pierce
> Into the height of love's rare Universe,
> Are chains of lead around its flight of fire.
> I pant, I sink, I tremble, I expire!
>
> (Ll. 588-591)

The lines contain certain echoes from the *Phaedo* and the *Phaedrus*. Words, like the earthly element of the soul (cf. *Phaedo*), drag down the ascent of the soul into the Platonic heaven as pictured in the myth of the charioteer in the *Phaedrus*.

Fragments Connected with *Epipsychidion*

> And Socrates, the Jesus Christ of Greece,
> And Jesus Christ Himself, did never cease
> To urge all living things to love each other,
> And to forgive their mutual faults, and smother
> The Devil of disunion in their souls.
>
> (Ll. 33-37)

The reference to Socrates's urging mortals to smother the disunion in their souls is of course a direct allusion to Aristophanes's speech in the *Symposium* (191d), which Shelley combines with the Christian notion by the interpolation of the word "Devil"; for the association of Socrates and Jesus, see page 323, *infra*.

> I love you!—Listen, O embodied Ray
> Of the great Brightness; I must pass away
> While you remain, and these light words must be
> Tokens by which you may remember me.
> Start not—the thing you are is unbetrayed,
> If you are human, and if but the shade
> Of some sublimer Spirit . . .
>
> (Ll. 38-44)

A variation of the eternal-versus-transient theme in Platonism. The description of Emilia as an "embodied Ray of the great Brightness" has affinities with the Neoplatonic emanation from the One (cf. l. 479).

> If any should be curious to discover
> Whether to you I am a friend or lover,
> Let them read Shakespeare's sonnets, taking thence
> A whetstone for their dull intelligence.
>
> (Ll. 97-100)

The reference here is to love of persons of the same sex which Shelley undertook to explain in his *Discourse on the Manners of the Antients,* written to explain the presence of it in Plato's *Symposium.* Compare Shelley's statement in the *Discourse:*

It may blunt the harshness of censure also to reflect that in the golden age of our own literature a certain sentimental attachment towards persons of the same sex was not uncommon. Shakespeare has devoted the impassioned and profound poetry of his sonnets to commemorate an attachment of this kind, which we cannot question was wholly divested of any unworthy alloy.

> . . . or let them guess
> How Diotima, the wise prophetess,
> Instructed the instructor, and why he
> Rebuked the infant spirit of melody
> On Agathon's sweet lips, which, as he spoke
> Was as the lovely star when morn has broke
> The roof of darkness, in the golden dawn
> Half-hidden, and yet beautiful.
>
> (Ll. 101-108)

Shelley here advises his reader who seeks to know the character of his love for Emilia, whether he be her friend or lover, to read, besides Shakespeare, Diotima's discourse to Socrates on the true nature of Ideal Love and Beauty (*Symposium,* 201d-212c). Likewise Shelley refers to Socrates's philosophic refutation of Agathon's poetic description of love (*Symposium,* 205b ff.), which impressed Shelley (cf. *Prince Athanase,* commentary on Fragment 3, ll. 55-68 *supra,* p. 228). For another indication of the importance of the *Symposium* for this poem, see the statement of his intention to write a Symposium on this theme (Letter to John Gisborne, October 22, 1821, Julian *Works,* X, 333).

> Death cannot part us—we must meet again . . .
>
> (L. 179)

See commentary on lines 130-137, *supra,* pages 283-284.

> Wherever beauty on the earth's bare [?] breast
> Lies like the shadow of thy soul—till we
> Become one being with the world we see. . .
>
> (Ll. 184-186)

Emilia, after being identified with Intellectual Beauty on earth, now becomes the source itself of the shadows of beauty on earth. Shelley here is fusing the Plotinian conception of emanation with his own desire to mingle with Emilia in such a far-reaching embrace that the world itself and they are one.

Adonais

June, 1821

As Shelley regarded the *Adonais* as his "least imperfect" poem, so the Platonism of the poem may be considered as the clearest and purest statement of it found in Shelley. Even as the meeting with Emilia evoked the *Symposium* to express his love, so the death of Keats evoked the *Phaedo,* which Shelley had read and partially translated in 1820, for the expression of his elegiac grief which could find comfort only in the Platonic immortality of the spirit which leaves a world full of empty shadows and of sorrows such as Keats had suffered at the hands of his reviewers. By associating Keats's spirit rather than woman with Platonic Immortality and Intellectual Beauty, Shelley attained a purer expression of Platonism more in harmony with Plato's own philosophy. The Platonism of the poem consists briefly in contrasting the two realms of Keats's life, the temporal and the eternal. Mortality is simply an illusion like all the phenomena of nature; it is only in death that we really live and the soul finds its true home in the Platonic reality above and beyond the physical world. The poem is an inextricable fusion of Plato's metaphysical view of the ideal and temporal world as stated in the *Republic.* It is restated in terms of immortality versus mortality in the *Phaedo,* and in terms of Intellectual Beauty, immanent and transcendent, versus the transient shadows in the *Symposium* and the *Phaedrus.* Shelley read all of these dialogues with the exception of the *Symposium* in 1820, and this concentrated reading in Plato supplied him with sufficient thought and imagery to express Keats's immortality. These Platonic themes are sometimes developed separately, but in the last stanzas of the poem they are blended into a perfect amalgam of Platonism. Shelley, like Plato, saw clearly the unity of Being, Immortality, and Beauty in rearing a fitting monument to Keats's genius. In his life Keats lived amid the shadows of Beauty, in unprofitable strife with phantoms, in a world whose blindness, ignorance, and falsehood were exhibited in the reviewers' treatment of his soul and poetry; in his death he has become united with the true essence of Intellectual Beauty, which will shine for him in all the vivid and unfading and imageless reality which Plato ascribed to it. Keats, who because of his devotion to Beauty in his earthly life knew something of its reality, will in death become a portion of Eternal Beauty, which he made more lovely. Thus Shelley, as in the case of Emilia, evaluates Keats's life and death by refracting them through Platonic concepts which truly do justice to the poet's genius and make his physical death a glorious and joyous occasion, transmuting our sorrow into ecstasy by giving us a glimpse of his soul amid the white radiance of Eternity.

These ideas and emotions, however, are not refracted entirely through the prism of Plato; the sources of *Adonais* are multiple. Professor White has pointed out how closely parallel Shelley's poem is to Petrarch's *Triumphs* which interpret Laura's death in terms of Plato's conception of perfect Eternity versus the transient procession of shadows in this earthly life (*Shelley,* II, 294-295). Again, the Plotinian theory of emanation is rather prominent in the relation of the One and the Many, in Keats's being made one with Nature and the Eternal. Furthermore, the conception of the power and plastic shaping of the world by Nature, which in the poem is equivalent to Intellectual Beauty, is ultimately derived from Cudworth's Plastic Nature, which is adapted from Plato's divine creator who stamps upon matter the eternal forms and shapes them in accordance with Ideal Beauty. Shelley, as we have seen (pp. 115-116, 120, 157, 160), found this doctrine in Coleridge and in other sources. Finally, as in the case of *Epipsychidion,* the poem is a passionate expression of the natural Platonism in his own soul, of his intense belief in the immortality of poetry and Beauty. Shelley fused all three kinds of Platonism into a pure organic unity which, as seen in the fifty-second stanza, is one of the loveliest expressions of the quintessence of Platonism in English poetry.

> Ἀστὴρ πρὶν μὲν ἔλαμπες ἐνὶ ζῳοῖσιν Ἐῷος,
> νῦν δὲ θανὼν λάμπεις Ἕσπερος ἐν φθιμένοις. —Plato

In his study of Shelley's symbolism W. B. Yeats has shown that "the most important, the most precise of all Shelley's symbols, the one he uses with the fullest knowledge of its meaning, is the Morning and Evening Star" (*Ideas of Good and Evil,* pp. 128-133). Shelley's conscious association of the theme of his poem with Plato is seen in his choice of Plato's epigram for the motto of the poem. Shelley, who translated this epigram (*vide infra,* p. 508), saw in it the epitome of Platonic immortality. (For the incorrect accents of the epigram in the Pisan text, see *Notebook of the Shelley Society,* First Series, No. 2 [London, 1888], p. 17.)

> Forget the Past, his fate and fame shall be
> An echo and a light unto eternity!
>
> (Ll. 8-9)

The theme of immortality is stated in the first stanza; its development will take Platonic character as the poem goes on.

> Lament anew, Urania!—He died . . . .
>
> (L. 29)

The substitution of Urania for the Cyprian in Bion's poem is probably for reasons of meter and for its symbolic value as a name for Platonic Immortality and Love. For Urania in Shelley as synonymous with Plato's Aphrodite Urania, see White, *The Best of Shelley*, page 525, where Professor White points out that Urania's musical qualities are not found in Plato's conception but are added by Shelley from Milton's conception, "mistress of Celestial song."

> And others came . . . Desires and Adorations,
> Winged Persuasions and veiled Destinies,
> Splendours, and Glooms, and glimmering Incarnations
> Of hopes and fears, and twilight Phantasies . . .
>
> (Ll. 109-112)

Though this passage reveals a direct influence of Moschus's *Lament for Bion*, it also contains the nucleus of a Neoplatonic notion that may have reached Shelley through his reading of Drummond (*vide supra*, pp. 148-149, 86-89).

> Out of her secret Paradise she sped,
> Through camps and cities rough with stone, and steel,
> And human hearts, which to her aery tread
> Yielding not, wounded the invisible
> Palms of her tender feet where'er they fell . . . .
>
> (Ll. 208-212)

These lines are a direct echo of the description of Love in Agathon's speech:

For Love walks not upon the earth, nor over the heads of men, which are not indeed very soft; but he dwells within, and treads on the softest of existing things, having established his habitation within the souls and inmost nature of Gods and men; not indeed in all souls—for wherever he chances to find a hard and rugged disposition, there he will not inhabit, but only where it is most soft and tender. Of needs must he be the most delicate of all things, who touches lightly with his feet, only the softest parts of those things which are the softest of all. (*Symposium,* 195e, Shelley's translation)

Shelley also made use of this passage in *Prometheus Unbound,* I, 772-775.

> Nor let us weep that our delight is fled
> Far from these carrion kites that scream below;
> He wakes or sleeps with the enduring dead;
> Thou canst not soar where he is sitting now.—
> Dust to the dust! but the pure spirit shall flow
> Back to the burning fountain whence it came,
> A portion of the Eternal, which must glow
> Through time and change, unquenchably the same,
> Whilst thy cold embers choke the sordid hearth of shame.
>
> (Ll. 334-342)

Beginning with this stanza Shelley develops the Platonic theme of immortality. This stanza is an epitome of *Phaedo,* 80-81, where the body dissolves to dust and the spirit returns to its immortal source, here described by Shelley as a "burning fountain." (See also Shelley's translation of *Spirit of Plato,* where the same conception is repeated.) The Platonism of this passage is refracted through the Plotinian doctrine of emanation of souls from the One (*vide supra,* pp. 86-88). Professor Beach says of the imagery here, "This image of the soul as fire derived from a burning fountain is used by Plotinus, . . . 'as if from universal fire one should be a vast and another a diminutive fire; while in the meantime all the various gradations would proceed from universal fire, or rather from that which is the source of this general fire'" (J. W. Beach, *The Concept of Nature in Nineteenth Century English Poetry* [New York, 1936], p. 265). For other instances, see *Enneads,* I, vi, 3; II, ix, 3. This conception, however, got into the Platonic tradition (see Beach, *op. cit.,* p. 590 n. 39), and Shelley may have absorbed this imagery from the Platonic tradition rather than a direct reading of Plotinus. In particular Shelley may have been attracted to the Plotinian doctrine of emanation and the fountain from Coleridge's poetry, where they figure prominently (*vide supra,* pp. 160-162; *Religious Musings,* ll. 402-410, 414-415; *Destiny of Nations,* ll. 15-29). Shelley had previously expressed this idea in a passage in the *Essay on Christianity* (1816-1817): "The unobscured irradiations from the fountain fire of all goodness shall reveal all that is mysterious and unintelligible until the mutual communications of knowledge and of happiness throughout all thinking natures constitute a harmony of good that ever varies and never ends. This is Heaven . . .

when the benignant principle unt[rammel]led and uncontrolled, visits in the fulness of its power the universal frame of things" (Julian *Works,* VI, 235-236). For a study of effluence in Shelley, see O. W. Firkins, *Power and Elusiveness in Shelley,* pages 156-170.

> Peace, peace! he is not dead, he doth not sleep—
> He hath awakened from the dream of life—
> 'Tis we, who lost in stormy visions, keep
> With phantoms an unprofitable strife,
> And in mad trance strike with our spirit's knife
> Invulnerable nothings.—*We* decay
> Like corpses in a charnel; fear and grief
> Convulse us and consume us day by day,
> And cold hopes swarm like worms within our living clay.
>
> (Ll. 343-351)

Professor White states that "the idea that death may be life and life death had doubtless been encountered by Shelley in his reading of Plato's *Gorgias*" (*Shelley,* II, 612). Shelley may have known the content of *Gorgias,* 492e, from the indirect Platonic tradition, but he could not have read the *Gorgias,* for Hogg recommended this dialogue to Shelley in a letter dated June 15, 1821, and Shelley started on it after this date, as his letter of October 20, 1821, shows (*vide supra,* p. 69).

For the Platonic philosophy in these lines, see commentary on the Platonism of the poem, *supra* pages 291-292. "The dream of life," the "stormy visions," the "phantoms" are variant echoes of Shelley's Platonically influenced philosophy that this world is an illusion, an unreal phantom of a transcendent and eternal Reality. The portrait of mortality here may contain echoes from *Republic,* 520d and 586c.

> He has outsoared the shadow of our night . . . .
>
> (L. 352)

An expression of mortality in terms of the Platonic metaphor of shadow (*vide supra,* p. 204), or, astronomically, the "cone of night." Compare Plotinus's statement about the impossibility of a star's being "darkened by night at that great distance above the earth's shadow" (*Enneads,* II, iii, 5).

> He is made one with Nature: there is heard
> His voice in all her music, from the moan
> Of thunder, to the song of night's sweet bird;
> He is a presence to be felt and known

In darkness and in light, from herb and stone,
Spreading itself where'er that Power may move
Which has withdrawn his being to its own;
Which wields the world with never-wearied love,
Sustains it from beneath, and kindles it above.

(Ll. 370-378)

Shelley here describes the Eternal of which Keats's soul has become a portion. The Eternal is conceived in terms of Nature (l. 370) and Power (l. 375), which, if compared with Shelley's *Hymn to Intellectual Beauty*, shows that the Eternal, Nature, and Power are variant facets of Intellectual Beauty. Intellectual Beauty here is presented in its immanent and transcendent character; it sustains the world from beneath and kindles it from above with eternal love; thus it is shown that the Platonic Beauty in these lines is also synonymous with Love.

He is a portion of the loveliness
Which once he made more lovely: he doth bear
His part, while the one Spirit's plastic stress
Sweeps through the dull dense world, compelling there
All new successions to the forms they wear;
Torturing th' unwilling dross that checks its flight
To its own likeness, as each mass may bear;
And bursting in its beauty and its might
From trees and beasts and men into the Heaven's light.

(Ll. 379-387)

The Platonism in these lines is an echo of the Platonic tradition rather than of Plato himself. In the *Timaeus* the divine Creator fashioned the world after the eternal pattern; in his account of creation Plato says that "the universal nature," while receiving all things,

never departs at all from her own nature, and never in any way, or at any time, assumes a form like that of any of these things which enter into her; she is the natural recipient of all impressions, and is stirred and informed by them, and appears different from time to time by reason of them. But the forms which enter into and go out of her are like the likenesses of real existences modeled after their patterns in a wonderful and inexplicable manner. . . . fire is that part of her nature which from time to time is inflamed, and water that which is moistened, and that the mother substance becomes earth and air, in so far as she receives the impressions of them. (*Timaeus*, 50-51)

This conception of the elements being merely affections of space produced by the impression of Platonic forms was fused in the Platonic tradition with the Lucretian *daedala tellus,* the artificer earth, and appears in Cudworth's treatise *The True Intellectual System of the Universe* as Plastic Nature, which orders and disposes the world, permeating and molding it, even down to the lowest animals and plants. In describing the relation of Plastic Nature to God, Cudworth says it has "a certain dull and obscure idea of that which it stamps and prints upon matter." This notion was taken up by philosophy and poetry and appears in attractive form in a considerable number of Shelley's readings (*vide supra,* pp. 116, 120, 157, 160). In particular it appears along with the Platonic conception that mind pervades and animates the whole universe in Lord Monboddo's *Antient Metaphysics,* which Shelley read in 1820 (see Vol. I, Book II, chaps. vi, xvii). Furthermore, Wordsworth and Coleridge gave beautiful poetic expression to Plastic Nature, and a comparison of Shelley's lines in *Adonais* with their versions of this doctrine makes it likely that Shelley absorbed this poetical idea from his contemporary poets whom he read and admired. Shelley therefore refracts the Platonism of these lines, not from Plato himself, even though he had read the *Timaeus* and a summary of it in 1818, but from the Platonic tradition.

The Spirit here is also conceived in terms of an immanent Intellectual Beauty (see commentary on lines 370-378, *supra*). In line 385 the phrase "as each mass may bear" is an echo in the Platonic tradition of the recalcitrant matter upon which Plato's Demiourgos in the *Timaeus* stamps the impress of the Platonic forms. It is suggested that it is this recalcitrant, unwilling, rebellious character of the material world that accounts for the evil in this world (*vide supra,* pp. 235-237).

> And many more, whose names on Earth are dark
> But whose transmitted effluence cannot die
> So long as fire outlives the parent spark,
> Rose, robed in dazzling immortality.
> "Thou art become as one of us," they cry;
> "It was for thee yon kingless sphere has long
> "Swung blind in unascended majesty,
> "Silent alone amid an Heaven of Song.
> "Assume thy winged throne, thou Vesper of our throng!"
>   (Ll. 406-414)

For a similar conception of the association with the souls of the great, see *Apology,* 41. The words "Vesper of our throng" in line 414 are a direct allusion to Plato's epigram which Shelley used as the motto of the poem. In the first rough draft of his translation (*MS Shelley adds. e. 8,* p. 145) Shelley used the word *Vesper,* which he later changed to *Hesperus.*

> The One remains, the many change and pass;
> Heaven's light forever shines, Earth's shadows fly;
> (Ll. 460-463)
> Life, like a dome of many-coloured glass,
> Stains the white radiance of Eternity . . . .

Shelley's statement of the essence of Platonism and the imagery through which he expresses it constitute the best epigrammatic expression of Platonism in English poetry. Shelley knew the doctrine both from such sources of Platonism as Petrarch's *Triumphs,* which constitutes a beautiful dramatization of the Platonic theme, Life and Death (*vide supra,* p. 158, and White, *Shelley,* II, 294-295, 630-631); and from its metaphysical development in the *Parmenides,* which was included in the tenth volume of the Bipont edition brought to Italy; or from the sixth book of the *Republic,* which Shelley read in 1820 and of which he wrote to Hogg in a letter dated October 20, 1821: "Do you know the πολιτεια and especially the sixth book of it?" (*Shelley at Oxford,* p. 64). In view of this it is likely that the doctrine was fresh in Shelley's mind from his reading both of Plato and of Petrarch's *Triumphs,* for "in this brilliant image," says Professor White, "Shelley condensed almost the whole spirit of Petrarch's *Triumphs*" (*Shelley,* II, 294). Shelley transmutes this Platonic doctrine into poetry thus: The first line is a beautiful epigrammatic statement of the doctrine itself, without resort to imagery; it is in fact a translation of Plato's own words. In the second line Shelley restates this doctrine in terms of Plato's own imagery and metaphor; in the sixth and seventh books of the *Republic* Plato expresses the doctrine of the One and the Many in terms of original and shadow, and light and darkness. Shelley here fuses both of these conceptions, applying in a chiastic order the image of light to the One and that of shadow to the Many. Then Shelley translates the One into Heaven and the Many into Earth, substituting poetical for metaphysical terminology. Thus far Shelley is following Plato directly. The third and fourth lines express the Platonic thought of the first two lines anew through an image which Shelley fashioned out of his own imagination and traditional imagery. A study of the poet's imagery shows that it "presents mental phenomena in terms of the physical, physical phenomena in terms of the mental, and even fuses matter and spirit in the same image" (White, *Shelley,* II, 130). In lines 462-463 Shelley has fashioned an image which combines all three:

he interprets Platonic metaphysics in terms of physical imagery; he interprets physical phenomena (Life) in terms of Platonic metaphysics; and finally he fuses both of these into an image which is polar in character, interpreting the mental and physical in terms of each other. The imagery in which Shelley chose to express this is partly derived from the operations of his own mind, partly from traditional imagery. In the preface to *Prometheus Unbound* we have the notion of the One and the Many expressed as "Every man's mind . . . is the mirror upon which all forms are reflected, and in which they compose one form." In *A Defence of Poetry* the image of the *Adonais* appears as "The drama . . . is as a prismatic and manysided mirror, which collects the brightest rays of human nature and divides and reproduces them from the simplicity of these elementary forms, and touches them with majesty and beauty, and multiplies all that it reflects, and endows it with the power of propagating its like wherever it may fall" and "the mirrors of the gigantic shadows which futurity casts upon the present." Thus we see that the imagery is born in Shelley's own mind. But it is also clothed in traditional imagery. Plotinus speaks of the soul's "giving forth, without any change in itself, images or likenesses of itself like one face caught by many mirrors" (*Enneads,* I, i, 8). In Dante's *Divine Comedy,* which Shelley read, we find "Behold now the height and amplitude of the Eternal Worth, seeing it hath made itself so *many* mirrors in which it breaks, while remaining *one* in itself, as before" (*Paradiso,* xxix, 142-145). Furthermore, in Southey's *Thalaba,* one of Shelley's favorite poems (*vide supra,* p. 153) we find

> The many-coloured domes
> Yet wore one dusky hue.

Out of his own operations of the mind and the traditional imagery of the dome, which is extensively used in Romantic poetry (see Knight, *The Starlit Dome,* pp. 127, 179, 183, 201-203), Shelley's imagination shaped a new image to express the Platonic metaphysical doctrine. The operations of his mind in shaping this imagery are subtle. He integrates the images in a chiastic order,

Heaven's light	versus	Earth's shadows
Life, a dome of many-coloured glass	versus	the white radiance of eternity

"Heaven's light" is restated as "the white radiance of Eternity," which is placed last so that the line may end in the poetic symbol of the One, rather than that of the Many. "Earth's shadows" (which ends line 461)

is restated in terms of a new symbol; Earth is restated as Life, as natural
an equation as Eternity is for Heaven; "shadows" is restated as "a
dome of many-coloured glass." Shelley here is thinking of the Earth
rather than of Life, for the Earth is a sphere, a conception which
is as old as Pythagoras and Plato. In the *Republic* (616-617) Plato speaks
of concentric whorls fitted into one another. Of these spherical whorls,
one of which is the Earth, Plato says, "that of the greatest was spangled,
that of the seventh, brightest, that of the eighth took its colour from the
seventh which shone upon it." Here we have the ultimate origin of
Shelley's notion that the crystalline dome of the sphere of the Earth imparts its many colors to another. Shelley, who completed the reading of
the *Republic* in 1820, may have retained this conception in his mind and
evoked it in fashioning an image for Platonism itself. In the Songs of
the Moon to the Earth in the *Prometheus Unbound* (IV, 459-463) Shelley
speaks of the moon as a "crystal" paramour and the Earth as a

> Green and azure sphere which shinest
> With a light which is divinest
> Among all the lamps of Heaven,

a conception which is repeated with variation in *Hellas,* Prologue, lines
20-23.

　　Out of this Platonic conception of the earth as a spangled crystalline
sphere, the commonplace imagery of the dome in Romantic poetry, Shelley fashioned a new image to symbolize Life and its "shadows," which
he already had described in his *Sonnet* as

> 　　the painted veil which those who live
> Call Life: though unreal shapes be pictured there,
> And it but mimic all we would believe
> With colours idly spread.

　　Shelley expresses in *Adonais* this same philosophy of the illusory
nature of Life in terms of a new and more brilliant imagery. Finally,
to make this "dome of many-coloured glass" consonant with Platonic
philosophy, Shelley makes use of the verb *stain,* which emphasizes
the notion of the pollution of the earthly in the *Phaedo* (cf. *Prometheus
Unbound,* II, iii, 13-14). If Shelley had not used this verb with its
Platonic connotation of the earthly, the image would be pointless; for
otherwise the "dome of many-coloured glass" would reflect only a
kaleidoscopic prettiness on the white surface of Eternity's radiance. Thus
Shelley fashioned his own image to express brilliantly the Platonic meta-

physics of the One and the Many. (Cf. Raphael Demos, "The One and the Many," *Philosophical Essays for Alfred North Whitehead* [London, New York, 1936], pp. 41-66.) It fuses poetry and metaphysics as no one else except Donne has in English poetry.

> —Die,
> If thou wouldst be with that which thou dost seek!
> (Ll. 464-465)

This is an echo of *Phaedo*, 68b, where the philosopher is yearning to die so that his soul might return to its pristine purity.

> That Light whose smile kindles the Universe,
> That Beauty in which all things work and move,
> That Benediction which the eclipsing Curse
> Of birth can quench not, that sustaining Love
> Which through the web of being blindly wove
> By man and beast and earth and air and sea,
> Burns bright or dim, as each are mirrors of
> The fire for which all thirst; now beams on me,
> Consuming the last clouds of cold mortality.
> (Ll. 478-486)

Intellectual Beauty, immanent in the world, transfigures Shelley in an ecstasy which purges him of all mortality. In this ecstasy Shelley fuses Platonic Immortality, Beauty, Love, as in his other poems. Compare commentary on *Epipsychidion*, lines 21-32, *supra*, pages 281-282, where line 480 of *Adonais* is a variant of *Epipsychidion*, line 25.

> Whilst, burning through the inmost veil of Heaven,
> The soul of Adonais, like a star,
> Beacons from the abode where the Eternal are.
> (Ll. 493-495)

The poem ends with another allusion to Plato's epigram,

> Now, having died, thou art as Hesperus, giving
> New splendour to the dead.

With the "veil of Heaven," compare *Epipsychidion*, line 472, and *Unfinished Drama*, lines 24, 239. It is of interest to note that in *The Choice*, written by Mary shortly after Shelley's death, Mary, in referring to Shelley, says:

> "Thou shin'st the evening star among the dead"
> (R. Glynn Grylls, *Mary Shelley*, p. 300, l. 6).

Hellas

Autumn of 1821

The Platonism in this poem appears mostly in the utterances of the Wandering Jew, who improvises on the Platonic theme of Appearance and Reality. The Greek revolution is used as an occasion to evoke all that Greece meant to Shelley and to the world, and this mood inevitably led him to Plato, who represented to Shelley the best that had been thought and said. The allusions to him and his thought in this poem are numerous. What part Plato plays in the thought and emotion of this poem may be seen in a newly published fragment from the *Prologue to Hellas:*

> And as one thought of Plato's mind outlives
> The Palaces of Athens, and with light
> Gilds their oblivion—so . . .
>
> (*Verse and Prose, From the Manuscripts of Percy Bysshe Shelley,* ed. Sir John C. E. Shelley-Rolls and Roger Ingpen [London, 1934], p. 48)

> That green and azure sphere, that earth inwrapt
> Less in the beauty of its tender light
> Than in an atmosphere of living spirit
> Which interpenetrating all the . . .
>
> (Prologue, ll. 20-23)

For the world soul, see commentary on *Queen Mab,* pages 176-178, *supra.*

> The curtain of the Universe
> Is rent and shattered.
>
> (Prologue, ll. 52-53)

The curtain is a variant of the Platonic veil (cf. *Prometheus Unbound,* IV, 58).

> For this I felt—by Plato's sacred light,
> Of which my spirit was a burning morrow—
>
> (Prologue, ll. 94-95)

As has been noted in the history of the Platonic tradition, Christianity saw in Platonism a foreshadowing of its own doctrines (*vide supra,* p. 93). Shelley shares this view. In *The Moral Teaching of Jesus Christ* he writes, "The doctrines of Jesus Christ though excellent are not new. The immortality of the soul was already a dogma, familiar from all antiquity to every nation of the earth except the Jews. Plato said all that could be said on this subject. . . ." In *Hellas* Shelley repeats this view. In the last sentence he has in mind Plato's *Phaedo,* which he had recently read and in part translated.

> By Greece and all she cannot cease to be.
> Her quenchless words, sparks of immortal truth,
> Stars of all night—her harmonies and forms,
> Echoes and shadows of what Love adores . . .
>   (Prologue, ll. 96-99)

The art and literature of Greece are viewed as images of Ideal Beauty and Love. The reference to Love's adoring forms is to the Love in the *Symposium* which contemplates "forms" (cf. *Prometheus Unbound,* I, 748-750, and III, iii, 51-56, where Shelley uses "forms" for Plato's theory of Ideas). For Shelley, Greece was the best image in the history of the Platonic Intellectual Beauty. Here as in the rest of the poem Shelley refracts the glory of Greece in Platonic theories and images.

> When virtuous spirits through the gate of Death
> Pass triumphing over the thorns of life,
> Sceptres and crowns, mitres and swords and snares,
> Trampling in scorn, like Him and Socrates.
>   (Prologue, ll. 152-155)

Shelley associates here Socrates's martyrdom with that of Christ, a frequent association in the history of the Platonic tradition. For the association of Socrates with Christ, see *Epipsychidion,* Fragments, lines 33-34.

> He, I, and all things shall compel—enough.
> Silence those mutineers—that drunken crew,
> That crowd about the pilot in the storm.
>   (Ll. 190-192)

This image is directly taken over from *Republic,* 488.

> Worlds on worlds are rolling ever
> From creation to decay,
> Like the bubbles on a river
> Sparkling, bursting, borne away.
>   (Ll. 197-200)

For the Platonism in these lines, see Shelley's own note on this stanza: "The first stanza contrasts the immortality of the living and thinking beings which inhabit the planets, and, to use a common and inadequate phrase, *clothe themselves in matter,* with the transience of the noblest manifestations of the external world." Shelley's phrase in italics refers to the language and thought of the *Phaedo.* Miss Winstanley sees in this song the influence of Plato's *Statesman,* 170 ff., with its successions of births and deaths and the change of ages. However, see commentary on *Prometheus Unbound,* II, v, 98-103, *supra,* pages 251-253.

> But they are still immortal
> Who, through birth's orient portal
> And death's dark chasm hurrying to and fro,
> Clothe their unceasing flight
> In the brief dust and light
> Gather'd around their chariots as they go;
> New shapes they still may weave,
> New Gods, new laws receive,
> Bright or dim are they, as the robes they last
> On Death's bare ribs had cast.
>
> (Ll. 201-210)

* The Platonic view of immortality and transmigration in these lines contains a direct echo from the argument of Cebes in the *Phaedo,* wherein he states that the soul may pass through many bodies, just as the weaver may outlive many coats (*Phaedo,* 87-88). See commentary on *The Witch of Atlas,* ll. 97-104, pp. 272-273, *supra.* A new fragment of this passage reveals a variant expression of the Platonism of these lines as contained in the original draft:

> But thy spirit is immortal
> Which beholds them as they flow
> All who through Birth's orient portal
> And Death's dark gate pass to and fro
> Live in those mists—all on whom
> Thy   secret breath has blown
> Will now behold thee, 'tis their doom
> To be a portion everyone
> Of thee—Thou art thyself alone.
>
> (*Shelley, Verse and Prose,* p. 50)

> But many-headed insurrection stands
> Divided in itself, and soon must fall.
>
> (Ll. 334-335)

Shelley is echoing here Plato's description of man as the "many-headed beast" in *Republic*, 588c (cf. letter to Leigh Hunt, November 3, 1819, Julian *Works*, X, 113).

> But Greece and her foundations are
> Built below the tide of war,
> Based on the crystalline sea
> Of thought and its eternity . . . .
> (Ll. 696-699)

Shelley applies here the Platonic distinction of the temporal versus the eternal, which is the central metaphysical idea of the poem, to the thought of Greece, which is eternal, above and beyond the fate of things which are characterized by flux. Greece is viewed in terms of her thought rather than her temples, citadels, marts, and other earthly edifices which decay; it is thought alone which transcends this fate. Just as in the *Adonais* Shelley created a unique image to express the Platonic philosophy of the One and the Many (see commentary, *supra*, pp. 298-301), so in these lines Shelley is also fashioning a new image to express the Platonic conception of the eternal and the transient. This time he uses the sea as a Platonic symbol. The Eternity of thought is symbolized by the diaphanous calm of the blue Mediterranean, which he describes in the *Ode to the West Wind* (ll. 29-42) as

> Thou who didst waken from his summer dreams
> The blue Mediterranean, where he lay,
> Lulled by the coil of his crystalline streams,
>
> Beside a pumice isle in Baiae's bay,
> And saw in sleep dim palaces and towers
> Quivering within the wave's intenser day,
>
> All overgrown with azure moss and flowers
> So sweet, the sense faints picturing them! Thou
> For whose path the Atlantic's level powers
>
> Cleave themselves into chasms, while far below
> The sea-blooms and the oozy woods which wear
> The sapless foliage of the ocean, know
>
> Thy voice, and suddenly grow grey with fear,
> And tremble and despoil themselves: O, hear!

This description of the crystalline calm of the blue Mediterranean, whose tideless depths are contrasted with its disturbed surface, shows that Shelley chose such a sea to symbolize the calm crystal-clear radiance ("the wave's intenser day") of Eternity. Another example of Shelley's use of crystalline with the sea is found in lines 489-490:

> . . . convulsed
> To its crystalline depths that stainless sea . . .

And still another:

> From their crystalline mines below
> The storms that never see the sun . . .

which is found among the fragments of *Prometheus Unbound* (Shelley, *Verse and Prose*, p. 143). The word "stainless" strikingly recalls "Stains the white radiance of Eternity" in the image of the *Adonais*, line 463. Shelley's use of "a crystalline sea" is thus a partial parallel to the image in *Adonais*.

> Thou art an adept in the difficult lore
> Of Greek and Frank philosophy . . . .
> (Ll. 741-742)

Ahasuerus, adept in Greek philosophy, is appropriately made the mouthpiece of the Platonic thought in lines 768 ff. Inasmuch as Ahasuerus also appears in *Queen Mab,* which is influenced by French philosophy, he is described as adept in French philosophy as well.

> Sultan! talk no more
> Of thee and me, the future and the past;
> But look on that which cannot change—the One
> The unborn and the undying. Earth and ocean,
> Space, and the isles of life or light that gem
> The sapphire floods of interstellar air,
> This firmament pavilioned upon chaos,
> With all its cressets of immortal fire,
> Whose outwall, bastioned impregnably
> Against the escape of boldest thoughts, repels them
> As Calpe the Atlantic clouds—this Whole
> Of suns, and worlds, and men, and beasts, and flowers,
> With all the silent or tempestuous workings
> By which they have been, are, or cease to be,
> Is but a vision;—all that it inherits
> Are motes of a sick eye, bubbles and dreams;
> Thought is its cradle and its grave, nor less
> The future and the past are idle shadows

Of thought's eternal flight—they have no being;
Nought is but that it feels itself to be.

. . . .

Mistake me not! All is contained in each.
Dodona's forest to an acorn's cup
Is that which has been or will be, to that
Which is—the absent to the present. Thought
Alone, and its quick elements, Will, Passion,
Reason, Imagination, cannot die;
They are what that which they regard appears,
The stuff whence mutability can weave
All that it hath dominion o'er,—worlds, worms,
Empires, and superstitions. What has thought
To do with time, or place, or circumstance?
                    (Ll. 766-785, 792-802)

Ahasuerus's speech contains the essence of Platonism which Shelley expressed in *Adonais*, lines 460-463, and *Hellas*, lines 696-699. This speech reveals clearly the influence of Prospero's final soliloquy in *The Tempest*, Shelley's favorite play. Though the famous similar passage in *The Tempest* reveals indirect Platonic influence, it is pessimistic. Shelley, using the same language, obviously refutes it Platonically.

Ahasuerus bases his prophecy of triumph on Platonic reality, whereas Mahmud bases it on the relative and ever-changing world of time and space, which is not real but a phantom. The world and all its elements, Time with its flux, are but an illusion, an unsubstantial vision or phantom of the One which cannot change and is unborn and undying. The thought and phraseology here is an expansion of the One and the Many in *Adonais*, lines 460-461. Shelley fills his realm of the Many with an array of poetic imagery which enhances the Beauty that permeates the world; yet beautiful as the images are, they are but shadows of the One described with Platonic adjectives. Even Time with its Past and Future is, like Plato's description of it, but the fleeting image of Eternity (*Timaeus*, 37d). The philosophy here is once more Shelley's Platonic philosophy of the Reality of Being and the illusory nature of the world of time and space.

            If Greece must be
        A wreck, yet shall its fragments reassemble,
        And build themselves again impregnably
            In a diviner clime,
        To Amphionic music on some Cape sublime,

Which frowns above the idle foam of Time.
(Ll. 1002-1007)

The Platonic conception here is a variant of that in lines 696-699 (see commentary, *supra*, pp. 305-306).

Burst, like morning on dream, or like Heaven on death
Through the walls of our prison;
And Greece, which was dead, is arisen!
(Ll. 1057-1059)

The freedom of Greece is expressed in terms of the Platonic immortality of the *Phaedo;* "the walls of our prison" are an allusion to *Phaedo,* 62b, 67d, 82e.

The world's great age begins anew,
The golden years return,
The earth doth like a snake renew
Her winter weeds outworn . . . .
(Ll. 1060-1063)

Miss Winstanley sees in these lines the idea of the alternation of the periods of order and disorder as pictured in *Statesman,* 270. Yet the note which Shelley added to explain the chorus shows that it comes directly from Virgil's *Fourth Eclogue.* Shelley no doubt has infused into this chorus the Platonic immortality as applies to the freedom of Greece. (For a bibliography of the "Golden Age" in classical literature, see W. C. Greene, *Moira* [Cambridge, Mass., 1944], pp. 402-403).

Guides the sphere which is its prison,
Like an angelic spirit pent
In a form of mortal birth,
Till, as a spirit half-arisen
Shatters its charnel, it has rent,
In the rapture of its mirth,
The thin and painted garment of the Earth . . .
(Fragment written for *Hellas,* ll. 28-34)

The conception of the soul in these lines echoes in phrase and thought *Phaedo,* 62b; the "painted garment" is a variant of the Platonic "painted veil" (see commentary on *Sonnet, supra,* pp. 230-231).

Mutability

1821

I

The flower that smiles to-day
    To-morrow dies;
All that we wish to stay
    Tempts and then flies.
What is this world's delight?
Lightning that mocks the night,
    Brief even as bright.

II

Virtue, how frail it is!
    Friendship how rare!
Love, how it sells poor bliss
    For proud despair!
But we, though soon they fall,
Survive their joy, and all
    Which ours we call.

III

Whilst skies are blue and bright,
    Whilst flowers are gay,
Whilst eyes that change ere night
    Make glad the day;
Whilst yet the calm hours creep,
Dream thou—and from thy sleep
    Then wake to weep.

For the philosophic doctrine of mutability, see commentary *supra,* pages 194-195. Shelley here makes a personal application of the Platonic doctrine of mutability; he does not complement it with an affirmation in Platonic permanence.

Sonnet: To the Republic of Benevento

1821

Staining that Heaven with obscene imagery
Of their own likeness. What are numbers knit
By force or custom? Man who man would be,
Must rule the empire of himself; in it
Must be supreme, establishing his throne
On vanquished will, quelling the anarchy
Of hopes and fears, being himself alone.

(Ll. 8-14)

In lines 8-9 Shelley is echoing the Platonic image of *Adonais*, lines 462-463 (see commentary *supra*, pp. 298-301); the degradation of humanity by tyranny constitutes the obscene imagery which stains the radiance of Eternity. Shelley here applies his image to the evils of tyranny.

The remaining lines voice an ideal of Shelley, which is analogous to Plato's definition of Justice in the *Republic*, 433, and the myth of the *Phaedrus*, 247 ff.

To ——: "One word is too often profaned"

1821

> I can give not what men call love,
>   But wilt thou accept not
> The worship the heart lifts above
>   And the Heavens reject not:
> The desire of the moth for the star,
>   Of the night for the morrow,
> The devotion to something afar
>   From the sphere of our sorrow?

(Ll. 9-16)

An expression of Platonic adoration and yearning for a transcendent ideal which received full expression in *Epipsychidion*. See commentary on *Epipsychidion*, lines 149-159, pages 284-285, *supra*.

SHELLEY'S READINGS IN PLATO AND THE PLATONIC TRADITION, 1822

DIRECT PLATONISM: *Gorgias*
INDIRECT PLATONISM: Spinoza

PLATONISM IN SHELLEY'S POETRY WRITTEN IN 1822

Charles the First

Begun at close of 1819; resumed in January and laid aside by June, 1822

> . . . and the knaves, to
> marshal them, join in a procession to Bedlam, to entreat the
> madmen to omit their sublime Platonic contemplations, and
> manage the state of England.

(Sc. ii, ll. 60-63)

Archy, the Court fool, voices his judgment concerning the wise and godly, a judgment of the man in the street about Platonic contemplations which was also known in Plato's own day (*Republic*, 495c). See commentary on "Platonic reveries," *supra*, pages 137-138.

> Which spurs to rage the many-headed beast.
> (ii, 118)

See commentary on *Hellas*, 334-335, *supra*, pages 304-305.

> A commonwealth like Gonzalo's in the play,
> Gynaecocoenic and pantisocratic.
> (ii, 363-364)

This is another reference to *The Tempest* and its discussion of a Platonic utopia in Act II, scene i, lines 153-175 (cf. *Republic*, 449d ff.). The word *pantisocratic* has a contemporary allusion to Southey's and Coleridge's Platonically inspired Pantisocracy, which they planned to found in America (see *Peter Bell the Third*, Part VI, 126 n., and commentary *supra*, p. 263).

> *Archy.* Ay, I am the physician of whom Plato prophesied,
> who was to be accused by the confectioner before a jury of
> children, who found him guilty without waiting for the
> summing-up, and hanged him without benefit of clergy.
> (ii, 387-390)

This passage is a direct allusion to *Gorgias*, 464d-e: "Cookery simulates the disguise of medicine, and pretends to know what food is the best for the body; and if the physician and the cook had to enter into a competition in which children were the judges, or men who had no more sense than children, as to which of them understands the goodness or badness of food, the physician would be starved to death" (cf. *Gorgias*, 521e-522a). Upon receipt of a letter from Hogg recommending the *Gorgias*, Shelley immediately devoted himself to the reading of it (for Hogg's and Shelley's correspondence on the *Gorgias* of Plato, *vide supra*, pp. 68-70).

> . . . England, is a nest
> Of cradling peace built on the mountain tops,—
> To which the eagle spirits of the free,
> Which range through heaven and earth, and scorn the storm
> Of time, and gaze upon the light of truth,
> Return to brood on thoughts that cannot die
> And cannot be repelled.
> (iv, 49-55)

The Platonic theme of the immortality of thought which Shelley stated in *Hellas*, lines 696-699, is repeated here.

The Triumph of Life
Spring and early summer of 1822

The Platonism of this poem, like that of most of Shelley's other great Platonic poems, is a mixture of natural, direct, and indirect Platonism. Shelley's poem is essentially concerned with depicting the Platonic status of mortality and Life. His talent for natural Platonism fashions a new symbol to express the soul's unhappiness and illusion since "the eclipsing Curse of birth." Life is depicted as a chariot in a procession which never ascends to the Platonic empyrean because its charioteer is a symbol of the pollution, brutality, and blindness of mortality. The direct Platonism of the poem is manifest in Shelley's inclusion of Plato in the procession of the great which follows the chariot. Plato influences the philosophy of the poem both directly and indirectly through Petrarch's *Triumphs,* which are a poetically attractive restatement of Plato's philosophy (see White, *Shelley,* II, 294-295). As Professor White has shown (*Shelley,* II, 630-631), these poems of Petrarch influenced not only *Adonais* but also *The Triumph of Life.*

The Platonism of *The Triumph of Life* centers largely on the Platonic rise and fall of Rousseau. To understand the Platonism of this episode one must keep in mind Plato's account in the *Phaedrus* of the charioteer of the soul who starts on a heavenward journey to Platonic Beauty; mortality, however, weighs heavy as the chariot ascends, and eventually the soul is toppled in headlong flight to the earth. Shelley expressed this search for Platonic beauty and the attendant frustrations of mortality in a letter to Gisborne dated June 18, 1822 (Julian *Works,* X, 401). Shelley, who had experienced this in his own life and expressed it in *Alastor* and *Prince Athanase,* saw the same Platonic frustration in Rousseau's life. *The Triumph of Life* portrays this Platonic aspiration for Ideal Beauty in the figure of Rousseau, a captive of life following in the procession of the chariot, which symbolizes Aphrodite Pandemos (see John Todhunter, "Notes on 'The Triumph of Life,'" *The Shelley Society's Papers,* First Series, No. 1, Part I, 78). Rousseau addresses Shelley and unfolds the story of his vision of "A Shape all light," which is the Shelleyan Intellectual Beauty of *The Witch of Atlas* (see White, *Shelley,* II, 370), with all her traditional Platonic symbols of the cave, the fountain, and the crystal glass from which only a few chosen spirits may drink. Rousseau drank of it, but the vision of the heavenly was supplanted by a new one symbolical of the earthly. As a result he was soon caught in the earthly triumphal procession of the car of Life, and the phantoms of the earthly supplanted the shining vision of Beauty. Maddened and disillusioned, he had dropped by the wayside, where he was found by the poet. Though the theme of the complete poem is irrecoverable and the apparent theme of the fragment could only be that of an episode in the complete poem, it may be that this scene is another version of the theme of *Alastor* and *Prince Athanase* and expresses the Platonic experience which Plato stated in the *Phaedrus,* and Shelley in his own life and poetry. If so, it is ironical that Shelley's last great poem should have the same theme as his earliest, *Alastor,* for both poetically express the search and failure to attain a Platonic ideal.

> Swift as a spirit hastening to his task
> Of glory and of good, the Sun sprang forth
> Rejoicing in his splendour . . . .
>> (Ll. 1-3)

In the *Republic* (507-509c) Plato represents the Sun as the offspring and symbol of the Good. Shelley, who refers to this book of the *Republic* in his letter to Hogg dated October 20, 1821, shows here the influence of Plato's metaphysical image.

> So came a chariot on the silent storm . . . .
>> (L. 86)

For the chariot as a Platonic image, see commentary *supra,* page 312.

> All but the sacred few who could not tame
> Their spirits to the conquerors—but as soon
> As they had touched the world with living flame,
>
> Fled back like eagles to their native noon . . . .
>> (Ll. 128-131)

The sacred few, who include Plato, are characterized by Platonic qualities; their souls are at home only in the pure realms from which they came. The imagery here is probably an echo of Plato's epitaph, which Shelley translated as

> Eagle! why soarest thou above that tomb?
> To what sublime and star-y-paven home
> Floatest thou?—
> I am the image of swift Plato's spirit,
> Ascending Heaven—Athens doth inherit
> His corpse below.

"First, who art thou?"—"Before thy memory,

"I feared, loved, hated, suffered, did and died,
And if the spark with which Heaven lit my spirit
Had been with purer nutriment supplied,

"Corruption would not now thus much inherit
Of what was once Rousseau,—nor this disguise
Stained that which ought to have disdained to wear it . . . ."

(Ll. 199-205)

For the conception of Rousseau as a pursuer of the Platonic ideal and his corruption, see commentary on the Platonic character of the poem, *supra,* pages 134-136, 312-313.

"The great, the unforgotten,—they who wore
Mitres and helms and crowns, or wreaths of light,
Signs of thought's empire over thought—their lore

"Taught them not this, to know themselves . . . ."

(Ll. 209-212)

"Signs of thought's empire over thought" may refer to the Platonic philosopher who thinks not about the earthly but about thought itself (*Republic,* 511).

Line 212 is a translation of Γνῶθι σαυτόν (*Protagoras,* 343b), which is the summation of Socrates's philosophical activity.

—"Let them pass,"
I cried, "the world and its mysterious doom

"Is not so much more glorious than it was,
That I desire to worship those who drew
New figures on its false and fragile glass

"As the old faded."—"Figures ever new
Rise on the bubble, paint them as you may;
We have but thrown, as those before us threw,

"Our shadows on it as it passed away.
But mark how chained to the triumphal chair
The mighty phantoms of an elder day . . ."

(Ll. 243-253)

Mortality here is conceived of as the projections of figures on the false and fragile glass of the world. This image is analogous to the image in *Adonais,* lines 462-463, where Life is compared to a dome of many-coloured glass which stains Eternity.

"All that is mortal of great Plato there
Expiates the joy and woe his master knew not:
The star that ruled his doom was far too fair,

"And life, where long that flower of Heaven grew not,
Conquered that heart by love, which gold, or pain,
Or age, or sloth, or slavery, could subdue not."
(Ll. 254-259)

The reason why Plato and not Socrates is chained to the car of Life
is to be explained by the fact that Socrates did not yield to Alcibiades's
offer of male love (*Symposium,* 217b ff.), whereas Plato is said by tradition to have had male lovers. Shelley has here specifically in mind the account of Plato's male lover in Diogenes Laertius's *Life of Plato,* which
was contained in the first volume of Shelley's Bipont edition of Plato
and in which Shelley found the epigrams of Plato which he translated in
1820-1821 (*vide infra,* pp. 508-509).

If we connect line 256,

The star that ruled his doom was far too fair,

with Diogenes Laertius's account of Plato's love for a youth named Aster
(i.e., Star), we see not only the reason for Plato's enslavement but also
the meaning and significance of line 256 in the poem. Diogenes Laertius says:

Aristippus in his fourth book *On the Luxury of the Ancients* says that he
[Plato] was attached to a youth named Aster, who joined him in the study
of astronomy, as also to Dion, who has been mentioned above, and, as some
aver, to Phaedrus too. His passionate affection is revealed in the following
epigrams which he is said to have written upon them:
Star-gazing Aster, would I were the skies,
To gaze upon thee with a thousand eyes. . . .
(III, 29, Loeb Library Translation)

Thus it was only physical love which conquered Plato's heart, which
neither gold, pain, age, sloth, nor slavery could subdue. That is why
Shelley is careful to specify that only what is mortal of great Plato is in
the company of those enslaved to the Chariot of Life; his spirit, as Shelley
knew and perhaps alluded to in line 131, did not belong to this realm.
Although Shelley had tried his best to explain male love to the modern
world in his *Discourse on the Manners of the Antient Greeks Relative
to the Subject of Love,* in his own heart he did not put Plato on the same
plane as his master Socrates, who was above and beyond the "joy and
woe" of this type of love. His tacit disapproval of Plato's loves is also

seen in the fact that when Shelley translated Plato's epigrams to his lovers, Aster and Agathon, he changed their names in the title of the poems to Stella and Helena (*vide infra*, p. 508-509). It is thus a tribute to Shelley's independent moral judgment to condemn Plato, who was the father of his philosophy of idealism and the inspirer of some of his best poetry. (For a similar attitude toward Plato, see Petrarch, *De remediis utriusque fortunae*, I, 69.) In the opinion of Shelley, Plato made the same mistake as Rousseau; he pursued Intellectual Beauty in the form of earthly loves. Both are illustrations of Shelley's reasons why "the wise, the great," are chained to the car, explained in lines 214-215:

> ". . . for the morn of truth they feigned, deep night
> "Caught them ere evening."

> "And near him walk the   twain,
> The tutor and his pupil, whom Dominion
> Followed as tame as vulture in a chain."
>   (Ll. 260-262)

These spirits in the procession of the great are Diotima and Socrates, who appear in the *Symposium* as tutor and pupil. Shelley was so impressed with Diotima's instruction of Socrates in the true meaning of Love that he speaks of it in a fragment of the *Epipsychidion* (ll. 101-103) thus:

> or let them guess
> How Diotima, the wise prophetess,
> Instructed the instructor . . . .

This identification is made sure if we connect the phrase

> whom Dominion
> Followed as tame as vulture in a chain

with line 255,

> Expiates the joy and woe his master knew not.

Socrates's high-minded refusal of Alcibiades's offer of male love in the *Symposium* is the reason why Dominion follows him as tame as a vulture in a chain.

In *The Triumph of Life* Shelley put himself on record as to the moral purity of Socrates. If these lines are read in the context of Shelley's statements in the letter to Leigh Hunt written on November 3, 1819, they receive increased illumination (*vide infra*, pp. 365-367). This tribute to Socrates's self-control brings the question of why he follows in the procession. In lines 128-136 Shelley speaks of the sacred few of Athens and Jerusalem who were included among the captives. There is no doubt but that these sacred few are Socrates and Jesus. This inconsistency may be due to the fact that this section is incomplete—"in so unfinished a state," says Mary, "that I arranged it in its present form with the greatest difficulty"—and consequently lacked Shelley's revision. Shelley perhaps included Socrates in the procession for the same reason that he included men like Bacon, Gregory, and John, and men divine, because they are a part of the mortal pageant of great figures rather than because of any mortal error, as in the case of Plato.

> "Though it was now broad day, a gentle trace
> Of light diviner than the common sun
> Sheds on the common earth, and all the place
>
> "Was filled with magic sounds woven into one
> Oblivious melody, confusing sense
> Amid the gliding waves and shadows dun . . . ."
>
> (Ll. 337-342)

The approach of "A Shape all light" (line 352) is prefaced by the infusion in the world of the light of Intellectual Beauty. Shelley's description of this "Shape" fits in with his other descriptions of Asia, Emilia, the Witch of Atlas, and the Beauty in *Adonais,* whose smiling light kindles the Universe.

> there stood
>
> "Amid the sun, as he amid the blaze
> Of his own glory, on the vibrating
> Floor of the fountain, paved with flashing rays,—
>
> "A Shape all light, which with one hand did fling
> Dew on the earth, as if she were the dawn,
> And the invisible rain did ever sing
>
> "A silver music on the mossy lawn;
> And still before me on the dusky grass,
> Iris her many-coloured scarf had drawn:
>
> "In her right hand she bore a crystal glass,
> Mantling with bright Nepenthe; the fierce splendour
> Fell from her as she moved under the mass

"Of the deep cavern, and with palms so tender,
Their tread broke not the mirror of its billow."
(Ll. 348-362)

As Professor White shows, this vision is Intellectual Beauty as presented by Shelley in *The Witch of Atlas.* "The cave, the fountain (the 'burning Fountain' of *Adonais,* whence all beauty arises and to which it returns), the crystal glass which she offers to a few chosen spirits, the effect of its contents and of her presence, are all clearly recognizable properties of Shelley's beautiful Witch" (*Shelley,* II, 370).

"And underneath ethereal glory clad
The wilderness, and far before her flew
The tempest of the splendour, which forbade

"Shadow to fall from leaf and stone . . . ."
(Ll. 442-445)

For the intense light of Platonic Beauty in Shelley, see commentary on lines 337-342, *supra,* page 317.

The grove
"Grew dense with shadows to the inmost covers,
The earth was grey with phantoms, and the air
Was peopled with dim forms, . . .

I became aware
"Of whence those forms proceeded which thus stained
The track in which we moved. After brief space,
From every form the beauty slowly waned;

"From every firmest limb and fairest face
The strength and freshness fell like dust, and left
The action and the shape without the grace

"Of life.
(Ll. 480-483, 516-523)

The light of Intellectual Beauty gives way to the shadows of mortality and Life which supplant Rousseau's first vision. Shelley here is depicting the Platonic pattern of the eternal and transient through the imagery of light and shadow, which symbolize Reality and Appearance. The close relation of this imagery to the Platonism of *Adonais,* lines 460-463, is seen in Shelley's use of "stained" (l. 517), which contributes greatly to the Platonic character of the image in *Adonais* (see commentary *supra,* pp. 298-301). The imagery of light and darkness in *The Triumph of Life* lacks the clear-cut beauty of the lines in *Adonais,* but it embodies the same Platonic philosophy.

Zucca

January, 1822

Too happy Earth! over thy face shall creep
    The wakening vernal airs, until thou, leaping
From unremembered dreams, shalt   see
No death divide thy immortality.
                                (Ll. 13-16)

The doctrine of *Phaedo*, 71-73, is associated with cycles of nature.

I loved—oh, no, I mean not one of ye,
    Or any earthly one, though ye are dear
As human heart to human heart may be;—
    I loved, I know not what—but this low sphere
And all that it contains, contains not thee,
    Thou, whom, seen nowhere, I feel everywhere.
From Heaven and Earth, and all that in them are,
    Veiled art thou, like a   star.
                                (Ll. 17-24)

These lines to Jane Williams are a variant expression of the Platonic
Love which Shelley expresses for Emilia in *Epipsychidion*, lines 149-159
(see commentary *supra,* pp. 284-286). The poet discovers that the earthly
realm, though beautiful and dear, does not contain the perfect Reality
that his Platonic soul seeks. The transcendent character of Platonic
Beauty is emphasized in these lines, and Reality, as in the other poems, is
seen only through the Platonic veil.

The Magnetic Lady to Her Patient

1822

For the Platonic basis of this poem, see A. E. Taylor's note on
Timaeus, 70e ff.: "A serious alteration in health modifies the behaviour
of the blood and animal spirits. The modification may often be discovered from the patient's dreams when they would go undetected in
waking life, because the more massive movements due to peripheral
stimulations mask them. This was the foundation for the practice, common a century ago, of hypnotizing a patient and calling on him to diag-
nose his condition and prescribe for himself in the hypnotized state. (See
the description of the process in Shelley's poem *The Magnetic Lady
to Her Patient,* which refers to an experiment of this kind made on
himself.)" (A. E. Taylor, *A Commentary on Plato's Timaeus* [Oxford,
1928], p. 509). In her Journal entry for Monday, June 29, 1818, Mary

wrote, "Read the 'Magnetick Lady [Ben Jonson].'" The present poem, though written later, may reflect a possible reading and influence of this play on Shelley.

Lines:
"When the Lamp is shattered"
1822

> As music and splendour
> Survive not the lamp and the lute . . .
> (Ll. 9-10)

These lines are a direct echo of the thought of *Phaedo*, 86c.

With A Guitar, To Jane
1822

> And now, alas! the poor sprite is
> Imprisoned, for some fault of his,
> In a body like a grave.—
> (Ll. 37-39)

The imagery here is an echo of *Phaedo*, 62b, 67d, 82e, and *Cratylus*, 400b-c (cf. *Hellas*, l. 1058; Fragment written for *Hellas*, ll. 28-34).

> The artist who this idol wrought
> To echo all harmonious thought . . .
> (Ll. 43-44)

The Platonism of these lines has been clearly brought out in Dr. Garnett's note on Mr. Palgrave's emendation: "He [Mr. Palgrave] ingeniously conjectures *viol* for *idol* in the couplet:—

> "The artist who this *idol* wrought,
> To echo all harmonious thought."

But *idol* is used in the Platonic sense, and the guitar spoken of as the instrument by which harmonious thought, otherwise abstract and impalpable to the senses, is *imaged* forth (εἴδωλον)" (*Relics of Shelley* [London, 1862], pp. 97-98; cf. "I shall endeavour to . . . unveil the inmost idol of the error," Julian *Works*, X, 243, and *Epipsychidion*, ll. 267-268).

> Died in sleep, and felt no pain
> To live in happier form again . . .
> (Ll. 55-56)

The immortality of the soul is associated here, as in the *Epipsychidion* and *Adonais*, with Shelleyan love.

Commentary on the Platonism of Shelley's Prose and Letters

A. Prose Works[10]

A STUDY OF SHELLEY'S direct Platonism has shown that his compositions written shortly after periods of intense Platonic reading, such as in the years 1817, 1818, and 1820, reflect almost immediately an immense amount of Platonism. The same should be the case with Shelley's compositions written after his reading of Plato at Oxford. As we have seen in Hogg's account of Shelley's enthusiasm for Plato at Oxford, Shelley read a considerable number of Plato's dialogues and enthusiastically discussed their doctrines. Yet we have no corresponding reflection of this Platonism in Shelley's poetry written in 1812 and 1813. Shelley's refraction of this Platonism must have been in a volume of "moral and metaphysical essays" which he wrote at Keswick in 1811-1812. It is known that Shelley continued his studies in London and Keswick. As Professor White has pointed out: "From December 11, 1811, until the beginning of February he was engaged on no less than five literary projects, all but one of which were completed, or nearly completed, by the latter date" (*Shelley*, I, 191). One of these projects was a volume of essays which he mentions in a letter to his publisher Stockdale, dated August 1, 1811: "I am at present engaged in completing a series of moral and metaphysical essays—perhaps their copyright would be accepted in lieu of part of my debt?" (Julian *Works*, VIII, 137). We hear more of these essays in a letter to Elizabeth Hitchener dated December 26, 1811. "I do not proceed with my poem: the subject is not *now* to my mind. I am composing some essays which I design to publish in the summer" (Julian *Works*, VIII, 225). From another letter to Miss Hitchener, dated January 2, 1812, we learn that he had already written about 150 pages of the essays. These essays, which Shelley intended to publish at Dublin, were not published; what happened to the manuscript is not known. The loss of these moral and metaphysical essays leaves a big gap in the Platonism of Shelley. If we note Shelley's moral and metaphysical views at Oxford as revealed in Hogg's account, we can conjecture that the moral and metaphysical

[10] For the dating of Shelley's prose essays and fragments, see J. A. Notopoulos, "The Dating of Shelley's Prose," *PMLA*, LVIII (1943), 477-498.

content of these essays would have been largely Platonic in character, as is seen in the idealistic tone of his letters to Elizabeth Hitchener at the time. They would contain reflections of Shelley's enthusiastic study of Plato at Oxford and an elaboration of the Platonic idealism in Shelley's philosophical discussions there. If these essays survived, we should probably have as full an expression of Platonism as we find in Shelley's compositions written after his reading of the *Symposium, Phaedrus, Phaedo,* and *Republic* in Italy.

SHELLEY'S READING IN PLATO AND THE PLATONIC TRADITION, 1810-1813

See pages 172, 173-174, *supra.*

PLATONISM IN SHELLEY'S PROSE WRITTEN IN 1812

An Address to the Irish People
January, 1812

I wish to impress upon your minds, that without virtue or wisdom, there can be no liberty or happiness . . . .

(Julian *Works,* V, 235)

Shelley shares with Socrates the conviction that virtue (ἀρετή) and wisdom (σοφία) are the foundations of private and public good (see *Apology,* 30b).

A Letter to Lord Ellenborough
1812

In the name of justice, what answer is there to these questions? The answer which Heathen Athens made to Socrates, is the same with which Christian England must attempt to silence the advocates of this injured man— "He has questioned established opinions."

(Julian *Works,* V, 284)

This marks the first appearance in Shelley of Socrates as the prototype of a fearless liberal, as martyr and victim of the prejudices of society. Shelley had read the *Apology* at Oxford and uses the portrait of Socrates in this dialogue as a parallel in his defence of Eaton, who was sentenced for publishing Paine's *Age of Reason.*

Socrates was poisoned because he dared to combat the degrading superstitions in which his countrymen were educated. Not long after his death,

Athens recognized the injustice of his sentence; his accuser Melitus was condemned, and Socrates became a demigod.

(Julian *Works*, V, 289)

Compare commentary on preceding excerpt. The information for the
condemnation of Melitus comes not from Plato but from Diogenes
Laertius's *Lives of the Philosophers*, II, 43, which appears in Shelley's
reading for 1814. It is likely that Shelley found this information reflected in a handbook or in his readings in the Platonic tradition.

This belief [that Jesus was something divine], rolling through the lapse
of ages, acquired force and extent . . . .

(Julian *Works*, V, 290)

After the word "ages" Shelley added in *Queen Mab*, "met with the
reveries of Plato and the reasonings of Aristotle, and. . . ." With "the
reveries of Plato," compare commentary on the same phrase in Shelley's
notes to *Queen Mab, supra*, pages 137-138.

I mean not to compare Mr. Eaton with Socrates or Jesus. . . . But I will
assert that should a second Jesus arise among men; should such a one as
Socrates again enlighten the earth, lengthened imprisonment and infamous
punishment . . . would effect, what hemlock and the cross have heretofore
effected, and the stain on the national character, like that on Athens and
Judaea, would remain indelible . . . ; like the murder of Socrates, it [Eaton's
sentence] would secure the execration of every age.

(Julian *Works*, V, 291-292)

The association of Socrates and Jesus is also found in a fragment
On the Moral Teaching of Christ, in *The Triumph of Life*, line 134,
in the Prologue to *Hellas*, line 155, and in particular in "Socrates, the
Jesus Christ of Greece," *Fragments Connected with Epipsychidion*,
line 33.

SHELLEY'S READING IN PLATO AND THE PLATONIC TRADITION, 1814-1815

See page 189, *supra*.

PLATONISM IN SHELLEY'S PROSE WRITTEN IN 1814

A Refutation of Deism
Spring of 1814

An interesting aspect of the influence of Platonism on this essay is
Shelley's use of the form and dialectical technique of a Platonic dialogue.

Shelley was probably influenced in this by his reading of Berkeley's philosophical dialogues. Some of the doctrines of Eusebes and Theosophus ultimately go back to Plato, though Shelley probably met these doctrines in reading literature influenced by the Platonic tradition.

> . . . when we recollect . . . that the Theists, Anaxagoras, Pythagoras and Plato, vainly endeavoured by that human reason, which is truly incommensurate to so vast a purpose, to establish among philosophers the belief in one Almighty God, the creator and preserver of the world . . .
>
> (Julian Works, VI, 29-30)

Shelley has in mind here either the history of ancient theism in Cicero's *De natura deorum* or the account of it in Sir William Drummond's *Academical Questions,* both of which appear in his reading at this time (*vide supra,* pp. 83, 147-148). In Drummond's treatise in a dialogue between Hylus, Theophilus, and Eugenius, Hylus rejects the deistic systems of Plato and the other philosophers of antiquity as having been founded upon conjecture (*vide supra,* pp. 149-150).

> In creating the Universe, God certainly proposed to himself the happiness of his creatures. It is just, therefore, to conclude that he left no means unemployed, which did not involve an impossibility to accomplish this design. In fixing a residence for this image of his own Majesty, he was doubtless careful that every occasion of detriment, every opportunity of evil should be removed.
>
> (Julian Works, VI, 32-33)

The thought here is that of *Timaeus,* 29e-30c, though Shelley is reflecting it indirectly. The *Timaeus* with its doctrine of the Demiourgos and his creation, in which evil is accounted for by the flaw in the material upon which this creator imposes the pattern of Platonic forms, had a great influence on the Platonic tradition as found in Shelley's reading (*vide supra,* pp. 296-297).

> For to assert that the Creator is the author of all good, and the creature the author of all evil . . .
>
> (Julian Works, VI, 33)

See commentary above and Plato's argument in *Republic,* 379c, a passage which Shelley translated later (*vide infra,* p. 496).

> If there is motion in the Universe, there is a God. The power of beginning motion is no less an attribute of mind than sensation or thought.
>
> (Julian Works, VI, 45-46)

The argument here ultimately stems from *Phaedrus*, 245c; *Laws*, 895; *Theaetetus*, 153d (see J. B. Skemp, *The Theory of Motion in Plato's Later Dialogues* [Cambridge, 1942]). Shelley may have found this argument in any number of the philosophical sources he was reading at this time— Cicero's *Tusculan Disputations*, Drummond's *Academical Questions*, Lord Monboddo's *Of the Origin and Progress of Language*—all of which discuss Plato's theism.

Every thing which begins to exist must have a cause: every combination, conspiring to an end, implies intelligence.

(Julian *Works*, VI, 46)

For the ultimate source of this doctrine which permeates later religious and philosophic thought, see *Philebus*, 26e, 30d, and *Timaeus*, 28a-c. Shelley could have found it in almost any of his philosophical readings at this period.

The Assassins
August-September, 1814

All that was wonderful and lovely was collected in this deep seclusion. The fluctuating elements seemed to have been rendered everlastingly permanent in forms of wonder and delight. . . . No spectator could have refused to believe that some spirit of great intelligence and power had hallowed these wild and beautiful solitudes to a deep and solemn mystery.

(Julian *Works*, VI, 158-160)

For this foreshadowing of Shelley's Intellectual Beauty and Shelley's gradual abandonment of the doctrine of Necessity in *Queen Mab*, see commentary on *Hymn to Intellectual Beauty*, *supra*, pages 203-204.

SHELLEY'S READING IN PLATO AND THE PLATONIC TRADITION, 1816

See pages 195-196, *supra*.

PLATONISM IN SHELLEY'S PROSE WRITTEN IN 1816

On the Punishment of Death
Ca. 1816

That that within us which thinks and feels, continues to think and feel after the dissolution of the body, has been the almost universal opinion of mankind, and the accurate philosophy of what I may be permitted to term the modern Academy. . . .

(Julian *Works*, VI, 185)

The Platonic conception of immortality in this statement is made explicit by Shelley's reference to the Academy.

The philosopher is unable to determine whether our existence in a previous state has affected our present condition, and abstains from deciding whether our present condition will affect us in that which may be future. That, if we continue to exist, the manner of our existence will be such as no inferences nor conjectures, afforded by a consideration of our earthly experience can elucidate, is sufficiently obvious.

(Julian *Works*, VI, 186)

For Shelley's views on immortality, see pages 21-22, 175-176, *supra*.

Persons of energetic character, in communities not modelled with philosophical skill to turn all the energies which they contain to the purposes of common good . . .

(Julian *Works*, VI, 188)

A reference to the ideal state in the *Republic*.

Essay on Christianity
End of 1816 or early 1817

The Stoic the Platonist and the Epicurean, the Polytheist the Dualist and the Trinitarian, differ infinitely in their conceptions of its [God's] meaning. They agree only in considering it the most awful and most venerable of names, as a common term devised to express all of mystery or majesty or power which the invisible world contains.

(Julian *Works*, VI, 229)

The reference to the Platonist's conception of God reflects no specific doctrine in Plato. It forms a part of Shelley's general interest in Deism at this period.

Whosoever is no deceiver or destroyer of his fellowmen . . . may walk among his species, deriving from the communion with all which they contain of beautiful or of majestic, some intercourse with the Universal God.

(Julian *Works*, VI, 231)

Shelley here is approaching something of the Platonic interrelation of the Beautiful, the Good, and the Divine.

. . . the Power which models, as they pass, all the elements of this mixed universe to the purest and most perfect shape which it belongs to their nature to assume.

(Julian *Works*, VI, 235)

This description, which fits that of the Demiourgos in the *Timaeus*, 53a ff., is basically the same Power as appears in the *Hymn to Intellectual Beauty;* the conception is stated metaphysically rather than poetically as in the *Hymn.*

The unobscured irradiations from the fountainfire of all goodness shall reveal all that is mysterious and unintelligible until the mutual communications of knowledge and of happiness throughout all thinking natures constitute a harmony of good that ever varies and never ends. This is Heaven . . . when the benignant principle unt[rammel]led and uncontrolled, visits in the fulness of its power the universal frame of things.

(Julian *Works*, VI, 235-236)

Here we have in full bloom Plotinus's doctrine of emanation from the One (*vide supra*, pp. 86-88). This doctrine is transmuted into beautiful poetry in Coleridge's *Religious Musings*, lines 402-410, 414-415, and in his *Destiny of Nations*, lines 15-30. Since Shelley read Coleridge's poems in 1815, Coleridge may seriously be considered one of the sources of this Plotinian doctrine in Shelley. Shelley transmuted this doctrine in poetry in *Adonais*, where in lines 338-341 it appears as

> but the pure spirit shall flow
> Back to the burning fountain whence it came,
> A portion of the Eternal, which must glow
> Through time and change, unquenchably the same . . . .

See commentary on these lines, *supra*, pages 294-295.

. . . man by resembling God fulfils most accurately the tendencies of his nature. . . .

(Julian *Works*, VI, 239)

For Plato's similar notion of imitation of the divine, see *Theaetetus*, 176b.

Every human mind has, what Lord Beacon calls its "idola specus," peculiar images which reside in the inner cave of thought.

(Julian *Works*, VI, 241)

The reference is to Lord Bacon's *Novum Organum*, Aphorism 53, which Shelley read in 1815, and *De aug. scien. Lib.* V. c. 4. Bacon's "idola specus" directly refers to Plato's myth of the Cave in the *Republic*, 514 ff., where the chained prisoners behold before them the shadows of the passing images which are symbolical of the realm of sense and opinion. The passage forms one of the best examples of the indirect Platonic tradition in Shelley. It is of interest to note the appearance of this symbol in *Mont Blanc*, which was also written in 1816:

In the still cave of the witch Poesy,
Seeking among the shadows that pass by
Ghosts of all things that are, some shade of thee . . .

See commentary *supra*, pages 210-211. For the cave of thought, see *Ode to Liberty*, XVIII, 1; *Cenci*, II, ii, 89; *Julian and Maddalo*, line 573; *Laon and Cythna*, IX, 203; *Prometheus Unbound*, I, 659; and *Speculations on Metaphysics* (Julian *Works*, VII, 64). All these examples show that Plato's Cave became for Shelley a regular symbol for the mind, even when it has no direct connection with the metaphysical context of Plato's myth. Shelley was very fond of creating symbols or finding them in nature or in literary tradition to express the complexity of mind. We have an insight into the way Shelley's mind worked with respect to the image of the Cave in an excerpt from his notebook which Mary quoted in her note on *Prometheus Unbound:*

I find in one of his manuscript books some remarks on a line in the *Oedipus Tyrannus*, which shows at once the critical subtlety of Shelley's mind, and explains his apprehension of those "minute and remote distinctions of feeling, whether relative to external nature or the living beings which surround us," which he pronounces, in the letter quoted in the note to the *Revolt of Islam*, to comprehend all that is sublime in man.

"In the Greek Shakespeare, Sophocles, we find the image,

Πολλὰς δ' ὁδοὺς ἐλθόντα φροντίδος πλάνοις:

a line of almost unfathomable depth of poetry; yet how simple are the images in which it is arrayed!

Coming to many ways in the wanderings of careful thought.

If the words ὁδούς and πλάνοις had not been used, the line might have been explained in a metaphorical, instead of an absolute sense, as we say "ways and means," and "wanderings" for error and confusion. But they meant literally paths or roads, such as we tread with our feet; and wanderings, such as a man makes when he loses himself in a desert, or roams from city to city, as Oedipus, the speaker of this verse, was destined to wander, blind and asking charity. What a picture does this line suggest of the mind as a wilderness of intricate paths, wide as the universe, which is here made its symbol; a world within a world which he, who seeks some knowledge with respect to what he ought to do, searches throughout, as he would search the external universe for some valued thing which was hidden from him upon its surface."

In reading Shelley's poetry, we often find similar verses, resembling, but not imitating, the Greek in this species of imagery; for, though he adopted the style, he gifted it with that originality of form and colouring which sprung from his own genius.

This testament of Mary sheds light on Shelley's imagery of the cavern of the mind. Shelley took Plato's myth of the Cave and saw in it exactly what he saw in Sophocles's image. Shelley's image has no Neoplatonic connotations, as some writers think. He simply gifts Plato's image "with that originality of form and colouring which sprung from his own genius." Shelley's use of the stream in the *Speculations on Metaphysics* (Julian *Works*, VII, 64) is simply a variant imagery of nature to express the same meaning that he saw in Plato's Cave and Sophocles's "ways in the wanderings of careful thought."

To judge truly of the moral and philosophical character of Socrates it is not necessary to determine the question of the familiar Spirit which it is supposed that he believed to attend him. . . . the connection of the instance of Jesus Christ with the established religion of the country in which I write renders it dangerous to subject oneself to the imputation of introducing new gods or abolishing old ones, nor is the duty of mutual forbearance sufficiently understood to render it certain that the metaphysician and the moralist, even tho he carefully sacrifice a cock to Esculapius, may not receive something analogous to the bowl of hemlock for the reward of his labours.

(Julian *Works*, VI, 242)

This passage shows Shelley's familiarity with Plato's *Apology* and *Phaedo*. For the familiar Spirit which attended Socrates, see *Apology*, 40a-b; for the imputation of introducing new gods or abolishing old ones, see *Apology*, 26b-27d; for the sacrifice of a cock to Asclepius and the bowl of hemlock, see *Phaedo*, 117-118. For Shelley's association of Socrates with Jesus, see commentary *supra*, page 323. Shelley's interest in the daemon of Socrates is also shown in his note *On the Daemon of Socrates*, and in his letter to Horace Smith, June 29, 1822 (Julian *Works*, X, 410; *vide infra*, pp. 505-507.

This [Luke 4:18] is an enunciation of all that Plato and Diogenes have speculated upon the equality of mankind. They saw that the great majority of the human species were reduced to the situation of squalid ignorance . . . for the purpose of purveying for the luxury of a few, and contributing to the satisfaction of their thirst for power. . . . Plato wrote the scheme of a republic in which law should watch over the equal distribution of the external instruments of unequal power: honours, property. . . .

(Julian *Works*, VI, 244)

For the similarity of the doctrines of Christ and Plato, see Shelley's fragment *The Moral Teaching of Jesus Christ*. Shelley refers in this passage specifically to the fourth book of Plato's *Republic*, where the subjects he mentions are discussed.

Among true and real friends all is common . . . .

(Julian *Works*, VI, 245)

The proverb κοινὰ γὰρ τὰ τῶν φίλων is found in the *Phaedrus*, 279c; *Republic*, 424a, 449c; *Lysis*, 207c; and *Laws*, 739c. It is likely, however, that Shelley is translating here from Diogenes Laertius's *Life of Diogenes*, VI, 72: κοινὰ δὲ τὰ τῶν φίλων, "friends share all property in common." Shelley quotes from Diogenes Laertius's life of the philosopher shortly after this passage in the *Essay*. For an illustration of this in Shelley's life, see *The Letters of Mary W. Shelley*, edited by F. L. Jones, I, 7 note 2; *Harriet and Mary. Being the Relations between Percy Bysshe Shelley, Mary Shelley, and Thomas Jefferson Hogg*, edited by Walter Sidney Scott (London, 1944).

The only perfect and genuine republic is that which comprehends every living being.

(Julian *Works*, VI, 245)

This statement has thematic reference to Plato's *Republic*.

Before a man can be free and equal and truly wise he must cast aside the chains of habit and superstition, he must strip sensuality of its pomp and selfishness of its excuses, and contemplate actions and objects as they really are. He will discover the wisdom of universal love. . . . He will consider Ευγενειας δε και δοξας προσκοσμηματα κακιας ειναι, μονην τε ορθην πολιτειαν ειναι την εν κοσμω.

(Julian *Works*, VI, 246)

On the surface Shelley seems to be alluding to Plato's doctrines. Yet as the quotation, which has hitherto been unidentified, shows, Shelley has reference to Diogenes's philosophy, which is partially based on Plato's *Republic*. The quotation comes from Diogenes Laertius's *Life of Diogenes*, VI, 72; the full quotation runs εὐγενείας δὲ καὶ δόξας [καὶ τὰ τοιαῦτα πάντα διέπαιζε] προσκοσμήματα κακίας εἶναι [λέγων]· μόνην τε ὀρθὴν πολιτείαν εἶναι τὴν ἐν κόσμῳ. The translation for this is: "He would ridicule good birth and fame and all such distinctions, calling them showy ornaments of vice. The only true commonwealth was, he said, that which is as wide as the universe" (Loeb Classical Library). The translation of this unidentified quotation in Julian *Works*, VI (Notes), 368, is inaccurate. Leigh Hunt in the preface to *The Masque of Anarchy*, 1832, says, "I was looking the other day into a Diogenes Laertius that belonged to him, and almost the first passage I met with thus marked was a saying of the biographer's namesake, in which birth and honours

are treated with contempt." Shelley's copy of Diogenes Laertius passed
along with that of Plato's *Republic* into Leigh Hunt's library (see *The
Correspondence of Leigh Hunt* [London, 1862], I, 222).

Permit, therefore, the spirit of this benignant principle to visit your intellectual frame, or, in other words become just and pure. . . . The Universal
Harmony or Reason which makes your passive frame of thought its dwelling
in proportion to the purity and majesty of its nature, will instruct you if ye
are willing to attain that exalted condition, in what manner to posess [*sic*]
all the objects necessary for your material subsistence. . . . The man who has
fewest bodily wants approaches nearest to the divine nature.

(Julian Works, VI, 248)

Shelley here is on common ground with the Pythagorean doctrine as
expressed in *Phaedo*, 67a, 81. In fact Shelley's statement can be considered a summary of the *Phaedo*.

On the Doctrines of Christ

End of 1816 or early 1817

The most eminent philosophers of Greece had long been familiarized to
the boldest and most sublime speculations on God, on the visible world, and
on the moral and intellectual Nature of Man. The universality and unity of
God, the omnipotence of the mind of man, the equality of human beings and
the duty of internal purity, is either asserted by Pythagoras, Plato, Diogenes,
Zeno, and their followers, or may be directly inferred from their assertions.

(Julian Works, VII, 145)

The theme is the same as that in the *Essay on Christianity* (Julian
Works, VI, 244), a fact which supports Forman's view that this fragment
belongs to the *Essay*. The source of Shelley's view is partially his own
reading of these philosophers and partially reflections of his reading of
their doctrines as they are found in Diogenes Laertius's *Lives of the
Philosophers* (see lives of Diogenes, Zeno, Pythagoras, Plato). Shelley,
as we have seen, read Diogenes Laertius in 1814, and it is possible that
Rickman sent him a copy of Diogenes Laertius when Shelley requested
him on December 24, 1812, to send him Epicurus and Pythagoras, who
are included in the *Lives of the Philosophers*. In this passage the reference to Plato's doctrines of the equality of human beings and the duty
of internal purity is of course to the *Republic* and *Phaedo*.

Speculations on Metaphysics, III: *Difficulty of Analyzing the Human Mind*
1816

But thought can with difficulty visit the intricate and winding chambers which it inhabits. It is like a river whose rapid and perpetual stream flows outwards;—like one in dread who speeds through the recesses of some haunted pile, and dares not look behind. The caverns of the mind are obscure, and shadowy. . . .

(Julian *Works,* VII, 64)

For the Platonic image of caverns of the mind, see commentary on Shelley's statement, "Every human mind has, what Lord Bacon calls its 'idola specus,' peculiar images which reside in the inner cavern of thought," *supra,* pages 327-329.

Speculations on Morals, I: *Plan of a Treatise on Morals*
1816

It is necessary that material happiness produced by the common efforts, and preserved by the common care, should be distributed according to the just claims of each individual . . . .

(Julian *Works,* VII, 72)

This allusion to Plato's *Republic* is the same as that expressed in *Essay on Christianity,* Julian *Works,* VI, 244 (see commentary *supra,* p. 329).

An essay on the progressive excellence perceptible in the expressions—of Solomon, Homer, Bion and the Seven Sages, Socrates, Plato, Theodorus, Zeno, Carneades, Aristotle, Epicurus, Pythagoras, Cicero, Tacitus, Jesus Christ, Virgil, Lucan, Seneca, Epictetus, Antoninus . . . etc.

(Julian *Works,* VII, 72)

The list here reflects Shelley's reading of Diogenes Laertius's *Lives of the Philosophers,* where most of the above philosophers are discussed, and other classical reading found in Shelley's reading lists for 1814-1816. In view of the collocation of the names of Socrates and Plato with the rest of the philosophers found in Diogenes Laertius, it is evident that Shelley's intended essay would have discussed the writings of Plato and the thought of Socrates as found in the *Lives of the Philosophers* rather than in Plato's dialogues.

SHELLEY'S READING IN PLATO AND THE PLATONIC TRADITION, 1817

See pages 211-212, *supra*.

PLATONISM IN SHELLEY'S PROSE WRITTEN IN 1817

Note on the Banquet of Plato

Ca. August, 1817

The wonderful description of Love in Plato, Sympos. p. 214—particularly 214 l. 8—*l. ultima et passim* 218.

I should say in answer, that 'Ἔρως neither loved nor was loved, but is the cause of Love in others—a subtlety to beat Plato. *Agathon*, a poem

(Julian *Works*, VII, 160)

For a discussion of this note, see pages 382, 555, *infra*.

An Address to the People on the Death of Princess Charlotte

November 11-12, 1817

The Athenians did well to celebrate, with public mourning, the death of those who had guided the republic with their valour and their understanding, or illustrated it with their genius.

(Julian *Works*, VI, 74)

For the relation of this to Shelley's reading and translation of a portion of the *Menexenus*, see page 486, *infra*.

On Godwin's Mandeville

December, 1817

It is the genuine doctrine of "Political Justice" presented in one perspicuous and impressive view, and clothed in such enchanting melody of language, as seems, scarcely less than the writings of Plato, to realize those lines of Milton:—

(Julian *Works*, VI, 221)

Shelley reflects here his recent reading of the *Symposium*. For a similar comparison of *Mandeville* with Plato, see Shelley's letter to Godwin, December 7, 1817. For the Platonism in this novel, see page 147, *supra*.

SHELLEY'S READING IN PLATO AND THE PLATONIC TRADITION, 1818

See page 229, *supra*.

PLATONISM IN SHELLEY'S PROSE WRITTEN IN 1818

On Rhododaphne, or The Thessalian Spell
December, 1817—February, 1818

We sit with Plato by old Ilissus under the sacred Plane tree among the sweet scent of flowering sallows. . . . This it is to be a scholar; this it is to have read . . . Plato.

(Julian *Works*, VI, 273-274)

Shelley refers to the opening scene of the *Phaedrus,* which he read at Marlow, and speaks of his admiration for Peacock's scholarship, which played an important part in Shelley's reading of Plato (*vide supra*, pp. 44-47).

He there meets an old man who tells him that the flower he wears is the profane laurel-rose which grows in Larissa's unholy gardens, that it is impious to wear it in the temple of Love. . . . Anthemion enters the hall of the palace where, surrounded by sculptures of divine workmanship, he sees the earthly image of Uranian Love.

(Julian *Works*, VI, 275)

For the influence of the theme of Aphrodite Urania and Pandemos in Peacock's *Rhododaphne* on Shelley's *Prince Athanase*, see pages 51-52, *supra.*

Plato says, with profound allegory, that Love is not itself beautiful, but seeks the possession of beauty . . . .

(Julian *Works*, VI, 275)

Shelley here refers to *Symposium*, 201, a section which influenced him considerably (see *Epipsychidion* and *The Sensitive Plant*, ll. 76-77).

On the Symposium, Or Preface to the Banquet of Plato, A Fragment
July-August, 1818

For the text of the Preface and a discussion of Shelley's translation of the *Symposium,* see pages 402-403, 381-401, *infra.* The Preface gives us Shelley's own conception of Plato: he was both a poet and a philosopher, a reformer and an artist in language; his excellence consists in intuition; he embodied all that Shelley himself aspired to be. Behind this picture of Plato we see the yearnings and aspirations of Shelley's own soul and the strong ties that bound him to Plato's philosophy. In the Preface Shelley singles out Plato, who from now on appears to him as a god (*vide supra*, p. 66), as his ideal philosopher and the *Symposium* as the artistic masterpiece of Plato, a dialogue which exhibits the perfect fusion of philosophy, poetry, and artistry of language. As the commentary shows, this dialogue had the greatest influence on Shelley's poetry and prose.

For the association of Bacon with Plato and an explanation of Plato's "sophisms" and enthusiasm as the peculiar property of a poem, see Julian *Works,* II, 174; X, 26, 371; IX, 320-321; VII, 265; and pages 137-138, *supra.*

A Discourse on the Manners of the Antient Greeks Relative to the Subject of Love
July-August, 1818

Shelley wrote this essay to serve as a preface to his translation of the *Symposium* (*vide infra,* pp. 383-386). The influence of the *Symposium* is evident in the following passages:

> This object, or its archetype, forever exists in the mind, which selects among those who resemble it, that which most resembles it; and instinctively fills up the interstices of the imperfect image, in the same manner as the imagination moulds and completes the shape in clouds, or in the fire, into the resemblances of whatever form, animal, building etc., happens to be present to it.
>
> (*Infra,* p. 408)

Shelley is restating here Plato's theory of ideas and their relation to particulars as set forth in *Symposium,* 210-211; the archetype is grasped by mind alone, whereas the particulars in the world of time and space are imperfect images of this intellectual archetype. Thus far Shelley is in harmony with Plato; however, he interpolates an element which changes the Platonic complexion of the passage. Shelley makes poetic imagination play an integrating role between the particular and its Platonic archetype, whereas Plato stresses reason and makes the archetype not a mental concept but a transcendental, objective essence.

> . . . love, which is rather the universal thirst for a communion not merely of the senses, but of our whole nature, intellectual, imaginative, and sensitive . . .
>
> (*Infra,* p. 408)

Shelley is reshaping here a Platonic doctrine (*Symposium,* 207a ff.) in the image of his own nature (*vide supra,* page 22). Plato defined love as "the desire for the everlasting possession of the good." This desire for immortality is achieved through generation in the physical, spiritual, and intellectual realms. Shelley retains all the basic features of this Platonic doctrine with the exception of substituting Shelleyan sympathy in the place of desire for immortality; he also adds "imaginative and sensitive," which are characteristic of the poetic rather than the philosophic nature.

1st. That the person selected as the subject of this gratification should be as perfect and beautiful as possible, both in body and in mind; so that all sympathies may be harmoniously blended, and the moments of abandonment be prepared by the entire consent of all the conscious portions of our being. . . .

(Infra, p. 410)

Shelley echoes here the sentiment of Pausanias, in *Symposium,* 181:

Thus, not all love, nor every mode of love is beautiful, or worthy of commendation, but that alone which excites us to love worthily . . . . choosing in early youth as the objects of their love those in whom the intellectual faculties have begun to develop. (Shelley's translation)

. . . it will not be difficult to conceive the almost involuntary consequences of a state of abandonment in the society of a person of surpassing attractions, when the sexual connection cannot exist, to be such as to preclude the necessity of so operose and diabolical a machination as that usually described. This is the result apparently alluded to by Plato.

(Infra, p. 411)

Shelley defends the passion of homosexuality from the vulgar notions held about it by showing that Plato conceives it as involving higher elements which ennoble it.

The Coliseum
November 25, 1818

The influence of the *Symposium,* which Shelley had translated in July, and the *Discourse on the Manners of the Antient Greeks Relative to the Subject of Love* is evident in this fragment, which was inspired by a visit to the Coliseum on November 25, 1818. In her preface to the 1840 edition Mary Shelley says:

Shelley had something of the idea of a story in this. The stranger was a Greek, nurtured from infancy exclusively in the literature of his progenitors,— and brought up as a child of Pericles might have been; and to heighten the resemblance, Shelley conceived the idea of a woman, whom he named Diotima, who was his instructress and guide. In speaking of his plan, this was the sort of development he sketched; but no word more was written than appears in these pages.

(Julian *Works*, V, ix)

Just as Shelley had planned to write a poem about Agathon (see *Note on the Banquet of Plato*), so this fragment was intended to be a tale about Diotima, to whom Shelley refers in *Prince Athanase*, Fragment 3, lines 60-68; *Epipsychidion*, Fragments, lines 102-103; and *The Triumph of Life*, lines 260-262 (see commentary *supra*, pp. 228, 290, 316). This fragment contains echoes of her instruction of Socrates in *Symposium*, 199c-212b. The stranger who was nurtured from infancy on Greek literature is the counterpart of Shelley, whose enthusiasm and appreciation of Greek literature appear in the introduction to the *Discourse on the Manners of the Antient Greeks Relative to the Subject of Love.*

A nursling of man's art . . . transformed by the enchantment of Nature into a likeness of her own creations, and destined to partake their immortality!

(Julian *Works*, VI, 303)

This is but a variation of the poet's function as expressed in *Prometheus Unbound*, I, 743-749:

> He will watch from dawn to gloom
> The lake-reflected sun illume
> The yellow bees in the ivy-bloom,
> Nor heed nor see, what things they be;
> But from these create he can
> Forms more real than living man,
> Nurslings of immortality!

See commentary *supra*, pages 243-245.

"And this is Love. This is the religion of eternity, whose votaries have been exiled from among the multitude of mankind. O Power!" cried the old man, lifting his sightless eyes towards the undazzling sun, "thou which interpenetratest all things, and without which this glorious world were a blind and formless chaos, Love, Author of Good, God, King, Father! Friend of these thy worshippers! Two solitary hearts invoke thee, may they be divided never. . . . It is thine to unite, to eternize; to make outlive the limits of the grave those who have left among the living, memorials of thee."

(Julian *Works*, VI, 304)

This invocation to Love shows the influence of the speech of Aristophanes with its theme of the union of the two parts of the same soul (191d) and the speech of Diotima in which love "eternizes," i.e., is the seeking of something immortal in mortality (206c; cf. 208a-209e). This passage also contains a variant expression of the plastic interpenetration of Intellectual Beauty in this world, which appears in *Adonais*, lines 375-378 (see commentary on these lines, *supra*, p. 296).

> . . . that mystery, death, is a change which neither for ourselves nor for others is the just object of hope or fear. We know not if it be good or evil, we only know, it is. . . . We have no knowledge, if death be a state of sensation, of any precaution that can make those sensations fortunate, if the existing series of events shall not produce that effect.
>
> (Julian *Works*, VI, 305)

There is a reminiscence here of the thought and phraseology of *Apology*, 40c-e.

Ἔρως, *On Love*

Latter part of 1818

> . . . what is Love? It is that powerful attraction towards all that we conceive, or fear, or hope beyond ourselves, when we find within our own thoughts the chasm of an insufficient void, and seek to awaken in all things that are, a community with what we experience within ourselves . . . . there is something within us which, from the instant that we live, more and more thirsts after its likeness.
>
> (Julian *Works*, VI, 201)

Shelley's definition of love is similar to the more compact statement of it in the *Discourse on the Manners of the Antient Greeks Relative to the Subject of Love* (*vide supra*, p. 335). Here is an expression of Shelley's desire for sympathy and understanding, which is fused with Platonic love, the thirst of the soul after its own likeness (cf. *Symposium*, 189c-193d, 210-211). Shelley entitled this essay "Ἔρως, On Love," as Mary's transcript shows (*MS. Shelley adds. d. 8*, p. 148). The Greek portion of the title indicates that the essay was written shortly after the translation of the *Symposium*.

> We dimly see within our intellectual nature a miniature as it were of our entire self, . . . the ideal prototype of every thing excellent and lovely that we are capable of conceiving as belonging to the nature of man. . . . a soul within our soul that describes a circle around its proper Paradise. . . . The discovery of its antitype; the meeting with an understanding capable of clearly estimating our own; . . . this is the invisible and unattainable point to which Love tends; and to attain which, it urges forth the powers of man to arrest the faintest shadow of that, without the possession of which there is no rest.
>
> (Julian *Works*, VI, 201-202; text based on *MS. Shelley adds. d. 8*, pp. 149-150)

In this passage we have a reflection of two Platonic doctrines: the intellectual nature of Love and Beauty and the notion that Love is the union of two complementary parts of a once united soul, which is the theme of Aristophanes's speech in the *Symposium*. The Platonic nature of this Love is seen in its description as "ideal prototype," "antitype," "fainted shadow," which are Platonic terms for the Ideas and their shadows on earth. Since this fragment was written before *Epipsychidion*, we have here a foreshadowing of the Platonic conception which Shelley uses to express his love for Emilia. For the association of the words "miniature," "soul within our soul" with the title *Epipsychidion*, see commentary *supra*, pages 279-280.

On the Revival of Literature
1818-1819

In the refinements of the scholastic philosophy, the world seemed in danger of losing the little real wisdom that still remained as her portion; . . . Plato, the wisest, the profoundest, and Epicurus, the most humane and gentle among the ancients, were entirely neglected by them. Plato interfered with their peculiar mode of thinking concerning heavenly matters. . . .

(Julian Works, VI, 214)

Their neglect of Plato adds fuel to Shelley's antipathy toward the scholastics, and he regards the Middle Ages as an age of the tyranny of the church over the mind of man.

Shelley's Reading in Plato and the Platonic Tradition, 1819

See page 232, *supra*.

Platonism in Shelley's Prose Written in 1819
On the Daemon of Socrates
Memor. Lib. I
1819

Socrates' demon; one form of augury.

Socrates made a distinction between things subject to divination and things not subject to it. He said—a supernatural force has sway over the greatest things in all human undertakings (p. 5) and that the uncertainty belonging to them all, is the intervention of that power, or rather, that all events except those which the human will modifies, are modified by the divine will.

(Julian Works, VII, 266; text based
on MS. Shelley adds. d. 6, p. 1)

For a commentary of this fragment, which is based on Xenophon's *Memorabilia*, see pages 505-506, *infra*.

On Life
1819

The most refined abstractions of logic conduct to a view of life, which . . . strips, as it were, the painted curtain from this scene of things.

(Julian Works, VI, 194)

Shelley's philosophy of the illusory and unreal nature of life is stated here in the same Platonic imagery of the "painted veil" (*vide supra*, pp. 180, 231).

But I was discontented with such a view of things [materialism] as it afforded; man is a being of high aspirations, "looking both before and after," whose "thoughts wander through eternity," disclaiming alliance with transience and decay; incapable of imagining to himself annihilation; existing but in the future and the past. . . . Whatever may be his true and final destination, there is a spirit within him at enmity with nothingness and dissolution.

(Julian Works, VI, 194)

The influence of the *Phaedo* on Shelley's philosophy is shown not only here but in a similar statement in a letter to Horace Smith, dated April 11, 1822: "the doctrines of the French, and Material Philosophy, are as false as they are pernicious" (Julian *Works*, X, 378) (cf. "Plato . . . taught also a moral and intellectual system of doctrine, comprehending at once the past, the present, and the future condition of man" [Julian *Works*, VII, 127]).

The Moral Teaching of Jesus Christ
November, 1819

Doctrines of reform were never carried to so great a length as by Jesus Christ. The republic of Plato and the Political Justice of Godwin are probable and practical systems in the comparison.

The doctrines of Jesus Christ though excellent are not new. The immortality of the soul was already a dogma, familiar from all antiquity to every nation of the earth except the Jews. Plato said all that could be said on this subject; and whoever had aspired to excel this mighty mind, ought to have sought their information from undoubted sources. . . . The idea of forgiveness of injuries, the error of revenge, and the immorality and the inutility of punishment considered as punishment (for these [are] correlative doctrines) are stated by Plato in the first book of the Republic. . . .

(Julian *Works*, VI, 255-256; with additional lines from the text of this fragment as printed in Shelley, *Verse and Prose*, p. 111)

For Shelley's view of the affinities of Socrates and Jesus, see commentary on *A Letter to Lord Ellenborough* (Julian *Works*, V, 291-292); *Essay on Christianity* (Julian *Works*, VI, 242, 244); *On the Doctrines of Christ* (Julian *Works*, VII, 145), *supra*, pp. 323, 329, 331.

The trial of Richard Carlile, who was convicted for publishing Paine's *Age of Reason* and Palmer's *Principles of Nature*, stirred in Shelley a reaction against Christianity. A contributing factor to this reaction was Shelley's anger against a reviewer in the *Quarterly Review* who attacked Socrates and stated that there is "no philosophy so deep as the philosophy of Christianity" (*vide infra*, pp. 365-367). Shelley shows that Plato and his philosophy had prior validity and similarity to Christ's views. Shelley refers to Plato's teaching on the immortality of the soul *(Phaedo, passim)* and punishment *(Republic, 335, 379c)* as proof of his statement. Shelley had been reading the *Republic* and had translated parts of the second and third books. A parallel is found in Fragment VII of the translations from the *Republic*, where he says: "Plato's doctrine of punishment as laid down, p. 146, is refuted by his previous reasonings.—p. 26." For the references, see notes on Fragment VII, pages 496, 564, *infra*. These references and citations to the doctrines of Plato reveal Shelley's intimate knowledge of the *Republic*, which he was reading in 1819.

Prose Fragment [See Addendum, p. 494, *infra*]
1819-1820

In addition, when you would distinguish a philosophical [disposition] nature from one which is not, [consider] observe . . . whether it be servile or liberal; for all things a narrow littleness of [soul spirit] soul is the most $\begin{Bmatrix} \text{inauspicious} \\ \text{adverse} \end{Bmatrix}$ to a mind aspiring to embrace that comprehensive circle of divine & human nature beyond which nothing exists. . . . A cowardly & illiberal disposition is incapable of participating in the doctrines of true philosophy? Assuredly. But $\begin{Bmatrix} \text{he who is} \\ \text{the modest} \end{Bmatrix}$ free spirited [& gold despising] a despiser of wealth, neither insolent nor cowardly, would surely neither be nor unjust? Surely not. And [in the consideration] thus [by it] you may [discover] distinguish a philosophical man from one that is not so by observing from early youth whether its disposition is just & $\begin{Bmatrix} \text{gentle} \\ \text{[mild]} \end{Bmatrix}$ or savage desire;

... The true aspirant after knowledge ought from his earliest youth to affect

entire truth . . . { He / [Thou] } who { s / ha[ve] } been impelled toward knowledge

& { a / [its] } kindred discipline, seeks the ⌈sens⌉ pleasures of the soul [as within] as ⌈it⌉ they exists within itself, & omit the pursuit of bodily enjoyments; if indeed he be truly a philosopher & not a fictitious resemblance of that character. . . . Such a person must be temperate, & in no manner a lover of money; [for those things] for those things for the sake of which others devote their whole ⌈attention⌉ powers at whatever expense to obtain wealth, he disregards;

to ⌈any to⌉ him least of all mankind { could / [would] } there be any motive for accumulating wealth.

> (Shelley MS 2 pp. 4to—, Pforzheimer Collection, Peck, *Shelley, His Life and Work*, II [Appendix O], 433-434)

This portrait of a philosopher is largely Platonic. It has so many direct echoes from Plato's *Republic* (especially sections 475-476, 480, 484b, 485-487, 490, 494, 498) that it is evident that Shelley wrote this fragment when these sections in the *Republic* were fresh in his mind.

A Philosophical View of Reform
December 23, 1819—May 26, 1820

... the influence which is moved not but moves . . .

> (Julian *Works*, VII, 20)

Shelley is probably reflecting the doctrine of *Phædrus,* 245c, a dialogue which he finished reading on May 2, 1820 (see "A Refutation of Deism," Julian *Works*, VI, 45-46).

Morals and politics can only be considered as portions of the same science, with relation to a system of such absolute perfection as Christ and Plato and Rousseau and other reasoners have asserted. . . . Equality in possessions must be the last result of the utmost refinements of civilization. . . .

> (Julian *Works*, VII, 42-43)

Shelley is referring here to Plato's *Republic,* where morals and politics are portions of the same science and where community of property is essential in the ideal state. Shelley voices the same view in the *Essay on Christianity* (see commentary *supra,* pp. 330-331).

SHELLEY'S READING IN PLATO AND THE PLATONIC TRADITION, 1820

See page 265, *supra*.

PLATONISM IN SHELLEY'S PROSE WRITTEN IN 1820

Una Favola

1820

This fragment is of interest for Shelley's Platonism because of its similarity to the Platonic theme of *Alastor*. The youth in this tale, like the poet in *Alastor*, pursues a Love which is false. This quest involves the usual Shelleyan veiled women who are symbolic of Platonic abstractions.

They sang with such sweetness that perhaps the harmony of the spheres, to which the stars dance, is not so sweet. (Translation by R. Garnett)

(Julian *Works*, VI, 283)

For the Platonic music of the spheres, see page 173, *supra*.

On a Future State

1820

When you can discover . . . the music of the broken lyre, seek life among the dead.

(Julian *Works*, VI, 207)

This image, which is also repeated in *Lines: When the Lamp Is Shattered*, lines 9-10, is a direct echo of *Phaedo*, 86c, which Shelley read in 1820.

On a Passage in Crito

1821

For Shelley's reading of the *Crito* and the date of this note, see pages 502-503, *infra*.

Indeed, your city cannot subsist, because the laws are no longer of avail.

(Julian *Works*, VII, 265)

The reference is to *Crito*, 50b.

. . . when those who deserve to be nourished in the Prytanea at the public expense . . .

(Julian *Works*, VII, 265)

The reference is to *Apology*, 36d (see Sterling Dow, "The Guardians, Socrates, and Board 'in Prytaneion,'" *Classical Weekly*, XXXVII [1944], 130-132).

Although you have inflicted an injustice on me, which is sufficient, according to the opinions of the multitude, to authorise me to consider you and me as in a state of warfare . . .

(Julian *Works*, VII, 265)

The reference is to *Crito*, 49b.

. . . it would . . . be . . . delightful to me to die, surrounded by my friends, secure of the inheritance of glory, and escaping, after such a life as mine, from the decay of mind and body which must soon begin to be my portion should I live.

(Julian *Works*, VII, 265)

See Medwin, *Life of Shelley*, page 435, for an almost exact repetition of this passage. For its importance in the dating of this fragment, see page 502, *infra*.

The passage as a whole refers to the *Phaedo* and not to the *Crito*, the former being a dialogue which Shelley had translated in part in 1820. It alludes to the opening and closing scene of the dramatic death of Socrates and to the central doctrine of the *Phaedo*, the corrupt nature of the body.

Such are the arguments, which overturn the sophism placed in the mouth of Socrates by Plato.

(Julian *Works*, VII, 265)

For Shelley's association of Plato with sophisms, a reflection of the influence of French philosophy on Shelley, see pages 137-138, *supra*. For a similar statement of Plato's sophisms, see Preface to Shelley's translation of the *Symposium* and Shelley's note on the *Banquet* of Plato, *supra*, pages 402, 461. The recalcitrant tone shown in this note reveals Shelley's independence of mind and his consciousness of differences between his beliefs and those of Plato. This critical spirit shows that he is not a passive admirer of Plato.

On the Devil and Devils
1821

Plato following his master, Socrates, who had been struck with the beauty and novelty of the theistical hypothesis, as first delivered by the tutor of Pericles, supposed the existence of a God, and accommodated a moral system of the most universal character, including the past and present and the future condition of man, to the popular supposition of the moral superintendence of this one intellectual cause. . . . These hypotheses, though rude enough, are in no respect very absurd and contradictory. The refined speculations respecting the existence of external objects, by which the idea of matter is suggested, to which Plato has the merit of first having directed the attention of the thinking part of mankind. . .

(Julian *Works*, VII, 88)

The tutor of Pericles is Anaxagoras (see *Phaedrus*, 270a), of whom Socrates says, " I was delighted to think that I had found in Anaxagoras a teacher of the cause of things quite to my mind . . ."(*Phaedo*, 97d). This delight, however, turns into a disappointment when Socrates discovers that Anaxagoras by mind means a material substance.

Although Shelley had read the *Phaedo* in the original, he is also echoing Sir William Drummond's *Academical Questions*, as the following quotations show: "Plato, in speaking of the primary matter, from which modern philosophers have borrowed their doctrine concerning material substance, observes, *that it is a question dubiously to be understood, and difficult to be comprehended*" (I, 41); "Plato in the Phaedo has censured him [Anaxagoras] with much severity *for not using mind, and not seeking any causes in the order and government of the world, but aerial, aetherial, aquatic, and many other absurd causes.* Nevertheless Plato had acknowledged Anaxagoras to be a theist" (I, 214). For another discussion of the theism of Plato, see Lord Monboddo, *Antient Metaphysics*, Introduction and I, 230.

But the Greek Philosophers abstained from introducing the Devil. They accounted for evil by supposing that what is called matter is eternal, and that God in making the world, made not the best that he, or even inferior intelligence could conceive; but that he moulded the reluctant and stubborn materials ready to his hand, into the nearest arrangement possible to the perfect archetype existing in his contemplation.

(Julian *Works*, VII, 88-89)

Shelley here is referring to Plato's account in *Timaeus*, 28 ff., as is also evident from his reference to "the Platonic scheme" (Julian *Works*, VII, 90). Plato's doctrine in the *Timaeus*, of the Demiourgos who looks to the archetype of ideas in his creation and imposes form on recalcitrant matter, which is the cause of evil in the world, is one of the most influential ideas in the Platonic tradition (*vide supra*, pp. 92-93, 235-237). Shelley, however, may not be referring to the *Timaeus* itself, but to Lord Monboddo's *Antient Metaphysics*, Vol. I, Book II, chapter 1, which discusses the *Timaeus* and Plato's views on matter; compare *ibid.*, Vol. VI, Book III, chapter 7.

Is it possible that Socrates seriously believed that Aesculapius would be propitiated by the offering of a cock?

(Julian *Works*, VII, 91)

This is a direct allusion to *Phaedo*, 118, which Shelley read in 1820. For an echo of this incident, see *Essay on Christianity*, Julian *Works*, VI, 242 (*vide supra*, p. 329).

"In Egypt the Serpent was an hieroglyphic of eternity."

(Julian *Works*, VII, 103)

For commentary, see pages 186-188, *supra*.

A Defence of Poetry
February 22?—March 12?, 1821

The Platonism in this essay goes deeper than incidental borrowing. Plato no less than Peacock had attacked poetry, and the defense of poetry in Shelley's essay must be interpreted as an answer to both. But Shelley rejects Plato's attack on art in the tenth book of the *Republic*, only to accept Plato's view of poetry in the *Ion* and the *Phaedrus*. Plato offered Shelley two contradictory views of poetry: in the *Republic* Plato attacks not only bad poets but poetry itself, yet in the *Ion* and *Phaedrus* he states that poetry is an emanation of divinity. Shelley's defense makes use of the latter thesis to attack the former. In order to understand Shelley's defense of poetry we must understand Plato's attack on art in the tenth book of the *Republic*. This may be regarded from two points of view: (1) the standard of perfection in art being such and such, all the works which fall short of it are bad, or (2) all art is bad because it has no standards. One might maintain the first view because the art of Plato's day failed to come up to the standard of perfection. It is wrong, however, to think that Plato attacked only bad art. Plato's fundamental view about art is as follows: In sense perception the objects that we perceive are ambiguous and contradictory, and the emotions we experience in their perception are equally various and conflicting. Nothing can be valuable which is not organized by a standard of its own. This standard is supplied both for perceptions and emotions by philosophy and ultimately in both cases by the Idea of the Good. A work of art claims to be something other than a mere recording of sense perceptions and a mere feeling of perceptions. The artist selects, but qua artist he has no standard of selection except pleasure (ἡδονή). His services may be valuable in so far as the pleasure he provides may for the undeveloped man sugar the pill of logical or moral instruction. But if we turn to art for an independent standard of artistic excellence, then we are in a state of logical and moral delusion. Plato's real position in art is stated in the *Republic*, 603a10-603b1: "This, then, was what I wished to have agreed upon when I said that poetry, and in general the mimetic art, produces a product that is far removed from truth in the accomplishment of its task, and associates with the part in us that is remote from intelligence, and is its companion and friend for no sound and true purpose." The essence then of Plato's attack is that the artist has no standard. Shelley's defense rests essentially on Plato's view of poetry as something divine (see *Ion* and *Phaedrus,* 245a, a passage to which Shelley refers in his letter to Peacock dated August 16, 1818). "Poetry," he says, "is indeed something divine. It is at once the centre and circumference of knowledge; it is that which comprehends all science, and that to which all science must be referred." This is Shelley's reply to Plato's attack in the *Republic*.

Woven into the texture of Shelley's essay are all the fundamental doctrines of Plato about Intellectual Beauty, immortality, the relative and absolute world. Poetry for Shelley is philosophy itself: "a poet," he says, "participates in the eternal, the infinite, and the one." Poetry has for Shelley the same function as Eros in the *Symposium:* it is an intermediary daemon between man and the divine; like Love it leads us from the earthly to the divine; it strips the world of the veil of unreality and enables us to see the Ideal Beauty. In his essay Shelley has refracted all the rays of the Platonism that had previously appeared in his poetry through the prism of poetry; the doctrines of the *Symposium,* the *Phaedrus,* and the *Ion,* and the metaphysics of the *Republic* all emerge in the essay with Shelleyan coloration. Poetry, says Shelley, "strips the veil of familiarity from the world, and lays bare the naked and sleeping beauty, which is the spirit of its forms"; it "purges from our inward sight the film of familiarity which obscures from us the wonder of our being." Thus poetry, like philosophy, reveals reality and Intellectual Beauty. It "makes immortal all that is best and most beautiful in the world"; it "redeems from decay the visitations of the divinity in Man"; it "defeats the curse which binds us to be subjected to the accident of surrounding impressions" (cf. "Sweet Benediction in the eternal Curse," *Epipsychidion,* l. 25, and "That Benediction which the eclipsing Curse," *Adonais,* l. 480); "what were the scenery of this beautiful Universe which we inhabit; what were our consolations on this side of the grave, and what were our aspirations beyond it, if Poetry did not ascend to bring light and fire from those eternal regions?" In all these statements we see the Platonic immortality of the *Phaedo,* which, as seen in *Adonais* and *Epipsychidion,* is always an attribute of Ideal Beauty. Furthermore, poetry "creates for us a being within our being." What is this but the Platonic soul as described in *Epipsychidion* and the fragment *On Love?* Poetry for Shelley is the Platonic quest for beauty in all the planes of life, the physical, moral, and intellectual. In this essay the cloud of Shelley's own mind is "discharging its collected lightning" from Plato into a vast, comprehensive, and all-inclusive conception of the nature of poetry. Although Shelley does not unify all these Platonic strands, nevertheless we see in all of them a restatement of the Platonic philosophy that Shelley expressed in his poetry. Poetry, like Shelley's Platonic women, is but the means by which Intellectual Beauty finds expression in the world of time and space. As Professor White puts it, ". . . poetry is to Shelley simply the voice of Intellectual Beauty, . . . Intellectual Beauty is itself the sum of all true Imagination conceivable and inconceivable, . . . the individual human imagination flows from this fountain and back into it and is the nearest human contact with the Divine" (*Shelley,* II, 278).

Even though Plato and Shelley do not agree as to the nature of poetry, they do agree about the use of poetry in the regeneration of man. Poetry, Shelley maintains, improves man morally and awakens the human spirit. "The great secret of morals," says Shelley, "is love; or a going out of our own nature, and an identification of ourselves with the beautiful which exists in thought, action, or person, not our own. A man, to be greatly good, must imagine intensely and comprehensively; he must put himself in the place of another and of many others. . . . The great instrument of moral good is the imagination; and poetry administers to the effect by acting upon the cause." Like Shelley, Plato recognizes the propaedeutic power of poetry in the habituation of moral feeling. "Let our artists," says Plato, "rather be those who are gifted to discern the true nature of beauty and grace; then will our youth dwell in a land of health, amid fair sights and sounds, and receive the good in everything; and beauty, the effluence of fair works, shall flow into the eye and ear, like a health-giving breeze from a purer region, and insensibly draw the soul from earliest years into likeness and sympathy with the beauty of reason" (*Republic,* 401). By supplanting reason with imagination Shelley makes poetry not a mere stage at a certain level of education, but education itself. Thus Plato and Shelley agree as to the function of poetry in education, but differ as to the primacy of reason or imagination in the educational process.

In Shelley's conception of poetry we also see a similarity to Plotinus. Like Keats's soul in *Adonais*, poetry is to Shelley a portion of the Eternal which flows from and returns to this fountain, bringing with it "the light and fire from those eternal regions." Shelley has woven into his conception of poetry the Plotinean theory of emanation which he expresses in *Adonais* and in particular in the *Essay on Christianity* (*vide supra*, pp. 294-295). Furthermore, Shelley's view of art is Plotinian rather than Platonic. As we have seen in *A Discourse on the Manners of the Antient Greeks*, he restates Plato's theory of Ideas and their relation to particulars in terms of imagination rather than reason (*vide supra*, pp. 335-336). He bases poetry on imagination rather than on reason; imagination is an active creative agent which synthesizes rather than analyzes.

This conception reappears in *A Defence of Poetry* as "Poetry enlarges the circumference of the imagination by replenishing it with thoughts of ever new delight, which have the power of attracting and assimilating to their own nature all other thoughts, and which form new intervals and interstices whose void for ever craves food."

The affinities of this view of poetry with Plotinus rather than Plato are marked, though in the absence of proof we must be cautious about deducing any derivative relation, for if Shelley's essay shows anything clearly, it shows his own creative powers of thought. Dean Inge has pointed out how Plotinus in *Enneads,* V, viii, 1; ix, 2, 11, "agrees with Philostratus, who in an epoch-making passage [*Vit. Apoll.,* VI, 19] says that great works of art are produced not by imitation (the Aristotelian μίμησις) but by imagination (φαντασία), 'a wiser creator than imagination [*sic*, imitation], for imitation copies what it has seen, imagination what it has not seen'" (W. R. Inge, *The Philosophy of Plotinus,* II, 215, quoted in P. E. More, *Hellenistic Philosophies,* p. 185). Plotinus, unlike Plato, does not view the artist as one who imitates imitations (cf. *Republic,* 596e ff.). The question which Plotinus asked and answered was, as More points out, "Why . . . did not Plato, taught by his own technique, understand that the great artist has his eye fastened not on nature or manufactured objects as on an opaque veil, but is really looking through these to the Ideas behind the curtain? Why did he not see that the artist is no slave of nature, but at once her lover and, as it were, her corrector and finisher, and more truly a maker than he who fashions works of utility with his hands?" (More, *Hellenistic Philosophies,* p. 185). The answer which Shelley gave to Plato is the same as that Plotinus gave to Plato, and in so doing we may also apply to Shelley

More's appraisal of Plotinus's theory of art: " . . . he justified Platonism as the artist's philosophy *par excellence.*"

Yet the influence of direct Platonism on the essay is great. Shelley had translated the *Symposium* and had read in the preceding year Plato's *Phaedo, Phaedrus,* and *Republic.* In acknowledging the receipt of Peacock's essay which provoked the composition of his own essay, Shelley wrote, "I was at that moment reading Plato's *Ion,* which I recommend you to reconsider." This statement gives us an insight into Shelley's Platonic frame of mind in writing the essay. Coupled with such indirect Platonism as is found in Sir Philip Sidney's *Defence of Poesie* (for Shelley's quotation from this in the Journal, see R. Glynn Grylls, *Mary Shelley,* p. 274), the dialogues of Plato which Shelley read form an important contribution to the color of phraseology and the texture of Shelley's thoughts. Shelley found in Plato a kindred spirit, despite their differences of outlook on poetry. He used the treasure of Plato's dialogues in the spirit of the statement in the *Essay on Christianity:* "Among true and real friends all is common." As this introduction and the following detailed analysis of Platonic passages show, the Platonism in this essay represents the high-water mark of Shelley's Platonism.

Reason is to imagination . . . as the shadow to the substance. . . .

(Julian *Works,* VII, 109)

Shelley's sentence is Platonic only in the imagery used (cf. *Republic,* 510a). Compare "as the shadow is less vivid than the substance," Julian *Works,* VII, 125.

Man is an instrument over which a series of external and internal impressions are driven, like the alternations of an ever-changing wind over an Aeolian lyre, which move it by their motion to ever-changing melody.

(Julian *Works,* VII, 109)

This conception of man has certain affinities with Plato's conception of man as the instrument of divine expression in the *Ion,* but Shelley may only be echoing here Coleridge's lines:

> And what if all of animated nature
> Be but organic Harps diversely fram'd,
> That tremble into thought, as o'er them sweeps
> Plastic and vast, one intellectual breeze,
> At once the Soul of each, and God of all?
> (*The Eolian Harp,* ll. 44-48)

A child at play by itself will express its delight by its voice and motions. . . .

(Julian *Works*, VII, 110)

Compare " In the youth of the world, men dance and sing and imitate natural objects . . ." (Julian *Works*, VII, 111).

In these lines we may have a direct echo of a passage in Plato's *Laws* which Shelley transcribed in the notebook containing the rough draft of *A Defence of Poetry*. See Shelley's *Prose in the Bodleian Manuscripts*, edited by A. H. Koszul (London, 1910), page 122: "On ff. 88 v. rev. and 87 rev. Shelley transcribed the delightful passage in Plato's *Leges* (ii. 653-654) which contrasts the disordinate cries and motions of children and animals with the human aspirations after rhythm and harmony, and attributes the latter to the teaching of the Muses, Apollo and Dionysos."

A poet participates in the eternal, the infinite, and the one; as far as relates to his conceptions, time and place and number are not.

(Julian *Works*, VII, 112)

Shelley is creating his poet in the image of the Platonic philosopher (cf. *Symposium*, 211a).

Language, colour, form, and religious and civil habits of action, are all the instruments and materials of poetry; they may be called poetry by that figure of speech which considers the effect as a synonyme of the cause. But poetry in a more restricted sense expresses those arrangements of language, and especially metrical language, which are created by that imperial faculty, whose throne is curtained within the invisible nature of man.

(Julian *Works*, VII, 113)

Plato makes the same distinction in *Symposium*, 205c.

The distinction between poets and prose writers is a vulgar error. . . . Plato was essentially a poet—the truth and splendour of his imagery, and the melody of his language, is the most intense that it is possible to conceive. He rejected the measure of the epic, dramatic and lyrical forms, because he sought to kindle a harmony in thoughts divested of shape and action, and he forbore to invent any regular plan of rhythm which should include, under determinate forms, the varied pauses of his style. Cicero sought to imitate the cadence of his periods, but with little success.

(Julian *Works*, VII, 114)

This appraisal of Plato as a poet is a variant expression of a similar conception in Shelley's *Preface to the Banquet of Plato* (see commentary *supra*, pp. 334-335). Shelley shares with Sidney the belief that the distinction between poetry and prose is only nominal, and both cite Plato to prove this point. It is possible that Shelley also met with the same conception in Aristotle's *Poetics,* 1451b, a work which is mentioned in Hogg's correspondence with Shelley in 1817 (see Scott, *The Athenians,* pp. 37-38, 43); a reference to Aristotle's definition of comedy, apparently in Shelley's writing, found at the end of Claire Clairmont's Diary for March 7, 1819, to August 1, 1820 (see R. Glynn Grylls, *Claire Clairmont,* p. 252), along with a quotation from Aeschylus's *Prometheus Bound* and a Latin translation of a Greek epigram (*A.P.,* IX, 549), also suggests a possible reading of Aristotle's treatise. The reference to Plato's rejection of poetic forms probably refers to Plato's burning of his youthful poetical compositions after hearing Socrates. This incident is mentioned in Diogenes Laertius's *Life of Plato,* III, 5, which Shelley had read.

... it [poetry] acts in a divine and unapprehended manner. . . .

(Julian *Works,* VII, 116)

This is Plato's doctrine in the *Ion* (see commentary *supra,* p. 346, on the influence of Plato's doctrine on Shelley's conception of poetry).

The beauty of the internal nature cannot be so far concealed by its accidental vesture. . . .

(Julian *Works,* VII, 117)

The phrase "accidental vesture" is a variant of Shakespeare's "muddy vesture of decay" (*Merchant of Venice,* IV, ii, 64), which expresses the status of the body in comparison with the soul in Plato's philosophy (see *Phaedo,* 65-67, 81). Shelley also uses it in this sense in *Fiordispina,* line 79: "When, once of mortal [vesture] disarrayed. . . ."

Few poets of the highest class have chosen to exhibit the beauty of their conceptions in its naked truth and splendour; and it is doubtful whether the alloy of costume, habit, etc., be not necessary to temper this planetary music for mortal ears.

(Julian *Works,* VII, 117)

Shelley is applying to poetry the Platonic conception of Beauty. Intellectual Beauty is so intensely bright that she must be seen through a veil (cf. *Prometheus Unbound,* II, v, 55; *Epipsychidion,* ll. 21-32; and see commentary on these lines, *supra,* pp. 249-250, 281-282). Similarly, the beauty of Poetry is so insupportable in its pristine purity that it needs the alloy of costume or habit to temper it for mortal eyes. The alloy of costume or habit here is of course the body, the "mortal vesture" of the *Phaedo* (*vide supra,* pp. 174, 308), which is synonymous with Shelley's use of the veil. A parallel for the planetary music of poetry is found in Sidney's *The Defence of Poesie:* ". . . you cannot heare the Planet-like Musicke of *Poetrie*" (*The Complete Works of Sir Philip Sidney,* ed. Albert Feuillerat [Cambridge, 1923], III, 45). For the music of the spheres, see commentary *supra,* page 173.

> The whole objection, however, of the immorality of poetry rests upon a misconception of the manner in which poetry acts to produce the moral improvement of man.
>
> (Julian Works, VII, 117)

Shelley is referring here to Plato's charges of immorality in poetry (see *Republic,* 379 ff.).

> But Poetry acts in another and diviner manner. . . . Poetry lifts the veil from the hidden beauty of the world, and makes familiar objects be as if they were not familiar; it reproduces all that it represents, and the impersonations clothed in its Elysian light stand thenceforward in the minds of those who have once contemplated them, as memorials of that gentle and exalted content which extends itself over all thoughts and actions with which it coexists. The great secret of morals is love; or a going out of our own nature, and an identification of ourselves with the beautiful which exists in thought, action, or person, not our own.
>
> (Julian Works, VII, 117-118)

For the Platonism in these lines, see commentary *supra,* pages 347-348.

> The sacred links of that chain have never been entirely disjoined, which descending through the minds of many men is attached to those great minds, whence as from a magnet the invisible effluence is sent forth, which at once connects, animates, and sustains the life of all.
>
> (Julian Works, VII, 124)

These lines are found in f. 60 rev. of the Bodleian notebook containing a draft of the essay. Koszul, who edited this draft of the essay, says: "There is a blank of a few lines at the top of f. 60 rev., and a note at the bottom says: 'This is the language of Plato'" (*Shelley's Prose in the Bodleian Manuscripts,* ed. A. H. Koszul, p. 83 n. 3). This acknowledgment by Shelley of the Platonic language in these lines must be connected with Fragments I and II in Koszul's Appendix of unpublished drafts and notes for *A Defence of Poetry* (pp. 121-122), which are not, as Koszul thinks, variant fragments composed by Shelley but actually Shelley's translation of *Ion,* 533d3-534b7, of which the above lines are a summary. As will be shown (*vide infra,* p. 482), the translation of these two passages was made earlier than Shelley's translation of the *Ion* and was intended for use in this essay. For the important role which the *Ion* plays in Shelley's thought in the essay, see commentary *supra,* page 347.

The Past, like an inspired rhapsodist, fills the theatre of everlasting generations with their harmony.

(Julian *Works,* VII, 125)

Shelley here uses Plato's picture of Ion, the inspired rhapsodist (*Ion,* 535d-e), and Agathon and applies it to the Past. Cf. *infra,* p. 417.

At a certain period after the prevalence of doctrines founded upon those promulgated by him, the three forms into which Plato had distributed the faculties of mind underwent a sort of apotheosis, and became the object of the worship of Europe.

(Julian *Works,* VII, 126)

The three faculties of mind are the appetitive, the spirited, and the rational, as discussed by Plato in the *Republic,* 435a ff. They constitute the Platonic soul, and their influence on subsequent thought has been profound. This and the following references to the *Republic* show the impression which its reading in 1820 had made on Shelley.

Listen to the music, unheard by outward ears. . . .

(Julian *Works,* VII, 126)

An allusion to the Platonic music of the spheres (*vide supra,* p. 173).

The principle of equality has been discovered and applied by Plato in his Republic, as the theoretical rule of the mode in which the materials of pleasure and power produced by the common skill and labour of human beings ought to be distributed among them.

(Julian *Works,* VII, 127)

The reference is to the *Republic,* 416e, 420a, 422d, 464, 543. This doctrine was a favorite of Shelley, as may be seen from his reference to it in *The Essay on Christianity* (Julian *Works,* VI, 244), *The Speculation on Morals* (Julian *Works,* VII, 72), and *A Philosophical View of Reform* (Julian *Works,* VII, 42-43).

Plato, following the doctrines of Timaeus and Pythagoras, taught also a moral and intellectual system of doctrine, comprehending at once the past, the present, and the future condition of man.

(Julian *Works,* VII, 127)

This statement is also echoed in *On the Devil and Devils* as "Plato ... supposed the existence of a God, and accommodated a moral system of the most universal character, including the past the present and future condition of man, to the popular supposition of the moral superintendence of this one intellectual cause" (Julian *Works*, VII, 88; cf. VI, 194; and commentary *supra*, pp. 344-345).

Love, which found a worthy poet in Plato alone of all the antients, has been celebrated by a chorus of the greatest writers of the renovated world. . . .
(Julian *Works*, VII, 128)

The reference of course is to the *Symposium* and in particular to the speeches of Agathon and Diotima and Socrates which Shelley admired and praised. Compare *Prince Athanase*, Fragment 3, lines 60-68; *Epipsychidion*, Fragments, lines 101-108; *Note on the Banquet of Plato;* Letter to Godwin dated December 7, 1817 (Julian *Works*, IX, 260).

There are two modes or degrees of pleasure, one durable, universal and permanent; the other transitory and particular.
(Julian *Works*, VII, 132)

For a discussion of these two kinds of pleasure, see *Republic*, 583a, 585c, 586-587.

Poetry is not like reasoning, a power to be exerted according to the determination of the will. A man cannot say, "I will compose poetry." The greatest poet even cannot say it: for the mind in creation is as a fading coal, which some invisible influence, like an inconstant wind, awakens to transitory brightness.
(Julian *Works*, VII, 135)

Shelley transposes Plato's thought in *Ion*, 533d-535a; *Apology*, 22c; *Phaedrus*, 245a, in terms of an original and brilliant image. For Shelley's talent for creating natural Platonic imagery, see commentary on *Adonais*, lines 462-463, pages 298-301, *supra*.

It is as it were the interpenetration of a diviner nature through our own. . . . Poetry redeems from decay the visitations of the divinity in Man.
(Julian *Works*, VII, 136-137)

For Shelley's Platonic view of poetry here, see commentary *supra*, pages 347-348.

. . . it strips the veil of familiarity from the world, and lays bare the naked and sleeping beauty, which is the spirit of its forms.
(Julian *Works*, VII, 137)

Shelley assigns to poetry a function similar to that of art in Plotinus's philosophy (see commentary *supra,* pp. 349-350). For Shelley poetry lifts "the veil of life" and enables us to see Intellectual Beauty.

Poetry, as has been said, in this respect differs from logic, that it is not subject to the controul of the active powers of the mind. . . .
> (Julian *Works,* VII, 138)

This is a restatement of Plato's conception of poetry in the *Ion.*

The persons in whom this power resides, may often . . . have little apparent correspondence with that spirit of good of which they are the ministers. . . . Poets are the hierophants of an unapprehended inspiration. . . .
> (Julian *Works,* VII, 140)

Shelley restates once more with kaleidoscopic variety Plato's conception of poetry in the *Ion.*

Poets are the unacknowledged legislators of the world.
> (Julian *Works,* VII, 140)

For poets as the acknowledged legislators of the Greek world, see *Republic,* 599e, and James Adam's remark on this passage (*The Republic of Plato* [Cambridge, 1902], II, 399).

Fragments

Poetry is the medicinal honey of those bees, who feed upon the sweetest dew of the softest flowers of thought.
> (Koszul, *Shelley's Prose in the Bodleian Manuscripts,* Fragment III
> [Appendix], p. 122)

This is an elaboration of Plato's image in *Ion,* 534, the translation of which as found in the Bodleian notebook reads: "For Poets tell us that flying like bees, and wandering over the gardens and meadows and the honey flowing fountains of the Muses they return to us laden with sweet melodies, and they speak truth: for a poet is a thing aetherially light; winged and sacred. . . ."

. . . it [poetry] . . . is the Serpent which clasps eternity.
> (Koszul, *Shelley's Prose* . . . , III, 122)

For commentary, see pages 186-188, *supra.*

B. Letters

Letter to Elizabeth Hitchener
June 20, 1811

. . . then do I suppose . . . that neither will soul perish; that in a future existence it will lose all consciousness of having formerly lived elsewhere, will begin life anew, possibly under a shape of which we have no idea.

(Julian *Works*, VIII, 108)

Shelley's letters to Elizabeth Hitchener are full of statements about the immortality of the soul. If we compare these statements with Shelley's enthusiasm for Plato's doctrine of immortality as shown in Hogg's account of Shelley at Oxford (*vide supra*, pp. 32, 35-36), we can be fairly certain that these statements show the profound influence of Plato's *Phaedo*. They also give us a clue as to what might have been the Platonic content of the metaphysical and moral essays which Shelley was writing in the latter part of 1811 (*vide supra*, pp. 321-322).

Letter to Elizabeth Hitchener
June 25, 1811

You have witnessed *one* suspension of intellect in dreamless sleep. . . . you witness another in Death.

(Julian *Works*, VIII, 115)

Compare commentary *supra*. The argument here is tangent to *Apology*, 40.

Letter to Elizabeth Hitchener
October [15?], 1811

But thou art a sister of *my soul, he* is its brother. . . .

(Julian *Works*, VIII, 158)

See commentary on *Epipsychidion, supra*, pages 279-281.

Letter to Elizabeth Hitchener
November 12, 1811

. . . how beautiful does death appear, what a release from the crimes and miseries of mortality!

(Julian *Works*, VIII, 184)

An echo of Plato's *Phaedo*, 66-68.

Letter to Elizabeth Hitchener
November 24, 1811

So much for real [false?] and so much for true love. The one perishes
with the body whence on earth it never dares to soar, the other lives with the
soul which was the exclusive object of its homage.

(Julian *Works*, VIII, 201)

This marks the first appearance of the Platonic conception of Earthly
and Heavenly Love in Shelley. Later it developed into a major theme
in Shelley's Platonism. Shelley is reflecting here either the influence of
the reading of the *Symposium* at Eton with Dr. Lind or his acquaintance
with Plato's doctrine in his Oxford reading. The Platonic doctrine here
is mingled with the conception of the immortality of the soul as developed in the *Phaedo*.

... must not *that* (the soul) without which a flower cannot be a flower *exist*,
when the earthly flower hath perished?

(Julian *Works*, VIII, 202)

Shelley's argument here is based on the Platonic metaphysical argument of the relation of the particular to the Idea: the Idea of Beauty remains when the particular flower which embodied it has perished.

I will say, then, that all Nature is animated. .... *Perhaps* the animative
intellect of all this is in a constant rotation of change, perhaps a future state
is no other than a different mode of terrestrial existence to which we have
fitted ourselves in this mode. Is there any probability in this supposition?
On this plan, *congenial* souls must meet; because, having fitted themselves
for nearly the same mode of being, they cannot fail to be *near* each other.

(Julian *Works*, VIII, 202)

It is of interest to note how many of Shelley's later poetic ideas are
found in nuclear form in Shelley's early letters (see commentary on
Epipsychidion, supra, p. 279). The Platonism in this passage consists
of three distinct Platonic doctrines merged into one conception: the world
soul, immortality, and the quest of the soul for its counterpart. Shelley
gave poetic expression to the first two notions in *Queen Mab* (see commentary on *Queen Mab*, I, 180-185, 188-190, 264-277, *supra*, pp. 180-181).
The last conception is also expressed in a poem written in the same period
as this letter:

> Congenial minds will seek their kindred soul,
> E'en though the tide of time has roll'd between;

They mock weak matter's impotent control,
And seek of endless life the eternal scene.

> (*Posthumous Fragments of Margaret Nichol-*
> *son: Fragment, Supposed to be an Epitha-*
> *lamium of Francis Ravaillac and Charlotte*
> *Cordé,* ll. 42-45)

Letter to Elizabeth Hitchener
November 26, 1811

Everything which relates simply to this clay-formed dungeon is comparatively despicable. . . .

> (Julian *Works*, VIII, 204)

Compare "For the imoral [*sic*] 'never to be able to die, never to escape from some shrine as chilling as the clay-formed dungeon which now it inhabits,' is the future punishment which I believe in" (*Shelley at Oxford* [London, 1944], p. 16). The sentiment as well as the image come from *Phaedo*, 62b, 82e.

Letter to Elizabeth Hitchener
December 11, 1811

Thus then I am led to love a being, not because it stands in the physical relation of *blood* to me, but because I discern an intellectual relationship.

> (Julian *Works*, VIII, 211)

This is one of the most important and fundamental statements of Shelley's Platonism, for it shows that the Platonism of his later great poems is a mood in his own soul awakened to articulation by contact with Plato's philosophy. This statement is the philosophical nucleus of the *Epipsychidion* (see Shelley's letter to Gisborne dated October 22, 1821 [Julian *Works*, X, 333]). Shelley's statement in this early letter illustrates what Professor White has pointed out in the case of *Queen Mab*: "The ideas which the poem was written to express were mainly ideas that Shelley had held for several years already and that he was to continue to hold, with surprisingly little modification, for the rest of his life" (*Shelley*, I, 292-293). Shelley's own life and poems are a search for the Platonic goal stated in this letter.

Every day makes me feel more keenly that our being is eternal.

> (Julian *Works*, VIII, 213)

For commentary, see page 357, *supra*.

Letter to Elizabeth Hitchener
January 7, 1812

I find you begin to doubt the eternity of the soul: I do not.—More of that hereafter.

(Julian *Works*, VIII, 238)

Compare the following letter and commentary *supra*, page 357.

Letter to Elizabeth Hitchener
January 20, 1812

You have said no more of the immortality of the soul. Do you not believe it? I do; but I cannot tell you why in a letter—at least, not clearly.

(Julian *Works*, VIII, 251)

For commentary, see page 357, *supra*.

Letter to Thomas Hookham, Jr.
December 17?, 1812

Shelley orders "Plato (with a translation)."

(Julian *Works*, IX, 35)

For the order of Plato, see page 41, *supra*.

Letter to William Godwin
December 7, 1817

Clifford's character as mere beauty is a divine and soothing contrast; and I do not think, if perhaps, I except (and I know not if I ought to do so) the speech of Agathon in the Symposium of Plato—that there ever was produced a moral discourse more characteristic of all that is admirable and lovely in human Nature . . . than that of Henrietta to Mandeville.

(Julian *Works*, IX, 260)

For the Platonism in Godwin's *Mandeville*, see page 147, *supra*. For Shelley's enthusiasm for the speech of Agathon in Plato's *Symposium*, which he read in 1817, see *Prince Athanase*, Fragment 3, line 65; *Note on the Banquet of Plato; Prometheus Unbound*, I, 772-775; and *Epipsychidion*, Fragments, lines 101-108; and commentary on these references (pp. 228, 244-245, 290, *supra*).

Letter to John and Maria Gisborne
July 16, 1818

I am employed just now, having little better to do, in translating into my fainting and inefficient periods the divine eloquence of Plato's Symposium;

only as an exercise or perhaps to give Mary some idea of the manners and feelings of the Athenians—so different on many subjects from that of any other community that ever existed.

(Julian *Works*, IX, 312)

For Shelley's translation of the *Symposium*, see pages 381-401, *infra*.

Letter to Thomas Love Peacock
July 25, 1818

I have lately found myself totally incapable of original composition. I employed my mornings, therefore, in translating the "Symposium," which I accomplished in ten days. Mary is now transcribing it, and I am writing a prefatory essay.

(Julian *Works*, IX, 314-315)

The letter shows Shelley's pride in becoming such an accomplished student of Greek that he could translate the *Symposium* in ten days. For his envy of Peacock's Platonic scholarship, see Shelley's remarks in his review of Peacock's *Rhododaphne*. For the prefatory essay and the translation, see pages 383-386, *infra*. For Peacock's reply to this letter of Shelley, see page 383, *infra*.

Letter to William Godwin
July 25, 1818

I have been constantly occupied in literature but have written little—except some translations from Plato in which I exercised myself in the despair of producing anything original. The Symposium of Plato, seems to me, one of the most valuable pieces of all antiquity whether we consider the intrinsic merit of the composition or the light which it throws on the inmost state of manners and opinions among the antient Greeks. I have occupied myself in translating this, and it has excited me to attempt an Essay upon the cause of some differences in sentiment between the Antients and Moderns, with respect to the subject of the dialogue.

(Julian *Works*, IX, 317)

In this letter Shelley is more formal in his statements about the translation. The letter is intended for an ideologist like Godwin. For the translation and the essay, see pages 383-386, *infra*.

Letter to Thomas Love Peacock
August 16, 1818

I have translated, and Mary has transcribed the "Symposium," as well as my poem [*Rosalind and Helen*]; and I am proceeding to employ myself on a discourse, upon the subject of which the "Symposium" treats, considering the subject with reference to the difference of sentiments respecting it, existing between the Greeks and modern nations: a subject to be handled with that delicate caution which either I cannot or I will not practise in other matters, but which here I acknowledge to be necessary. Not that I have any serious thought of publishing either this discourse or the "Symposium," at least till I return to England, when we may discuss the propriety of it.

(Julian *Works*, IX, 320)

There is a change of emphasis in this letter from that of July 25, which Shelley wrote to Peacock. In the first letter he mentions only the translation; in the second letter the emphasis is on the subject matter and the need of explanation with tact. Shelley's intention to consult Peacock about the publication is indicative of his respect for Peacock's scholarship.

What a wonderful passage there is in "Phaedrus"—the beginning, I think, of one of the speeches of Socrates in praise of poetic madness, and in definition of what poetry is, and how a man becomes a poet.

(Julian *Works*, IX, 320-321)

The "Bacchic fury" required for the treatment of Peacock's projected nympholeptic tale reminds Shelley of Plato's remarks on madness in the *Phaedrus,* which he read on August 4 and 5, 1818.

In his Memoirs of Shelley's life, where this letter was first published, Peacock points out that the passage to which Shelley refers in his letter is *Phaedrus*, 245a, which he translates in a note. This letter is important not only for evidence of Shelley's reading of the *Phaedrus* at this period but for a foreshadowing of Shelley's Platonic view of poetry in *A Defence of Poetry* (see commentary *supra*, p. 346).

Letter to Byron
October 17, 1818

My dear Lord B.

I am so dreadfully sleepy that I cannot come tonight. Will you have the goodness to send us—the "Fudge Family" the "Quarterly" and my Plato. . . .

Truthfully [Gratefully?] Yours
P. B. SHELLEY

Between sleep and awake
Oct. 17, 1818.

(White, *Shelley*, II, 460)

The letter is interesting for revealing another of Shelley's efforts to have his friends and intimates share his Platonic enthusiasm, for example, his sending of his copy of the *Phaedo* to Gisborne in November, 1820 (Julian *Works*, X, 220). Immediately upon the receipt of his Plato, Shelley commenced reading the *Republic* (*vide supra*, p. 62). For the influence of Shelley's enthusiasm for Plato on Byron, see page 60, *supra*.

Letter to Thomas Love Peacock
November 7, 1818

You know I always seek in what I see the manifestation of something beyond the present and tangible object.

(Julian *Works*, IX, 340)

For a commentary, see pages 18-21, 61, *supra;* see also Julian *Works*, VIII, 211, and X, 333.

Letter to Thomas Love Peacock
November 9, 1818

There is one refuge from the despondency of this contemplation. The material part indeed of their works must perish, but they survive in the mind of man, and the remembrances connected with them are transmitted from generation to generation. The poet embodies them in his creations, the systems of philosophers are modelled to gentleness by their contemplation, opinion, that legislator, is infected with their influence; men become better and wiser. . . .

(Julian *Works*, IX, 347)

There is an echo in this statement of Plato's view in *Symposium*, 209, and *Republic*, 401.

Letter to Thomas Love Peacock
January 24, 1819

You see how ill I follow the maxim of Horace, at least in its literal sense: "Nil admirari . . ." Fortunately Plato is of my opinion and I had rather err with Plato than be right with Horace.

(Julian *Works*, X, 26)

Shelley is referring to Plato's view of poetry as divine madness in *Phaedrus*, 245a, as a defense of his poetic outburst over the effect of nature on the Greek poets. Shelley considered admiration and enthusiasm as the peculiar property of a poet. For Horace's *nil admirari*, see *Epistles*, I, 6. Shelley is adapting here Cicero's statement in *Tusculan Disputations*, I, 39: "errare me hercule malo cum Platone . . . quam cum istis vera sentire." This became a favorite and often repeated credo of Shelley (see Julian *Works*, X, 226, 234, 404, II, 174; White, *Shelley*, II, 602 n. 63, on the entry in Claire Clairmont's Journal, November 8, 1820; Medwin, *op. cit.*, p. 443; Trelawny, *The Recollections of Shelley and Byron*, II, 199).

Letter to Maria Gisborne
October 13 or 14, 1819

. . . one of my chief [objects] in Italy being the observing in statuary and painting the degree in which, and the rules according to which, that ideal beauty of which we have so intense yet so obscure an apprehension, is realised in external forms.

(Julian *Works*, X, 94)

Shelley is applying to works of art his philosophy of the relation of the world of nature to Intellectual Beauty. The works of art are an obscure yet intense image of Ideal Beauty (see commentary *supra*, pp. 246-247).

Letter to Leigh Hunt
November 3, 1819

Tyrants, after all, are only a kind of demagogues; they must flatter the great Beast.

(Julian *Works*, X, 113)

This is a direct reference to Plato's statement in *Republic*, 493a, 588c. Although, as the Journal shows, Shelley had been reading the *Republic* at the time of the composition of this letter, he also found a specific reference to "the great Beast" in a provocative review of Aristophanes's *Clouds*, which he read in the *Quarterly Review* (April, 1819, pp. 288-289). For an account of this review, see pages 365-367, *infra*.

But in the case of attacking any of the aristocratical Deists the risk of defeat would be great, and the chances of success small.

(Julian *Works*, X, 113)

Shelley adds the following note on the word *aristocratical*: "This word is not used in a bad sense; nor is the word aristocracy susceptible of an ill signification. Oligarchy is the term for the tyrannical monopoly of the few."

This note has reference to the use of these terms in Plato's *Republic*, 445d, 544c-e, 550 ff.

"Nor was Mr. Carlile's defence a model of sublime and dignified eloquence like the Apology of Socrates as given in Plato."

(Julian *Works*, X, 115)

Though Shelley states this is an imaginary reply of the jury in condemning Carlile, the statement reflects his own appraisal of Plato's *Apology*.

In a late number of the Quarterly Review I observe an attack on the character of Socrates, which appearing to proceed from the pen of an accomplished scholar gave me the severer pain. A portion of Cumberland's Observer is dedicated to the same purpose of defaming that illustrious person by taking advantage against him of a change which has been operated in certain conventional notions of morals, which he is accused, but as I feel myself prepared to prove, falsely accused of having violated. I concieve [sic] him to have been the author of some of the most elevated truths of ethical philosophy; to have been to the science of the conduct of men in their social relations, what Bacon was to the science of the classification of the material world, and metaphysics. I concieve [sic] him personally to have presented a grand and simple model of much of what we can concieve, [sic] and more than in any other instance we have seen realized, of all that is eminent and excellent in man. I concieve [sic] that many of those popular maxims which under the name of Christianity have softened the manners of modern Europe are channels derived from the fountain of his profound yet overflowing mind. These sentiments are with me a kind of religion; yet how wickedly absurd I should be if I should go from study to study of all the Greek scholars in London and Cambridge, and excite them to seize upon the author of the article on the Grecian Philosophy, and carry him off to some solitary dungeon, and instead of arguments give him bread and water, and then publish a violent tirade against him and his opinions. I have a strong inclination if my health will permit me to take the more unchristian method of presenting the same subject to the public—without any disrespect to Aristophanes or his learned translator—in a very different point of view.

(Julian *Works*, X, 116; text based on *The Shelley Correspondence in the Bodleian Library*, ed. R. H. Hill, p. 21)

The article to which Shelley refers in the *Quarterly Review* is "View of Grecian Philosophy.—The Clouds, etc.," found in the issue of April, 1819, which also contained an unfavorable review of Shelley's *Laon and Cythna* and *The Revolt of Islam*.[11] This lengthy article, which Hogg also noticed, and Shelley's reaction to which he anticipated (*The Athenians*, pp. 58-59), is significant for Shelley's indirect Platonism, for it gives an elaborate historical review of Presocratic and Platonic philosophy.

[11] See White, *The Unextinguished Hearth* (Durham, N. C., 1938), p. 143 n. 4. For Peacock's reaction to this article, see Halliford *Works*, IX, 58-59. For Hogg's reaction, see Scott, *The Athenians*, p. 59.

However, this is only incidental to the reviewer's purpose, which is to prove that the true portrait of Socrates is not to be found in Plato or Xenophon but in Aristophanes's *Clouds,* translated by Cumberland, to whom Shelley refers in his letter as the "learned translator."[12] The reviewer traces the rise of the sophists and gives an account of their aims and methods. Then he tries to show how Aristophanes chose Socrates as the central figure of a satire against the sophists, their errors and pernicious system of public education. Then follows a historical account of Socrates which presents his life, thought, and teachings in an unfavorable light. It is this picture which provoked the indignation of Shelley.

The particular charge which angered Shelley most was that of homosexuality, alluded to by the *Quarterly Review* but openly discussed by Cumberland in the *Observer,* No. 77.[13] Shelley's statement about the false accusation brought about by "a change which has been operated in certain conventional notions of morals" is a reference to a subject which he had just dealt with in his essay *A Discourse on the Manners of the Antient Greeks Relative to the Subject of Love.* According to Cumberland it was Socrates's vice and corruption which form the justification for Aristophanes's attack in the *Clouds.* He considers Socrates not the admired master of morality in the pages of Plato and Cicero, but the fountain of corruption. The school of Socrates was detrimental to the morals of youth. It was, says Cumberland, "in such public disrepute on account of the infamous characters of many of his disciples, and of the disgraceful attachments he was known to have" (*Observer,* III, 158). Then he illustrates this statement with a list of such students as Alcibiades: "the stories of Socrates's attachment to him are such as need not be enlarged upon" (p. 160). On the authority of Aristoxenus, "a man of the most candid character," he also stigmatizes Socrates "for his guilty connections in his

---

[12] Richard Cumberland (1732-1811), the grandson of the classical scholar Richard Bentley, wrote a periodical paper called the *Observer,* an imitation of the *Spectator* (*The Observer: Being a Collection of Moral, Literary and Familiar Essays*⁴ [London, 1791], 5 vols.). Among his essays in the *Observer* were those on Aristophanes, the *Clouds* of Aristophanes (Nos. 75-77), and the other Greek comic poets. These essays and translations of the fragments of Greek comic poets were later reprinted as the second volume of Chalmers's *British Essayists.* Alexander Fraser Tytler (Lord Woodhouselee) quoted and commended Cumberland's translation of two Greek comic fragments (IV, 115; V, 145) in his *Essay on the Principles of Translation* (1791, 1797) (pp. 90-95 of the Everyman's Library edition of the *Essay*). Encouraged by this, Cumberland completed his translation of the *Clouds,* of which he had given a specimen in *Observer,* No. 141, and dedicated it to the author of the *Essay on the Principles of Translation.* The translation of the *Clouds* was first published in 1798 and reprinted in 1812 in Mitchell's *Aristophanes.* In his Dedication Cumberland reaffirms the interpretation of the play which he had given in his essays in the *Observer.*

[13] *Quarterly Review,* XXI (1819), 296; *Observer*⁴, III, 155-163.

youth with his preceptor Archelaus" (p. 161). Cumberland collects (and believes in) these charges to show that Aristophanes was not singular in his attack on Socrates. He vindicates the character of Aristophanes from collusion with Socrates's accusers, as stated by Aelian in *Variae historiae*, II, 13, and shows that Aristophanes was right in attacking such an immoral man. The charge in the *Quarterly Review* and Cumberland's *Observer* was a modern echo of Polycrates's pamphlet accusing Socrates of immorality, and it is now thought by some scholars that Plato wrote Alcibiades's eulogy of Socrates in the *Symposium* and the *Gorgias* as a reply to Polycrates's slander (see *The Symposium of Plato*,[2] edited by R. G. Bury [Cambridge, 1932], Introduction, pp. xviii, xxi; Jean Humbert, *Polycrates, l'accusation de Socrate, et le Gorgias* [Paris, 1930]). Shelley's answer to the slanders against Socrates constitutes a modern defense against the deeply rooted prejudice in England which considered Plato as a mirror of the ancient immorality of male love (see Peacock's and Hogg's letters and the reasons for Mary's omission of many sections of Shelley's translation of the *Symposium, infra*, pp. 388-390). Though Shelley does not enter the lists to disprove these charges, we find his categorical answer in *The Triumph of Life*. There he shows Plato as enslaved to the Chariot of Life on account of his love for a youth named Aster, to whom he wrote the epigram which Shelley translated as *Stella* (for commentary on ll. 254-259, 260-262 of *The Triumph of Life, vide supra*, pp. 315-317). Shelley refers to Plato's enchainment in the Chariot of Life as expiating

> the joy and woe his master knew not . . .

and in lines 261-262 he speaks of Socrates,

> whom Dominion
> Followed as tame as vulture in a chain. . . .

Thus Shelley finally gave his answer to the modern charges against Socrates and "presented the subject to the public" in *The Triumph of Life*. In this letter he disproves the charges by painting a vivid portrait of the greatness and achievement of Socrates which is matched only by his account of Plato's genius in the Preface to his translation of the *Symposium*. For Socrates as the source of many of the doctrines of Christianity, see Shelley's statement noted in commentary on pages 323, 340-341, *supra*. This point is specifically aimed at the reviewer who asserts, "There is no philosophy so deep as the philosophy of Christianity" (p. 313).

Letter to Leigh Hunt
November, 1819

I have only translated . . . the "Symposium" of Plato, which is the delight and astonishment of all who read it; I mean the original, or so much of the original as is seen in my translation, not the translation itself.

(Julian *Works*, X, 130)

In line with his exhortation to Hunt to pursue original creation and not translation, Shelley speaks modestly of his translation as a veil of the original. For Hunt's interest in Plato, see *The Athenians*, pages 49-50.

Letter to John Gisborne
November, 1820

I send you the Phaedon and Tacitus.

(Julian *Works*, X, 220)

For an account of Shelley's reading and partial translation of the *Phaedo* in 1820, see pages 64-65, *supra*, and pages 514-515, *infra*.

Letter to Thomas Love Peacock
November 15?, 1820

I have been reading nothing but Greek and Spanish. Plato and Calderon have been my gods.

(Julian *Works*, X, 223)

For an account of Shelley's reading of Plato at this period, see pages 63-66, *supra*.

Letter to Clara Mary Jane Clairmont
November, 1820

My verses please so few persons that I make much of the encouragement of the few, whose judgment . . . I should say with Shakespeare and Plato "outweighed a whole theatre of others."

(Julian *Works*, X, 226)

Shelley probably refers to *Republic*, 476b, where Plato states that only the minority are able to appreciate the nature of the beautiful (*vide infra*, p. 548, note on p. 433, l. 38).

Letter to Thomas Love Peacock
February 15, 1821

. . . your anathemas against poetry itself excited me to a sacred rage, or *caloëthes scribendi* of vindicating the insulted Muses.

(Julian *Works*, X, 234)

Shelley here has reference to poetry as divine madness (see his letter to Peacock, Julian *Works*, IX, 320-321, where he refers to *Phaedrus*, 245a).

I was at that moment reading Plato's "Ion," which I recommend you to reconsider. Perhaps in the comparison of Platonic and Malthusian doctrines, the *mavis errare* of Cicero is a justifiable argument . . . .
(Julian *Works*, X, 234)

For Shelley's reading and translation of the *Ion*, see pages 462-467, *infra;* for the importance of its influence on Shelley's *A Defence of Poetry*, see page 346, *supra*. The *mavis errare* of Cicero is "errare me hercule malo cum Platone . . . quam cum istis vera sentire" (*Tusculan Disputations*, I, 39; cf. Julian *Works*, X, 26, and commentary *supra*, pp. 363-364).

Letter to Charles Ollier
February 22

I shall endeavour to . . . unveil the inmost idol of the error.
(Julian *Works*, X, 243)

The imagery here is Shelley's elaboration of the idols of ignorance in Plato's myth of the Cave, *Republic*, 514 (cf. *Epipsychidion*, ll. 267-268; *With a Guitar, to Jane*, l. 43).

Letter to Thomas Medwin
August 22, 1821

I think you must have put up by mistake a MS. translation of the "Symposium" of Plato; if so, pray contrive to send it me.
(Julian *Works*, X, 317)

See page 385, *infra*. For the discovery of the MS, see Julian *Works*, X, 413.

Letter to Thomas Jefferson Hogg
October 20, 1821

For the text and commentary on this letter and Hogg's letter to which this is a reply, see pages 68-70, *supra*.

Letter to John Gisborne
October 22, 1821

The Epipschydion [*sic*] is a mystery—As to real flesh and blood, you know that I do not deal in those articles; you might as well go to a gin-shop for a

leg of mutton, as expect any thing human or earthly from me. I desired
Ollier not to circulate this piece except to the Σύνετοι, and even they, it
seems are inclined to approximate me to the circle of a servant girl and her
sweetheart. But I intend to write a Symposium of my own to set all this
right.

(Julian *Works*, X, 333)

See commentary on *Epipsychidion*, pages 276-277, *supra*. Shelley dedicated his *A Refutation of Deism* (1814) to Συνετοῖσιν (to the intelligent,
to the wise), a phrase found in Pindar's *Olympian Odes*, 2, 85, which Shelley read (see Forman, *Notebooks of Shelley*, II, 111-112, for excerpt from
the second Pythian). William Cherubini, taking up a suggestion of
Rossetti, interprets *The Triumph of Life* as Shelley's intended "Symposium" ("Shelley's 'Own Symposium': *The Triumph of Life*," *SP*, XXXIX
[1942], 559-560). For Peacock's fondness for this phrase from Pindar, see
The Athenians, p. 39.

What Godwin is compared with Plato and Lord Bacon we well know.

(Julian *Works*, X, 334)

This is an interesting revelation as to the position which Godwin
occupied in Shelley's mind at a time when he was reading Plato enthusiastically. It marks a considerable change from his earlier years when
Godwin was Shelley's god. For his attitude toward Plato and Bacon,
see Julian *Works*, II, 174; and Claire Clairmont's Diary, November 8,
1820: "I had rather be damned with Plato & Lord Bacon than go to
Heaven with Paley and Malthus."

I read the Greek Dramatists and Plato forever.

(Julian *Works*, X, 334)

See pages 63-66, 368, *supra*.

You are right about Antigone—how sublime a picture of a woman! . . .
Some of us have in a prior existence been in love with an Antigone, and that
makes us find no full content in any mortal tie."

(Julian *Works*, X, 334)

An appraisal of Sophocles's Antigone in terms of the Platonic doctrine of the pre-existence of the soul in the *Phaedo*.

Letter to John Gisborne
April 10, 1822

Perhaps all discontent with the *less* (to use a Platonic sophism) supposes
the sense of a just claim to the *greater*.

(Julian *Works*, X, 371)

For a commentary on this passage, see page 73, *supra.* Shelley is probably referring to *Phaedo,* 70e: "I mean to say, for example, that anything which becomes greater must become greater after being less. True. And that which becomes less must have been once greater and then have become less." Shelley read the *Phaedo* in 1820.

For the association of "sophism" with Plato, see pages 137-138, *supra,* and Julian *Works,* VII, 161, 265.

Letter to Clara Mary Jane Clairmont
April 11, 1822

My mind agitates the prison which it inhabits. . . .

(Julian *Works,* X, 375-376)

The image and the conception here are derived from *Phaedo,* 62b, 67d, 82e; cf. *With a Guitar, To Jane,* ll. 37-39; *Hellas,* l. 1058; Fragment written for *Hellas,* l. 28.

Letter to John Gisborne
June 18, 1822

It [the *Epipsychidion*] is an idealized history of my life and feelings. I think one is always in love with something or other; the error, and I confess it is not easy for spirits cased in flesh and blood to avoid it, consists in seeking in a mortal image the likeness of what is perhaps eternal.

(Julian *Works,* X, 401)

See commentary on *Epipsychidion,* pages 276-277, *supra.*

Letter to Horace Smith
June 29, 1822

I am glad that my good genius said *refrain.*

(Julian *Works,* X, 410)

A direct reference to the divine sign or daemon of Socrates (*Apology,* 40).

Letter to Mary Shelley
July 4, 1822

I have found the translation of the "Symposium."

(Julian *Works,* X, 413)

See Julian *Works,* X, 317, and page 385, *infra.*

Part III

SHELLEY'S TRANSLATIONS
FROM PLATO:
A CRITICAL EDITION

The Text of Shelley's Translations from Plato

THE NEED OF a critical edition of Shelley's translations from Plato has long been a desideratum in Shelleyan scholarship. In a note contributing several textual emendations to Shelley's translation of the *Symposium* Farrington says, "The text of Shelley's original works has been thoroughly canvassed in recent years. . . . his translations would appear to have escaped attention. It is true that Buxton Forman in his edition of the Prose Works quotes once or twice from the Greek of the *Symposium*. But he cannot have made any close comparison between Shelley's version and the original."[1] The Julian edition of Shelley's works marks the first real advance in attaining a satisfactory edition of Shelley's translations. The discovery of the transcript of Shelley's translation of the *Symposium* which Mary Shelley made for the printers not only added sections omitted in the 1840 edition but also furnished a better text. Yet even this edition suffers from textual inaccuracies, inadequate collation with the manuscript, and omissions. In the Julian edition the *Discourse on the Manners of the Antient Greeks Relative to the Subject of Love* appears as an unfinished fragment of Shelley's prose. Yet, as Shelley's own letters at the time of its composition reveal, it is actually Shelley's prefatory essay to his translation of the *Symposium*. Mrs. Shelley published the *Discourse* in the 1840 edition as a fragment, deleting the substance of the essay for the same reasons which led her to censor Shelley's translation of the dialogue. The full text of the *Discourse* was found among the manuscripts belonging to Sir John C. E. Shelley-Rolls and first printed by him and Ingpen in 1931 in a privately printed edition of *The Banquet* limited to 100 copies. With the kind permission of the Bodleian Library, which has put at the editor's disposal a microfilm of the manuscript of the *Discourse*, Mary's transcript of Shelley's translation of the *Symposium*, a fragment of the *Ion*, versions of Plato's epigrams, and some other unpublished Shelley-Plato material,[2] the editor is able to offer a considerably improved text of Shelley's translation and notes on Plato, with respect both to completeness and fidelity to the *ipsissima verba* of Shelley.

---

[1] "The Text of Shelley's Translation of the 'Symposium' of Plato," *MLR*, XIV (1919), 325.

[2] For Sir John C. E. Shelley-Rolls's gift of Shelley manuscripts, see *The Bodleian Record*, II (1946), 144-145.

This is only one among several reasons which call for a new edition of Shelley's translations from Plato. The editor hopes to throw considerable light on Shelley's translation of the *Ion*. This translation contains several large lacunae which in the 1840 edition were filled by interpolated sections marked by brackets. Unfortunately, some of the brackets were omitted by the printers of the *editio princeps* with the result that we do not know which is Shelley's own version. To add to the difficulties, we, have another version of Shelley's translation of the *Ion* in a transcript which Claire Clairmont made. Buxton Forman first published it along with the 1840 version in his edition of Shelley's works in 1880 without making a thorough study of the relation of the two versions. With the discovery of a fragment of Shelley's translation of the *Ion,* the editor hopes to throw light on the relation of the two versions and on the exact position of the missing brackets in the *editio princeps*. As a result the present edition contains a text on the *Ion* which carries further the reconstruction of Shelley's complete translations from Plato.

Shelley's translations from Plato have suffered not only from deletions but from textual errors as well. The text is far from satisfactory, although it has been improved by access to the manuscripts, many of which are transcriptions by Mary from Shelley's manuscripts. Yet there remains room for improvement in the text of Shelley, as Locock, Farrington, and the present writer have pointed out.[3] It is now known that many of the errors in the text and translation are not Shelley's own but are due to Mary's transcription of Shelley's manuscripts; Shelley's handwriting has been notoriously difficult for editors to decipher.[4] The editor's basis for the detection of the errors has been a systematic and complete comparison of the transcript of Shelley's translation of the *Symposium* and his other translations with the Bipont text of Plato's works which Shelley used in his translation, containing Ficino's Latin translation, which Shelley consulted frequently in the interpretation and rendering of the Greek. As a result of this comparison the present edition offers a considerably improved text over previous editions.

In the present text the editor has made some necessary changes in the punctuation of the manuscripts and the 1840 edition, which does

[3] C. D. Locock, *An Examination of the Shelley Manuscripts in the Bodleian Library* (Oxford, 1903), pp. 1-2; Benjamin Farrington, "The Text of Shelley's Translation of the 'Symposium' of Plato," *MLR*, XIV (1919), 325; J. A. Notopoulos, "Note on the Text of Shelley's Translation of the 'Symposium,'" *MLR*, XXXIV (1939), 421-422; Notopoulos, "Notes on the Text of Shelley's Translations from Plato," *MLN*, LVI (1941), 536-541.

[4] See H. S. Salt, *A Shelley Primer*, The Shelley Society's Publications, First Series, No. 4 (London, 1887), pp. 117-118.

not follow strictly the punctuation of the manuscripts. The editor has kept the text and spelling of Shelley's manuscripts except in instances where a comparison of Mary's transcription with the Greek text shows errors in transcribing Shelley's manuscripts or where the corrections of the transcript and interpolations in the 1840 edition are essential for intelligibility. All such instances have been noted in the *apparatus criticus,* where all textual variants and emendations are discussed. Changes from the manuscripts other than errors in transcribing have been indicated by brackets, which also indicate a deletion or addition in the manuscript reading necessary for sense. Shelley's inconsistencies, such as "neither . . . or" (which occurs very frequently) and "neither . . . nor," have been retained.

The present edition goes beyond the mere matter of text. It investigates such problems as the date and history of the translations; it makes a study of Shelley's translations of Plato's epigrams, whose number has been considerably increased by recent discoveries; it gives an appraisal of Shelley's theory and practice of translation, and his skill as a translator. Such an evaluation involves a detailed study of the accuracy of his translations, and this necessitates an appendix listing Shelley's errors, variations from the Greek as well as his own interpolations. The felicities of his translation are for the most part left in silence. Finally, this present edition of Shelley's translations was undertaken as an essential step in the proper evaluation of Shelley as a Platonist, in determining the relation of Shelley's translation from Plato to the re-creation of Platonism in his own thought, and in bringing about a greater understanding of Shelley's importance in the history of the Platonic tradition.

MRS. SHELLEY'S REMARKS ON
SHELLEY'S TRANSLATIONS FROM PLATO

FROM

PREFACE TO *ESSAYS, LETTERS FROM ABROAD, TRANSLATIONS AND FRAGMENTS*, 1840

THE FRAGMENTS[1] that follow form an introduction to *The Banquet* or *Symposium* of Plato—and that noble piece of writing follows; which for the first time introduces the Athenian to the English reader in a style worthy of him. No prose author in the history of mankind has exerted so much influence over the world as Plato. From him the Fathers and commentators of early Christianity derived many of their most abstruse notions and spiritual ideas. His name is familiar to our lips, and he is regarded even by the unlearned as the possessor of the highest imaginative faculty ever displayed by man—the creator of much of the purity of sentiment which in another guise was adopted by the founders of chivalry—the man who endowed Socrates with a large portion of that reputation for wisdom and virtue, which surrounds him evermore with an imperishable halo of glory.

With all this, how little is really known of Plato! The translation we have is so harsh and un-English in its style, as universally to repel. There are excellent abstracts of some of his dialogues in a periodical publication called the *Monthly Repository;* and the mere English reader must feel deeply obliged to the learned translator. But these abstracts are defective from their very form of abridgment; and, though I am averse to speak disparagingly of pages from which I have derived so much pleasure and knowledge, they want the radiance and delicacy of language with which the ideas are invested in the original, and are dry and stiff compared with the soaring poetry, the grace, subtlety, and infinite variety of Plato. They want, also, the dramatic vivacity, and the touch of nature, that vivifies the pages of the Athenian. These are all found here. Shelley commands language splendid and melodious as Plato, and renders faithfully the elegance and the gaiety which make the *Symposium* as amusing as it is sublime. The whole mechanism of the drama, for such in some sort it is,—the enthusiasm of Apollodorus, the sententiousness of Eryximachus, the wit of Aristophanes, the rapt and

---

[1] Small portions of these and other essays were published by Captain Medwin in a newspaper. Generally speaking, his extracts are incorrect and incomplete. I must except the "Essay on Love" and "Remarks on some of Statues in the Gallery of Florence," however, as they appeared there, from the blame of these defects.

golden eloquence of Agathon, the subtle dialectics and grandeur of aim of Socrates, the drunken outbreak of Alcibiades,—are given with grace and animation. The picture presented reminds us of that talent which, in a less degree, we may suppose to have dignified the orgies of the last generation of free-spirited wits,—Burke, Fox, Sheridan, and Curran. It has something of license,—too much, indeed, and perforce omitted; but of coarseness, that worst sin against our nature, it has nothing.

Shelley's own definition of Love follows; and reveals the secrets of the most impassioned, and yet the purest and softest heart that ever yearned for sympathy, and was ready to give its own, in lavish measure, in return. *The Coliseum* is a continuation to a great degree of the same subject. Shelley had something of the idea of a story in this. The stranger was a Greek,—nurtured from infancy exclusively in the literature of his progenitors,—and brought up as a child of Pericles might have been; and to heighten the resemblance, Shelley conceived the idea of a woman, whom he named Diotima, who was his instructress and guide. In speaking of his plan, this was the sort of development he sketched; but no word more was written than appears in these pages. . . .

I do not know why Shelley selected the *Ion* of Plato to translate. Probably because he thought it characteristic; that it unfolded peculiar ideas, and those Platonic, with regard to poetry; and gave insight into portions of Athenian manners, pursuits, and views which would have been otherwise lost to us. We find manifestations here of the exceeding partiality felt by the Greeks for every exhibition of eloquence. It testifies that love of interchanging and enlarging ideas by conversation, which in modern society, through our domestic system of life, is too often narrowed to petty objects, and which, from their fashion of conversing in streets and under porticoes, and in public places, became a passion far more intense than with us. Among those who ministered exclusively to this taste were the rhapsodists; and among rhapsodists, Ion himself tells us, he was the most eminent of his day; that he was a man of enthusiastic and poetic temperament, and abundantly gifted with the power of arranging his thoughts in glowing and fascinating language, his success proves. But he was singularly deficient in reason. When Socrates presses on him the question of, whether he as a rhapsodist is as well versed in nautical, hippodromic, and other arts as sailors, charioteers, and various artisans? he gives up the point with the most foolish inanity. One would fancy that practice in his pursuit would have caused him to reply, that though he was neither mariner nor horseman, nor practically skilled in any other of the pursuits in question, yet that he had consulted men versed in them; and enriching his mind with the knowledge afforded by adepts in all arts, he was better qualified by study and by his gift of language and enthusiasm to explain these, as they form a portion of Homer's poetry, than any individual whose knowledge was limited to one subject only. But Ion had no such scientific view of his profession. He gives up point after point, till, as Socrates observes, he most absurdly strives at victory, under the form of an expert leader of armies. In this, as in all the other of Plato's writings, we are perpetually referred, with regard to the enthusiastic and ideal portion of our intellect, to something above and beyond our sphere, the inspiration of the God—the influence exercised over the human mind, either through the direct agency of the deities, of our own half-blind memory of divine knowledge acquired by the soul in its antenatal state. Shelley left [the] *Ion* imperfect—I thought it better that it should appear as a whole—but at the same time have marked with brackets the passages that have been added; the rest appears exactly as Shelley left it.

Respect for the name of Plato as well as that of Shelley, and reliance on the curiosity that the English reader must feel with regard to the sealed book of the Ancient Wonder, caused me to include in this volume the fragment of *Menexenus,* and passages from *The Republic.* In the first we have another admirable specimen of Socratic irony. In the latter the opinions and views of Plato enounced in *The Republic,* which appeared remarkable to Shelley, are preserved, with the addition, in some instances, of his own brief observations on them.

INTRODUCTION TO SHELLEY'S TRANSLATION OF
THE BANQUET OF PLATO

HISTORY OF THE TRANSLATION

SEVERAL READINGS possibly preceded the translation itself, which was the culmination of Shelley's interest in the *Symposium*. In discussing Shelley's masters at Eton, Thomas Medwin speaks of "Dr. Lind . . . with whom Shelley says he read the *Symposium*."[1] This statement is open to doubt. "Medwin's statement," says Professor White, "seems to be a conclusion from the lines he quotes from 'Prince Athanase' showing Prince Athanase and Zonoras reading the *Symposium* together. The journal of Shelley and Mary shows that Shelley read the *Symposium* at the time of writing 'Prince Athanase,' which accounts for the lines more convincingly than Medwin's supposition."[2] It is a moot point whether Shelley is giving in *Prince Athanase* a biographical incident with Dr. Lind at Eton, or associating his reading of the *Symposium* in 1817 with the memory of Dr. Lind. Medwin, who was himself very much interested in Shelley's Platonism, may be actually recording Shelley's own statement made to him on the occasion of his showing interest in Shelley's manuscript of the translation in 1821.[3]

We have no specific evidence that Shelley read the *Symposium* in the interval between this possible reading at Eton and the reading of it in 1817. At Oxford he may have read it in Sydenham's translation.[4] His interest in this dialogue must have been constantly stimulated by the great influence which it had on authors like Apuleius (the story of Psyche), Spenser, Wieland, Godwin, Rousseau, and others whom Shelley read during the interval of 1812-17.[5] This is shown by the fact that the first work of Plato which Shelley read in the original was the *Symposium*. As has been shown, the most important factor in prompting Shelley to read this dialogue in 1817 was his friendship with Peacock, who was largely responsible for steering him to the beauty of classical literature. Shelley's admiration of Peacock's *Rhododaphne,* which is a poetic expression of the doctrine of Platonic Love, is evident from the fact that even after Shelley read the *Symposium* he modeled the plot of his *Prince Athanase* after *Rhododaphne*.[6] The *Symposium* appears in Shelley's and

---

[1] Medwin, *op. cit.,* p. 33.   [2] White, *Shelley,* I, 576.   [3] Julian *Works,* X, 317.
[4] Cf. Hogg, *op. cit.,* I, 121; for the influence of one of the doctrines of the *Symposium* on Shelley at this time, see letter to Elizabeth Hitchener, November 24, 1811, and *supra,* pages 358-359.
[5] *Vide infra,* pp. 606-615.
[6] *Vide supra,* pp. 51-52.

Mary's Journal both in the list of books read by Shelley in 1817 and in one lone entry for Wednesday, August 13: "Shelley writes; reads Plato's *Convivium*." The page references to Agathon's speech in "Note on the *Banquet* of Plato"[7] show that the text used by Shelley was the Bipont edition of Plato's works; these page references, moreover, show that Shelley read the dialogue in the original, though he made use of Ficino's juxtaposed Latin translation. The impression which this dialogue left on him is evident not only in *Prince Athanase* and the "Note on the *Banquet* of Plato" but also in his decision to translate it. An opportunity was presented when Shelley settled at Bagni di Lucca and found himself "totally incapable of original composition." His letters to various friends gave variant expressions of this condition.[8] He therefore chose the "exercise" of translation as a stepping stone to poetic creation. As the entries in the Journal show, the translation was a work of inspiration:

Thursday, July 9 (1818) . . . Shelley translates the "Symposium."

Friday, July 10 . . . Shelley translates the "Symposium."

Sunday, July 12 . . . Shelley translates the "Symposium," and reads a part of it to me.

Monday, July 13 . . . Shelley translates the "Symposium."

Tuesday, July 14 . . . Shelley translates the "Symposium"; he reads a part to me.

Wednesday, July 15 . . . Shelley translates the "Symposium."

Thursday, July 16 . . . Shelley translates the "Symposium" and reads Herodotus.

Friday, July 17 . . . Shelley finishes the translation of the "Symposium," and reads Herodotus.

Monday, July 20 . . . Shelley finishes correcting the "Symposium," and I begin to transcribe it. . . . Shelley reads Herodotus.[9]

The entire translation therefore was, as Shelley himself states, the result of ten mornings' work, two of which were devoted to corrections.[10]   Yet

---

[7] *Vide infra*, p. 555.

[8] Julian *Works*, IX, 312, 314, 317.

[9] *Shelley and Mary*, 297-302.

[10] Julian *Works*, IX, 315. There is no entry for its translation on July 11. Shelley speaks of finishing it in ten days, a statement which is corroborated by Mary in a letter to Mrs. Gisborne (*vide infra*, page 385); there are eight entries in the Journal noting Shelley's translation and one day for revising it. This would leave July 11 as one of the days Shelley was occupied in the translation. Between the seventeenth and twentieth Shelley may have read the translation over aloud several times, as Mary tells in her letter to Leigh Hunt (see *The Letters of Mary W. Shelley*, ed. F. L. Jones, II, 140). Mary's transcript is now in the Bodleian Library (*MS. Shelley adds. d. 8*, pp. 55-146). Whether Shelley's original manuscript has survived is not known. It is not included among the Shelley manuscripts in the Bodleian.

as Mary later wrote to Leigh Hunt, "this was no hasty translation," for Shelley read it over aloud several times. The speed of the translation shows that Shelley was already familiar with the text from the previous reading in 1817, and, as passages in the translation show, he made considerable use of Ficino's version when he was unable to understand the Greek. The translation was a careful work of love and enthusiasm rather than *limae labor*.

Some time shortly after the completion of the translation Shelley wrote the preface. This preface is mainly a tribute to Plato's "surpassing graces of the composition" and "remarkable intuitions." It breaks off, however, in the midst of the beginning of an analysis of the dialogue. Shelley's failure to finish this preface was no doubt the result of his decision to be content with the introductory essay he had just written which was less conventional and more expressive of his desire to have Plato better understood. This introduction was called *A Discourse on the Manners of the Antient Greeks Relative to the Subject of Love*.

Shelley's letters to his friends written during and after the completion of the translation show that the communication to the English language of the surpassing graces of the composition was not the only motive in his decision to translate the dialogue. In a letter to Thomas Love Peacock he says:

I have translated, and Mary has transcribed the "Symposium". . . . I am proceeding to employ myself on a discourse, upon the subject of which the "Symposium" treats, considering the subject with reference to the difference of sentiments respecting it, existing between the Greeks and modern nations: a subject to be handled with that delicate caution which either I cannot or I will not practice in other matters, but which here I acknowledge to be necessary. Not that I have any serious thought of publishing either this discourse or the "Symposium," at least till I return to England, when we may discuss the propriety of it.[11]

Other letters to Godwin and John and Maria Gisborne express the same sentiment with slight variation.[12]   Peacock's letter in reply sheds light on the status of Plato in English education and society. "You have done well," he says, "in translating the *Symposium,* and I hope you will succeed in attracting attention to Plato, for he certainly wants patronage in these days, when philosophy sleeps and classical literature seems destined to participate in its repose."[13]   This lack of patronage is evident from the

[11] Julian *Works,* IX, 320.
[12] *Ibid.,* IX, 312, 317.
[13] Halliford *Works,* VIII, 202-203.

fact that Plato does not appear in the set papers of the school of *Literae Humaniores* at Oxford until 1847.[14] The reason for this is partly seen in Hogg's own letter to Shelley recommending him to read the *Gorgias*. "Plato," he remarks, "is unfortunately little read, even by scholars, which is much to be regretted. . . . That he should be shunned at Universities is natural enough, for reasons which he himself gives in the dialogue in question."[15] This attitude of Shelley's contemporaries toward Plato disturbed Shelley; one of the main objects in translating the dialogue and in writing the prefatory essay was to explain to Mary and, if the translation were ever published, to the English world the subject of homosexuality, which formed a barrier to a true understanding of the Greek mind and prevented a true appreciation of Plato's genius. Shelley saw clearly that a prerequisite for a true understanding and enjoyment of the *Symposium* is the recognition of differences between ancient and modern society with respect to love. The *Symposium,* Shelley saw, could not be truly appreciated or understood because of the subject of homosexuality which is present in many of the speeches and in particular in the speech of Alcibiades where he exalts Socrates by contrasting his own base homosexual attempt on Socrates (an episode which Mary deleted in the course of publication) with Socrates's noble and pure conduct. It was Shelley's aim to prevent the historical context of differences in manners between two societies from obscuring our vision of Plato's values and the enjoyment of his artistry. With characteristic courage he plunged into a subject where the English feared to tread, and daringly explored and discussed in a frank and objective manner the subject of homosexuality. Whatever we may think of the armory of his arguments, it is clear now that Shelley, in this as in many other respects, was far ahead of his time. Whoever reads or teaches the *Symposium* in these days can appreciate the modern outlook in Shelley's aim, which was "to induce the reader to cast off the cloak of his self-flattering prejudices and forbid the distinction of manners . . . interfere with his delight or his instruction."[16] The essay is not an academic introduction to the *Symposium,* and if the undeleted text had not waited until 1931 for a limited publication it would have rendered signal service to the understanding of a subject in Plato which is still indelicate to modern society. With the complete publication now of both translation and prefatory essay we can appreciate Shelley's contribution to the Platonic tradition

[14] Geoffrey Mure, "Oxford and Philosophy," *Philosophy*, XII (1937), 296-297.

[15] *Shelley and Mary*, p. 642. Cf. M. L. Clarke, *Greek Studies in England, 1700-1830* (Cambridge, 1945), pp. 112-122; *infra*, pp. 395-396.

[16] *Vide infra*, p. 413.

both as an artistic translator and as an interpreter of Plato to modern society. His insistence that we not allow differences in the temporal ways of life to prejudice our view of Plato's value or genius *sub specie aeternitatis* is still of value today.

Shelley's immediate object was the conversion of Mary, for whom he translated the *Symposium;* he wanted to give her "some idea of the manners and feelings of the Athenians—so different on many subjects from that of any other community that ever existed."[17]   Mary's conversion was aided not only by Shelley's reading to her the portions of the translation that he completed from day to day, but also by her transcription of the translation, which she started, as the Journal shows, on July 20, when Shelley finished correcting the manuscript of his translation, and completed on August 6.   How completely successful Shelley was in his purpose is seen in Mary's letter to Maria Gisborne on August 17, 1818. "Shelley," she writes, "translated the Symposium in ten days (an anecdote for Mr. Bielby). . . . It is a beautiful piece of writing,—I think you will be delighted with it—It is true that in many particulars it shocks our present manners, but no one can be a reader of the works of antiquity unless they can transport themselves from these to other times, and judge not by our but by their morality."[18]   Mary carried out her promise of delighting Mrs. Gisborne.   The entries in the Journal for August 27 and 28, 1818, read: ". . . Read the 'Symposium' to Mrs. Gisborne. . . . Finish reading the 'Symposium' to Mrs. Gisborne."   The translation went the rounds of the Shelley circle.   Claire Clairmont's Diary shows that she read Shelley's translation of the *Symposium* on August 14, 15, and 16, 1819.   No doubt it was read by other friends of Shelley, for, missing the translation, he wrote to Medwin on August 22, 1821, "I think you must have put up by mistake a MS. translation of the 'Symposium' of Plato; if so, pray contrive to send it me."[19]   In his last letter, July 4, 1822, he wrote Mary, "I have found the translation of the 'Symposium.' "[20]   The search for the missing manuscript gives us an inkling of Shelley's concern for his translation.   He wanted to publish the translation, but he realized the difficulties that beset its publication.   In his letter to Peacock on August 16, 1818, he wrote that he did not have any serious thought of publishing either the prefatory essay or the translation itself until he

[17] Julian *Works*, IX, 312.

[18] *The Letters of Mary W. Shelley*, ed. F. L. Jones, I, 56. Mr. Bielby was an Englishman whom the Shelleys met in Italy (see Mary's entry in the Journal for May 17, 1818: "Walk out with Mrs. Gisborne and Mr. Beilby" [*sic*]).

[19] Julian *Works*, X, 317.

[20] *Ibid.*, X, 413.

returned to England and discussed its propriety with Peacock. In view of the prejudice on the subject he realized it was a daring venture, and later in 1821 when an interval had elapsed he weakened with respect to publication even of the translation itself. In reporting his Platonic translations to Hogg on October 20, 1821, he writes, "I . . . have translated the *Symposium* . . . but have no intention of publishing it."[21] It is evident from this that Shelley himself would not have sanctioned the later deletions either in the translation or the prefatory essay. Shelley's intellectual honesty was incapable of such compromises with the conventional society of his England.

The history of the manuscript until its final publication in 1840 forms a veritable odyssey.[22] Upon Shelley's death and Mary's return to England Peacock took charge of the negotiations with Sir Timothy Shelley, her father-in-law. Wishing to obliterate the memory of Shelley, Sir Timothy agreed to give Mary £100 per annum, but with the proviso that she should cease bringing her husband's name before the public. Mary, however, without the knowledge of Peacock, who was carrying on negotiations through Mr. Whitton, the solicitor of Sir Timothy Shelley, got Leigh Hunt's brother John to issue an edition, limited to five hundred copies, of a collection of Shelley's unpublished poems, which was published as Shelley's *Posthumous Poems*, 1824.[23] It was her intention to include in this volume Shelley's translations from Plato. In a letter to Mrs. Hunt dated November 27, 1823, she writes, ". . . I have been hitherto fully occupied in preparing Shelley's MS.—it is now complete, and the poetry alone will make a large volume. Will you tell Hunt that he need not send any of the MS. that he has (except the Essay on Devils . . .) as I have recopied all the rest."[24] An advertisement for the volume appeared in December, 1823, at the end of Byron's *Don Juan*, XII-XIV, 1823. Listed among works being prepared for publication, it reads:

In one vol. 8 vo. The Posthumous Works of the late Percy B. Shelley, Esq. Containing: The Witch of Atlas, Julian and Maddalo; Triumph of Life; Alastor, or the Spirit of Solitude. Translations:—The Cyclop, a Silenic

[21] Scott, *Shelley at Oxford*, p. 64.

[22] This account is largely based on information given in Roger Ingpen, *Shelley in England* (Boston, New York, 1917), pp. 580-587, 618-623; *The Letters of Mary W. Shelley*, ed. F. L. Jones.

[23] R. Glynn Grylls, *Mary Shelley* (Oxford, 1938), p. 185; see also *The Letters of Mary W. Shelley*, ed. F. L. Jones, I, 264.

[24] *The Letters of Mary W. Shelley*, ed. F. L. Jones, I, 281; for a list of the MSS which Mary had asked from Hunt, see *ibid.*, I, 264-265.

drama from Eurypides [sic]; Homer's Hymn to Mercury; The Symposium and Ion of Plato, etc. Letters from Italy; and smaller poems.[25]

The size of the publication, however, made it necessary for the prose translations to appear in a separate volume which had to be abandoned because Mr. Whitton objected to "any further publication of the writings as intended to annoy" the Shelley family. To insure this, Whitton demanded that the manuscripts of the works to form the volume should be removed from Mary's possession. Mary complied and handed all manuscripts, with the exception of the *Symposium* and *Ion,* to Peacock, who became their custodian. On August 18, 1824, he wrote to Whitton:

I have received from Mrs. Shelley the original MSS which were to have composed the prose volume.

There are two translations from Plato which she cannot immediately procure from a person to whom she had lent them, and who (if I recollect rightly, having mislaid her note) is out of town.

She assures me that they shall not be printed, and that they shall be sent to me as soon as she can obtain them.[26]

Just who it was to whom Mary gave the manuscripts of the *Symposium* and *Ion* is not known. It may have been Hazlitt, Charles or Mary Lamb, the Novello family, the Gliddons, Basil Montagu, John Howard Payne, Washington Irving, or Coleridge, who were Mary's friends in London at this time.[27] Mary no doubt kept her word and returned the manuscripts to Peacock when they were returned by the person to whom she had lent them.[28]

Upon the death of Mr. Whitton in July, 1832, Mr. Gregson became the new solicitor for Sir Timothy Shelley. In 1835 when Edward Moxon offered Mary £600 for an edition of Shelley's works, she tried once more to publish her husband's work. Finally in 1838 she was granted permission, with certain stipulations, to publish the collected edition of Shelley's poetry and prose. After the volume of poetry was published in the early months of 1839 Mary made arrangements with Moxon in May

[25] Ingpen, *op. cit.,* p. 577 n. 2.

[26] *Ibid.,* p. 583.

[27] R. Glynn Grylls, *op. cit.,* pp. 183-184; R. M. Smith, *The Shelley Legend* (New York, 1945), p. 15; for Mary's friendship with Payne and Irving, see *The Letters of Mary W. Shelley,* ed. F. L. Jones, II, Appendix II.

[28] Though the publication of the translation was indefinitely postponed, Mary made use of Shelley's translation of a part of Agathon's speech (*Symposium,* 197d4-197e3) in an article entitled "The Loves of the Poets," *Westminster Review,* No. XXII, October, 1829, pp. 472-473 (see *The Letters of Mary W. Shelley,* ed. F. L. Jones, II, 19). Mary also published Shelley's translation of an epigram of Plato in an annual, *Album Wreath and Literature,* II, (1834), 57 (*vide infra,* p. 567).

for the publication of Shelley's prose. In publishing the prose volume Mary turned to Leigh Hunt for help. In August, 1839, she wrote to him, "I am about to publish a vol. of Prose of Shelleys. . . . I want your advice on several portions of it,—especially with regard to the translation of the Symposium."[29] This translation presented certain problems with respect to the publication. The permission to publish the works of Shelley at this time involved a certain amount of censorship. This is evident in the letter of Mary to Hunt on December 12, 1838: "Moxon wants me to leave out the sixth part [of *Queen Mab*] as too atheistical."[30] It is evident from this that the publication of Shelley's works at this time required the omission of all that might be offensive to English taste. We have a typical reaction to what was offensive in the *Symposium* in the opinion expressed by the Reverend Dr. Folliott in Peacock's novel *Crotchet Castle* (1831):

> I am aware, sir, that Plato, in his Symposium, discourseth very eloquently touching the Uranian and Pandemian Venus: but you must remember that, in our Universities, Plato is held to be little better than a misleader of youth; and they have shown their contempt for him, not only by never reading him . . . , but even by never printing a complete edition of him.[31]

Though Mary herself, as her letter to Mrs. Gisborne shows, shared Shelley's liberal views on this problem of the *Symposium,* it is evident that she did not have a free hand in the matter. No doubt she had to comply with certain conditions laid down by Moxon, the publisher, to whose judgment Sir Timothy Shelley probably left all questionable matters, among which were certainly the episode in Alcibiades's confession, and the greater part of *A Discourse on the Manners of the Antient Greeks Relative to the Subject of Love.* We get a picture of Mary's editorial troubles in conforming to these conditions in her letters to Leigh Hunt. To Mary mutilation of her husband's work was a Procrustean torture. She writes to Hunt concerning an essay in the volume: "You see I have scratched out a few lines which might be *too shocking*—and yet I hate to *mutilate.* . . . It is *my* duty to publish every thing of Shelley."[32] When it came to the *Symposium,* Mary's troubles with the homosexual

[29] *The Letters of Mary W. Shelley,* ed. F. L. Jones, II, 136.

[30] *Ibid.,* II, 127. In the review of the 1840 edition Mary was criticized for this: "There is still, on the Editor's part, an evident reluctance in producing certain portions of these written documents—an attempt to soften, and temporize, and explain away, wholly at variance with the frank and uncompromising spirit of her husband" (*Athenaeum,* No. 633, Dec. 14, 1839, p. 939).

[31] Halliford *Works,* IV, 95; cf. Clarke, *op. cit.,* p. 113.

[32] *The Letters of Mary W. Shelley,* ed. F. L. Jones, II, 139.

phraseology and episode of the dialogue, and her compromises, appear in a newly published letter to Leigh Hunt:

[Putney] Thursday [? October, 1839]

Dear Hunt

You have puzzled me much. What you *said* convinced me. You said: "Do as Mills,(a) who has just phrased it so that the common reader will think common love is meant—the learned alone will know what is meant." Accordingly I read the Phaedrus(b) & found less of a veil even than I expected—thus I was emboldened to leave it so that our sort of civilized love should be understood—Now you change all this back into friendship—which makes the difficulty as great as ever. I wished in every way to preserve as many of Shelley's own *words* as possible—& I was glad to do so under the new idea which you imparted—but your alterations puzzle me mightily—I do not like *not* to abide by them—yet they destroy your own argument that different sexes would be understood & thus all is in confusion.

Accordingly I have left some & not others(c)—where you seemed very vehement—& your p. 192(d) I have altered and omitted as you mention—but I could not bring myself to leave the word *love* out entirely from a treatise on Love. With regard to your verbal corrections—this was no hasty translation—Shelley read it over aloud several times—so some things that look uncouth, I suppose he thought, as you phrase it *more Greek*—and I like to leave it as he left it as much as possible.

After all the beauty of the piece consists in Agathon's, Socrates, & Alcibiades speeches—the rest are of minor importance. It is puzzling—*That's a fact* as the Americans say. . . .

Ever truly Ys.
M W Shelley[33]

This letter brings to light not only Mary's knowledge and understanding of the *Symposium* but also her fidelity to Shelley's own words under trying circumstances. She saved the text from Hunt's confusing

---

[33] *Ibid.*, II, 139-140. I append the following notes to elucidate certain points and references in the letter, which is quoted with the kind permission of the University of Oklahoma Press and that of the custodian of the Luther A. Brewer-Leigh Hunt collection in the State University of Iowa Libraries.

ᵃ The reference is to J. S. Mill's translations of large sections of the *Protagoras, Gorgias,* and *Phaedrus* which appeared in the *Monthly Repository*, n.s. VIII (1834). Mary praised these abstracts in her preface to the 1840 edition, yet thought them stylistically inferior to Shelley's translations.

ᵇ The reference is to Mill's translation of a portion of the *Phaedrus* which offered Mary a guide as to the translation of the troublesome word ἔρως.

ᶜ For Mary's substitution of *friendship* for *love* and *friend* for *lover* in the text of the 1840 edition, *vide infra,* pages 542 ff.

ᵈ The reference is to the galleys, for it does not refer to the manuscript or the 1840 edition.

suggestion and verbal changes which in many instances would have vitiated the translation as far as it is a translation of the Greek. The letter also throws light on *A Discourse on the Manners of the Antient Greeks Relative to the Subject of Love,* which appears as a separate fragment. The reasons which compelled its mutilation are the same as those affecting the *Symposium.* The essay finally appeared complete[34] as a prefatory essay to the translation of the *Symposium* in a limited edition in 1931.[35] Now at last we are able to understand the paradox of an essay which did not discuss what Shelley set out to do and a translation which omitted the very portions which the prefatory essay intended to discuss.

SHELLEY AS A TRANSLATOR OF PLATO

An appraisal of Shelley's translation of the *Symposium* and other works of Plato cannot be separated from his views on reading a language in the original and the value and standards of translation. Shelley's reading of Plato in the original is not merely of academic importance. It reveals the channel through which one creative mind affects another. To understand this one must read Shelley's own words on the difference between grasping thought in the original language in which it was written and grasping it through translation. Writing to a lady who loved Greek, Shelley said:

It is probable that you will be earnest to employ the sacred talisman of language. . . . You desire to enjoy the beauties of eloquence and poetry—to sympathise in the original language with the institutors and martyrs of ancient freedom. The generous and inspiriting examples of philosophy and virtue, you desire intimately to know and feel . . . clothed in the very language of the actors,—that language dictated by and expressive of the passions and principles that governed their conduct. . . . What is a translation of Homer into English? A person who is ignorant of Greek need only look at "Paradise Lost," or the tragedy of "Lear" translated into French, to obtain an analogical conception of its worthless and miserable inadequacy. Tacitus, or Livius, or Herodotus, are equally undelightful and uninstructive in transla-

[34] Mary thought of *A Defence of Poetry* as "the only entirely finished & corrected prose essay left by him" (*The Letters of Mary W. Shelley,* ed. F. L. Jones, II, 138). Ingpen thinks that the essay is incomplete. The last paragraph of the essay, however, shows clearly that Shelley had finished with the subject of the essay and that he was deliberately making for the reader the transition to the reading of the translation of the *Banquet.*

[35] *Plato's Banquet, Translated from the Greek, A Discourse on the Manners of the Antient Greeks Relative to the Subject of Love, Also A Preface to the Banquet, Revised and enlarged by Roger Ingpen, From MSS in the possession of Sir John C. E. Shelley-Rolls, Bart.* Printed for private circulation, MCMXXXI, One hundred copies Only, Printed at the Curwen Press, Plaistow, Lond.

tion. You require to know and be intimate with those persons who have acted a distinguished part to benefit, to enlighten . . . humankind.[36]

He gave the perfect answer for the inadequacy of translation in *A Defence of Poetry*.

Sounds as well as thoughts have relation both between each other and towards that which they represent, and a perception of the order of those relations has always been found connected with a perception of the order of those relations of thoughts. Hence the language of poets has ever affected a certain uniform and harmonious recurrence of sound, without which it were not poetry. . . . Hence the vanity of translation; it were as wise to cast a violet into a crucible that you might discover the formal principle of its colour and odour, as seek to transfuse from one language into another the creations of a poet.[37]

Despite this acknowledged inadequacy of translation Shelley was a prolific and good translator; he was constantly translating great thinkers and poets from all languages. He served a considerable time as an apprentice in translation before he attempted the *Symposium*. We first hear of his translation of a section of Aristotle's *Ethics* in the spring of 1811, then in 1813 of a treatise of Buffon.[38] In the same year he translated two essays of Plutarch, Περὶ σαρκοφαγίας, in order to enlighten people on the value of vegetarianism;[39] he translated, as we shall see, the opening section of Plato's *Menexenus* in 1817, and was occupied at various intervals from 1813 to 1821 in translating Spinoza. In January, 1818, Shelley busied himself with a translation of the *Hymns* of Homer, to which he returned at a later date.[40] In this we may see the influence of Peacock, whose translations of a number of choral lyrics from Greek

[36] Julian *Works*, X, 267; cf. *The Athenians* (London, 1943), p. 42. It is conjectured that this lady is Claire Clairmont.

[37] Julian *Works*, VII, 114; cf. "Such is a liberal translation of this astonishing Chorus; it is impossible to represent in another language the melody of the versification; even the volatile strength and delicacy of the ideas escape in the crucible of translation, and the reader is surprised to find a *caput mortuum*" (Julian *Works*, IV, 323 n.; cf. *ibid.*, X, 130). Medwin reports the following remark of Shelley: "Shelley always says that reading Dante is unfavourable to writing, from its superiority to all possible compositions. Whether he be the first or not, he is certainly the most untranslatable of all poets. You may give the meaning; but the charm, the simplicity,—is lost. You might as well clothe a statue, as attempt to translate Dante. He is better, as an Italian said, 'nudo che vestito'" (Thomas Medwin, *Journal of the Conversations of Lord Byron* [London, 1824], p. 161).

[38] Hogg, *op. cit.*, I, 264; cf. *Shelley at Oxford*, pp. 48-50. Carlos Baker, "Shelley's Translation from Aristotle," *MLN*, LXI (1946), 405-406; Kenneth N. Cameron, "Shelley and Aristotle," *Notes and Queries*, CXC (1940), 80.

[39] Julian *Works*, IX, 81-82.

[40] Entry in Journal for January 20, 1818: "Shelley translates Homer's Hymns"; Julian *Works*, X, 187; *Shelley at Oxford*, p. 56.

tragedies Shelley admired.[41] All these translations reveal that Shelley undertook translation to advocate ideas and causes in which he believed, or to re-create artistically some work in another language. His translation of the *Symposium* was undertaken in part for both of these reasons, as his letters and his Preface to the translation reveal.

Yet the translation of the *Symposium* was the result of a complex set of factors, some of which he consciously expresses and some of which he implies. Shelley's life at Bagni di Lucca was one of solitude. He read much, rode amid the magnificent scenery, and took delight in watching the atmosphere, but with all this he was not creative.[42] He chose as a stepping stone to poetic creation the translation of Plato's *Symposium*. "I am employed just now," he says, "having little better to do, in translating into my fainting and inefficient periods the divine eloquence of Plato's Symposium."[43] Bacchylides's remark, "Poet is heir to poet now as of yore; for in sooth 'tis no light task to find the gates of virgin song"[44] illustrates Shelley's dependence on Plato at this time. His whole mind was filled with this new enthusiasm. The philosopher-poet was all that Shelley himself hoped to be. "Plato," he says, "exhibits the rare union of close and subtle logic, with the Pythian enthusiasm of poetry, melted by the splendour and harmony of his periods into one irresistible stream of musical impressions, which hurry the persuasions onward, as in a breathless career. His language is that of an immortal spirit, rather than a man."[45] This intense admiration is but a reflection of Shelley's own aspiration. "The mind," he says, "becomes that which it contemplates."[46] It can be said of Shelley also that his mind became that which he was translating. In transmuting "the surpassing graces of the composition" into English Shelley was choosing a method to ignite a similar process in his own soul. Thus translation served another purpose for Shelley; it ignited the creative process, which, as Shelley confessed, was incapable of original composition at the time.

Shelley called the translation an "exercise." It remains now to examine the propaedeutic value of this exercise for future poetic creation. Few poets today translate in order to become better poets, yet with Shel-

[41] Peacock, *op. cit.*, II, 336; see Halliford *Works*, VII, Appendix I.

[42] Julian *Works*, IX, 314.

[43] *Ibid.*, IX, 312. Cf. "I have only translated the 'Cyclops' of Euripides when I could absolutely do nothing else" (*Ibid.*, X, 130).

[44] Frag. 5 (Snell).

[45] Julian *Works*, VII, 161; cf. "Plato was essentially a poet—the truth and splendour of his imagery, and the melody of his language, is the most intense that it is possible to conceive" (*ibid.*, VII, 114).

[46] *Prince Athanase*, Frag. 2, l. 15.

ley translating was, like Eros in the *Symposium,* an intermediary between inertia and poetic creation. Shelley is unique among the poets in the English language in recognizing the value of Greek translation as a propaedeutic for poetry. His many translations from the Greek have a significance which has not been recognized. An attempt therefore will be made to point out the close relation of translation with the poetic process.

The translation of the *Symposium* into English was for Shelley an exercise involving certain fundamental facts underlying all translation from the Greek. The value of translation lies fundamentally in the activity of mind, for translation is an activity which takes place in connection with thought. As the Greek word λόγος shows, thought involves both the content or meaning and the formal expression of this in language. Translation never concerns itself merely with the formal expression of language. Before Shelley could translate the formal expression of the *Symposium,* he had to understand the meaning itself. The activity of mind involved in being compelled, as Shelley inevitably was in translating, to understand, digest, and assimilate the meaning behind language is the best way to assimilate the greatness of another mind. Being forced to assimilate the same insight which a first-rate mind has, and then to understand the expression of this insight in the conceptual language of the author's language is an activity of the mind which lies at the very heart of re-creation. This self-imposed, obligatory analysis of meaning often leads to an awakening of similar but unrealized values within us; it often stimulates our own creation through the inspiration, taste, judgment, and appreciation which translation imparts. All this can be strikingly illustrated in the compositions which Shelley wrote after the translation of the *Symposium.*[47]

The second stage involved in the activity of translating is the re-creative process of transmuting the form in which meaning is expressed. As the first stage in translation involves a re-creative exercise in the assimilation of meaning, so the second stage involves a re-creative activity in form. The translation, say of the *Symposium,* from Greek into English is an exercise involving certain fundamental facts underlying all translation. The first of these is grammar; in translating the *Symposium* Shelley had to know some grammar, not so much as a set of rules but as form, the living anatomy of thought. But even with a knowledge of grammar Shelley, before translating, had to understand the nature of the leap from Greek into English. Is this leap an imitation of the form of

[47] *Vide supra,* pp. 229-320, 334-356, *infra,* 615-623, *passim.*

Greek by the form of the English? But translation, as Shelley himself shows, is not exactly imitation because the English is not a copy of Greek; it has a nature and character all its own, differing in its rhythm, connotation and denotation of words, idiom, color, emotion, and a multitude of other *differentia*. Translation is more like an equation $(a + b)$ $(a + b) = a^2 + 2ab + b^2$. The meaning is identical on both sides of the equation though the form of the expression is different. Identity of "meaning" expressed through the difference of "form" is the essence of translation from Greek into English. It is this re-creation of form which is a creative factor in the art of translation. With some knowledge of grammar as the foundation of translation, and with a feeling of English prose artistry, Shelley attempted the *Symposium*. In the storehouse of English artistry Shelley sought for *le mot juste* to express the thought, the phrase, the emotion he met in the Greek of the *Symposium*. He had to find in English a natural, idiomatic counterpart for the sensuous or abstract quality of its words, the color of its phrase, and its rhythm, which he described as "poetry melted by the splendour and harmony of his periods into one irresistible stream of musical impressions." This feeling for language, one of Shelley's great talents, furnished him with possible suggestions from which he had to choose. Aristophanes in the *Frogs* shows Aeschylus and Euripides challenging each other in the "weight" of words. Shelley as a translator had to know instinctively the weight of words, what quantity goes to make up quality. A word also has color, whether it be of sense, thought, or psychological distinction. Shelley had to choose words for their color in his translation. Furthermore, he had to choose a counterpart rhythm in English. Rhythm of phrase and thought is the most difficult element in translation. The inability to equate the Greek rhythm by some natural counterpart in English is where most translations suffer. In Shelley's translation English rhythm is an inborn quality.[48] The "exercise" of translation therefore was for Shelley a re-creation akin to poetry. The intimate relation of translation and poetry is acknowledged by Shelley himself; Medwin writes: "'There is no greater mistake than to suppose,' I use Shelley's own words,—'that the knowledge of a language is all that is required in a translator. He must be a poet, and as great a one as his original, in order to do justice to him.'"[49] Thus we can see that Shelley's undertaking of the translation of the *Symposium* was the best possible prepara-

[48] "Shelley's Symposium is in parts exquisite in point of language and rhythm" (*Quarterly Review*, CXII [October, 1862], 307).
[49] Medwin, *op. cit.*, p. 385.

tion for a renewal of poetic creation, and therefore a light kindled from a poet's fire shines through it.

Shelley's translation of the *Symposium* cannot be appraised solely on the basis of accurate classical scholarship. Shelley's own standards and character as a translator must also be taken into consideration. The great number of translations which he made not only from the Greek but also from other languages shows that he considered himself a translator as well as a poet. Medwin records that Shelley was conscious of his talent for translation and once told him that he considered turning to translation in view of his lack of success in original composition.[50] In his translations Shelley kept in mind the English reader who knew no Greek; therefore the spirit rather than the letter was his aim. Medwin, in speaking of him as a translator, said, ". . . another of the canons of Shelley was that translations are intended for those who do not understand the originals, and that they should be purely English."[51] Shelley, who considered Plato as the master of prose style, must have considered the existing translations like those of Taylor, which Coleridge described as "difficult Greek transmuted into incomprehensible English," inadequate.[52] His description of Plato's prose style in the preface to the *Banquet* shows Shelley's awareness of the inadequacy of any English translation of this dialogue. Furthermore, there was a general apathy toward Plato in England at this time, which is evident not only in the picture given in Peacock's *Crotchet Castle*[53] but also by John Stuart Mill, who gives us the appropriate background for an understanding of Shelley's contribution to Platonic scholarship in the early nineteenth century:

Considering the almost boundless reputation of the writings of Plato, not only among scholars, but (upon their authority) among nearly all who have any tincture of letters, it is a remarkable fact, that of the great writers of antiquity, there is scarcely any one who, in this country at least, is not merely so little understood, but so little read. Our two great "seats of learning," of which no real lover of learning can ever speak but in terms of indignant disgust, bestow attention upon the various branches of classical acquirement in exactly the reverse order to that which would be observed by persons who valued the ancient authors for what is valuable in them: namely, upon the mere niceties of the language *first;* next, upon a few of the poets; next, (but at a great distance,) some of the historians; next (but at a still greater interval,) the orators; last of all, and just above nothing, the philosophers. An English book-

[50] *Ibid.*, p. 249.
[51] *Ibid.*, p. 246.
[52] *Memorials of Coleorton*, ed. William Knight (Edinburgh, 1887), II, 107.
[53] Halliford *Works*, IV, 85; cf. p. 31, *supra;* Clarke, *op. cit.*, pp. 112-122.

seller, by the aid of a German scholar, recently produced an excellent edition of Plato; the want of sale for which, by the way, is said to have been one of the causes of his insolvency. But with the exception of the two dialogues edited by Dr. Routh [*Euthydemus* and *Gorgias,* Oxford, 1784], we are aware of nothing to facilitate the study of the most gifted of Greek writers, which has ever emanated from either of the impostor-universities of England; and of the young men who have obtained university honours during the last ten years, we are much misinformed if there be six who have even looked into his writings. If such be the neglect of the best parts of classical learning among those whose special vocation and whose positive duty it is to cultivate them, what can be expected from others?[54]

In view of the neglect of Plato in the universities, the lack of interest and of adequate translations of Plato, Shelley's attempt to present to the English reader the beauty of Plato's language and thought is worthy of the praise which Peacock gave to Shelley.[55] In calling Shelley a Platonist we must not neglect to enroll his name in the long list of those who enriched the Platonic tradition, *honoris causa.* In translating the *Symposium* he gave to the English readers a Plato they had not seen before; he anticipated by almost half a century the renascence of Plato in England through Jowett's translations and Pater's studies. His translation of the *Symposium* presented to the Greekless reader of Plato the first poetic transcription of his style. Mrs. Shelley is not exaggerating when she says of Shelley's translation of the *Symposium,* ". . . for the first time [it] introduces the Athenian to the English reader in a style worthy of him."[56] In order to appreciate the truth of this statement one has only to read an example of the harsh and un-English translations and abridgments of the period, with which Mrs. Shelley contrasts Shelley's translations. The following example is chosen at random from *The Works of Plato* translated from the French with notes by M. Dacier, a work which Shelley read at Oxford: "Socrates is an impious Man; with a criminal Curiosity he pretends to penetrate in all that passes in the Heavens, and

[54] The *Monthly Repository,* N.S. VIII (1834), 89; cf. the remarks of the reviewer of Thomas Taylor's *Plato* in the *Edinburgh Review* (XIV [1809], 188-189): "It is remarkable that England has contributed very little service towards the promotion of classical learning. None of the lettered nations of Europe . . . are so badly supplied with translations, in their own language, of the prose classics. . . . The *Socraticae chartae* . . . are abandoned for the Choruses of Euripides." For the neglect of Plato in England and English universities, see *Correspondence of Thomas Gray,* ed. Paget Toynbee and Leonard Whibley (Oxford, 1935), III, 1295; MP, XLI (1943), 103, 106-107.

[55] *Vide supra,* p. 383.

[56] Julian *Works,* V, viii; cf. the review of the 1840 edition in the *Athenaeum,* No. 633, Dec. 14, 1839, p. 984: " 'The Banquet of Plato' . . . like all of Shelley's translations conveys vividly the spirit of the original."

to fathom what's contain'd in the Bowels of the Earth. He has a way of giving the Ascendant to Injustice; and is not content to reserve these Secrets to himself, but communicates them to others."[57] The Greek of this passage (*Apology,* 19b) reads simply: "Socrates is guilty and over-does it, investigating the things below the earth and in the heavens, and making the weaker argument the stronger, and teaching others these same things."

A comparison of Shelley's translation of the *Symposium* with any other translation of his time shows how outstanding it is. Shelley's translation has been described with justice as "the poetry of a philosopher rendered by the prose of a poet"; it "may rank as one of Shelley's major works."[58] He gave the world a Plato good enough to be included in Van Doren's excellent *Anthology of World Prose,* about which a reviewer says: "The greatest single piece of translation is Shelley's radiant version of the *Banquet.*"[59] For this service to the Platonic tradition (which is unrecognized) Shelley ranks among its torchbearers in English literature.

Shelley's translation is, like his poems, a reflection of the man. Hogg has given us a vivid picture of Shelley as a translator:

Bysshe, a king in intellect, had always at his command a short and royal road to knowledge. It seemed to a superficial observer, that he rejected and despised the grammar and the dictionary, and all ordinary aids of a student; this to a certain extent was the case, but to a certain extent only; he was impatient of such tardy methods of progression; nevertheless he sometimes availed himself of them, and when he condescended to be taught, like a mere mortal, which assuredly he was not, his eagle glance, his comprehensive grasp, his inconceivable quickness, and miraculous powers and faculty of apprehension, enabled him to seize and to master in minutes what his less highly gifted fellow-learners acquired in hours, or days, or weeks.[60]

This accounts for the merits as well as the defects in Shelley's translations. The criterion of his translation is entirely poetic, revealing a poetic grasp which in its flight often outsoars strict textual accuracy. The translation reveals the keen insight into Plato which he had and which other translators, even if possessed of a greater scholarship, lacked. We have another insight into Shelley's manner of translating in a letter to Hogg on the

[57] *The Works of Plato Abridg'd . . .* In Two Volumes. Illustrated with notes. By M. Dacier. Translated from the French by several Hands. London, 1739. II, 12-13.

[58] R. Glynn Grylls, *Claire Clairmont* (London, 1939), p. 98.

[59] Clifton Fadiman, *New York Herald-Tribune Books,* Sunday, June 30, 1935. Shelley's versions of the *Symposium* and *Ion* were also chosen for the Everyman's Library edition of *Five Dialogues of Plato Bearing on Poetic Inspiration.*

[60] Hogg, *op. cit.,* II, 61-62; cf. *ibid.,* I, 84-86, 358-359; Medwin, *op. cit.,* pp. 75, 268 269.

subject of using Scapula, the Greek lexicon, in translating. He writes,
". . . nor have I summoned courage to accept Scapula as my mentor and
guide thro' the bowers of Greek delight. Might I not, by a confidence
in Scapula, lose the end while busied about the means; and exchange
the embraces of a living and tangible Calypso for the image of a Penelope,
who, though wise, can never again be young."[61] It is this dislike of the
lexicon in which the spirit would spend itself in thumbing pages that
led Shelley to rely often on Ficino's Latin translation, juxtaposed to the
Greek text in his Bipont edition of Plato. Shelley was more familiar
with Latin[62] than with Greek and accordingly made considerable use
of Ficino's version. A comparison of his translation with the Bipont text
shows that Shelley often would not look at the Greek but resort to the
Latin version for the meaning of the Greek. This is evident not only
in the case of a phrase but of entire paragraphs. On the other hand, the
speed with which Shelley made his translation shows that he did not
always understand or follow Ficino; he would often take a guess as to
the meaning. A detailed comparison of his translation with the Bipont
text, as shown in the appendix of errors in Shelley's translation,[63] leads
to these conclusions: (1) Shelley knew Greek well, but was frequently
careless; (2) he followed the Greek text where he could, but when he
did not understand it he made use of Ficino, whose Latin translation
often forms the basis of his own version; (3) he did not always follow
or understand Ficino. The errors in translation consist of those made
in following Ficino, who is not always exact; of those which are the
result of Shelley's misunderstanding of the Greek or Ficino; or, as more
often is the case, of those resulting from speed in translating and effort
to get artistic effects; and finally of minor errors which are unimportant
as far as the meaning is concerned but which are not an exact, accurate
translation of the Greek text.[64]

[61] Julian *Works*, IX, 254; this is an answer to Hogg's letter recommending the use of
Scapula's lexicon; see *The Athenians*, pp. 37-39, 42; *Shelley at Oxford*, p. 56; cf. Stephen
MacKenna in his translation of Plotinus: "The present translator has not thought of his
probable readers as glossary-bound pedants but as possessed of the living vision which can
follow a stream of thought by the light of its own vivid movement" (Plotinus: *The
Ethical Treatises* [London and Boston, 1926], I, 115).

[62] Evidence of this is the fact that in the Journal he records the reading of twelve hundred pages of Livy in seventeen days (*Shelley and Mary*, p. 65).

[63] *Vide infra*, pp. 572-603.

[64] With respect to Shelley's errors it is well to keep in mind Jowett's remark about
errors in his own translation: "It is not that I do not *know* these elementary things; but
the effort of making the English harmonious is so great, that one's mind is insensibly
drawn away from the details of the Greek" (quoted by Benjamin Farrington in "Shelley's Translations from the Greek," *Dublin Magazine*, III [1928], 9).

A great many of Shelley's errors in translation, however, are not his own. A comparison of the translation with that of the Bipont text of the Greek shows that many apparently meaningless sentences and obvious errors are the result of Mary's transcription of Shelley's manuscript, written in a hand that has been notoriously difficult for editors to decipher.[65]

In general, however, a survey of the errors which Shelley made in translating the *Symposium* and other works of Plato shows that he was not a scientifically careful, patient, and exact scholar of Plato. His impatience with grammar and lexicon, the unusual speed of the translation which required only eight days, his reliance on Ficino, and his effort to make the translation idiomatic and its language harmonious and inspired account for the errors. His translation sometimes sacrificed accuracy in order to achieve harmony, beauty, and vividness, qualities which Shelley consciously strove to impart to his version.

Yet what Shelley may have lost in accuracy he amply compensated in style of translation. His translation, inaccuracies apart, is the best English version of the dialogue. Dowden says of it: "The translation of the 'Banquet,' not always exact in scholarship, has much of the vivid life, the grace of movement, and the luminous beauty of Plato."[66] A comparison of Shelley's version with those of his own day, like Thomas Taylor's, which John Stuart Mill characterized as "full of faults, and often with difficulty understood even by those who can read the original,"[67] shows that the difference is one of light and shadow; if one compares it with the English translation of Dacier's Plato which Shelley used at Oxford, he will realize Shelley's genius as a translator. A comparison of Shelley's version even with that of Jowett finds Shelley not without points of superiority. Shelley has superb passages of prose transcending Jowett, who, though a great scholar, is not the equal of Shelley in the

[65] See J. A. Notopoulos, "Notes on the Text of Shelley's Translations from Plato," *MLN*, LVI (1941), 536-541. For a description of Shelley's MSS, see Trelawny's Description of Shelley, from the Williams-Trelawny Notebook: "his manuscripts are so interlined & erased as scarcely to be legible"; see also Peck, *op. cit.*, II, 408.

[66] Dowden, *op. cit.*, II, 219. Léon Robin, one of the great Plato scholars of our day, pays unique tribute to Shelley's translation by using it as an aid in his own version for the Budé series: "J'ai utilisé une traduction anglaise, incomplète, parfois inexacte, mais souvent très fine, du poète Shelley" (*Platon oeuvres complètes*, Tome IV, 2ᵉ partie. *Le Banquete*. Texte établi et traduit par Léon Robin, Paris, 1924. Notice, p. cxxi). Another tribute to Shelley's translation is seen in the fact that Paul Shorey, another great Plato scholar, uses it for quotation in *What Plato Said* (Chicago, 1933), p. 45 (see also p. 51).

[67] *Monthly Repository*, N.S. VIII (1834), 91; see also *Quarterly Review*, CXII (Oct., 1862), 307: "Taylor . . . is frequently deficient both in style and accuracy"; Clarke, *op. cit.*, pp. 117-119.

felicities of the English language. In comparing Jowett's and Shelley's translations no less competent a Greek scholar than Farrington remarks:

It would be vain to seek to excuse Shelley . . . from ignorance of some elementary things; but at the same time it is easy to exaggerate the importance of his blunders . . . and if we may suppose that Shelley had less difficulty in making English harmonious, he certainly had greater success. The defect of Jowett's *Plato* lies, not in his scholarship, but in the fact that his prose never soars; it has no wings. . . . Nor is it only in the more exalted passages, such as the simile of the magnet in the *Ion*, or the speeches of Agathon or Socrates in the *Symposium*, that the superiority of Shelley manifests itself; in lighter moments also he bears off the palm. Jowett, for instance, somehow imparts to his Alcibiades the atmosphere, together with the locutions of an English undergraduate, while Shelley's Alcibiades carries about him, with something of a Byronic air and with an incommunicable verve and charm and freshness, the atmosphere of an accomplished man of the world, a spoilt darling of the gods.

Furthermore, Farrington points out, Shelley's version surpasses Jowett's even in trivial phrases, e.g.:

Jowett: Concerning the things about which you ask to be informed, I believe that I am not ill-prepared with an answer.
Shelley: I think that the subject of your enquiries is still fresh in my memory.[68]

The excellence of Shelley's translation is apparent in the fact that it reads like prose-poetry. Shelley came to the translation with a Platonic understanding of some of its thought and therefore a greater talent and sensitivity in appreciating Plato's artistic qualities, which, he says, he despairs of having rendered. Shelley was conscious of his limitations. He tells his friends that he presents no more than an "imperfect shadow." Shelley, however, succeeded in transmuting the style of the Greek into English with fitting art; the color of Shelley's words matches the brilliant and varying shades of Plato's style. Agathon's speech is polyphonic prose in English, and the speeches of the other characters match the character of the speakers as in Plato: Socrates's speech is expressed with majesty, whereas that of Aristophanes flies on the wings of amusement. Shelley's excellence in transmuting a scene, a mood, a thought in appropriate rhythm is one of the most distinguished features of his translation. Shel-

---

[68] Farrington, *op. cit.*, p. 9. See also Shelley's and Jowett's rendering of *Symposium*, 217e3-4: "τὸ λεγόμενον, οἶνος ἄνευ τε παίδων καὶ μετὰ παίδων ἦν ἀληθής," which Shelley translates as "the proverb . . . wine tells truth, whether with or without youth," while Jowett renders it as "the proverb . . . 'In vino veritas,' whether with boys, or without them."

ley matches the quality and mood of each speaker with its appropriate rhythm; he transmutes this rhythm with an unerring touch, as may be seen in his version of the ascent toward Beauty. It is these qualities, evident to one who has the Greek before him and compares the styles, which stamp Shelley's version, if not as the most accurate, at least as that which most re-creates in poetical prose many qualities of Plato's style.[69]

The translation of the *Symposium* constitutes one of the most important sources of Shelley's Platonism. It is valuable not only for itself but for its permeating influence on Shelley's prose, poetry, and way of life. The allusions to it in his poetry and prose are unparalleled in number and importance.[70] An examination of Shelley's poetry shows that Shelley's Platonism can be traced mostly to this work of Plato. Consequently his translation of it marks the birth of an intellectual love which became in Shelley's life "a light kindled from a leaping fire."

[69] Shelley belongs to that rare class of English translators which is represented by Stephen MacKenna, for whose view of translation, see *Plotinus: The Ethical Treatises*, I, 114-116. For an appraisal of his translation of Plotinus, see E. S. Batt *Intertraffic: Studies in Translation* (London, 1943), pp. 137-142.

[70] *Vide supra*, pp. 229-320, 334-356., *passim*.

THE BANQUET
TRANSLATED FROM PLATO
ON THE SYMPOSIUM
OR PREFACE TO THE BANQUET OF PLATO

A FRAGMENT

PLATO is eminently the greatest among the Greek philosophers, and from him, or, rather, perhaps through him, from his master Socrates, have proceeded those emanations of moral and metaphysical knowledge, in which a long series and an incalculable variety of popular superstitions have sheltered their absurdities from the slow contempt of mankind. Plato exhibits the rare union of close and subtle logic, with the Pythian enthusiasm of poetry, melted by the splendour and harmony of his periods into one irresistible stream of musical impressions, which hurry the persuasions onward, as in a breathless career. His language is that of an immortal spirit, rather than a man. Lord Bacon is, perhaps, the only writer, who, in these particulars, can be compared with him: his imitator, Cicero, sinks in the comparison into an ape mocking the gestures of a man. His views into the nature of mind and existence are often obscure, only because they are profound; and though his theories respecting the government of the world, and the elementary laws of moral action, are not always correct, yet there is scarcely any of his treatises which do not, however stained by puerile sophisms, contain the most remarkable intuitions into all that can be the subject of the human mind. His excellence consists especially in intuition, and it is this faculty which raises him far above Aristotle, whose genius, though vivid and various, is obscured in comparison with that of Plato.

The dialogue entitled the Banquet was selected by the translator as the most beautiful and perfect among all the works of Plato. He despairs of having communicated to the English language any portion of the surpassing graces of the composition, or having done more than present an imperfect shadow of the language and the sentiment of this astonishing production.

[The dialogue intitled the Banquet]. It is called εϱωτιϰος, or a discussion upon Love, and is supposed to have taken place at the house of Agathon, at one of a series of festivals given by that poet, on the occasion of his gaining the prize of tragedy at the Dionysiaca. The account of the debate on this occasion is supposed to have been given by Apollodorus, a pupil of Socrates, many years after it had taken place, to a companion who was curious to hear it. This Apollodorus appears, both from the style in which he is represented in this piece, as from a passage in the *Phaedon,* to have been a person of an impassioned and enthusiastic disposition; to borrow an image from the Italian painters, he seems to have been the St. John of the Socratic groups. The drama (for [so] the lively distinction of characters and the various and well-wrought circumstances of the story almost entitle it to be called) begins by Socrates persuading Aristodemus to sup at Agathon's, uninvited. The whole of this introduction affords the most lively conception of refined Athenian manners. Socrates after having paused to   Eryximachus the physician proposes the subject of the discourse by relating that Phaedrus, one of the company, had . . .

[UNFINISHED]

A DISCOURSE ON THE MANNERS
OF THE ANTIENT GREEKS
RELATIVE TO THE SUBJECT OF LOVE

THE PERIOD which intervened between the birth of Pericles and the death of Aristotle, is undoubtedly, whether considered in itself or with reference to the effects which it had produced upon the subsequent destinies of civilised man, the most memorable in the history of the world. What was the combination of moral and political circumstances which produced so unparalleled a progress during that short period in literature and the arts;—why that progress, so rapid and so sustained, so soon recieved a check, and became retrograde,—are problems left with the wonder and conjectures of posterity. The wrecks and fragments of those subtle and profound minds, like the ruins of a fine statue, obscurely suggest to us the grandeur and perfection of the whole. Thier very language—a type of the understandings of which it was the creation and the image—in variety, in simplicity, in flexibility, and in copiousness, excells every other language of the western world. Their sculptures are such as we, in our presumption, assume to be the models of ideal truth and beauty, and to which no artist of modern times can produce forms in any degree comparable. Their paintings, according to Pliny and Pausanias, were full of delicacy and harmony; and some even were powerfully pathetic, so as to awaken, like tender music or tragic poetry, the most overwhelming emotions. We are accustomed to concieve of the painters of the sixteenth century, as those who have brought thier art to the highest perfection, probably because none of the antient paintings have been preserved. For all the inventive arts maintain, as it were, a sympathetic connection between each other, being no more than various expressions of one internal power, modified by different circumstances, either of an individual, or of society. The paintings of that period would probably bear the same relation as is confessedly borne by the sculptures to all succeeding ones. Of their music we know little; but the effects which it is said to have produced, whether they be attributed to the skill of the composer, or the sensibility of his audience, are far more powerful than any which we experience from the music of our own times; and if, indeed, the melody of their compositions were more tender and delicate, and inspiring, than the melodies of some modern European nations, their superiority in this art must have been something wonderful, and wholly beyond conception.

Their poetry seems also to maintain a very high, though not so disproportionate a rank, in the comparison. Perhaps Shakespeare, from the variety and comprehension of his genius, is to be considered, on a whole, as the greatest individual mind, of which we have specimens remaining. Perhaps Dante created imaginations of greater loveliness and energy than any that are to be found in the antient literature of Greece. Perhaps nothing has been discovered in the fragments of the Greek lyric poets equivalent to the sublime and chivalric sensibility of Petrarch.—But, as a poet, Homer must be acknowledged to excel Shakespeare in the truth, the harmony, the sustained grandeur, the satisfying completeness of his images, their exact fitness to the illustration, and that to which they belong[s]. Nor could Dante, deficient in conduct, plan, nature, variety, and temperance, have been brought into comparison with these men, but for those fortunate isles, laden with golden fruit, which alone could tempt any one to embark in the misty ocean of his dark and extravagant fiction.

But, omitting the comparison of individual minds, which can afford no general inference, how superior was the spirit and system of their poetry to that of any other period! So that, had any genius equal in other respects to the greatest that ever enlightened the world, arisen in that age, he would have been superior to all, from this circumstance alone—that his conceptions would have assumed a more harmonious and perfect form. For it is worthy of observation, that whatever the poets of that age produced is as harmonious and perfect as possible. If a drama, for instance, were the composition of a person of inferior talent, it was still homogeneous and free from inequalities; it was a whole, consistent with itself. The compositions of great minds bore throughout the sustained stamp of their greatness. In the poetry of succeeding ages the expectations are often exalted on Icarean wings, and fall, too much disappointed to give a memory and a name to the oblivious pool in which they fell.

In physical knowledge Aristotle and Theophrastus had already—no doubt assisted by the labours of those of their predecessors whom they criticise—made [advances] worthy of the maturity of science. The astonishing invention of geometry, that series of discoveries which have enabled man to command the elements and foresee future events, before the subjects of his ignorant wonder, and has opened as it were the doors of the mysteries of nature, had already been brought to great perfection. Metaphysics, the science of man's intimate nature, and logic, or the grammar and elementary principles of that science, recieved from the latter philosophers of the Periclean age a firm basis. All our more exact philosophy is built upon the labours of these great men, and many of the words which we employ in metaphysical distinctions were invented by them to give accuracy and system to their reasonings. The science of morals, or the voluntary conduct of men in relation to themselves or others, dates from this epoch. How inexpressibly bolder and more pure were the doctrines of those great men, in comparison with the timid maxims which prevail in the writings of the most esteemed modern moralists. They were such as Phocion, and Epaminondas, and Timoleon, who formed themselves on their influence, were to the wretched heroes of our own age.

Their political and religious institutions were more difficult to bring into comparison with those of other times. A summary idea may be formed of the worth of any political and religious system, by observing the comparative degree of happiness and of intellect produced under its influence. And whilst many institutions and opinions, which in antient Greece were obstacles to the improvement of the human race, have been abolished among modern nations, how many pernicious superstitions and new contrivances of misrule, and unheard of complications of public mischief, have not been invented among them by the ever-watchful spirit of avarice and tyranny!

The modern nations of the civilized world owe the progress which they have made—as well in those physical sciences in which they have already excelled their masters, as in the moral and intellectual enquiries, in which, with all the advantage of their experience of the latter, it can scarcely be said that they have yet equalled them,—to what is called the revival of learning; that is, the study of the writers of the age which preceded and immediately followed the government of Pericles, or of subsequent writers, who were, so to speak, the rivers flowing from those immortal fountains. And though there seems to be a principle in the modern world, which, should circumstances analogous to those which modelled the intellectual resources of the age to which we refer, into so harmonious a proportion, again arise, would arrest and perpetuate them, and consign their results to a more equal, extensive, and lasting improvement of the condition of man—though justice and the true meaning of human society is, if not more accurately, more generally understood; though perhaps men know more, and therefore are more, as a mass, yet this principle has never been called into action, and requires indeed a universal and almost appalling change in the system of existing things. The study of modern history is the study of kings, financiers, statesmen, and priests. The history of antient Greece is the study of legislators, philosophers, and poets; it is the history of men, compared with the history of titles. What the Greeks were, was a reality, not a promise. And what we are and hope to be, is derived, as it were, from the influence and inspiration of these glorious generations.

Whatever tends to afford a further illustration of the manners and opinions of those to whom we owe so much, and who were perhaps, on the whole, the most perfect specimens of humanity of whom we have authentic record, were infinitely valuable. Let us see their errors, their weaknesses, their daily actions, their familiar conversation, and catch the tone of their society. When we discover how far the most admirable community ever formed, was removed from that perfection to which human society is impelled by some active power within each bosom, to aspire, how great ought to be our hopes, how resolute our struggles! For the Greeks of the Periclean Age were widely different from us. It is to be lamented that no modern writer has hitherto dared to show them precisely as they were. Barthelemy cannot be denied the praise of industry and system; but he never forgets that he is a Christian and a Frenchman. Wieland, in his delightful novels, makes indeed a very tolerable Pagan, but cherishes too many political prejudices, and refrains from diminishing the interest of his romances by painting sentiments in which no European of modern times can possibly sympathize. There is no book which shows the Greeks precisely as they were; they seem all written for children, with the caution that no practice or sentiment, highly inconsistent with our present manners, should be mentioned, lest those manners should recieve outrage and violation. But there are many to whom the Greek language is inaccessible, who ought not to be excluded by this prudery to possess an exact and comprehensive conception of the history of man; for there is no knowledge concerning what man has been and may be, from partaking of which a person can depart, without becoming in some degree more philosophical, tolerant, and just.

One of the chief distinctions between the manners of antient Greece and modern Europe, consisted in the regulations and the sentiments respecting sexual intercourse. Whether this difference arises from some imperfect influence of the doctrines of Jesus Christ, who alledges the absolute and unconditional equality of all human beings, or from the institutions of chivalry, or from a certain fundamental difference of physical nature existing in the Celts, or from a combination of all or any of these causes, acting on each other, is a question worthy of voluminous investigation. The fact is, that the modern Europeans have in this circumstance, and in the abolition of slavery, made an improvement the most decisive in the regulation of human society; and all the virtue and the wisdom of the Periclean age arose under other institutions, in spite of the diminution which personal slavery and the inferiority of women, recognized by law and by opinion, must have produced in the delicacy, the strength, the comprehensiveness, and the accuracy of their conceptions, in moral, political, and metaphysical science, and perhaps in every other art and science.

The women, thus degraded, became such as it was expected that they should become. They possessed, except with extraordinary exceptions, the habits and the qualities of slaves. They were probably not extremely beautiful; at least there was no such disproportion in the attractions of the external form between the female and male sex among the Greeks, as exists among the modern Europeans. They were certainly devoid of that moral and intellectual loveliness with which the acquisition of knowledge and the cultivation of sentiment animates, as with another life of overpowering grace, the lineaments and the gestures of every form which it inhabits. Their eyes could not have been deep and intricate from the workings of the mind, and could have entangled no heart in soul-enwoven labyrinths.

Let it not be imagined that because the Greeks were deprived of its legitimate object, [they] were incapable of sentimental love; and that this passion is the mere child of chivalry and the literature of modern times. This object, or its archetype, forever exists in the mind, which selects among those who resemble it, that which most resembles it; and instinctively fills up the interstices of the imperfect image, in the same manner as the imagination moulds and completes the shapes in clouds, or in the fire, into the resemblances of whatever form, animal, building, etc., happens to be present to it. Man is in his wildest state a social being: a certain degree of civilization and refinement ever produces the want of sympathies still more intimate and complete; and the gratification of the senses is no longer all that is sought in sexual connexion. It soon becomes a very small part of that profound and complicated sentiment, which we call Love, which is rather the universal thirst for a communion not merely of the senses, but of our whole nature, intellectual, imaginative and sensitive; and which, when individualised, becomes an imperious necessity, only to be satisfied by the complete or partial, actual or supposed, fulfilment of its claims. This want grows more powerful in proportion to the developement which our nature recieves from civilization; for man never ceases to be a social being. The sexual impulse, which is only one, and often a small part of those claims, serves, from its obvious and external nature, as a kind of type or expression of the rest, as common basis, an acknowledged and visible link. Still it is a claim which even derives a strength not its own from the accessory circumstances which surround it, and one which our nature thirsts to satisfy. To estimate this, observe the degree of intensity and durability of the love of the male towards the female in animals and savages; and acknowledge all the duration and intensity observable in the love of civilised beings beyond that of savages to be produced from other causes. In the susceptibility of the external senses there is probably no important difference.

Among the antient Greeks the male sex, one half of the human race, recieved the highest cultivation and refinement; whilst the other, so far as intellect is concerned, were educated as slaves, and were raised but few degrees in all that related to moral or intellectual excellence above the condition of savages. The gradations in the history of man present us with a slow improvement in this respect. The Roman women held a higher consideration in society, and were esteemed almost as the equal partners with their husbands in the regulation of domestic economy and the education of their children. The practices and customs of modern Europe are essentially different from and incomparably less pernicious than either, however remote from what an enlightened mind cannot fail to desire as the future destiny of human beings.

From this distinction arose that difference of manners which subsists between the antient Greeks and the modern Europeans. They both had arrived at that epoch of refinement, when sentimental love becomes an imperious want of the heart and of the mind. The senses of both sought with the same impatient eagerness that gratification upon which the perpetuity of our species depends. In modern Europe the sexual and intellectual claims of love, by the more equal cultivation of the two sexes, so far converge towards one point, as to produce, in the attempt to unite them, no gross violation in the established nature of man.

Among the Greeks these feelings, being thus deprived of their natural object, sought a compensation and a substitute. The men of Greece corresponded in external form to the models which they have left as specimens of what they were. The firm yet flowing proportion of their forms, the winning unreserve and facility of their manners, the eloquence of their speech, in a language which is itself music and persuasion; their gestures animated at once with the delicacy and the boldness which the perpetual habit of persuading and governing themselves and others; and the poetry of their religious rites, inspired into their whole being, rendered the youth of Greece a race of beings something widely different from that of modern Europe. If my observation be correct, the word καλος (beautiful) is more frequently applied to the male sex, whilst ευειδης (handsome) denoted the attractiveness of a female. Whether the cause is to be sought in the climate, in the original constitution of the peculiar race of the Greeks, or in the institutions and system of society, or in the mutual action of these several circumstances, such is the effect. And as a consequence of those cause[s], beautiful persons of the male sex became the object of that sort of feelings, which are only cultivated at present as towards females.

An enlightened philosophy, although it must condemn the laws by which an indulgence in the sexual instinct is usually regulated, suggests, however, the propriety of habits of chastity in like manner with those of temperance. It regards the senses as but a minute and subordinate portion of our complicated nature, and it deems the pleasures to be derived from their exercise such as are rather weakened, not enhanced, by repetition, especially if unassociated with some principle from which they may participate in permanency and excellence. Few characters are more degraded than that of an habitual libertine; that is a person who is in the custom of seeking a relief from the impulse of the sexual instinct, divested of those associated sentiments which in a civilized state, precede, accompany, or follow such an act.

The act itself is nothing. The sources of condemnation to be pronounced against the indulgence in this gratification are twofold.

1st as it regards the complicated and arbitrary distinctions of society; and the other as it regards the indestructible laws of human nature.

With respect to the first, the one general law applicable to all other actions is applicable also to this:—that nothing is to be done, which, including your own being in the estimate, will produce, on the whole, greater pain than pleasure. In this sense adultery, seductions, etc., until mankind shall have enough. With respect to the second, the following propositions may be established as applications of this general law.

1st. That the person selected as the subject of this gratification should be as perfect and beautiful as possible, both in body and in mind; so that all sympathies may be harmoniously blended, and the moments of abandonment be prepared by the entire consent of all the conscious portions of our being; the perfection of intercourse consisting, not perhaps in a total annihilation of the instinctive sense, but in the reducing it to as minute a proportion as possible, compared with those higher faculties of our nature, from which it[s] derives a value.

2dly. Temperance in pleasure. This prevents the act which ought always to be the link and type of the highest emotions of our nature from degenerating into a diseased habit, equally pernicious to body and mind. Everyone will recollect Mrs. Shandy's clock; and after the customary smile has past, cannot but be shocked at the picture it affords of the brutal prostitution of the most sacred impulses of our being.

3dly. This act ought to be indulged *according to nature*. A volume of definitions and limitations belong to this maxim, which here may be passed over.

To apply these propositions to the Greeks. The passion which their poets and philosophers described and felt seems inconsistent with this latter maxim, in a degree inconcievable to the imagination of a modern European. But let us not exaggerate the matter. We are not exactly aware,—and the laws of modern composition scarcely permit a modest writer to investigate the subject with philosophical accuracy,—what that action was by which the Greeks expressed this passion. I am persuaded that it was totally different from the ridiculous and disgusting conceptions which the vulgar have formed on the subject, at least except among the more debased and abandoned of mankind. It is impossible that a lover could usually have subjected the object of his attachment to so detestable a violation or have consented to associate his own remembrance in the beloved mind with images of pain and horror. If we consider the facility with which certain phenomena connected with sleep, at the age of puberty, associate themselves with those images which are the objects of our waking desires; and even that in some persons of an exalted state of sensibility, that a similar process may take[s] place in reverie, it will not be difficult to concieve the almost involuntary consequences of a state of abandonment in the society of a person of surpassing attractions, when the sexual connection cannot exist, to be such as to preclude the necessity of so operose and diabolical a machination as that usually described. This is the result apparently alluded to by Plato.[1] That it could seldom have approached to a resemblance the vulgar imputation, with even among the more gross and unrefined Romans, I appeal to a passage of Petronius, well known to every scholar, in which Giton, the pathic, is represented to talk the language of a woman recieving pleasure from the embraces of Encolpius. This, even as a piece of meretricious flattery, is wholly inconsistent with the vulgar notion.

But let us not measure the Greeks of the age to which I refer, with our own feeble conceptions of the intensity of disinterested love; or according to the horrible commentary which the imitation of their manners by the licentious Romans who had contributed to the overthrow of the Republic, produced upon the text. Probably there were innumerable

[1] *Phaedrus.*

instances among that exalted and refined people, in which [it] never [happened] any circumstance happens the lover and his beloved by which natural modesty was wronged. The lover appeased his physical instinct with his wife or his slave; or was engrossed in such lofty thoughts and feelings as admitted of no compromise between them and less intense emotions. Thus much is to be admitted, that, represent this passion as you will, there is something totally irreconcilable in its cultivation to the beautiful order of social life, to an equal participation in which all human beings have an indefeasible claim, and from which half of the human race, by the Greek arrangement, were excluded. This invidious distinction of human kind, as a class of beings [of] intellectual nature, into two sexes, is a remnant of savage barbarism which we have less excuse than they for not having totally abolished.

The action by which this passion was expressed, taken in its grossest sense, is indeed sufficiently detestable. But a person must be blinded by superstition to conceive of it as more horrible than the usual intercourse endured by almost every youth of England with a diseased and insensible prostitute. It cannot be more unnatural, for nothing defeats and violates nature, or the purposes for which the sexual instincts are supposed to have existed, than prostitution. Nor is it possible that the society into which the one plunges its victim should be more pernicious than the other. Nothing is at the same time more melancholy and ludicrous than to observe that the inhabitants of one epoch[s] or of one nation[s], harden themselves to all amelioration of their own practices and institutions and soothe their consciences by heaping violent invectives upon those of others; while in the eye of sane philosophy their own are no less deserving of censure. If it be enquired how an individual ought to act in the   —the reply is—make the best of a bad matter.

The ideas suggested by Catullus, Martial, Juvenal and Suetonius never occur among the Greeks; or even among those Romans, who, like Lucretius, Virgil, Horace, imitated them. The Romans were brutally obscene; the Greeks seemed hardly capable of obscenity in a strict sense. How innocent is even the Lysistrata of Aristophanes compared with the infamous perversions of Catullus! The earlier dramatic English writers are often frightfully obscene, exceeding even the Romans. I should consider obscenity to consist in a capability of associating disgusting images with the act of the sexual instinct. Luxury produced for the Romans what the venereal disease did for the writers of James, and after the redeeming interval over which Milton presided the effects of both were united, under Charles II, to infect literature.

It may blunt the harshness of censure also to reflect that in the golden age of our own literature a certain sentimental attachment towards persons of the same sex was not uncommon. Shakespeare has devoted the impassioned and profound poetry of his sonnets to commemorate an attachment of this kind, which we cannot question was wholly divested of any unworthy alloy. Towards the age of Charles 2^d it is said that this romantic friendship degenerated into licentiousness and this latter age bears the same relation to the former as the first of the Roman Empire, to . . .

Thus far the translator has thought it his duty to overstep the jealous limits between what the learned and the unlearned know of the Greeks; and to indicate a system of reasoning which may enable the reader to form a liberal, consistent, and just judgement of the peculiarities of their domestic manners. This slight sketch was undertaken to induce the reader to cast off the cloak of his self-flattering prejudices and forbid the distinction of manners, which he has endeavored to preserve in the translation of the ensuing piece, interfere with his delight or his instruction.

THE BANQUET
TRANSLATED FROM PLATO

THE PERSONS OF THE DIALOGUE

APOLLODORUS

A FRIEND OF APOLLODORUS

GLAUCO

ARISTODEMUS

SOCRATES

AGATHON

PHAEDRUS

PAUSANIAS

ERYXIMACHUS

ARISTOPHANES

DIOTIMA

ALCIBIADES

Apollodorus. I think that the subject of your enquiries is still fresh in my memory; for yesterday, as I chanced to be returning home from Phaleros, one of my acquaintance, seeing me before him, called out to me from a distance, jokingly, "Apollodorus, you Phalerian, will you not wait a minute?"—I waited for him, and as soon as he overtook me, "I have just been looking for you, Apollodorus," he said, "for I wished to hear what those discussions were on Love, which took place at the party, when Agathon, Socrates, Alcibiades, and some others met at supper. Some one who heard of them from Phoenix, the son of Philip, told me that you could give a full account, but he could relate nothing distinctly himself. Relate to me, then, I entreat you, all the circumstances. I know you are a faithful reporter of the discussions of your friend; but first tell me, were you present at the party or not?"

"Your informant," I replied, "seems to have given you no very clear idea of what you wish to hear, if he thinks that these discussions took place so lately as that I could have been of the party."—"Indeed I thought so," replied he.—"For how," said I, "O Glauco! could I have been present? Do you not know that Agathon has been absent from the city many years? But since I began to converse with Socrates, and to observe each day all his words and actions, three years are scarcely past. Before this time I wandered about wherever it might chance, thinking that I did something, but being, in truth, a most miserable wretch, not less than you are now, who believe that you ought to do anything rather than practice the love of wisdom."—"Do not cavil," interrupted Glauco, "but tell me, when did this party take place?"

"Whilst we were yet children," I replied, "when Agathon first gained the prize of tragedy, and the day after that on which he and the chorus made sacrifices in celebration of their success."—"A long time ago, it seems. But who told you all the circumstances of the discussion? Did you hear them from Socrates himself?" "No, by Jupiter, but the same person from whom Phoenix had his information, one Aristodemus, a Cydathenean,—a little man who always went about without sandals. He was present at this feast, being, I believe, more than any of his contemporaries, a lover and admirer of Socrates. I have questioned Socrates concerning some of the circumstances of his narration, who confirms all that I have heard from Aristodemus."—"Why then," said Glauco, "why not relate them, as we walk, to me? The road to the city is every way convenient, both for those who listen and those who speak."

Thus as we walked, I gave him some account of those discussions concerning Love; since, as I said before, I remember them with sufficient accuracy. If I am required to relate them also to you, that shall willingly be done; for, whensoever either I myself talk of philosophy, or listen to others talking of it, in addition to the improvement which I conceive there arises from such conversation, I am delighted beyond measure; but whenever I hear your discussions about monied men and great proprietors, I am weighed down with grief, and pity you, who, doing nothing, believe that you are doing something. Perhaps you think that I am a miserable wretch; and, indeed, I believe that you think truly. I do not think, but well know, that you are miserable.

Companion. You are always the same, Apollodorus—always saying some ill of yourself and others. Indeed, you seem to me to think every one miserable except Socrates, beginning with yourself. I do not know what could have entitled you to the surname of the "Madman," for, I am sure, you are consistent enough, forever inveighing with bitterness against yourself and all others, except Socrates.

Apollodorus. My dear friend, it is manifest that I am out of my wits from this alone—that I have such opinion as you describe concerning myself and you.

Companion. It is not worth while, Apollodorus, to dispute now about these things; but do what I entreat you, and relate to us what were these discussions.

Apollodorus. They were such as I will proceed to tell you. But let me attempt to relate them in the order which Aristodemus observed in relating them to me. He said that he met Socrates washed, and, contrary to his usual custom, sandalled, and having enquired whither he went so gaily dressed, Socrates replied, "I am going to sup at Agathon's; yesterday I avoided it, disliking the crowd, which would attend at the prize sacrifices then celebrated; today I promised to be there, and I made myself so gay, because one ought to be beautiful to approach one who is beautiful. But you, Aristodemus, what think you of coming uninvited to supper?" "I will do," he replied, "as you command." "Follow then, that we may, by changing its application, disarm that proverb, which says, *To the feasts of the good, the good come uninvited.* Homer, indeed, seems not only to destroy, but to outrage the proverb; for, describing Agamemnon as excellent in battle, and Menelaus but a faint-hearted warrior, he represents Menelaus as coming uninvited to the feast of one braver and better than himself."—Aristodemus hearing this, said, "I also am in some danger, Socrates, not as you say, but according [to] Homer, of approaching like an unworthy inferior the banquet of one more wise and excellent than myself. Will you not, then, make some excuse for me? for, I shall not confess that I came uninvited, but shall say that I was invited by you."—"As we walk together," said Socrates, "we will consider together what excuse to make—but let us go."

Thus discoursing, they proceeded. But as they walked, Socrates, engaged in some deep contemplation, slackened his pace, and, observing Aristodemus waiting for him, he desired him to go on before. When Aristodemus arrived at Agathon's house he found the door open, and it occurred, somewhat comically, that a slave met him at the vestibule, and conducted him where he found the guests already reclined. As soon as Agathon saw him, "You arrive just in time to sup with us, Aristodemus," he said; "if you have any other purpose in your visit, defer it to a better opportunity. I was looking for you yesterday, to invite you to be of our party; I could not find you anywhere. But how is it that you do not bring Socrates with you?"

But he turning round, and not seeing Socrates behind him, said to Agathon, "I just came hither in his company, being invited by him to sup with you."—"You did well," replied Agathon, "to come; but where is Socrates?"—"He just now came hither behind me; I myself wonder where he can be."—"Go and look, boy," said Agathon, "and bring Socrates in; meanwhile, you, Aristodemus, recline there near Eryximachus." And he bade a slave wash his feet that he might recline. Another slave, meanwhile, brought word that Socrates had retired into a neighbouring vestibule, where he stood, and, in spite of his message, refused to come in.—"What absurdity you talk!" cried Agathon; "call him, and do not leave him till he comes."—"Leave him alone, by all means," said Aristodemus; "it is customary with him sometimes to retire in this way and stand wherever it may chance. He will come presently, I do not doubt; do not disturb him."—"Well, be it as you will," said Agathon; "as it is, you boys, bring supper for the rest; put before us what you will, for I resolved that there should be no master of the feast. Consider me and these my friends, as guests, whom you have invited to supper, and serve them so that we may commend you."

After this they began supper, but Socrates did not come in. Agathon ordered him to be called, but Aristodemus perpetually forbade it. At last he came in, much about the middle of supper, not having delayed so long as was his custom. Agathon (who happened to be reclining at the end of the table, and alone,) said, as he entered, "Come hither, Socrates, and sit down by me; so that by the mere touch of one so wise as you are, I may enjoy the fruit of thy meditations in the vestibule; for, I well know, you would not have departed till you had discovered and secured it."

Socrates, having sate down as he was desired, replied, "It would be well, Agathon, if wisdom were of such a nature as that when we touched each other, it would overflow of its own accord, from him who possesses much to him who possesses little; like the water in the two chalices, which will flow through a flock of wool from the fuller into the emptier, until both are equal. If wisdom had this property, I should esteem myself most fortunate in reclining near to you. I should thus soon be filled, I think, with the most beautiful and various wisdom. Mine, indeed, is something obscure, and doubtful, and dreamlike. But yours is radiant, and has been crowned with amplest reward; for though you are yet so young, it shone forth from you, and became so manifest yesterday, that more than 30,000 Greeks can bear testimony to its excellence and loveliness."—"You are laughing at me, Socrates," said Agathon; "but you and I will decide this controversy about wisdom by and bye, taking Bacchus for our judge. At present turn to your supper."

After Socrates and the rest had finished supper, and had reclined back on their couches, and the libations had been poured forth, and they had sung hymns to the God, and all other rites which are customary had been performed, they turned to drinking. Then Pausanias made this kind of proposal. "Come, my friends," said he, "in what manner will it be pleasantest for us to drink? I must confess to you that, in reality, I am not very well from the wine we drank last night and I have some need of intermission. I suspect that most of you are in the same condition, for you were here yesterday. Now, consider how we shall drink most easily and comfortably."

" 'Tis a good proposal, Pausanias," said Aristophanes, "to contrive, in some way or other, to place moderation in our cups. I was one of those who were drenched last night."—Eryximachus, the son of Acumenus, hearing this, said: "I am of your opinion; I only wish to know one thing —whether Agathon is in the humour for hard drinking?"—"Not at all," replied Agathon; "I confess that I am not able to drink much this evening."—"It is an excellent thing for us," replied Eryximachus—"I mean myself, Aristodemus, Phaedrus, and these others—if you, who are such invincible drinkers, now refuse to drink. I ought to except Socrates, for he is capable of drinking everything or nothing; and whatever we shall determine will equally suit him. Since, then, no one present has any desire to drink much wine, I shall perhaps give less offence if I declare the nature of drunkenness. The science of medicine teaches us that drunkenness is very pernicious; nor would I willingly choose to drink immoderately myself, or counsel another to do so, especially if he had been drunk the night before."—"Yes," said Phaedrus, the Myrinusian, interrupting him, "I have been accustomed to confide in you, especially in your directions concerning medicine; and I would now willingly do so, if the rest will do the same." All then agreed that they would drink at this present banquet not for drunkenness but for pleasure.

"Since, then," said Eryximachus, "it is decided that no one shall be compelled to drink more than he pleases, I think that we may as well send away the flute-player to play to herself; or, if she likes, to the women within. Let us devote the present occasion to conversation between ourselves, and if you wish, I will propose to you what shall be the subject of our discussions." All present desired and entreated that he would explain. —"The exordium of my speech," said Eryximachus, "will be in the style of the 'Melanippe' of Euripides, for the story which I am about to tell belongs not to me, but to Phaedrus. Phaedrus has often indignantly complained to me, saying— 'Is it not strange, Eryximachus, that there are innumerable hymns and paeans composed for the other Gods, but that not one of the many poets who spring up in the world has ever composed a verse in honour of Love, who is such and so great a God? Nor any one of those accomplished sophists, who, like the famous Prodicus, have celebrated the praise of Hercules and others, [has] ever celebrated that of Love; but what is more astonishing, I have lately met with the book of some philosopher, in which salt is extolled on account of its utility, and many other things of the same nature are in like manner celebrated with elaborate praise. That so much serious thought is expended on such trifles, and that no man has dared to this day to frame a hymn in honour of Love, who being so great a deity, is thus neglected, may well be sufficient to excite my indignation.'

"There seemed to me some justice in these complaints of Phaedrus; I propose, therefore, at the same time, for the sake of giving pleasure to Phaedrus, and that we may on the present occasion do something well and befitting us, that this God should receive from those who are now present the honour which is most due to him. If you agree to my proposal, an excellent discussion might arise on the subject. Every one ought, according to my plan, to praise Love with as much eloquence as he can. Let Phaedrus begin first, both because he reclines the first in order, and because he is the father of the discussion."

"No one will vote against you, Eryximachus," said Socrates, "for how can I oppose your proposal, who am ready to confess that I know nothing on any subject but love? Or how can Agathon, or Pausanias, or even Aristophanes, whose life is one perpetual ministration to Venus and Bacchus? Or how can any other whom I see here? Though we who sit last are scarcely on an equality with you; for if those who speak before us shall have exhausted the subject with their eloquence and reasonings, our discourses will be superfluous. But in the name of Good Fortune, let Phaedrus begin and praise Love." The whole party agreed to what Socrates said, and entreated Phaedrus to begin.

What each then said on this subject, Aristodemus did not entirely recollect, nor do I recollect all that he related to me; but only the speeches of those who said what was most worthy of remembrance. First, then, Phaedrus began thus:—

"Love is a mighty deity, and the object of admiration, both to Gods and men, for many and for various claims; but especially on account of his origin. For that he is to be honoured as one of the most ancient of the Gods, this may serve as a testimony, that Love has no parents, nor is there any poet or other person who has ever affirmed that there are such. Hesiod says, that first 'Chaos was produced; then the broad-bosomed Earth, to be a secure foundation for all things; then Love.' He says that after Chaos these two were produced, the Earth and Love. Parmenides, speaking of generation, says:—'But he created Love before any of the Gods.' Acusileus agrees with Hesiod. Love, therefore, is universally acknowledged to be among the eldest of things. And in addition to this, Love is the author of our greatest advantages; for I cannot imagine a greater happiness and advantage to one who is in the flower of youth than an amiable lover, or to a lover than an amiable object of his love. For neither birth, nor wealth, nor honours, can awaken in the minds of men the principles which should guide those who from their youth aspire to an honourable and excellent life, as Love awakens them. I speak of the fear of shame, which deters them from that which is disgraceful; and the love of glory which incites to honourable deeds. For it is not possible that a state or private person should accomplish, without these incitements, anything beautiful or great. I assert, then, that should one who loves be discovered in any dishonourable action, or tamely enduring insult through cowardice, he would feel more anguish and shame if observed by the object of his passion, than if he were observed by his father or his companions, or any other person. In like manner, one who is the object of love is especially grieved to be discovered by his lover in any dishonourable act. If then, by any contrivance, a state or army could be composed of lovers and the beloved, it is beyond calculation how excellently they would administer their affairs, refraining from any thing base, contending with each other for the acquirement of fame, and exhibiting such valour in battle as that, though few in numbers, they might subdue all mankind. For should a lover desert the ranks or cast away his arms in the presence of his beloved, he would suffer far acuter shame from that one person's regard, than from the regard of all other men. A thousand times would he prefer to die, rather than desert the object of his attachment, and not succour him in danger.

"There is none so worthless whom Love cannot impel, as it were, by a divine inspiration, towards virtue, even so that he may through this inspiration become equal to one who might naturally be more excellent; and, in truth, as Homer says: The God breathes vigour into certain heroes —so Love breathes into those who love, the spirit which is produced from himself. Not only men, but even women who love, are those alone who willingly expose themselves to die for others. Alcestis, the daughter of Pelias, affords to the Greeks a remarkable example of this opinion; she alone being willing to die for her husband, and so surpassing his parents in the affection with which love inspired her towards him, as to make them appear, in the comparison with her, strangers to their own child, and related to him merely in name; and so lovely and admirable did this action appear, not only to men, but even to the Gods, that, although they conceded the prerogative of bringing back the spirit from death to few among the many who then performed excellent and honourable deeds, yet, delighted with this action, they redeemed her soul from the infernal regions: so highly do the Gods honour zeal and devotion in love. They sent back indeed Orpheus, the son of Oeagrus, from Hell, with his purpose unfulfilled, and, showing him only the spectre of her for whom he came, refused to render up herself. For Orpheus seemed to them, not as Alcestis, to have dared die for the sake of her whom he loved, and thus to secure to himself a perpetual intercourse with her in the regions to which she had preceded him, but like a cowardly musician, to have contrived to descend alive into Hell; and, indeed, they appointed as a punishment for his cowardice, that he should be put to death by women.

"Far otherwise did they regard Achilles, the son of Thetis, whom they sent to inhabit the islands of the blessed. For Achilles, though informed by his mother that his own death would ensue upon his killing Hector, but that if he refrained from it he might return home and die in old age, yet preferred revenging and honouring his beloved Patroclus; not to die for him merely, but to disdain and reject that life which he had ceased to share. Therefore the Gods honoured Achilles beyond all other men, because he thus preferred his friend to all things else. Aeschylus talks nonsense when he says, that Patroclus was beloved by Achilles, who was more beautiful, not only than Patroclus, but than all the other heroes, who was in the freshness of youth, and beardless, and according to Homer, much younger than his friend. But in truth the species of devotion in love which he exhibited is that which the Gods chiefly honour. Far more do they love and admire and crown with rewards the beloved who cherishes his lover, than the lover who cherishes his beloved; for the lover is diviner than the beloved, he is inspired by the God. On this account have they rewarded Achilles more amply than Alcestis; permitting his spirit to inhabit the islands of the blessed. Hence do I assert that Love is the most ancient and venerable of deities, and most powerful to endow mortals with the possession of happiness and virtue, both whilst they live and after they die."

Thus Aristodemus reported the discourse of Phaedrus; and after Phaedrus, he said that some others spoke, whose discourses he did not well remember. When they had ceased, Pausanias began thus:—

"Simply to praise Love, O Phaedrus, seems to me too bounded a scope for our discourse. If Love were one, it would be well. But since Love is not one, I will endeavour to distinguish which is the Love whom it becomes us to praise, and having thus discriminated one from the other, will attempt to render him who is the subject of our discourse the honour due to his divinity. We all know that Venus is never without Love; and if Venus were one, Love would be one; but since there are two Venuses, of necessity also must there be two Loves. For assuredly are there two Venuses; one, the eldest, the daughter of Uranus, born without

a mother, whom we call the Uranian; the other younger, the daughter
of Jupiter and Dione, whom we call the Pandemian;—of necessity must
there also be two Loves, the Uranian and Pandemian companions of these
Goddesses. It is becoming to praise all the Gods, but the attributes which
fall to the lot of each may be distinguished and selected. For any particular action whatever, in itself is neither good nor evil; what we are
now doing—drinking, singing, talking, none of these things are good
in themselves, but the mode in which they are done stamps them with
its own nature; and that which is done well, is good, and that which is
done ill, is evil. Thus, not all love, nor every mode of love is beautiful,
or worthy of commendation, but that alone which excites us to love
worthily. The Love, therefore, which attends upon Venus Pandemos
is, in truth, common to the vulgar, and presides over transient and fortuitous connexions, and is worshipped by the least excellent of mankind:
the votaries of this deity regard women as equally objects of love with
men; they seek the body rather than the soul, and the ignorant rather
than the wise, disdaining all that is honourable and lovely, and considering how they shall best satisfy their sensual necessities. This Love is
derived from the younger Goddess, who partakes in her nature both of
male and female. But the attendant on the other, the Uranian, whose
nature is entirely masculine, is the Love who inspires us with affection
towards men, and exempts us from all wantonness and libertinism. Those
who are inspired by this divinity seek the affections of that sex which
is endowed by nature with greater excellence and vigour both of body
and mind. And it is easy to distinguish those who especially exist under
the influence of this power, by their choosing in early youth as the objects
of their love those in whom the intellectual faculties have begun to de-
velope: in preference to mere youths. For those who begin to love in
this manner, seem to me to be preparing to pass their whole life together
in a community of good and evil, and not ever lightly deceiving those
who love them, to be faithless to their vows. There ought to be a law
that none should love mere youths; so much serious affection as this
deity enkindles should not be doubtfully bestowed; for the body and
mind of those so young are yet unformed, and it is difficult to foretell
what will be their future tendencies and power. The good voluntarily
impose this law upon themselves, and those vulgar lovers ought to be
compelled to the same observance, as we deter them with all the power
of the laws from the love of free matrons. For these are persons
whose shameful actions embolden those who observe their importunity
and intemperance, to assert, that it is dishonourable to serve and gratify

the objects of our love. But no one who does this gracefully and according to law, can justly be liable to the imputations of blame.

"The law as it relates to love in other cities may be easily understood, for it is plainly defined. Here and in Lacedaemon it is various. In Elis and in Beotia, where men are yet unskilled in philosophy and the use of language, the law simply declares that it is honourable to serve those we love: nor has any legislator either of ancient or modern times considered it dishonourable for this reason I imagine, because unaware of these distinctions, they were unwilling to throw obstacles in their own way by a vain attempt to dissuade the youth wholly from this practice. In Ionia and many other places, which are subject to the Barbarians, the law declares this affectionate service to be shameful. For not only this species of love, but philosophy and the practice of the gymnastic exercises, are represented as dishonourable by the tyrannical governments under which the Barbarians live. For I imagine it would little conduce to the benefit of the governors, that the governed should be disciplined to lofty thoughts and to unity and communion of stedfast friendship, of which admirable effects the tyrants of our own country have also learned that Love is the author. For the love of Harmodius and Aristogiton, strengthened into a firm friendship, dissolved the tyranny. Wherever, therefore, it is declared dishonourable in any case to serve and benefit lovers, that law is a mark of the depravity of the legislator, the avarice and tyranny of the rulers, and the cowardice of those who are ruled. Wherever it is simply declared to be honourable without distinction of cases, such a declaration denotes dulness and want of subtlety of mind in the authors of the regulation. Here the degree[s] of praise or blame to be attributed by law to this practice is far better regulated; but it is yet difficult to determine the cases to which they should refer.

"It [is] evident, however, for one in whom this passion is enkindled, it is more honourable to love openly than secretly; and most honourable to love the most excellent and virtuous, even if they should be less beautiful than others. It is honourable for the lover to exhort and sustain the object of his love in virtuous conduct. It is considered honourable to attain the love of those whom we seek, and the contrary shameful; and to facilitate this attainment, the law has given to the lover the permission of acquiring favour by the most extraordinary devices, which if a person should practise for any purpose besides this, he would incur the severest reproof of philosophy. For if any one desirous of accumulating money, or ambitious of procuring power, or seeking any other advantage, should, like a lover, seeking to acquire the favour of his beloved, employ prayers and entreaties in his necessity, and swear such oaths as lovers swear, and sleep before the threshold, and offer to subject himself to such slavery as no slave even would endure; he would be frustrated of the attainment of what he sought, both by his enemies and friends; these reviling him for his flattery, those sharply admonishing him, and taking to themselves the shame of his servility. But there is a certain grace in a lover who does all these things, and the law declares that he alone may do them without dishonour. It is commonly said that the Gods accord pardon to the lover alone if he should break his oath, and that there is no oath by Venus. Thus as our law declares, both Gods and men have given to lovers all possible indulgence.

"Considering these things, how admirable a thing in the state is love, and the affection and the facility of lovers towards each other! But since on the other hand the fathers of those who are the objects of love command their masters not to suffer them to converse with their lovers, and their comrades reproach them, if they perceive any intimacy of that kind, and those who are old do not reproach the censurers as if they censured unjustly; considering these things I say, one might think that this species of service and attachment were held to be dishonourable.

"The affair, however, I imagine, stands thus: As I have before said, Love cannot be considered in itself as either honourable or dishonourable: if it is honourably pursued, it is honourable; if dishonourably, dishonourable: it is dishonourable basely to serve and gratify a worthless person; it is honourable honourably to serve a person of virtue. That Pandemic lover who loves rather the body than the soul, is worthless, nor can be constant and consistent, since he has placed his affections on that which has no stability. For as soon as the flower of the form, which was the sole object of his desire, has faded, then he departs and is seen no more; bound by no faith or shame of his many promises and persuasions. But he who is the lover of virtuous manners is constant during life, since he has placed himself in harmony and desire with that which is consistent with itself.

"The[se] two classes of persons our law directs us to distinguish with careful examination, so that we may serve and converse with the one and avoid the other; determining, by that inquiry, by what the lover is attracted, and for what the object of his love is dear to him. On the same account it is considered dishonourable to be inspired with love at once, lest time should be wanting to know and approve the character of the object. It is considered dishonourable to be captivated by the allurements of wealth and power, or terrified through injuries to yield up the affections, or not to despise in the comparison with an unconstrained choice all political influence and personal advantage. For no circumstance is there in wealth or power so invariable and consistent, as that no generous friendship can ever spring up from amongst them. Our law therefore has left one method by which the beloved may gratify his lover. We have a law with respect to lovers which declares that it shall not be considered servile or disgraceful, though the lover should submit himself to any species of slavery for the sake of his beloved. The same opinion holds with respect to those who undergo any degradation for the sake of virtue. For it is esteemed among us, that if any one chooses to serve and obey another for the purpose of becoming more wise or more virtuous through the intercourse that might thence arise, such willing slavery is not the slavery of a dishonest flatterer. Through this law we should consider in the same light a servitude undertaken for the sake of love as one undertaken for the acquirement of wisdom or any other excellence, if indeed the devotion of a lover to his beloved is to be considered a beautiful thing. For when the lover and the beloved have once arrived at the same point, the province of each being distinguished; the one serving and gratifying his beloved, now his indeed in all things in which it were not unjust to serve him; the one conceding to his lover, the author of his wisdom and virtue, whatever it were not honourable to refuse; the one able to assist in the cultivation of the mind and in the acquirement of every other excellence; the other yet requiring education, and seeking the possession of wisdom; then alone, by the union of these conditions, and in no other case, is it honourable for the beloved to yield up his affections to his lover. In this servitude alone there is no disgrace in being deceived and defeated of the object for which it was undertaken; whereas every other is disgraceful, whether we are deceived or no. For if any one favours his lover for his wealth, and is deceived in the advantage which he expected, his lover turning out to be poor instead of rich, his conduct is not the less base; for such an one has already shown that for the sake of money he would submit in anything to any one. On the same principle, if any one favours another, believing him to be virtuous, for the sake of becoming better through the intercourse and affection for his lover, and is deceived; his lover turning out to be worthless, and far from the possession of virtue; yet it is honourable to have been so deceived. For such an one seems to have submitted to the servitude of Love, because he would endure anything from any one for the sake of becoming more virtuous and wise; a disposition of mind eminently beautiful.

"This is that Love who attends on the Uranian deity, and is Uranian; the author of innumerable benefits both to the state and to individuals, and by the necessity of whose influences both the lover and the beloved are disciplined into the zeal of virtue. All other Loves are the attendants on Venus Pandemos. So much, although unpremediated, is what I have to deliver on the subject of love, O Phaedrus."

Pausanias having ceased (for so the learned teach me to denote the changes of the discourse), Aristodemus said that it came to the turn of Aristophanes to speak; but [that] it happened that, from repletion or some other cause, he had an hiccup which prevented him; so he turned to Eryximachus, the physician, who was reclining close beside him, and said—"Eryximachus, it is but fair that you should cure my hiccup, or speak instead of me until it is over."—"I will do both," said Eryximachus; "I will speak in your turn, and you, when your hiccup has ceased, shall speak in mine. Meanwhile, if you hold your breath some time, it will subside. If not, gargle your throat with water; and if it still continues, take something to stimulate your nostrils, and sneeze; do this once or twice, and even though it should be very violent it will cease."— "Whilst you speak," said Aristophanes, "I will follow your directions."— Eryximachus then began:—

"Since Pausanias, beginning his discourse excellently, placed no fit completion and developement to it, I think it necessary to attempt to fill up what he has left unfinished. He has reasoned well in defining Love as of a double nature. The science of medicine, to which I have addicted myself, seems to teach me that the love which impels towards those who are beautiful, does not subsist only in the souls of men, but in the bodies also of those of all other living beings which are produced upon earth, and, in a word, in all things which are. So wonderful and mighty is this divinity, and so widely is his influence extended over all divine and human things! For the honour of my profession, I will begin by adducing a proof from medicine. The nature of the body contains within itself this double Love. For that which is healthy and that which is diseased in a body differ and are unlike: that which is unlike, loves and desires that which is unlike. Love, therefore, is different in a sane and in a diseased body. Pausanias has asserted rightly that it is honourable to gratify those things in the body which are good and healthy, and in this consists the skill of the physician; whilst those which a[re] bad and diseased, ought to be treated with no indulgence. The science of medicine, in a word, is a knowledge of the love affairs of the body, as they bear relation to repletion and evacuation; and he is the most skilful physician who can trace in those operations the good and evil love, can make the one change places with the other, and attract love into those parts from which he is absent, or expel him from those which he ought not to occupy. He ought to make those things which are most inimical, friendly, and excite them to mutual love. But those things are most inimical, which are most opposite to each other: cold to heat, bitterness to sweetness, dryness to moisture. Our progenitor, Aesculapius, as the poets inform us, (and indeed I believe them,) thro' the skill which he possessed to inspire Love and concord in these contending principles, established the science of medicine.

"The gymnastic arts and agriculture, no less than medicine, are exercised under the dominion of this God. Music, as any one may perceive, who yields a very slight attention to the subject, originates from the same source; which Heraclitus probably meant, though he could not express his meaning very clearly in words, when he says, 'One though apparently differing, yet so agrees with itself, as the harmony of a lyre and a bow.' It is great absurdity to say that an harmony differs, and can exist between things whilst they are dissimilar; but probably he meant that from sounds which first differed, like the grave and the acute, and which afterwards agreed, harmony was produced according to musical art. For no harmony can arise from the grave and the acute whilst yet they differ. But harmony is symphony: symphony is, as it were, concord. But it is impossible that concord should subsist between things that differ, so long as they differ. Between things which are discordant and dissimilar there is then no harmony. A rhythm is produced from that which is quick, and that which is slow, first being distinguished and opposed to each other, and then made accordant; so does medicine, no less than music, establish a concord between the objects of its art, producing love and agreement between adverse things.

"Music is then the knowledge of that which relates to Love in harmony and rhythm. In the very system of harmony and rhythm, it is easy to distinguish love. The double Love is not distinguishable in music itself; but it is required to apply it to the service of mankind by rhythm and harmony, which is called poetry, or the composition of melody; or by the correct use of songs and measures already composed, which is called discipline; then one can be distinguished from the other, by the aid of an extremely skilful artist. And the better love ought to be honoured and preserved for the sake of those who are virtuous, and that the nature of the vicious may be changed through the inspiration of its spirit. This is that beautiful Uranian love, the attendant of the Uranian muse: the

Pandemian is the attendant of Poly[hy]mnia; to whose influence we should only so far subject ourselves, as to derive pleasure from it without indulging to excess; in the same manner as, according to our art, we are instructed to seek the pleasures of the table, only so far as we can enjoy them without the consequences of disease. In music, therefore, and in medicine, and in all other things, human and divine, this double Love ought to be traced and discriminated; for it is in all things.

"Even the constitution of the seasons of the year is penetrated with these contending principles. For so often as heat and cold, dryness and moisture, of which I spoke before, are influenced by the more benignant Love, and are harmoniously and temperately intermingled with the seasons, [they] bring maturity and health to men, and to all other animals and plants. But when the evil and injurious Love assumes the dominion of the seasons of the year, destruction is spread widely abroad. Then pestilence is accustomed to arise, and many other blights and diseases fall upon animals and plants: and hoar frosts, and hails, and mildew on the corn, are produced from that excessive and disorderly love, with which each season of the year is impelled towards the other; the motions of which and the knowledge of the stars, is called astronomy. All sacrifices, and all those things in which divination is concerned (for these things are the links by which is maintained an intercourse and communion between the Gods and men) are nothing else than the science of preservation and right government of Love. For impiety is accustomed to spring up, so soon as any one ceases to serve the more honourable Love, and worship him by the sacrifice of good actions; but submits himself to the influences of the other, in relation of his duties towards his parents, and the Gods, and the living, and the dead. It is the object of divination to distinguish and remedy the effects of these opposite Loves; and divination is therefore the author of the friendship of Gods and men, because it affords the knowledge of what in matters of Love is lawful or unlawful to men.

"Thus every species of Love possesses collectively a various and vast, or rather universal power. But Love which incites to the acquirement of its objects according to virtue and wisdom, possesses the most exclusive dominion, and prepares for his worshippers the highest happiness through the mutual intercourse of social kindness which it promotes among them, and through the benevolence which he attracts to them from the Gods, our superiors.

"Probably in thus praising Love, I have unwillingly omitted many things; but it is your business, O Aristophanes, to fill up all that I have left incomplete; or, if you have imagined any other mode of honouring the divinity; for I observe your hiccup is over."

"Yes," said Aristophanes, "but not before I applied the sneezing. I wonder why the harmonious construction of our body should require such noisy operations as sneezing; for it ceased the moment I sneezed." —"Do you not observe what you do, my good Aristophanes?" said Eryximachus; "you are going to speak, and you predispose us to laughter, and compel me to watch for the first ridiculous idea which you may start in your discourse, when you might have spoken in peace."—"Let me unsay what I have said, then," replied Aristophanes, laughing. "Do not watch me, I entreat you; though I am not afraid of saying what is laughable (since that would be all gain, and quite in the accustomed spirit of my muse) but lest I should say what is ridiculous."—"Do you think to throw your dart, and escape with impunity, Aristophanes? Attend, and what you say be careful you maintain; then, perhaps, if it pleases me, I may dismiss you without question."

"Indeed, Eryximachus," proceeded Aristophanes, "I have designed that my discourse should be very different from yours and that of Pausanias. It seems to me that mankind are by no means penetrated with a conception of the power of Love, or they would have built sumptuous temples and altars, and have established magnificent rites of sacrifice in his honour; he deserves worship and homage more than all the other Gods, and he has yet received none. For Love is of all the Gods the most friendly to mortals; and the physician of those wounds, whose cure would be the greatest happiness which could be conferred upon the human race. I will endeavour to unfold to you his true power, and you can relate what I declare to others.

"You ought first to know the nature of man, and the adventures he has gone through; for his nature was anciently far different from that which it is at present. First, then, human beings were formerly not divided into two sexes, male and female; there was also a third, common to both the others, the name of which remains, though the sex itself has disappeared. The androgynous sex, both in appearance and in name, was common both to male and female; its name alone remains, which labours under a reproach.

"At the period to which I refer, the form of every human being was round, the back and the sides being circularly joined, and each had four arms and as many legs; two faces fixed upon a round neck, exactly like each other; one head between the two faces; four ears, and two organs of generation; and everything else as from such proportions it is easy to conjecture. Man walked upright as now, in whatever direction he pleased; and when he wished to go fast he made use of all his eight limbs, and proceeded in a rapid motion by rolling circularly round,—like tumblers, who, with their legs in the air, tumble round and round. We account for the production of three sexes by supposing that, at the beginning, the male was produced from the Sun, the female from the Earth; and that sex which participated in both sexes, from the Moon, by reason of the androgynous nature of the Moon. They were round, and their mode of proceeding was round, from the similarity which must needs subsist between them and their parent.

"They were strong also, and had aspiring thoughts. They it was who levied war against the Gods; and what Homer writes concerning Ephialtus and Otus, that they sought to ascend heaven and dethrone the Gods, in reality relates to this primitive people. Jupiter and the other Gods debated what was to be done in this emergency. For neither could they prevail on themselves to destroy them, as they had the Giants, with thunder, so that the race should be abolished; for in that case they would be deprived of the honours of the sacrifices which they were in the custom of receiving from them; nor could they permit a continuance of their insolence and impiety. Jupiter, with some difficulty having devised a scheme, at length spoke. 'I think,' said he, 'I have contrived a method by which we may, by rendering the human race more feeble, quell the insolence which they exercise, without proceeding to their utter destruction. I will cut each of them in half; and so they will at once be weaker and more useful on account of their numbers. They shall walk upright on two legs. If they show any more insolence, and will not keep quiet, I will cut them up in half again, so they shall go about hopping on one leg.'

"So saying, he cut human beings in half, as people cut eggs before they salt them, or as I have seen eggs cut with hairs. He ordered Apollo to take each one as he cut him, and turn his face and half his neck towards the operation, so that by contemplating it he might become more cautious and humble; and then to cure him, Apollo turned the face round, and drawing the skin upon what we now call the belly, like a contracted pouch, and leaving one opening, that which is called the navel, tied it in the middle. He then smoothed many other wrinkles, and moulded the breast with much such an instrument as the leather-cutters use to smooth the skins upon the block. He left only a few wrinkles in the belly, near the navel, to serve as a record of its former adventure. Immediately after this division, as each desired to possess the other half of himself, these divided people threw their arms around and embraced each other, seeking to grow together; and from this resolution to do nothing without the other half, they died of hunger and weakness: when one half died and the other was left alive, that which was thus left sought the other and folded it to its bosom; whether that half were an entire woman (for we now call it a woman) or a man; and thus they perished. But Jupiter, pitying them, thought of another contrivance, and placed the parts of generation before. Since formerly when these parts were exposed they produced their kind not by the assistance of each other, but like grasshoppers, by engendering upon the earth. In this manner is generation now produced, by the union of male and female; so that from the embrace of a man and woman the race is propagated, but from those of the same sex no such consequence ensues.

"From this period, mutual Love has naturally existed in human beings; that reconciler and bond of union of their original nature, which seeks to make two, one, and to heal the divided nature of man. Every one of us is thus the half of what may be properly termed a man, and like a *psetta*[1] cut in two, is the imperfect portion of an entire whole, perpetually necessitated to seek the half belonging to him. Those who are a section of what was formerly one man and woman, are lovers of the female sex, and most of the adulterers, and those women who fall in love with men and intrigue with them, belong to this species. Those women who are a section of what in its unity contained two women, are not much attracted by the male sex, but have their inclinations principally engaged by their own. And the *Hetairistriae*[2] belong to this division. Those who are a section of what in the beginning was entirely male seek the society of males; and before they arrive at manhood, such being portions of what was masculine, are delighted with the intercourse and familiarity of men. These are the youths who, being of a more manly nature, promise the fairest harvest of future excellence. Some attach to them the reproach of libertinism and immodesty, but without justice; for they do not seek an intercourse with men from any immodesty but from the impulses of a generous, aspiring and manly nature. A great proof of which is that such alone ever attain to political power. When they arrive at manhood they still only associate with those of their own sex; and they never engage in marriage and the propagation of the species from sensual desire but only in obedience to the laws. It would be sufficient to them if they lived for ever unmarried in the mutual society of their equals.

[1] Shelley is here transliterating ψῆττα, sole or flounder; see D'Arcy Wentworth Thompson, *A Glossary of Greek Fishes* (London, 1947), pp. 294-295.

[2] Shelley is here transliterating ἑταιρίστριαι, homosexual women.

"Such as I have described is ever an affectionate lover and a faithful friend, delighting in that which is in conformity with his own nature. Whenever, therefore, any such as I have described are impetuously struck, through the sentiment of their former union, with love and desire and the want of community, they are ever unwilling to be divided even for a moment. These are they who devote their whole lives to each other, with a vain and inexpressible longing to obtain from each other something they know not what; for it is not merely the sensual delights of their intercourse for the sake of which they dedicate themselves to each other with such serious affection; but the soul of each manifestly thirsts for, from the other, something which there are no words to describe, and divines that which it seeks, and traces obscurely the footsteps of its obscure desire. If Vulcan should stand over the couch of these persons thus affected as they were reclining together, with his tools, and should say to them, 'My good people, what is it that you want with one another?' And if, while they were hesitating what to answer, he should proceed to ask, 'Do you not desire the closest union and singleness to exist between you, so that you may never be divided night or day? If so, I will melt you together, and make you grow into one, so that both in life and death ye may be undivided. Consider, is this what you desire? Will it content you if you become that which I propose?' We all know that no one would refuse such an offer, but would at once feel that this was what he had ever sought; and intimately to mix and melt and to be melted together with his beloved, so that one should be made out of two.

"The cause of this desire is, that according to our original nature, we were once entire. The desire and the pursuit of integrity and union is that which we all love. First, as I said, we were entire, but now we have been divided through our own wickedness, as the Arcadians by the Lacedaemonians. There is reason to fear, if we are guilty of any additional impiety towards the Gods, that we may be cut in two again, and may go about like those figures painted on the columns, divided through the middle of our nostrils, as thin as *lispae*.[3] On which account every man ought to be exhorted to pay due reverence to the Gods, that we may escape so severe a punishment, and obtain those things which Love, our general and commander, incites us to desire; against whom let none rebel by exciting the hatred of the Gods. For if we continue on good terms with them, we may discover and possess those lost and concealed objects of our love; a good-fortune which now befalls to few. Nor let

[3] Shelley is here transliterating λίσπαι, dice cut in two by friends, each of whom kept half as a tally.

Eryximachus take up that expression as if I alluded to Pausanias and Agathon, for probably they who are manly by nature, are to be ranked among those fortunate few.

"I assert, then, that the happiness of all, both men and women, consists singly in the fulfilment of their Love, and in that possession of its objects by which we are in some degree restored to our antient nature. If this be the completion of felicity, that must necessarily approach nearest to it, in which we obtain the possession and society of those whose natures most intimately accord with our own. And if we would celebrate any God as the author of this benefit, we should justly celebrate Love with hymns of joy; who, in our present condition, brings good assistance in our necessity, and affords great hopes, if we persevere in piety towards the Gods, that he will restore us to our original state, and confer on us the complete happiness alone suited to our nature.

"Such, Eryximachus, is my discourse on the subject of Love; different indeed from yours, which I nevertheless entreat you not to turn into ridicule, that we may not interrupt what each has separately to deliver on the subject."

"I will refrain at present," said Eryximachus, "for your discourse delighted me. And if I did not know that Socrates and Agathon were profoundly versed in the science of love affairs, I should fear that they had nothing new to say, after so many and such various imaginations. As it is, I confide in the fertility of their geniuses."—"Your part of the contest, at least, was strenuously fought, Eryximachus," said Socrates, "but if you had been in the situation in which I am, or rather shall be, after the discourse of Agathon, like me, you would then have reason to fear, and be reduced to your wits' end."—"Socrates," said Agathon, "wishes to confuse me with the enchantments of his wit, sufficiently confused already with the expectation I see in the assembly in favour of my discourse."—"I must have lost my memory, Agathon," replied Socrates, "if I imagined that you could be disturbed by a few private persons, after having witnessed your firmness and courage in ascending the rostrum with the actors, and in calmly reciting your compositions in the presence of so great an assembly as that which decreed you the prize of tragedy." —"What then, Socrates," retorted Agathon, "do you think me so full of the theatre as to be ignorant that the judgement of a few wise is more awful than that of a multitude of others, to one who rightly balances the value of their suffrages?"—"I should judge ill indeed, Agathon," answered Socrates, "in thinking you capable of any rude and unrefined conception, for I well know that if you meet with any whom you consider wise, you esteem such alone of more value than all others. But we are far from being entitled to this distinction, for we were also of that assembly, and to be numbered among the rest. But should you meet with any who are really wise, you would be careful to say nothing in their presence which you thought they would not approve—is it not so?"—"Certainly," replied Agathon.—"You would not then exercise the same caution in the presence of the multitude in which they were included?"—"My dear Agathon," said Phaedrus, interrupting him, "if you answer all the questions of Socrates, they will never have an end; he will urge them without conscience so long as he can get any person, especially one who is so beautiful, to dispute with him. I own it delights me to hear Socrates discuss; but at present, I must see that Love is not defrauded of the praise, which it is my province to exact from each of you. Pay the God his due, and then reason between yourselves if you will."

"Your admonition is just, Phaedrus," replied Agathon, "nor need any reasoning I hold with Socrates impede me; we shall find many future opportunities for discussion. I will begin my discourse then, first having defined what ought to be the subject of it. All who have already spoken seem to me not so much to have praised Love, as to have felicitated mankind on the many advantages of which that deity is the cause; what he is, the author of these great benefits, none have yet declared. There is one mode alone of celebration which would comprehend the whole topic, namely, first to declare what are those benefits, and then what he is who is the author of those benefits, which are the subject of our discourse. Love ought first to be praised, and then his gifts declared. I assert, then, that although all the Gods are immortally happy, Love, if I dare trust my voice to express so awful a truth, is the happiest, and most excellent, and the most beautiful. That he is the most beautiful is evident; first, O Phaedrus, from this circumstance, that he is the youngest of the Gods; and, secondly, from his fleetness, and his repugnance to all that is old; for he escapes with the swiftness of wings from old age; a thing in itself sufficiently swift, since it overtakes us sooner than there is need; and which Love, who delights in the intercourse of the young, hates, and in no manner can be induced to enter into community with. The ancient proverb, which says that like is attracted by like, applies to the attributes of Love. I concede many things to you, O Phaedrus, but this I do not concede, that Love is more ancient than Saturn and Iapetus. I assert that he is not only the youngest of the Gods, but invested with everlasting youth. Those ancient deeds among the Gods recorded by Hesiod and

Parmenides, if their relations are to be considered as true, were produced not by Love, but by Necessity. For if Love had been then in Heaven, those violent and sanguinary crimes never would have taken place; but there would ever have subsisted that affection and peace, in which the Gods now live, under the influence of Love.

"He is young, therefore, and being young is tender and soft. There were need of some poet like Homer to celebrate the delicacy and tenderness of Love. For Homer says, that the Goddess Calamity is delicate, and that her feet are tender. 'Her feet are soft,' he says, 'for she treads not upon the ground, but makes her path upon the heads of men.' He gives as an evidence of her tenderness, that she walks not upon that which is hard, but that which is soft. The same evidence is sufficient to make manifest the tenderness of Love. For Love walks not upon the earth, nor over the heads of men, which are not indeed very soft; but he dwells within, and treads on the softest of existing things, having established his habitation within the souls and inmost nature of Gods and men; not indeed in all souls—for wherever he chances to find a hard and rugged disposition, there he will not inhabit, but only where it is most soft and tender. Of needs must he be the most delicate of all things, who touches lightly with his feet only the softest parts of those things which are the softest of all.

"He is then the youngest and the most delicate of all divinities; and in addition to this, he is, as it were, the most moist and liquid. For if he were otherwise, he could not, as he does, fold himself around everything, and secretly flow out and into every soul. His loveliness, that which Love possesses far beyond all other things, is a manifestation of the liquid and flowing symmetry of his form; for between deformity and Love there is eternal contrast and repugnance. His life is spent among flowers, and this accounts for the immortal fairness of his skin; for the winged Love rests not in his flight on any form, or within any soul the flower of whose loveliness is faded, but there remains most willingly where is the odour and radiance of blossoms, yet unwithered. Concerning the beauty of the God, let this be sufficient, though many things must remain unsaid. Let us next consider the virtue and power of Love.

"What is most admirable in Love is, that he neither inflicts nor endures injury in his relations either with Gods or men. Nor if he suffers any thing does he suffer it through violence, nor doing anything does he act it with violence, for Love is never even touched with violence. Every one willingly administers every thing to Love; and that which every one voluntarily concedes to another, the laws, which are the kings of the republic, decree that it is just for him to possess. In addition to justice, Love participates in the highest temperance; for if temperance is defined to be the being superior to and holding under dominion pleasures and desires; then Love, than whom no pleasure is more powerful, and who is thus more powerful than all persuasions and delights, must be excellently temperate. In power and valour Mars cannot contend with Love: the love of Venus possesses Mars; the possessor is always superior to the possessed, and he who subdues the most powerful must of necessity be the most powerful of all.

"The justice and temperance and valour of the God have been thus declared;—there remains to exhibit his wisdom. And first, that, like Eryximachus, I may honour my own profession, the God is a wise poet; so wise that he can even make a poet one who was not before: for every one, even if before he were ever so undisciplined, becomes a poet as soon as he is touched by Love; a sufficient proof that Love is a great poet, and well skilled in that science according to the discipline of music. For what any one possesses not, or knows not, that can he neither give nor teach another. And who will deny that the divine poetry, by which all living things are produced upon the earth, is not harmonized by the wisdom of Love? Is it not evident that Love was the author of all the arts of life with which we are acquainted, and that he whose teacher has been Love, becomes eminent and illustrious, whilst he who knows not Love, remains forever unregarded and obscure? Apollo invented medicine, and divination, and archery, under the guidance of desire and Love; so that Apollo was the disciple of Love. Through him the Muses discovered the arts of literature, and Vulcan that of moulding brass, and Minerva the loom, and Jupiter the mystery of the dominion which he now exercises over Gods and men. So were the Gods taught and disciplined by the love of that which is beautiful; for there is no love towards deformity.

"At the origin of things, as I have before said, many fearful deeds are reported to have been done among the Gods, on account of the dominion of Necessity. But so soon as this deity sprang forth from the desire which forever tends in the Universe towards that which is lovely, then all blessings descended upon all living things, human and divine. Love seems to me, O Phaedrus, a divinity the most beautiful and the best of all, and the author to all others of the excellencies with which his own nature is endowed. Nor can I restrain the poetic enthusiasm which takes possession of my discourse, and bids me declare that Love is the divinity who creates peace among men, and calm upon the sea, the windless silence of storms, repose and sleep in sadness. Love divests us of all alienation from each other, and fills our vacant hearts with overflowing sympathy; he gathers us together in such social meetings as we now delight to celebrate, our guardian and our guide in dances, and sacrifices, and feasts. Yes, Love who showers benignity upon the world, and before whose presence all harsh passions flee and perish; the author of all soft affections; the destroyer of all ungentle thoughts; merciful, mild; the object of the admiration of the wise, and the delight of Gods; possessed by the fortunate, and desired by the unhappy, therefore unhappy because they possess him not; the father of grace, and delicacy, and gentleness, and delight, and persuasion, and desire; the cherisher of all that is good, the abolisher of all evil; our most excellent pilot, defence, saviour and guardian in labour and in fear, in desire and in reason; the ornament and governor of all things human and divine; the best, the loveliest; in whose footsteps everyone ought to follow, celebrating him excellently in song, and bearing each his part in that divinest harmony which Love sings to all things which live and are, soothing the troubled minds of Gods and men. This, O Phaedrus, is what I have to offer in praise of the Divinity; partly composed, indeed, of thoughtless and playful fancies, and partly of such serious ones, as I could well command."

No sooner had Agathon ceased, than a loud murmur of applause arose from all present; so becomingly had the fair youth spoken, both in praise of the God, and in extenuation of himself. Then Socrates, addressing Eryximachus, said, "Was not my fear reasonable, son of Acumenus? Did I not divine what has, in fact, happened,—that Agathon's discourse would be so wonderfully beautiful, as to pre-occupy all interest in what I should say?"—"You, indeed, divined well so far, O Socrates," said Eryximachus, "that Agathon would speak eloquently, but not that, therefore, you would be reduced to any difficulty."—"How, my good friend, can I or any one else be otherwise than reduced to difficulty, who speak after a discourse so various and so eloquent, and which otherwise had been sufficiently wonderful, if, at the conclusion, the splendour of the sentences, and the choice selection of the expressions, had not struck all the hearers with astonishment; so that I, who well know that I can never say anything nearly so beautiful as this, would, if there had been any escape, have run away for shame. The story of Gorgias came into my mind, and I was afraid lest in reality I should suffer what Homer describes; and lest Agathon, scaring my discourse with the head of the eloquent Gorgias, should turn me to stone for speech-lessness. I immediately perceived how ridiculously I had engaged myself with you to assume a part in rendering praise to Love, and had boasted that I was well skilled in amatory matters, being so ignorant of the manner in which it is becoming to render him honour, as I now perceive myself to be. I, in my simplicity, imagined that the truth ought to be spoken concerning each of the topics of our praise, and that it would be sufficient, choosing those which are the most honourable to the God, to place them in as luminous an arrangement as we could. I had, therefore, great hopes that I should speak satisfactorily, being well aware that I was acquainted with the true foundations of the praise which we have engaged to render. But since, as it appears, that our purpose has been, not to render Love his due honour, but to accumulate the most beautiful and the greatest attributes of his divinity, whether they in truth belong to it or not, and that the proposed question is not how Love ought to be praised, but how we should praise him most eloquently, my attempt must of necessity fail. It is on this account, I imagine, that in your discourses you have attributed everything to Love, and have described him to be the author of such and so great effects as, to those who are ignorant of his true nature, may exhibit him as the most beautiful and the best of all things. Not, indeed, to those who know the truth. Such praise has a splendid and imposing effect, but as I am unacquainted with the art of rendering it, my mind, which could not foresee what would be required of me, absolves me from that which my tongue promised. Farewell, then, for such praise I can never render.

"But if you desire, I will speak what I feel to be true; and that I may not expose myself to ridicule, I entreat you to consider that I speak without entering into competition with those who have preceded me. Consider, then, Phaedrus, whether you will exact from me such a discourse, containing the mere truth with respect to Love, and composed of such unpremeditated expressions as may chance to offer themselves to my mind."—Phaedrus and the rest bade him speak in the manner which he judged most befitting.—"Permit me, then, O Phaedrus, to ask Agathon a few questions, so that, confirmed by his agreement with me, I may proceed."—"Willingly," replied Phaedrus, "ask."—Then Socrates thus began:—

"I applaud, dear Agathon, the beginning of your discourse, where you say, we ought first to define and declare what Love is, and then his works. This rule I particularly approve. But, come, since you have given us a discourse of such beauty and majesty concerning Love, you are able, I doubt not, to explain this question, whether Love is the Love of something or nothing? I do not ask you of what parents Love is; for the enquiry, of whether Love is the love of any father or mother, would be sufficiently ridiculous. But if I were asking you to describe that which a father is, I should ask, not whether a father was the love of any one, but whether a father was the father of any one or not; you would undoubtedly reply, that a father was the father of a son or daughter; would you not?"—"Assuredly."—"You would define a mother in the same manner?"—"Without doubt."—"Yet bear with me, and answer a few more questions, for I would learn from you that which I wish to know. If I should enquire, in addition, is not a brother, through the very nature of his relation, the brother of some one?"—"Certainly."—"Of a brother or sister is he not?"—"Without question."—"Try to explain to me then the nature of Love; Love is the love of something or nothing?"—"Of something, certainly."

"Observe and remember this concession. Tell me yet farther, whether Love desires that of which it is the Love or not?"—"It desires it, assuredly."—"Whether possessing that which it desires and loves, or not possessing it, does it desire and love?"—"Not possessing it, I should imagine."—"Observe now, whether it does not appear, that, of necessity, desire desires that which it wants and does not possess, and no longer desires that which it no longer wants: this appears to me, Agathon, of necessity to be; how does it appear to you?"—"It appears so to me also." —"Would any one who was already illustrious, desire to be illustrious; would any one already strong, desire to be strong? From what has already been conceded, it follows that he would not. If any one already strong, should desire to be strong; or any one already swift, should desire to be swift; or any one already healthy, should desire to be healthy, it must be concluded that they still desired the advantages of what they already seemed possessed. To destroy the foundation of this error, observe, Agathon, that each of these persons must possess the several advantages in question, at the moment present to our thoughts, whether he will or no. And, now, is it possible that those advantages should be at that time the objects of his desire? For, if any one should say, being in health, 'I desire to be in health'; being rich, 'I desire to be rich, and thus still desire those things which I already possess,' we might say to him, 'You, my friend, possess health, and strength, and riches; you do not desire to possess now, but to continue to possess them in the future; for, whether you will or no, they now belong to you. Consider then, whether, when you say that you desire things present to you, and in your own possession, you say anything else than that you desire the advantages to be for the future also in your possession.' What else could he reply?"

—"Nothing, indeed."—"Is not Love, then, the love of that which is not within its reach, and which cannot hold in security, for the future, those things of which it obtains a present and transitory possession?"—"Evidently."—"Love, therefore, and every thing else that desires anything, desires that which is absent and beyond his reach, that which it has not, that which is not itself, that which it wants; such are the things of which there are desire and love."—"Assuredly."

"Come," said Socrates, "let us review your concessions. Is Love anything else than the love first of something; and, secondly, of those things of which it has need?"—"Nothing."—"Now, remember of those things you said in your discourse, that Love was the love—if you wish I will remind you. I think you said something of this kind, that all the affairs of the Gods were admirably disposed through the love of the things which are beautiful; for there was no love of things deformed; did you not say so?"—"I confess that I did."—"You said what was most likely to be true, my friend; and if the matter be so, the love of beauty must be one thing, and the love of deformity another."—"Certainly."—"It is conceded, then, that Love loves that which he wants but possesses not?" —"Yes, certainly."—"But Love wants and does not possess beauty?"— "Indeed it must necessarily follow."—"What, then! call you that beautiful which has need of beauty and possesses not?"—"Assuredly no."— "Do you still assert, then, that Love is beautiful, if all that we have said be true?"—"Indeed, Socrates," said Agathon, "I am in danger of being convicted of ignorance, with respect to all that I then spoke."—"You spoke most eloquently, my dear Agathon; but bear with my questions yet a moment. You admit that things which are good are also beautiful?" —"No doubt."—"If Love, then, be in want of beautiful things, and things which are good are beautiful, he must be in want of things which are good?"—"I cannot refute your arguments, Socrates."—"You cannot refute truth, my dear Agathon: to refute Socrates is nothing difficult.

"But I will dismiss these questionings. At present let me endeavour, to the best of my power, to repeat to you, on the basis of the points which have been agreed upon between me and Agathon, a discourse concerning Love, which I formerly heard from the prophetess Diotima, who was profoundly skilled in this and many other doctrines, and who, ten years before the pestilence, procured to the Athenians, through their sacrifices, a delay of the disease; for it was she who taught me the science of things relating to Love.

"As you well remarked, Agathon, we ought to declare who and what is Love, and then his works. It is easiest to relate them in the same order, as the foreign prophetess observed when, questioning me, she related them. For I said to her much the same things that Agathon has just said to me—that Love was a great deity, and that he was beautiful; and she refuted me with the same reasons as I have employed to refute Agathon, compelling me to infer that he was neither beautiful or good, as I said—'What then,' I objected, 'O Diotima, is Love ugly and evil?'—'Good words, I entreat you,' said Diotima; 'do you think that every thing which is not beautiful, must of necessity be ugly?'—'Certainly.'—'And every thing that is not wise, ignorant? Do you not perceive that there is something between ignorance and wisdom?'—'What is that?'—'To have a right opinion or conjecture. Observe, that this kind of opinion, for which no reason can be rendered, cannot be called knowledge; for how can that be called knowledge, which is without evidence or reason? Nor ignorance, on the other hand; for how can that be called ignorance which arrives at the persuasion of that which it really is? A right opinion is something between understanding and ignorance.'—I confessed that what she alledged was true.—'Do not then say,' she continued, 'that what is not beautiful is of necessity deformed, nor what is not good is of necessity evil; nor, since you have confessed that Love is neither beautiful or good, infer, therefore, that he is deformed or evil, but rather something intermediate.'

" 'But,' I said, 'Love is confessed by all to be a great God.'—'Do you mean, when you say all, all those who know, or those who know not, what they say?'—'All collectively.'—'And how can that be, Socrates?' said she laughing; 'how can he be acknowledged to be a great God, by those who assert that he is not even a God at all?'—'And who are they?' I said.—'You for one, and I for another.'—'How can you say that, Diotima?'—'Easily,' she replied, 'and with truth; for tell me, do you not own that all the Gods are beautiful and happy? or will you presume to maintain that any God is otherwise?'—'By Jupiter, not I!'—'Do you not call those alone happy who possess all things that are beautiful and good?' —'Certainly.'—'You have confessed that Love, through his desire for things beautiful and good, possesses not those materials of happiness.'— 'Indeed such was my concession.'—'But how can we conceive a God to be without the possession of what is beautiful and good?'—'In no manner, I confess.'—'Observe, then, that you do not consider Love to be a God.'—'What then,' I said, 'is Love a mortal?'—'By no means.'—'But what, then?'—'Like those things which I have before instanced, he is neither mortal or immortal, but something intermediate.'—'What is that, O Diotima?'—'A great Daemon, Socrates; and every thing daemoniacal hold[s] an intermediate place between what is divine and what is mortal.'

" 'What is his power and nature?' I inquired.—'He interprets and makes a communication between divine and human things, conveying the prayers and sacrifices of men to the Gods, and communicating the commands and directions concerning the mode of worship most pleasing to them, from Gods to men. He fills up that intermediate space between these two classes of beings, so as to bind together, by his own power, the whole universe of things. Through him subsist all divination, and the science of sacred things as it relates to sacrifices, and expiations, and disenchantments, and prophecy, and magic. The divine nature cannot immediately communicate with what is human, but all that intercourse and converse which is conceded by the Gods to men, both whilst they sleep and when they wake, subsists through the intervention of Love; and he who is wise in the science of this intercourse is supremely happy, and participates in the daemoniacal nature; whilst he who is wise in any other science or art, remains a mere ordinary slave. These daemons are, indeed, many and various, and one of them is Love.

" 'Who are the parents of Love?' I enquired.—'The history of what you ask,' replied Diotima, 'is somewhat long; nevertheless I will explain it to you. On the birth of Venus the Gods celebrated a great feast, and among them [came] Plenty, the son of Metis. After supper, Poverty, observing the profusion, came to beg, and stood beside the door. Plenty being drunk with nectar, for wine was not yet invented, went out into Jupiter's garden, and fell into a deep sleep. Poverty wishing to have a child by Plenty, on account of her low estate, lay down by him, and from his embraces conceived Love. Love is, therefore, the follower and servant of Venus, because he was conceived at her birth, and because by nature he is a lover of all that is beautiful, and Venus was beautiful. And since Love is the child of Poverty and Plenty, his nature and fortune participate[s] in that of his parents. He is for ever poor, and so far from being delicate and beautiful, as mankind imagine, he is squalid and withered; he flies low along the ground, and is homeless and unsandalled; he sleeps without covering before the doors, and in the unsheltered streets; possessing thus far his mother's nature, that he is ever the companion of Want. But, inasmuch as he participates in that of his father, he is for ever scheming to obtain things which are good and beautiful; he is fearless, vehement, and strong; a dreadful hunter, for ever weaving some new contrivance; exceedingly cautious and prudent, and full of resources; he is also, during his whole existence, a philosopher, a powerful enchanter, a wizard, and a subtle sophist. And, as his nature is neither mortal nor immortal, on the same day when he is fortunate and successful, he will at one time flourish, and then die away, and then, according to his father's nature, again revive. All that he acquires perpetually flows away from him, so that Love is never either rich or poor, and holding for ever an intermediate state between ignorance and wisdom. The case stands thus:—no God philosophizes or desires to become wise, for he is wise; nor, if there exist any other being who is wise, does he philosophize. Nor do the ignorant philosophize, for they desire not to become wise; for this is the evil of ignorance, that he who has neither intelligence, nor virtue, nor delicacy of sentiment, imagines that he possesses all those things sufficiently. He seeks not, therefore, that possession of whose want they are not aware.'—'Who, then, O Diotima,' I enquired, 'are philosophers, if they are neither the ignorant nor the wise?'—'It is evident, even to a child, that they are those intermediate persons, among whom is Love. For Wisdom is one of the most beautiful of all things; Love is that which thirsts for the beautiful, so that Love is of necessity a philosopher, philosophy being an intermediate state between ignorance and wisdom. His parentage accounts for his condition, being the child of a wise and well-provided father, and of a mother both ignorant and poor.

" 'Such is the daemoniacal nature, my dear Socrates; nor do I wonder at your error concerning Love, for you thought, as I conjecture from what you say, that Love was not the lover but the beloved, and thence, well concluded that he must be supremely beautiful; for that which is the object of Love must indeed be fair, and delicate, and perfect, and most happy; but Love inherits, as I have declared, a totally opposite nature.'— 'Your words have persuasion in them, O stranger,' I said; 'be it as you say. But this Love, what advantages does he afford to men?'—'I will proceed to explain it to you, Socrates. Love being such and so produced as I have described, is, indeed, as you say, the love of things which are beautiful. But if any one should ask us, saying: O Socrates and Diotima, why is Love the love of beautiful things? Or, in plainer words, what does the lover of that which is beautiful, love in the object of his love, and seek from it?'—'He seeks,' I said, interrupting her, 'the property and possession of it.'—'But that,' she replied, 'might still be met with another question, What has he, [who] possesses that which is beautiful?'— 'Indeed, I cannot immediately reply.'—'But if, changing the beautiful for good, any one should enquire,—I ask, O Socrates, what is that which he who loves that which is good, loves in the object of his love?'—'To be in his possession,' I replied.—'And what has he, who has the possession of good?'—'This question is of easier solution: he is happy.'—'Those who are happy, then, are happy through the possession; and it [is] useless to enquire what he desires, who desires to be happy; the question seems to have a complete reply. But do you think that this wish and this love are common to all men, and that all desire, that [that] which is good should be for ever present to them?'—'Certainly, common to all.'—'Why do we not say then, Socrates, that every one loves? if, indeed, all love perpetually the same thing? But we say that some love, and some do not.'—'Indeed I wonder why it is so.'—'Wonder not,' said Diotima, 'for we select a particular species of love, and apply to it distinctively the appellation of that which is universal.'—

" 'Give me an example of such a select application.'—'Poetry; which is a general name signifying every cause whereby anything proceeds from that which is not, into that which is; so that the exercise of every inventive art is poetry, and all such artists poets. Yet they are not called poets, but distinguished by other names; and one portion or species of poetry, that which has relation to music and rhythm, is divided from all others, and known by the name belonging to all. For this is alone properly called poetry, and those who exercise the art of this species of poetry, poets. So, with respect to Love. Love is indeed universally all that earnest desire for the possession of happiness and that which is good; the greatest and the subtlest love, and which inhabits the heart of every human being; but those who seek this object through the acquirement of wealth, or the exercise of the gymnastic arts, or philosophy, are not said to love, nor are called lovers; one species alone is called Love, and those alone are said to be lovers, and to love, who seek the attainment of the universal desire through one species of Love, which is peculiarly distinguished by the name belonging to the whole. It is asserted by some, that they love, who are seeking the lost half of their divided being. But I assert, that Love is neither the love of [the] half or of the whole, unless, my friend, it meets with that which is good; since men willingly cut off their own hands and feet, if they think that they are the cause of evil to them. Nor do they cherish and embrace that which may belong to themselves, merely because it is their own; unless, indeed, any one should choose to say, that that which is good is attached to his own nature and is his own, whilst that which is evil is foreign and accidental; but love nothing but that which is good. Does it not appear so to you?'—'Assuredly.'—'Can we then simply affirm that men love that which is good?' —'Without doubt.'—'What, then, must we not add, that, in addition to loving that which is good, they love that it should be present to themselves?'—'Indeed that must be added.'—'And not merely that it should be

present, but that it should ever be present?'—'This also must be added.'
" 'Love, then, is collectively the desire in men that good should be
for ever present to them.'—'Most true.'—'Since this is the general definition of Love, can you explain in what mode of attaining its object,
and in what species of actions, does Love peculiarly consist?'—'If I knew
what you ask, O Diotima, I should not have so much wondered at your
wisdom, or have sought you out for the purpose of deriving improvement from your instructions.'—'I will tell you,' then she replied: 'Love
is the desire of generation in the beautiful, both with relation to the
body and the soul.'—'I must be a diviner to comprehend what you say,
for, being such as I am, I confess that I do not understand it.'—'But I
will explain it more clearly. The bodies and the souls of all human
beings are alike pregnant with their future progeny, and when we arrive
at a certain age, our nature impells us to bring forth and propagate.
This nature is unable to produce in that which is deformed, but it
can produce in that which is beautiful. The intercourse of the male
and female in generation, a divine work, through pregnancy and production, is, as it were, something immortal in mortality. These things
cannot take place in that which is incongruous; for that which is deformed is incongruous, but that which is beautiful is congruous with
what is immortal and divine. Beauty is, therefore, the Fate, and the
Juno Lucina to generation. Wherefore, whenever that which is pregnant with the generative principle, approaches that which is beautiful,
it becomes transported with delight, and is poured forth in overflowing
pleasure, and propagates. But when it approaches that which is deformed, it is contracted and sad[ness], it is repelled and checked and
does not produce, but retains unwillingly that with which it is pregnant. Wherefore, to one pregnant, and, as it were, already bursting
with the load of his desire, the impulse towards that which is beautiful
is intense, on account of the great pain of retaining that which he has
conceived. Love, then, O Socrates, is not as you imagine the love of
the beautiful.'—'What, then?'—'Of generation and production in the
beautiful.'—'Why then of generation?'—'Generation is something eternal
and immortal in mortality. It necessarily, from what has been confessed,
follows, that we must desire immortality together with what is good,
since Love is the desire that good be for ever present to us. Of necessity
Love must also be the desire of immortality.'

"Diotima taught me all this doctrine in the discourse we had together
concerning Love; and in addition, she enquired, 'What do you think,
Socrates, is the cause of this love and desire? Do you not perceive how

all animals, both those of the earth and of the air, are affected when they desire the propagation of their species, affected even to weakness and disease by the impulse of their love; first, longing to be mixed with each other, and then seeking nourishment for their offspring, so that the feeblest are ready to contend with the strongest in obedience to this law, and to die for the sake of their young, or to waste away with hunger, and do or suffer anything so that they may not want nourishment. It might be said that human beings do these things through reason, but can you explain why other animals are thus affected through love?'—I confessed that I did not know.—'Do you imagine yourself,' said she, 'to be skilful in the science of Love, if you are ignorant of these things?'—'As I said before, O Diotima, I come to you, well knowing how much I am in need of a teacher. But explain to me, I entreat you, the cause of these things, and of the other things relating to Love.'—'If,' said Diotima, 'you believe that Love is of the same nature as we have mutually agreed upon, wonder not that such are its effects. For the mortal nature seeks, so far as it is able, to become deathless and eternal. But it can only accomplish this desire by generation, which for ever leaves another new in place of the old. For, although each human being be severally said to live, and be the same from youth to old age, yet, that which is called the same, never contains within itself the same things, but always is becoming new by the loss and change of that which it possessed before; both the hair, and the flesh, and the bones, and the entire body.

" 'And not only does this change take place in the body, but also with respect to the soul. Manners, morals, opinions, desires, pleasures, sorrows, fears; none of these ever remain unchanged in the same persons; but some die away, and others are produced. And, what is yet more strange [is] that not only does some knowledge spring up, and another decay, and that we are never the same with respect to our knowledge, but that each several object of our thoughts suffers the same revolution. That which is called meditation, or the exercise of memory, is the science of the escape or departure of knowledge; for, forgetfulness is the going out of knowledge; and meditation, calling up a new memory in the place of that which has departed, preserves knowledge; so that, tho' for ever displaced and restored, it seems to be the same. In this manner every thing mortal is preserved: not that [it] is constant and eternal, like that which is divine; but that in the place of what has grown old and is departed, it leaves another new like that which it was itself. By this contrivance, O Socrates, does what is mortal, the body and all other things, partake of immortality; that which is immortal, is immortal in another manner. Wonder not, then, if every thing by nature cherishes that which was produced from itself, for this earnest Love is a tendency towards eternity.'

"Having heard this discourse, I was astonished, and asked, 'Can these things be true, O wisest Diotima?' And she, like an accomplished sophist, said, 'Know well, O Socrates, that if you only regard that love of glory which inspires men, you will wonder at your own unskilfulness in not having discovered all that I now declare. Observe with how vehement a desire they are affected to become illustrious and to prolong their glory into immortal time, to attain which object, far more ardently than for the sake of their children, all men are ready to engage in any dangers, and expend their fortunes, and submit to any labours and incur any death. Do you believe that Alcestis would have died in the place of Admetus, or Achilles for the revenge of Patroclus, or Codrus for the kingdom of his posterity, if they had not believed that the immortal memory of their actions, which we now cherish, would have remained after their death? Far otherwise; all such deeds are done for the sake of ever-living virtue, and this immortal glory which they have obtained; and inasmuch as any one is of an excellent nature, so much the more is he impelled to attain this reward. For they love what is immortal.

" 'Those whose bodies alone are pregnant with this principle of immortality are attracted by women, seeking through the production of children what they imagine to be happiness and immortality and an enduring remembrance; but they whose souls are far more pregnant than their bodies, conceive and produce that which is more suitable to the soul. What is suitable to the soul? Intelligence, and every other power and excellence of the mind, of which all poets, and all other artists who are creative and inventive, are the authors. The greatest and most admirable wisdom is that which regulates the government of families and states, and which is called moderation and justice. Whosoever, therefore, from his youth feels his soul pregnant with the conception of these excellencies, is divine; and when due time arrives, desires to bring forth; and wandering about, he seeks the beautiful in which he may propagate what he has conceived; for there is no generation in that which is deformed; he embraces those bodies which are beautiful rather than those which are deformed, in obedience to the principle within him which is ever seeking to perpetuate itself. And if he meets, in conjunction with loveliness of form, a beautiful, generous and gentle soul, he embraces both at once, and immediately undertakes to educate this object of his love, and is inspired with an overflowing persuasion to declare what is virtue, and what he ought to be who would attain to its possession, and what are the duties which it exacts. For, by the intercourse with, and as it were, the very touch of that which is beautiful, he brings forth and produces what he had formerly conceived; and nourishes and educates that which is thus produced together with the object of his love, whose image, whether absent or present, is never divided from his mind. So that those who are thus united are linked by a nobler community and a firmer love, as being the common parents of a lovelier and more enduring progeny than the parents of other children. And every one who considers what posterity Homer and Hesiod and the other great poets have left behind them, the sources of their own immortal memory and renown, or what children of his soul Lycurgus has appointed to be the guardians, not only of Lacedaemon, but of all Greece; or what an illustrious progeny of laws Solon has produced, and how many admirable achievements, both among the Greeks and Barbarians, men have left as the pledges of that love which subsisted between them and the beautiful, would choose rather to be the parent of such children than those in an human shape. For divine honours have often been rendered to them on account of such children, but on account of those in human shape, never.

" 'Your own meditation, O Socrates, might perhaps have initiated you in all these things which I have already taught you on the subject of Love. But those perfect and sublime ends, to which these are only the means, I know not that you would have been competent to discover. I will declare them, therefore, and will render them as intelligible as possible: do you meanwhile strain all your attention to trace the obscure depth of the subject. He who aspires to love rightly, ought from his earliest youth to seek an intercourse with beautiful forms, and first to make a single form the object of his love, and therein to generate intellectual excellencies. He ought, then, to consider that beauty in whatever form it resides is the brother of that beauty which subsists in another form; and if he ought to pursue that which is beautiful in form, it would be absurd to imagine that beauty is not one and the same thing in all forms, and would therefore remit much of his ardent preference towards one, through his perception of the multitude of claims upon his love. In addition, he would consider the beauty which is in souls more excellent than that which is in form. So that one endowed with an admirable soul, even though the flower of his form were withered, would suffice him as the object of his love and care, and the companion with whom he might seek and produce such conclusions as tend to the improvement of youth; so that it might be led to observe the beauty and the conformity which there is in the observation of its duties and the laws, and to esteem little the mere beauty of the outward form. The lover would then conduct his pupil to science, so that he might look upon the loveliness of wisdom; and that contemplating thus the universal beauty, no longer like some servant in love with his fellow would he unworthily and meanly enslave himself to the attractions of one form, nor one subject of discipline or science, but would turn towards the wide ocean of intellectual beauty, and from the sight of the lovely and majestic forms which it contains, would abundantly bring forth his conceptions in philosophy; until, strengthened and confirmed, he should at length steadily contemplate one science, which is the science of this universal beauty.

"'Attempt, I entreat you, to mark what I say with as keen an observation as you can. He who has been disciplined to this point in Love, by contemplating beautiful objects gradually, and in their order, now arriving at the end of all that concerns Love, on a sudden beholds a beauty wonderful in its nature. This it is, O Socrates, for the sake of which all the former labours were endured. It is eternal, unproduced, indestructible; neither subject to encrease nor decay: not, like other things, partly beautiful and partly deformed; not at one time beautiful and at another time not; not beautiful in relation to one thing and deformed in relation to another; not here beautiful and there deformed; not beautiful in the estimation of one person and deformed in that of another; nor can this supreme beauty be figured to the imagination like a beautiful face, or beautiful hands, or any portion of the body, nor like any discourse, or any science. Nor does it subsist in any other thing that lives or is, either in earth, or in heaven, or in any other place; but it is eternally uniform and consistent, and monoeidic with itself. All other things are beautiful through a participation of it, with this condition, that although they are subject to production and decay, it never becomes more or less, or endures any change. When any one, ascending from a correct system of Love, begins to contemplate this supreme beauty, he already touches the consummation of his labour. For such as discipline themselves upon this system, or are conducted by another beginning to ascend through these transitory objects which are beautiful, towards that which is beauty itself, proceeding as on steps from the love of one form to that of two, and from that of two, to that of all forms which are beautiful; and from beautiful forms to beautiful habits and institutions, and from institutions to beautiful doctrines; until, from the meditation of many doctrines, they arrive at that which is nothing else than the doctrine of the supreme beauty itself, in the knowledge and contemplation of which at length they repose.

" 'Such a life as this, my dear Socrates,' exclaimed the stranger prophetess, 'spent in the contemplation of the beautiful, is the life for men to live; which if you chance ever to experience, you will esteem far beyond gold and rich garments, and even those lovely persons whom you and many others now gaze on with astonishment, and are prepared neither to eat or drink so that you may behold and live for ever with these objects of your love! What, then, shall we imagine to be the aspect of the supreme beauty itself, simple, pure, uncontaminated with the intermixture of human flesh and colours, and all other idle and unreal shapes attendant on mortality; the divine, the original, the supreme, the self consistent, the monoeidic beautiful itself? What must be the life of him who dwells with and gazes on that which it becomes us all to seek? Think you not that to him alone is accorded the prerogative of bringing forth, not images and shadows of virtue, for he is in contact not with a shadow but with reality; with virtue itself, in the production and nourishment of which he becomes dear to the Gods, and if such a priviledge is conceded to any human being, himself immortal.'

"Such, O Phaedrus, and my other friends, was what Diotima said. And being persuaded by her words, I have since occupied myself in attempting to persuade others, that it is not easy to find a better assistant than Love in seeking to communicate immortality to our human natures. Wherefore I exhort every one to honour Love; I hold him in honour, and chiefly exercise myself in amatory matters, and exhort others to do so; and now and ever do I praise the power and excellence of Love, in the best manner that I can. Let this discourse, if it pleases you, Phaedrus, be considered as an encomium of Love; or call it by what other name you will."

The whole assembly praised his discourse, and Aristophanes was on the point of making some remarks on the allusion made by Socrates to him in a part of his discourse, when suddenly they heard a loud knocking at the door of the vestibule, and a clamour as of revellers, attended by a flute-player.—"Go, boys," said Agathon, "and see who is there: if they are any of our friends, call them in; if not, say that we have already done drinking."—A minute afterwards, they heard the voice of Alcibiades in the vestibule excessively drunk and roaring out:—"Where is Agathon? Lead me to Agathon!"—The flute-player, and some of his companions, then led him in, and placed him against the door-post, crowned with a thick crown of ivy and violets, and having a quantity of fillets on his head.—"My friends," he cried out, "hail! I am excessively drunk already, but I'll drink with you, if you will. If not, we will go away after having crowned Agathon, for which purpose I came. I assure you that I could not come yesterday, but I am now here with these fillets round my temples, that from my own head I may crown his head who, with your leave, is the most beautiful and wisest of men. Are you laughing at me because I am drunk? Aye, I know what I say is true, whether you laugh or not. But tell me at once, whether I shall come in, or no. Will you drink with me?"

Agathon and the whole party desired him to come in, and recline among them; so he came in, led by his companions. He then unbound his fillets that he might crown Agathon, and though Socrates was just before his eyes, he did not see him, but sat down by Agathon, between Socrates and him, for Socrates moved out of the way to make room for him. When he sate down, he embraced Agathon and crowned him; and Agathon desired the slaves to untie his sandals, that he might make a third, and recline on the same couch. "By all means," said Alcibiades, "but what third companion have we here?" And at the same time turning round and seeing Socrates, he leaped up and cried out:—"O Hercules! what have we here? You, Socrates, lying in ambush for me wherever I go! and meeting me just as you always do, when I least expected to see you! And, now, what are you come here for? Why have you chosen to recline exactly in this place, and not near Aristophanes, or any one else who is, or wishes to be ridiculous, but have contrived to lie down beside the most beautiful person of the whole party?"—"Agathon," said Socrates, "see if you cannot defend me. I declare my love for this man is a bad business: from the moment that I first began to love him I have never been permitted to converse with, or so much as to look on any one who is beautiful. If I do, he is so jealous and suspicious that he does the most extravagant things, and hardly refrains from beating me. I entreat you to prevent him from doing anything of that kind at present. Procure a reconciliation: or, if he perseveres in attempting any violence, I entreat you to defend me, for I am seriously alarmed at the fury of his amatory impulse."—"Indeed," said Alcibiades, "I will not be reconciled to you; I shall find another opportunity to punish you for this. But now," said he, addressing Agathon, "lend me some of those fillets, that I may crown the wonderful head of this fellow, lest I incur the blame, that having crowned you, I neglected to crown him who conquers all men with his discourses, not yesterday alone as you did, but ever."

Saying this he took the fillets, and having bound the head of Socrates, and again having reclined, said: "Come, my friends, you seem to be sober enough. You must not flinch, but drink, for that was your agreement with me before I came in. I choose as president, until you have drunk enough—myself. Come, Agathon, if you have got a great goblet, fetch it out. But no matter, that wine-cooler will do; bring it, boy!" And observing that it held more than eight cups, he first drank it off, and then ordered it to be filled for Socrates, and said:—"Observe, my friends, I cannot invent any scheme against Socrates, for he will drink as much as any one desires him, and not be in the least drunk." Socrates, after the boy had filled up, drank it off; and Eryximachus said:—"Shall we then have no conversation or singing over our cups, but drink down stupidly, just as if we were thirsty?" And Alcibiades said:—"Ah, Eryximachus, I did not see you before; hail, you excellent son of a wise and excellent father!"—"Hail to you also," replied Eryximachus, "but what shall we do?"—"Whatever you command, for we ought to submit to your directions; a physician is worth an hundred common men. Command us as you please."—"Listen then," said Eryximachus; "before you came in, each of us had agreed to deliver as eloquent a discourse as he could in praise of Love, beginning at the right hand; all the rest of us have fulfilled our engagement; you have not spoken, and yet have drunk with us: you ought to bear your part in the discussion; and having done so, command what you please to Socrates, who shall have the priviledge of doing so to his right-hand neighbour, and so on to the others."—"Indeed, there appears some justice in your proposal, Eryximachus, though it is rather unfair to induce a drunken man to set his discourse in competition with that of those who are sober. And, besides, did Socrates really persuade you that what he just said about me was true, or do you not know that matters are in fact exactly the reverse of his representation? For I seriously believe that, should I praise in his presence, be he God or man, any other beside himself, [that] he would not keep his hands off me."—"Good words I entreat you," said Socrates—"I charge you by Neptune," cried Alcibiades, "to keep quiet, I assure you that I will praise no one beside yourself in your presence."

"Do so, then," said Eryximachus; "praise Socrates if you please."—"What!" said Alcibiades, "shall I attack him, and punish him before you all?"—"What have you got into your head now," said Socrates; "are you going to expose me to ridicule, and to misrepresent me? Or what are you going to do?"—"I will only speak the truth; will you permit me on this condition?"—"I not only permit, but exhort you to say all the truth you know," replied Socrates. "I obey you willingly," said Alcibiades; "and if I advance anything untrue, do you, if you please, interrupt me, and convict me of misrepresentation, for I would never willingly speak falsely. And bear with me if I do not relate things in their order, but just as I remember them, for it is not easy for a man in my present condition to enumerate systematically all your singularities.

"I will begin the praise of Socrates by comparing him to a certain statue. Perhaps he will think that this statue is introduced for the sake of ridicule, but I assure you that it is necessary for the illustration of truth. I assert, then, that Socrates is exactly like those Silenuses that sit in the sculptors' shops, and which are carved holding flutes or pipes, but which, when divided in two, are found to contain withinside the images of the Gods. I assert that Socrates is like the satyr Marsyas. That your form and appearance are like these Satyrs, I think that even you will not venture to deny; and how like you are to them in all other things, now hear. Are you not scornful and petulant? If you deny this, I will bring witnesses. Are you not a piper, and far more wonderful a one than he? For Marsyas, and whoever now pipes the music that he taught (for that music which is of Heaven is described as being taught by Marsyas) enchants men through the power of the mouth. For if any musician, be he skilful or not, awakens this music, it alone enables him to retain the minds of men, and from the divinity of its nature makes evident those who are in want of the Gods and initiation. You differ only from Marsyas in this circumstance, that you effect without instruments, by mere words, all that he can do. For when we hear Pericles, or any other accomplished orator, deliver a discourse, no one, as it were, cares anything about it. But when any one hears you, or even your words related by another, though ever so rude and unskilful a speaker, be that person a woman, man or child, we are struck and retained, as it were, by the discourse clinging to our mind.

"If I was not afraid that I am a great deal too drunk, I would confirm to you by an oath the strange effects which I assure you I have suffered from his words, and suffer still; for when I hear him speak, my heart leaps up far more than the hearts of those who celebrate the Corybantic mysteries; my tears are poured out as he talks, a thing I have seen happen to many others beside myself. I have heard Pericles and other excellent orators, and have been pleased with their discourses, but I suffered nothing of this kind; nor was my soul ever on those occasions disturbed and filled with self-reproach, as if it were slavishly laid prostrate. But this Marsyas here has often affected me in the way I describe, until the life which I lead seemed hardly worth living. Do not deny it, Socrates; for I well know that if even now I chose to listen to you, I could not resist, but should again suffer the same effects. For, my friends, he forces me to confess that while I myself am still in want of many things, I neglect my own necessities, and attend to those of the Athenians. I stop my ears, therefore, as from the Syrens, and flee away as fast as possible, that I may not sit down beside him and grow old in listening to his talk. For this man has reduced me to feel the sentiment of shame, which I imagine no one would readily believe was in me; he alone inspires me with remorse and awe. For I feel in his presence my incapacity of refuting what he says, or of refusing to do that which he directs; but when I depart from him, the glory which the multitude confers overwhelms me. I escape, therefore, and hide myself from him, and when I see him I am overwhelmed with humiliation, because I have neglected to do what I have confessed to him ought to be done; and often and often have I wished that he were no longer to be seen among men. But if that were to happen, I well know that I should suffer far greater pain; so that where I can turn, or what I can do with this man, I know not. All this have I and many others suffered from the pipings of this satyr.

"And observe [how] like he is [to] what I said, and what a wonderful power he possesses. Know that there is not one of you who is aware of the real nature of Socrates; but since I have begun, I will make him plain to you. You observe how passionately Socrates affects the intimacy of those who are beautiful, and how ignorant he professes himself to be; appearances in themselves excessively Silenic. This, my friends, is the external form with which, like one of those sculptured Sileni, he has clothed himself; for if you open him, you will find within admirable temperance and wisdom. For he cares not for mere beauty, but despises more than any one can imagine all external possessions, whether it be beauty or wealth, or glory, or any other thing for which the multitude felicitates the possessor. He esteems these things and us who honour them, as nothing, and lives among men, making all the objects of their admiration the playthings of his irony. But I know not if any one of you have ever seen the divine images which are within, when he has been opened and is serious. I have seen them, and they are so supremely beautiful, so golden, so divine, and wonderful, that every thing which Socrates command[s] surely ought to be obeyed, even like the voice of a God.

"On our first intimacy I imagined that Socrates was in love with me on account of my beauty, and was determined to seize so favourable an opportunity, by conceding to him all that he required, of learning from him all that he knew: for I imagined that my beauty was something irresistable and extraordinary. As soon as I perceived this I sent away the servant, who was accustomed to be present at our meetings, and remained with him alone: for I will tell you the whole truth, therefore now attend; and do you, Socrates, if I say anything that is false, interrupt and refute me. Well, he and I were now alone together and I thought that he would then say all that a lover is accustomed to say in solitude to his beloved, and was rejoiced. But nothing of this kind passed, and after spending the day with me, and talking just as usual, he went away. After this I invited him to exercise with me in gymnastic exercises, hoping that something might arise out of this; and we were very often stript and wrestled together with no other person present. What is the use of more words? Everything failed; and since I could not succeed thus I resolved having once taken it into hand to assail him with more powerful temptations; and now I have once begun I will tell all.

"I invited him to supper, actually laying plots for him as a lover would for his beloved. At first he would not accept my invitation, at last being persuaded he came and went away immediately after supper. I was ashamed that time of what I had undertaken and let him go. But laying my plan a second time, I protracted the conversation after supper far into the night, and when he motioned to depart, I prevailed on him to remain, alledging the lateness of the hour. He composed himself to sleep on the couch next to mine on which he had supped: and no one else slept in the house beside ourselves. So much as this I could relate without difficulty to any one; but I cannot proceed further without reminding you of the proverb that, wine tells truth, whether with or without youth. I cannot pass over, though I have undertaken to praise Socrates, so proud and scornful a deed. Besides I am like one bitten by a viper, who they say will not tell his misfortune to any, but those who are bitten in the same manner, since they alone knowing what it is, will pardon him for whatever he dares to do or say under the mitigation of his pain. I then, bitten by something more keen and vehement than the keenest of all things by which any one ever was bitten, wounded in my very heart and soul, or whatever else you choose to call it, by the words of philosophy which pierce more sharply than a viper's tooth, when they seize on a fresh and not ungenerous spirit, and instigate it to say or do anything, seeing Phaedrus, and Agathon, and Eryximachus, and Pausanias, and Aristodemus, and Aristophanes, and Socrates himself, and the rest of our companions; for ye are all participators with me in the sacred madness and bacchic enthusiasm of philosophy, am willing that you should hear all. Pardon, I entreat you, what then was done and now is said. Let the servants, or if any other prophane and unrefined person is present, close their ears with impenetrable gates.

Well, my friends, as soon as the attendants had withdrawn and the lamp was extinguished I determined to hesitate no longer but plainly to speak my mind. Touching him, therefore, I said:—"Socrates are you asleep?"—"Not I," said he.—"Do you know what I have been thinking of?"—"Well, what is it?"—"Why," said I, "I esteem you to be the only lover worthy of me, but I imagine that although you feel such tenderness for me as lovers feel, you are ashamed to confess your sentiments. Being such as I am, I should consider myself indeed unwise if I were not prepared to make every return you can desire to your preference, as I would willingly gratify you, not only in this, but in every thing else that my fortune and connexion can command; for it has been my earliest ambition to become as virtuous and accomplished as possible, nor can I conceive any companion or guide more excellent than you to conduct me in the path of its attainment; and not conceding all that such a man as you could desire, I should more dread the reproaches of the wise, than conceding it, the idle clamours of the multitude."—Hearing this, Socrates said ironically and just in his way:—"My dear Alcibiades, if what you say of me be true, and if there be any power in me through which you may become better, you must see methinks some very uncommon beauty in me, very different from that loveliness which is so conspicuous in yourself. If you seek my intercourse for the sake of this, and would exchange your beauty against mine, you design no doubt to gain considerably by me: you would possess that which is truly beautiful instead of the opinion and appearance of beauty, gold instead of molten brass. But my dear friend, observe lest you be deceived in me, and I be indeed nothing. The vision of the understanding then grows keen when the radiance of youth first wanes in the eyes, and yours are yet far from this."—Hearing this I said: "My sentiments are such as I have expressed. I have said nothing that I do not mean. Do you only determine what is best for yourself and me."—"This is well," he replied, "for the future we will consider what is best to be done; both concerning what you propose, and concerning all other things."—After this conversation I believed and hoped that my words had wounded him as with a weapon, so rising from my couch and permitting him to say no more, and casting this garment around us both (for it was winter) I lay the whole night with my arms around this truly divine and wonderful being, upon that very old cloak that he has got on now. I know, Socrates, that you cannot deny what I alledge. He despised and contemptuously neglected that beauty which I had thus exposed to his rejection, O Judges, for you shall be judges of the insolence of Socrates: know then, by all the Gods and Goddesses, I swear that I awoke and arose from as unimpassioned an embrace as if I had slept with my father or my elder brother! And after this what think you was the contest of my mind feeling that I had been thus dishonoured, and yet loving the courage, and temperance and wisdom with which I found this man endowed, so excellently as I had not believed could have fallen to the lot of any human being. So that I could neither persevere in my indignation against, or deprive myself of an intercourse with him, or discover any attraction with which I might entice him to my society. For I knew that he was less vulnerable by money than Ajax by iron, and that resource alone with which I had endeavoured to captivate him, had already failed me. I became the prey of doubt and trouble, and enslaved to this man far more than any other was ever enslaved, I wandered about disconsolately. Such as I have declared was the event of what I attempted.

"Some time after this, we were fellow-soldiers, and had our mess together in the camp before Potidaea. Socrates there overcame not only me, but everyone beside, in endurance of toils: when, as often happens in a campaign, we were reduced to few provisions, there were none who could sustain hunger like Socrates; and when he had plenty, he alone seemed to enjoy our military fare. He never drank much willingly, but when he was compelled, he conquered all even in that to which he was least accustomed; and what is most astonishing, no person ever saw Socrates drunk either then or at any other time. In the depth of winter (and the winters there are excessively rigid), he sustained calmly incredible hardships: and amongst other things, whilst the frost was intolerably severe, and no one went out of their tents, or if they went out, wrapt themselves up carefully, and put fleeces under their feet, and bound their legs with hairy skins, Socrates went out only with the same cloak on that he usually wore, and walked barefoot upon the ice; more easily, indeed, than those who had sandalled themselves so delicately: so that the soldiers thought that he did it to mock their want of fortitude. It would indeed be worth while to commemorate all that this brave man did and endured in that expedition. In one instance he was seen early in the morning, standing in one place wrapt in meditation; and as he seemed not to be able to unravel the subject of his thoughts, he still continued to stand as enquiring and discussing within himself, and when noon came, the soldiers observed him, and said to one another—'Socrates has been standing there thinking, ever since the morning.' At last some Ionians came to the spot, and having supped, as it was summer, bringing their blankets, they lay down to sleep in the cool; they observed that Socrates continued to stand there the whole night until morning, and that, when the sun rose, he saluted it with a prayer and departed.

"I ought not to omit what Socrates is in battle. For in that battle after which the generals decreed to me the prize of courage, Socrates alone of all men was the saviour of my life, standing by me when I had fallen and was wounded, and preserving both myself and my arms from the hands of the enemy. On that occasion I entreated the generals to decree the prize, as it was most due, to him. And this, O Socrates, you cannot deny, that [while] the generals, wishing to conciliate a person of my rank, desired to give me the prize, you were far more earnestly desirous than the generals that this glory should be attributed not to yourself, but me.

"But to see Socrates when our army was defeated and scattered in flight at Delius, was a spectacle worthy to behold. On that occasion I was among the cavalry, and he on foot, heavily armed. After the total rout of our troops, he and Laches retreated together; I came up by chance, and seeing them, bade them be of good cheer, for that I would not leave them. As I was on horseback, and therefore less occupied by a regard of my own situation, I could better observe than at Potidaea the beautiful spectacle exhibited by Socrates on this emergence. How superior was he to Laches in presence of mind and courage! Your representation of him on the stage, O Aristophanes, was not wholly unlike his real self on this occasion, for he walked and darted his regards around with a majestic composure, looking tranquilly both on his friends and enemies; so that it was evident to every one, even from afar, that whoever should venture to attack him would encounter a desperate resistance. He and his companion thus departed in safety; for those who are scattered in flight are pursued and killed, whilst men hesitate to touch those who exhibit such a countenance as that of Socrates even in defeat.

"Many other and most wonderful qualities might well be praised in Socrates; but such as these might singly be attributed to others. But that which is unparalleled in Socrates, is, that he is unlike, and above comparison, with all other men, whether those who have lived in ancient times, or those who exist now. For it may be conjectured, that Brasidas and many others are such as was Achilles. Pericles deserves comparison with Nestor and Antenor; and other excellent persons of various times may, with probability, be drawn into comparison with each other. But to

such a singular man as this, both himself and his discourses are so uncommon, no one, should he seek, would find a parallel among the present
or the past generations of mankind; unless they should say that he resembled those with whom I lately compared him, for, assuredly, he and
his discourses are like nothing but the Sileni and the Satyrs. At first I
forgot to make you observe how like his discourses are to those Satyrs
when they are opened, for, if any one will listen to the talk of Socrates,
it will appear to him at first extremely ridiculous; the phrases and expressions which he employs, fold around his exterior the skin, as it
were, of a rude and wanton Satyr. He is always talking about great
market-asses, and brass-founders, and leather-cutters, and skin-dressers;
and this is his perpetual custom, so that any dull and unobservant person
might easily laugh at his discourse. But if any one should see it opened,
as it were, and get within the sense of his words, he would then find
that they alone of all that enters into the mind of man to utter, had a
profound and persuasive meaning, and that they were most divine; and
that they presented to the mind innumerable images of every excellence,
and that they tended towards objects of the highest moment, or rather
towards all, that he who seeks the possession of what is supremely beautiful and good, need regard as essential to the accomplishment of his
ambition.

"These are the things, my friends, for which I praise Socrates, as well
as those which I complain of in him, for I have mixed up in my discourse
the peculiar scorn with which he treated me. Not that I have been the
only object of his contempt, but Charmides, the son of Glauco, and
Euthydemus, the son of Diocles, are deceived in the same manner, imagining that he was their lover, whilst in fact they vainly pursued him
as the object of theirs. As to you, Agathon, take my advice; do not let
him cheat you. Be admonished, by my sufferings to take care, and not
according to the proverb, like a fool grow wise by your own experience."

Alcibiades having said this, the whole party burst into laughter at the
frankness with which he seemed to confess that he was still in love with
Socrates; and Socrates said, "You seem to be sober enough, Alcibiades,
else you would not have made such a circuit of words, only to hide the
main design for which you made this long speech, and which, as it were,
carelessly, you just throw in at the last; now, as if you had not said all
this for the mere purpose of dividing me and Agathon? You think that
I ought to love you and no one else, and that Agathon ought to be loved
by you and no one else. I have found you out; it is evident enough for
what design you invented all this Satyrical and Silenic drama. But, my

dear Agathon, do not let his device succeed. I entreat you to permit no one to throw discord between us."—"No doubt," said Agathon, "he sate down between us only that he might divide us; but this shall not assist his scheme, for I will come and recline near you."—"Do so," said Socrates, "come, there is room for you close under me."—"Oh, Jupiter!" exclaimed Alcibiades, "what I endure from that man! He thinks to subdue [me] every way; but, at least, I pray you, let Agathon recline between us."—"Impossible," said Socrates, "you have just praised me; I ought to praise him sitting at my right hand. If Agathon reclines under you, he will not praise me before I praise him. Now, my dear friend, allow the young man to receive what praise I can give him. I have a great desire to pronounce his encomium."—"Quick, quick, Alcibiades," said Agathon, "I cannot stay here, I must change my place, or Socrates will not praise me." "This is just like him," said Alcibiades, "when Socrates is present it is impossible to catch hold of any of those who are beautiful. I entreat you to observe how easily he found out a plausible pretext for this beautiful Agathon to come and lie down by him."— Agathon then arose to take his place near Socrates.

He had no sooner reclined than there came in a number of revellers— for some one who had gone out had left the door open—and took their places on the vacant couches, and everything became full of confusion; and no order being observed, every one was obliged to drink a great quantity of wine. Eryximachus, and Phaedrus, and some others, said Aristodemus, went home to bed; that, for his part, he went to sleep on his couch, and slept long and soundly—the nights were then long—until the cock crew in the morning. When he awoke he found that some were still fast asleep, and others had gone home, and that Aristophanes, Agathon, and Socrates had alone stood it out, and were still drinking out of a great goblet which they passed round and round. Socrates was disputing between them. The beginning of their discussion Aristodemus said that he did not recollect, because he was asleep; but it was terminated by Socrates forcing them to confess, that the same person is able to compose both tragedy and comedy, and that the foundations of the tragic and comic arts were essentially the same. They, rather convicted than convinced, went to sleep. Aristophanes first awoke, and then, it being broad daylight, Agathon. Socrates, having put them to sleep, went away, Aristodemus following him; and coming to the Lyceum he washed himself, as he would have done anywhere else, and after having spent the day there in his accustomed manner, went home in the evening.

SHELLEY'S NOTE ON THE BANQUET OF PLATO

THE WONDERFUL description of Love in Plato, Sympos. p. 214—particularly 214, l. 8——l. ultima, et passim 218.

I should say in answer, that 'Ἔρως neither loved nor was loved, but is the cause of Love in others—a subtlety to beat Plato.

Agathon, a poem.

[1817.]

SHELLEY'S TRANSLATION OF THE ION OF PLATO

SHELLEY'S TRANSLATION of the *Ion* is not only another manifestation of his interest in Plato but is also important for the influence it has had on Shelley's theory of the nature and function of poetry. Shelley refers to his reading of the dialogue in his letter to Peacock, February 15, 1821, wherein he tells him that he delayed answering his essay on the *Four Ages of Poetry* because he was, at the moment of its arrival, reading Plato's *Ion*, which he recommended to him.[1] His only other reference to the dialogue is in a letter to Hogg, dated October 20, 1821: "I read the tragedies, Homer and Plato perpetually: and have translated the *Symposium*, the *Ion*, and part of the *Phaedon*."[2]

From these references it is evident that we have February 15, 1821, and October 20, 1821, as the *termini post quem* and *ante quem* for the reading and translation of the *Ion*. It is likely that Shelley read the *Ion* in January, 1821, between the composition of the *Epipsychidion* (February 1-14?) and that of *A Defence of Poetry* (February 22-March 12?, 1821), which contains direct allusions to the dialogue. Farrington, in his study of Shelley's translations from the Greek, noting the difference in quality of translation between the Plato translations and that of the *Cyclops* and *Homeric Hymns,* assigns the *Ion* to the Plato translation period of 1818 at Bagni di Lucca.[3] The dating of the dialogue on the basis of the quality of translation is too subjective. In support of the 1821 date we have the allusions to the *Ion* in Shelley's compositions of the same year. In *A Defence of Poetry,* Shelley shows the influence of the *Ion*, which he had just finished reading, in such statements as "The sacred links of that chain have never been entirely disjoined, ... whence as from a magnet the invisible effluence is sent forth."[4] As this doctrine appears for the first time in Shelley's writings and immediately after the reading of the *Ion,* it is reasonable to infer that Shelley had not read the dialogue before 1821.

Further evidence for this date is to be found in Medwin's record of one of Shelley's beliefs. Inasmuch as Medwin's stay with Shelley covers the interval between November, 1821, and March, 1822, it is likely that Medwin's evidence is applicable to this period in Shelley's life. Medwin

---

[1] Julian *Works*, X, 234.

[2] Scott, *Shelley at Oxford*, p. 64.

[3] Benjamin Farrington, "Shelley's Translations from the Greek," *Dublin Magazine*, III (1928), 11.

[4] Julian *Works*, VII, 124; cf. *The Four Ages of Poetry and A Defence of Poetry,* ed. H. F. B. Brett-Smith (Oxford, 1923, Percy Reprints No. 3), xxi-xxii, notes on pp. 40 l. 27, 42 l. 11, 55 l. 1.

reports: "It was one of his fanciful notions, that what we call talent, is in some degree magnetic, or epidemic, that spirits catch from each other a particle of the *mens divinior*. Such an idea, if not to be found in Plato, is worthy of him."[5] There can be no doubt that Shelley expounded the doctrine after reading the *Ion*, which contains the nucleus of such an idea in its analogy of poetic inspiration to the magnetic quality of "the stone called magnet by Euripides, and Heraclea by the people."[6]

Medwin furnishes us with another piece of evidence to support the 1821 date in a paper which appeared in the *New Monthly and London Magazine*, excerpted from the *Polar Star*, V (July–October, 1830): "Byron and Shelley on the Character of Hamlet, By An Eye Witness."[7] The eyewitness, who is thought to be Medwin, reports a conversation between Byron and Shelley which may have taken place in one of the Pisan meetings, at which Medwin took notes. In this paper Shelley replies to Byron, "Are you then so orthodox in any thing as to think Shakspeare a man of no art or thought—a prophet of poetry, possessed by a spirit unintelligible to himself?" This doctrine of the *Ion* appearing as it does here as an utterance of Shelley reflects Shelley's development and application of a notion which he absorbed in his reading and translation of the dialogue.

Finally Claire Clairmont, who made a transcript of Shelley's translation of the *Ion*, corroborates and supplements the above evidence for the date. Claire Clairmont had witnessed with the Shelleys on December 21, 1820, a performance of Sgricci, whose poetic readings and improvisations attracted Shelley and his circle. Seeing perhaps in Sgricci the modern counterpart of the rhapsode Ion, Claire Clairmont, either echoing a comment of Shelley or reflecting her knowledge of the *Ion*, says in her diary entry for December 21, 1820: "It seemed not the work of a human mind, but as if he were the instrument played upon by the superhuman inspiration of a god."[8] These echoes of the *Ion* in Shelley's close associates at Pisa as well as the influence of it in his writings of 1821 establish

[5] Thomas Medwin, *Memoir of P. B. Shelley* (London, 1833), p. 38; cf. Thomas Medwin, *Journal of Conversations of Lord Byron: Noted During a Residence with his Lordship at Pisa In the Years 1821 and 1822* (London, 1824), p. 233: "Shelley, who was present, observed:—'Poets are sometimes the echoes of words of which they know not the power,—the trumpet that sounds to battle, and feels not what it inspires.' " This sentiment emanates from Shelley's reading of the *Ion*.

[6] *Plato's Ion, or Of the Iliad*, Shelley's translation in *The Prose Works of Percy Bysshe Shelley*, ed. Harry Buxton Forman (London, 1880), III, 263, l. 15.

[7] W. E. Peck, *op. cit.*, II, 421-432. The date of this, if the author is Medwin, is fixed by the interval of his stay with Shelley and Byron.

[8] Dowden, *op. cit.*, II, 366; cf. *The Letters of Mary W. Shelley*, ed. F. L. Jones, II, 122-123.

conclusively the date for the reading and translation of the dialogue.

Mary's transcription of Shelley's translation of the *Ion* occupied pages 27-53 of the notebook containing transcriptions of Shelley's prose *(MS. Shelley adds. d. 6)*. As the contents list (p. 114) of this MS shows, the translation followed Shelley's observations in the Florence Gallery (pp. 1-27). The translation of the *Ion* no longer remains in this notebook. It was probably used as copy by the printer for the 1840 edition of Shelley's prose. Mrs. Shelley, who first published the translation in the *Essays, Letters from Abroad, Translations and Fragments,* 1840, says of the translation: "Shelley left *Ion* imperfect. I thought it better that it should appear as a whole—but at the same time have marked with brackets the passages that have been added; the rest appears exactly as Shelley left it." The brackets to which Mrs. Shelley refers were unfortunately not carefully placed in the 1840 edition by the printer; there are two such brackets marking the introduction of the added passages, but there are no brackets to mark where they end. Thus it is not known where the interpolated sections end and where Shelley's own version begins.

The textual difficulties of the *Ion* are complicated not only by the bracket problem but also by the fact that there exists another version of Shelley's translation made by Claire Clairmont.[9] Shelley was himself a veritable magnet of Greek and Platonism. Claire Clairmont is to be included among his converts to Greek and Plato. Like Harriet and Mary she took up the study of Greek to please Shelley, and in her diary for September 21-26, 1814, we have entries about her study of Greek. Shelley also interested her in Plato, for in her entry for April 23, 1818, she refers to Plato's *Republic*. She read Shelley's translation of Plato's *Symposium* April 14-16, 1819, and refers to an incident in it in her entry for July 3, 1820. Her interest in the *Ion* is foreshadowed in her entry for December 21, 1820, where she refers to the central thought of the *Ion*. In view of this interest in Plato it is quite natural that she should have been interested in making a transcription of Shelley's translation, either of her own accord or at Shelley's request. It was probably sent or taken by Shelley on his frequent visits to Claire while she was living at this period at Casa Bojti in Florence. This would account for the fact that Mary found only the first version among Shelley's MSS, whereas Claire's transcription, which reached Forman, was unknown both to Mary and Dowden.

[9] First published by Forman, *op. cit.,* III, 251-288; see *ibid.,* p. 250, for a discussion of the Clairmont Transcript. For Shelley's intellectual attraction to Claire, see Smith, *The Shelley Legend,* pp. 4, 222, and for Forman and Claire's MSS, *ibid.,* pp. 285-287.

The problem of the relation of the two versions was first examined by H. B. Forman, who collated the two versions in establishing the text of the *Ion* translation in his 1880 edition of Shelley's writings. The conclusion of Forman's investigation is that

Miss Clairmont's transcript, which is old-looking enough to have been written during Shelley's lifetime, was made when the rough MS. was less confused and imperfect than when Mrs. Shelley performed her labour of love; and I have no doubt that the transcript is wholly from Shelley's notes. If, as I also feel sure, Mrs. Shelley's text of that part where there is a gap in the transcript was *not* meant to be included within one of the missing brackets, it results that we have the whole dialogue from Shelley's hand, and that the imperfections found in 1839 were the result of the same fortuitous circumstances which left the text of Shelley's other works a matter of gradual growth.[10]

A re-examination of the evidence shows that the 1840 version is later than the Clairmont transcript. This conclusion is established by the following considerations. A comparison of the variants of the two texts shows that, while the Clairmont transcript is closer to the Greek, the 1840 version is the result of a later revision, for its variants show an attempt on Shelley's part to make the translation less literal and more in harmony with his ideal of translation. The felicitous word in English is preferred to the exact translation of the Greek, and a lengthy passage is compressed to several lines which express the same idea with complete sacrifice of the literal. For example, the Clairmont transcript of *Ion* (534d1-4) reads *that we their auditors, may acknowledge that such absurd persons cannot possibly be the authors of the excellent and admirable things which they communicate; but that God himself is he who speaks and that they are merely the organs of his voice.* This version, which is close to the Greek, is compressed in the 1840 version to *that we, their auditors, may acknowledge that those who write so beautifully, are possessed, and address us, inspired by the God.* In the case of variants consisting of single words we find again that while the Clairmont transcript is closer to the Greek, the 1840 version is more idiomatic English. For example, the Clairmont variant is *conjecture,* which is a direct translation of εἰχάσαι (*Ion,* 532c5); the 1840 variant is *suggest.* The Clairmont variant *any other one great sculptor* is again close to the Greek τινὸς ἀνδριαντοποιοῦ ἑνὸς (*Ion,* 533b2); the 1840 variant is *any other great sculptor.*

[10] Forman, *op. cit.,* p. 250. Forman's conjecture that the gap in the transcript was not included within the missing brackets has been corroborated by the discovery of Shelley's own MS. of this portion. *Vide infra,* p. 466.

Furthermore, a comparison of the Clairmont transcript with *MS. Shelley adds. c. 4,* foll. 258ʳ-9ᵛ, which is an earlier draft of the one from which Mary made her transcription for the 1840 version, brings out the same conclusion as a study of the variants of the two texts. The Clairmont transcript for ἄρχοντι (*Ion,* 540b5) reads *for the governor.* The MS originally read *the governor,* which Shelley then crossed out, writing above it *the ruler,* the reading of the 1840 text.

Thus it can now be definitely established that the 1840 text is a later revision of the Clairmont transcript. When Mary and Claire came to transcribe the later and earlier versions respectively, they both found lacunae in their manuscript which they noted. These can be accounted for by the fact that some sections of loose sheets were lost in both versions. If we can determine the precise points in the 1840 version where the printer's brackets marked the end of Mary's interpolations in the 1840 text and supply the text in these gaps from Shelley's earlier version of the translation in the Clairmont transcript, we shall have a complete text of Shelley's translation of the *Ion.*

Both versions reveal large gaps; one in the Clairmont transcript and two in the 1840 text. In the Clairmont transcript Claire indicates that there was a gap in the translation: *And when Homer introduces. . . . Certainly* (p. 276, l. 14—p. 280, l. 5, Forman; 538b7-540a5, Burnet's edition of Plato, *Scriptorum Classicorum Bibliotheca Oxoniensis*). *MS. Shelley adds. c. 4,* foll. 258ʳ-9ᵛ, which contains the translation of *Ion* 538a7-540c6, enables us now not only to fill in the gap in the Clairmont transcript but also to limit the size of the first gap in the 1840 text which began with *Ion* 534d5. The MS furthermore shows that Shelley left the quotations from Homer blank and that it was Mary who added in the 1840 text both the Greek text and Pope's translation of these passages.

In the 1840 version we have two gaps in the text where the two beginning brackets occur: one at *Tynnichus the Chalcidean* (p. 284, l. 5, 1840; 534d5, Burnet), and another at *But what a woman should* (p. 295, l. 18, 1840; 540c6, Burnet). It is possible to determine the limits where the brackets begin and end in the 1840 version by the following rules: (1) where the 1840 version and the Clairmont transcript resemble each other closely, there we have *ipso facto* evidence that there is no interpolation in the 1840 version; (2) where the two versions are far apart in their reading, we have *ipso facto* evidence that there is an interpolation by Mrs. Shelley, a fact already corroborated by the occurrence of Mrs. Shelley's two brackets at the beginning of passages in the 1840 text which differ widely from the Clairmont transcript.

Applying now the criteria for determining the interpolations in the 1840 version, we find that the Clairmont transcript and the 1840 version agree very closely from the beginning of the dialogue to *Tynnichus the Chalcidean* (p. 284, l. 5, 1840; p. 265, l. 15, Forman; 534d5, Burnet). From here to *respect to it* (p. 290, l. 9, 1840; p. 275, l. 10, Forman; 538a7, Burnet), where the text of *MS. Shelley adds. c. 4,* foll. 258ʳ-9ᵛ begins, the 1840 text and the Clairmont transcript differ widely. The printer's bracket marking the close of the first passage added by Mrs. Shelley ought therefore to have come just before the words *respect to it,* for from here to Socrates's speech *And when Homer introduces Hecamede* (p. 290, l. 25, 1840; p. 276, l. 14, Forman; 538a7 Burnet), where the Clairmont transcript contains a gap, the 1840 text and the Clairmont transcript are almost identical in their readings. Thus the first interpolation in the 1840 edition extends from page 284, line 5 to page 290, line 9 (534d5-538a7, Burnet).

The beginning of the second interpolation is marked with a bracket in the 1840 text at the beginning of Socrates's speech *But what a woman should say* (p. 295, l. 18, 1840; p. 282, l. 4, Forman; 540c6, Burnet). It marks the beginning of the second passage interpolated by Mary to fill a lacuna which extended to the end of the dialogue. That this is the extent of the second lacuna is evident from the following: from Socrates's speech *you will not assert* (p. 294, l. 15, 1840; p. 280, l. 7, Forman; 540a5, Burnet), where the Clairmont transcript begins after the gap noted, to *no, indeed* (p. 295, l. 17, 1840; p. 282, l. 2, Forman; 540c6, Burnet) the Clairmont transcript and the 1840 version, despite variants, are in close agreement; from where the bracketed passage added by Mary begins to the end of the dialogue, exclusive of the last three lines, the 1840 version is so different from the Clairmont transcript that it is evident that Mary's interpolated passage extended to the end of the dialogue. Furthermore, the last three lines of the translation belong to the 1840 text, for the Clairmont transcript omits their translation.

Thus it can be shown that by using the similarity and dissimilarity of the two versions we have a criterion for establishing two lacunae in the MS which Mary used for her version. By filling in these two lacunae from Shelley's earlier version in the Clairmont transcript we have, with the exception of the Homer quotations, Shelley's organic whole translation of the *Ion.*

ION, OR OF THE ILIAD
Translated from Plato

SOCRATES and ION

Socrates. Hail to thee, O Ion! from whence returnest thou amongst us now?—from thine own native Ephesus?

Ion. No, Socrates; I come from Epidaurus and the feasts in honour of Aesculapius.

Socrates. Had the Epidaurians instituted a contest of rhapsody in honour of the God?

Ion. And not in rhapsodies alone; there were contests in every species of music.

Socrates. And in which did you contend? And what was the success of your efforts?

Ion. I bore away the first prize at the games, O Socrates.

Socrates. Well done! You have only to consider how you shall win the Panathenaea.

Ion. That may also happen, God willing.

Socrates. Your profession, O Ion, has often appeared to me an enviable one. For, together with the nicest care of your person and the most studied elegance of dress, it imposes upon you the necessity of a familiar acquaintance with many and excellent poets, and especially with Homer, the most admirable of them all. Nor is it merely because you can repeat the verses of this great poet that I envy you, but because you fathom his inmost thoughts. For he is no rhapsodist who does not understand the whole scope and intention of the poet and is not capable of interpreting it to his audience. This he cannot do without a full comprehension of the meaning of the author he undertakes to illustrate; and worthy indeed of envy are those who can fulfil these conditions.

Ion. Thou speakest truth, O Socrates. And indeed I have expended my study particularly on this part of my profession. I flatter myself that no man living excels me in the interpretation of Homer; neither Metrodorus of Lampsacus, nor Stesimbrotus the Thasian, nor Glauco, nor any other rhapsodist of the present times can express so many various and beautiful thoughts upon Homer as I can.

Socrates. I am persuaded of your eminent skill, O Ion. You will not, I hope, refuse me a specimen of it?

Ion. And indeed it would be worth your while to hear me declaim upon Homer. I deserve a golden crown from his admirers.

Socrates. And I will find leisure some day or other to request you to favour me so far. At present I will only trouble you with one question. Do you excel in explaining Homer alone or are you conscious of a similar power with regard to Hesiod and Archilochus?

Ion. I possess this high degree of skill with regard to Homer alone and I consider that sufficient.

Socrates. Are there any subjects upon which Homer and Hesiod say the same things?

Ion. Many, as it seems to me.

Socrates. [Whether] Do you demonstrate these things better in Homer or Hesiod?

Ion. In the same manner, doubtless; inasmuch as they say the same words with regard to the same things.

Socrates. But with regard to those things in which they differ— Homer and Hesiod both treat of divination, do they not?

Ion. Certainly.

Socrates. Do you think that you or a diviner would make the best exposition respecting all that these poets say of divination, both as they agree and as they differ?

Ion. A diviner probably.

Socrates. Suppose you were a diviner, do you not think that you could explain the discrepancies of those poets on the subject of your profession, if you understand their agreement?

Ion. Clearly so.

Socrates. How does it happen then that you are possessed of skill to illustrate Homer and not Hesiod or any other poets in an equal degree? Is the subject-matter of the poetry of Homer different from all other poets? Does he not principally treat of war and social intercourse; and of the distinct functions and characters of the brave man and the coward, the professional and private person; the mutual relations which subsist between the Gods and men, together with the modes of their intercourse, the phaenomena of Heaven, the secrets of Hades, and the origin of Gods and heroes? Are not these the materials from which Homer wrought his poem?

Ion. Assuredly, O Socrates.

Socrates. And the other poets, do they not treat of the same matter?

Ion. Certainly, but not like Homer.

Socrates. How? Worse?

Ion. Oh, far worse.

Socrates. Then Homer treats of them better than they?

Ion. Oh Jupiter!—how much better!

Socrates. Amongst a number of persons employed in solving a problem of arithmetic might not a person know, my dear Ion, which had given the right answer?

Ion. Certainly.

Socrates. The same person who had been aware of the false one or some other?

Ion. The same clearly.

Socrates. That is, some one who understood arithmetic?

Ion. Certainly.

Socrates. Among a number of persons giving their opinions on the wholesomeness of different foods [whether] would one person be capable to pronounce upon the rectitude of the opinions of those who judged rightly and another on the erroneousness of those which were incorrect, or would the same person be competent to decide respecting them both?

Ion. The same evidently.

Socrates. What would you call that person?

Ion. A physician.

Socrates. We may assert then universally that the same person who is competent to determine the truth is competent also to determine the falsehood of whatever assertion is advanced on the same subject; and it is manifest that he who cannot judge respecting the falsehood or unfitness of what is said upon a given subject is equally incompetent to determine upon its truth or beauty.

Ion. Assuredly.

Socrates. The same person would then be competent or incompetent for both?

Ion. Yes.

Socrates. Do you not say that Homer and the other poets, and among them Hesiod and Archilochus, speak of the same things but unequally, one better and the other worse?

Ion. And I speak truth.

Socrates. But if you can judge of what is well said by the one you must also be able to judge of what is ill said by another, inasmuch as it expresses less correctly.

Ion. It should seem so.

Socrates. Then, my dear friend, we should not err if we asserted that Ion possessed a like power of illustration respecting Homer and all other poets; especially since he confesses that the same person must be esteemed a competent judge of all those who speak on the same subjects; inasmuch as those subjects are understood by him when spoken of by one, and the subject-matter of almost all the poets is the same.

Ion. What can be the reason then, O Socrates, that when any other poet is the subject of conversation I cannot compel my attention, and I feel utterly unable to declaim anything worth talking of, and positively go to sleep; but when any one makes mention of Homer my mind applies itself without effort to the subject; I awaken as if it were from a trance and a profusion of eloquent expressions suggest themselves involuntarily?

Socrates. It is not difficult to conjecture the cause of this, my dear friend. You are evidently unable to declaim on Homer according to art and knowledge; for did your art endow you with this faculty, you would be equally capable of exerting it with regard to any other of the poets. Is not poetry, as an art or a faculty, a thing entire and one?

Ion. Assuredly.

Socrates. The same mode of consideration must be admitted with respect to all arts which are severally one and entire. Do you desire to hear what I understand by this, O Ion?

Ion. Yes, by Jupiter, Socrates, I am delighted with listening to you wise men.

Socrates. It is you who are wise, my dear Ion; you rhapsodists, actors, and the authors of the poems you recite. I, like an unprofessional and private man, can only speak the truth. Observe how common, vulgar, and level to the comprehension of any one is the question which I now ask relative to the same consideration belonging to one entire art. Is not painting an art whole and entire?

Ion. Yes.

Socrates. Are there not and have there not been many painters both good and bad?

Ion. Certainly.

Socrates. Did you ever know a person competent to judge of the paintings of Polygnotus, the son of Aglaophon, and incompetent to judge of any other painter; who, on the compositions of the works of other painters being exhibited to him, was wholly at a loss, and very much inclined to go to sleep, and lost all faculty of reasoning on the subject; but when his opinion was required of Polygnotus or any one single painter you please, awoke, paid attention to the subject, and discoursed on it with great eloquence and sagacity?

Ion. Never, by Jupiter!

Socrates. Did you ever know any one very skilful in determining the merits of Daedalus, the son of Metion, Epius, the son of Panopus, Theodorus the Samian, or any other great sculptor, who was immediately at a loss and felt sleepy the moment any other sculptor was mentioned?

Ion. I never met with such a person certainly.

Socrates. Nor do I think that you ever met with a man professing himself a judge of poetry and rhapsody, and competent to criticise either Olympus, Thamyris, Orpheus, or Phemius of Ithaca, the rhapsodist, who, the moment he came to Ion the Ephesian, felt himself quite at a loss, utterly incompetent to judge whether he rhapsodised well or ill.

Ion. I cannot refute you, Socrates, but of this I am conscious to myself: that I excel all men in the copiousness and beauty of my illustrations of Homer, as all who have heard me will confess, and with respect to other poets I am deserted of this power. It is for you to consider what may be the cause of this distinction.

Socrates. I will tell you, O Ion, what appears to me to be the cause of this inequality of power. It is that you are not master of any art for the illustration of Homer but it is a divine influence which moves you, like that which resides in the stone called Magnet by Euripides, and Heraclea by the people. For not only does this stone possess the power of attracting iron rings but it can communicate to them the power of attracting other rings; so that you may see sometimes a long chain of rings and other iron substances attached and suspended one to the other by this influence. And as the power of the stone circulates through all the links of this series and attaches each to each, so the Muse communicating through those whom she has first inspired to all others capable of sharing in the inspiration the influence of that first enthusiasm, creates a chain and a succession. For the authors of those great poems which we admire do not attain to excellence through the rules of any art but they utter their beautiful melodies of verse in a state of inspiration and, as it were, *possessed* by a spirit not their own. Thus the composers of lyrical poetry create those admired songs of theirs in a state of divine insanity, like the Corybantes, who lose all control over their reason in the enthusiasm of the sacred dance; and, during this supernatural possession, are excited to the rhythm and harmony which they communicate to men; like the Bacchantes who, when possessed by the God, draw honey and milk from the rivers in which, when they come to their senses, they find nothing but simple water. For the souls of the poets, as poets tell us, have this peculiar ministration in the world. They tell us that these souls, flying like bees from flower to flower and wandering over the gardens and the meadows and the honey-flowing fountains of the

Muses, return to us laden with the sweetness of melody; and arrayed as they are in the plumes of rapid imagination they speak truth. For a poet is indeed a thing ethereally light, winged, and sacred, nor can he compose anything worth calling poetry until he becomes inspired and as it were mad; or whilst any reason remains in him. For whilst a man retains any portion of the thing called reason he is utterly incompetent to produce poetry or to vaticinate. Thus those who declaim various and beautiful poetry upon any subject, as for instance upon Homer, are not enabled to do so by art or study; but every rhapsodist or poet, whether dithyrambic, encomiastic, choral, epic, or iambic, is excellent in proportion to the extent of his participation in the divine influence and the degree in which the Muse itself has descended on him. In other respects poets may be sufficiently ignorant and incapable. For they do not compose according to any art which they have acquired but from the impulse of the divinity within them; for did they know any rules of criticism according to which they could compose beautiful verses upon one subject they would be able to exert the same faculty with respect to all or any other. The God seems purposely to have deprived all poets, prophets, and soothsayers of every particle of reason and understanding, the better to adapt them to their employment as his ministers and interpreters; and that we, their auditors, may acknowledge that those who write so beautifully are possessed and address us inspired by the God. A presumption in favour of this opinion may be drawn from the circumstance of Tynnichus the Chalcidian having composed no other poem worth mentioning except the famous poem which is in everybody's mouth, perhaps the most beautiful of all lyrical compositions and which he himself calls a gift of the Muses. I think you will agree with me that examples of this sort are exhibited by the God himself to prove that those beautiful poems are not human nor from man but divine and from the Gods; and that poets are only the inspired interpreters of the Gods, each excellent in proportion to the degree of this inspiration. This example of the most beautiful of lyrics having been produced by a poet in other respects the worst seems to have been afforded as a divine evidence of the truth of this opinion.—Do you not think with me, Ion?

Ion. By Jupiter, I do. You touch as it were my soul with your words, O Socrates. The excellent poets appear to me to be divinely commissioned as interpreters between the Gods and us.

Socrates. Do not you rhapsodists interpret the creations of the poets?

Ion. We do.

Socrates. You are then the interpreters of interpreters?

Ion. Evidently.

Socrates. Now confess the truth to me, Ion, and conceal not what I ask of you.—When you recite some passage from an epic poem which excites your audience to the highest degree; when for instance you sing of Ulysses leaping upon the threshold of his home, bursting upon the assembled suitors, and pouring forth his arrows before his feet; or of Achilles rushing upon Hector; or when you represent some pathetic scene relating to Andromache, Hecuba, or Priam, do you then feel that you are in your senses or are you not then as it were out of yourself; and is not your soul transported into the midst of the actions which it represents, whether in Ithaca or in Troy, or into whatever other place may be the scene of the passage you recite?

Ion. How justly you conjecture my sensations, O Socrates, for I will not conceal from you that when I recite any pathetic passage my eyes overflow with tears, and when I relate anything terrible or fearful my hair lifts itself upright upon my head and my heart leaps with fear.

Socrates. How then, O Ion, can we call that man anything but mad who arrayed in a many coloured robe and crowned with a golden crown weeps in the midst of festivity and sacrifice; who surrounded by twenty thousand admiring and friendly persons, and thus secure from all possibility of injury or outrage, trembles with terror?

Ion. No indeed, to speak the truth, O Socrates.

Socrates. Do you know too that you compel the greater number of your auditors to suffer the same affections with yourself?

Ion. And I know it well. For I see every one of them upon their seats aloft weeping and looking miserable; indeed it is of importance to me to observe them anxiously, for whilst I make them weep I know that my profits will give me occasion to laugh, but if I make them laugh it is then my turn to weep for I shall receive no money.

Socrates. Know then that the spectator represents the last of the rings which derive a mutual and successive power from that Heracleotic stone of which I spoke. You, the actor or rhapsodist, represent the intermediate one and the poet that attached to the magnet itself. Through all these the God draws the souls of men according to his pleasure, having attached them to one another by the power transmitted from himself. And as from that stone so a long chain of poets, theatrical performers, and subordinate teachers and professors of the musical art, laterally connected with the main series, are suspended from the Muse itself as from the origin of the influence. We call this inspiration and our expression indeed comes near to the truth; for the person who is an agent in this universal and reciprocal attraction is indeed possessed, and some are attracted and suspended by one of the poets who are the first rings in this great chain and some by another. Some are possessed by Orpheus, some by Musaeus, and many, among whom you may be numbered, my dear friend, by Homer. And so complete is his possession of you that you doze and are at a loss when any one proposes the verses of any other poet as the subject of recitation; but no sooner is a single passage of this poet recited than you awaken and your soul dances within you and dictates words at will. For it is not through art or knowledge that you illustrate Homer but from a divine influence and election, like the Corybantes who hear no sound except that penetrating melody which proceeds from the Deity by whom they are possessed, and although mad in other respects, are capable of accommodating their words and their dress to the rhythm of that music. Hence, O Ion, you have a power of speech respecting Homer alone, and this is the cause which you sought why that power is united to Homer; it is by a divine election and not through art that you have attained so singular an excellence in panegyrizing and illustrating this Poet.

Ion. You speak well, O Socrates. Yet I should be surprised if you had eloquence enough to persuade me that when I praise Homer I am mad and possessed. I think you would change your opinion if you once heard me declaim.

Socrates. And indeed I desire to hear you, but just answer me one question. On what subjects does Homer speak well—not on every one I imagine?

Ion. Be assured, O Socrates, that he speaks ill on none.

Socrates. And does Homer never speak anything respecting which you may happen to be ignorant?

Ion. There are indeed subjects spoken of by Homer which I do not understand.

Socrates. Does not Homer speak copiously and in many places of various arts—such for instance as charioteering? If you do not remember the passages I will quote the verses to you.

Ion. Allow me. I remember them well.

Socrates. Recite me those then in which Nestor warns his son Antilochus to beware of the turn in the course at the horse race given at the funeral of Patroclus.

Ion.   [. . . and warily proceed,
         A little bending to the left-hand steed;
         But urge the right, and give him all the reins;

While thy strict hand his fellow's head restrains,
And turns him short; till, doubling as they roll,
The wheel's round nave appears to brush the goal.
Yet, not to break the car or lame the horse,
Clear of the stony heap direct the course.]

Socrates. Enough. Now Ion, which would be the best judge of whether Homer had given right directions on this subject or not—a physician or a charioteer?

Ion. A charioteer certainly.

Socrates. For what reason? Because it belongs to his art to determine?

Ion. Because it belongs to his art.

Socrates. For the God has attached to every art the knowledge of the peculiar things which relate to it. The rules for steering a ship would never teach us anything in medicine?

Ion. Certainly not.

Socrates. Nor could we deduce from the art of medicine any rules for architecture.

Ion. We could not.

Socrates. Thus with regard to all arts: we can infer nothing from the rules of one to the subject of another. Permit me this one question— you allow a distinction of arts?

Ion. Certainly.

Socrates. Do you understand it in the sense that I do? I say that arts are distinct one from the other inasmuch as they are the sciences of different things.

Ion. So I understand it.

Socrates. We cannot establish any distinction between science the objects of which are the same. For instance, we both know that the fingers of our hand are five in number; and if I should ask you whether we acquire this knowledge through the same science, that is arithmetic, or by two different sciences, you would say by the same.

Ion. Certainly.

Socrates. Now answer the question I was just going to propose. Is it not true of all arts that one class of things must be known by one single art and that the knowledge of other classes belongs to other arts, separately and distinctly considered; so that if the art ceases to be the same the subject must also become different?

Ion. So it should appear, O Socrates.

Socrates. No one, therefore, who is ignorant of any part can be competent to know rightly what to say or to do with respect to it.

Ion. Certainly not.

Socrates. To return to the verses which you just recited—do you think that you or a charioteer would be better capable of deciding whether Homer had spoken rightly or not?

Ion. Doubtless a charioteer.

Socrates. For you are a rhapsodist and not a charioteer.

Ion. Yes.

Socrates. And the art of reciting verses is different from that of driving chariots?

Ion. Certainly.

Socrates. And if it is different it supposes a knowledge of different things.

Ion. Certainly.

Socrates. And when Homer introduces Hecamede, the concubine of Nestor, giving Machaon who was wounded a posset to drink, he speaks thus:

> [Tempered in this, the nymph of form divine,
> Pours a large portion of the Pramnian wine;
> With goats'-milk cheese, a flavorous taste bestows,
> And last with flour the smiling surface strews.],

does it belong to the medical or the rhapsodical art to determine whether Homer speaks rightly on this subject?

Ion. To the medical.

Socrates. And when he says:

> [She plunged, and instant shot the dark profound:
> As, bearing death in the fallacious bait,
> From the bent angle sinks the leaden weight.],

does it belong to the rhapsodical or the piscatorial art to determine whether he speaks rightly or not on the subject?

Ion. Manifestly to the piscatorial art.

Socrates. Consider if you are not inspired to make some such demand as this to me: Come, Socrates, since you have found in Homer a complete and fit description of these arts, assist me also in the enquiry as to his competence in determining on the subject of soothsayers and divination; and how far he speaks well or ill on such subjects; for he often treats of them in the Odyssey, and especially when he introduces

Theoclymenus, the soothsayer of the Melampodides, prophesying to the Suitors:

> [O race to death devote! with Stygian shade
> Each destined peer impending Fates invade;
> With tears your wan distorted cheeks are drowned,
> With sanguine drops the walls are rubied round;
> Thick swarms the spacious hall with howling ghosts,
> To people Orcus, and the burning coasts.
> Nor gives the sun his golden orb to roll,
> But universal night usurps the pole.]

Often too in the Iliad, as at the battle at the walls; for he there says:

> [A signal omen stopped the passing host,
> Their martial fury in their wonder lost.
> Jove's bird on sounding pinions beats the skies,
> A bleeding serpent of enormous size
> His talons trussed, alive and curling round,
> He stung the bird, whose throat received the wound;
> Mad with the smart, he drops the fatal prey,
> In airy circles wings his painful way,
> Floats on the winds and rends the heaven with cries:
> Amidst the host the fallen serpent lies.]

I assert, it belongs to a soothsayer both to observe and to judge respecting such appearances as these.

Ion. And you assert the truth, O Socrates.

Socrates. And you also, my dear Ion. For we have both in our turn recited from the Odyssey and the Iliad passages relating to vaticination, to medicine, and the piscatorial art; and as you are more skilled in Homer than I can be do you now make mention of whatever relates to the rhapsodist and his art; for a rhapsodist is competent above all other men to consider and pronounce on whatever has relation to his art—

Ion. Or with respect to every thing else mentioned by Homer.

Socrates. Do not be so forgetful as to say everything. A good memory is particularly necessary for a rhapsodist.

Ion. And what do I forget?

Socrates. Do you not remember that you admitted the art of reciting verses was different from that of driving chariots?

Ion. I remember.

Socrates. And did you not admit that being different the subjects of its knowledge must also be distinct?

Ion. Certainly.

Socrates. You will not assert that the art of rhapsody is that of universal knowledge; a rhapsodist may be ignorant of some things.

Ion. Except, perhaps, such subjects as we now discuss, O Socrates.

Socrates. What do you mean by *such* subjects, besides those which relate to other arts? And with which among them do you profess a competent acquaintance, since not with all?

Ion. I imagine that the rhapsodist has a perfect acquaintance with what is becoming for a man to speak, what for a woman; what for a slave, what for a free man; what for the ruler, what for the governed.

Socrates. How! do you think that a rhapsodist knows better than the pilot what the captain of a ship in a tempest ought to say?

Ion. In such a circumstance I allow that the pilot would know best.

Socrates. Has the rhapsodist or the physician the clearer knowledge of what ought to be said to a sick man?

Ion. In that case the physician.

Socrates. But you assert that he knows what a slave ought to say?

Ion. Certainly.

Socrates. To take for example—in the driving of cattle a rhapsodist would know much better than the herdsman what ought to be said to a slave engaged in bringing back a herd of oxen that had run wild?

Ion. No indeed.

Socrates. Perhaps you mean that he knows much better than any housewife what ought to be said by a workman about the dressing of wool?

Ion. No! No!

Socrates. Or by a general animating his soldiers to battle?

Ion. The rhapsodist is not unacquainted with such matters.

Socrates. What! is rhapsody the military art?

Ion. I should know what it became a general to say.

Socrates. Very likely, if you have studied tactics. You may be at the same time a musician and horse-breaker, and know whether horses are well or ill broken; now if I asked you, O Ion, by which of these two arts you judged respecting these horses, what would be your reply?

Ion. By that of horse-breaking.

Socrates. And in relation to any judgments you might pronounce upon musical performers you would profess yourself a musician, not a horse-breaker.

Ion. Certainly.

Socrates. If then you possess any knowledge of military affairs do you possess it in your character of general or rhapsodist?

Ion. I see no difference between a general and a rhapsodist.

Socrates. How! no difference? Are not the arts of generalship and recitation two distinct things?

Ion. No, they are the same.

Socrates. Must he who is a good rhapsodist be also necessarily a good general?

Ion. Infallibly, O Socrates.

Socrates. And must a good general be also a good rhapsodist?

Ion. That does not follow.

Socrates. But you are persuaded at least that a good rhapsodist is a good general.

Ion. Assuredly.

Socrates. But you are the first rhapsodist in Greece?

Ion. By far.

Socrates. And consequently best general?

Ion. Be convinced of it, O Socrates.

Socrates. Why then, by all the Gods, O Ion, since you are at once the best rhapsodist and the greatest general among the Greeks, do you content yourself with wandering about rhapsodizing from city to city and never place yourself at the head of your armies? Do you think the Greeks have so great a need of one to recite verses to them in a golden crown and none whatever of a general?

Ion. Our own city, O Socrates, is subjected to yours and can give no employment in that branch of the art; and Athens and Sparta are so strongly persuaded of the competence of their own citizens that I doubt whether they would entrust me with a command.

Socrates. My dear Ion, do you know Apollodorus of Cyzene?

Ion. Which Apollodorus?

Socrates. Him whom the Athenians entrusted with a command, although a foreigner; Phanosthenes the Andrian and Heraclides the Clazomenian, likewise foreigners, were also promoted to many civil and military trusts in Athens on account of their reputation. Why should they not honour and elect Ion the Ephesian as their general, if he should be considered equal to the situation?—you Ephesians were originally Athenians and Ephesus is a city inferior to none.—But you are in the wrong, Ion, if you are serious in your pretence of being able to illustrate Homer by art and knowledge. For after having promised to explain a multiplicity of subjects mentioned by Homer and assuring me that you knew them well you now deceive me; and although I give you every opportunity you are still found wanting even with respect to that very subject of which you profess yourself fully master. Like Proteus you assume a multiplicity of shapes until at last escaping through my fingers, that you may avoid giving me any proof of your skill in Homer, you suddenly stand before me in the shape of a general. If now you have deceived me in your promise of explaining Homer in your quality of a professor in the science of rhapsody, you act unjustly by me; but if the various and beautiful expressions which at times you can employ are, according to my view of the subject, suggested by the influence of the divine election whilst you are possessed as it were by the spirit of Homer, and you are in yourself ignorant and incompetent, I absolve you from all blame. Take your choice, whether you prefer to be considered inspired or unjust.

Ion. There is a great difference between these two imputations, O Socrates; the former is far more honourable.

Socrates. It is better both for you and for us, O Ion, to say that you are the inspired and not the learned eulogist of Homer.

Fragments of Translation from the *Ion*

In fragments I-II of the Appendix to *A Defence of Poetry* in Koszul's *Shelley's Prose in the Bodleian Manuscripts* (London, 1910), pages 121-122, we find Shelley's translation of a continuous passage of the *Ion* (533d3-534a6, 534a7-b7). The text of this passage differs from that in the 1840 and Clairmont texts. The inferior quality of translation of this passage and its position in the notebook containing *A Defence of Poetry* show that Shelley translated it as he was reading or after reading the *Ion*. As was his practice with quotations in notebooks, he intended to make use of this passage in his own composition. The finish of the translation of this passage in the 1840 text shows that the translation of the *Ion* was made later.

I[1]

f. 91 v rev. For a divine power moves you, as that of the magnet;
in pencil which not only can draw iron rings to itself but can endow
them with a similar power of attraction to draw other rings,
until a long chain of rings is attached to each other; and
all is attached to the stone itself.—Thus poetry, being itself
divinely inspired, communicates this inspiration to others,
until a long chain is made every link of which is a human
spirit and the first [link] of which is attached to that of
f. 91 rev. the [poet]. For no poets are excellent from their art, but
when they sing those beautiful poems, they are inspired
and possessed by a higher power. And as the Corybants
dance in being mad; so poets being mad make those beautiful poems and possessed with the divinity bacchanalize
so soon as the[y] [arrive?] at harmony and rhythm; like
those Menads who in their orgasm find milk and honey
in the rivers and when they are in their senses find it no
more.

II

f. 89 v rev. For Poets tell us that flying like bees, and wandering over
the gardens and the meadows and the honey flowing fountains of the Muses they return to us laden with sweet melodies, and they speak truth: for a poet is a thing aetherially
light; winged and sacred; nor can he make poetry before
he becomes divinely inspired and out of his senses; and
until understanding be no longer in him. So long as he has
this posses[sion] a man is incapable of producing poetry
and vatication.

[1] Brackets indicate doubtful readings or editorial additions.

Fragments on the *Ion*

The manuscript of this unpublished fragment *(MS. Shelley adds. d. 6, p. 1)* is found in a notebook which contained Shelley's translation of the *Ion*. The notes follow the translation of the *Ion*, directly after the note on "Memor. Lib. I," as may be seen from the contents page of this notebook *(MS. Shelley adds. d. 6, p. 114)*. The date therefore is very likely January, 1821. These notes on the *Ion* reveal that Shelley, as in his other notes on Plato, is not a blind follower of Plato, but rather exercises his own independent judgment. In view of Peacock's attack on poetry we see in these notes a sensitive reaction to Plato's criticism of Tynnichus. In "a sophism here" we find another instance of Shelley's criticism of Plato for sophisms. (See *On a Passage in Crito*, Julian *Works*, VII, 161-162.) It is difficult to determine whether the numbering of the notes refers to the pages of his text or his translation or to the chapters in the *Ion*. Note 6 definitely refers to *Ion* 534d5, while note 5 refers to *Ion* 535c6. Note 4 refers to *Ion* 534a ff., a passage which impressed Shelley. Note 10 refers to *Ion* 537d ff. It is not clear in note 8 to what passage in the *Ion* Shelley imputes the phrase "Baconic philosophy," but it likely refers to 536a ff.

Mary Shelley, in transcribing the various fragments which she found in the notebook containing *Notes on Sculptures*, listed the Plato material as follows *(MS. Shelley adds. d. 6, p. 114)*:

7. Translation of Plato's "Ion or the Iliad.". 27
8. 9. 53-54
10. Extracts translated from Plato's Republic. 54
                  Plat[o]
9. In one sense utility expresses the means. 54
    But it w^d be almost impossible to build your city in such a situation. . 54
    But with this system of life some are not contented. 56
    At first we must improve on the composers. 58

The order is not chronological but thematic. Fragment 9 is both listed with Fragment 8 (Notes on "Ion") and then the first line of it is again listed under "Plat[o]," followed by the first lines of the first three extracts in Shelley's translations from the *Republic*. It is quite clear that Mary, in grouping Fragment 9 with the Platonic material and especially following the notes on the *Ion*, thought it had some connection with Plato. The connection with the *Ion* becomes clear when it is realized that Shelley, in the notes to *Ion*, objects to Plato's treatment of Tynnichus and Ion. He read the final passages in the *Ion* with Peacock's *The Four Ages of Poetry* fresh in his mind. Plato shows that the poet is useless when it comes to teaching one the practical arts. Shelley associated this thought with Peacock's similar point on the uselessness of poetry in a practical world. Fragment 9 therefore is an answer both to Plato and to Peacock and consequently it may be included, as Mary does, with the comments on the *Ion*.

Fragment 9, which subsequently was woven in the argument of *A Defence of Poetry* (Julian *Works,* VII, 132, ll. 5 ff.), is with some textual variations an even earlier version of the one which Forman printed as an early draft of the passage in *A Defence of Poetry* (Julian *Works,* VII, 356-357). It stems both from the *Ion* and *The Four Ages of Poetry.*

Fragments on the *Ion*

1

(Notes to Ion) 4. A godsend, we should say.

5. Why the example of Tynnichus is not conclusive. It is rather an exception, than a rule; great poets, though not always good, or reasonable, men, have always been persons of marked and singular power both of character and countenance.

6. A sophism here. Tears did not indicate grief and horror; fear this had both their source in sensibility, which had no reference to the self of the person thus. 8. Baconic philosophy.

10^2 Science and art confounded here.

2

In one sense utility expresses the means for producing and preserving the most intense, and durable, and universal pleasure, and has relation to our actual being. And in this sense whatever tends to enlarge our imagination is useful. In another, it expresses the means of banishing the importunity of the wants of our animal nature, & surrounding us with security; and of conciliating such a degree of mutual forbearance between men, as may spring from motives consistent with their own present and manifest advantages. The author of the 4 ages of Poetry employs it entirely in the latter sense.

MENEXENUS, OR THE FUNERAL ORATION. A FRAGMENT

THE *MENEXENUS*, even though a minor dialogue of Plato, was very popular in the eighteenth century, a fact which may account for Shelley's attraction to it.[1] Shelley's translation of the introduction of the *Menexenus* (234a-236d) is concerned with Socrates's meeting Menexenus, who has just arrived from the senate house. The council has met for the appointment of a speaker who is to give the funeral oration on those Athenians who died in the last war. Shelley's translation stops at the point where Socrates is about to give a funeral oration which he had learned from Aspasia. In *An Address to the People on the Death of Princess Charlotte*, by the Hermit of Marlow, 1817, composed on the eleventh and twelfth of November, 1817,[2] we have a passage which throws light on the translation. "The Athenians," says Shelley, "did well to celebrate, with public mourning, the death of those who had guided the republic with their valour and their understanding, or illustrated it with their genius."[3] This allusion may reflect the reading of either Thucydides, II, 35-47, which is in the list of books read by Shelley in 1815[4] or the *Menexenus* of Plato. The probabilities are that the allusion is drawn from a recent reading of the *Menexenus* at Marlow, where he read Plato under the influence of Hogg and Peacock.[5] The reading of the *Menexenus* at Marlow may therefore be a clue to the date of the translation. The translation is fairly accurate, and was probably made from the Bipont text. It is important for showing Shelley's reading even of the minor dialogues of Plato, and if Mary is reflecting Shelley's own reason in the Preface of the 1840 edition, it may have been regarded by Shelley as an "admirable specimen of Socratic irony."

[1] See *MP*, XLI (1943), 105, 109.

[2] Julian *Works*, VI, 354.

[3] *Ibid.*, VI, 74.

[4] White, *Shelley*, II, 541.

[5] Hogg, *op. cit.*, I, 121-122. The influence of the *Menexenus* on *An Address to the People on the Death of Princess Charlotte*, by the Hermit of Marlow, 1817, makes it probable that this short dialogue was among those listed in Mary's entry in the Journal for February 23, 1817: "Shelley reads 'Waverly,' 'Tales of my Landlord,' and several of the works of Plato." In view of the amount of reading listed for that day it is likely that this dialogue was read in translation, possibly in Ficino's translation in the Bipont edition of Plato's works.

MENEXENUS, OR THE FUNERAL ORATION

A FRAGMENT

SOCRATES *and* MENEXENUS

Socrates. Whence comest thou, O Menexenus? from the forum?

Menexenus. Even so; and from the senate-house.

Socrates. What was thy business with the senate? Art thou persuaded that thou hast attained to that perfection of discipline and philosophy, from which thou mayest aspire to undertake greater matters? Wouldst thou, at thine age, my wonderful friend, assume to thyself the government of us who are thine elders, lest thy family should at any time fail in affording us a protector?

Menexenus. If thou, O Socrates, shouldst permit and counsel me to enter into public life, I would earnestly endeavour to fit myself for the attempt. If otherwise, I would abstain. On the present occasion, I went to the senate-house, merely from having heard that the senate was about to elect one to speak concerning those who are dead. Thou knowest that the celebration of their funeral approaches?

Socrates. Assuredly. But whom have they chosen?

Menexenus. The election is deferred until to-morrow; I imagine that either Dion or Archinus will be chosen.

Socrates. In truth, Menexenus, the condition of him who dies in battle is, in every respect, fortunate and glorious. If he is poor, he is conducted to his tomb with a magnificent and honourable funeral, amidst the praises of all; if even he were a coward, his name is included in a panegyric pronounced by the most learned men; from which all the vulgar expressions, which unpremeditated composition might admit, have been excluded by the careful labour of leisure; who praise so admirably, enlarging upon every topic remotely, or immediately connected with the subject, and blending so eloquent a variety of expressions, that, praising in every manner the state of which we are citizens, and those who have perished in battle, and the ancestors who preceded our generation, and ourselves who yet live, they steal away our spirits as with enchantment. Whilst I listen to their praises, O Menexenus, I am penetrated with a very lofty conception of myself, and overcome by their flatteries. I appear to myself immeasurably more honourable and generous than before, and many of the strangers who are accustomed to accompany me, regard me with additional veneration, after having heard these relations; they seem to consider the whole state, including me, much more worthy of admiration, after they have been soothed into persuasion by the orator.

The opinion thus inspired of my own majesty will last me more than three days sometimes, and the penetrating melody of the words descends through the ears into the mind, and clings to it; so that it is often three or four days before I come to my senses sufficiently to perceive in what part of the world I am, or succeed in persuading myself that I do not inhabit one of the islands of the blessed. So skilful are these orators of ours.

Menexenus. Thou always laughest at the orators, O Socrates. On the present occasion, however, the unforeseen election will preclude the person chosen from the advantages of a preconcerted speech; the speaker will probably be reduced to the necessity of extemporising.

Socrates. How so, my good friend? Every one of the candidates has, without doubt, his oration prepared; and if not, there were little difficulty, on this occasion, of inventing an unpremeditated speech. If, indeed, the question were of Athenians, who should speak in the Peloponnesus; or of Peloponnesians, who should speak at Athens, an orator who would persuade and be applauded, must employ all the resources of his skill. But to the orator who contends for the approbation of those whom he praises, success will be little difficult.

Menexenus. Is that thy opinion, O Socrates?

Socrates. In truth it is.

Menexenus. Shouldst thou consider thyself competent to pronounce this oration, if thou shouldst be chosen by the senate?

Socrates. There would be nothing astonishing if I should consider myself equal to such an undertaking. My mistress in oratory was perfect in the science which she taught, and had formed many other excellent orators, and one of the most eminent among the Greeks, Pericles, the son of Xantippus.

Menexenus. Who is she? Assuredly thou meanest Aspasia.

Socrates. Aspasia, and Connus the son of Metrobius, the two instructors. From the former of these I learned rhetoric, and from the latter music. There would be nothing wonderful if a man so educated should be capable of great energy of speech. A person who should have been instructed in a manner totally different from me; who should have learned rhetoric from Antiphon the son of Rhamnusius, and music from Lampses, would be competent to succeed in such an attempt as praising the Athenians to the Athenians.

Menexenus. And what shouldst thou have to say, if thou wert chosen to pronounce the oration?

Socrates. Of my own, probably nothing. But yesterday I heard

Aspasia declaim a funeral oration over these same persons. She had heard, as thou sayest, that the Athenians were about to choose an orator, and she took the occasion of suggesting a series of topics proper for such an orator to select; in part extemporaneously, and in part such as she had already prepared. I think it probable that she composed the oration by interweaving such fragments of oratory as Pericles might have left.

Menexenus. Rememberest thou what Aspasia said?

Socrates. Unless I am greatly mistaken. I learned it from her; and she is so good a schoolmistress, that I should have been beaten if I had not been perfect in my lesson.

Menexenus. Why not repeat it to me?

Socrates. I fear lest my mistress be angry, should I publish her discourse.

Menexenus. O, fear not. At least deliver a discourse; you will do what is exceedingly delightful to me, whether it be of Aspasia or any other. I entreat you to do me this pleasure.

Socrates. But you will laugh at me, who, being old, attempt to repeat a pleasant discourse.

Menexenus. O no, Socrates; I entreat you to speak, however it may be.

Socrates. I see that I must do what you require. In a little while, if you should ask me to strip naked and dance, I shall be unable to refuse you, at least, if we are alone. Now, listen. She spoke thus, if I recollect, beginning with the dead, in whose honour the oration is supposed to have been delivered.

INTRODUCTION TO SHELLEY'S TRANSLATION OF
FRAGMENTS FROM THE REPUBLIC

SHELLEY FIRST READ this important work of Plato at Oxford in a French translation.[1] He probably read part of it again at Marlow, if the references to it in the *Essay on Christianity*[2] and a note reflect a recent reading. His statement in a note written in 1818 is indicative of the value which Shelley placed on this work:

The Republic, though replete with considerable errors of speculation, is, indeed, the greatest repository of important truths of all the works of Plato. This, perhaps, is because it is the longest. He first, and perhaps last, maintained that a state ought to be governed, not by the wealthiest, or the most ambitious, or the most cunning, but by the wisest. The method of selecting such rulers and the laws by which such a selection [is made] must correspond with and arise out of the moral freedom and[3]

Further evidence of Shelley's interest in this work at this period is seen in Claire's Journal for April 23, 1818,[4] when she writes, "Walk with Shelley and the *Chicks* in the public Gardens. . . . Plato excluded Homer from his republic because he said it made its readers tolerate war." Claire may be echoing a conversation with Shelley or Wieland's *Aristippus,* which she was reading at the time.

An incentive for Shelley's commencement of the reading of the *Republic* in the original in 1818 may have been the summary of the dialogue in Barthélemy's *Travels of Anacharsis the Younger,* an epitome of Greek civilization, which Shelley enthusiastically read at Bagni di Lucca from June 22 through July 6.[5] The desire to read the *Republic* in the original seized Shelley in October, 1818, while he was visiting Byron at Venice. Shelley, who had loaned his copy of Plato to Byron, hoping to interest him in Plato, wrote a note to him on October 17: "I am so dreadfully sleepy that I cannot come to-night. Will you have the goodness to send us . . . my Plato."[6] The Plato was duly returned. On October 20 Mary wrote in her Journal, "Shelley begins the 'Republic' of Plato." Entries in the Journal for November 7 and 9 show that Shelley

[1] Hogg, *op. cit.,* I, 121; the French translation was either *La République,* traduite par De la Pillonnière (London, 1726), or *La République,* traduite du Grec, par J. Grou, 2 vols. (Amsterdam, 1763).

[2] *Vide supra,* pp. 329-331.

[3] This was published as a note in Shelley's preface to the *Symposium.* It is, however, a separate note in the manuscript. *Vide infra,* pp. 564-565.

[4] Pforzheimer MS; cf. White, *op. cit.,* I, 670-671.

[5] *Vide supra,* pp. 132-133.

[6] White, *op. cit.,* II, 460.

continued his reading of the *Republic* at Ferrara and Rome. The reading was discontinued until the Shelleys' arrival at Florence; entries in the Journal for October 9, 10, 24, 28 and November 2, 6, 7, 8 and 9, 1819, record Shelley's reading of the *Republic*. The reading of the *Republic* may have continued later in the year, for Mary neglected the Journal because of the birth of Percy Florence on November 12. However, it is likely that Shelley discontinued the reading of the *Republic* during December, 1819, and January, 1820, for the Journal entries record mostly the reading of the Bible and Sophocles. The *Republic* was again taken up in 1820, when it was completed and so noted in Mary's list of Shelley's readings for that year. The first entry for its reading in this year occurs on September 4; however, Shelley's reading of it may have started earlier, for after one more entry for its reading on September 9, Mary lists other readings of his for the remainder of the year. The impression which this reading of the *Republic* made on Shelley is seen in his letter to Hogg dated October 20, 1821.

Do you know the πολιτεια, and especially the sixth book of it? His speculations on civil society are surely the foundations of true politics, and if ever the world is to be arranged on another System than that of the several members of it destroying, and tormenting one another for the pleasures of sense, or from the force of habit and imitation, it must start from such principles.[7]

The *Republic* constitutes along with the *Symposium* the most important of Plato's dialogues which influenced Shelley. The *Republic* satisfied Shelley's passion for reforming the world; the *Symposium* satisfied Shelley the poet and artist.

A reflection of Shelley's interest in this work of Plato is seen in his translation of the fragments from the *Republic*. These fragments comprise twenty passages, "the opinions and views of Plato enounced in the *Republic*, which" according to Mary, "appeared remarkable to Shelley . . . with the addition, in some instances, of his own observations on them."[8] Mary gives no date of composition for these fragments. Internal

---

[7] Scott, *Shelley at Oxford*, p. 64.

[8] Julian *Works* V, xii–xiii. Mary transcribed Shelley's translations of these fragments in a notebook (*MS. Shelley adds. d. 6*, p. 2) which, as the contents list (p. 114) shows, followed the translation of the *Ion* and occupied pages 54–68 of the notebook (*vide supra*, p. 483). Mary entitled these fragments "Extracts translated from Plato's Republic." Only a portion of the first fragment survives and, with the exception of the first few words of the first three fragments in the contents list, all the remaining fragments no longer remain in the notebook. The MS shows no textual variants from the fragments as printed in the 1840 edition. Though these fragments follow the translation of the *Ion* in the contents list, they are not chronologically later, for Mary arranged the Platonic material, as the 1840 edition shows, in such a way that fragments follow the more complete translations.

evidence, however, gives us sure clues as to the approximate date of these translations. Appended to the translation of Fragment XV (*Republic*, 401b-c) is the following comment:

The monstrous figures called Arabesques,—however in some of them is to be found a mixture of a truer and simpler taste—, which are found in the ruined palaces of the Roman Emperors, bear, nevertheless, the same relation to the brutal profligacy and killing luxury which required them, as the majestic figures of Castor and Pollux, and the simple beauty of the sculpture of the frieze of the Parthenon, bear to the more beautiful and simple manners of the Greeks of that period. With a liberal interpretation, a similar analogy might be extended into literary composition.[9]

The reference to the statues of Castor and Pollux makes it appear that the translation cannot have been made earlier than March 20, 1819. On that date Claire Clairmont notes in her diary: "We drive to Monte Cavallo and admire the fountain and the horses of Castor and Pollux for some time." In a letter to Peacock from Rome written on March 23, 1819, Shelley also tells of his visit to the fountain on the Quirinal:

On each side on an elevated pedestal stand the statues of Castor and Pollux, each in the act of taming his horse, which are said, but I believe wholly without authority, to be the work of Phidias and Praxiteles. These figures combine the irresistible energy with the sublime and perfect loveliness supposed to have belonged to their divine nature.[10]

Thus if we assume that the comment was simultaneous with the translation, the fragments from the *Republic* were translated sometime in March or April, 1819. One important piece of evidence appears in support of this date. It appears that Shelley finished the first book of the *Republic*, begun in Venice, and completed the second and third books before October and November of 1819, when Mary's Journal records readings of the *Republic* on October 9, 10, 24, 28, November 2, 6, 7, 8, and 9, 1819. It is likely that Shelley had got as far as the ninth book of the *Republic* in these readings, for in a letter dated November 3, 1819, he writes, "Tyrants, after all, are only a kind of demagogues; they must flatter the Great Beast"; and in a note to this letter he writes, "This word [aristocratical] is not used in a bad sense; nor is the word aristocracy susceptible of an ill signification. Oligarchy is the term for the tyrannical monopoly of the few."[11] The reference is clearly to *Republic*, 588c (Book IX),

[9] *Ibid.*, VII, 262.
[10] *Ibid.*, X, 43.
[11] *Ibid.*, X, 113.

where Plato compares the animal in man to a "many-headed beast" which tyrants flatter; furthermore, the note in this letter specifically alludes to the eighth book of the *Republic*. If then Shelley had got in November, 1819, as far as the ninth book, it is likely that he composed the fragments at a much earlier date when he was reading the second and third books; this period would then be in March or April, a date strongly supported by the reference to the horses of Castor and Pollux.

On the other hand, a case may be made for October or November of 1819 as the date of the composition of these fragments. On October 13 and 20 Mary records that Shelley visits the Gallery. The visit probably brought to Shelley memories of sculpture at Rome. In favor of this latter date is the evidence in the fragment *The Moral Teaching of Jesus Christ*. The closing sentence of this fragment reads, "The idea of forgiveness of injuries, the error of revenge, and the immorality and inutility of punishment considered as punishment (for these [are] correlative doctrines), are stated by Plato in the first book of the Republic."[12] The reference to the first book of the *Republic* finds a parallel in the seventh fragment of Shelley's translation from the *Republic*: "Plato's doctrine of punishment as laid down, p. 146, is refuted by his previous reasoning—p. 26." The similarity of sentiments about Christ in *The Moral Teaching of Jesus Christ* and in the letter to Leigh Hunt about the trial of Richard Carlile (written November 5, according to Mary's Journal entry) shows that *The Moral Teaching of Jesus Christ* was written in November, 1819. The cross-reference to Plato's view of punishment in both fragments supports the latter part of October or early November, 1819, as the date of the composition of the fragments from the *Republic*. Although this editor previously favored the latter date,[13] he is now inclined to favor the earlier date of March or April, 1819. As the specific page references in the seventh fragment show, the text which Shelley used in translating the fragments from the *Republic* was E. Massey, *Platonis de Republica* (Cambridge, 1713).[14] Shelley had left in England the sixth and seventh volumes of the Bipont edition which contained the *Republic*.

The fragments are in the order in which they occur in the second and third books of the *Republic*. The choice of passages reveals examples of important truths, which Shelley translated not for publication but, as his translation of two passages of the *Ion* shows,[15] as statements of

---

[12] *Shelley, Verse and Prose*, ed. Sir John C. E. Shelley-Rolls and Roger Ingpen (London, 1934), p. 111.

[13] See *MLR*, XXXIV (1939), 246. [14] *Vide infra*, p. 564.

[15] *Vide supra*, p. 482; cf. passage from Plato's *Laws* in Koszul, *Shelley's Prose in the Bodleian Manuscripts*, pp. 121-122.

truths or ideas to be used later in his own work. These fragments reveal that for Shelley Plato was a source of ideas, some of which he absorbed, others of which he criticized, noting resemblances and differences from his own views. Besides Fragment VII, another example of the use that Shelley made of these passages in his later work is found in *A Defence of Poetry* (1821).

The principle of equality had been discovered and applied by Plato in his Republic, as the theoretical rule of the mode in which the materials of pleasure and of power produced by the common skill and labour of human beings ought to be distributed among them. The limitations of this rule were asserted by him to be determined only by the sensibility of each, or the utility to result to all.[16]

This passage is based on the *Republic*, 369, which Shelley translated in the first fragment. The direct relationship of this passage in *A Defence of Poetry* to Shelley's own translation of it reveals concretely the debt that Shelley owed to Plato and the use he made of his reading of Plato. Shelley, here as before, carried the stage of translation over into re-creation.

ADDENDUM

A re-examination of a prose fragment of Shelley first published by Peck (*Shelley, His Life and Work*, II, 433-434) Shows that it is a translation of a section from the sixth book of the *Republic* (485b10-486b12). A comparison with the text of the *Republic* shows that Peck reversed the order of the two pages in the manuscript (Shelley MS 2 pp. 4to Pforzheimer Collection). If the section commencing with the words *And what is to be found more intimately* and ending with *for accumulating wealth* is placed at the beginning of the fragment, we have a continuous translation of Plato's passage. The date of this translation, on the evidence of the reading of the *Republic* in the Journal, is 1819 or 1820. For the new text, *vide infra*, pp. 500-501.

[16] Julian *Works*, VII, 127.

FRAGMENTS
FROM THE REPUBLIC OF PLATO

I.—But it would be almost impossible to build your city in such a situation that it would need no imports.—Impossible.—Other persons would then be required, who might undertake to conduct from another city those things of which they stood in need.—Certainly.—But the merchant who should return to his own city, without any of those articles which it needed, would return empty handed. It will be necessary, therefore, not only to produce a sufficient supply, but such articles, both in quantity and in kind, as may be required to remunerate those who conduct the imports. There will be needed then more husbandmen, and other artificers, in our city. There will be needed also other persons who will undertake the conveyance of the imports and the exports, and these persons are called merchants. If the commerce which these necessities produce is carried on by sea, other persons will be required who are accustomed to nautical affairs. And, in the city itself, how shall the products of each man's labour be transported from one to another; those products, for the sake of the enjoyment and the ready distribution of which, they were first induced to institute a civil society?—By selling and buying, surely.—A market and money, as a symbol of exchange, arise[s] out of this necessity.—Evidently.—When the husbandman, or any other artificer, brings the produce of his labours to the public place, and those who desire to barter their produce for it do not happen to arrive exactly at the same time, would he not lose his time, and the profit of it, if he were to sit in the market waiting for them? Assuredly. But, there are persons who, perceiving this, will take upon themselves the arrangement between the buyer and the seller. In constituted civil societies, those who are employed on this service, ought to be the infirm, and unable to perform any other; but, exchanging on one hand for money, what any person comes to sell, and giving the articles thus bought for a similar equivalent to those who might wish to buy.

II.—*Description of a frugal enjoyment of the goods of the world.*

III.—But with this system of life some are not contented. They must have beds and tables, and other furniture. They must have scarce ointments and perfumes, women, and a thousand superfluities of the same character. The things which we mentioned as sufficient, houses, and clothes, and food, are not enough. Painting and mosaic-work must be cultivated, and works in gold and ivory. The society must be enlarged in consequence. This city, which is of a healthy proportion, will not suffice, but it must be replenished with a multitude of persons, whose occupations are by no means indispensable. Huntsmen and mimics, persons whose occupation it is to arrange forms and colours, persons whose trade is the cultivation of the more delicate arts, poets and their ministers, rhapsodists, actors, dancers, manufacturers of all kinds of instruments and schemes of female dress, and an immense crowd of other ministers to pleasure and necessity. Do you not think we should want schoolmasters, tutors, nurses, hair-dressers, barbers, manufacturers and cooks? Should we not want pig-drivers, which were not wanted in our more modest city, in this one, and a multitude of others to administer to other animals, which would then become necessary articles of food,—or should we not?—Certainly we should.—Should we not want physicians much more, living in this manner than before? The same tract of country would no longer provide sustenance for the state. Must we then not usurp from the territory of our neighbours, and then we should make aggressions, and so we have discovered the origin of war; which is the principal cause of the greatest public and private calamities.—C. ii.

IV.—And first, we must impose upon the composers of fabulous histories in verse, to compose them according to the rules of moral beauty; and those not composed according to the rules must be rejected; and we must persuade mothers and nurses to teach those which we approve to their children, and to form their minds by moral fables, far more than their bodies by their hands.—Lib. ii.

V.—On the Danger of the Study of Allegorical Composition (in a Large Sense) for Young People

For a young person is not competent to judge what portions of a fabulous composition are allegorical and what literal; but the opinions produced by a literal acceptation of that which has no meaning, or a bad one, except in an allegorical sense, are often irradicable.—Lib. ii.

VI.—God then, since he is good, cannot be, as is vulgarly supposed, the cause of all things; he is the cause, indeed, of very few things. Among the great variety of events which happen in the course of human affairs, evil prodigiously overbalances good in everything which regards men. Of all that is good there can be no other cause than God; but some other cause ought to be discovered for evil, which should never be imputed as an effect to God.—L. ii.

VII.—*Plato's doctrine of punishment as laid down, p. 146, is refuted by his previous reasonings.*—p. 26.

VIII.—The Unchangeable Nature of God

Do you think that God is like a vulgar conjuror, and that he is capable for the sake of effect, of assuming, at one time, one form, and at another time, another? Now, in his own character, converting his proper form into a multitude of shapes, now deceiving us, and offering vain images of himself to our imagination? Or do you think that God is single and one, and least of all things capable of departing from his permanent nature and appearance?

IX.—The Permanency of What Is Excellent

But everything, in proportion as it is excellent, either in art or nature, or in both, is least susceptible of receiving change from any external influence.

X.—Against Superstitious Tales

Nor should mothers terrify their children by these fables, that Gods go about in the night-time, resembling strangers, in all sorts of forms: at once blaspheming the Gods, and rendering their children cowardly.

XI.—The True Essence of Falsehood and Its Origin

Know you not, that that which is truly false, if it may be permitted me so to speak, all, both Gods and men, detest?—How do you mean?— Thus: No person is willing to falsify in matters of highest concern to himself concerning those matters, but fears, above all things, lest he should accept falsehood.—Yet, I understand you not.—You think that I mean something profound. I say that no person is willing in his own mind to receive or to assert a falsehood, to be ignorant, to be in error, to possess that which is not true. This is truly to be called falsehood, this ignorance and error in the mind itself. What is usually called falsehood, or deceit in words, is but a voluntary imitation of what the mind itself suffers in the involuntary possession of that falsehood, an image of later birth, and scarcely, in a strict and complete sense, deserving the name of falsehood.—Lib. ii.

XII.—Against a Belief in Hell

If they are to possess courage, are not those doctrines alone to be taught, which render death least terrible? Or do you conceive that any man can be brave who is subjected to a fear of death? that he who believes the things that are related of hell, and thinks that they are truth, will prefer in battle, death to slavery, or defeat?—Lib. iii.—*Then follows a criticism on the poetical accounts of hell.*

XIII.—On Grief

We must then abolish the custom of lamenting and commiserating the death of illustrious men. Do we assert that an excellent man will consider it anything dreadful that his intimate friend, who is also an excellent man, should die?—By no means, *(an excessive refinement)*. He will abstain then from lamenting over his loss, as if he had suffered some great evil?—Surely.—May we not assert in addition, that such a person as we have described suffices to himself for all purposes of living well and happily, and in no manner needs the assistance or society of another? that he would endure with resignation the destitution of a son, or a brother, or possessions, or whatever external adjuncts of life might have been attached to him? and that, on the occurrence of such contingencies, he would support them with moderation and mildness, by no means bursting into lamentations, or resigning himself to despondence?—Lib. iii.

Then he proceeds to allege passages of the poets in which opposite examples were held up to approbation and imitation.

XIV.—The Influence of Early Constant Imitation

Do you not apprehend that imitations, if they shall have been practised and persevered in from early youth, become established in the habits and nature, in the gestures of the body, and the tones of the voice, and lastly, in the intellect itself?—C. iii.

XV.—On the Effect of Bad Taste in Art

Nor must we restrict the poets alone to an exhibition of the example of virtuous manners in their compositions, but all other artists must be forbidden, either in sculpture, or painting, or architecture, to employ their skill upon forms of an immoral, unchastened, monstrous, or illiberal type, either in the forms of living beings, or in architectural arrangements. And the artist capable of this employment of his art, must not be suffered in our community, lest those destined to be guardians of the society, nourished upon images of deformity and vice, like cattle upon bad grass, gradually gathering and depasturing every day a little, may ignorantly establish one great evil, composed of these many evil things, in their minds.—C. iii.

The monstrous figures called Arabesques,—however in some of them is to be found a mixture of a truer and simpler taste—, which are found in the ruined palaces of the Roman Emperors, bear, nevertheless, the same relation to the brutal profligacy and killing luxury which required them, as the majestic figures of Castor and Pollux, and the simple beauty of the sculpture of the frieze of the Parthenon, bear to the more beautiful and simple manners of the Greeks of that period. With a liberal interpretation, a similar analogy might be extended into literary composition.

XVI.—AGAINST THE LEARNED PROFESSIONS

What better evidence can you require of a corrupt and pernicious system of discipline in a state, than that not merely persons of base habits and plebeian employments, but men who pretend to have received a liberal education, require the assistance of lawyers and physicians, and those too who have attained to a singular degree *(so desperate are these diseases of body and mind)* of skill. Do you not consider it an abject necessity, a proof of the deepest degradation, to need to be instructed in what is just or what is needful, as by a master and a judge, with regard to your personal knowledge and suffering?

What would Plato have said to a priest, such as his office is, in modern times?—C. iii.

XVII.—ON MEDICINE

Do you not think it an abject thing to require the assistance of the medicinal art, not for the cure of wounds, or such external diseases as result from the accidents of the seasons (ἐπετείων), but on account of sloth and the superfluous indulgences which we have already condemned; thus being filled with wind and water, like holes in earth, and compelling the elegant successors of Aesculapius to invent new names, flatulences, and catarrhs, &c., for the new diseases which are the progeny of your luxury and sloth?—L. iii.

XVIII.—THE EFFECT OF THE DIETETIC SYSTEM

Herodicus being paedotribe (παιδοτρίβης, *Magister palaestrae*), and his health becoming weak, united the gymnastic with the medical art, and having condemned himself to a life of weariness, afterwards extended the same pernicious system to others. He made his life a long death. For humouring the disease, mortal in its own nature, to which he was subject, without being able to cure it, he postponed all other purposes to the care of medicating himself, and through his whole life was subject to an access of his malady, if he departed in any degree from his accustomed diet, and by the employment of this skill, dying by degrees, he arrived at an old age.—L. iii.

Aesculapius never pursued these systems, nor Machaon or Podalirius. They never undertook the treatment of those whose frames were inwardly and thoroughly diseased, so to prolong a worthless existence, and bestow on a man a long and wretched being, during which they might generate children in every respect the inheritors of their infirmity.—L. iii.

XIX.—Against What Is Falsely Called "Knowledge of the World"

A man ought not to be a good judge until he be old; because he ought not to have acquired a knowledge of what injustice is, until his understanding has arrived at maturity: not apprehending its nature from a consideration of its existence in himself; but having contemplated it distinct from his own nature in that of others, for a long time, until he shall perceive what an evil it is, not from his own experience and its effects within himself, but from his observations of them as resulting in others. Such a one were indeed an honourable judge, and a good; for he who has a good mind, is good. But that judge who is considered so wise, who having himself committed great injustices, is supposed to be qualified for the detection of it in others, and who is quick to suspect, appears keen, indeed, as long as he associates with those who resemble him; because, deriving experience from the example afforded by a consideration of his own conduct and character, he acts with caution; but when he associates with men of universal experience and real virtue, he exposes the defects resulting from such experience as he possesses, by distrusting men unreasonably and mistaking true virtue, having no example of it within himself with which to compare the appearances manifested in others; yet such a one finding more associates who are virtuous than such as are wise, necessarily appears, both to himself and others, rather to be wise than foolish.—But we ought rather to search for a wise and good judge; one who has examples within himself of that upon which he is to pronounce.—C. iii.

XX.—Those who use gymnastics unmingled with music become too savage, whilst those who use music unmingled with gymnastics, become more delicate than is befitting.

XXI.—Shelley's Translation of Republic 485b10-486b12

And what is to be found more intimately connected with wisdom than truth? Nothing. Can then the same nature [but] be at once philosophical & prone to falsehood! By no means. The true aspirant after knowledge ought from his earliest youth to affect entire truth. Certainly whenever { the affections / [certain persons] } violently impel a person to a certain particular { course of life / [tendency] } we know that their strength is by so much the more remiss to any other tendency [in proportion as] their stream having been diverted into another channel. Certainly. { He / [Those] } who { s / ha[ve] } been impelled toward knowledge & { a / [its] } kindred discipline, seeks the [sens] pleasures of the soul [as within] as [it] they exists within itself, & omit the pursuit of bodily enjoyments; if indeed he be truly a philosopher & not a fictitious resemblance of that character. Of necessity it must be so. Such a person must be temperate, & in no manner a lover of money; [for those things] for those things for the sake of which others devote their whole [attention] powers at whatever expense to obtain wealth, he disregards; to [any to] him least of all mankind $\begin{Bmatrix} \text{could} \\ [\text{would}] \end{Bmatrix}$ there be any motive for accumulating wealth. In addition, when you would distinguish a philosophical [disposition] nature from one which is not, [consider] observe —what 3—whether it be servile or liberal; for all things a narrow littleness of [soul spirit] soul is the most $\begin{Bmatrix} \text{inauspicious} \\ \text{adverse} \end{Bmatrix}$ to a mind aspiring to embrace that comprehensive circle of divine & human nature beyond which nothing exists. For how [large] small $\begin{Bmatrix} \text{the} \\ [\text{a}] \end{Bmatrix}$ space $\begin{Bmatrix} \text{which} \\ [\text{would}] \end{Bmatrix}$ human life occupy in an intellect accustomed to the magnificent spectacle afforded by the contemplation of all time and all existence. Small indeed replies he. Could such a one consider death as terrible? Surely not. A cowardly & illiberal disposition is incapable of participating in the doctrines of true philosophy? Assuredly. But $\begin{Bmatrix} \text{he who is} \\ \text{the modest} \end{Bmatrix}$ free spirited [& gold despising] a despiser of wealth, neither insolent nor cowardly, would surely neither be nor unjust? Surely not. And [in the consideration] thus [by it] you may [discover] distinguish a philosophical man from one that is not so by observing from early youth whether its disposition is just & $\begin{Bmatrix} \text{gentle,} \\ [\text{mild}] \end{Bmatrix}$ or savage desire.

NOTE ON THE REPUBLIC

The Republic, though replete with considerable errors of speculation, is indeed the greatest repository of important truths of all the works of Plato—this perhaps is because it is the longest. He first, and perhaps last, maintained that a state ought to be governed, not by the wealthiest, or the most ambitious, or the most cunning, but by the wisest. The method of selecting such rulers, and the laws by which such a selection [is made] must correspond with and arise out of the moral freedom and

NOTE ON REPUBLIC 587e

A legitimate ruler is 729 times happier than a tyrant—how much better is he? Let the Legitimate ruler be[ing] 729, the tyrant is x and [his vaster] y his happiness;

$$729 \times x = y$$

$$
\begin{array}{r}
729 \\
729 \\
\hline
6561 \\
1458 \\
5103 \\
\hline
531441
\end{array}
$$

ON A PASSAGE IN CRITO

ALTHOUGH SHELLEY had read the *Crito* in an English translation of Dacier's edition of Plato at Oxford,[1] this note is the result of a reading of the dialogue in the original in 1821. If the report of Medwin's conversations with Shelley[2] is to be trusted, Shelley's note *On a Passage in Crito* can be dated sometime during Medwin's first visit with Shelley at Pisa, October 22, 1820, to March 15, 1821, or his visit of November 15, 1821, and after. Recollecting an incident in one of these visits, Medwin says, "I have often heard him say that he wished to die young—and he one day opened Plato and read, 'It would be delightful to me to die surrounded by my friends—secure of the Inheritance of glory and escaping after *such* an existence as mine, from the decay of mind and body that must soon be my portion.'"[3] This remark, however, is not to be found in Plato but in Shelley's *On a Passage in Crito,* where it is found in almost the identical words which Medwin quotes. It is obvious that Shelley had not been reading Plato, but his own note on the *Crito* or perhaps some notebook which contained this Platonic passage. *On a Passage in Crito* may be dated therefore within the period of Medwin's visit with Shelley in Pisa. The variant repetition of a phrase in this note in a canceled paragraph of a section of *Fragments on Metaphysics and Morals,* dated in 1821,[4] and the direct reference to Socrates's death in the *Phaedo,* which Shelley read in 1820, make it likely that Shelley read the *Crito* and wrote the note in the 1821 portion of Medwin's visit. If Shelley read the *Crito* in the folio edition of Plato,[5] then he may have written the fragment sometime between May 8 and November 1, 1821, when he was at Bagni di Pisa.[6] Shelley had sent the first volume of his Bipont edition, which contained the *Crito* as well as the *Phaedo,* to John Gisborne sometime in November, 1820.[7] However, Shelley missed this volume and had substituted for it, by October 20, 1821, "a folio *Plato,* whose incredible contractions and abominable inaccuracy torment me to

---

[1] *Vide supra,* p. 33.

[2] See H. B. Forman's introduction to Thomas Medwin's *Revised Life of Shelley* (Oxford, 1913) and *Prose Works* (London, 1880), I, xvi, where he calls Medwin "a well-intentioned narrator with an essentially inexact turn of mind."

[3] Thomas Medwin, *The Revised Life of Percy Bysshe Shelley,* ed. H. B. Forman, p. 435.

[4] Koszul, *Shelley's Prose in the Bodleian Manuscripts,* p. 145 n. 2; cf. J. A. Notopoulos, "The Dating of Shelley's Prose," *PMLA,* LVIII (1943), 488.

[5] Scott, *Shelley at Oxford,* p. 64.

[6] Cf. White, *op. cit.,* II, 289-290, 611 n. 2.

[7] Julian *Works,* X, 220.

death."[8]   This description of the folio fits either the folio edition of Stephanus (Paris, 1578), or more likely the cheaper Lugd. fol. 1590 or Francof. 1602, popular though inaccurate reprints of Stephanus's edition.[9] It is likely, therefore, that Shelley read the *Crito* in this text.

[8] Scott, *Shelley at Oxford,* p. 64.
[9] Cf. J. W. Moss, *A Manual of Classical Bibliography*[2] (London, 1837), II, 423-427.

ON A PASSAGE IN CRITO

[It is well known that when Socrates was condemned to death, his friends made arrangements for his escape from prison and his after security; of which he refused to avail himself, from the reason, that a good citizen ought to obey the laws of his country. On this Shelley makes the following remarks—]

THE reply is simple.

Indeed, your city cannot subsist, because the laws are no longer of avail. For how can the laws be said to exist, when those who deserve to be nourished in the Prytanea at the public expense, are condemned to suffer the penalties only due to the most atrocious criminals; whilst those against, and to protect from whose injustice, the laws were framed, live in honour and security? I neither overthrow your state, nor infringe your laws. Although you have inflicted an injustice on me, which is sufficient, according to the opinions of the multitude, to authorise me to consider you and me as in a state of warfare; yet, had I the power, so far from inflicting any revenge, I would endeavour to overcome you by benefits. All that I do at present is, that which the peaceful traveller would do, who, caught by robbers in a forest, escapes from them whilst they are engaged in the division of the spoil. And this I do, when it would not only be indifferent, but delightful to me to die, surrounded by my friends, secure of the inheritance of glory, and escaping, after such a life as mine, from the decay of mind and body which must soon begin to be my portion should I live. But, I prefer the good, which I have it in my power yet to perform.

Such are the arguments, which overturn the sophism placed in the mouth of Socrates by Plato. But there are others which prove that he did well to die.

ON THE DAEMON OF SOCRATES

This fragment, which was first published by H. Buxton Forman in his edition of Shelley's *Prose Works* (1880), was found in Shelley's MS notebook containing the *Notes on Sculptures in Rome and Florence,* which were composed in 1819. Another unpublished manuscript of this note was found among the manuscripts given to the Bodleian by Sir John C. E. Shelley-Rolls (*MS. Shelley adds. d. 6,* p. 1). It differs slightly from Forman's text. The notes on the sculpture in Rome were composed in March, 1819; for the Journal entries for March 8, 9, and 10 read, "Visit the Museum of the Vatican. . . . Shelley and I go to the Villa Borghese. . . . Visit the Capitol, and see the most divine statues."[1] The notes on the sculpture in Florence were written in October, 1819, for Mary records in the Journal for October 13 and 20, "He [Shelley] spends the morning at the Gallery. . . . Shelley visits the Galleries." The eighth note probably belongs to the sculpture seen in Florence, for the preceding note refers to Giovanni da Bologna's (1529?-1608) famous statue of Mercury, which is now in the Bargello, Florence, and the ninth note refers to an urn in the Uffizi Gallery in Florence.[2] The eighth note reads "A most admirable ox in bronze." Forman says "this note is followed in the MS Note-book by one on the Demon of Socrates—a memorandum of a thought which would seem to have occurred to Shelley while in the Gallery among the statues."[3] This fragment therefore was composed sometime in October, 1819.

Forman thinks that this is a Platonic fragment, for he says, "This will be found among the Platonic fragments." However, Shelley's fragment *On the Daemon of Socrates* is not based on his reading of Plato, but rather, as the title in the Bodleian manuscript shows, on his reading of Xenophon's *Memorabilia.* The source of Shelley's remarks, "Socrates' demon; one form of augury. Socrates made a distinction between things

---

[1] Julian *Works,* X, 37.

[2] Giovanni da Bologna's statue of Mercury was at one time in the Villa Medici, R'ome, but was removed to the Palazzo Riccardi, Florence, about 1780. It must, however, be taken into consideration that Shelley perhaps saw a contemporary small replica of the Mercury by Giovanni da Bologna in Rome, for such exists, but it seems likely that he was referring to a statue. The urn mentioned by Shelley in the ninth note may be identified by the inscription. It is published in the *Inscriptiones Graecae,* Vol. XIV: *Inscriptiones Italiae et Siciliae* (Berlin, 1890), No. 347 (among the would-be Roman objects). It was first recorded in Florence in the seventeenth century. The ox in note eight cannot be precisely identified, though there are many bronze statuettes of oxen in Florence that Shelley could have seen. The writer is indebted to the staff of the Metropolitan Museum for the above information.

[3] Forman, *Shelley's Prose Works* (London, 1876-1880), III, 50 n. 1.

subject to divination, and things not subject to it" is in the very first chapter of Book One of Xenophon's *Memorabilia*. Shelley's notation "p. 5" as the page of Xenophon for a remark of Socrates enables us to find the exact place and text of Xenophon's *Memorabilia* which he used. In Appendix F of the second volume of Peck's *Shelley, His Life and Work* we have Shelley's notes in his copy of Xenophon. In volume VIII of *Xenophontis quae exstant opera, Graece & Latine, ex editionibus Schneideri et Zeuneii.* Edinburgi: E Prelo Academico. Impensis Guglielmi Laing MDCCCXI, Peck notes the following:

Page 2, straight line down left margin opposite passage, lines 14-15: ὁυτοί τε γὰρ ὑπολαμζάνουσιν, οὐ τοὺς ὄρνιθας running over to

Page 3, and concluding with οὕτως ἐνόμιζεν, the first three lines on this page being marked by straight line in margin at right.[4]

This marked passage is found in the first chapter of the first book of the *Memorabilia*, where Socrates's daemon and its relation to augury are discussed. Among the box of books that arrived at Bagni di Lucca in June, 1818, was Xenophon's *Memorabilia*, entries for the reading of which by Shelley occur in the Journal on June 13, 14, 15, 16 and 17, 1818.

[4] Peck, *op. cit.*, II, 350. The Greek is printed as found in Peck's text; it is an inaccurate transcription of οὖτοί τε γὰρ ὑπολαμβάνουσιν οὐ τοὺς ὄρνιθας.

ON THE DAEMON OF SOCRATES
Memor. Lib. I

Socrates' demon; one form of augury.

Socrates made a distinction between things subject to divination, and things not subject to it. He said—a supernatural force has sway over the greatest things in all human undertakings (p. 5), and that the uncertainty belonging to them all, is the intervention of that power, or rather that all events except those which the human will modifies, are modified by the divine will.

SHELLEY'S TRANSLATIONS OF PLATO'S EPIGRAMS

SHELLEY, who thought that "Plato was essentially a poet," translated a number of epigrams attributed by tradition to Plato. His enthusiasm for Plato the poet starts at Oxford, where he published, along with some other Greek epigrams, a translation of an epigram of Plato (*Anth. Pal.,* IX, 39; Diogenes Laertius, *Life of Plato,* III, 33). The translation appeared in the *Oxford University and City Herald* on March 9, 1811.[1] This marks the first appearance of Shelley as a translator of Plato.

The date of the translation of five of the remaining six epigrams of Plato is probably 1820 or 1821. A clue to their date of composition is found when it becomes apparent that all these epigrams are found in Diogenes Laertius's *Life of Plato,* III, 29, 32-33, 44. Shelley read this in 1814, but it is not likely that he translated the epigrams then. An examination of the Bipont edition of Plato shows that the first volume contains Diogenes Laertius's *Life of Plato,* and it is likely that Shelley used his own copy of the Bipont edition rather than the Palatine Anthology as the text for the translation. Though we first hear of Shelley's reading Plato in the Bipont edition in 1817 and though he translated one of several epigrams of Plato found in Apuleius's *Apologia,* which he read in 1816,[2] it is likely that the translation of the rest of Plato's epigrams dates from 1820-1821, when Medwin tells of Shelley's interest in Plato's Epigram on Aster (*To Stella*), which he had used on the title-page of *Adonais.* Medwin, who stayed with Shelley from October 22, 1820, to March 15, 1821, relates how Plato's Epigram on Aster happened to be mentioned. Medwin asked Shelley if he could render it; whereupon Shelley rendered it in English and Medwin in Latin.[3] This interest in Plato's epigrams suggests that the translation of the other epigrams was made shortly before or after. We have evidence in *The Triumph of Life,* written in 1822, of Shelley's interest in Plato's epigrams in this period. Line 256 in *The Triumph of Life:*

"The star that ruled his doom was far too fair"

has direct reference to this epigram in Diogenes Laertius's *Life of Plato.* In this life of Plato the epigram is quoted as a poem which Plato wrote to a youth named Aster, who, according to Diogenes Laertius, was Plato's lover. It is because of this mortal weakness that Plato, in the poem, is

---

[1] D. F. MacCarthy, *Shelley's Early Life* (London, 1872), p. 62; *vide infra,* pp. 566-567; White, *Shelley,* I, 110; Smith, *The Shelley Legend,* p. 43.

[2] Hogg, *op. cit.,* I, 122; *vide infra,* pp. 509, 568.

[3] Medwin, *op. cit.,* pp. 349-350. For Shelley's and Medwin's classical discussions and translations from the Greek, see *ibid.,* pp. 242-243.

chained to the car of Life, whereas Socrates, who was above male love, is exempt from this servitude (for commentary on ll. 254-262 of *The Triumph of Life, vide supra,* pp. 315-317). Thus the Epigram of Plato, cited in the *Apologia* of Apuleius, which Shelley translated in 1816, was interpreted in 1822 in the context of Diogenes Laertius's account of Plato's lovers. Furthermore, the close sequence of the epigrams in the text of Diogenes Laertius suggests Shelley's interest in the group as a whole rather than isolated translations scattered over many years. This translation in a group may be reflected in Mary's publication of the Epigram on Aster along with three other epigrams of Plato in the 1839 edition of Shelley's poems. Of these *Circumstance,* the title of which was given by Forman, is a paraphrase of a distich epigram of Plato (Diogenes Laertius, III, 33; *Anth. Pal.,* IX, 44); the last four lines of the poem are Shelley's own conclusion. *The Spirit of Plato* is a translation of Plato's epitaph (Diogenes Laertius, III, 44; *Anth. Pal.,* VII, 62); *Kissing Helena* is a translation of Diogenes Laertius, III, 32 (*Anth. Pal.,* V, 78), in which Shelley has substituted *Helena* for the name *Agathon.*[4]

Besides these four epigrams Shelley also translated several other epigrams of Plato which have only recently been published. Of these "Translated, From an Epigram of Plato cited in the Apologia of Apuleius" was first published in the Boston *Herald,* Monday, December 21, 1925, by Dr. Peck from the Shelley MS notebook at Harvard.[5] It is, in Shelley's own words, "Translated, from an epigram of Plato, cited in the Apologia of Apuleius." As Dr. Peck has shown,[6] the date of composition is 1816, the same time that Shelley wrote *Verses Written on Receiving a Celandine in a Letter from England.* A different version of this epigram appears in *Laon and Cythna,* IX, lines 321-324. Shelley's fondness for this epigram of Plato is attested by the fact that he made another version of this epigram in the following year.

The most recent discovery of another epigram of Plato completely rounds out Shelley's translation of most of Plato's epigrams found in Diogenes Laertius's *Life of Plato.* It is a translation of Diogenes Laertius, III, 32 (*Anth. Pal.,* V, 79-80), which consists of two versions of the same theme. By translating both, Shelley showed how closely he followed the text of Diogenes Laertius. Shelley's translation of this epigram was found among the Shelley manuscripts in the possession of Sir John C. E. Shelley-Rolls (*MS. Shelley adds. e.8.,* p. 146; *e.9.,* p. 318) and published in 1934, in *Shelley, Verse and Prose.*

[4] For the reasons for this change, *vide supra,* p. 316. For Shelley's unpublished version of this epigram *Kissing Agathon, vide infra,* pp. 511, 568-569.

[5] *Vide infra,* p. 568.

[6] Peck, *op. cit.,* I, 207 n. 37; Boston *Herald, loc. cit.*

Shelley's translations of Plato's epigrams are not a literal but a poetic transcript which aims, like all of Shelley's translations, to make the Greek "legible—a quality much to be desired in translations."[7]

Addendum

An examination of *MS. Shelley adds. e. 8*, pp. 142-147; *e. 9*, pp. 318-319, which contain most of Shelley's translations of Plato's epigrams, corroborates the date of composition given above. The epigrams which occupy pages 142, 144-147 are in reverse position, for Shelley used the notebook upside down. An analysis of these pages shows the following contents:

Page 142 contains a rough draft of *Epipsychidion*, lines 574-575, then in the center, framed in parallel lines, *To Stella* followed by *Epipsychidion*, lines 576-579.

Page 143 contains *Epipsychidion*, lines 575 (variants), 541-542, 577.

Page 144 contains the epigrams *Circumstance* and *Kissing Helena*.

Page 145 contains a very illegible canceled draft of *To Stella* and *Ye Gentle Visitations of Calm Thought*.

Page 146 contains *To Zanthippe* and the opening lines of *Kissing Agathon*.

Page 147 contains *Spirit of Plato* and *Kissing Agathon* (see frontispiece).

Page 318 contains version Vb of *To Zanthippe*.

Page 319 contains Shelley's transcription of the Greek text of *Spirit of Plato* and *Note on Republic 587e* (for date, *vide infra*, p. 565).

The *terminus post quem* of these epigrams is 1819, Mary's date for *Ye Gentle Visitations of Calm Thought;* the position of *To Stella* on page 142, framed in the midst of lines 574-579 of *Epipsychidion*, shows that the *terminus ante quem* is the first two weeks of February, 1821, when *Epipsychidion* was composed. Medwin's account of Shelley's interest in *To Stella* favors a date of composition coinciding with his stay with Shelley, October 22, 1820, to the beginning of February, 1821.

[7] Julian *Works*, X, 187.

SHELLEY'S TRANSLATIONS OF EPIGRAMS ATTRIBUTED TO AND ABOUT PLATO

I.—VENUS AND THE MUSES

The Queen of Love once threat'ning vow'd,
Unless the Nine her sway allow'd,
That Cupid's never-erring dart
Should quickly pierce them to the heart.
When they: "On Mars your menace try,
The little urchin we defy."

II.—TO STELLA

Thou wert the morning star among the living,
    Ere thy fair light had fled—
Now, having died, thou art as Hesperus, giving
    New splendour to the dead.

III.—TRANSLATED,

FROM AN EPIGRAM OF PLATO, CITED IN THE APOLOGIA OF APULEIUS.

Sweet Child, thou star of love and beauty bright,
    alone thou lookest on the midnight skies;
Oh! That my spirit were yon Heaven of light
    To gaze upon thee with a thousand eyes.

IIIa.—VERSION OF SAME EPIGRAM IN *Laon and Cythna,* IX, lines 321-324.

"Fair star of life and love," I cried, "my soul's delight,
Why lookest thou on the crystalline skies?
O, that my spirit were yon Heaven of night,
Which gazes on thee with its thousand eyes!"

IV.—KISSING AGATHON

Kissing Agathon, together
With the kiss, my spirit was
Upon my lips and there I kept it—
For the poor thing had come thither
As if it were departing.

IVa.—ANOTHER VERSION

> Kissing Helena, together
> With the kiss, my soul beside it
> Came to my lips and there I kept it,—
> For the poor thing had wandered thither,
> To follow where the kiss should guide it,
> O cruel I! to intercept it.

V.—TO ZANTHIPPE

> Here catch this apple, girl, and if thou lovest me
> Give me thy virgin flower, in return—
> And [if thou] still refusest—[this apple keep.]
> [Look at it well, and if thou sayest this cannot be,]
> This child of the green tree
> Will teach how brief is beauty.

Va.—ANOTHER VERSION

> W^{d}st thou have
> This [unregarded thing]
> [I throw]   [hand to] thee
> Oh cast me not away, as I have it,
> [For both our youths are withering] . . . while we ban?

Vb.—ANOTHER VERSION

> Here catch this apple, fill it dearest
> With the fresh beauty which thou wearest
> [Clothe it in and then return it]
> Ah that can never be. [gather?]
> Think how soon its bloom is withered.

VI.—CIRCUMSTANCE

> A man who was about to hang himself,
> Finding a purse of gold then threw away his rope,
> The owner, coming to reclaim his pelf,
> The halter found and used it. So is hope
> Changed for despair—one laid upon the shelf,
> We take the other. Under Heaven's high cope
> Fortune is God. All you endure and do—
> Depends on circumstance as much as you.

VII.—SPIRIT OF PLATO

Eagle! why soarest thou above that tomb?
To what sublime and star-ypaven home
　　　Floatest thou?—
I am the image of swift Plato's spirit,
Ascending Heaven—Athens doth inherit
　　　His corpse below.

NOTE ON SHELLEY'S MISSING TRANSLATION
OF THE PHAEDO

TO COMPLETE the account of Shelley as a translator of Plato all the available evidence should be collected concerning his missing translation of the *Phaedo*. Hogg has given us a picture of Shelley's enthusiastic reading of this dialogue at Oxford in an English translation of Dacier's French version. "Shelley," says Hogg, "was never weary of reading, or of listening to me whilst I read, passages . . . from the *Phaedo*, and he was vehemently excited by the striking doctrines which Socrates unfolds, especially by that which teaches that all our knowledge consists of reminiscences of what we had learned in a former existence."[1] An illustration of this vehement excitement about the *Phaedo* is seen in Hogg's account of Shelley questioning a mother with a young infant on Magdalen Bridge, "Will your baby tell us anything about pre-existence, madam?"[2]

Although the *Phaedo* influenced Shelley considerably in the ensuing years, there is no evidence that he read the Dialogue in the original until many years later. In the preface to the *Banquet*, Shelley writes, "This Apollodorus appears, both from the style in which he is represented in this piece, as well as from a passage in the *Phaedon*, to have been a person of an impassioned and enthusiastic disposition." This detailed knowledge of a small episode at the beginning of the *Phaedo* (59a) may indicate the commencement of its reading sometime in 1817 or 1818. However, it is not until 1820 that we know that Shelley read the dialogue. Mary lists it among the books read by Shelley in 1820 and its reading appears in a specific entry. On May 9 Mary writes, "Shelley reads 'Phaedon,' having read 'Phaedrus' "; no other entries appear for the *Phaedo* but it must have been finished by September 4, when she lists a reading of the *Republic*. Shelley's reaction to this dialogue is evident from his sending it to John Gisborne in November, 1820,[3] Shelley showed his interest in this dialogue not only by the many references to its doctrine in his compositions of 1820 and 1821[4] but by translating a portion of it as well. In his letter to Hogg dated October 20, 1821, where he lists his Platonic activities, Shelley writes, "I . . . have translated the *Symposium*, the *Ion*, and part of the

[1] Hogg, *op. cit.*, I, 73.

[2] *Ibid.*, I, 147-148; cf. pp. 142-146.

[3] Julian *Works*, X, 220. Shelley perhaps sent to Gisborne the first volume of the Bipont edition containing, besides the *Phaedo*, the *Euthyphro*, *Apology*, and *Crito*. This may account for his reading the *Crito* in the folio edition of Plato which he describes in a letter to Hogg on October 22, 1821; see Julian *Works*, VII, 312.

[4] *Vide supra*, pp. 265-310, 342-356, *passim*.

Phaedon."[5]   The inclusion of the *Phaedo* along with the other two translations is indicative of the importance Shelley attached to this dialogue. It is not known whether he made the translation concurrently with or after the reading. At any rate, the date of its translation is not that as stated in the order of reference in the letter, for it is evident that the order is one of completion versus incompletion of translation. It is very probable that Shelley had made the translation prior to his sending away his copy of the *Phaedo* to Gisborne; it may be that the sending of his copy to Gisborne accounts for his failure to complete the translation. The manuscript of the *Phaedo* translation has not survived, or Mary would have included it in her lists of fragment translations from Plato in her edition of 1840. It was possibly loaned to Medwin, who took considerable interest in Shelley's translations.[6] Its loss leaves a gap in our knowledge of Shelley's translations from Plato, but its mention by Shelley shows once more the truth about all of Shelley's translations, namely, that if he loved a work of another great mind, he made it all the more his own through translation.

[5] Scott, *Shelley at Oxford*, p. 64.
[6] See Julian *Works*, X, 317; Medwin, *op. cit.*, pp. 349, 242-243; also Medwin's use of Shelley's MSS not accessible to Mary (Julian *Works*, VI, 375).

Notes on the Text

Mrs. Shelley's Remarks on the Translations from Preface to *Essays, Letters from Abroad, Translations and Fragments,* 1840. Titles of Plato's Dialogues and other books italicized in the present edition are generally in quotation marks in the 1840 edition, though these are sometimes omitted.

Page	Line	
378	5	*Fathers* 1845; *fathers* 1840.

378   16   *abstracts*. These abstracts are by J. S. Mill. Cf. *Autobiography* (New York, 1874): "... the writings ... which I published from 1832 to 1834 amount to a large volume. This, however, includes abstracts of several of Plato's Dialogues, with introductory remarks, which though not published until 1834, had been written several years earlier" (pp. 197-198). They appeared in the *Monthly Repository,* N.S. VIII (1834), 89-99, 203-211, 404-420, 633-646, 691-710, 802-815, 829-842. The abstracts contain introductions and translations of the significant sections of the *Protagoras, Phaedrus,* and *Gorgias.* It is of interest to note that the *Monthly Repository* was edited at this time by Leigh Hunt, Shelley's and Mary's friend who had taken an interest in Shelley's Platonism. Leigh Hunt recommended to Mary Mill's method in circumventing in his translation the references to homosexuality in Plato. See *The Letters of Mary W. Shelley,* ed. F. L. Jones, II, 139.

378   Note 1   The extracts published by Captain Medwin, to which Mrs. Shelley refers in her note, are two from *A Discourse on the Manners of the Antient Greeks Relative to the Subject of Love* which appeared in the *Athenaeum,* September 15 and September 29, 1832.

379   3   *us* omitted 1840; added in 1845 edition.

379   6   *license* 1840; *license* J(ulian *Works*).

Page   Line
379   14-15 *and to heighten the resemblance, Shelley conceived* 1845; *and the greater the resemblance, since Shelley conceived* 1840. Forman conjectures that the change is Mrs. Shelley's own.

380   13 Probably Mrs. Shelley wrote "left the *Ion*" (cf. her previous reference to "the *Ion*," *supra*, p. 379, line 19); *left Ion* 1840.

On the Symposium
Or Preface to the Banquet of Plato

Shelley's manuscript of the *Preface to the Banquet of Plato* is included among the manuscripts given to the Bodleian by Sir John Shelley-Rolls *(MS. Shelley adds. e. 6*, pp. 60-65) and follows the *Discourse* in the notebook. It is in his own hand, and in some places it is so worked over that the version is illegible. The Preface was first published by Mrs. Shelley in *Essays, Letters from Abroad, Translations and Fragments*, 1840.

The Republic perha canceled in MS at the top of page 60.

402   Title *Or Preface to the Banquet of Plato* omitted in MS.

402   1 Shelley has a line from the word *Plato* proceeding along the left margin and ending with *The dialogue* in the first line. It is evident that Shelley intended the Preface to start with the second paragraph.

402   2 *and from him or rather perhaps, through him from his master* MS, 1840; *and from, or, rather, perhaps through him, his master* 1845.

402   3 *science* canceled before *and metaphysical.*

402   3 *science* canceled and *knowledge* substituted.

402   3-4 *knowledge* in MS; *knowledge* on 1840.

402   5 *contem* canceled before *the slow.*

402   6 *Plato's language is rather that* canceled before *Plato exhibits.*

402   6 *manifested in himself* canceled and *exhibits* substituted.

402   6 *ever* [?] canceled before *close.*

402   7 *moulded* canceled and *melted* substituted.

402   7 *of* canceled before *harmony* and *and* substituted.

402   8 *language* canceled and *periods* substituted.

402   8 *impressions which even in spite of the puerile sophisms* can-

Page   Line

celed before *which hurry.* Above these canceled words is written and then canceled *Lord Bacon is perhaps the only writer that can in other.*

402   9   *to the end* canceled before *as in a breathless.*

The MS is interlined as follows:

Lord B canceled
His language is that of an immortal
        Lord Bacon is perhaps the only writer who
spirit rather than a man. His views
in these particulars can [ought written above it] be com-
        pared with him
into the nature of mind and existence
his imitator Cicero [is in the poem canceled before sinks]
        sinks in
not also are canceled before are often obscure
        the comparison into an ape mocking the
only because they are profound
gestures of a man
and though his theories respecting.

402   16   *such as I can assent to* canceled and *correct* substituted.

402   17   *in* canceled before *which.*

402   21   *obscured* MS; *obscure* 1840, J.

402   23   Shelley's note on the *Republic,* which Mary added to the word *Plato,* does not belong to this Preface. *Vide supra,* page 501.

402   26   *slight* canceled before *imperfect* in MS.

402   26   *its sublime and lovely* canceled before *the language.*

402   28   The manuscript reads as follows:
        The dialogue intitled the Banquet
        It is called εϱωτιϰος *or a discussion*
        upon Love

A line in the margin leads from *It* to *The,* which is underlined twice, in the line above. It indicates a transposition between the first and second paragraphs in the manuscript.

402   30   *in a series* MS with *one of* written above.

402   30   *tragic* canceled before *poet.*

402   31   *The persons present, some of the most eminent literary characters at Athens* canceled before *The account.*

Page	Line	
402	33	*the* canceled before *it had.*
403	1	*his* canceled before *the style.*
403	1	*as from* MS; *as well as from* 1840.
403	1	*the* canceled before *passage* and *a* substituted.
403	4	*groups* MS; *group* 1840.
403	4	*Phaedrus is represented as complaining* canceled before *The drama.*
403	4	*such* canceled and *so* substituted.
403	5	*the characters* MS; *character* 1840.
403	8	*discourse* [?] canceled before *of this.*
403	8	*is the playground* [?] and several other illegible words are canceled before *affords* (possibly *effects*).
403	9-11	*Socrates . . . had;* first published in the revised and enlarged edition of *Plato's Banquet* edited by Roger Ingpen.
403	9	after *paused to* there is a gap followed in the next line, which ends page 64, by *Ph* canceled. Then on the next page there follows for fourteen lines Shelley's note on the *Republic.* After a gap of several lines there follows *Eryximachus the physician.*

A Discourse on the Manners of the Antient Greeks
Relative to the Subject of Love

The text is that of the original manuscript found in two separate note-books of Shelley which were in the possession of Sir John C. E. Shelley-Rolls, and are now in the Bodleian Library (*MS. Shelley adds. e. 6,* pp. 45-59; *e. 11,* pp. 17-41). It was published for the first time in its entirety in *Plato's Banquet, Translated from the Greek, A Discourse on The Manners of the Antient Greeks Relative to the Subject of Love, Also A Preface to the Banquet, Revised and Enlarged by Roger Ingpen, From MSS in the possession of Sir John C. E. Shelley-Rolls, Bart.* Printed for private circulation, MCMXXXI, One Hundred Copies Only, Printed at the Curwen Press, Plaistow, London.

HISTORY OF TEXT. Medwin printed two extracts from the *Discourse* in the *Athenaeum;* first extract, *The period which, supra,* page 404, line 1, to *extravagant fiction,* page 405, line 15, in the issue for September 15, 1832; second extract from *mind, supra,* page 408, line 22, to *social being,* page 408, line 38, in the issue for September 29, 1832. He included both of these extracts in *The Shelley Papers*, 1833, under the title *The Age of Pericles, with Critical Notices of the Sculpture in the Florence Gallery* and *Reflection on Love*. The text of Medwin differs in many places from Mrs. Shelley's text and from the manuscript.

Mrs. Shelley in a footnote added to the essay in the 1840 edition says, "Shelley named this essay *A Discourse on the Manners of the Ancients, relative to the subject of Love*. It was intended to be a commentary on the *Symposium*, or *Banquet of Plato*, but it breaks off at the moment when the main subject is about to be discussed." For the reason which compelled her to suppress a part of the essay, see pages 388-390, *supra*. Mary transcribed the unpublished portion of the essay in an interleaved copy of the *Essays, Letters from Abroad, etc.* (cf. Preface, p. vii, of *The Banquet of Plato* in the Ingpen edition). The part printed in the 1840 edition begins on page 404, line 1, and ends with *human beings*, page 409, line 20. The title of the *Discourse* in the 1840 edition is *Essay on the Literature, the Arts, and the Manners of the Athenians, A Fragment*. The text in the present edition is collated with *MS. Shelley adds. e. 6*, pp. 45-59; *e. 11*, pages 17-41.

Page	Line	
404	Title	The title in the MS reads, *A Discourse of the manners of the Antient Greeks relative to the subject of Love; of* was changed afterward to *on*.
404	1	*a* canceled before *period*.
404	1-2	*birth of Pericles* and *Aristotle* canceled, but no substitute supplied in MS.
404	2	*with* canceled before *in itself*.
404	3	*had* MS; *has* 1840, Ingpen.
404	3	illegible word canceled before *destinies* and *subsequent* substituted.
404	6	*une* canceled before *unparalleled*.
404	6	*short* MS; omitted 1840.
404	7	*met with dwindled into* canceled before *so soon*.
404	7	*recieved* MS spelling throughout with one exception.
404	8	*which* canceled after *problems*.
404	8	*with* [?] MS; *to* 1840, Ingpen.
404	9	*conjectures* MS; *conjecture* 1840, Ingpen.
404	9	*those* changed to *the* before *wrecks*.

Page	Line	
404	9	*that* changed to *those* before *subtle*.
404	9-10	*mighty philosophers & poets* canceled and *subtle & profound minds* substituted below.
404	10	[illegible word] *which* [*obscurely*] in MS before *like*.
404	11	*their* is generally spelled *thier* throughout the MS.
404	12	*understandings* MS, 1840; *understanding* 1833.
404	13	*excells* MS; *excels* 1840, Ingpen.
404	14	*It is* [*can express*] *is capable of the subtlest distinctions & the most majestic combinations of thought* canceled before *Thier sculptures*.
404	14-15	*we in our presumption* MS, 1840; *in our perception* 1833.
404	16	*with all* canceled before *no artist*.
404	16	*any thing comp* canceled and *forms* substituted.
404	17	*if* canceled before *according*.
404	17	*according to Pliny and Pausanias* MS, 1840; *Pliny and* omitted 1833.
404	18	*even* omitted 1833.
404	19	*to* 1840; omitted MS.
404	19	*produce* canceled and *awaken* substituted.
404	20	*And if* canceled before *We are*.
404	20	*concieve of* MS; *conceive* 1840; *consider* 1833.
404	20	*paintings* canceled and *painters* substituted.
404	21	*thier* MS, 1840; *the* 1833.
404	22	*it is probable only* canceled and *probably* substituted.
404	22	*of the* canceled before *have been*.
404	23	*For all* MS, 1840; *All,* 1833.
404	25	*the* canceled before *different*.
404	25	*the* canceled before *individual* and *an* substituted.
404	26	*the* canceled before *society*.

Page	Line	
404	26	*and* canceled and a new paragraph begins with *The paintings* MS; *and the paintings* 1840, Ingpen; *The painting* 1833.
404	28	*succeeding* MS, 1840; *successive* 1833.
404	29	*stat* canceled before *said*.
404	30	*hearer* canceled and *audience* substituted.
404	30	*are far* MS, 1840; *were far* 1833.
404	32	*thier* changed to *the*.
404	33	illegible word canceled above *modern*.
404	34	*superiority* MS, 1840; *progress* 1833.
404	36	After *conception,* the following passage, a first draft of the next paragraph, is canceled in the MS with an oblique line running through. The words in brackets are canceled with a line through them.

Thier poetry [if I make two exceptions] seems to maintain [the, illegible canceled word, superiority] a very high tho not so disproportionate rank in the company; for though Shakespeare from the variety & comprehension of his genius [seems higher] considered as [an] whole is to be exempted from a comparison with all other men & though perhaps Dante has created imaginations which in themselves have greater [beginning of an illegible word] loveliness & energy than any [to be found in the literature of Greece & though the tenderness & sublime sensibility of Petrarch find no rival in the fragments] yet considered as a mere poet Homer must be acknowledged to excel Shakespeare in the truth & harmony and picturesque fitness of his images—in the entire fulness & satisfaction [illegible word] [of his expressi] which they preserve in all thier parts [to exceed Shakespeare], and [in the] Dante in conduct and plan & nature & variety & temperance, & every thing but those [green & hesperian] majestic & beautiful fortunate isles laden with golden fruit which [gleam thro] succour those who voyage the ocean of his dark & extravagant fiction.

At this point in the manuscript (page 21) there is a calculation:

$$6$$
$$18\tfrac{1}{2}$$
$$16\tfrac{1}{2}$$

$$41 \quad 0$$

Page   Line

> *Few specimens of their lyrical poetry remain, but Anacreon*
> *& the fragments of Simonides Sappho & Alcaeus teach us to*
> *hesitate in preferring except obscure relics these the profound*
> *[illegible word smudged] & chivalric sensibility of Petrarch,*
> *the only lyric poet who can enter into comparison with them.*
> *Their [poetry too] dramatic poetry too.*

404   36   *also* added in MS above; omitted 1840, Ingpen.

404   36   *very* MS, 1840; omitted 1833.

405   2   *as [the greatest in]* canceled after *considered.*

405   2   *as* canceled and *on* substituted before *a whole; the whole* 1840, Ingpen; *on the whole* omitted 1833.

405   2   *to be* canceled and *as* substituted before *the greatest.*

405   3   two illegible words canceled and *specimens remaining* substituted.

405   4   *energy* MS, 1840; *beauty* 1833.

405   6   *is to be found* canceled and *has been discovered* substituted.

405   6   *lyrical* canceled before *fragments.*

405   6   *of* canceled before *of the.*

405   7   *chivalric* MS, 1840; *chivalrous* 1833.

405   8   *man* canceled before *poet.*

405   10   *and that to which* MS; *and to that to which* 1840, Ingpen.

405   11   *belongs* MS; *belong* 1840, Ingpen.

405   11   *as muc and* canceled after *belongs.*

405   11   *enter into a con* canceled before *deficient.*

405   12   illegible word canceled after *with* and *these men* [?] substituted.

405   12   *with these men* omitted 1833.

405   15   With *fiction* ends the excerpt, *The Age of Pericles,* published by Medwin.

405   16-18   brackets canceled before *But* and after *period.*

405   18-19   *to the* canceled before *in other.*

Page	Line	
405	20	*them* canceled and *all* substituted.
405	21	*all* canceled before *his conceptions.*
405	22-23	For [*it is remarkable in the writers poetry poets of that age*] *that* [*all they*] *produced is as* [*entire*] canceled and *For it is worthy of observation that whatever* [*the*] *poets of that age produced is as harmonious* substituted.
405	23-24	*There are none of those inequalities in the compositions which are obser* canceled before *If a drama.*
405	23	*the* canceled and *a* substituted before *drama.*
405	24	*genius* canceled and *talent* substituted.
405	26	*If* canceled before *The compositions.*
405	26	*greater* canceled before *great.*
405	27	*times* canceled and *ages* substituted.
405	27-28	*In the poetry . . . & fall* canceled in MS by an oblique line.
405	28	*feelings* canceled and *expectations* substituted.
405	28	*the* canceled before *often.*
405	31	*science* canceled and *knowledge* substituted.
405	31	*had already* canceled before *& Theophrastus.*
405	33	*placed such from whom* [?] canceled before *made.*
405	33	*advances* 1840; not in MS.
405	34	*had already even brought I consider on which rests* canceled before *that series.*
405	34	*by that* canceled before *which have.*
405	36	*has* MS; *which have* 1840.
405	37	*ap* canceled before and an illegible word after *been.*
405	38	*Metaphysics* canceled before *Metaphysics.*
406	1	*founded on* canceled and *built upon* substituted.
406	1	illegible word canceled before *words.*
406	3	*Their moral* canceled before *The science.*
406	9	*of* canceled before *were.*

Page	Line	
406	10	*were* MS; *are* 1840.
406	12	*concieved* canceled and *formed* substituted.
406	14	*of ens.* canceled before *institutions.*
406	17	*have not been invented by the ever* canceled before **unheard of.**
406	17	*systems* canceled before *of public.*
406	19	illegible word *impostures* canceled and *avarice & tyranny* substituted.
406	20	*There seems indeed in* canceled before *The modern.*
406	20	*all* canceled before *the civilized.*
406	21	*in the common arts of life as well as in* canceled before *as well.*
406	22	*their* MS, 1845; *the* 1840.
406	22	*as* or *is* [?] before *in the moral.*
406	22	*imp* canceled before *enquiries.*
406	23	*they* canceled and *it* substituted.
406	26	*writers* canceled before *subsequent.*
406	28	*This age* canceled before *And though.*
406	28	*modern nations* canceled before *the modern.*
406	29	*such* canceled before *circumstances.*
406	29	*as these* canceled before *analogous.*
406	30	*writers to whom we refer* canceled before *intellectual.*
406	31	*prolong* canceled before *& perpetuate.*
406	32	*& consign* canceled before *& consign.*
406	33	*though* canceled before *though.*
406	34	*is* MS; *are* 1840.
406	35	*yet this prin* canceled before *though perhaps.*
406	36	*these principles* MS with *these* altered to *this.*
406	37	*almost* MS, 1845; *an almost* 1840.

Page	Line	
406	37	*What the Greeks were . . . glorious generations* follows in the MS (page 28) directly after *existing things* but the passage is enclosed in lines and the word *insert* indicates that it is to follow *of titles* in the next sentence.
406	39	*study* canceled and *history* substituted before *of antient*.
407	4	*The Romans—In the Roman literature and their language appears to have been at first only a dialect of the Greeks—* canceled after *generations*.
407	4	*it is to be lamented that* canceled before *Whatever tends*.
407	4	*an* canceled before *a*.
407	9	*that the most* canceled before *how far*.
407	10	*society* canceled before *was*.
407	10	*men who were hard* [?] canceled before *community*.
407	10	*formed* or possibly *framed* MS; *framed* 1840.
407	10	*perfection* canceled before *that*.
407	10	*which* canceled before *to which*.
407	13	*& the were* canceled before *It is*.
407	14	*we have* canceled before *no modern*.
407	14	*Greeks* canceled after *them*.
407	15	*are* canceled and *were* substituted.
407	15	*Anac* canceled above *Barthelemy*.
407	15	*Barthelemy* MS; *Barthélemi* 1840.
407	16	*can* canceled before *forgets*.
407	17	*European* canceled and *Frenchman* substituted.
407	18	illegible word canceled before *cherishes*.
407	20	*European* canceled before *of modern* but no word substituted.
407	22	*idea* canceled and *practice or sentiment* substituted.
407	24	*recieve* MS.
407	26	*to possess* MS; *from possessing* 1840.
407	27	*&* canceled and *for* substituted.

Page	Line	
407	27	*the* canceled before *what.*
407	28	*fro* canceled before *without.*
407	29	*sharpsighted to estimate in just scales the past the present &* *the future. Until such a book is written the just* canceled after *just.*
407	30	*antient & modern* canceled and *the* substituted before *manners.*
407	31	illegible word canceled and *consisted in* substituted.
407	32	*the* canceled and *some* substituted.
407	33	*alledges* MS; *alleges* 1840.
407	35	*a* canceled and *certain* substituted.
407	37	*it* canceled before *acting.*
408	1	*were produced from* canceled and *arose under* substituted.
408	2	*evil, effects* canceled and *diminution* substituted.
408	2	*fundame* canceled and *personal* substituted.
408	2	*of* canceled before *& the inferiority.*
408	3	*by opinion* MS; *opinion* 1840.
408	5	*in whatever other* canceled before *perhaps.*
408	7	*It is probable that* canceled before *The women.*
408	7-8	*that they should* MS; *they would* 1840.
408	8	*had [the] except in extraordinary instances* altered without cancellation to *possessed except with extraordinary exceptions.*
408	10	*certain certainly bore no such* canceled before *there was* and *at least* substituted.
408	12	*divested* canceled and *devoid* substituted.
408	13	*harmony* canceled and *loveliness* substituted.
408	13	*boundless* canceled before *acquisition.*
408	14	*with* canceled before *as with.*
408	15	*lineaments which* canceled after *grace.*
408	15	illegible word canceled and *lineaments* substituted.

Page	Line	
408	15	*the* canceled and *every* substituted before *form*.
408	16	*it inhabits* MS; *they inhabit* 1840.
408	17	*spirit* canceled and *mind* substituted.
408	20	*these greeks* canceled before *that were*.
408	20	*that were* MS; *they were* 1840.
408	21	*a mere* canceled after *passion is*.
408	21	*the sent* canceled before *the literature*.
408	22	*because the Greeks had no* [*objects*] [*could* [?] *have*] *natural objects* [*for*] *of this sentiment* canceled before *This object*.
408	22	*for ever ex* canceled before *or its*.
408	22	*imagination* canceled and *mind* substituted.
408	22	Medwin's excerpt *Reflection on Love* begins with *the mind;* the opening sentence reads: *The mind selects among those who most resemble it, that which is most its archetype and instinctively*. . . .
408	25	*with as* canceled before *the imagination*.
408	25	*by an involuntary operation* canceled and *moulds* substituted.
408	25	*of the* canceled and *in* substituted.
408	26	*resemblances* MS, 1845; *resemblance* 1840; *a resemblance* 1833.
408	27	*being* MS, 1840; *animal* 1833.
408	30	*all that is sought in sexual connexion* MS, 1840; *all that is desired* 1833.
408	30	*appetite* canceled and *senses* substituted.
408	32	*that* canceled and *the* substituted before *universal*.
408	34	*can only* canceled before *becomes*.
408	35	*real or imag* [?] canceled and *complete or partial* substituted.
408	35	*actual* omitted 1833.
408	36	*becomes* canceled and *grows* substituted.
408	38	*& the worthlessness* canceled before *for man*.

Page	Line	
408	38	Medwin's excerpt *Reflection on Love* ends with the word *being*.
408	38	*It is difficult to believe that* [*this*] *through And though, when individualised it seldom* [illegible word above] *if ever fails of producing together with the disappointment the* [*internal*] *moral ruin of its possessor, yet if cultivated as a universal sentiment & particularly. And though* canceled before *The sexual impulse.*
408	40	*of basis* canceled before *type.*
408	40	*as common* MS; *a common* 1840.
409	1	*with* canceled before *which.*
409	3	[*it is*] *surround* [*ded*] *it* MS.
409	3	After *satisfy* the MS (page 37) continues directly with *Among the antient Greeks the male sex one half of it. . . .* At the bottom of the page, however, begins a section *To estimate this . . . no important difference* which continues also at the bottom of pages 38 and 39, all of which are separated by lines from the rest of the text. This passage probably belongs, as Ingpen has edited it, directly after *satisfy.*
409	3-4	*As a proof of this only observe* canceled and *To estimate all this* substituted.
409	4	*which* canceled and *of* substituted before *the love.*
409	5	*& dec* [. . . ?] *ed from the intensity* canceled before *& acknowledge.*
409	8	several illegible words canceled after *difference.*
409	9	*In the harmonious progress of human society such* canceled before *Among the antient Greeks.*
409	10	*recieved* MS.
409	13	*history* MS; *society* 1840, Ingpen.
409	15	*society* MS; *history* 1840, Ingpen.
409	15	*considered* canceled and *esteemed* substituted.
409	17	The text at this point reads with the following interlineation: *practices & customs with respect to the* [*interest*] *different from & incomparably less pernicious than*

Page   Line

The [*manners of*] *modern Europe are essentially* [*superior to both in*] *either, however*
[*remote from what an enligh*] *tened mind cannot* [*much they leave to be des*] *fail to desire as the future destiny of human beings.* An illegible phrase is written over the words *human beings.*

409	20	The part of the essay published by Mrs. Shelley in 1840 ends with the word *beings.*
409	21	*difference* canceled and *distinction* substituted.
409	21	*which considered largely in part one of manners* canceled before *that difference.*
409	22	*both had* MS; *had both* Ingpen.
409	23	*ci* canceled before *refinement.*
409	24	*understanding* canceled and *mind* substituted.
409	26	*But in modern Europe. But among their claim are more harmoniously united* canceled before *In modern.*
409	26-27	*sexual & moral* canceled and *sexual & intellectual* substituted.
409	28	*united as to* canceled before *converge.*
409	28	*as* canceled before *in.*
409	29	*any* canceled before and *vi* after *no.*
409	30	*this passion was deprived of its natural object* canceled before *these feelings.*
409	32	*were* canceled and *corresponded* substituted.
409	32	*as* MS; *us as* Ingpen.
409	33	*estimate & pen* [?] canceled and *firm yet flowing* substituted.
409	34	*grace* canceled and *unreserve* substituted.
409	36	*the boldness* MS; *boldness* Ingpen.
409	37	faint illegible word added above *of governing.*
410	2	*The epithet beautiful now scarcely applied but the female sex, was then appropriate to the male* canceled before *Whether the cause.* At the bottom of the next page (41) the passage is reworked as *If my observation . . . of a female.* In this

Page	Line	
		passage the Greek words are without accents and *beautiful* is not enclosed in parentheses.
410	2	*a female* MS; *the female* Ingpen.
410	5	*any one* canceled before *the mutual*.
410	5	*Richardson that fine observer of the human heart has made Lovelace express his contempt for the pleasure of the mere act of sexual intercourse* canceled after *effect*. Then after a gap on page 41, which contains a watermark, there is canceled: *And from the anomalous consequence* [illegible word] Then below there is written in bold calligraphy, Mrs. Müller.
410	5-6	*the* canceled before *consequence* and *as a* substituted.
410	6	*this* changed to *those*.
410	6	*distinction* canceled and *cause* substituted; *causes* Ingpen.
410	6	*the male* canceled before *beautiful*.
410	7	Shelley wrote *that* and *those* in the same word before *sort*.
410	7	*in those* canceled before *at present*.
410	7	*as* MS; omitted Ingpen.
410	8	*the most excellent* canceled after *females*.
410	9	*That these feelings* canceled and *An enlightened* substituted.
410	9	After *philosophy* Shelley has an insertion mark and on the opposite page (page 44, which is filled with a drawing) he inserts *in like manner with those of temperance*. This phrase was intended to precede *suggests to us the propriety of habits of chastity* canceled after *philosophy*.
410	9	*may* canceled and *must* substituted.
410	11	*usually* MS; omitted Ingpen.
410	11-12	*in like manner . . . temperance* inserted here by Ingpen.
410	12	*as but* MS; *but as* Ingpen.
410	13	*this comp* canceled before *our complicated*.
410	14	*such as are rather* MS; *as are* Ingpen.

Page	Line
410	14	*as* canceled before *such; than* before *not.*

410   15   *a* canceled before *some.*

410   16   *of greater* canceled before *permanency* and above there is written *from which they may* and below *they may participate* [?] *in.*

410   16   *In* MS; omitted Ingpen.

410   16   *Lastly The sexual instinct, in its gratification reduces itself to a point without extent & but for the ideas impressions which precede accompany or follow it* canceled after *excellence.*

410   17   *The mere act of the sexual instinct divested of the associated sentiments which precede accompany or follow it is* [*an imaginary point; totally only valuable is such as into—which seldom be sought*] *is a circumstance wholly unimportant, except as its* canceled after *libertine* with an inverted *v.* The phrase in brackets is canceled with a line drawn through.

410   18   *habit* canceled and *custom* substituted.

410   18   *a* before *relief* in MS; omitted Ingpen.

410   18   *impulse* MS; *impulses* Ingpen.

410   20   [*The mode in which he resorts to such this indulgence has a complicated is reprehensible in many*] *The degree of criminality attached to the mode in which he resorts to this gratification must vary* [*varies* first version] *according to* [*the established modes institutions*] *a multitude of circumstances extant.* [*In Greece it was*] *the highest degree of criminality was concieved to attach, & the wrong depending on opinion did consequently attach to adultery. The sentiment of its being preferable to educate those children of which a man is the exciting physical cause, united with* [*the*] *a reluctance that* [*the*] *his female companion should be the* [*cause of pleas*] *source of pleasure to another (simply a narrow & an envious motive) yet remain in force as the cause of the high penalties attached to adultery.* [*Seduction*] *The seduction of young virgins, a crim[e], which the consequences attached to it express even a darker stain, has ever been regarded as a high offence.* This passage, which begins after *an act*, is canceled with a line running down the length of pages 46-47.

Page	Line	

After *high penalties attached to adultery* Shelley has inserted the following sentence between the lines of the text: *They seem to [be depend.] depend on elementary feelings in [the] animals as well as men & like revenge avarice perverseness & pride, are found weak in proportion to the extent in intellectual cultivation.*

410   21   *It's the mode in which [it] a person resorts to this* canceled after *nothing.*

410   22   illegible word canceled after *against.*

410   23   *one* canceled and *1st* substituted.

410   24   *nature* canceled and *laws* substituted.

410   24   *the* canceled before *human.*

410   25   illegible word, *amoral* [?], written above *law.*

410   25   *oth* [?] canceled after *all.*

410   28   *ec* [?] MS; *etc* Ingpen.

410   29   *enough* MS; *arrived* Ingpen.

410   29   *the same law applies with this par attended with this particular all wanting* canceled after *second, the.*

410   30   illegible word canceled and *applications* substituted.

410   32-33 *there may be a harmony of* canceled in MS after *so that.*

410   35   *nature* canceled and *being* substituted.

410   35   *this* [?] before *intercourse.*

410   37   *those* MS; *the* Ingpen.

410   38   *its derives* MS before which Shelley added *from.*

410   38   *a* MS; *its* Ingpen.

411   2   *first smile has* canceled before *customary.*

411   8   *The G* canceled before *To apply.*

411   9   *some* canceled before *poets.*

411   8-9   *This [habitual] passion [seems]* MS. *This* changed perhaps to *The.*

Page	Line	
411	9	*practised* deleted and *felt* substituted.
411	10	*inconcievable* MS.
411	11	After *European* the following false starts are canceled: *There may. It will not. It ought. But let us not confound the Greeks with the Romans, what when they.*
411	11	At the top of page 51 of the manuscript over the line *But let us not exaggerate the matter* is written *Phaedrus*.
411	11	*That some acts of* canceled before *We are not*.
411	13	*affair* canceled and *subject* substituted.
411	13	*that* MS; *the* Ingpen's reading of MS.
411	15	*totally* MS with the first three letters canceled.
411	15	*the [vulgar conception] ridiculous & [vulgar] disgusting* MS.
411	15	*[of the] vulgar [on the subject]* MS with *which* written over *of the*.
411	18	[illegible word] *ever* canceled before *have* and *usually* substituted.
411	19	*image* canceled and *own remembrance* substituted.
411	20	*reflected how easy in an exalted state of the external* canceled before *consider*.
411	23	*perhaps* canceled and *that* substituted under it.
411	24	two illegible words canceled before *a similar* and *that* substituted.
411	24	*takes* MS over which is added *may*.
411	27	*to be* canceled before *when*.
411	29	*concieved* canceled before *described*.
411	29	After *Plato* Shelley wrote *x Phaedrus*.
411	29-31	*That it could have been nothing resembling the vulgar imputation [& that] with even among* MS; *seldom have approached to a resemblance* added as a variant with *resembling* changed to *resemblance*.
411	33	*made* canceled and *represented* substituted.

Page	Line	
411	33	*which* canceled before *recieving*.
411	34	*embraces* MS; *embrace* Ingpen.
411	34	*of* canceled before *Encolpius*.
411	36	[*It is known* [?] *that Theocritus & Aristophanes contain refine some gross allusions to the vulgar idea. But I know. But*] *all this* [*reprove* ?] *if it is to be admitted it as you might is I must* [illegible word] *refine* [?] *it as you wish, is something totally irreconcilable with the beautiful harmony of social feelings.* After this sentence there is a line horizontally across page 53. Then the text begins with *But let us not.*
411	40	*of their* [?] *manners* canceled before *Probably*.
412	1	*it* MS; *there* Ingpen.
412	1-3	The MS reads *it never happened any circumstance happens the lover & his beloved by which natural modesty was wronged.* Ingpen silently emends *it* to *there* and *happens* to *between*.
412	3	*man physical instinct* canceled before *lover*.
412	3	*gratified* canceled and *appeased* substituted.
412	6	*It is* MS with *Thus much* written over it.
412	10	*This* MS; *The* Ingpen.
412	11	[*man*] *kind* MS with *human* written over.
412	11	The MS originally read *as* [?] *was* [?] *intellectual being;* then *a class of being* was inserted above it and *being* changed to *nature*. Ingpen emends the text to *as a class of beings* [*of*] *intellectual nature*.
412	15	*sufficiently* canceled before *blinded*.
412	17	*the* canceled before *youth* and *almost every* added.
412	17	*cold* [?] canceled before *prostitute* and *insensible* added. Ingpen reads it as *insensate*.
412	19	*the*[*se*] MS.
412	23	*a person that two different periods or* canceled before *the inhabitants*.

Page	Line	
412	23	*these different epochs or of different nations* MS, then *one* substituted for *these different* and *one* for *different*.
412	24	*equally* canceled and *their own* substituted.
412	25	*their own* canceled before *institutions*.
412	26	*nat* canceled after *others*.
412	27	*no less* MS; illegible word written above.
412	27	*what* canceled and *how* substituted.
412	28	blank after *in the* in MS.
412	28	two illegible words after *reply is.* Ingpen reads *make.*
412	28	*a* MS; *the* Ingpen.
412	28	*As to the distinction which endless legislators have set up between debauchery of [a] different kinds, if* canceled at top of page 57 after *matter,* followed by the paragraph beginning *Thus far the translator. . . . This slight sketch was.* Then a line is drawn across the page and the words *The ideas. . . . Greeks seemed* fill the rest of page 57. Page 58 commences with *undertaken to induce . . . delight or his instruction* continuing the paragraph which begins *Thus far the translator.* After the word *instruction* a horizontal line is drawn across page 58 and the words *hardly capable of obscenity* continue. It is evident that Shelley intended to use *Thus far the translator . . . or his instruction* as his concluding paragraph for the two paragraphs: *The ideas suggested . . . of the Empire* fit directly, as Ingpen has arranged them, after *a bad matter.*
412	30	*or* MS; *nor* Ingpen.
412	30	*those* MS; *the* Ingpen.
412	31	*and* before *Horace,* Ingpen; omitted MS.
412	31	*Greeks were* canceled before *Romans were.*
412	32	*true* canceled and *strict* substituted.
412	33	*the* canceled before *even.*
412	34	*perversions* MS; *diversions* Ingpen.
412	34	*dramatic English* MS; *English dramatic* Ingpen.
412	35	*are* canceled in MS.

Page	Line	
412	36	*come from* canceled and *consist in* substituted.
412	36	*from* [illegible word] *influence of luxury* canceled before *of associating.*
412	36	(*which by a few of the human kind bear no witness to sure reason on no days or perhaps* [?]. The interlinear sentence, which is very illegible, seems incomplete.
412	37	*& power* canceled before *produced.*
412	38	*elder* canceled before *writers.*
412	38	*of James* ends page 58. Page 59 begins with *It may blunt.* After the words *Empire to* there is a line drawn across the page and there follows:

to infect literature

the effects of both—were were united under Charles 2
& after the redeeming interval over which Milton
[presided & Charles the 2] presided

Ingpen has edited them as belonging after the words *writers of James* on the preceding page.

Page	Line	
413	1	*The violence* canceled before *It may.*
413	1	*blunt* MS; *be* Ingpen.
413	2	*passionate* canceled and *sentimental* substituted.
413	3	*also* canceled after *Shakespeare.*
413	6	*sensual* canceled and *any unworthy* substituted.
413	6	[*In*] *the* [*age of Charles the*] 2ᵈ *bears the same relation* canceled before *Towards.*
413	7	*& this* MS; *The* Ingpen.
413	7	*this latter age as compared* canceled before *this latter age bears.*
413	8	*first of the Roman Empire, to* MS; *first Romans of the Empire to* [*the Republic*] Ingpen.
413	10	*much* canceled and *far* substituted.
413	10	*translator of* [*the ensuing piece*] MS.
413	12	*judgement* canceled and *reasoning* substituted.
413	13	*degree of answer due to the* canceled before *peculiarities*

Page	Line	

413 14 [*prevent the preconceived notions of a*] *show* [?] [*prevent*] canceled before *induce.*

413 15 *recieve such p.* canceled before *forbid.*

413 16 *he has* written over *we have* MS; *the author has* Ingpen.

413 17 *interfere* MS; *to interfere* Ingpen.

Ingpen says "The following passage occurs in the same notebook [*MS. Shelley adds. e. 11,* page 52] as that which contains the *Discourse* to which it evidently belongs, although it is detached from the rest of the MS."

In the human world, one of the commonest expressions of love is sexual intercourse, & in describing the deepest effects of abstract love the author could not avoid the danger of exciting some ideas connected with this mode of expression. In this he has exposed himself to the danger of awakening ludicrous or unauthorized images; but in obedience to an impulse.

THE BANQUET

TRANSLATED FROM PLATO

Editio princeps and other editions and reprints of Shelley's translations from Plato:

1. *Essays, Letters from Abroad, Translations and Fragments,* by Percy Bysshe Shelley, edited by Mrs. Shelley. London: E. Moxon, 1840. 2 vols. Printed by Bradbury and Evans, Printers, Whitefriars, London (for a description, see Forman, *The Shelley Library* [London, 1886], pp. 117-121). For reviews of this work, see *The Letters of Mary W. Shelley,* ed. F. L. Jones, II, 143 n. 1.

2. *Idem,* Philadelphia, Pa.: Lea and Blanchard, 1840. 2 vols. Printed by Haswell, Barrington, and Haswell.

3. *Idem,* A New Edition, London: E. Moxon, 1845 (for a description, see Forman, *The Shelley Library,* pp. 121-122).

4. *Idem,* combined with royal octavo edition of *The Works of Percy Bysshe Shelley,* edited by Mrs. Shelley in a single volume, 1847, 1850, 1853, 1854, 1874.

5. *Standard Library. Comprising The Indicator and the Companion, by Leigh Hunt. The Poetical Works of Charles Lamb. Tales from Shakespeare, by Charles Lamb. The Poems of William Shakespeare. Essays, Letters from Abroad, &c by P. B. Shelley.* London: William Tegg and Co., 1850. Forman says of this edition, "I can find no difference but the

want of title-page between this issue of the prose volume of Shelley and the issue of 1845,—even the paper seems to be the same" (Forman, *The Shelley Library*, p. 79).

6. *Essays, Letters from Abroad, Translations and Fragments*. A New Edition. London: E. Moxon, 1852. 2 vols. (for a description, see Forman, *The Shelley Library*, p. 123).

7. *The Prose Works of Percy Bysshe Shelley*, edited by H. B. Forman, London: Reeves & Turner, 1880.

8. *The Banquet of Plato, and Other Pieces Translated and Original by Percy Bysshe Shelley*, with an Introduction by Henry Morley. London and New York, 1887, 1905. See also Cassell's National Library, vol. 80, 1886.

9. *The Banquet of Plato*, translated by Percy B. Shelley. Decorations by Bruce Rogers. Chicago: Way and Williams, 1895. 75 copies.

10. *The Prose Works of Percy Bysshe Shelley*, from Original Editions, Edited, Prefaced, and Annotated by Richard Herne Shepherd. London: Chatto & Windus, 1888, 1906. 2 vols.

11. *The Banquet of Plato*, translated by P. B. Shelley. Boston: Houghton Mifflin Co., limited edition of 440 copies, 1908.

12. *Five Dialogues of Plato Bearing on Poetic Inspiration*. Introduction by A. D. Lindsay. Everyman's Library. London: J. M. Dent & Sons Ltd., 1910. Contains *Ion* and *Symposium* translated by Percy Bysshe Shelley.

13. *Julian Edition of the Complete Works of Percy Bysshe Shelley*. London & New York: Ernest Benn, Ltd., and Charles Scribner's Sons, 1926-1930. Volume VII, edited by Roger Ingpen, contains for the first time Shelley's complete translation of *The Banquet*.

14. *Plato's Banquet, Translated from the Greek, A Discourse on the Manners of the Antient Greeks Relative to the Subject of Love, Also a Preface to the Banquet, Revised and Enlarged by Roger Ingpen from MSS in the possession of Sir John C. E. Shelley-Rolls, Bart.* Printed for private circulation, 1931. One Hundred Copies Only. Printed at the Curwen Press, Plaistow, London.

15. *Plato's Banquet*, translated by P. B. Shelley, in *An Anthology of World Prose*, edited by Carl Van Doren. New York: Reynal & Hitchcock, 1935, pp. 220-252.

16. *The Symposium, On Love, Or, The Banquet: A Dialogue of Plato*, translated by Percy Bysshe Shelley. Mount Vernon, New York: The Peter Pauper Press, n.d.

The Text of Shelley's Translation of *The Banquet*

Shelley's original manuscript of the translation and Mrs. Shelley's transcript which he corrected are not among the Shelley manuscripts which Sir

John Shelley-Rolls gave to the Bodleian (see the *Bodleian Library Record,*
II [1946], 144-145). The only known manuscript is Mrs. Shelley's transcription which was used as copy for the printers of the 1840 edition (Bradbury
and Evans, Whitefriars, London). This transcript is now in the Bodleian and
catalogued as *MS. Shelley adds. d. 8,* pp. 55-150. This transcript was used as
the text of the Julian edition and the privately printed and limited edition of
Mr. Ingpen. A comparison of the MS of the transcript with these editions
shows some inaccuracies and a large number of textual variants not recorded
in both editions. Since this transcript does not contain Shelley's corrections
in his own handwriting, it must be a revised transcription. The transcript
shows that the punctuation of the 1840 edition does not follow that of the
copy. Furthermore, the transcript shows many deletions and substitutions,
most of which are the result of the censorship of the translation by Mrs. Shelley and Leigh Hunt. Most of the corrections are in ink, but a few are in
pencil. Much more of the transcript is censored than is shown in the comparison of the transcript and the 1840 edition. Some variants between the
transcript and the 1840 and 1845 texts show that Mrs. Shelley may have made
the corrections in proof. In the following notes the transcript is referred to as
T; Mary's and Hunt's alterations of the text of the transcript as TA; the respective editions of *Essays, Letters from Abroad, etc.,* as 1840 and 1845; the
text of the Julian edition as J; the text of the privately printed edition of Mr.
Ingpen as I. The author's changes are signed J. A. N.

Page	Line	
414	1	*enquiries* T; *inquiries* 1840, 1845, J.
414	6	*wished* T, 1840; *wish* 1845, J.
414	9	*it* canceled and *of them* substituted in T; *it* 1840, 1845, J.
414	12	*friend* T; *friends* 1840.
415	2	*that* canceled and *that on which* substituted in T; *that on which* 1840, J.
415	10	*his* T, 1840; *this* 1845, J.
415	12	*but* T, 1840; *but from* 1845, J.
415	18	*that* canceled and *which* substituted in T; *which* 1840, J.
415	32	*opinion* T; *opinions* 1840.
416	12	*braver and better* T; *better and braver* 1840, J.
416	13-14	*Homer* T; *to Homer* 1840, J.
416	31	*thither* changed to *hither* in T; *hither* 1840, J.

Page	Line	
416	40	*Leave him alone* T, 1840; *Let him alone,* 1845, J.
417	14	*thy* T; *your* 1840, J.
417	28	*30,000* T; *thirty thousand* 1840, J.
417	30	*by and bye* T, 1840; *by and by* 1845, J.
417	38-39	*some need of intermission* T; *need of some intermission* 1840, J.
418	3	*Acumenius* T, 1840, J; *Acumenus* Farrington; cf. page 437, line 25, *supra.*
418	14	*willingly choose* T; *choose* 1840, J. The reading of T is right for *willingly* renders ἑκών (176d2) of the Greek text.
418	26	*discussions* T; *discussion* 1840.
418	28	*Menalippe* T, 1840, J. This is an error in transcription of *Melanippe,* Μελανίππην (177a3).
418	35	*have* T, 1840, 1845, J; should read *has.* The Julian *Works* note here is in error, for *have* is the reading both of the 1840 and 1845 editions.
418	39	*celebrated* T, 1840; *extolled* 1845, J. The error in the Julian *Works* note has been corrected in the Ingpen edition.
419	36	*eldest* T; *oldest* 1840, J; cf. page 421, line 40, *supra, the eldest.*
419	39	*loving friend* written in pencil over *amiable lover* and *lover* in T.
420	1	*men* T, 1840; *human beings* TA.
420	1-20	Line drawn through the center of page in T indicating intention to cancel this section. Subsequently the passage underwent verbal paraphrase in the 1840 edition.
420	7	*loves* T, 1840; *loves his friend* TA.
420	9	*passion* T, 1840; *affection* TA.
420	11	*manner, one who is the object of love is especially grieved* T; *manner among attached friends one who is the object of affection* TA; *manner among warmly attached friends, a man is especially grieved* 1840.

Page	Line	
420	12	*lover* T; *friend* TA, 1840. For Mary's substitution of *friendship* for *love* in the text, see *The Letters of Mary W. Shelley*, ed. F. L. Jones, II, 139-140.
420	13	*composed of lovers and the beloved* T; *composed by friends bound by strong attachment* TA, 1840.
420	18	*a lover* T; *one friend* TA, 1840.
420	18-19	*his beloved* T; *another* TA; *the other* 1840.
420	21	*the object of his attachment* T, 1840, *his friend* TA.
420	32	*so* canceled before *as* in T.
421	14	*Greeks* T, 1840; this is an error in the transcription of *Gods*, which is the translation of θεοί (180a2).
421	15-23	*Aeschylus . . . with the God* bracketed in T and omitted 1840.
421	17	*Achilles* canceled before *Patroclus* in T.
421	23	*by the God* T; *by* canceled and *with* written over it.
421	24	*they rewarded* T; *the Gods rewarded* 1840, J.
422	15-16	*regard women . . . men, they* T; canceled and omitted 1840.
422	22	*towards men* T; canceled and omitted 1840.
422	23-24	*of that sex which is endowed* T; *of those who are endowed* TA, 1840.
422	27	*develope* T; *develop* 1840.
422	28	*in preference to mere youths* T; canceled and omitted 1840.
422	32	*love mere youths* T; *love the very young* TA, 1840.
422	38	*persons* T; *the persons* 1840.
422 l. 40-423 l. 1		*it is dishonourable to serve and gratify the objects of our love* T, 1840; *love [it is] dishonourable* TA.
423	1	*does this* T, 1840; *loves* TA.
423	3-13	*The law . . . species of love* canceled and omitted 1840.
423	7	*or modern* T; *or of modern* 1840.
423	10-11	*this practice* T; *the practice* 1840.
423	13	*For not only this species of love* T; *Not only friendship* TA, 1840.

Page	Line	
423	17	*stedfast* T, 1840, 1845; *steadfast* J.
423	22	*lovers* T; *friends* TA, 1840.
423	26	*degrees* T; *degree* J.A.N.
423	27	*to this practice* T; canceled and omitted 1840.
423	27	*is far* T; *are far* 1840, J.
423	30	*It evident* T; *It is evident* 1840, J.
423	30	*this passion* T; *passion* TA, 1840.
423	36	*the law* T; *opinion* TA, 1840.
424	3	*threshold* of [space] T, with *of* canceled.
424	8	*and the law declares* T; *so that he* TA, 1840.
424	13-20	*Considering these things . . . dishonourable* T; canceled and omitted 1840.
424	30	*or shame* T; *nor shame* 1840, J.
424	34	*The* T; *These* 1840, J.
424	34	*persons our law directs us to distinguish* T; *persons which we ought to distinguish* TA; *persons we ought to distinguish* 1840.
424	36	*the lover* T; *a man* TA (canceled), 1840.
424	38	*as* before *dishonourable* 1845, J; omitted T, 1840.
425	5-6	*Our law . . . his lover* T; canceled and omitted 1840.
425	7	*a law* T; *a belief* TA; *an opinion* 1840.
425	11	*For* T; *And also* TA, 1840.
425	14	*law* T; canceled and omitted 1840.
425	19-23	*the one serving . . . to refuse* T; no cancellation in T but omitted 1840.
425	27	*his affections to his lover* T, with the second *his* canceled and *the* substituted; *the affections to the lover* 1840.
425	30-34	*For if any one favours . . . to any one,* T; omitted 1840; *In the same way if any one pretends to be the friend of another for his wealth and is deceived in the advantage which he ex-*

pected, his friend turning out to be poor instead of rich, this [*his?*] *conduct is not the less base; for such an one has already shewn that for the sake of money he would submit in anything to any one.* TA.

425   34   *favours another* T; *seeking the friendship of any* [*man?*] TA; *seeks the friendship of another* 1840.

425   35-36   *the intercourse and affection of his lover* T; *such intercourse and affection* TA, 1840; *the intercourse and affection for his lover* J.

425   36   *lover* T; *friend* TA, 1840.

425   38   *For such an* T; canceled and changed to *Thus* [*with love*] *in love of any one seems to have* [*been deceived*] submitted.

425   38   *an one* T; *a one* 1840.

425   38-39   *to the servitude of Love* T; *to a kind of servitude in love* 1840.

425   39   *from any one* T; omitted 1840.

425   40-41   *a disposition of mind eminently beautiful* T, 1840; *such a disposition of mind is eminently beautiful* TA.

426   3   *both the lover and the beloved* T; *mankind is* TA; *those who love* 1840.

426   9   *that it happened* T; *it happened* 1840, J.

426   12   *hiccup* throughout the text of T; *hiccough* 1840.

426   17   *continues* T; *continue* 1840.

426   22   *developement* T; *development* 1840.

426   25   *which* canceled after *who* in T.

426   25   *all* canceled before *those* in T.

426   37   *which a bad* T; *which are bad* 1840.

427   1   *trace in those operations the good* T, J; *trace those operations of the good* 1840.

427   17   *an harmony* T, J; *a harmony* 1840.

427   31   *system. In* T, 1840; *rhythm. In* Forman, Farrington. The Julian note is in error as to the reading of T here.

Page	Line	
427	33	*system* T, 1840, J; *system* should be emended to *rhythm*, for it is the same error in the transcription of *rhythm*, the translation of ῥυθμῷ (187d1).
428	1	*attendant on* T, 1840; *attendant of* 1845, J.
428	1	*Polymnia* T; *Polyhymnia* 1840. *Polymnia* is an error in transcription.
428	12	*bring* T; *they bring* 1840.
428	26	*in relation of* T; *in relation to* 1840, J.
429	29	*then* T; *there* 1840.
429	37-38	*two organs of generation* T; canceled and deleted 1840.
430	10	*Ephialtus* T, 1840, J; *Ephialtes* Forman. Though *Ephialtes* is the correct transliteration of Ἐφιάλτης, it is evident that Shelley, on the analogy of Otus (Ὦτος), wrote *Ephialtus,* in ignorance of the nominative ending of Ἐφιάλτου (190b7).
430	18-19	*desired silence* T, 1840, J. Mr. Farrington says of this rendering, "Obviously Shelley wrote 'having devised a scheme.' The words *scheme* and *silence* would be readily confused in Shelley's script." His emendation should now be accepted, for a comparison of it with Ficinio's version of μόγις δὴ ὁ Ζεὺς ἐννοήσας λέγει (190c6), which he translated as *Tandem sententiam suam explicuit,* shows that Shelley, at a loss how properly to render ἐννοήσας, translated Ficino's *sententiam suam explicuit* as *devised a scheme.*
430	25	*so they* T, 1840, J; it is possible that Shelley's MS read "so that they shall go," etc. (cf. *so that*, p. 430, l. 30, *supra*), and that in the transcription *that* was omitted.
431	1	*and* canceled before *when* in T.
431	3-4	*whether . . . call* canceled in T. Pages 90-91 of T *(But Jupiter . . . even for a moment)* are canceled and were originally not intended for publication. They were published later with certain deletions and changes.
431	5-8	*and placed . . . upon the earth* T; bracketed and omitted 1840.
431	10-11	*but from . . . ensues* T; omitted 1840.
431	11	*consequence* T; *consequences* J.

Page   Line
431   12   *in* T; *between* 1840.

431   16   *pselta* T, 1840; *psetta* Farrington. This word, which is the
                 transliteration of ψῆτται (191d4), sole or flounder, explains
                 ψήττα λίψαι (for ψῆτται λίσπαι?), which is found in the
                 Journal entry for April 28, 1819. Probably the dinner for
                 the day consisted of thin sole or flounder and the *Symposium*
                 offered the terminology for the menu. Shelley rendered
                 ψῆτται (191d4), λίσπαι (193a7), *as thin as lispae.*

431   23   *Naetenstriae* T; this is an error in transcription for *Hetairis-*
                 triae ἑταιρίστριαι (191e5).

431   24-37   *Those who are . . . of their equals* T; bracketed in T with
                 cancellation in several phrases; omitted 1840.

432   1-2   The following words are canceled in T: *such as I have de-*
                 scribed [two illegible words canceled above]; *lover; with his*
                 own nature.

432   5   *even* T; omitted 1840 but not canceled in T.

432   13-15   *should stand over the couch of these persons thus affected as*
                 they were reclining together, with his tools, and should say
                 to them T; *should say to persons thus affected* TA, 1840.

432   28   *dwindled to our own weakness* T; *dwindled through our own*
                 weakness 1840, J; *dwindled* is very likely an error in the tran-
                 scription of *divided* (cf. *divided through,* p. 432, l. 31, *supra*),
                 which Shelley may have actually written, following Ficino's
                 scissi fuimus for διῳκίσθημεν (193a2). Furthermore, *weak-*
                 ness is likely an error in the transcription of *wickedness,*
                 which is a closer rendering of Ficino's *inustitiam* and of the
                 Greek ἀδικίαν (193a2).

432   29   *Lacaedemonians* T; *Lacedaemonians* J.A.N., cf. *Lacedaemon,*
                 p. 448, l. 13, *supra.*

432   32   *this as lispae* T; *thin as lispae* 1840.

432   36   *exiting* T; *exciting* 1840.

432 l. 38-   *Nor let Eryximachus . . . fortunate few* T; canceled and
433 l. 3   omitted 1840.

433   6   *are* T; *were* 1840.

433   6   *antient* T; *ancient* 1840.

Page	Line	
433	36	*judgement* T; *judgment* 1840.
433	38	*suffrages.* There is a note on this word at the bottom of page 96 of T: *Shakespeare.* Leigh Hunt added later in pencil [*Milton* P (or?) *Fit audience find, though few*], a quotation from *Paradise Lost,* VII, 31. The note is not Mrs. Shelley's, as claimed by the Julian note, but a transcription of Shelley's own note. Shelley wrote to Claire Clairmont in November, 1820, "My verses please so few persons that I make much of the encouragement of the few, whose judgment . . . I should say with Shakspeare and Plato 'outweighed a whole theatre of others'" (Julian *Works,* X, 226).
434	13	*his rights* canceled before *the praise* T.
434	31	*and his repugnance* T; *and from his repugnance* 1840.
434	38	*Japetus* T; *Jupiter* 1840, J. *Japetus* is right, for it is a transliteration of Ἰαπετοῦ (195b7).
435	17	*and hard* T; *a hard* 1840.
436	19	*not harmonized* T, 1840, J. Forman suspects *not* and deletes it in his edition, but it should stand, for Shelley rendered by it the negative μὴ οὐχί (197a2).
437	4	*sacrifizes* T; *sacrifices* 1840.
437	5-14	Mrs. Shelley quotes these lines from Shelley's translation in her article "The Loves of the Poets," *Westminster Review,* XXII (1829), 472-473; cf. *The Letters of Mary W. Shelley,* ed. F. L. Jones, II, 19. The text of her quotation varies a little from that of the 1840 edition.
437	25	*Acumenius* T; *Acumenus* Farrington.
437	30	*otherwise than* written above and between *be* and *reduced.*
437	38	*scaring* T; *scanning* 1840, 1845, J.
438	10	*that our* T; *our* 1840, J.
438	26	*preceeded* T; *preceded* 1840.
438	38	*The* T; *Then* 1840.
439	1	*enquiry* T, 1840; *inquiry* 1845, J.
439	9	*enquire* T, 1840; *inquire* 1845, J.

Page	Line	
439	27	*what they* T; *which they* 1840, J.
439	36	*in future* T, 1840; it is likely that Shelley wrote *in the future* as the phrase *for the future* shows (cf. p. 439, l. 40, *supra*).
440	10	*remember of* T, 1840, J; any question as to whether *of* should be left in the text is settled by remembering that Shelley is here translating literally ἀναμνήσθητι, τίνων ἔφησθα ἐν τῷ λόγῳ (201a2); cf. also *judge of* in *Ion,* page 471, line 31, *supra.*
441	17	*alledged* T and throughout text; *alleged* 1840.
441	20	*or good* T; *nor good* 1840.
441	39	*or immortal* T; *nor immortal* 1840; cf. pages 442, line 40— 443, line 1, *supra.*
442	1	*hold* T; *holds* 1840.
442	2	*inquired* T, 1840.
442	18	*enquired* T; *inquired* 1840.
442	21	*came* 1840; omitted T.
442	30	*participates* T; *participate* 1840.
443	5	*cause* canceled and *case* substituted in T.
443	12	*they are* T; *he is* 1840.
443	12	*enquired* T, 1840, 1845, J.
443	35	*that possesses* T; *who possesses* 1840, correct translation of the Greek. Cf. *he who has the possession of,* page 443, line 39, *supra.*
444	1	*it useless* T; *it is useless* 1840.
444	2	*enquire* T, 1840, 1845, J.
444	4	*that which* T; *that that* 1840.
444	10	*application* T; *appellation* 1840, J. The correct reading of the 1840 text makes it evident that Mrs. Shelley caught an error in transcription. *Application* appears in the next line of the text.
444	16	*rhythm* canceled and rewritten as *rythm* in T.
444	22	*human* canceled and changed to *living;* cf. *human being,* page 446, line 8, *supra.*

Page	Line	
444	26-27	*contracted and sadness, it is repelled and checked and does not produce* T; *contracted by sadness and being repelled and checked, it does not produce* 1840.
444	29	*of half or* T; *of the half nor* 1840, J.
445	8	*then she replied* T; *she replied* 1840, J.
445	14	*impells* T; *impels* 1840.
445	21	*immortal* T, 1845, J; *mortal* 1840.
445	28	*whose soul is* is written above *one* and then canceled.
445	39	*enquired* T, 1840, 1845, J.
446	28	*strange* T; *strange is* 1840.
446	32	*departure of memory* T, 1840; *departure of knowledge* Farrington.
446	34	*tho'* T; *though* 1840.
446	36	*is* T; *it is* 1840.
447	11	*in any* T; *in many* 1840.
447	31	*excellencies* T, 1840; *excellences* 1845, J.
447	33	*beautiful* T, 1840; *excellent* TA.
447	35	*he embraces* T, 1840; *And thus in his love for women* before *he embraces* TA.
447	36	*within him which is* T; *which is within him, which is* 1840, J.
448	6-7	*So that* deleted in T; *And so with the friendship between those who are united* [illegible word] *love of the beautiful* TA.
448	8	*love* T, 1840; *affection* TA.
448	8	*endearing* T, 1840; *enduring* Farrington.
448	18	*an human* T; *a human* 1840.
448	30	*excellencies* T, 1840; *excellences* 1845, J.
448	38	*his form* T; *the form* TA, 1840.
449	3	*The lover* T; *The wise friend* TA; *He* 1840.

Page	Line	
449	6	*like some servant in love with his fellow* T, with illegible phrase substituted and then canceled; omitted 1840.
449	7	*one form, nor* T; *one form; in love nor one ordered in friendship* TA; *one form in love nor* 1840.
449	12	*once* T; *one* 1840.
449	26-27	*or any* T; *nor any* 1840.
449	27	*other thing* T; *other* 1840.
450	13-14	*the self consistent* T; omitted 1840. As the words *the original, the supreme, the self consistent* are not in the Greek, it seems that Shelley tried out various renditions of μονοειδές (211e4) before he finally settled on the *monoeidic beautiful* without deleting, as is the case in many of his MSS, his previous attempts. In view of this and the Greek text the words *the original, the supreme, the self consistent* should be bracketed. Yet in view of Shelley's occasional interpolations in his translation of Plato (cf. *infra*, p. 590, note on *Ion*, p. 473, l. 2, *supra*) the words may be considered as an exegetical interpolation of Shelley (cf. *consistent, and monoeidic with itself*, p. 449, l. 29, *supra*).
451	6	*his head* T; *his* 1840.
451	8	*Aye* T; *Ay* 1840.
451	16	*sate* T; *sat* 1840.
451	25	*to lie down* T; *to take your place* TA, 1840.
451	26	*beautiful* T; *delightful* TA, 1840.
451	27	*love* T; *friendship* TA, 1840.
451	28	*love* T; *know* TA, 1840.
451	29-30	*look on any one who is beautiful* T; *look upon any one else* TA, 1840.
451	34-35	*for I am seriously alarmed at the fury of his amatory impulse* T; canceled and omitted 1840.
452	17	*an hundred* T; *a hundred* 1840.
452	31	*that he* T; *he* 1840.
452	32-34	*Good words . . . presence* T; *But I assure you, Socrates, I will praise no one beside yourself in your presence* TA, 1840.

Page	Line	
453	11	*sculptor's* T; *sculptors'* 1840.

453   12   *in* T, 1840; *into* 1845, J.

453   14   *satyrs* T, 1845, J; *satyr's* 1840.

453   18-21   *For Marsyas, and whoever now pipes the music that he taught, for that music which is of heaven and described as being taught by Marsyas, enchants men through the power of the mouth. For if any musician* . . . T, 1840. "There can hardly be a doubt," says Forman, "that *is* [*described*] should be in the place of *and.* The sense of the original would then be rendered: now the sentence has no construction, and does not render the sense." An examination of the Greek text shows that Forman is right. Inasmuch as the subject of *enchants men* is *Marsyas and whoever now pipes the music that he taught,* it is best to follow the Greek and take the phrase *for that music . . . by Marsyas* as epexegetic of *whoever now . . . he taught.* If the epexegetic sentence is enclosed in parentheses, Shelley's text becomes clear. Finally, *heaven* should be capitalized, for it refers to the music of Olympus (215c3), who was taught by Marsyas. Shelley did not understand that Olympus is a person and not an abstraction in this context.

454   20   *who like he is to* T; *how like he is to* 1840; *who* is obviously an error in transcribing *how.*

454   26   *those sculptured* T; *the sculptured* 1840, J.

454   37   *command* T; *commands* 1840, J.

455   2   *As soon as I thought I perceived* T, J, with *I thought* faintly canceled in T. Here Shelley made two variants for διανοηθείς (217a6), which were incorporated in T.

455   22   *motioned to depart* T, J. The Greek here is ἐβούλετο (217d5), which Shelley translated as *wanted,* mistakenly transcribed as *motioned.*

455   28   *pround* T [*sic*]; [*forward*] J; *proud* I. The Greek here is ἔργον ὑπερήφανον (217e5), which Ficino translated as *superbum & invictum facinus.* Shelley follows Ficino's version closely.

455   35   *chose* T; probably an error in transcription for *choose.*

Page	Line	
456	28	*mountain brass* T. *Mountain* is meaningless here. This is clearly an error in transcription for *molten brass*, by which Shelley translates χαλκείων (219a1). Cf. Shelley's use of this phrase in a letter to John and Maria Gisborne, dated May 26, 1820: "flowing not like the words of Sophocles, with honey, but *molten brass* and iron" (Julian *Works*, X, 176).
456	29	*you be* T; *you have been* J.
456	38	*as casting* T, J. Shelley's sentence is confused as it stands. If *as* is emended to *and*, the sentence follows the Greek. It is obvious that *as* is an error in transcription of Shelley's *&* in the MS.
457	7	*contest of my mind* T, J. *Contest* here may be an error in the transcription of *state*, which is closer to διάνοιαν. (219d3); if *contest* is retained, it can be understood only as bringing out the force of the "polar" particles μέν, δέ in the phrase ἡγούμενον μὲν ἠτιμάσθαι, ἀγάμενον δὲ τὴν τούτου φύσιν (219d3-4).
457	14	*Ajax by wine,* T, J. Shelley must have written *iron* here, translating σιδήρῳ (219e2), which was confused in the transcription. It is to be noted that Shelley translates elsewhere in the text the Greek for *wine* correctly. We have a corroboration for the reading of *iron* in the text of *The Diary of Clara Mary Jane Clairmont.* Claire Clairmont read Shelley's translation of the *Symposium* August 14-16, 1819. In her entry for July 3, 1820, she refers to this passage and says, "Alcibiades tells us he had thoughts of trying to seduce Socrates by gold but he knew him to be more invulnerable to that, than was Achilles to steel." Though she mistakes Achilles for Ajax, she reveals the true reading of Shelley's text here to be *iron.*
457	19	*Sometime after this* T, J; *At one time* TA, 1840.
457	40	*enquiring* T, 1840, J.
458	13	*that the generals* T, 1840; *that while the generals* 1845, J.
458	14	*gave* T; *desired to give* TA, 1840.
458	16	*at scattered* T; *and scattered* 1840.

Page	Line	
458	17	*Delius* T, 1840, J. Shelley may have written *Delium* in the MS, or if he did write *Delius* he did so through ignorance of the nominative of Δηλίου (220e8).
458	22	*that* T; *than* 1840, J.
458	23	*emergence* T; *emergency* 1840.
458	29	*resistence* T; *resistance* 1840.
458	33	*might well* T, 1840; *could well* 1845, J.
458	39	*Antenor* canceled before *Nestor* in T.
459	1-2	*discourses are so uncommon* T, 1840, J; *discourses being so uncommon* 1845.
459	2	*parrallel* T; *parallel* 1840.
459	5	*Sileni* T, 1845, J; *Silen* 1840.
459	10 ff.	at the bottom of page 146 of the manuscript there is a penciled note in Mary's hand: [This passage would make an excellent motto, or preparation, for the discourse].
459	13	*easily* canceled lightly before *laugh* in T.
459	14-33	*(within the sense . . . Alcibiades)* deleted in T.
459	22-30	*as well as . . . own experience* T; canceled and omitted 1840.
459	31	*burst into laughter* T; *burst into a laugh* 1840, J.
459	31-32	*at the frankness* T; *at his frankness* TA, 1840.
459	32-33	*with which he seemed to confess that he was still in love with Socrates* T; canceled and omitted 1840.
459	38-39	*ought to love you and no one else, and that Agathon ought to be loved by you and no one else* T; *ought to be your friend, and to care for no one else* TA, 1840.
460	4	*recline* T; *sit* TA, 1840.
460	5	*close under me* T; *by me* TA, 1840.
460	7	*subdue every way* T, 1840, J; "Insert *me* after subdue," Farrington.
460	7	*recline* T; *remain* TA, 1840.
460	9	*reclines under you* T; *is placed beside you* TA, 1840.

Page	Line	
460	10	*he will not praise me, before I praise him* T; *will he not praise me before I praise him?* 1840, J.
460	14-17	*This is just like him . . . lie down by him* T; canceled and omitted 1840.
460	35	*Aristophanes first awoke* T, 1840; "This looks like a mere slip for 'fell asleep.'" Farrington.

Note on *The Banquet of Plato*

First published by Mr. Richard Garnett in *Relics of Shelley* (London: Edward Moxon & Co., 1862), page 77, and is assigned by him to 1817.

With respect to the date 1817, Garnett says, ". . . the dates appended to these fragments are usually conjectural, but no important error will have been committed" (p. 74). In view of the *Symposium's* appearing in Shelley's reading for 1817, Garnett's date may stand.

| 461 | 3 | Ἔρως; *sic* in Garnett's text. |
| 461 | 4 | *is the cause,* Garnett; *in the cause* J, which is no doubt a misprint. |

The page references in the note are to the Bipont text of the *Symposium* (Πλάτων / *Platonis Philosophi / Quae Exstant / Graece Ad Editionem Henrici Stephani / Accurate Expressa / Cum Marsilii Ficini Interpretatione / Accedit Varietas Lectionis /* Studiis Societatis Bipontinae / Biponti / Ex Typographia Societatis, 12 vols., 1781-1787). They all refer to the speech of Agathon: page 214 = 195c7 (Stephanus pagination in J. Burnet's edition of Plato, *Scriptorum Classicorum Bibliotheca Oxoniensis*), page 214, line 8 = 195e1, Ἔρωτα ὅτι ἁπαλός... l. ultima = 196a1-2 πρὸς δὲ τούτοις ὑγρὸς τὸ εἶδος. οὐ γὰρ ἂν οἷός τ' ἦν, page 218 = 197b7-197e2 ἐπειδὴ δ' ὁ Θεός... συμπάντων τε θεῶν καὶ...

For the influence of this passage on Shelley's poetry, cf. *Prometheus Unbound*, I, 772-775; *Adonais*, ll. 208-216. It is believed that "*Agathon*, a poem" indicates that Shelley intended to write a poem using Agathon of the dialogue as the subject. *Prince Athanase*, whose original title was *Pandemos and Urania*, is another example of the *Symposium's* offering inspiration and thematic material for Shelley's poetry.

Ion, or Of the Iliad

First published in *Essays, Letters from Abroad, Translations, etc.*, 1840. For the history of the text of this translation, cf. pages 462-467, *supra.*

Manuscripts: Cf. pages 464-466, *supra.* Mr. Buxton Forman possessed Claire Clairmont's transcript of Shelley's translation which he used in his edition of this dialogue in 1880. The Clairmont transcript is designated in the following notes by C, while Forman's edition is referred to as F.

Page	Line	
468	2	*Ephesus* 1840; *spheres* C.
468	3	*Aesculapius* 1840; *Epidaurus of the Aesculapians* C.
468	5	*Epidaurians* 1840; *Aesculapians* C.
468	11	*at* 1840; *of* C.
468	16	*person* 1840; *persons* C.
468	21	*thoughts* 1840; *thought* C.
468	27-28	*I flatter myself that no man living* 1840; *and I flatter myself that no human being* C.
468	35	*admirers* 1840; *descendants* C; the reading of C is closer to the text of the Greek.
469	10	*Whether do you demonstrate* etc. 1840; Shelley translated here correctly the first word of the sentence, πότερον (531a1), by *whether,* but as he read on and got to its correlative ἤ *or,* he forgot to delete *whether,* which is superfluous in the English translation of πότερον . . . ἤ. That Shelley knew how to render πότερον...ἤ idiomatically is seen on page 469, line 3, *supra:* "Do you excel in explaining Homer alone *or* are you" etc. Cf. also page 470, line 6, *supra.* In view of this, *whether* should be bracketed not only here but also on page 470, lines 11-15, *supra;* "Among a number of persons giving their opinions on the wholesomeness of different foods, *whether* would one person be capable . . . *or* would" etc. where Shelley must also have forgotten to delete the unnecessary literal translation of πότερον.
469	10-11	*Whether do you demonstrate these things better in Homer or Hesiod?* 1840; *Whether do you illustrate these subjects better for Homer or in Hesiod* C.
469	14	*regard* 1840; *respect* C.
469	15	*treat* 1840; *speak* C.
469	22	*those* 1840; *these* F.
469	23	*understand* 1840; *understood* C.
469	23	*agreement* 1840, F; *argument* 1845; the reading of 1840 is closer to the Greek text.

Page	Line	
469	26	*any other poets* 1840; *any of the other poets* C.
469	27	*from all* 1840; *from that of all* C.
469	28	*treat* 1840; *deal* C.
469	31	*men* 1840; *man* F.
470	3	*which* 1840; *who* F.
470	6	*who* 1840; *as* F.
470	11	*persons* 1840; *people* C.
470	11	*opinions* 1840; *opinion* C.
470	12	*whether* 1840; for the bracket, see note on text reading of page 469, line 10, *supra* page 556.
470	22	*unfitness* 1840; *emptiness* C.
470	26	*would then* 1840; *then would* F.
470	33	*But if you can judge of* 1840; *Yet if you can judge* F.
470	34	*judge of* 1840; *judge* F.
470	34-35	*it expresses* 1840; *it is expressed* F.
471	1	*and* 1840; *if* C.
471	5	*talking of* 1840; *hearing* F.
471	5	*positively* 1840; *I instead* C.
471	7	*as if it were* 1840; *as it were* C.
471	8	*suggest* 1840; *conjecture* C, which is closer to the Greek text.
471	12	*and* 1840; *or* F.
471	27-29	*Yes . . . bad* C; omitted 1840.
471	31	*to judge of* 1840; *to judge the merit of* F.
471	32-33	*to judge of any other painter; who, on the compositions of the works of other painters* 1840; *to judge the production of any other painter; who, on the supposition of the works of other painters,* C.
472	1	*Epius,* 1840; *Epeius* F.
472	1	*Panopus* 1840; *Panopeus* F.

Page	Line	
	Page	Line
472	2-3	*any other great sculptor, who was immediately at a loss,* 1840; *any other one great sculptor, who immediately was at loss* C.
472	4	*met* 1840; *will* C.
472	6	*rhapsody* 1840; *melody* C.
472	9	*judge* 1840; *determine* C.
472	12	*and with* 1840; *and that with* F.
472	16	*It is that you are not master of* 1840; *It is not that you are master of* F, J.
472	18	*magnet* 1840, F; *Magnet* 1845.
472	19	*stone* 1840; *stone itself* F.
472	22	*attached* 1840, cf. *attached,* page 482, line 16, *supra; attracted* C.
472	31	*admired* 1840, cf. *admirable things,* also page 558, *infra,* text reading of page 473, lines 21-22; *divine* C.
472	33	*the sacred* 1840; *their sacred* C.
472	37	*souls of the poets* 1840; *souls of poets* C.
473	2	*rapid* 1840; *vapid* C.
473	21-22	*and that we . . . the God,* 1840; *that we their auditors, may acknowledge that such absurd persons cannot possibly be the authors of the excellent and admirable things which they communicate; but that God himself is he who speaks and that they are merely the organs of his voice.* C. With these words the text of the Clairmont transcript begins to differ considerably from the 1840 text. After *God* in the 1840 text appears Mrs. Shelley's first bracket, marking the beginning of the first passage she interpolated to supply a lacuna in the MS from which she made her transcript of the *Ion.*
477	2	Printer's brackets, marking the end of the first passage interpolated by Mrs. Shelley to fill the lacuna in the MS, must have come just before the words *with respect to it;* cf. page 467, *supra.*
477	2	MS. *Shelley adds. c.* 4, foll. 258^r-9^v starts with the words *with respect to it.*

Page	Line	
477	4	The MS always abbreviates *Soc.*
477	4	*With reference to H* MS, then *with reference* canceled.
477	5-6	*better capable of deciding whether Homer had spoken rightly or not?* 1840, MS; *better able to decide whether Homer had treated this subject correctly* C.
477	10	*For* canceled in MS, then *and* substituted.
477	13	*And if it is different it supposes* 1840; *And if the arts which you profess are different they suppose* C.
477 l. 15-479 l. 3		A gap in the Clairmont transcript begins here and ends with *Certainly;* cf. page 466, *supra.*
477	16	*Heca Kamede* [?] canceled in MS.
477	17	*who was wounded* MS; omitted 1840.
477	17	*and he speaks* 1840; *and speaking* canceled in MS then *he speaks* added.
477	18	There is a blank in the MS for this and the remaining quotations from Homer.
477	25	*The* 1840; *To the* MS.
477	31	*or not?* 1840; *or not on the subject* MS.
477	31	*respecting* canceled in MS and *on* substituted.
477	33	*whether* 1840; *if* MS.
477	33	*impelled* [or *compelled?*] canceled in MS and *inspired* substituted.
477	33	*put* [?] canceled in MS and *make* substituted.
477	33	*question* canceled in MS and *demand* substituted.
477	34	*Know o* canceled in MS and *Come* substituted.
477	34	*found Just.* MS; Shelley changed an illegible word to *found* and *Just* was associated with it.
477	35	*a complete description of these arts* [?] *sic* MS; then *complete description* canceled in MS and *& fit description* substituted.
477	35	*then you will investigate also* canceled in MS before *assist me also in;* after the words *also in* the following is canceled

Page   Line

in the MS: *the enquiry as to the institution of a criticism into the degree of knowledge that he [has] developes of soothsayers & divination.*

477   35   *enquiry* MS; *inquiry* 1840.

477   36   *competence on the subject of* 1840; *competence in determining on matters the subject of* MS, with *matters* canceled.

478   1   *Theoclymenus the Soothsayer of the Melampians,* 1840; *the soothsayer Theoclymenus of the Melampodides* MS.

478   22   an illegible word is canceled and followed by *fisherman* [?] at the top of MS p. 259.

478   22   *I assert, it belongs* 1840; *Such things as these I assert that it belongs* MS, with the first two words canceled.

478   23   *these* canceled in MS and *such* substituted.

478   25   *we have* 1840; *we have both* MS.

478   26   *Iliad, passages* 1840; *Iliad whatcon re passages* MS, with the second and third words canceled.

478   28   *do you now make mention of* 1840; *you have not omitted* MS, canceled and *do you now [tell] make mention* written above.

478   29   *for a rhapsodist is competent* 1840; *competent as you are* MS, with *you are* canceled and *for a rhapsodist is* written above.

478   29   *to rhapsody* MS, with *his art* written above.

478   31   *Ion* 1840; *Soc.* MS.

478   31   *any* canceled before *every* in MS.

478   32   *Socrates* 1840; *Ion* MS.

478   36   *distinct* MS, then canceled and *different* substituted.

478   36   *different* 1840; *distinct* MS.

479   3   The portion omitted from Clairmont transcript ends with *Certainly;* cf. page 466, *supra.*

479   4   *is that* 1840; *is the art* C.

479   5   *a rhapsodist may be ignorant of some things.* 1840, MS; *There are subjects on which a rhapsodist may be ignorant?* C.

Page	Line	

479   7   *besides those* 1840, MS; *since you except* C.

479   8   *and if the rhapsodist you have* MS, with the words after *and* canceled and *with* substituted.

479   8   *them* 1840, MS; *these* C.

479   8-9   *profess to a complete* MS, with *to* and *complete* canceled.

479   10-12   *I imagine . . . governed* 1840; *I imagine that the rhapsodist has a competent knowledge of the varieties of human character and situation and the various expressions of them; he knows what is probable and becoming for a man to say and for a woman, for the slave, for the freeman, for the governor, for the governed* C.

479   10   *The conduct & theory of character* canceled in MS and *I imagine that the rhapsodist has a perfect kno acquaintance with the* substituted; the words *kno* and *with the* are also canceled.

479   11   *speak* 1840; *speaks* MS.

479   12   *the governor* MS, then canceled for *the ruler,* which is also the reading of the 1840 edition.

479   12   *for him who is governed* MS; *him who is* is then canceled and *the* substituted.

479   13-14   *What with* MS then canceled for *How do you think the rhapsodist knows better than the pilot,* with *a pilot* changed to *the pilot.*

479   13   *think that a* 1840; *assert that the* C.

479   14   *in a tempest* 1840; *labouring in a tempest* C.

479   15   *that* canceled in MS and *such a* substituted.

479   15   *might* canceled in MS and *would* substituted.

479   16   *better judge of what* canceled in MS after *physician.*

479   16   *clearest* 1840; *clearer* MS; *secret* C.

479   17   *a sick* 1840; *the sick* M.

479   18   *So as* [?] *as that goes* canceled in MS before *In that case.*

479   19   *still* canceled in MS before *assert.*

Page	Line	
479	19	an illegible word canceled in MS before *a slave*.
479	20	*Certainly* 1840; *I do* C.
479	21	*To take for example, in the driving of cattle* 1840; *To take your example, from cattle-driving* C.
479	21	*As for* canceled in MS before *example* and *To take for an* substituted.
479	21	*the instance of a herdsman* canceled in MS and *the driving of cattle* substituted; *the herdsman* 1840; *a herdsman* C.
479	21	*the rhapsodist* changed in MS to *a rhapsodist; a rhapsodist* 1840; *the rhapsodist* C.
479	23	*Bring* [?], followed by illegible word; *the* canceled in MS and *bringing back a herd oxen* [*sic*] substituted.
479	23	*had taken* changed in MS to *had run*.
479	23	*a slave engaged in bringing back a herd of oxen run wild* 1840; *his fellow slave engaged in alluring back a herd of oxen that had run wild* C.
479	23	The manuscript ends with *wild*.
479	24	*No, indeed* 1840; *I do not say that* C.
479	24	The bracket marking the beginning of the second interpolated passage by Mrs. Shelley begins directly after *No, indeed* and extends to the end of the dialogue; cf. page 467, *supra*.
481	17	The Clairmont transcript ends here; it is probable that the last two lines of the translation belong to the final passage interpolated by Mrs. Shelley.

Fragments I-II of the Appendix to *A Defence of Poetry* in Koszul's *Shelley's Prose in the Bodleian Manuscripts*

482	20	*act* in Koszul text; Shelley without a doubt wrote *art*, the translation of τέχνη.

Fragments on the *Ion*

485	2	Shelley first wrote *inclusive* and then changed the first letters to make the word *conclusive*.
485	10	*utility* MS; *Utility* Forman.

Page	Line	
485	10	*preserving* MS; *fixing* Forman.
485	12	*actual being* MS; *intellectual being* Forman.
485	12-13	*And in this sense . . . is useful,* omitted Forman.
485	14-15	*nature, & surrounding us with security* MS; *nature; and surrounding us with security and tranquility of life, destroying the grosser desires, superstition, etc.* Forman.
485	15	*and of conciliating* MS; *and conciliating* Forman.
485	17	*advantages* MS; *advantage* Forman.
485	17	*the 4 ages* MS; *The Four Ages* Forman.
485	18	The MS ends with *sense* and is followed directly by Fragment 10 *(from Plato's republic)—But it would be almost impossible* etc.

Menexenus, or the Funeral Oration. A Fragment

First published in *Essays, Letters from Abroad, Translations and Fragments,* 1840.

487	9	*Thou* 1840; *If thou* 1845, J.
487	9	*life. I* 1840; *life, I* 1845.

Fragments from the *Republic* of Plato

First published in *Essays, Letters from Abroad, Translations and Fragments,* 1840.

Manuscript: *vide supra,* page 483.

495	Title	*Fragments from the Republic of Plato* 1840; *Extracts translated from Plato's Republic. MS. Shelley adds. d. 6, p. 114.*
495	1-6	On page 2 of this notebook the first fragment is entitled *from Plato's republic* preceded by the canceled words *I believe.* In this notebook the fragment extends to *return emp* (l. 6).
495	4-5	*merchant* 1840; *merchants,* MS.
495	30	Forman prints this caption in italics; roman type, 1840.
496	17	The notation *C.* xi at the end of the fragment seems to be an error in transcribing *C.* ii, for *C.* xi does not refer to chapter XI; the section translated in the second fragment belongs to Book II, chapters XIII-XIV (373a-e7). But since Shelley

Page   Line

used Massey's text (see note on Fragment VII), and the text does not contain chapter subdivisions, Shelley could have written *C*. ii only for Book II. He uses *C*[*aput*] as well as *L*[*iber*] for *Book;* cf. Fragments XIV-XVI, XIX.

496   18   *improve* 1840, MS. *Shelley adds. d. 6*, p. 114; *impose* Farrington.

496   37-38   Forman prints this comment in italics; roman type, 1840.

496   38   *P. 26.* 1840; *p. 26.*
            The edition to which these page references refer is E. Massey, *Platonis de Republica*, Cambridge, 1713. Page 146 in this edition = 379d6-380c3 in Burnet's edition of the *Republic (Scriptorum Classicorum Bibliotheca Oxoniensis)*, and page 26 = 335a1-335d11. According to Shelley, Plato's doctrine that punishment is remedial (*Republic* 380), is contradicted by Plato's reasoning in *Republic* 335b where Socrates proves by analogy to the other arts that to hurt a human being is to make him worse in respect of human excellence. From Leigh Hunt's letter to Elizabeth Kent, Florence, June 2, 1824, we find that Shelley's copy of the *Republic* passed to him after Shelley's death. In describing his library he says, "Second Shelf: . . . Plato's *Republic*, Diogenes Laërtius' *Lives of the Philosophers* (these two works belonged to dear S.)" (*Correspondence of Leigh Hunt* [London, 1862], I, 222).

498   35-36   The 1840 text is punctuated thus: *The monstrous figures called Arabesques, however in some of them is to be found a mixture of a truer and simpler taste, which* etc.

499   10-11   The remark in the parenthesis is not found in the Greek text (405a). It turns out to be a parenthetic remark which Shelley, as in the other fragments (cf. Fragments XIII, XVIII), interpolated in the text. It should therefore be italicized, as are the rest of his interpolated remarks.

499   20   επητειην 1840, J. The Greek is either the transcriber's or the printer's error for ἐπετείων (405c9) of Massey's text. Shelley here omits Greek accents, as was his custom.

499   22   *this* 1840; *thus* 1845, J.

Note on the Republic

Mary included this note as part of Shelley's Preface to the *Symposium*. An examination of the MS of this Preface (*MS. Shelley adds. e. 6*, pp. 60-65), however, shows that it does not belong to the Preface. The word *Plato* carries no indication of a footnote; furthermore, the note is found on page 65 of the MS, immediately after the words *Socrates, after having paused to,* which are found at the bottom of page 64. The Preface is continued on page 65 after a brief space at the end of the note marked by an asterisk. Since Shelley began page 60 with the canceled words *The Republic perha* followed in the next line by *On the Symposium,* it is evident that the note was separate; but since it was found imbedded within the pages containing the Preface to the *Symposium,* Mary included it as part of the text. The date of this note is 1818.

Page	Line	
501	1	*error, is perhaps* canceled in MS before *considerable.*
501	7	*selection is made, must* 1840; *selection must* MS.
501	7-8	*refinement of the people* after *freedom and* 1840; omitted in MS.

Note on Republic 587e

This previously unpublished note is found in *MS. Shelley adds. e. 9.,* p. 319, which contains besides this note the Greek text of Plato's epigram (Diogenes Laertius, III, 44; *Anthologia Palatina,* VII, 62) which Shelley translated (*MS. Shelley adds. e. 8.,* p. 147). Shelley finished the tenth and last book of the *Republic* at the end of 1820, and the last entry for its reading in the Journal is September 9, 1820. Since this note is on a passage at the end of Book IX of the *Republic,* the date of this note is sometime toward the end of 1820.

To understand Shelley's equation one must keep in mind Plato's argument, which is well set forth by Shorey (*What Plato Said* [Chicago, 1933], pp. 246-247).

The tyrant is at the third remove from the oligarch and the oligarch is the third from the king or aristocrat. The superficial ratio is three times, or nine. But if we look below the surface and probe the tyrant's misery in all its depth, we must cube the number and admit that the kingly man is more happy in the ratio of 729 to 1—an apt number to measure the nights and days that round out the years of mortal life.

Shelley expressed this in an algebraic equation with the tyrant represented by x and the vaster happiness of the legitimate ruler by y. Since he set out to compute the value of y, which could be solved only by another simultaneous equation with the same values for x and y, he meets with failure, which he solves with poetic logic by squaring 729!

| 501 | 2 | *Leg. L. R. 729* canceled in MS before *Let.* |
| 501 | 2-3 | What Shelley intended to write was "and y his vaster happiness." *Goodness* canceled in MS before *happiness.* |

Page   Line
501   4   *3* canceled in MS before 729. In the computation of the
               squaring of 729 Shelley writes by the side of the computation
               the carry over figures.

On a Passage in Crito

First published in *Essays, Letters from Abroad, Translations and Fragments,* 1840.

Mrs. Shelley added the note in brackets; Forman omits this note but adds,
"Wherein Socrates refuses to escape from prison and death, alleging that a
good citizen ought to obey his country's laws."

504   20   *but delightful* 1840; *be delightful,* Medwin.

504   22   *such a life* 1840, *such an existence,* Medwin.

504   22-23   *which must soon begin to be my portion should I live.* 1840;
               that must soon be my position. Medwin.

On the Daemon of Socrates
Note on Memor. Lib. I

507   1   *Memor. Lib. I* MS; *Mem. on. L. I.* Forman.

507   2   *demon; one form of augury* MS; *daemon a form of Augury*
               Forman.

507   3-4   *divination, and things* MS; *divination and those* Forman.

507   6   *intervention* MS; *introduction* Forman.

Shelley's Translations of Epigrams Attributed to and about Plato

I. *Venus and the Muses*

D. F. MacCarthy has shown in his account of Shelley's early life
that while at Oxford he published in the *Oxford University and City
Herald* (January 5, 12, and March 9, 1811) a series of epigrams from
the *Greek Anthology,* most of them signed with the letter "S." One of
these epigrams, a poem attributed to Plato (*Anthologia Palatina,* IX,
39), appeared on March 9 in the *Oxford University and City Herald.* The
Oxford University and City Herald was published at this time by Munday and Slatter. It was John Munday who was the printer of the *Posthumous Fragments of Margaret Nicolson* and in whose bookshop copies
of *The Necessity of Atheism* were prominently displayed. MacCarthy,
after an examination of all the evidence, concludes that all these epigrams
were written by the same person. "The signature attached to them," he
says, "the time at which they appeared, the journal in which they were
published, and the course of his studies at this time, all create an amount
of presumptive evidence that justify [*sic*] me in offering them here as

having in all probability been written by Shelley" (*Shelley's Early Life, from Original Sources* [London, 1872], p. 58). His conclusion was corroborated by an independent examination of these epigrams by Florian Asanger in *Percy Bysshe Shelleys Sprach-Studien, Seine Uebersetzungen aus dem Lateinischen und Griechischen* (Bonn, 1911), pages 119-125. The text of the epigram appears on page 62 of MacCarthy's work under the title *"Venus and the Muses,"* "From the same" [i.e., the *Greek Anthology*] and is signed "Versificator."

II. *To Stella*

The Julian edition states that this epigram was first published in *Shelley's Poetical Works,* 1839. Professor Nitchie has shown, however, that Shelley's version of this epigram was first published along with two other poems in an annual edited by John Francis, *Album Wreath of Music,* II (1834), 57 (Elizabeth Nitchie, "Shelley in 'Frasers' and the 'Annuals,'" *Times Literary Supplement,* August 26, 1939, p. 503). Mary's transcript of this epigram and the other poems published in the annual was in the hands of Mr. W. T. Spencer in 1936. The editor of *The Album Wreath* had access either to this transcript or to one similar to it. A comparison of the text in the annual with that of the 1839 edition shows some variants (see Elizabeth Nitchie, "Variant Readings in Three of Shelley's Poems," *MLN,* LIX [1944], 274-277). The Greek original appears on the title page of

ADONAIS

AN ELEGY ON THE DEATH OF JOHN KEATS,
AUTHOR OF ENDYMION, HYPERION ETC.

BY

PERCY B. SHELLEY

Αστὴρ πρὶν μὲν ἔλαμπες ενι ζώοισιν εῶος·
Νυν δε θανῶν, λάμπεις ἔσπερος εν φθίμενοις [*sic*].

PISA

WITH THE TYPES OF DIDOT
MDCCCXXI

Medwin says in connection with this epigram, "Plato's epigram on Aster, which Shelley had applied to Keats, happened to be mentioned . . . and I asked Shelley if he could render it. He took up the pen and improvised:

> Thou wert a morning star among the living,
> Ere thy fair light was fled;

Now, having died, thou art as Hesperus, giving
New splendour to the dead."
(*Life of Shelley,* ed. Forman [Oxford, 1913], pp. 349-350.)

Forman suggests that Shelley's version as printed by Medwin may be a genuine variant. The variants in the manuscript (*MS. Shelley adds. e. 8,* pp. 142-145), the 1834, 1839, and Medwin versions are:

Page   Line

511   1   *the* MS, 1834, 1839; *a* Medwin.

511   1   *amongst* 1834; *among* MS, 1839, Medwin.

511   2   *new* 1834; *fair* MS, 1839, Medwin; *dear* canceled in MS.

511   2   *had* MS, 1834, 1839; *was* Medwin.

511   3   *Thou* canceled before *Now; the* [illegible word] canceled before *Hesperus* and *as* substituted in MS.

511   4   *even The* canceled before *splendour* in MS.

Shelley's translation has been set to music by H. Buxton Forman and appears on the title page of *The Shelley Library, An Essay in Bibliography* (London, 1866).

III. Translated, From an Epigram of Plato, cited in the Apologia of Apuleius

The text of the epigram is that of the manuscript, which is reproduced here by the kind permission of Dr. Keyes D. Metcalf, Librarian of Harvard College and Director of the University Library. Dr. Peck found the manuscript of this translation in the Shelley MS Notebook at Harvard (Harv. MS. 258. 3. f.), which was procured by E. A. Silsbee from Claire Clairmont and willed to the Harvard Library in 1902 (Smith, *The Shelley Legend,* pp. 284-287). It was first published in the Boston *Herald,* Monday, December 21, 1925, page 12. The poem was also reprinted in a private edition of thirty copies in *The Light of the Dead: a newly discovered poem / by Percy Bysshe Shelley / Printed by Edward Henry Blakeney at his / Private Press,* Winchester: 1927 (cf. *An Account of An Exhibition of Books and Manuscripts of Percy Bysshe Shelley with Something of Their Literary History, Their Present Condition and Their Provenance* [Austin, Texas, 1935], p. 36).

Star of Love, the title of this poem in the Julian *Works,* is that of Dr. Peck, for in the manuscript it is entitled, in Shelley's own words, "Translated, From an Epigram of Plato, cited in the Apologia of Apuleius."

IIIa. Version of same epigram in *Laon and Cythna,* IX, lines 321-324.

IV. *Kissing Agathon*

This unpublished epigram is found in *MS. Shelley adds. e. 8,* p. 147 and is a translation of Plato's epigram in Diogenes Laertius, III, 32

MS OF SHELLEY'S TRANSLATION OF AN EPIGRAM OF PLATO
(in Shelley MS Notebook at Harvard)

The legend below reads: "Shelley came in from his study and showed them this. They were delighted—C. remembers it."

(*Anthologia Palatina*, V, 78). It follows Shelley's version of Diogenes
Laertius, III, 44 (*Anthologia Palatina*, VII, 62). For the date *vide infra*,
pp. 508-509. The epigram has no title in the manuscript. Shelley began
this version at the bottom of *MS. Shelley adds. e. 8*, p. 146, which contains Shelley's versions of the epigrams *To Zanthippe*, but stopped after
the first few phrases.

Page   Line

511   2 *soul* canceled in MS and *spirit* substituted.

511   3 *upon the* canceled in MS before *my lips*.

511   4 *Kissing The* canceled in MS before *For the*.
               After line 4 Shelley canceled:
                   Lo   to
               Kissing Agathon together.
               With my kiss my spiri.
               He then rewrote line 4 as *For the poor thing came there.*

511   5 Canceled in the MS.

IVa. *Another Version*
        This epigram is found in *MS. Shelley adds. e. 8*, p. 144.

512   1 *Agathon* canceled and *Helena* substituted.

512   2 *the kiss* MS; *my kiss,* 1839; *spirit was arose* canceled and
               soul substituted; *did* [several illegible words] canceled and
               beside it written above.

512   3 *upon* canceled and *came to* substituted.

512   5 *As if it were about to cross* [?] canceled; *lead* canceled and
               guide substituted.

V. *To Zanthippe*
        Plato wrote two epigrams on this theme of the apple as a symbol
of short-lived beauty. They are both found in Diogenes Laertius, III,
32 (*Anthologia Palatina*, V, 79, 80). Shelley made one version of the
first epigram in *MS. Shelley adds. e. 8*, p. 146, lines 1-10 (= II, 3, p.
146, *Verse and Prose from Manuscripts of Percy Bysshe Shelley*), and
two versions of the second epigram, the first version of which is combined with the first epigram (ll. 10-18). The second version is found
in *MS. Shelley adds. e. 9*, p. 318 (= IV, page 212, *Verse and Prose
from Manuscripts of Percy Bysshe Shelley*). *MS. Shelley adds. e. 8*, p.
146 also contains (ll. 18-25) a rough draft of the beginning of the epigram on *Kissing Agathon*, and thus shows the same date of composition
for all these epigrams.
        The epigrams *To Zanthippe* were first published in *Verse and Prose
of Shelley*, edited by Sir John C. E. Shelley-Rolls and Roger Ingpen
(London, 1934), pages 9, 140-141. The present text differs from the
Shelley-Rolls and Ingpen edition in presenting a detailed transcription
of the manuscripts and excerpting from the chaotic condition of the

manuscript such lines and phrases as may be said to give the essence
of the Plato epigrams. No attempt is made at determining the meter,
rhyme, or length of line, for Shelley's draft had not reached such a stage.
Cancellations in the text are indicated by brackets.

MS. Shelley adds. e. 8, p. 146.

3.
To Zanthippe

1 Here catch this apple girl, & if thou lovest me
  Give me thy virgin flower, in return—
  [If thou thou then refusest still,—oh think]
                  consider

  [And if thou still denyest that this can ever be]
5 And [if thou] still refusest—[this apple keep] [illegible word]
  [Look at it well,—and if thou sayest this cannot be]
             this child of the green tree
  [How brief its youth youth's]
  [Look but]

10 Will teach how brief is beauty w^dst thou have
  This [disreg unregarded thing] [hand to] thee
  [I throw]
  [Like this] Oh cast me not away, as I have it, [for we to-
  gether?]
  [For both our youths are withering while]

15 Are   [both]   [are not]
  [Are not our we withering], while We ban?
  [Are both love-flames]—dying withering together.
  [flows? love-flames   to my lips]
  With love & youth are withering [my life soul]

20 Kissing Agathon,   [my soul]
  [For to my With the kiss & with]
             [spirit came]
  With the kiss   [my soul arose]
             [I held my soul]

25 [For] On
     MS. Shelley adds. e. 9, p. 318.

1 [Here take this apple—if you love me take it]
    and
  [And   virgin beauty make it]
                fill it

> *And if thou say*   [*take it*], *dearest*
>   *you*
> *Here catch this apple,*   [*if sweetest, take it*]
>
> 5 [*If you love me true,*   *make it*]
>   *With fresh*
>   [*A fresh*]
>   [*And*] *the beauty which thou wearest* [*it*]
>   [*Clothe it in in, & then return it*]
>   *Ah that can never be.* [*oh gather it?*]
>   *Think how soon its bloom is withered*
>
> 10 *Kiss*

VI. *Circumstance*

The manuscript is found in *MS. Shelley adds. e. 8,* p. 144. Title given by Forman.

512   2 *a purse of gold* canceled in MS; *purse* 1839.

512   3 *Another* canceled over *The owner.*

512   4 *The halter found and used it* canceled in MS.

512   5 *Changed* canceled in MS.

512   7 *we* canceled and *you* substituted in MS.

VII. *Spirit of Plato*

This epigram is found in *MS. Shelley adds. e. 8,* p. 147. It carries no title, but at the top of the page Shelley has drawn the figure of an eagle. This page also contains a rough draft of Shelley's translation of another epigram of Plato (Diogenes Laertius, III, 32, *Anthologia Palatina,* V, 78); and it follows in the notebook Shelley's translation of Plato's epigram *To Zanthippe* (*MS. Shelley adds. e. 8,* p. 146). Shelley has also transcribed the Greek text of this epigram, as usual without accents, on *MS. Shelley adds. e. 9,* p. 319, which also contains Shelley's *Note on Republic, 587e* (*vide supra,* p. 565.). If the translation was made about the same time as the transcription of the Greek, the date of this epigram as well as *To Zanthippe* and *Anthologia Palatina,* V, 78 is the end of 1820. For a facsimile, see frontispiece.

513   2 *And* canceled in MS and *To* written above.

513   3 *seekest* canceled in MS before *thou,* and *ascendest* substituted, which in turn is canceled for *Floatest.*

513   4 *high* canceled in MS and *swift* substituted.

513   5 *Ascending Heaven* canceled in MS for *Climbing Olympus' Heavens* with *Climbing Olympus',* which is a translation of ἀποπταμένης ἐς Ὄλυμπον, also canceled. *doth* MS; *does* 1839.

Shelley's Errors in Translation, Variants from the Greek, and Interpolations in His Translations from Plato[1]

The Banquet

Page	Line	
414	2-3	*returning home from Phaleros:* going up to town from my house in Phalerum.
414	12	*faithful reporter:* the most proper.
414	15	*if he thinks:* if you suppose.
415	29	*forever:* should be in the previous clause, "you are always like that in your way of speech."
416	2	*I avoided it:* I evaded him.
416	12	omits the translation of θυσίαν ποιουμένου: who was offering sacrifice.
416	14	omits the translation of ἄκλητον: unbidden.
416	19	*Thus discoursing, they proceeded:* After some such conversation, he told me, they started off.
416	24	*already reclined:* about to dine.
416	44	*till he comes:* not in the Greek; Shelley follows Ficino's version: *neque demittas, quo usque venerit.*
417	4-5	*for I am resolved that there should be no master of the feast:* now that you have no one to direct you (a method I have never tried before). Shelley omits the translation of the clause ὅ . . . ἐποίησα.
417	8-9	*Agathon ordered him to be called, but Aristodemus perpetually forbade it:* though Agathon ever and anon gave orders that they should go and fetch him, my friend would not allow it.

[1] The translation used in corrections is, unless otherwise specified, that of Plato's *Works* in the Loeb Classical Library.

Page	Line	
417	11-12	*at the end of the table:* in the lowest place.
417	17	*as he was desired:* added by Shelley.
417	22	*until both are equal:* added by Shelley.
417	26	*amplest reward:* expansive.
417	28	*excellence and loveliness:* added by Shelley.
417	32-33	*had reclined back on their couches:* κατακλινέντος, "reclined," refers to Socrates's taking his place in the seat and then dining; it does not refer to the entire company.
417	40	*last night:* yesterday.
418	9	omits ἡμεῖς μὲν γὰρ ἀεὶ ἀδύνατοι: we, of course, are known weaklings.
418	13	*nature of drunkenness:* add "the true nature" (J.A.N.).
418	16	*drunk the night before:* still heavy from a bout of the day before.
418	17	*confide in you:* obey you.
418	22	*I think:* I next propose that.
418	23	*flute-player:* omits "who came in just now."
418	31	*innumerable:* omit.
418	33	*who is such:* so ancient.
418	35	*celebrated:* writing in prose (R. G. Bury, *The Symposium of Plato,*[2] Cambridge, 1932).
419	2	*may well be sufficient to excite my indignation:* not in the Greek; Shelley follows Ficino's *nonne indignum est?*
419	4-5	*for the sake of giving pleasure to Phaedrus:* I am not only desirous of obliging him *with a contribution of my own;* Shelley omits italicized phrase.
419	10	omits ἐπιδέξια (Bipont text), which Ficino renders as *quam dexterrime.*
419	24-25	*First, then, Phaedrus began thus:* First then, as I said, he told me that the speech of Phaedrus began with points of this sort.

Page	Line	
419	28-29	*For that he is to be honoured as one of the most ancient of the Gods:* that Love was a great god, among men and gods a marvel; Shelley follows Ficino's *mirandus*.
419	39	*amiable:* honourable.
420	8	*insult:* supply "at another's hands."
420	16	*in battle:* supply "side by side."
421	3-5	*and thus to secure to himself a perpetual intercourse with her in the regions to which she had preceded him:* added by Shelley.
421	12	*revenging and honouring:* rescue . . . and avenged. Shelley mistook τιμωρήσας for τιμήσας here.
421	31	*When they had ceased:* Shelley omits οὓς παρεὶς, which he passed over.
421	33	Shelley follows Ficino in omitting νῦν δὲ οὐ γάρ ἐστιν εἷς: but, you see, he is not one.
421	34	*I will endeavour to distinguish:* it would be more correct to have it previously announced.
422	5	*may be distinguished and selected:* try to describe. Shelley follows Ficino's *distinguenda*.
422	13-14	*presides over transient and fortuitous connexions:* functions promiscuously (*Plato's Symposium or Supper, Newly Translated into English* [by Francis Birrell and Shane Leslie], Introduction by Shane Leslie. London: The Fortune Press [1928]).
422	19	*partakes in her nature:* in origin.
422	22	*and exempts us from all wantonness and libertinism:* and secondly, is the elder, untinged with wantonness.
422	29-31	*seem to me to be preparing to pass their whole life together in a community of good and evil, and not ever lightly deceiving those who love them, to be faithless to their vows:* are prepared to be always with them and share all with them as long as life shall last: they will not take advantage of a boy's green thoughtlessness to deceive him and make a mock of him by running straight off to another.

Page	Line	
422	35	*tendencies and power:* vicious or virtuous in body or soul.
422	37-38	*with all the power of the laws:* with all our power.
423	7-11	*nor has any legislator either of ancient or of modern times considered it dishonourable for this reason I imagine, because unaware of these distinctions, they were unwilling to throw obstacles in their own way by a vain attempt to dissuade the youth wholly from the practice:* no one whether young or old will call it shameful, in order, I suppose, to save themselves the trouble of trying what speech can do to persuade the youths; for they have no ability for speaking.
423	26-28	*Here the degree[s] of praise or blame to be attributed by law, to this practice, is far better regulated:* In our city we have far better regulations, which, as I said, are not so easily grasped.
423	30	*for one in whom this passion is enkindled:* to one who reflects (J.A.N.).
424	9	*without dishonour:* after this Shelley omits the translation of ὡς πάγκαλον . . . διαπραττομένου, as compassing a most honourable end.
424	14	*facility:* added by Shelley.
424	20	*dishonourable:* add "here," i.e., in Athens.
424	32-33	*placed himself in harmony and desire with that which is consistent with itself:* whereas the lover of a nature that is worthy abides throughout life, as being fused into one with the abiding.
424	39	*time:* time, the generally approved touchstone.
425	2-3	*in the comparison with an unconstrained choice:* added by Shelley.
425	9	omits δεῖ δὴ τὼ νόμω τούτω συμβαλεῖν: Let us compare the two rules.
425	32-33	*for such an one has already shown:* supply "his character."
425	33-34	*in anything to anyone:* Shelley omits τοῦτο δὲ οὐ καλόν, this is not honourable.
425	38	Shelley omits: δοκεῖ γὰρ αὖ...δεδηλωκέναι, this youth is also held to have discovered his nature.

Page	Line	
425	40	*for the sake of becoming more virtuous and wise; a disposition of mind eminently beautiful:* he would make anyone the object of his utmost ardour for the sake of virtuous improvement; and this by contrast is supremely honourable. Thus by all means it is right to bestow this favour for the sake of virtue.
426	7-8	*for so the learned teach me to denote the changes of discourse:* this is the balanced way in which I have been taught by the wise to speak [Jowett].
426	11	*who was reclining close beside him:* whose place was next below him.
426	19	*Whilst you speak, . . . I will follow your directions:* the sooner you speak the better [Bury].
426	35-36	Shelley has omitted the clause καλὸν χαρίζεσθαι . . . ἀκολάστοις αἰσχρόν, that it is right to gratify good men, base to gratify the dissolute.
426	37-38	*whilst those which are bad and diseased, ought to be treated with no indulgence:* but it is a disgrace to do aught but disappoint the bad and the sickly parts, if one aims at being adept.
427	7	*dryness to moisture:* supply "and the rest of them."
427	20	*according:* by.
427	32-37	*the double Love is not distinguishable in music itself; but it is required to apply it to the service of mankind by rhythm and harmony, which is called poetry, or the composition of melody; or by the correct use of songs and measures already composed, which is called discipline; then one can be distinguished from the other, by the aid of an extremely skilful artist:* in the actual system of harmony or rhythm we can easily distinguish these love matters; as yet the double Love is absent: but when we come to the application of rhythm and harmony to social life, whether we construct what are called "melodies," or render correctly, by what is known as "training," tunes and measures already constructed, we find here a certain difficulty and require a good craftsman. Shelley here paraphrases Ficino's version.
427	37	omits πάλιν γὰρ ἥκει ὁ αὐτὸς λόγος, round comes the same conclusion.

Page	Line	
427	37-39	*And the better love ought to be honoured and preserved for the sake of those who are virtuous, and that the nature of the vicious may be changed through the inspiration of the spirit:* well-ordered men, and the less regular only so as to bring them to better order, should be indulged in this Love, and this is the sort we should preserve. The phrase *and that the nature . . . spirit* is added by Shelley.

428 6-7 *this double Love ought to be traced and discriminated:* we must be on the watch as far as may be for either sort of love.

428 9 *contending principles:* two principles (J.A.N.).

428 10-11 *are influenced by the more benignant Love:* when brought together by the orderly love.

428 11 *are harmoniously and temperately intermingled with the seasons:* and taking on a temperate harmony as they mingle.

428 13 After *plants* Shelley omits καὶ οὐδὲν ἠδίκησεν, are guilty of no wrong.

428 14 *is spread widely abroad:* great destruction and wrong does he wreak.

428 17-18 *with which each season of the year is impelled towards the other:* added by Shelley, probably expanding Ficino's *proveniunt.*

428 23 *right government of Love:* cure of Love. Shelley was influenced in his translation by Ficino's *custodiam.*

428 24-25 *and worship him by the sacrifice of good actions:* or to honour and prefer him in all our affairs.

428 33-34 *exclusive dominion:* add "here on earth and in heaven above."

429 5 *predispose us to laughter:* Shelley follows Ficino's version of γελωτοποιεῖς, *risum contra te moves.* Should be "you are buffooning."

429 22 after *mortals* add "he succours mankind."

429 22 *physician of those wounds.* Cf. G. Burges's note in the Bohn translation of the dialogue (III, 508 n. 59): "healer of those (wounds): This is Shelley's happy introduction of the very word required here and which has led me to suggest τραυμάτων for τούτων."

Page	Line	
429	37	After *faces* Shelley omits ἐναντίοις κειμένοις, which looked opposite ways.
429	38	*easy:* added by Shelley.
430	28	*eggs cut:* Shelley follows Ficino's text ὠὰ.
431	1	*weakness:* general indolence.
431	10-11	*but from those of the same sex no such consequence ensues:* and also, if male met with male they might have satiety of their union and a relief, and so might turn their hands to their labours and their interest to ordinary life.
431	12	*From this period:* from such early times [Bury].
431	15	*the half of what:* the indenture of a man [Jowett].
431	18	omits ὁ δὴ τότε ἀνδρόγυνον ἐκαλεῖτο, which was then called man-woman [J.A.N.].
431	27	*familiarity:* general word for the specific details of the Greek.
431	27-28	*These are the youths who, being of a more manly nature, promise the fairest harvest of future excellence:* these are the finest boys and striplings, for they have the most manly nature.
432	12-13	*and traces obscurely the footsteps of its obscure desire:* darkly hinting. Shelley follows Ficino's version closely: *affectum insitum vestigiis signat obscuris.*
432	18-20	*If so . . . undivided:* not a translation but a compression of the Greek.
432	32	*as thin as lispae:* thus become like tokens of split dice. *Vide supra,* page 547, note on page 431, line 16.
432	37-38	*those lost and concealed objects of our love:* of discovering our proper favourites.
433	1	*take up that expression:* ridiculing my discourse. Shelley follows Ficino in omitting the force of κωμῳδῶν.
433	12	*great hopes:* supply "for the future."
433	13	omits ἰασάμενος, heal.
433	17-18	*that we may not interrupt what each has separately to deliver on the subject:* for we want to hear what the others will say in their turn—I rather mean the other two, since Agathon and Socrates are left.

Page	Line	
433	23	*I confide in the fertility of their geniuses:* my confidence is unshaken.
433	27-28	*to confuse me with the enchantments of his wit, sufficiently confused already with the expectation I see in the assembly in favour of my discourse:* to throw a spell over me, . . . so that I may be flustered with the consciousness of the high expectations the audience has formed of my discourse.
433	33-34	*in calmly reciting your compositions in the presence of so great an assembly:* how you sent a straight glance at that vast assembly to show that you meant to do yourself credit with your production.
433	37-38	*to one who rightly balances the value of their suffrages:* to one who is intelligent [J.A.N.].
434	14	*pay:* supply "each of you."
434	32	*of wings:* added by Shelley.
434	34	*who delights in the intercourse of the young:* added by Shelley.
435	3	*those violent and sanguinary crimes:* no gelding or fettering of each other.
435	5	*under the influence of Love:* ever since Love has reigned over the gods.
435	22	*of all the divinities:* added by Shelley.
435	23	*moist and liquid:* supple of form [Birrell and Leslie].
435	27	*liquid and flowing symmetry:* fit proportion and pliancy.
435	28	*contrast and repugnance:* war with one another.
435	31	*most willingly:* added by Shelley.
436	11	omits ὅσον...ἐλλείπειν, and here I must try my best to be adequate.
436	14	omits ἐν κεφαλαίῳ, I speak summarily.
436	16	*in that science according to the discipline of music:* in all composing that has to do with music.
436	26	*that of moulding brass:* metal-work.

Page	Line	
436	27-28	*the mystery of the dominion which he now exercises over Gods and men:* in the pilotage of gods and men.
436	28-30	*So were the Gods taught and disciplined by the love of that which is beautiful; for there is no love towards deformity:* Hence also those dealings of the gods were contrived by Love—clearly love of beauty—astir in them, for Love has no concern with ugliness.
437	2-3	*and fills our vacant hearts with overflowing sympathy:* draws intimacy on. The phrase is typically Shelleyan.
437	5	*showers benignity upon the world:* who brings meekness [J.A.N.] *Benignity* is a favorite word with Shelley.
437	5-6	*before whose presence all harsh passions flee:* who banishes harshness [J.A.N.]. Cf. *Ode to the West Wind* for the phraseology and sentiment here:

> from whose unseen presence the leaves dead
> Are driven, like ghosts from an enchanter fleeing . . .

Page	Line	
437	9	*desired by the unhappy:* desired by those who have no share.
437	9-10	*therefore unhappy because they possess him not:* treasured of such as good share have got.
437	10	*grace:* luxury.
437	12	*defence:* a shipmate [Birrell and Leslie].
437	14	*the best, the loveliest:* supply "leader."
437	26-27	*as to preoccupy all interest in what I say:* and I be hard put to it.
437	38-39	*lest Agathon, scaring my discourse with the head of the eloquent Gorgias, should turn me to stone for speechlessness:* I was afraid that Agathon at the end of his speech would hurl the head of the terrible-speaking Gorgias and gorgonize me into stone for my lack of eloquence [Birrell and Leslie].
438	14	*my attempt must of necessity fail:* added by Shelley.
438	37	*This rule:* Those opening words.
439	8	*for I would learn from you that which I wish to know:* so that you may better grasp my meaning.

Page	Line	
440	1-3	*Is not Love, then, the love of that which is not within its reach, and which cannot hold in security, for the future, those things of which it obtains a present and transitory possession:* would you not define this desire of an object which he does not hold or have as the wish for the continued presence and preservation of what he does hold? [Birrell and Leslie].
440	39	Shelley omits ὅν ἐκείνη ἔλεγε λόγον . . . ὅπως ἂν δύνωμαι, I will try and follow up the points on which Agathon and I have just agreed by narrating to you all on my own account, as well as I am able, the speech she delivered to me.
441	7	*Good words, I entreat you:* peace, for shame. Shelley follows Ficino's *dic meliora.*
441	14-15	*for how can that be called ignorance which arrives at the persuasion of that which it really is:* for what hits on the truth cannot be ignorance.
441	28	*and with truth:* omit.
442	10	*disenchantments:* incantations.
442	32	*he flies low along the ground:* on the bare ground always he lies with no bedding. Shelley follows Ficino's *volans,* which is not in the Greek.
442	38	*exceedingly cautious and prudent, and full of resources:* eager, fertile of wisdom [Birrell and Leslie].
444	1	*the possession:* i.e., of good things.
444	2	*what he desires:* for what end.
444	3	omits ἀληθῆ λέγεις, εἶπον ἔγω, "Quite true," I said.
444	10	omits τὰ δὲ ἄλλα ἄλλοις καταχρώμεθα ὀνόμασιν, there are other names that we commonly abuse.
444	14	omits ἀληθῆ λέγεις, That is true.
444	19	omits ἀληθῆ λέγεις ἔφην, "Quite true," I said.
444	21-22	*which inhabits the heart of every human being:* an expansion of παντί, all-ensnaring [Bury].
445	5	*in what species of actions, does Love peculiarly consist?:* and what is the behaviour whose eagerness and straining are to be termed love?

Page	Line	
445	11	*being such as I am:* not in the Greek.
445	13	*with their future progeny:* not in the Greek.
445	14	*impells:* yearns.
445	22	*Juno:* added by Shelley. The Greek is Εἰλείθυια, of which the Roman equivalent is Lucina.
445	23	*with the generative principle:* added by Shelley.
445	26	*by sadness:* pain. Shelley follows Ficino's *tristitia.*
445	27	*unwillingly:* distressfully [Birrell and Leslie].
445	29-31	*the impulse towards that which is beautiful is intense, on account of the great pain of retaining that which he has conceived:* the phrase *the impulse . . . beautiful* is a translation of ποίησις, which was the reading of Shelley's text; the better reading in modern texts is πτόησις, flutter.
445	33	omits εἶεν...ἦν δ' ἐγώ, Be it so, I said.
445	39	*in addition:* one time.
446	2-3	*affected even to weakness and disease by the impulse of their love:* they are all sick and amorously disposed.
446	23	omits "blood."
446	31	follows Ficino in translating μελέτη, *meditatio.*
446	34-35	*tho' for ever displaced and restored:* added by Shelley.
447	18	*which they have obtained:* added by Shelley.
447	33-34	*what he has conceived:* added by Shelley.
447	40	*is inspired with an overflowing persuasion to declare:* a typical Shelleyan touch for εὐπορεῖ λόγων, he is resourceful in discoursing.
448	5-6	*whose image:* added by Shelley.
448	10	omits ζηλῶν, envying.
448	12	omits εἰ...βούλει, or only look.
448	12	*of his soul:* added by Shelley.
448	12-13	*to be the guardians:* saviours [Birrell and Leslie].

Page	Line	
448	16	*as the pledges of that love which subsisted between them and the beautiful:* esteemed . . . for the number of goodly deeds shown forth in them, the manifold virtues they begot.
448	21-23	*Your own meditation, O Socrates, might perhaps have initiated you in all these things which I have already taught you on the subject of Love:* into these love-matters even you, Socrates, might haply be initiated.
448	23	*those perfect and sublime ends:* the rites and revelations.
448	23-24	*are only the means:* i.e., for the properly instructed.
448	26-27	*to trace the obscure depth of the subject:* try . . . to follow.
448	28	*beautiful forms:* beautiful bodies.
448	30	omits ἐάν...ὁ ἡγούμενος: if his conductor guides him aright.
448	34-35	*and would therefore remit much of his ardent preference towards one, through his perception of the multitude of claims upon his love:* he must make himself a lover of all beautiful bodies, and slacken the stress of his feeling for one by condemning it and counting it a trifle.
449	1-3	*the beauty and the conformity which there is in the observation of its duties and laws, and to esteem little the mere beauty of the outward form:* to contemplate the beautiful as appearing in our observances and our laws, and to behold it all bound together in kinship and so estimate the body's beauty as a slight affair. Shelley compresses into *conformity* the entire phrase "and to behold it . . . kinship."
449	6	*his fellow:* child.
449	8-9	*ocean of intellectual beauty:* "intellectual" added by Shelley; cf. *Hymn to Intellectual Beauty*, page 196, *supra*.
449	18	omits πρῶτον: First of all.
449	32-33	*correct system of Love:* by the right method of boy-loving ascends.
449	38	*forms:* bodies; omits "institutions."
449	39	*and from institutions:* from beautiful habits to [J.A.N].
450	4-5	*exclaimed the stranger prophetess:* the Mantinean woman. Shelley follows Ficino here.

Page   Line

450   5-6   *for men to live:* supply "if anywhere" [Birrell and Leslie], εἴπερ που ἄλλοθι.

450   13-14   *original . . . the supreme, the self-consistent:* not in the Greek.

450   14-15   *What must be the life of him who dwells with and gazes on that which it becomes us all to seek?:* Do you call it a pitiful life for a man to lead—looking that way, observing that vision by the proper means, and having it ever with him.

450   16-18   *Think you not that to him alone is accorded the prerogative of bringing forth, not images and shadows of virtue, for he is in contact not with a shadow but with reality; with virtue itself:* Do but consider, she said, that there only will it befall him, as he sees the beautiful through that which makes it visible, to breed not illusions but true examples of virtue, since his contact is not with illusion but with truth.

450   36-37   *say that we have already done drinking:* say we are not drinking but just about to retire.

451   11   *come in:* supply "on these terms," ἐπὶ ῥητοῖς.

451   12   omits ἀναθορυβῆσαι, all boisterously acclaimed him.

451   13-14   *and though Socrates was just before his eyes:* he so held them before his eyes that he failed to notice Socrates.

452   13   *stupidly:* simply [Birrell and Leslie].

452   14-15   *of a wise and excellent father:* the adjectives should be in the superlative degree.

452   32   *Good words:* come, enough of this. Shelley follows Ficino's *bona verba.*

452   38   *and to misrepresent me:* added by Shelley.

453   1   *I obey you willingly:* I will not delay talking [Birrell and Leslie]. Shelley follows Ficino's *parebo . . . quam libentissimus.*

453   6   omits εὐπόρως, fluently [J.A.N.].

453   7-8   *by comparing him to a certain statue:* by imagery [Birrell and Leslie].

453   8   *this statue:* this imagery [Birrell and Leslie].

Page	Line	
453	16	*Are you not scornful and petulant:* you are a busy mocker [Birrell and Leslie]. Shelley follows Ficino's *procax & contumeliosus* for ὑβριστής.
453	18-20	*For Marsyas, and whoever now pipes the music that he taught (for that music which is of Heaven is described as being taught by Marsyas) enchants men through the power of the mouth:* His lips indeed had power to entrance mankind by means of instruments; a thing still possible today for anyone who can pipe his tunes; for the music of Olympus's flute belonged, I may tell you, to Marsyas his teacher.
453	21	*be he skilful or not:* whether a fine flute-player or a paltry flute-girl.
453	25-26	*For when we hear Pericles, or any other accomplished orator:* when we hear any other person—quite an excellent orator perhaps.
453	29-30	*and retained, as it were, by the discourse clinging to our mind:* entranced.
453	31	*I am a great deal too drunk:* that I might appear to be absolutely tipsy.
454	3	*my friends:* not in the Greek.
454	5	omits βίᾳ, perforce.
454	28	*wisdom:* added by Shelley.
454	32-33	*lives among men, making all the objects of their admiration the playthings of his irony:* he spends his whole life in chaffing and making game of his fellow-men.
454	34	*divine:* added by Shelley on the basis of Ficino's *divinas . . . imagines.*
454	38	*on our first intimacy:* added by Shelley.
454	39-40	*was determined to seize so favourable an opportunity:* I supposed I had here a godsend and a rare stroke of luck.
455	11-12	*we were very often stript:* trained. Shelley here translates literally the force of συνεγυμνάζετο.
455	22	*motioned to depart:* wanted to go.
455	27	*wine tells truth, whether with or without youth:* note the rhyme; and *vide supra,* page 400 n. 68.

Page	Line	
455	28-29	*I cannot pass over, though I have undertaken to praise Socrates, so proud and scornful a deed:* I consider it dishonest, when I have started on the praise of Socrates, to hide his deed of lofty disdain.
455	32	*mitigation of:* not in the Greek.
455	33	*by something more keen and vehement:* by a more painful creature, in the most painful way that one can be bitten.
455	37	*not ungenerous:* not ungifted.
456	7	*touching him:* shaking him [J.A.N.]. Shelley follows Ficino's *tetigi*.
456	17	*companion or guide:* ally.
456	21	After *Alcibiades* Shelley omits κινδυνεύεις τῷ ὄντι οὐ φαῦλος εἶναι, you can really be no blockhead [Birrell and Leslie].
456	25	*If:* supply "on espying this."
456	38-39	*and casting this garment:* I wrapped my own coat about him.
457	1	*that very old cloak that he has got on now:* not in the Greek.
457	3	*which I had thus exposed to his rejection:* the very thing on which I prided myself.
457	7	*contest:* state.
457	17	*disconsolately:* not in the Greek.
457	17-18	*Such as I have declared was the event of what I attempted:* now all . . . this . . . had already happened to me.
457	22	omits ἀποληφθέντες: cut off [Bury].
457	24	*enjoy our military fare:* enjoy it to the full. Shelley follows Ficino's *mensaque militari*.
457	27	*either then or at any other time:* added by Shelley.
457	26-27	after the phrase *no person . . . time* Shelley omits τούτου . . . ἔσεσθαι, Of this power I expect we shall have a good test in a moment.
457	31-32	*put fleeces under their feet, and bound their legs with hairy skins:* after putting on our shoes we muffled up our feet with felt and little fleeces.

Page   Line
457   34   *so delicately:* added by Shelley.

457   34-35 *so that the soldiers thought that he did it to mock their want of fortitude:* the soldiers looked askance at him, thinking that he despised them.

457   37   Shelley omits ἅμα...ἐστήξοι, thus they waited to see if he would go on standing all night too.

458   7   *I ought not to omit what Socrates is in battle:* Then, if you care to hear of him in battle—for there also he must have his due.

458   17   *Delius:* Delium.

458   18   *heavily armed:* under arms.

458   26-27 *for he walked and darted his regards around with a majestic composure, looking tranquilly both on his friends and enemies:* he stepped along, as his wont is in our streets, "strutting like a proud marsh-goose, with ever a side-long glance," turning a calm sidelong look on friend and foe alike. Shelley follows Ficino's version.

458   32   *such a countenance as that of Socrates even in defeat:* who show this disposition in war.

459   8-10 *the phrases and expressions which he employs, fold around his exterior the skin, as it were, of a rude and wanton Satyr:* on the outside they are clothed with such absurd words and phrases—all, of course, the gift of a mocking satyr.

459   12   *this is his perpetual custom:* he seems always to be using the same terms for the same things.

459   14-16 *he would then find that they alone of all that enters into the mind of man to utter, had a profound and persuasive meaning:* first of all you will discover that they are the only speeches which have any sense in them.

459   26   *Diocles:* supply "and any number of others," καὶ ἄλλους πάνυ πολλούς.

460   19   *no sooner reclined:* was getting up in order to seat himself by Socrates.

460   19-20 *took their places on the vacant couches:* They marched straight into the party and seated themselves.

Page	Line	
460	29	*passed round and round:* from left to right.

460   30-31   *the beginning of their discussion Aristodemus said that he did not recollect, because he was asleep:* As to most of the talk, Aristodemus had no recollection, for he had missed the beginning and was also rather drowsy.

460   34-35   *They, rather convicted than convinced, went to sleep:* While they were being driven to this, and were feebly following it, they began to nod. Shelley's reading follows Ficino's *coacti potius quam persuasi.*

460   35   *Aristophanes first awoke:* the first to slumber [Birrell and Leslie]; *vide supra,* page 555, note on page 460, line 35.

460   37   *following him:* supply "as usual," ὥσπερ εἰώθει ἔπεσθαι.

460   37-39   *and coming to the Lyceum he washed himself, as he would have done anywhere else, and after having spent the day there in his accustomed manner, went home in the evening:* on arriving at the Lyceum, he washed himself, and then spent the rest of the day in his ordinary fashion; and so, when the day was done, he went home for the evening and reposed. Here Shelley follows the Bipont text, which is badly punctuated: καὶ ἐλθόντα εἰς Λύκειον, ἀπονιψάμενον ὥσπερ ἄλλοτε, τὴν ὅλην ἡμέραν διατρίβειν· καὶ οὕτω διατρίψαντα, εἰς ἑσπέραν οἴκοι ἀναπαύεσθαι.

The Ion

468   19   *Homer, the most admirable of them all:* the best and divinest poet of all.

468   22   *the whole scope and intention of the poet:* what the poet says.

468   29-30   *nor any other rhapsodist of the present times:* nor any one that the world has ever seen.

468   32   *I am persuaded of your eminent skill:* that is good news.

468   34-35   *hear me declaim upon Homer:* hearing how well I have embellished Homer.

468   35   *from his admirers* 1840: from the Homeridae. Shelley follows Ficino's *qui Homerum studiosi sunt.*

469   10-11   *[Whether] do you demonstrate these things better in Homer or Hesiod: vide supra,* page 556, note on page 469, line 10.

Page   Line
469   17   *or a diviner:* one of the good seers.

469   28-30   *social intercourse, and of the distinct functions and characters of the brave man and the coward, the professional and private person:* intercourse of men, good and bad, lay and professional.

469   32   *phaenomena:* happenings.

470   2-4   *Amongst a number of persons employed in solving a problem of arithmetic, might not a person know, . . . which had given the right answer:* when several people are talking about number, and one of them speaks better than the rest, I suppose there is someone who will distinguish the good speaker?

470   12   [*whether*]: *vide supra,* page 556, note on page 469 line 10.

470   19-21   *the same person who is competent to determine the truth, is competent also to determine the falsehood of whatever assertion is advanced on the same subject:* the same person will always distinguish, given the same subject and several persons talking about it, both who speak well and who badly.

470   23-24   *is equally incompetent to determine upon its truth or beauty:* will not distinguish the good one either, where the subject is the same.

470   34-35   *as it expresses less correctly:* a mistranslation of ὅτι χεῖρον λέγουσιν, you could distinguish also the inferiority of the worse speakers.

470 l. 40-   *inasmuch as those subjects are understood by him when*
471 l. 1   *spoken of by one:* added by Shelley.

471   7-8   *as if it were from a trance:* added by Shelley.

471   14   *Is not poetry, as an art or a faculty, a thing entire and one:* there is an art of poetry, I take it, as a whole, is there not?

471   16-17   *with respect to all arts which are severally one and entire:* when one has acquired any other art whatever as a whole.

471   21   omits βουλοίμην...λέγειν, I only wish you were right there.

471   23   *Observe how common, vulgar and level to the comprehension of any one, is the question which I now ask relative to the same consideration belonging to one entire art:* For in regard to this question I asked you just now, observe what a trifling commonplace it was that I uttered—a thing that any man might know—namely, that when one has acquired a whole art the inquiry is the same.

Page	Line	
471	25-26	*Is not painting an art whole and entire:* there is an art of painting as a whole.
472	6	*judge of poetry and rhapsody:* in fluting or harping or minstrelsy or rhapsodizing.
472	16	*inequality of power:* expansion of τοῦτο.
472	17	omits ὃ νυνδὴ ἔλεγον, as I was saying just now.
472	18	*stone:* stone itself.
472	20	omits ταὐτὸν τοῦτο ποιεῖν ὅπερ ἡ λίθος, able to do the very same thing as the stone.
472	23-24	*as the power of the stone circulates through all the links of this series:* and they all depend for this power on that one stone.
472	27-28	*which we admire:* added by Shelley.
472	30	*a spirit not their own:* added by Shelley.
472	30-31	*the composers of lyrical poetry:* Shelley here omits the opening phrase, πάντες γὰρ οἵ τε τῶν ἐπῶν ποιηταὶ οἱ ἀγαθοί, "all the good epic poets," and chooses for the subject the second phrase, καὶ οἱ μελοποιοὶ οἱ ἀγαθοὶ ὡσαύτως, "and the good lyric poets likewise."
472	36	*in which, when they come to their senses, they find nothing but simple water:* the phrases "in which, they find . . . water" are added by Shelley.
472	38-39	*They tell us that these souls, flying like bees from flower to flower:* tell us . . . that the songs they bring us are the sweets they cull from honey-dropping founts.
473	1-2	*arrayed as they are in the plumes of rapid imagination:* Shelley spun all this out of πετόμενοι, winging the air. The phrase is a variant of Till those bright plumes of thought, in which arrayed It over-soared this low and worldly shade . . . (*Epipsychidion*, ll. 15-16).
473	3	*ethereally:* added by Shelley.
473	4	*anything worth calling poetry:* added by Shelley.
473	7-9	*Thus, those who declaim various and beautiful poetry upon any subject, as for instance upon Homer, are not enabled to do so by art or study:* Seeing then that it is not by art that

they compose and utter so many fine things about the deeds of men—as you do about Homer—but by a divine dispensation.

473   18-20   *to have deprived all poets, prophets, and soothsayers of every particle of reason and understanding, the better to adapt them to their employment as his ministers and interpreters:* takes away the mind of these men and uses them as his ministers, just as he does soothsayers and godly seers.

473   27   *a gift of the Muses:* an invention of the Muses.

473   27-29   *I think you will agree with me that examples of this sort are exhibited by the God himself to prove that those beautiful poems:* For the god, as it seems to me, intended him to be a sign to us that we should not waver or doubt that these fine poems.

473   30-31   *each excellent in proportion to the degree of his inspiration:* according as each is possessed by one of the heavenly powers.

473   32   ἐξεπίτηδες omitted in the translation, the god of *set purpose* sang the finest of songs.

474   10   *is not your soul transported into the midst of the actions:* does your soul in an ecstasy suppose herself to be among the scenes.

474   19   after *sacrifice* omits the translation of μηδὲν ἀπολωλεκὼς τούτων, having been despoiled of none of his finery.

474   25-26   *For I see every one of them upon their seats aloft, weeping and looking miserable:* for I look down upon them from the platform and see them at such moments crying and turning awestruck eyes upon me and yielding to the amazement of the tale.

475   6-7   *when any one proposes the verses of any other poet as the subject of my recitation:* when anyone recites the work of another poet.

475   10   *by divine . . . election:* by divine dispensation; cf. page 475, line 16, and page 481, line 12, *supra*.

475   13-14   *accommodating their words and their dress to the rhythm of that music:* have plenty of gestures and phrases for that tune; omits τῶν δέ ἄλλων οὐ φροντίζουσιν, but do not heed any other.

Ficino's version here is: *ad eum concentum decentibus verbis & figuris abundant, alios vero contemnunt;* the 1840 edition here reads *and abound with verse and gestures for his songs alone, and care for no other,* which follows Ficino closely.

475   17-18   *an excellence in panegyrizing and illustrating this Poet:* this phrase is an expansion of 'Ομήρου... δεινὸς εἶ ἐπαινέτης, your skill in praising Homer.

475   32-33   *If you do not remember the passages, I will quote the verses to you:* If I can recall the lines, I will quote them to you.

477   33-37   *Consider if you are not inspired to make some such demand as this to me: Come, Socrates, since you have found in Homer a complete and fit description of these arts, assist me also in the enquiry as to his competence in determining on the subject of soothsayers and divination; and how far he speaks well or ill on such subjects:* Then please observe: suppose you were questioning me and should ask: "Since therefore, Socrates, you find it is for these several arts to appraise the passages of Homer that belong to each, be so good as to make out those also that are for the seer and the seer's art, and show me the sort of passages that come under his ability to distinguish whether they are well or ill done"; observe how easily and truly I shall answer you.

478   25-27   *For we have both in our turn recited from the Odyssey and the Iliad, passages relating to vaticination, to medicine and the piscatorial art:* now you must do as I did, and in return for my picking out from the *Odyssey* and the *Iliad* the kinds of passage that belong severally to the seer, the doctor, and the fisherman, you have now to pick out for me.

478   29-30   *for a rhapsodist is competent above all other men to consider and pronounce on whatever has relation to his art:* which he [a rhapsodist] should be able to consider and distinguish beyond the rest of mankind.

479   8   *do you profess:* does he profess.

479   21-23   *To take your example, in the driving of cattle a rhapsodist would know much better than a herdsman what ought to be said to a slave engaged in bringing back a herd of oxen that had run wild:* For instance, if the slave is a cowherd, you say the rhapsode will know what the other should say to pacify his cows when they get fierce, but the cowherd will not.

Page Line

480   19 *Be convinced of it O Socrates:* omits ταῦτά γε ἐκ τῶν Ὁμήρου μαθών, that I owe to my study of Homer.

481   5   *multiplicity of shapes:* a compression of στρεφόμενος ἄνω καὶ κάτω, twisting about this way and that.

481   13 *and incompetent:* added by Shelley.

Errors in translation and variants from the Greek in Shelley's translation of two passages in the *Ion* found in the notebook containing *A Defence of Poetry:*

Fragment I

482   13 *which:* after this word Shelley omits the translation of Εὐριπίδης... Ἡρακλείαν (533d3-4), which Euripides named a magnet, but most people call "Heraclea stone."

482   16-20 *Thus poetry, being itself divinely inspired, communicates this inspiration to others, until a long chain is made every link of which is a human spirit and the first [link] of which is attached to that of the [poet]:* In the same manner also the Muse inspires men herself, and then by means of these inspired persons the inspiration spreads to others, and holds them in a connected chain.

482   26 *find:* draw.

482   28 *more:* after this word Shelley omits the translation of καὶ τῶν μελοποιῶν...λέγουσι, that the soul of the lyric poets does the same thing, by their own report.

Fragment II

482   29 omits δήπουθεν, I believe.

482   32 *aethereally:* added by Shelley.

Menexenus

487   3   Shelley follows Ficino in omitting the force of μάλιστα, especially.

487   19 *fortunate:* added by Shelley.

487   25-26 *enlarging upon every topic remotely, or immediately connected with the subject:* ascribing to each both what he has and what he has not.

487   31-34 *I appear to my self immeasurably more honourable and generous than before, and many of the strangers who are*

Page   Line

accustomed to accompany me, regard me with additional
veneration, after having heard these relations: I . . . imagine
myself to have become all at once taller and nobler and more
handsome.   And as I am generally accompanied by some
strangers, who listen along with me, I become in their eyes
also all at once more majestic.

488   2-3   *and the penetrating melody of the words descends through*
the ears into the mind, and clings to it: so persistently does
the speech and voice of the orator ring in my ears.

488   3-4   *three or four days:* fourth or fifth day.

488   18   *contends for the approbation of those whom he praises:* in
the presence of the very men whom he is praising.

488   32-33   *should be capable of great energy of speech:* should be clever
at speaking.

488   34   *instructed in a manner totally different from me:* less well
taught than I.

488   35   *Antiphon the son of Rhamnusius:* Antiphon the Rhamnusian
[i.e., from the deme Rhamnus].

489   8-10   *I learned it from her; and she is so good a schoolmistress,*
that I should have been beaten if I had not been perfect in
my lesson: for I learnt it, to be sure, from her as she went
along, and I nearly got a flogging whenever I forgot.

489   17-18   *who, being old, attempt to repeat a pleasant discourse:* at my
age, seem to you to be playing like a child.

489   23-24   *in whose honour the oration is supposed to have been deliv-*
ered: added by Shelley.

Fragments of the Republic

495   I. 370e5-371d2.

495   2   *situation:* region.

495   3   *who might undertake to conduct:* who will bring in.

495   6   *needed:* supply παρ' ὧν . . . χρεία, from whom they procure what they themselves require.

495   6   omits ἦ γάρ; Δοκεῖ μοι, will he not? I think so.

495   7   *to produce:* supply "at home," οἴκοι.

Page	Line	
495	8-9	*to remunerate those who conduct the imports:* those of whom they have need.
495	9	omits πλειόνων γάρ, yes, more.
495	12	omits ἢ γάρ;...πάνυ γε, "are they not?" "Yes." "We shall also need traders, then." "Assuredly."
495	12-13	*which these necessities produce:* added by Shelley.
495	13	*other persons:* quite a number of others.
495	13-14	*accustomed to:* expert in.
495	14	omits συχνῶν μέντοι... τὶ δὲ δή, quite a number. But again.
495	15	*be transported from one to another:* share with one another.
495	22	*and the profit of it:* added by Shelley.
495	24-25	*the arrangement between the buyer and the seller:* expansion of διακονίαν.
495	25	*In constituted:* in well constituted.
495	33	*any other:* supply ἔργον, task.
495	27	omits αὐτοῦ γὰρ δεῖ μένοντας, they must wait there in the agora.
495	28-29	*for a similar equivalent:* added by Shelley.
495	30	II. 372a-e.
495	31	III. 373a-e7.
495	27	omits ὄψα, πέμματα, relishes, cakes.
495	35	*food:* shoes.
495	35	*mosaic-work:* embroidery. Shelley was probably influenced by Ficino's *varietatis artificia.*
495	35-36	omits καὶ πάντα τὰ τοιαῦτα κτητέον...ἔφη, procure . . . similar adornments.
495 l. 37- 496 l. 1		*This city, which is of a healthy proportion, will not suffice:* for that healthy state is no longer sufficient.
496	2	*Huntsmen:* the entire class of huntsmen.
496	7	*ministers to pleasure and necessity:* expansion of διάκονοι.

Page	Line	

496   8   *tutors:* omit.

496   8   *manufacturers:* cooks.

496   9-10   *which were not wanted in our more modest city:* there were none of these creatures in our former city, for we had no need of them.

496   10-11   *a multitude of others to administer to other animals, which would then become necessary articles of food:* other cattle in great numbers if they are to be eaten, shall we not?

496   13   omits πολύ γε, much.

496   14   omits ἢ πῶς λέγομεν...ἔφη, "Is that so or not?" "It is."

496   15   *our neighbours:* Shelley omits εἰ μέλλομεν ... τοσοῦτον μόνον, "if we are to have enough for pasture and ploughing, and they in turn of ours if they too abandon themselves to the unlimited acquisition of wealth, disregarding the limit set by our necessary wants." "Inevitably, Socrates." "We shall go to war as the next step, Glaucon—or what will happen?" "What you say," he said. "And we are not yet to speak," said I, "of any evil or good effect of war, but only to affirm that we have further discovered the origin of war, namely, from those things from which the greatest disasters, public and private, come to states when they come."

496   18   IV. 377b11-377c4.

496   19   *to compose them according to the rules of moral beauty:* We must begin, then, it seems, by a censorship over our story-makers, and what they do well we must pass.

496   24   V. 378d7-378e1.

496   27-29   *but the opinions produced by a literal acceptation of that which has no meaning, or a bad one, except in an allegorical sense, are often irradicable:* but whatever opinions are taken into the mind at that age are wont to prove indelible and unalterable.

496   30   VI. 379c2-c7.

496   31   *things:* supply τοῖς ἀνθρώποις, for mankind; Shelley also omits the phrase πολλῶν δὲ ἀναίτιος, but of many things not the cause.

Page	Line	
496	31-34	*Among the great variety of events which happen in the course of human affairs, evil prodigiously overbalances good in everything which regards men:* For good things are far fewer with us than evil.
496	35-36	*which should never be imputed as an effect to God:* and not in God.
496	37-38	VII. The edition to which these pages refer is E. Massey, *Platonis de Republica,* Cambridge, 1713; *vide supra,* page 564.
497	1	VIII. 380c1-d6.
497	2	*vulgar:* added by Shelley.
497	3	*for the sake of effect:* a mistranslation of ἐξ ἐπιβολῆς, by design.
497	5	*and offering vain images of himself to our imagination:* causing us to believe such things about him. Shelley follows literally Ficino's *vanasque de se nobis imagines offerentem.*
497	9	IX. 381b1-2.
497	13	X. 381e1-e6.
497	14	*that Gods:* certain gods.
497	15	*resembling strangers, in all sorts of forms:* strangers from all manner of lands.
497	17	XI. 382a4-c1.
497	19	*me:* omit.
497	20-21	*to falsify in matters of the highest concern to himself concerning those matters:* falsehood in the most vital part of themselves, and about the most vital concerns.
497	22	omits ἐκεῖ, there.
497	24	omits περὶ τὰ ὄντα, about realities.
497	24-25	*to possess that which is not true:* to have and hold the falsehood there.
497	25-26	*This is truly to be called falsehood, this ignorance and error in the mind itself:* is what all men would least of all accept, and it is in that case that they loathe it most of all.

Page   Line
497   26-30   *What is usually called falsehood, or deceit in words, is but a*
               voluntary imitation of what the mind itself suffers in the in-
               voluntary possession of that falsehood, an image of later birth,
               and scarcely, in a strict and complete sense, deserving the
               name of falsehood: a somewhat inaccurate paraphrase of the
               Greek, which runs: But surely it would be most wholly right,
               as I was just now saying, to describe this as in very truth
               falsehood—ignorance namely in the *soul* of the man deceived.
               For the falsehood in *words* is a copy of the affection in the
               soul, an after-rising image of it and not an altogether unmixed
               falsehood.

497   31   XII. 386a6-b6.

497   36   omits Μὰ Δία...Τί δέ, "No indeed, I do not," he replied.

498   1   XIII. 387d1-e7.

498   3   omits Ἀνάγκη...ἢ οὔ, "That necessarily follows," he said,
           "from the other." "Consider," said I, "whether we shall be
           right in thus getting rid of them or not."

498   9   *happily:* added by Shelley.

498   12-14   *and that, on the occurrence of such contingencies, he would*
               support them with moderation and mildness, by no means
               bursting into lamentations, or resigning himself to despond-
               ence: "Then he makes the least lament and bears it most
               moderately when any such misfortune overtakes him." "Cer-
               tainly." "Then we should be right in doing away with the
               lamentations of men of note," etc. Shelley has combined
               both sentences.

498   18   XIV. 395d1-3.

498   23   XV. 401b1-c3.

498   25   *virtue's manners:* omits ἢ μὴ παρ' ἡμῖν ποιεῖν, or else not
           write poetry among us.

498   26   *either in sculpture, or painting, or architecture:* added by
           Shelley.

498   28   *architectural arrangements:* omits μήτε ἐν ἄλλῳ μηδενὶ
           δημιουργουμένῳ, or in any other product of their art.

498   31   *deformity . . . like cattle:* added by Shelley.

Page   Line
498   33   *composed of these many evil things:* interpolated to explain
the general sense of the passage or explanatory of πολλά.
401c1.

499   5   XVI. 405a6-b4.

499   10-11   *(so desperate are these diseases of body and mind):* added by
Shelley as his own comment; *vide supra,* page 564.

499   12-14   *to need to be instructed in what is just or what is needful,
as by a master and a judge, with regard to your personal
knowledge and suffering?:* to have to make use of a justice
imported from others, who thus become your masters and
judges, from lack of such qualities in yourself?

499   17   XVII. 405c8-d4.

499   20   *and the superfluous indulgences which we have already condemned:* and such a regimen as we have described. Here
Shelley follows Ficino's error: *sed ob desidiam & quae in
victu supra damnavimus.*

499   24-25   *for the new diseases which are the progeny of your luxury
and sloth:* the phrase, with the exception of *for the diseases,*
is added by Shelley.

499   26   XVIII. 406a7-b8; 407c7-d8.

499   27   (παιδοτρίβης, *Magister palaestrae*): the Latin is not Ficino's
phrase, which is *exercitandorum magister iuvenum;* Shelley
transliterated paedotribe (cf. *Symposium,* page 431, lines 16,
23, page 432, line 32, *supra,* for other examples) and added
the Greek word with its Latin meaning, which he found on
looking the word up in Scapula's *Lexicon Graeco-Latinum*
(Julian *Works* IX, 254: "to accept Scapula as my mentor").

499   30   omits πῇ δή; ἔφη...ἦν δ' ἐγώ, "How so?" he said; . . .
said I.

499   32   *he postponed all other purposes to the care of medicating
himself:* lived through his days unfit for the business of life.

499   33-34   *through his whole life was subject to an access of his malady:*
suffering the tortures of the damned if he departed.

499   35   *dying by degrees:* struggling against death.

499   37   *Aesculapius never pursued these systems, nor Machaon or
Podalirius:* added by Shelley himself, who interpolates the

Page   Line

names of Machaon and Podalirius directly or indirectly from *Iliad*, II, 732, where they are mentioned as the sons of Aesculapius. An example of indirect source is Barthélemy's *Travels of Anacharsis*, III, 92, which Shelley read in 1818; *vide supra*, pages 132-133. Shelley takes the name Aesculapius (407c7) and then skips down to 407d4, τὰ δ' εἴσω... ἐπιχέοντα (407d4-6), "by diet and by gradual evacuations and infusions," etc. Shelley evidently was not translating but writing an introduction to or paraphrase of the passage.

500   4   XIX. 409b3-409d7.

500   5-7   *because he ought not to have acquired a knowledge of what injustice is, until his understanding has arrived at maturity:* a paraphrase of ὀψιμαθῆ γεγονότα τῆς ἀδικίας.

500   11-12   *from his observations of them as resulting in others:* a paraphrase of ἐπιστήμη.

500   12   *honourable judge:* noblest kind of judge.

500   14   *wise:* cunning.

500   17   *deriving experience from the example afforded by a consideration of his own conduct and character:* a paraphrase of "fixing his eyes on the patterns within himself."

500   19-20   *with men of universal experience and real virtue:* with the good and his elders.

500   20-21   *he exposes the defects resulting from such experience as he possesses:* he appears stupid.

500   22-23   *with which to compare the appearances manifested in others:* added by Shelley.

500   26-27   *one who has examples within himself of that upon which he is to pronounce:* added by Shelley, but contradicts what Plato says in 409b6.

On a Passage in Crito

504   7-8   *Indeed, your city cannot subsist, because the laws are no longer of avail:* cf. *Crito*, 50b2-5, ἢ δοκεῖ σοι... διαφθείρονται, or do you think that state can exist and not be overturned, in which the decisions reached by the courts have no force but are made invalid and annulled by private persons?

Page	Line	
504	8-9	*when those who deserve to be nourished in the Prytanea at the public expense:* cf. *Apology,* 36d6-7: πρέπει οὕτως ὡς τὸν τοιοῦτον ἄνδρα ἐν πρυτανείῳ σιτεῖσθαι, so fitting as that such a man be given his meals in the prytaneum.

| 504 | 13-15 | *Although you have inflicted an injustice on me, which is sufficient, according to the opinions of the multitude, to authorise me to consider you and me as in a state of warfare:* cf. *Crito,* 49b10-11, οὐδὲ ἀδικούμενον ἄρα ἀνταδικεῖν, ὡς οἱ πολλοὶ οἴονται, ἐπειδή γε οὐδαμῶς δεῖ ἀδικεῖν, and we ought not even to requite wrong with wrong, as the world thinks, since we must not do wrong at all. |

| 504 | 20-23 | *delightful for me to die . . . be my portion should I live:* cf. Medwin, *Life of Shelley,* page 435. |

Epigrams from Plato

1. *Venus and the Muses*
   This epigram is a translation of *Anthologia Palatina,* IX, 39, which attributes the epigram to Musicius, whereas Diogenes Laertius (III, 33) attributes it to Plato. Shelley's version is a paraphrase rather than a strict translation. A comparison with the Greek shows the following changes and errors in translation:

| 511 | 1-2 | *once threat'ning vow'd / Unless the Nine her sway allow'd:* Honour Aphrodite, ye maidens. |

| 511 | 3-4 | *That Cupid's never-erring dart / Should quickly pierce them to the heart / :* or I will arm Eros against you. |

| 511 | 6 | *The little urchin we defy:* your brat has no wings to fly to us. |

II. *To Stella*
   This epigram is a translation of *Anthologia Palatina* VII, 670 (Diogenes Laertius, III, 29). The translation is essentially accurate. Shelley expands πρίν into *ere thy fair light had fled,* and λάμπεις to *giving new splendour.*

III. *Translated, from an Epigram of Plato cited in the Apologia of Apuleius*
   This epigram is a translation of Apuleius's *Apologia,* 10 (*Anthologia Palatina,* VII, 669; Diogenes Laertius, III, 29). A comparison with the text shows that the translation is free.

| 511 | 1 | An expansion of ᾿Αστὴρ ἐμός. |

Page   Line

511   2   *alone* is added by Shelley.

511   3   *yon Heaven of light* is an expansion of οὐρανός.

IIIa. Version of same epigram in *Laon and Cythna*, IX, lines 321-324.

This is a paraphrase rather than a translation of Plato's epigram, which reads: "Thou lookest on the stars, my Star. Would I were heaven to look on thee with many eyes."

IV. *Kissing Agathon*

This epigram is a translation of *Anthologia Palatina*, V, 78 (Diogenes Laertius, III, 32).

511   5   *as if it were departing;* as if it were about to cross over.

IVa. *Another Version*

The version is an improvisation rather than a translation of the Greek. Helena is a substitute for Agathon in the Greek text. For the reasons for the substitution, *vide supra*, pages 315-316. Shelley expands the two lines of the Greek into six. The first three lines, with the exception of the change of the name, render accurately τὴν ψυχὴν 'Αγάθωνα, φιλῶν ἐπὶ χείλεσιν ἔσχον. Lines 4 and 5 do not correspond with the Greek but are rather a paraphrase, especially of διαβησομένη. The last line is added by Shelley.

V. *To Zanthippe*

This epigram is a translation of *Anthologia Palatina*, V, 79-80 (Diogenes Laertius, III, 32). Shelley combines both versions in the manuscript of his translation. A comparison of the first version with the Greek shows:

512   1   Shelley adds *girl* and does not render the force of ἑκοῦσα.

512   3-4 The Greek runs: "if thy thoughts be what I pray they are not."

512   5   *This child of the green tree* is expanded from τοῦτο.

512   5   Shelley in the first version (Va) paraphrases the second epigram (*Anthologia Palatina*, V, 80) with the exception of κἀγὼ καὶ σὺ μαραινόμεθα.

A comparison of the second version of the second epigram (Vb) with the Greek shows a wider variation:

512   1-2 *fill it dearest / With the fresh beauty which thou wearest /* is not in the Greek.

Page	Line	
512	4	*that can never be* is a vivid translation of εἰ δ' ἄρ' ὅ μὴ γίγνοιτο νοεῖς.
512	5	An accurate version of the Greek.

VI. *Circumstance*

This epigram is a translation of *Anthologia Palatina*, IX, 44 (Diogenes Laertius, III, 33). The last four lines are Shelley's own conclusion. The translation is quite accurate.

Page	Line	
512	1	An expansion of βροχόν.
512	3	Shelley translates χρυσόν by *purse*.
512	3	*coming to reclaim his pelf* is an expansion of οὐχ εὑρών.

VII. *Spirit of Plato*

This epigram is a translation of an epitaph on Plato, *Anthologia Palatina*, VII, 62 (Diogenes Laertius III, 44). The translation varies only slightly from the Greek.

Page	Line	
513	2	*To what sublime and star-ypaven home / Floatest thou? / :* tell me, why gazest thou at the starry home of the gods?
513	5	*inherit* is a free rendering of ἔχει.
513	5	*corpse:* earth-born body.

Appendix

Chronological Co-ordination of Shelley's Compositions Influenced by Plato
and Shelley's Reading in the Direct and Indirect Platonic Tradition

Date	Compositions of Shelley Showing Platonic Influence or Reference or Translation from Plato	Date	Reading of Plato in Translation* or in the Original	Date	Reading of Authors Influenced by the Platonic Tradition	For Platonism in These Authors, vide supra, pp.
Jan., 1810	Original Poetry by Victor and Cazire, I	1808-1810	Symposium	1804-1810?	Lucretius	82, 85
				1804-1810?	Albertus Magnus	91
				1804-1810?	Paracelsus	91, 111-112
1809-1810	Fragment: Supposed to be an Epithalamium of Francis Ravaillac and Charlotte Cordé			1810?	Southey, Curse of Kehama	152-155
1811	Epigram of Plato	1810-1811	Alcibiades I*	1810-1811	Dacier's Introduction to Plato	34
June 20, 25, Oct. 15? Nov. 12, 24, 26, Dec. 11, 1811	Letters to Elizabeth Hitchener		Alcibiades II*	1810-1811	Taylor's Introduction to Plato	29
			Theages*	1810-1811	Godwin's Political Justice	146-147
Jan. 7, 20, 1812	Letters to Elizabeth Hitchener		Euthyphro*	1811?	Pope	119-120
			Apology*	1810-1811	Locke	119
			Crito*	1811-1812	Berkeley	121-126
			Phaedo*	1811-1812?	Thomas Reid	127-128

Protagoras*	June, 1811	Southey, Curse of Kehama	152-155
Laches*	July, 1811	Erasmus Darwin	120-121
The Rivals*	1811	Lady Morgan, The Missionary	151-152
The Republic*	1811	Ensor, National Education	151
Parmenides?*	1811	Rousseau, Confessions	134-136
Cratylus?*	1811	Aristotle	82
Timaeus?*			
Banquet?*			
Ion?*			
Analysis, or excerpts or exposition of the Timaeus, Laws, Republic, Epistles, Symposium in Introductory Essay of Dacier's Plato			
	1812?	Milton's Prose Works	108-111
	1812?	Thomas Gray	121
	1812	Gibbon, Decline and Fall of the Roman Empire	131
	1812-1813	French Encyclopedists: Voltaire, Diderot	137-139
To Ireland	1812?		
The Retrospect: Cwm Elan	1812		
An Address to the Irish People	Jan., 1812		
Queen Mab	Aug., 1812- Feb. 19, 1813		

Date	Compositions of Shelley Showing Platonic Influence or Reference or Translation from Plato	Date	Reading of Plato in Translation* or in the Original	Date	Reading of Authors Influenced by the Platonic Tradition	For Platonism in These Authors, vide supra, pp.
1812-1815	The Daemon of the World			(1812-1813)	Cabanis, Rapports du Physique et du Moral de l'Homme	137-139
1812	A Letter to Lord Ellenborough			May-June, 1812	D'Holbach, Système de la Nature	137-139
Dec. 17?, 1812	Letter to Thomas Hookham, Jr.			1812	Sir William Drummond, Academical Questions	147-151
				1812	Godwin, Political Justice	146-147
				1813	Cicero's Philosophical Works	83-85
				1813?	Polybius	85
				1813	Plutarch	86
				1813-1819?	Petrarch	97-98
				1813?	Spinoza	114
				1813	Berkeley	121-126
				1813	Adam Smith, Theory of Moral Sentiments	131
				1813-1814	Dugald Stewart, Outlines of Moral Philosophy	128-129

Date	Work	Title/Author	Pages
1813-?		Erasmus Darwin, *Temple of Nature*	120-121
1813-?		Erasmus Darwin, *Zoönomia*	120-121
1813-?		Kant	145
1813-?		Lord Monboddo, *Of the Origin and Progress of Language*	129-131
1813-?		Sir William Drummond, *Academical Questions*	147-151
1814		Cicero, *Collectanea*	83-85
1814		Dante	95-97
1814		Diogenes Laertius	85-86
1814		Godwin, *Political Justice*	146-147
1814		Goethe	144-145
1814		Wordsworth, *The Excursion*	162-167
Sept. 14, 1814		Wordsworth, *The Excursion*	162-167
Sept. 15, Oct. 5, 1814		Coleridge, *Rime of the Ancient Mariner*	155-162
Sept. 17, 1814		Southey, *Curse of Kehama*	152-155
Sept. 20-24, 1814		Southey, *Thalaba*	152-155
Spring of 1814	*A Refutation of Deism*		
Aug.-Sept., 1814	*The Assassins*		

Date	Compositions of Shelley Showing Platonic Influence or Reference or Translation from Plato	Date	Reading of Plato in Translation* or in the Original	Date	Reading of Authors Influenced by the Platonic Tradition	For Platonism in These Authors, vide supra, pp.
				Oct. 7, 1814	Godwin, Political Science	146-147
				Oct. 14, 1814	Cicero, Collectanea	83-85
				Nov. 24-26, 1814	Wieland, Peregrinus Proteus, Agathon	139-144
				Nov. 29, 1814	Spenser, Faerie Queene	103-107
				Dec. 4, 1814	Diogenes Laertius	85-86
				1815	Cicero's Philosophic Dialogues	83-85
				1815	Vergil	83-85
				1815	Seneca's Works	85
1815	To— Δάχρυσι διοίσω πότμον ἄποτμον			Feb. 13, April 18, May 4-5, 10, 11, 1815	Seneca's Works	85
				1815	Augustine's Confessions	89-90
				1815	Bacon, Novum Organum	114-115
				1815	Spenser, Faerie Queene	103-107
				1815	Shakespeare's Plays	108
				March 14, 1815	Sir Thomas Browne, Religio Medici	118-119

Date	Shelley's Work	Date	Work Read	Pages
		1815	Milton, *Paradise Lost, Paradise Regained, Areopagitica, Lycidas, Comus*	108-111
		1815	Locke, *Essay on Human Understanding*	119
		1815	Gibbon, *Decline and Fall*	131
		Jan. 31, March 21, April 10, 1815	Gibbon, *Decline and Fall*	131
		1815	Rousseau, *Reveries*	134-136
		1815	Southey, *Curse of Kehama*	152-155
		1815	Coleridge, *Poems*	155-162
		1815	Wordsworth, *The Excursion*	162-167
		1815	Wordsworth, *Poems*	162-167
		1816	Lucretius	82, 85
		July 28, 29, 1816	Lucretius	82, 85
		1816	Lucian	85
		1816	Apuleius, *Apologia*	86
Autumn of 1815	*Alastor*			
Late in 1815 or early 1816	*Mutability*			
June 30, 1816	*Hymn to Intellectual Beauty*			
July 23, 1816	*Mont Blanc*			
1816	*Translated from an Epigram of Plato, Cited in the Apologia of Apuleius*			
1816	*On the Punishment of Death*			

Date	Compositions of Shelley Showing Platonic Influence or Reference or Translation from Plato	Date	Reading of Plato in Translation* or in the Original	Date	Reading of Authors Influenced by the Platonic Tradition	For Platonism in These Authors, vide supra, pp.
End of 1816 or early 1817	Essay on Christianity					
End of 1816 or early 1817	On the Doctrines of Christ			1816	Milton, Paradise Lost	108-111
				1816	Montaigne's Essays	112-114
				Sept. 22, 1816	Rousseau, Letters of Émile	134-136
				Sept. 29, Oct. 21, 22, Nov. 10-14, 1816	Lucian	85
1816	Speculations on Metaphysics, III			Oct. 18-27, Nov. 2-5, 7-10, 1816	Montaigne's Essays	112-114
				Nov. 15-22, 1816	Milton, Paradise Lost	108-111
				Nov. 15-23, 1816	Locke, Essay on Human Understanding	119
1816	Speculations on Morals, Julian Works, VII, 72			Nov. 25-26, 28-30, Dec. 1, 3-4, 1816	Gibbon, Decline and Fall	131

Date	Work	Source / Reading	Pages
Nov. 29-30, Dec. 1, 1816		Godwin, *Political Justice*	146-147
1816		Locke, *Essay on Human Understanding*	119
1816		Rousseau, *Letters of Émile*	134-136
1816		Rousseau, *Julie ou la Nouvelle Héloïse*	134-136
1816		Godwin, *Political Justice*	146-147
1816		Coleridge, *Lay Sermon*	155-162
1816		Peacock, *Headlong Hall*	49-54, 167-168
1817	*To Constantia, Singing*		
Feb. 23, 1817		"Several of the Works of Plato"	
1817	Translation of *Menexenus* (part)	*Menexenus*	
1817	*Fragment: Igniculus Desiderii*	*Apology? Republic?* (part?) *Phaedo?* (part?)	
1817	*Fragment: Amor Aeternus*	*Symposium*	
1817		Apuleius, *Story of Psyche*	86
Aug. 13, 1817	*Symposium*		
March 15?- Sept. 23, 1817	*Laon and Cythna*		
1817		*Phaedrus* (part)	

Date	Compositions of Shelley Showing Platonic Influence or Reference or Translation from Plato	Date	Reading of Plato in Translation* or in the Original	Date	Reading of Authors Influenced by the Platonic Tradition	For Platonism in These Authors, vide supra, pp.
Begun in summer of 1817, laid aside end of Sept, finished by Aug. 14, 1818	Rosalind and Helen			1817	Spenser, *Faerie Queene*	103-107
				April 13, 14, 23, 24, 25, 29; May 9, 13,15, 19-21, June 5-6, 14, July 10, 11, 22, 1817	Spenser, *Faerie Queene*	103-107
				May 9, 1817	Apuleius, *Story of Psyche*	86
Aug. ?, 1817	Note on Banquet of Plato					
Nov. 11-12, 1817	An Address to the People on the Death of Princess Charlotte			1817	Hume, *Essays*	126
				1817	Gibbon, *Decline and Fall*	131
				Aug. 5, 9, 13, 17, Dec. 24-31, 1817	Gibbon, *Decline and Fall*	131
Dec., 1817	Prince Athanase					
Dec., 1817	On Godwin's Mandeville			1817	Berkeley	121-126

Date	Writings	Date	Readings	Pages
		1817	Godwin, *Political Justice*	146-147
		Nov. 28?, 1817	Peacock, *Rhododaphne*	49-54, 167-168
Dec., 1817, or Feb. 18?, 1818	*On Rhododaphne*			
		Nov. 29, Dec. 1, 1817	Godwin, *Political Justice*	146-147
Dec. 7, 1817	Letter to Godwin	1817	Godwin, *Mandeville*	146-147
		Dec. 2, 1817	Godwin, *Mandeville*	146-147
		Dec. 12-14, 1817	Berkeley	121-126
		1817-1818?	Forsyth, *Principles of Moral Science*	151
		Dec., 1817-1818	Rousseau, *Discours sur les sciences et les arts*	134-136
		1817; Dec. 8, 1817	Coleridge, *Biographia Literaria*	155-162
		1817	Peacock, *Melincourt*	49-54, 167-168
1818	*Sonnet*	1818	Barthélemy, *Travels of Anacharsis the Younger*	132-133
July 9-20, 1818	Translation of the *Symposium*	July 9-20, 1818	*Symposium*	95-97
July 16, 1818	Letter to John and Maria Gisborne	1818	Gibbon, *Decline and Fall*	131

Date	Compositions of Shelley Showing Platonic Influence or Reference or Translation from Plato	Date	Reading of Plato in Translation* or in the Original	Date	Reading of Authors Influenced by the Platonic Tradition	For Platonism in These Authors, vide supra, pp.
July 25, 1818	Letter to T.L. Peacock			1818	Lucian, Works	85
July 25, 1818	Letter to W. Godwin			Jan. 6, 24, 1818	Vergil, Aeneid VI	83, 85
July-Aug., 1818	A Discourse on the Manners of the Antient Greeks Relative to the Subject of Love	Aug. 4-5, 1818	Phaedrus (part)	April, 1818	Wieland, Aristippus	139-144
Aug. 16, 1818	Letter to T. L. Peacock			April 19, 1818	Dante, Purgatorio	95-97
Sept. 5-Oct. 8, 1818	Prometheus Unbound, Act I			April 22, 1818	Dante, Paradiso	95-97
Oct., 1818	Lines Written Among the Euganean Hills			June 13-17, 1818	Xenophon, Memorabilia	82
Oct. 17, 1818	Letter to Byron	Oct. 20, Nov. 7, 9, 1818	Republic (part)	June 18, 20-21, 1818	Gibbon, Decline and Fall	131
Nov. 7, 9, 1818	Letters to T. L. Peacock			June 22-30, July 2, 5, 6, 1818	Barthélemy, Travels of Anacharsis the Younger	132-133

Date	Work	Plato	Date	Reading	Date	Page
Nov. 25, 1818	*The Coliseum*			Lucian, *Works*	Aug. 16, 1818	85
Dec., 1818	*Stanzas Written in Dejection Near Naples*			Winckelmann, *History of Art*	Dec. 24, 27, 29; 31, 1818, Jan. 2-3, March 14, 1818	144-145
Latter part of 1818	*Note on Republic*					
Autumn of 1818	*Julian and Maddalo*					
Winter of 1818	*Marenghi*					
Latter part of 1818	*On Love*					
1818-1819	*On the Revival of Literature*					
Jan. 24, 1819	Letter to Peacock			Lucretius	March 15, 16, 22, 1819	82, 85
March-April 6, 1819	*Prometheus Unbound,* Acts II-III	*Republic* (part)	1819	Lucretius	1819	82, 85
March-April, 1819	Translation of *Republic* (part)	*Republic*	Oct. 9, 10, 24, 28; Nov. 2, 6, 7, 8, 9, 1819			
May 4-Aug. 8, 1819	*The Cenci*	*Statesman?*	1819			

Date	Compositions of Shelley Showing Platonic Influence or Reference or Translation from Plato	Date	Reading of Plato in Translation* or in the Original	Date	Reading of Authors Influenced by the Platonic Tradition	For Platonism in These Authors, vide supra, pp.
Sept.-Dec., 1819	Love's Philosophy					
Oct. 13 or 14, 1819	Letter to Maria Gisborne			Oct. 20, 1819	Spenser	103-107
Oct. 24?, 1819	Peter Bell III					
1819	Song: To the Men of England					
Nov. 3, Nov. ?, 1819	Letters to Leigh Hunt					
Dec., 1819	Ode to Heaven					
1819	Ye Gentle Visitations of Calm Thought					
1819	On Life					
1819	On the Daemon of Socrates (Based on Xenophon's Memorabilia)					
Nov., 1819	The Moral Teaching of Jesus Christ					
Dec. 23, 1819- May 26, 1820	A Philosophical View of Reform					

1819-1820	Translation from *Republic* 485b10-486b12, in Peck, *op. cit.*, II, 433-434					
Close of 1819	*Prometheus Unbound, Act IV*					
March, 1820	*The Sensitive Plant*	Feb. 14, 16-17, 19, 1820	Reads Plato	1820	Lucretius	82, 85
				March 22, 26, April 1, 4, 1820	Godwin, *Political Justice*	146-147
Early 1820	*Ode to Liberty*	1820	*Phaedrus* (completed)	June 28-30; July 3-6, 8 1820	Lucretius	82, 85
June 15 or July 1, 1820	*Letter to Maria Gisborne*	May 2, 1820	Finishes *Phaedrus*			
1820	*The Cloud*	1820	*Phaedo* (completed)			
June 22, 1820	*To a Skylark*	May 9, 1820	"Reads Phaedon"	1820	Spinoza	114
Aug. 14-16, 1820	*The Witch of Atlas*	1820	*Republic* (completed)	Jan. 5, 8-9, 12, 15-16; March 17, 21-22, 26-31; April 1-2, 4-8; June 3, 1820	Spinoza	114
Aug. 17-25, 1820	*Ode to Naples*	Sept. 4, 9, 1820	*Republic* (completed)	1820	Locke	119
Oct. 22, 1820-Feb, 1821	*Epigrams of Plato*					
1820	*Hymn to Apollo*			1820	Lord Monboddo, *Antient Metaphysics*	129-131

Date	Compositions of Shelley Showing Platonic Influence or Reference or Translation from Plato	Date	Reading of Plato in Translation* or in the Original	Date	Reading of Authors Influenced by the Platonic Tradition	For Platonism in These Authors, vide supra, pp.
1820	*An Allegory*			Sept. 21, 22, 23; Oct. 1, 1820	Lord Monboddo, *Antient Metaphysics*	129-131
1820	*Fiordispina*					
1820	Translation of *Phaedo* (part)			1820	Gillies, *Greece*	131
1820	Note on *Republic, 587e*					
1820	*Una Favola*			Sept. 23; Oct. 1, 1820	Gillies, *Greece*	131
1820	*On a Future State*			1820	Godwin, *Political Justice*	146-147
Nov. 15?, 1820	Letter to Peacock					
Nov., 1820	Letter to Gisborne					
Nov., 1820	Letter to C. Clairmont					
Feb. 1-14?, 1821	*Epipsychidion*	April 19, 1821	"Reads Plato"	Jan. 31, 1821	Dante, *Vita Nuova*	95-97
Feb. 15, 1821	Letter to Peacock					
Feb. 22, 1821	Letter to Ollier					
Feb. 22?-March 12?, 1821	*A Defence of Poetry*					

April 19-June 8, 1821	Adonais	1821	Ion			
Finished by Nov. 6, 1821	Hellas	1821?	Crito	Sept. 1, 1821	Kant	145
1821	Mutability	1821?	Laws			
1821	Sonnet: To the Republic of Benevento	1821	Gorgias			
1821	To——One Word	1821?	Apology?	Nov. 15, 1821	Spinoza	141
1821	Fragments on the Ion	1821?	Timaeus?; or Timaeus of Locri, De anima mundi	End of 1821-1822	Goethe, Faust	144-145
1821	On a Passage in Crito					
1821	On the Devil and Devils			1821	Sir Philip Sidney, Defence of Poesie	107-108
Aug. 22, 1821	Letter to Medwin					
Oct. 20, 1821	Letter to Hogg					
Oct. 22, 1821	Letter to John Gisborne					

Date	Compositions of Shelley Showing Platonic Influence or Reference or Translation from Plato	Date	Reading of Plato in Translation* or in the Original	Date	Reading of Authors Influenced by the Platonic Tradition	For Platonism in These Authors, vide supra, pp.
Begun at close of 1819, resumed Jan. 8, and laid aside by June, 1822	Charles the First	1822	Gorgias	1822	Spinoza	114
Jan., 1822	The Zucca					
1822	The Magnetic Lady to Her Patient					
1822	Lines: When the Lamp is Shattered					
1822	With a Guitar, To Jane					
1822	Epitaph					
Spring and early summer of 1822	The Triumph of Life					
April 10, 1822	Letter to John Gisborne					
April 11, 1822	Letter to Claire Clairmont					

Index

All works cited are included in this index. Information as to place and date of publication may be found in the first citation. Editions of major works are listed under the title of the work; all other books, as well as articles, are listed under the name of the author. This index does not include the names in and thematic substance of either Shelley's translations of Plato or his own poetry and prose quoted in this book.

Planet, 261

Planetary rings, 12

Planets, motions of compared to dance, 110

Plastic nature: and plants, 116; history of concept of, 183; in Coleridge, 160; in Cudworth and Shelley, 116; in Diderot, 138; in Plato, 116; in Pope, 120; in Shelley's *Adonais,* 297; in Wordsworth, 164; *see also* 116, 130, 267, 273, 292, 350

"Plastic stress," 79

Plato:

PLATO

a creative force, 5; a discoverer, 5; and Christianity, 378; and reason, 28; and reform, 27; and the reflection of the eternal, 8; and the temporal, 8; as dynamic creator, 13; as mythopoeic artist, 277; as natural Platonist, 13; as poetic dreamer, 137; attack on art, 346; becomes identified with European philosophical tradition, 7, 9; chained to Car of Life, 315; changes Shelley's philosophy, 61 n. 142; conception of, in eighteenth century, 137; concepts not final, 5; condemned by Shelley for male love, 315-317, 509; contemporary of every thinker and poet, 81; creative spirit of, 8; definition of God, 24; dialectic, 22; dialogues as thought in process, 5; dialogues considered as art are finalities, 5; different facets of Plato in Platonic tradition, 9; discovers and reveals nature rather than creates it, 4; endows thought with variety of concepts and myths, 8; exemplifies creative and dynamic tradition, 9; formulation of thought, 8; fusion with Egyptian philosophy, 117; gives substance to Shelley, 61; grasping of truth through images, 5; hierarchy of values in, 28; his thought an image of the sun of Being, 5; hypotheses, images of Being, 5; ideal poet-philosopher for Shelley, 239; ideas constitute character and mentality of plastic tradition, 9; ideas of, as active causes, 9; images, 5; influences thought through variety of expression for each intuition, 8; Mary Shelley on, 378; neglect of, in England, 31, 57, 68, 120, 339, 367, 383-384, 395-396; notions concerning nature of essence, 8; on evil, 23, 236; on symbolism, 234-235; philosophy a midwifery,

5; philosophy an image of Being, 7; philosophy as partial images into realm of Being, 5; plastic interpenetration in civilization, 4; relation of intellect to soul, 27; "reveries" of, 137; symbolism in Plato's philosophy, 7, 23; sophisms of, 137; study of, at Oxford, 384; the personal Plato who images Reality, 8; the personal Plato, expressed through his master, friends, reaction to his society and times, 8; translations of, 120, 277; two contradictory views of poetry, 346; view of evil, 23

PLATONISM

a changing tradition, 9; a δύναμις, 9; activity in mind and history of Europe, 4; an impregnating force, 9; and intellect, 27; and science, 261; and will, 27; apprehension through degrees or levels, 3; as philosophy itself, 3; beauty of written Platonism, 8; characteristics of, 27; charting of three levels of, 9; complexity of, vii; confusion in discussion of, 3; degrees in, 12; deviations from, called spurious, 28; dialogues, a fusion of thought as process and thought as a thing, 8; dialogues, a "receptacle" of Plato's insights, 8; dialogues, an image of reality, 6; different types of, defined, 4; difficulty in determining nature of, 3; difficulty in pigeonholing poets and philosophers to levels of Platonism, 12; distinction between earthly and Uranian Aphrodite, 27; distinctions in planes of Being, 27; divided in levels for purposes of evaluation, 3-4; dogmatism of its judges, 28; εἰκασία in our conception of, 5; essence of, 307; eternal and temporal, 3; European philosophical tradition, a series of footnotes to Plato, 6; expression of, is both universal and particular, 8; gives substance to poetry, vii; grasps abstract thought with ordinary language, its concrete side with art, 8; historian of, 3-5; image and original, 4-5, 6, 8; imitation of, 12; informational, 79; involves an experience of recognition, 4; judges of, unaware of its real nature, 3; levels of, 4; molds other traditions, 9; movement of thought to apprehend truth, 5; natural Platonist in philosophy and literature, 9; nature of its eternal element,

4; not a mechanical standard of reference, vii; not an absolutism in thought, 5; not imitation of Plato, but lure of same beacon determines real Platonist, 7; of imitative tradition, 9; outburst of the spirit itself, 12; owes its influence to creative persuasion of Plato's thought, 9; philosophy viewed as fixed dogma, 28; Platonists who belong to all levels of Platonism, 13; poetical philosophy, vii; powers of illusion in service of reason, 27; problem of, viii; relations of levels of, 4; rhythm of appearance and disappearance, 9; shapes various facets of an epoch, 9; source of Plato's thought in the nature of things, 3; three levels of Platonism essential to understanding nature and function of Platonism, 3, 10; unity of insight, 27; view on man and nature, 27

PLATONISM: CONCEPTS, IMAGES, MOTIFS, MYTHS, SYMBOLS

See entries under Shelley: Concepts, Images, Motifs, Myths, Symbols

PLATONISM, DIRECT

dialogues, a dramatization of thought, 8; dialogues more than a passive image, 8, see also 79; defined, 3; image and original relations of indirect and direct Platonism, 9; in Bridges's *The Testament of Beauty*, 11-12; literal expression of, 3; not to be confused with natural or indirect Platonism, 8; the Platonism of the dialogues is the formulation in a fixed form of thought as living process, 8; Platonism of the dialogues, regarded by Plato as an image, 4; relation to philosophy, 4; relation to Plato, 4

PLATONISM, NATURAL

a form of philosophy, 7; apprehension of, a common privilege, 6; basic belief in dualism of temporal and eternal world, 18; colored by quality of seeker's soul, 19; common awareness of an immaterial reality behind this world, 19; creator first a discoverer, 5; difference between direct and natural Platonism, 7-8; defined, 3; endowed with a power of magnetism, 6; essential for understanding direct and indirect Platonism, 4; first expression of, 28; in Muirhead's *The Pla-

tonic Tradition in Anglo-Saxon Philosophy*, 7; intuitive grasp of, by poet, philosopher, theologian, 19; judges unaware of, 28; man's heart attuned to, 28; many Platonists before Plato, 6; natural Platonist shares Plato's thought, 6; not a static code of thought, 19; not identity with Plato, 6; relation of Being and Becoming, 6; relation to philosopher, 19, 25; relation to poet, 19, 25; relation to theologian, 19, 25; shares Plato's insight into the same realm of speculation, 4, 6; philosophic speculation, appropriate state of mind, 10; philosophy, the sun of its being, 10; poet symbolizes, through flesh and blood, 19; pursuit of ideal through the element of soul apprehending it, 25; source in human nature, 3; see also 204

PLATONIC TRADITION

a fusion of Platonism arising from its elements and the character of user, 9; a selective tradition, 9; adventure of Plato's ideas in thought and history, 9; an incarnate renascent spirit, 9; and Christianity, bibliography of, 89 n. 37; antipathy toward, and neglect of Plato, 31, 57, 68, 120, 137, 339, 367, 383-384, 395-396; anti-Platonic tradition in eighteenth-century France and England, 137 n. 196; as a tradition in mind and history of Europe, 3; as servile tradition without creative quality of the original, 9; at Alexandria, 9; authority of Plato dragged in to sanction doctrines plucked from his philosophy, 10; begins with Aristotle, 9; begins ultimately with writers prior to Plato, 81; bibliography of Platonism of Middle Ages, 91 n. 46; Cabalistic, 109; cannot be understood without reference to direct and natural Platonism, 10; careful scrutiny required, 10; Christianity canonized Platonism, 135, 160-161; confusions in, 131; complexity of, 78; defined, 3; feeds the imagination of the Middle Ages, 9; homosexual element in *Symposium* offensive to British, 57; image of direct Platonism, 4; imitation of direct Platonism, 9; in the eighteenth century, 119 ff.; in Epicureanism, 82; in French philosophers and Encyclopedists, 137-139; in Middle Ages, 91-95; in New Academy, 82; in progress of civili-

Magnetism, Man, Materialism, Mathematical relations, Matter, Metaphysics, Metempsychosis, Midwifery, Mind, Mortality, Mountain, symbol of, Mover, First, Muses, Music of the Spheres, Mutability, Mysticism, Myth, Nature, Necessity, Neoplatonism, Ocean, One, One and Many, Opinion, Organism, Pantisocracy, Perception, Perfection, Phantasms, Philosopher, Philosophy, Plastic nature, Plastic stress, Pleasure, Poet, Poetry, Politics, Polytheism, Pollution, Power, Pre-existence, Principle, Process, Prototype, Psyche, Purgation, Punishment, Reality, Reason, Receptacle, Relation, Relative World, Religion, Reminiscence, Retrogression, Romanticism, *scala naturae,* Sea, symbol of, Sensation, Sense perception, Senses, Shadow, symbol of, Shadow and original, Shadow and substance, Soul, Spindle of necessity, Spirit, Spirits, Stain, Stream, symbol of, Sun, simile of, Symbolism, Symbols, Temporal, Theism, Theology, Theophany, Thought, Tower, symbol of, Transcendence, Transmigration, Truth, Tyrant, Unity, Universe, Value, Veil, symbol of, Virtue, Will, Woman and boat, symbol of, Woman, Platonic, Word, World

INTELLECTUAL LIFE AND TRAITS

a follower of Berkeley, 123; and Boethius, 90; and Cabalism, 34; and Donne, 111 n. 99; and William Drummond of Hawthornden, 111 n. 99; and eighteenth-century philosophy, 237; and eighteenth-century thought, 125; and institutions, 27; and Lovelace, 111 n. 99; and soul-dissolving ecstasies, 26; and the French Revolution, 14; and the Renaissance, 103; and tyrants, 27; as *amator furiosus,* 26; capacity for seeing things separately, 175; complexity of his mind, 241; contact with the Renaissance, 103; continuity of classical influence after departure from Oxford, 38; creative process not strictly imitative, 17; desire for sympathy, 275, 278, 338; despised formal education, 40 n. 44; despised grammarians' approach to the classics, 40 n. 44; emotion and feeling in, 28; evolution in thought of, 125; interest in philosophy, 48 n. 77; mind of, 28; nature and temperament of, 40 n. 44; on French Encyclopedists, 138; on friendship, 54; on Lucretius, 49 n. 85; on poetry, 238; on the evils of classical learning, 40; paratactic mind of, 175; passion for reforming the world, 65; predominance of emotion over logic, 26; prodigious memory, 38; reaction against Christianity, 341; realizes un-Platonic error in his life, 73; sees no merit in the past except Athens, 43; "sensuous curtain," 16 n. 9; supplants reason with imagination, 348; thirst for communion with Beauty, 22

PLATO AND PLATONISM

a new amalgam of Platonism, 17; admiration of Plato, 392; analysis of Platonism, 81; and oral Platonism, 119; appraisal of Plato, 402; as a pseudo-Platonist, 25, 28; attainment of three levels of Platonism, 13; attitude toward Plato and Bacon, 370; begins study of Plato at Bagni di Lucca, 55; best appreciation of Plato as a natural Platonist in Shelley, 13; best laboratory for Platonic tradition, viii; calls Plato his god, 66, 368; child as true Platonist, 36; combines natural, direct, and indirect Platonism, 14; complexity of Platonism, vii; conception of Plato, 334; considers Plato essential for a good library, 63; considers Plato a prose master, 395; continuation of Platonism in Italy, 55; contrast in two periods of, 29; conversion of his soul to Platonism, 16; creative process and Platonism, 17; critics and Platonism, 17; dialogues rich in poetical thought and reform appealed to Shelley, 74; direct knowledge of Plato, 13; discovery of readings of dialogues through influence on his writings, 74; discussion of Plato at Oxford, 36; eclectic use of Platonism in poetic process, 74; enthusiasm for Plato, 48, 74; evidence for tracing study of Platonism, 29; explanations of differences from Plato, 25; Ficino-like enthusiasm for Plato, 60; finds in Plato an understanding spirit, 77; finds in Plato a sure guide to the attainment of his ideals, 76; formulas and concepts of Platonism express his natural Platonism, 16; graph of Platonic study, 76; high-water mark of study of Plato at Oxford, 36; Hogg on Shelley's reading of Plato, 47; identity, in difference, with Plato, 28;

PLATONISM, NATURAL

a latent force evoked by his maturing experience and contact with Platonism, 15; abstractions in, 21; an indwelling power in his soul, 15; an operation of his own mind, 14; and Absolute, 21; and Ideal Beauty, 18; and Ideal World, 18; and immortality of soul, 21; and Platonic love, 21; approaches Ideal through emotion and fantasy, 25; aroused by physical beauty, 206; awakened by

TEXTS, TRANSLATIONS, AND ABSTRACTS OF PLATO USED BY SHELLEY

TRANSLATION

WORKS: POETRY